Equals: National income	Gross National Product		Disposable Personal Income		Personal Consumption Expenditures		Year
	1972 Prices (billions of dollars)	Annual Real Rate of Growth	1972 Prices (billions of dollars)	Annual Real Rate of Growth	1972 Dollars (billions of dollars)	As a Percent of Disposable Personal Income	
84.8	315.7	6.6	229.5	—	215.1	94	**1929**
39.9	222.1	− 2.2	169.6	− 26.1	170.5	100	**1933**
71.4	319.8	7.8	229.8	35.4	219.8	96	**1939**
79.7	344.1	7.6	244.0	6.2	229.9	94	**1940**
102.7	400.4	16.3	277.9	6.6	243.6	88	**1941**
135.9	461.7	15.3	317.5	14.2	241.1	80	**1942**
169.3	531.6	15.1	332.1	4.6	248.2	75	**1943**
182.1	569.1	7.1	343.6	3.5	255.2	74	**1944**
180.7	560.4	− 1.5	338.1	− 1.6	270.9	80	**1945**
178.6	478.3	− 14.7	332.7	− 1.6	301.0	90	**1946**
194.9	470.3	− 1.7	318.8	− 4.2	305.8	96	**1947**
219.9	489.8	4.1	335.8	5.3	312.2	93	**1948**
213.6	492.2	.5	336.8	0.3	319.3	95	**1949**
237.6	534.8	8.7	362.8	7.7	337.3	93	**1950**
274.1	579.4	8.3	372.6	2.7	341.6	92	**1951**
287.9	600.8	3.7	383.2	2.8	350.1	91	**1952**
302.1	623.6	3.8	399.1	4.1	363.4	91	**1953**
301.1	616.1	− 1.2	403.2	1.0	370.0	92	**1954**
330.5	657.5	6.7	426.8	5.9	394.1	92	**1955**
349.4	671.6	2.1	446.2	4.5	405.4	91	**1956**
365.2	683.8	1.8	455.5	2.1	413.8	91	**1957**
366.9	680.9	− .4	460.7	1.1	418.0	91	**1958**
400.8	721.7	6.0	479.7	4.1	440.4	92	**1959**
415.7	737.2	2.2	489.7	2.1	452.0	92	**1960**
428.8	756.6	2.6	503.8	2.9	461.4	92	**1961**
462.0	800.3	5.8	524.9	4.2	482.0	92	**1962**
488.5	832.5	4.0	542.3	3.3	500.5	92	**1963**
524.9	876.4	5.3	580.8	7.1	528.0	91	**1964**
572.4	929.3	6.0	616.3	6.1	557.5	90	**1965**
628.1	984.8	6.0	646.8	4.9	585.7	91	**1966**
662.2	1,011.4	2.7	673.5	4.1	602.7	89	**1967**
722.5	1,058.1	4.6	701.3	4.1	634.4	90	**1968**
779.3	1,087.6	2.8	722.5	3.0	657.9	91	**1969**
810.7	1,085.6	− .2	751.6	4.0	672.1	89	**1970**
871.5	1,122.4	3.4	779.2	3.7	696.8	89	**1971**
963.6	1,185.9	5.7	810.3	4.0	737.1	91	**1972**
1,086.2	1,254.3	5.8	864.7	6.8	767.9	89	**1973**
1,160.7	1,246.3	− .6	857.5	− 0.8	762.8	89	**1974**
1,239.4	1,231.6	− 1.2	874.9	2.0	779.4	89	**1975**
1,379.2	1,298.2	5.4	906.8	3.6	823.1	91	**1976**
1,550.5	1,369.7	5.5	942.9	4.0	864.3	92	**1977**
1,760.3	1,438.6	5.0	988.8	4.9	903.2	91	**1978**
1,966.7	1,479.4	2.8	1,015.7	2.7	927.6	91	**1979**
2,116.6	1,475.0	− .3	1,021.6	0.6	931.8	91	**1980**
2,363.8	1,512.2	2.5	1,049.3	2.7	950.5	91	**1981**
2,446.8	1,480.0	− 2.1	1,058.3	0.9	963.3	91	**1982**
2,646.7	1,534.7	3.7	1,095.4	3.5	1,009.2	92	**1983**
2,959.4	1,639.0	6.8	1,169.5	6.8	1,062.6	91	**1984**

ECONOMICS

EC

ONOMICS

Richard B. McKenzie

Clemson University

Visiting Professor of American Business,
Washington University in St. Louis

Houghton Mifflin Company   Boston

Dallas   Geneva, Illinois   Lawrenceville, New Jersey   Palo Alto

Chapter Epigraphs

Chapter 1. Frank H. Knight, "Economics, Political Science, and Education," in *Freedom and Reform: Essays in Economics and Social Philosophy* (Indianapolis, Ind.: Liberty Press, 1982), p. 386.

Chapter 2. Lionel Robbins, *The Nature and Significance of Economic Science*, 2nd ed. (New York: Macmillan, 1973), p. 16.

Chapter 3. Friedrich A. Hayek, *Law, Legislation, and Liberty* (Chicago: University of Chicago Press, 1979) III, p. 74.

Chapter 4. John Locke, *The Second Treatise of Government*, ed. Thomas P. Peardon (New York: The Liberal Arts Press, 1954), pp. 32–33.

Chapter 5. Lewis Carroll, *Through the Looking Glass and What Alice Found There* (A number of modern sources are available.)

Chapter 6. Henry C. Wallich, "Honest Money," *Macroeconomics 1979: Readings on Contemporary Issues* (Ithaca, N.Y.: Cornell University Press, 1979), p. 43.

Chapter 7. David T. Bazelon, *The Paper Economy* (New York: Vintage Books, 1965), p. 73.

Chapter 8. Milton Friedman, *Dollars and Deficits: Inflation, Monetary Policy, and the Balance of Payments* (Englewood Cliffs, N.J.: Prentice-Hall, 1968), p. 165.

Chapter 9. Roger Leroy Miller, Raburn M. Williams, *The Economics of National Issues* (San Francisco: Canfield Press, 1972), p. 114.

Chapter 10. E. Ray Canterbery, *Economics on a New Frontier* (Belmont, Calif.: Wadsworth Publishing, 1968), p. i.

Chapter 11. Alvin H. Hansen, "The General Theory," in M. G. Mueller, ed., *Readings in Macroeconomics*, 2nd ed. (New York: Holt, Rinehart and Winston, 1971), p. 23.

Chapter 12. Walter W. Heller, "Ford's Budget and the Economy," *Wall Street Journal* (February 5, 1976), p. 18.

Chapter 13. Arthur Okun, *The Political Economy of Prosperity* (New York: W. W. Norton, 1970), p. 100.

Chapter 14. Darryl R. Francis, "The Role of Monetary Policy in Dealing with Inflation and High Interest Rates," *Federal Reserve Bank of St. Louis Review* (August 1974), p. 2.

(Continued at the end of the book.)

Cover painting: Frank Stella, "River of Ponds I." (11-color lithograph, 38 × 38 inches, 1970, edition: 78) Copyright 1970, Gemini G. E. L., Los Angeles.

Printed in the U.S.A.

Library of Congress Catalog Card Number: 85-71108

ISBN: 0-395-35526-5

ABCDEFGHIJ-RM-898765

Dedicated
to

Professor Hugh H. Macaulay

*E*very day, the media carry stories about the national, international, and local economies—how they work, or fail to work, to produce the goods and services people want. Whether the headlines are "unemployment," "inflation," "protectionism," "budget deficit," "tax reform," or "farm debt crisis," they indicate the prominent role economics has come to play in people's daily lives.

One central purpose in writing this text is to explore, with the aid of economic theory, the basic issues that underlie these headlines. Using theory as the "engine of analysis" to provide the necessary structure and methodology, this text applies it to the economic problems and policies of today. The intent is that students completing this text will have a better understanding of why inflation and unemployment occur, how the market power of a monopoly affects the way a market works, the power and the limits of governments to remedy economic problems, and other issues.

Consensus among economists has been hard to achieve in the 1980s. Old solutions have failed to work, new solutions have been proposed, and we are typically confronted by several quite different answers to any given question. But another central purpose of this text is to show students that a surprisingly small number of concepts, principles, and models are common to *any* proposed solution, and that the different views of different economists are more a matter of interpretation than of methodology.

The Text

With these central purposes in mind, *Economics* has been designed to be comprehensive and adaptable to most curricula, to be rich in applications, and to make economics easier to learn.

A text that is comprehensive, and adaptable to most curricula

Part I forms an introduction to macroeconomics (Parts II–V) or microeconomics (Parts VI–IX), so *Economics* is equally suited to a macro/micro sequence or a micro/macro sequence in the two-term principles course.

Preface

Macro

Parts II–IV form the core of the macro section, and treat money and monetary policy *before* covering national income and fiscal policy. Part IV ends with a thorough development of aggregate supply and demand, which was introduced first in Chapter 6. In Part V "Alternative Views of the Macroeconomy," monetarism, supply-side economics, and rational expectations theory are covered in three self-contained chapters. They are unified by reference to the aggregate supply/demand model, but each is complete in itself, allowing instructors to choose whether or not to assign any or all of these chapters.

Micro

Parts VI through VIII form the core of the micro section. Appendices treating indifference curves, isoquants, isocosts, and several other optional topics allow instructors to choose whether or not to cover them in their principles course. In Part IX, optional chapters covering market failures, government controls, agriculture, and public choice provide further flexibility in choosing specific areas of microeconomics applications.

A text that is rich in issues and applications

"Perspectives on Economics"—most written specifically for this text—draw on the experience and insight of a wide range of economists to illuminate current issues, applications, and historical background. Flat tax proposals, sexual discrimination, the federal deficit, and many other topics are covered. Informative, authoritative, and thought-provoking, these short essays show the many perspectives of economic analysis, and acquaint students with the kinds of questions economists ask, and some of the answers they propose.

A text that makes economics easier to learn

Right from Chapter 1, in which the concepts of scarcity and choice are clarified through an eyewitness account of life in a prisoner-of-war camp, abstract terms are presented in the context of realistic, integrated examples. All key terms are highlighted, defined immediately in the margins, and defined again in an alphabetical end-of-text glossary. In addition, the index indicates the page on which each term is initially defined in context.

Each chapter begins by asking the *central question* the chapter will provide answers to. *Key terms* are also previewed before the student encounters them in the text. All figures appear near the pertinent discussion of them in the text, and have full descriptive captions as well. Each chapter ends with a *summary, major conclusions*, and *discussion questions*.

Acknowledgments

Several of my colleagues helped bring economic issues to life by contributing articles for the boxed inserts in the text. For their assistance, I would like to thank (in order of first appearance): Delores T. Martin, Clark Nardinelli, Dennis Placone, Dwight R. Lee, N. Keith Womer, Thomas M. Humbert, William F. Shughart II, Clinton H. Whitehurst Jr., Bruce Yandle, Adele Ernst Wick, Catherine England, John Warner, Terry L. Anderson, Robert Valero, B. H. Robinson, Clifford M. Hardin, Cotton M. Lindsay, Edward L. Hudgins, Katsuro Sakoh, Laurence S. Moss, Russell Shannon, and Martin Schnitzer.

Finally, a word about Professor Hugh Macaulay, who will complete his thirty-seventh year of college and university teaching in 1986. He is the type of professor every student should have for their introductory economics course. Although he can barely be seen behind most normal size podiums, there are few professors who can stand higher in the minds of their students. His students may not always agree with him, but they are not able to ignore him or dismiss him. In and out of class, Professor Macaulay exudes excitement: for a new-found twist on an old argument, for an economist joke that he can turn on himself. By sheer example—by constantly putting his students first and giving of himself in helping his colleagues with their work at the expense of his own—Professor Macaulay has been a moral force among those who have known him. He is, simply stated, a person to be emulated. For this reason, I am proud to be able to dedicate this book to him.

Acknowledgments

Many reviewers read the manuscript of *Economics* at various stages of its development and offered valuable suggestions for its enrichment.

I appreciate the help of these reviewers.

Professor John E. Anderson
Eastern Michigan University

Professor Richard G. Anderson
Ohio State University

Professor Ronald G. Brandolini
Valencia Community College

Professor Wallace Broome
Community College of Rhode Island

Professor Marshall Colberg
Florida State University

Professor Douglas W. Copeland
Kansas State University

Professor Eleanor D. Craig
University of Delaware

Professor Lawrence Daellenbach
University of Wisconsin, La Crosse

Professor Mary Jane Gorman
Furman University

Professor A. R. Gutowsky
California State University, Sacramento

Professor Richard B. Hansen
University of Northern Iowa

Professor Roy B. Helfgott
New Jersey Institute of Technology

Professor Willard W. Howard
Maricopa County Community College, Phoenix College

Professor Maryann O. Keating
University of Notre Dame

Professor Anatoli Kuprianov
Virginia Polytechnic Institute and State University

Professor Patrick Lenihan
Eastern Illinois University

Professor James R. Marchand
University of Mississippi

Professor Kent W. Olson
Oklahoma State University

Professor Robert Payne
Portland Community College

Professor James T. Peach
New Mexico State University

Professor Stanley C. Sofas
Santa Barbara City College

Professor Richard A. Yach
Des Moines Area Community College

Instructor's Manual, prepared by the author. For each chapter, provides:
Chapter Objectives
Key Terms
Chapter Conclusions and Teaching Tips
Suggested Answers to all discussion questions in the text

Transparency Masters for every figure in the book and instructions for using the computerized Test Bank are also provided in the Instructor's Manual.

Test Bank, by Douglas W. Copeland, Kansas State University
Contains over 2,000 items in two separate files, A and B, providing two alternative sets of test items for each chapter.

Computerized Test Bank
Available for mainframes, minicomputers, and IBM PC, Apple II, and TRS-80 microcomputers.

Two-Color Overhead Transparencies
One hundred key figures from the text, reproduced on mylar for clear, legible projection.

Quadrant I
A computerized color graphics package that can generate virtually any graph commonly used in economics. Suitable for both classroom demonstration and for making custom overhead transparencies.

The Complete Teaching/Learning System

Economics,
The hardcover text.

Macroeconomics and **Microeconomics,** paperbacks.
Both volumes include chapters on introduction to economics, public choice economics, international trade and finance, comparative economic systems, and economic development.

Study Guide, by Douglas W. Copeland, Kansas State University.
For each chapter, provides:
Chapter Summary
Chapter Objectives
Review Terms and Concepts
Completion Exercises
Problems and Applications
True/False Questions
Multiple Choice Questions
Discussion Questions

xii

Suggested Outlines for One-Term Courses

Chapter	Macro Emphasis	Micro Emphasis	Public Policy Emphasis	Combined Macro-Micro
20. Cost and Producer Choice		■		■
21. Cost in the Short Run and the Long Run		■		■
22. Perfect Competition		■		■
23. Pure Monopoly		■		■
24. Imperfect Competition				
25. Business Regulation				
26. The Competitive Labor Market		■		■
27. Monopsonies and Unions		■		■
28. Rent, Interest, and Profit		■		
29. Poverty and Poverty Relief	□	□	■	
30. Market Failures: External Costs and Benefits		■	■	□
31. Government Controls: Price Controls and Consumer Protection			■	
32. Agriculture and Government Agricultural Policy			■	
33. Public Choice: The Economics of Government	□	□	■	□
34. International Trade		■	■	
35. International Finance		■		
36. Comparative Economic Systems			□	
37. Economic Growth and Development	□			

Contents in Brief

Contents

Part III
Money and Monetary Policy   145

Chapter 7
The Meaning and Creation of Money   147

Chapter 16
Rational Expectations   351

Part VI
Principles of Consumer Behavior and the Theory of Demand   371

Chapter 17
Principles of Individual Behavior   373

Chapter 25
Business Regulation   551

Part IX
Applications of Microeconomic Theory   679

Chapter 30
Market Failures: External Costs and Benefits   681

Chapter 31

Chapter 32

ECONOMICS

Introduction

Central Question

What is economics?

Key Terms

Market

Entrepreneur

Resources

Land

Labor

Capital

Technology

Scarcity

Economics

Theory

Positive economics

Normative economics

Microeconomics

Macroeconomics

Chapter 1

The Economic Way of Thinking

In economics in particular, education seems to be largely a matter of unlearning and "disteaching" rather than constructive action. A once famous American humorist observed that "it's not ignorance does so much damage; it's knowin' so derned much that ain't so." . . . It seems that the hardest things to learn and to teach are things that everyone already knows.

Frank H. Knight

Market: the process
by which buyers and
sellers determine what
they are willing to buy
and sell, on what
terms. That is, the
process by which
buyers and sellers
decide the prices and
quantities of goods to
be bought and sold.

*E*conomic systems spring from necessity. R. A. Radford, an American soldier who was captured and imprisoned during the Second World War, left a vivid account of the primitive market for goods and services that grew up in his prisoner-of-war camp.[1] A **market** is the process by which buyers and sellers determine what they are willing to buy and sell, on what terms. That is, it is the process by which buyers and sellers decide the prices and quantities of goods that are to be bought and sold. Because the inmates had few opportunities to produce the things they wanted, they turned to a system of exchanges based on the cigarettes, toiletries, chocolate, and other rations distributed to them periodically by the Red Cross.

The Red Cross distributed the supplies equally among the prisoners, but "very soon after capture . . . [the prisoners] realized that it was both undesirable and unnecessary, in view of the limited size and the equality of supplies, to give away or to accept gifts of cigarettes or food. Goodwill developed into trading as a more equitable means of maximizing individual satisfaction."[2] As the weeks went by, trade expanded and the prices of goods stabilized. A soldier who hoped to receive a high price for his soap found he had to compete with others who also wanted to trade soap. Soon shops emerged, and middlemen began to take advantage of discrepancies in the prices offered in different bungalows.

A priest, for example, found that he could exchange a pack of cigarettes for a pound of cheese in one bungalow, trade the cheese for a pack and a half of cigarettes in a second bungalow, and return home with more cigarettes than he had begun with. Although he was acting in his own self-interest, he had provided the people in the second bungalow with something they wanted—more cheese than they would otherwise have had. In fact, prices for cheese and cigarettes differed partly because prisoners had different desires, and partly because they could not all interact freely. In exploiting the discrepancy in prices, the priest moved the camp's store of cheese from the first bungalow, where it was worth less, to the second bungalow, where it was worth more. Everyone involved in the trade benefited from the priest's enterprise.

Entrepreneur: an
enterprising person
who discovers profit-
able opportunities and
organizes, directs, and
manages productive
ventures.

A few entrepreneurs in the camp hoarded cigarettes and used them to buy up the troops' rations shortly after issue—and then sold the rations just before the next issue, at higher prices. An **entrepreneur** is an enterprising person who discovers profitable opportunities and organizes, directs, and manages productive ventures. Though these entrepreneurs were pursuing their own private interest, like the priest, they were providing a service to the other prisoners. They bought the rations when people wanted to get rid of them and sold them when people were running short. The difference between the low price at which they bought and the high price at which they sold gave them the incentive they needed to make the trades, hold on to the rations, and assume the risk that the price of rations might not rise.

---

1. R. A. Radford, "The Economic Organization of a P.O.W. Camp," *Economica*, (November, 1945), pp. 180–201.
2. Ibid., p. 190.

Soon the troops began to use cigarettes as money, quoting prices in packs or fractions of packs. (Only the less desirable brands of cigarette were used this way; the better brands were smoked.) Because cigarettes were generally acceptable, the soldier who wanted soap no longer had to search out those who might want his jam; he could buy the soap with cigarettes. Even nonsmokers began to accept cigarettes in trade.

This makeshift monetary system adjusted itself to allow for changes in the money supply. On the day the Red Cross distributed new supplies of cigarettes, prices rose, reflecting the influx of new money. After nights spent listening to nearby bombing, when the nervous prisoners had smoked up their holdings of cigarettes, prices fell. Radford saw a form of social order emerging in these spontaneous, voluntary, and completely undirected efforts. Even in this unlikely environment, the human tendency toward mutually advantageous interaction had asserted itself.

Today markets for numerous new and used products spring up spontaneously in much the same way. At the end of each semester college students can be found trading books among themselves, or standing in line at the bookstore to resell books they bought at the beginning of the semester. Garage sales are now common in practically all communities. Indeed, like the priest in the POW camp, many people go to garage sales to buy what they believe they can resell—at a higher price, of course.

More than two hundred years ago, Adam Smith outlined a society that resembled these POW camp markets in his classic *Wealth of Nations*. Smith, considered the first economist, asked why markets arise and how they contribute to the social welfare. In answering that question, he defined the economic problem.

The Economic Problem

Our world is not nearly as restrictive as Radford's prison, but it is no Garden of Eden either. Most of us are constantly occupied in securing the food, clothing, and shelter we need to exist, to say nothing of those things we would only like to have—a tape deck, a night on the town. Indeed if we think seriously about the world around us, we can make two general observations.

First, the world is more or less fixed in size and limited in its resources. **Resources** are things used in the production of goods and services. There are only so many acres of land, gallons of water, trees, rivers, wind currents, oil and mineral deposits, trained workers, and machines that can be used in any one period to produce the things we need and want. We can plant more trees, find more oil, and increase our stock of human talent. But still there are limits on what we can accomplish with the resources at our disposal.

Economists group resources into four broad categories: land, labor, capital (also called investment goods), and technology. **Land** includes the surface area of the world and everything in nature—minerals, chemicals, plants—that is useful in the production process. **Labor** includes any way in which human energy, physical or mental, can be usefully expended.

Resources: things used in the production of goods and services.

Land: the surface area of the world and everything in nature—minerals, chemicals, plants—that is useful in the production process.

Labor: any way in which human energy, physical or mental, can be usefully expended.

Economists in History: Adam Smith (1723–1790)

"It is not from the benevolence of the butcher, the brewer, or the baker, that we expect our dinner, but from their regard to their own interest. We address ourselves, not to their humanity but to their self-love, and never talk to them of our own necessities but of their advantages."

When this passage from Adam Smith's *An Inquiry into the Nature and Causes of the Wealth of Nations* (1776) is taken out of context, as it so often is, it may convey a narrow and cynical view of human behavior. Understood in context, however, Smith's statement is merely a logical one. In a complex society, one simply cannot rely on the kindness of others for all one's wants and needs. People are charitable—at least most people are— but they have their limits. As Smith wrote, the individual "at all times stands in need of the cooperation and assistance of great multitudes [of people], while his whole life is scarcely sufficient to gain the friendship of a few persons . . . He will more likely prevail if he can interest their self-love in his favor, and show them that it is for their own advantage to do what he requires of them."

Smith saw the market as a means of enlisting cooperation among strangers. "Give me what I want and I will give you what you want" is the proposition that lies at the base of every market transaction. The butcher, the brewer, and the baker may not know their customers, but by pursuing their own interest, they provide the meat, beer, and bread that others need in order to put dinner on the table.

Prevailing opinion in Smith's time held that in a market exchange, one party profits at the expense of the other. Smith, however, reasoned that if both parties enter into an exchange *voluntarily*, and each gives up something of value for something else of value, both parties benefit. They may not be as well off as they would like to be, but their welfare has been improved by the transaction. Through trade, they have each obtained something they want but cannot produce themselves.

Smith's ideas also conflicted with the mercantilist philosophy of trade, which held that the unregulated pursuit of private interest would inevitably lead to disorder. In Europe in the seventeenth and eighteenth centuries, wages, prices, interest rates, employment, foreign trade, and the quality of goods and services were all strictly controlled by government. The object of this control was to ensure the ruling class's vision of social justice through the administration of what was produced and how it was produced and distributed. Yet to Smith, self-interest was obviously a constructive, coordinating force. In the drive to fulfill their own needs, self-interested people had to appeal to the interests of others. Self-interest is an incentive, a reason to cooperate and coordinate one's activities with others'.

Capital (investment goods): any output of a production process that is designed to be used later in other production processes. Includes plant and equipment.

Capital (investment goods) includes any output of a production process that is designed to be used later in other production processes. Plant and equipment—things produced to produce other things—are examples of these manufactured means of production. **Technology** is the knowledge of how resources can be combined in productive ways.

To this list some economists would add a fifth category, entrepreneurial talent. The entrepreneur is critical to the success of any economy, especially if it relies heavily on markets. Because entrepreneurs discover more effective and profitable ways of organizing resources to produce the goods and services people want, they are often considered a resource in themselves.

Critics of the market system saw profit as an unfair drain on workers' earnings, but Smith viewed it as an incentive, the reward that encourages the producer to meet the interests of others. He felt that competition among producers would keep profits and prices low, so consumers would not be overcharged. In Smith's words, self-interest acts like an "invisible hand," guiding individuals to work for the common interest in the pursuit of their own gain.

Smith saw government as necessary, but only to provide for national defense, for the administration of law and justice, and for certain essential public works that cannot be provided efficiently by the market, such as roads and education. He objected to further government involvement in the market for three reasons. First, government means collective decision making, which runs counter to the individual self-interest that is the foundation of the market system. To Smith, individual choices were important. Leaving decisions to the individual seemed the best way to ensure that good choices would be made.

Second, Smith argued that government restrictions on the market can prevent mutually beneficial trades and reduce the welfare of potential traders. Government-imposed tariffs on imports are a good example of this negative effect. Tariffs increase the price of imports, encouraging consumers to buy more domestic substitutes than they would otherwise, at a higher price. As a result, consumers get less for their dollar.

Third, Smith felt that businessmen would exploit any government power over the economy to further their own interests. He once wrote, "The proposal of any new law or regulations of commerce which comes from this order [of entrepreneurs], ought always to be listened to with great precaution, and ought never to be adopted till after having been long and carefully examined . . . with the most suspicious attention. It comes from an order of men . . . who have generally an interest to deceive and even to oppress the public. . . ." Businessmen, said Smith, seldom come together except to conspire against the public—that is, to restrict trade in their favor. He felt that the competition inherent in the market system would help to minimize such collusion.

Although he may never have used the word, Smith was well aware of the imperfections of the market system. He recognized the risk of monopoly, which he saw as an evil fostered primarily by government. And he acknowledged that the market often adjusts slowly to change and may fail to produce adequate quantities of certain goods without government intervention. *The Wealth of Nations* did not attempt to prove that the free market system is perfect. Rather, it was a classic statement of the relative merits of the market system, compared with the alternatives.

Our second general observation is that in contrast to the world's physical limitations, human wants abound. You yourself would probably like to have books, notebooks, pens, and a calculator; perhaps even a computer with 512K worth of memory and two double-sided disk drives. A stereo system, a car, more clothes, a plane ticket home, a seat at a big concert or ballgame—you could probably go on for a long time, especially when you realize how many basics, like three good meals a day, you normally take for granted.

In fact, most people want far more than they can ever have. One of the unavoidable conditions of life is the fundamental fact of scarcity.

Technology: the knowledge of how resources can be combined in productive ways.

Scarcity: the fact that we cannot all have everything we want all the time.

Scarcity is the fact that we cannot all have everything we want all the time. Put simply, there isn't enough of everything to go around. Consequently society must face several unavoidable questions:

1. What will be produced? More guns or more butter? More schools or more prisons? More cars or more art, more textbooks or more "Saturday night specials"?
2. How will those things be produced, considering the resources at our disposal? Shall we use a great deal of labor and little mechanical power, or vice versa?
3. Who will receive the goods and services produced? Shall we distribute them equally? If not, then on what other basis shall we distribute them?
4. Perhaps most important, how shall we answer all these questions? Shall we allow for individual freedom of choice, or shall we make all these decisions collectively?

These questions have no easy answers. Most of us spend our lives attempting to come to grips with them on an individual level. What should I do with my time today—study or walk through the woods? How should I study—in the library or at home with the stereo on? Who is going to benefit from my efforts—me or my mother, who wants me to succeed? Am I going to live by principle or by habit? Take each day as it comes or plan ahead? In a broader sense, these questions are fundamental not just to the individual but to all the social sciences, economics in particular. Scarcity is the root of economics. **Economics** is the study of how people cope with scarcity—with the pressing problem of how to allocate their limited resources among their competing wants so as to satisfy as many of those wants as possible.

Economics: the study of how people cope with scarcity—with the pressing problem of how to allocate their limited resources among their competing wants so as to satisfy as many of those wants as possible.

Markets like the one in the POW camp emerge in direct response to scarcity. Because people want more than is immediately available, they produce some goods and services for trade. By exchanging things they like less for things they like more, they reallocate their resources, enhancing their welfare as individuals.

The Scope of Economics

Beginning students often associate economics with a rather narrow portion of the human experience: the pursuit of wealth; money and taxes; commercial and industrial life. And critics often suggest that economists are oblivious to the aesthetic and ethical dimensions of human experience. Such criticism is not altogether unjustified. But increasingly, economists are expanding their horizons and applying the laws of economics to the full spectrum of human activities.

The struggle to improve one's lot is not limited to the attainment of material goals. Though most economic principles have to do with the pursuit of material gain, they can be relevant to aesthetic and humanistic goals as well. The appreciation of a poem or play can be the subject of economic inquiry. Poems and plays, and the time in which to appreciate them, are also scarce.

Jacob Viner, an economist active in the first half of this century, once defined economics as what economists do. Today economists study an increasingly diverse array of topics. As always, they are involved in describing market processes, methods of trade, and commercial and industrial patterns. But they also pay considerable attention to poverty and wealth; to racial, sexual, and religious discrimination; to politics and bureaucracy; to crime and crime law; and to revolution. There is even an economics of group interaction, in which economic principles are applied to marital and family problems. Thus though economists are still working on the conventional problems of inflation, unemployment, and international monetary problems, they are also studying the delivery of health care to the very young and the elderly, or of housing to the disadvantaged. In one way or another, today's economists are tackling a wide variety of subjects, from committee structure to the criminal justice system, ethics, voting rules, and the legislative process.

What is the unifying factor in these diverse inquiries? What ties them all together and distinguishes the economist's work from that of other social scientists? Economists take a distinctive approach to the study of human behavior. They employ a mode of analysis based on certain presuppositions about human behavior. For example, much economic analysis starts with the general proposition that people prefer more to less of those things they want; that they seek to maximize their welfare by making reasonably consistent choices in the things they buy and sell. These propositions enable economists to derive the "law of demand" (people will buy more of any good at a lower price than at a higher price, and vice versa), and many other principles of human behavior.

One purpose of this book is to describe this special approach in considerable detail—to develop in precise terms the commonly accepted principles of economic analysis, and to demonstrate how they can be used to understand a variety of problems, including pollution, unemployment, crime, and ticket scalping. In every case, economic analysis is useful only if it is based on a sound theory that can be evaluated in terms of real-world experience.

Developing and Using Economic Theories

The real world of economics is staggeringly complex. Each day millions of people engage in innumerable transactions, only some of them involving money, and many of them undertaken for contradictory reasons. To make sense of all these activities, economists turn to theory.

A theory is a model of how the world is put together, an attempt to uncover some order in the seemingly random events of daily life. Economic theory is abstract, but not in the sense that its models lack concreteness. On the contrary, good models are laid out with great precision. But economic theories are simplified models *abstracted from* the complexity of the real world. The economist deliberately concentrates on just a few outstanding features of a problem in an effort to discover the laws that govern their relationship. A **theory** is a set of abstractions about the real

Theory: a set of abstractions about the real world. An economic theory is a simplified explanation of how the economy, or part of the economy, functions or would function under specific conditions.

world. An economic theory is a simplified explanation of how the economy, or part of the economy, functions or would function under specific conditions.

Quite often the economist must also make unproved assumptions, called simplifying assumptions, about the parts of the economy under study. For example, in examining the effects of price and availability on the amount of food sold, the economist might assume that people eat only oranges and bananas in the model society in question. Such a simplifying assumption is permissible in constructing a model for two reasons. First, it makes the discussion more manageable. Second, it does not alter the problem under study or destroy its relevance to the real world.

As following chapters will reveal, economic theorizing is largely deductive—that is, the analysis proceeds from very general propositions (such as "more is preferred to less") to much more precise statements or predictions (for example, "the quantity purchased will rise when the price falls").[3] Economic theories sometimes vary in their premises and conclusions, but all develop through the following three steps.

First, a few very general premises or propositions are stated. "More is preferred to less" or "People will seek to maximize their welfare" are examples of such propositions. The premises tend to be so general that they are beyond dispute, at least for the economists developing the theory.

Second, logical deductions, which are tentative predictions about behavior, are drawn from the premises. From the premise "People will seek to maximize their welfare" we can deduce how people will tend to allocate their incomes, at certain prices. We can then conclude that they will purchase more of a good when its price falls. Mathematics and graphic analysis are often very useful in deducing the consequences of premises.

Third, the predictions are tested against observable experience. Theory may tell us that people buy more at lower prices than at higher prices, but the critical question is whether that prediction is borne out in the real world. Do people actually buy more apples when the price falls? Empirical tests require data to be carefully selected and statistically analyzed.

Empirical tests can never prove a theory's validity. The behavior that is observed—more apples purchased, for instance—may be caused by factors not considered in the theory. That is, the quantity of apples purchased may increase for some reason other than a drop in price. Empirical tests can only fail to disprove a theory. If a theory is repeatedly evaluated in different circumstances and is not disproven, however, its usefulness and general applicability increase. Economists have considerable confidence in the proposition that price and quantity purchased are inversely related because it has been repeatedly tested and found to be accurate.

Though a theory is not a complete and realistic description of the real world, a good theory should incorporate enough data to simulate real life. That is, it should provide some explanation for past experiences and

3. In contrast, inductive theorizing proceeds from very precise statements about observable relationships (such as "people are laid off when plants close") to much more general propositions (for example, "plant closings increase unemployment").

permit reasonably accurate predictions of the future. When you evaluate a new theory, ask yourself: Does this theory explain what has been observed? Does it provide a better basis for prediction than other theories?

Positive and Normative Economics

Economic thinking is often divided into two categories, positive and normative. **Positive economics** is that branch of economic inquiry that is concerned with the world as it is rather than as it should be. It deals only with the consequences of changes in economic conditions or policies. A positive economist suspends questions of values when dealing with issues like crime or minimum wage laws. The object is to predict the effect of changes in the criminal code or the minimum wage rate—not to evaluate the fairness of such changes. **Normative economics** is that branch of economic inquiry that deals with value judgments—with what prices, production levels, incomes, and government policies *ought* to be. A normative economist does not shrink from the question of what the minimum wage rate ought to be. To arrive at an answer, the economist weighs the results of various minimum wage rates on the groups affected by them—the unemployed, employers, taxpayers, and so on. Then, on the basis of value judgments of the relative need or merit of each group, the normative economist recommends a specific minimum wage rate. Of course, values differ from one person to the next. In the analytical jump from recognizing the alternatives to prescribing a solution, scientific thinking gives way to ethical judgment.

> **Positive economics:** that branch of economic inquiry that is concerned with the world as it is rather than as it should be. Deals only with the consequences of changes in economic conditions or policies.

> **Normative economics:** that branch of economic inquiry that deals with value judgments—with what prices, production levels, incomes, and government policies ought to be.

Microeconomics and Macroeconomics

The discipline of economics is divided into two main parts: microeconomics and macroeconomics. As the term *micro* (as in microscope) suggests, **microeconomics** is the study of the individual markets—for corn, records, books, and so forth—that operate within the broad national economy. When economists measure, explain, and predict the demand for specific products like bicycles and hand calculators, they are dealing with microeconomics. Much of the work of economists is concerned with microeconomic analysis—that is, with the interpretation of events in the marketplace and of personal choices among products.

> **Microeconomics:** the study of the individual markets—for corn, records, books, and so forth—that operate within the broad national economy.

Questions of interest to microeconomists include:

What determines the price of particular goods and services?

What determines the output of individual firms and industries?

What determines the wages workers receive? The interest rates lenders receive? The profits businesses receive?

How do government policies—like minimum wage laws, price controls, tariffs, and excise taxes—affect the price and output levels of individual markets?

Macroeconomics: the study of the national economy as a whole, or of its major components. Deals with the "big picture," not the details, of the nation's economic activity.

Economists are also interested in measuring, explaining, and predicting the performance of the economic system itself. To do so they study broad subdivisions of the economy, such as the total output of all firms that produce goods and services. **Macroeconomics** is the study of the national economy as a whole, or of its major components. It deals with the "big picture," not the details, of the nation's economic activity.

Instead of concentrating on how many bicycles or hand calculators are sold, macroeconomists watch how many goods and services consumers purchase in total, or how much money all producers spend on new plant and equipment. Instead of tracking the price of a particular good in a particular market, macroeconomics monitors the general price level or average of all prices. And instead of focusing on the wage rate and the number of people employed as plumbers or engineers, macroeconomists study incomes of all employees and the total number of people employed throughout the economy. In short, macroeconomics involves the study of national production, unemployment, and inflation. For that reason it is often referred to as aggregate economics.

Typical macroeconomic questions include:

What determines the general price level? The rate of inflation?

What determines national income and production levels?

What determines national employment and unemployment levels?

What effects do government monetary and budgetary policies have on the general price, income, production, employment, and unemployment levels?

What, if anything, can government do to combat inflation, unemployment, and recession?

These questions are of more than academic interest. The theories that have been developed to answer them can be applied to problems and issues of the real world. Throughout this book, as well as in specific chapters on topics like inflation, regulation and deregulation, and price controls and consumer protection, we will examine the practical applications of economic theory. In some basic way, scarcity—and the economic question of how to deal with it—touches all of us.

Summary and Extensions

Economics is a discipline best described as the study of human interaction in the context of scarcity. It is the study of how, individually and collectively, people use their scarce resources to satisfy as many of their wants as possible. The economic method is founded in a set of presuppositions about human behavior, on the basis of which economists construct theoretical models. A major purpose of this book is to describe the analytical tools economists use, and in that way to show how they study human behavior.

Major Conclusions

1. Economics can be defined as the study of human behavior in the context of scarcity. It is the study of how individuals, confronted by scarcity, allocate their resources among competing wants.
2. Economic thinking is founded on the assumption that people's needs and wants are limitless, but resources, goods, and services are scarce. Thus people must choose among the many things they want—they cannot have everything. Individually or collectively, they must decide what to produce, how to produce it, and for whom to produce it.
3. Resources are things useful in producing the goods and services people want. Economists divide resources into four categories: land, labor, capital, and technology.
4. Economists construct theories, or simplified models of the real world, in order to highlight the relationships among a few outstanding features of the economy.
5. Positive economics deals with the economy as it is, specifically with the consequences of a change in economic conditions or policy. Normative economics deals with value judgments, or with what economic policy and conditions ought to be.
6. Microeconomics is the study of individual markets, specifically their price levels, resource inputs, and product outputs. Macroeconomics is the study of economic activity across many markets, specifically the national price, output, employment, and unemployment levels.

Questions to Ponder

1. In the prison camp described on pages 6–7, rations were distributed equally. Why did trade within and among bungalows result?
2. Recall the priest who traded cigarettes for cheese, and cheese for cigarettes, so that he ended up with more cigarettes than he had initially. Did someone else in the camp lose by the priest's activities? How was the priest able to end up better off than when he began? What did his activities do to the price of cheese in the different bungalows?
3. Theories may be defective, but economists continue to use them. Why?
4. An introductory economics book could include theories more complex than those in this book. What might be the tradeoffs in dealing with more complex theories?
5. How can values influence scientific inquiry? How can value-free (positive) economic analysis affect the assessment of policy?

Central Question

Given the scarcity of resources and the limitlessness of human wants, how does society decide what to produce?

Key Terms

Cost

Production possibilities curve

Consumption goods

Private goods

Public goods

Specialization of labor

Economies of scale

Diseconomies of scale

Money

Comparative advantage

Circular flow of income

Chapter 2

Scarcity and Production Possibilities

Economics is the science which studies human behavior as a relationship between ends and scarce means which have alternative uses.
Lionel Robbins

*T*he last chapter introduced the basic economic problem: the conflict between unlimited human wants and limited resources. Using graphic analysis, this chapter examines the decisions that must be made individually and collectively as a result of the conflict. Two concepts, the production possibilities curve and the circular flow of income, are particularly important to the discussion.

The appendix at the end of this chapter outlines the basic features and uses of graphs. If you are unsure how to use or read graphs, turn to page 36 before reading further.

The Implications of Scarcity

Scarcity is a fact of life. Individually and collectively we cannot have all that we want; we are forced to live within our means. So the essential economic problem is this: Our ability to imagine the goods and services we would like to have far exceeds our ability to produce them—that is, to transform the resources at our disposal into the goods and services we want.

From the basic observation of scarcity, three conclusions flow. First, there is always more than one use for a resource. Time not spent studying can be used to farm, to run computers, or to raise a family. There is always something constructive for people (or machinery, or land) to do. Economically speaking, a person is unemployed because some barrier—distance or lack of skill—separates him or her from productive work, not because none exists. Technological change may eliminate the need for labor in a given industry, but it also frees labor to do other things, satisfy other wants.

Second, we must choose among alternative uses for resources. Choice is an inescapable, sometimes agonizing, part of the economic process. Whenever we do anything, we forgo the opportunity to do other things. If we go to a movie, we choose not to study. If we produce textiles, we forgo the chance to make machines or a variety of other products and services. And if we expand public education, we must do without extra police protection—or raise taxes and do without private goods. "You can't have your cake and eat it too" is a well-worn adage, but an economically apt one.

Third, every choice has a cost. Though often stated in dollars and cents, an item's cost is more accurately defined as the value of what could have been purchased instead. Dollars and cents are only a means of measuring this opportunity cost. **Cost** (or, more precisely, opportunity cost) is the value of the most highly preferred alternative not taken.

As long as resources are scarce and we can choose among them, everything we do will have a cost. There is a cost to studying, to producing textiles, and to providing public education. Although we talk about cost in terms of dollars and cents, cost itself will never be seen—can never be seen—for it is the option not taken, the value of what we could have done, but didn't.

Cost (opportunity cost): the value of the most highly preferred alternative not taken.

The Production Possibilities Curve

The limitations and choices inherent in the economy can be represented graphically. Assume that a nation can produce only two goods, guns (measured in numbers of guns) and butter (measured in pounds). Although this economy can produce only so much, choices among alternatives do exist. Resources can be shifted from one line of production to another, changing the combination of guns and butter produced. At one extreme, the nation can devote all its resources to making guns, producing no butter at all. Alternatively, it can make only butter. Or resources can be divided between the two production processes, yielding some combination of guns and butter. If all possible production combinations are plotted on a graph (with guns on the horizontal axis and butter on the vertical), the result is a production possibilities curve. A **production possibilities curve** (sometimes called a production possibilities frontier or a product transformation curve) is a graphical representation of the various combinations of goods that can be produced when all resources are fully and efficiently employed. It shows all the production combinations possible when all resources available are used in the most productive way possible, given the best known technology (see Figure 2.1).

Production possibilities curve (production possibilities frontier): a graphical representation of the various combinations of goods that can be produced when all resources are fully and efficiently employed.

Linear Production Possibilities Curves

The production possibilities curve can take several shapes, two of which are shown in Figure 2.1. All are downward sloping from left to right. (Such curves are said to have a *negative slope*—see the Appendix, page 36, for an explanation of the term *slope*.) Why? Suppose we are using all our resources to produce guns; that is, we are at point *a* in Figure 2.1, panel (a). Then the only way we can produce butter is to move some resources away from the production of guns. Such a shift necessarily means a cut in the number of guns produced. We move from point *a* to point *b*—upward and to the left.

The movement from *a* to *b* on the curve in Figure 2.1(a) can be seen as the cost of producing the butter. That is, the cost of the 80 pounds of butter gained is the *value* of the 50 guns given up. It is important to remember that cost is the value, not the number, of what is given up. In Figure 2.1(a), the slope of the curve, $-80/50$, or $-8/5$, is constant (because the curve is straight). Therefore the *number* of guns forgone for each additional unit of butter remains constant. The value of additional units of butter, in economic terms, does not necessarily remain constant, however.

In fact, as we move up along the curve, acquiring more butter and giving up more guns, the relative value of guns and butter is almost certain to change. As more guns are given up, they will be taken away from uses that are increasingly valuable. Hence the cost of additional units of butter will tend to rise as more are produced. At the same time, the relative value of the additional units of butter will tend to fall, since they will be

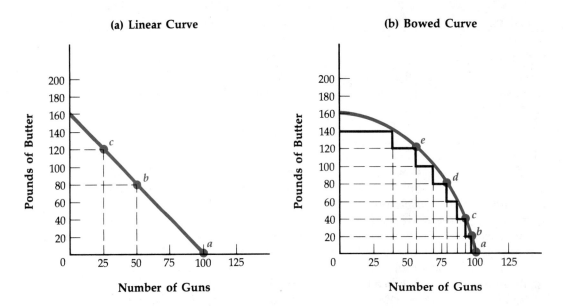

Figure 2.1. Production Possibilities Curves.
All production possibilities curves slope downward from the left to the right. When resources are fully and efficiently employed, more of one good, like guns, can be produced only by giving up some of another good, like butter.

A production possibilities curve that takes the form of a straight line—as in panel (a)—indicates that the number of goods that must be given up for a specific amount of a second good remains constant as production increases. A production possibilities curve that is bowed out—as in panel (b)—indicates that as production increases, more and more goods must be given up to gain the same amount of the second good.

used for less and less valuable purposes. Just how far up the curve we will go depends entirely on the relative values of the two commodities. If we stop at *c*, that is the point where additional units of butter are not worth their cost to us.

Bowed Production Possibilities Curves

The curve in Figure 2.1(b) is bowed out from (or, to use mathematical jargon, "concave to") the origin. What does such a shape imply? As the curve approaches the intersection on the vertical axis, it becomes flatter, or lower in slope. The number of guns that must be forgone for each additional unit of butter goes up progressively. When we moved from *a* to *b*, expanding our production of butter by 20 pounds, we gave up only 5 guns. If we move further up the curve from *b* to *c*, however, we must forgo significantly more guns than before—7 instead of 5—to get 20 more pounds of butter. Similarly, as we move up the curve from *c* to *d* and from *d* to *e*, we give up proportionally more guns for each 20 pounds of butter.

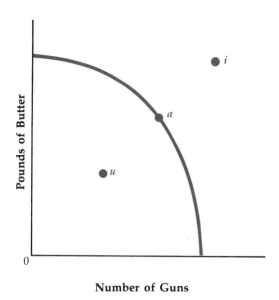

Figure 2.2. Maximizing Production.
Any point on a production possibilities curve (such as *a*) represents full and efficient use of resources. Points inside the production possibilities curve (such as *u*) represent incomplete or inefficient use of at least one resource. Points outside the curve (*i*, for instance) are beyond an economy's resources.

These increases in the number of units forgone stem from the tendency to use resources as efficiently as possible. As we divide up our resources between butter and guns, we put those resources that are better suited to butter production into the butter industry, and those better suited to guns into the gun industry. If we then want to increase butter production, we must move some resources from guns to butter. But we have already put the most suitable resources into butter; now we must add resources that are less suitable. Thus for each additional pound of butter, we must give up progressively more of our gun resources.

In Figure 2.1(b), the *cost* of producing each additional unit of butter increases for two reasons. First, as in Figure 2.1(a), the value of the guns forgone rises. Second, each time butter production is expanded, the resources transferred from guns will be less efficient for butter production; thus more and more guns must be given up.

Points Inside and Outside the Curve

The production possibilities curve assumes that resources are fully and efficiently employed. (That is, they are used where they will do the most good, in terms of what people want most.) If those two conditions are not met, then the economy will not be operating on the production possibilities curve, but at some point within it, like point *u* in Figure 2.2. At point *u*, fewer goods than possible are being produced. From such a point, we should be able to move to a point on the curve, like *a*, expanding the production of both guns and butter at the same time. In that respect, a movement from *u* to *a* is costless—nothing is forgone to increase production. Making sure that our economy is not functioning somewhere in the interior of the production possibilities curve, where resources are underutilized, is one of the major tasks for economic policymakers.

Points outside, or to the right of, the production possibilities curve are by definition impossible to achieve. To suggest, for instance, that we should choose to produce at a point like *i* is equivalent to saying that we should produce more than we are capable of producing (*i* stands for "impossible"). In the heat of debate, our political leaders sometimes seem to suggest just such impossible goals. Our production limitations (and the problems of choice) cannot be escaped. We cannot move to a point like *i* by printing more money. The additional dollars add nothing to our stock of real resources.

Partly because economists are constantly insisting that we recognize the obvious, economics is often referred to as the "dismal science." In fact we are generally either on or close to our production possibilities frontier. Getting more of one thing thus means giving up something else. We do have options, but they are options constrained by reality. To borrow the words of Ben Franklin, choices are as certain as death and taxes.

The Choice Between Investment and Consumption

Choices span the spectrum of goods and services. We must choose not only between the goods and services we can have today, but between current goods and services and those we can have in the future. When we choose an apple from our barrel, we also choose to have one less apple for the future. In the same way, our choices between capital or investment goods and consumption goods influence both our present and future incomes, and our consumption patterns over time. Recall from Chapter 1 that an investment or capital good is any output of a production process that is designed to be used in other production processes—for example, plant and equipment. Investment goods are manufactured means of production. A **consumption good** is any good that is produced to be used and enjoyed more or less immediately by its purchaser, like ice cream.

Consumption goods: goods that are produced to be used and enjoyed more or less immediately by their purchasers.

Figure 2.3 shows the economic consequences of various levels of investment. Assume that a nation's production possibilities curve is C_2I_3. Assume also that the nation chooses to produce at point *a*, representing C_1 consumption goods and I_1 investment goods. Several consequences follow from such a decision.

First, like consumption goods, investment goods come at a cost. That cost is the value of the consumption goods forgone, in this case, $C_2 - C_1$.

Second, investment goods are means of production; they add to a nation's stock of plant and equipment. As long as the level of investment—in this case, I_1—does more than replace old, worn-out plant and equipment, it increases future production capabilities. That is, because of the new

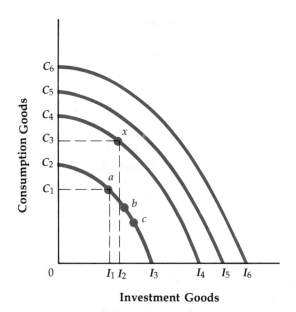

Figure 2.3. Investment Versus Consumption.
A nation's future production capability depends on the choices it makes between consumption and investment goods. The more investment goods it produces, the further to the right its production possibilities curve will shift. If a nation produces at point a on curve C_2I_2, its production possibilities curve will shift to C_4I_4. If it chooses point b, its curve will shift to C_5I_5; from point c, it will shift to C_6I_6.

plant and equipment, the nation's production possibilities curve will gradually shift to the right, perhaps to C_4I_4. This rightward shift of the production possibilities curve indicates economic growth.

Third, when the production possibilities curve shifts to the right, a nation's ability to afford consumption goods increases. When a nation that was producing initially at point a moves to point x, consumption increases from C_1 to C_3. Thus by forgoing a small amount of consumption goods $(C_2 - C_1)$ in the beginning, a nation gains a larger amount of consumption goods $(C_3 - C_2)$ in the future. This increased future consumption does not require a decrease in future investment. Investment increases too, from I_1 to I_2.

Fourth, this greater investment capability increases the potential for future growth. Every time investment increases, the production possibilities curve shifts further to the right—to C_5I_5, C_6I_6, and so on.

Fifth, the more a nation invests initially, the greater the shift in its future production possibilities. If a nation chooses to invest more than I_1—for example, choosing point b instead of point a on curve C_2I_3—its production possibilities curve will shift further to the right, perhaps to C_5I_5, than it would with I_1 investment. Choosing point c can cause the curve to shift still further, perhaps to C_6I_6. The more a nation invests initially, however, the more it must forgo in the way of consumption goods.

Thus a nation's long-term economic growth depends heavily on its ability to forgo current consumption in order to invest. Suppose three nations—A, B, and C—start out on the same production possibilities curve, C_2I_3. Simply by choosing different points on that curve—a, b, or c—they can end up with vastly different future production possibilities curves and future consumption patterns. What happens tomorrow depends critically on the choices made today.

Ideally, at what point should a nation produce initially: a, b, or c? At first it may seem that the answer is obviously c (and if not c, then b). But does the value of the future consumption gained exceed the value of the current consumption forgone? Not necessarily. If a nation chooses to produce at point a when it could have produced at point c, we must presume that its citizens do not value the benefits of future consumption as much as current consumption.

The position of the production possibilities curve also depends on the types of investment projects that are undertaken. A nation that merely duplicates existing plant and equipment, rather than improving them, will not do as well in the future as a nation that invests heavily in research and innovative technology. Of course innovation can be risky; not all new ideas are better ideas. Again the benefits of increased investment must be weighed against the cost to those who will pay for it.

In the United States, investment goods accounted for 14–16 percent of the total market value of all goods and services produced over the past two decades. That was higher than the percentage for economically stagnant Great Britain, but significantly lower than the percentage for dynamic Japan. During the early 1980s, the United States invested slightly less of its output (13 percent) in investment goods. The reasons cited most frequently for the drop in investment were the uncertainties produced by inflation; the reduced willingness of Americans to save (there can be no investment without saving); higher taxes; greater government regulation of industry; high interest rates; and reduced industry profits. In the mid-1980s, the decline in investment as a percentage of national output was reversed.

The Choice Between Private and Public Goods

Just as a society must decide between consumption and investment, it must choose between individual and collective consumption or investment. Politicians may be fond of so-called free lunch programs, and local officials may vie with each other for "federal handouts" with which to finance municipal projects. But these publicly funded goods are "free" only in a very limited sense. When a particular city receives federal funds, local taxpayers' federal income tax bills may not change very much. Nevertheless federal programs always involve a cost. One task of the economist is to spot that cost and bring it to the attention of decision makers.

Private goods: goods that are bought or produced and used by people as individuals or as members of small voluntary groups.

Figure 2.4 shows the production possibilities curve for private goods and public goods. **Private goods** are goods that are bought or produced and used by people as individuals or as members of small voluntary

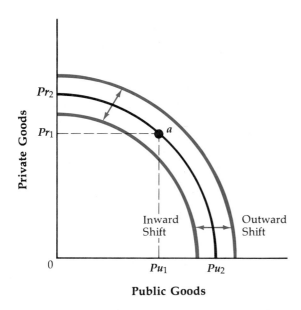

Figure 2.4. Public Versus Private Goods.
A nation's future production possibilities curve depends on the choices it makes between public and private goods. Production of some public goods—for example, pollution control devices or police protection—can shift the production possibilities curve outward. But production of other public goods—welfare assistance that discourages people from working or acquiring education, for example—can shift the production possibilities curve inward.

---

groups, like baseballs and food. **Public goods** are goods that are bought or produced and used by large groups of people or governments, like police protection or national defense. Public goods can benefit many people at once. As with other production possibilities curves, a society can operate at any point along the curve. Operating at point a will produce a combination of Pr_1 private goods and Pu_1 public goods. In this case, the cost of the public goods is the difference between Pr_2 and Pr_1 on the vertical axis. That is, to obtain Pu_1 public goods, we must give up $Pr_2 - Pr_1$ private goods. As individuals, we forgo so many cars, stereos, or computers to get missiles and water treatment plants instead.

Our choices between public and private goods can also (but do not necessarily) affect our nation's future production possibilities curve. The purchase of public goods can shift the curve in either direction. The curve may shift to the right, for instance, if government-provided goods allow the private sector to operate more efficiently, by reducing the costs businesses have to bear. Up to a point, police protection enables producers to devote more of their resources to production and investment and fewer to protecting their property from thieves and vandals. If government-provided goods increase the nation's stock of plant and equipment (for example, dams, hospitals, and sewer systems) or enhance people's ability to produce (through student loans, for example), the curve may shift to

Public goods: goods that are bought or produced and used by large groups of people or by governments.

the right. Government-enforced environmental controls may also have a positive effect, if they make producers and consumers more aware of the environmental costs of products, and thus less wasteful of resources.

Government-provided goods may shift the nation's production possibilities curve to the left, however, if they discourage people from working or reduce the resources available for production. If welfare allows people to remain out of work longer than they need to, for instance, it reduces the nation's production possibilities. Government-provided goods may also have a negative effect if, like taxes on the interest earned on savings accounts, they reduce people's incentive to save, increasing consumption at the expense of investment. Finally, government production of goods may be wasteful. If resources are idle or underutilized because of political maneuvering, fewer goods, public and private, will be produced than is possible.

The exact extent to which government affects the movement of the production possibilities curve has been the subject of considerable study by economists, but no consensus has been reached. This question can have no simple answer.

Shifting the Production Possibilities Curve

Given limited resources and unlimited wants, people have become quite creative in devising ways to get the most out of scarce resources and expand their production possibilities. Among the wide variety of techniques they have developed, several deserve to be mentioned.

Substitution of Resources

People have discovered new resources and substituted them where possible for scarce ones. Chemists developed fertilizers to increase the yield of farmland, freeing scarce land for other uses. Prospectors developed hydrocarbon fuels as a substitute for scarce human and animal energy. More recently scientists invented solar energy collectors to replace dwindling hydrocarbon fuels. The progressive substitution of nonhuman for human energy sources has increased society's production possibilities.

Cost Sharing

To share the cost of capital equipment ("spread the overhead") and the risk that must be assumed by investors, people have developed a variety of social structures, from families and cooperatives to corporations and insurance companies.

Specialization of labor: the process of dividing and assigning different production tasks to individuals with differing skills and talents.

Specialization of Labor

To increase the productivity of labor, people have learned to divide up the tasks of production, a process called specialization of labor. **Specialization of labor** is the process of dividing and assigning different production tasks to individuals with differing skills and talents. Specialization usually (but not always) increases production because when people concentrate on a limited number of tasks, they tend to become more proficient at them. They spend more time in actual production and less in shifting from one task to another. Specialization also reduces the duplication of tools that is necessary when people attempt to be self-sufficient.

Economies of Scale

Partly because it promotes specialization, production on a large, even massive, scale can reduce the cost per unit of production. **Economies of scale** are decreases in per unit cost due to an increase in the rate of production when the use of all resources is expanded. Economies of scale occur when an increase in resource inputs brings a proportionally greater increase in output during a given period of time. Large-scale production also allows the use of larger, faster, more efficient equipment. For example, if large computers can be fully used twenty-four hours a day, their speed—hundreds of thousands of calculations per second—makes up for their expense. When they are fully used, their cost per unit of calculation is less than the cost per unit of a desk-top calculator.

There are limits, of course, to a firm's ability to reduce costs by expanding its scale of operation. Beyond some point, expansion brings an increase in the cost of producing each unit, called a diseconomy of scale. **Diseconomies of scale** are increases in per unit cost due to an increase in the rate of production when the use of all resources is expanded. Diseconomies of scale occur when an increase in resource inputs is not matched by a proportionate increase in output. Diseconomies of scale are generally attributed to the communication problems that plague large, bureaucratic organizations. When those at the top of the organizational hierarchy lose touch with those at the bottom, the firm functions less efficiently.

Economies of scale: decreases in per-unit cost due to an increase in the rate of production when the use of all resources is expanded.

Diseconomies of scale: increases in per-unit cost due to an increase in the rate of production when the use of all resources is expanded.

Trade

As the priest in the POW camp found (see pages 6–7), the inconveniences associated with scarcity can be reduced by trade. Commerce allows people to exchange goods and services they value less for those they value more. It also increases people's opportunity to specialize, expand the scale of their operations, and take advantage of resulting economies of scale. But perhaps most important, trade allows people to capitalize on any advantage they may have in production cost.

Money as a Resource

In a very simple economy, barter (the exchange of goods for goods) is an acceptable means of trade. But it requires a double coincidence of wants. A person who has a good to sell, say pigs, must find someone who not only wants that particular good, but wants to give up something the pig

Economists in History: David Ricardo (1772—1823)

Delores T. Martin

At the beginning of the nineteenth century, English economic thought remained much as it had been in the preceding century. Since the publication of Adam Smith's classic treatise *An Inquiry into the Nature and Causes of the Wealth of Nations* (1776), many able economists had developed economic principles and applied them to the social problems of the day. But not until David Ricardo wrote his *Principles of Political Economy and Taxation* (1817) was Smith's classical theory seriously refined and advanced. In that work, Ricardo's great powers of abstraction and synthesis established a standard that permanently altered the method of economic analysis.

Ricardo had little formal education, but considerable native ability. At the age of twenty he became a stock broker; by his mid-twenties he had amassed a large fortune. Ricardo first encountered Smith's *Wealth of Nations* in 1799, while on vacation. Within ten years he was analyzing economic problems in pamphlets and the press. He quickly became one of the most influential economists of his time.

Ricardo was the first of the classical economists to formulate a theory of economic development. He recognized that invention and the formation of capital spurred industrial production. The pursuit of profit thus created seed money for development. Ricardo opposed the taxation of profits, arguing that it drained an economy's capacity for growth.

It was Ricardo's attack on protectionist trade policies that made his reputation. At that time Britain was attempting to export more than it

owner desires—chickens, perhaps. The time the pig farmer spends searching for a compatible trader is time that cannot be spent farming and producing.

Money was developed to make trading more efficient and to reduce the time spent looking for traders. Instead of searching for someone who wants pork and has chickens to sell, a pig farmer can sell his pigs for cash and use the cash to buy chickens. With the time he saves, he can produce more food. Money can serve as a medium of exchange because it is an accepted store of purchasing power. That is, people who want to postpone consumption can leave their money in a safe place, knowing that when they do want to spend it, it will still be valuable. **Money** is any generally accepted medium of exchange or trade that also serves as a store of purchasing power.

Money: any generally accepted medium of exchange or trade that also serves as a store of purchasing power.

Without money, people would have to save for future purchases by holding on to a variety of goods that could be used in trade. Their resources would be tied up in storage and would be unavailable for the production of other goods and services. Money, however, can be used productively while it is being stored for future use. A banker can lend it to someone who needs to buy a new machine, for instance. Thus money frees resources to be used in productive activity. It expands society's production possibilities frontier.

imported in order to accumulate hard currency. An elaborate system of tariffs and quotas supported this strategy. The so-called Corn Laws, for example, severely limited the importation of grain except in times of unusually high prices. But Ricardo demonstrated the mutual benefits of international exchange. His law of comparative advantage became the core of the classical free trade doctrine. "Under a system of perfectly free commerce," he wrote,

each country naturally devotes its capital and labour to such employments as are most beneficial to each. This pursuit of individual advantage is admirably connected with the universal good of the whole. By stimulating industry, by rewarding ingenuity, and by using efficaciously the peculiar powers bestowed by nature, it distributes labour most effectively and most economically: while, by increasing the general mass of produc-

tions, it diffuses general benefit, and binds together in one common tie of interest and intercourse, the universal society of nations throughout the civilized world. It is this principle which determines that wine shall be made in France and Portugal, that corn shall be grown in America and Poland, and that hardware and other goods shall be manufactured in England.[1]

Ricardo's influence on economic theory was enormous. As John Maynard Keynes put it in a biographical sketch, "Ricardo conquered England the way that the Holy Inquisition conquered Spain."[2]

1. David Ricardo, "On Foreign Trade," in *The Principles of Political Economy and Taxation* (Homewood, Ill.: Richard D. Irwin, 1963), pp. 70–71.
2. John Maynard Keynes, *Essays in Biography* (London: Macmillan, 1933), p. 143.

Taking Advantage of Comparative Advantage

One of the benefits of trade is that it allows people to capitalize on any advantages they may have in cost of production. Consider a world in which there are only two people, Fred and Harry. Let's imagine that they live on an island and that they can produce only two goods, coconuts and papayas. The table below shows how much each man can produce. In one hour Fred can produce four coconuts or eight papayas; Harry can produce six coconuts or twenty-four papayas. Harry is more productive than Fred in either case. Yet both can gain by specializing and trading with each other.

	Number of Coconuts Produced per Hour	Number of Papayas Produced per Hour
Fred	4	8
Harry	6	24

To see why, we must look at the relative cost of producing coconuts and papayas. If Fred produces four coconuts, he loses the opportunity to produce eight papayas. In other words, the cost of the four coconuts is eight papayas—or to put it another way, the cost of one coconut is two papayas. Fred would be better off if he could trade one coconut for more than two papayas, because two papayas is what he has to give up to produce the coconut.

From Harry's point of view, the cost of one coconut is four papayas. (To produce six coconuts, Harry has to give up twenty-four papayas.) If Harry could get a coconut for less than four papayas, he would be better off. He could produce four papayas, trade some for a coconut, and have some left over to eat.

The cost of producing coconuts may be summarized as follows:

$$\text{Fred: 1 coconut} = 2 \text{ papayas}$$

$$\text{Harry: 1 coconut} = 4 \text{ papayas}$$

Comparative advantage: a relatively lower cost of production, or the capacity to produce a product at a lower cost than a competitor, in terms of the goods that must be given up.

Fred can produce one coconut at less cost (in terms of the papayas that must be given up) than Harry can. Similarly, one papaya is less costly to produce (in terms of the coconuts that must be given up) for Harry than for Fred. In terms of the relative cost of production, Fred has a comparative advantage in the production of coconuts, and Harry has a comparative advantage in papaya production. A **comparative advantage** is a relatively lower cost of production, or the capacity to produce a product at a lower cost than a competitor, in terms of the goods that must be given up.

If Fred and Harry specialize in the fruits for which they have a comparative advantage and then trade with each other, each will benefit. Remember that Fred would be better off if he could trade one coconut for more than two papayas. Thus if he and Harry agree to an exchange at the rate of one coconut for three papayas, he will obviously benefit. He will produce one coconut, giving up two papayas in the process, but will get three papayas in return from Harry. Harry will also benefit. He can produce four papayas, giving up one coconut in the process, and trade three of those papayas to Fred for one coconut. Harry will end up with the same number of coconuts he would have had if he had produced coconuts instead of papayas, but he will have one papaya as well.

If both Fred and Harry are better off, their total production must have increased. Through specialization and trade Fred and Harry have cut their cost of production and moved closer to their joint production possibilities frontier. They have used scarce resources more efficiently than they would have otherwise.

The Circular Flow of Income

Circular flow of income: the integrated flow of resources, goods, and services between or among broad sectors of the economy, like producers, consumers, and government.

Trade not only enhances people's welfare, but increases their dependence on one another. This interdependence can be illustrated by what is called a circular flow diagram (see Figure 2.5). The **circular flow of income** is the integrated flow of resources, goods, and services between or among broad sectors of the economy, like producers, consumers, and government. In simplified form, this diagram shows the flow of resources, goods, and services between two sectors of the private economy, producers (bottom)

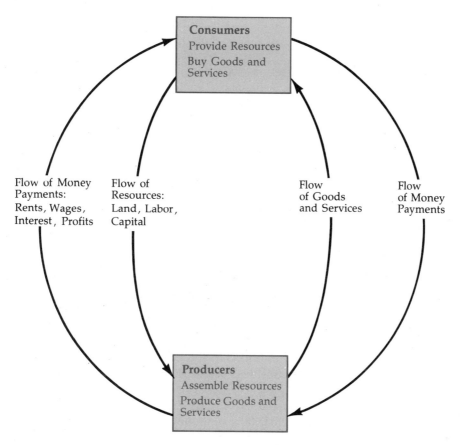

Figure 2.5. The Circular Flow of Income.
Consumers and producers generate opposing flows of resources and money payments for those resources, in the form of wages, rents, interest, and profits (left-hand side). In the same way, they generate opposing flows of goods and services and money payments for those goods and services (right-hand side).

and consumers (top). The consumers have two basic functions: to provide the resources (land, labor, and capital) needed by the producers and to consume the goods and services produced. The producers also have two basic functions: to assemble the necessary resources provided by consumers and to produce the goods and services consumers want. The integrated nature of the economy is symbolized by the arrows that represent the flows of resources, final products, and money payments to and from consumers and producers.

For a barter economy, the diagram would be even simpler. There would be only two arrows, one representing the flow of resources from the consumer to the producer, the other representing the flow of goods and services from the producer back to the consumer. In this primitive economy, the goods on the right-hand side of the diagram would trade for the resources on the left-hand side. The price of labor, for example, would be stated in so many gadgets produced, and the price of gadgets would be stated in so many hours of labor. Such a system would be extremely inefficient, for people would waste a great deal of time searching for beneficial trades.

Though money eases the difficulties of trading, it tends to obscure the interdependence of producers and consumers. When money is used for trade, producers secure their income from particular consumers, not caring whether those consumers work for them or provide them with resources. Laborers secure a money payment for their services from producers, which they use to buy goods from a variety of producers, not necessarily those they work for. Prices are stated in terms of dollars (or pounds sterling, or lira), and people may get the mistaken impression that their incomes are unrelated to production, except in a remote and tenuous way. After all, they don't get paid with the goods they produce.

Yet the two sectors are closely interrelated. The health of the business sector (producers) clearly depends on the expenditures made by the consuming sector. Without that flow of money payments from consumers, producers would be unable to pay for the resources they buy from consumers. Likewise, conditions in the consuming sector depend on the success of firms in the business sector. If the business sector cannot sell its goods and services, producers will not be able to pay workers' salaries. Thus an integrated, money-based trade can multiply the effects of disruptions in trade. If the circular flow of money is interrupted, production may slow, consumption may fall off, and laborers may be thrown out of work. Such interruptions in the circular flow, called recessions, are a subject of considerable concern to macroeconomists.

Figure 2.5 does not reflect the full complexity of the exchange relationships that exist among people. In the real world, the business sector has internal flows of its own. Producers funnel resources to other producers in the form of raw materials and investment goods like machinery. They make payments to each other in the form of money. A more realistic, though still incomplete description of the circular flow is contained in Figure 2.6. Producers have been divided into three representative groups: farmers, millers, and bakers. All three buy certain resources, like labor, from consumers. But in addition, the millers buy their basic resource, wheat, from the farmers, and the bakers buy their basic resource, flour, from the millers.

Actual trading arrangements are extraordinarily complex. Farmers, for example, must buy machinery to produce wheat. Farm equipment producers must buy metal, plastics, and hundreds of other resources to produce the machinery they sell to the farmers. Metal producers must buy equipment to process and finish their product. Both metal producers and equipment manufacturers must have food to live on. Furthermore, all these trades must be handled by a communications and transportation network that can deliver all the resources and products needed to the

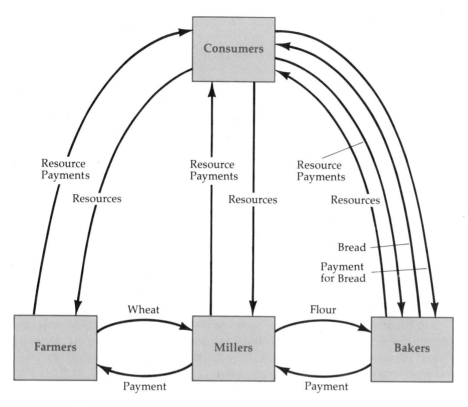

Figure 2.6. The Circular Flow of Income: A More Complicated Model.
Resources (goods and services) and money payments for them flow not just
between consumers and producers, but among producers as well. All producers
buy resources from households with money payments. Farmers, for instance,
receive resources from consumer households, for which they make money payments. But they also sell their wheat to millers, who make flour and sell it to
bakers—who then make bread and sell it to consumers.

appropriate destinations at the appropriate time. And traders must be able
to adjust their relationships to changes in consumer demand.

   Government further complicates the circular flow by drawing off money
in the form of taxes and then injecting it back into the circular flow in the
form of government purchases, for everything from planes to welfare
checks. There is also private saving, which channels purchasing power
through banks to consumers of cars, houses, and furniture and through
stock and bond markets to investors in inventory, plant, and equipment.
It is a wonder that the system works at all. The economy is an extraordinarily
complex web of fragile but productive interrelationships, all formed for
one overriding purpose: to make the most of society's production possibilities, given the inescapable fact of scarcity.

Summary and Extensions

Like scarcity, choice is pervasive. We must choose between a variety of goods and services, between public and private goods, between consumption and investment, and between old and new technology. The choices we make have huge consequences for both the present and the future. Our ability to grow and become more productive tomorrow depends on our willingness to save today. Greater future output does not necessarily imply greater welfare over time, however. Tomorrow's growth may not be worth today's sacrifice, in terms of consumption forgone.

Production possibilities curves can be useful in illustrating these and other choices we must make. But they can easily be misunderstood. The production possibilities curve may suggest that society's choices are more or less apparent: we simply have to plot the curve, observe the options, and choose. For several reasons, our economic difficulties cannot be solved so easily.

First, we lack a great deal of information about what our society can produce at the limit. If we produced only two goods, finding the production possibilities frontier might be relatively simple. But we produce millions of products, requiring many kinds of resources. The tradeoffs among those resources and the goods made from them are extraordinarily complex. Furthermore, we do not know very much about the quantity of existing resources. For instance, we do not know how much labor really exists in total, because we do not know how hard and long people are actually willing to work. The people who interact with one another in the labor market are the ones who know the answer to that question. Social scientists and policymakers may know something about the operation of the economy, but there is a great deal they do not and cannot know.

In short, though production possibilities curves help us to envision the types of choices we must make, the actual options open to us do not result from the curves, but from the economic process. They are the product of the millions of interrelated choices made daily by individuals, groups, and government. Our resources and our choices as to how those resources will be employed determine our production possibilities and our position on the production possibilities curve. In the next chapter we will see how people make choices through the market process and how, through the pricing system, they determine their society's production possibilities.

Major Conclusions

1. A decision to consume goods and services implies a decision to forgo investment goods. Since investment goods are used to produce other goods and services, the level of investment we choose will affect the position of our production possibilities curve in the future. In this way, current and future choices are inextricably related.
2. A decision to produce public goods is a decision to forgo private goods. The production of public goods can shift the future production possibilities curve to the left or right, depending on how those public goods affect people's tendency to produce, work, save, and invest.

3. People have devised a number of ways to improve the productivity of resources in the face of scarcity. They have developed substitute resources, organized to share costs, specialized their labor, and expanded in order to realize economies of scale. They have developed trading relationships based on comparative advantages in cost of production and used money to put idle resources to work. Trade increases production by encouraging the most efficient use of resources.

4. Circular flow diagrams show the economic interdependence of consumers and producers. Producers depend on consumer expenditures, and consumers depend on payment from producers for their land, labor, and capital.

1. What determines the shape and position of a nation's production possibilities curve?

2. Suppose a nation is producing at some point inside the production possibilities curve. If the government implements a policy that moves the nation onto the production frontier, is there a cost to the additional goods produced?

3. Suppose a nation's yearly purchase of investment goods is less than its yearly loss of investment goods through wear and tear. What will happen to the nation's production possibilities curve?

4. Evaluate the following statement: "Greater investment today will enable this nation to produce more in the future. It will reduce the cost of future investment and enable us to grow even faster in the future. Our government should therefore devise a policy that will stimulate business investment."

5. Does a nation's production possibilities curve depend on its distribution of wealth and income? On the existence and distribution of property rights? On the level of taxation and type of tax levied?

6. Suppose that Joan's and Terry's hourly production rates for squashes and turnips are as follows:

Questions to Ponder

Case I	Squashes	Turnips
Joan	10	50
Terry	40	800

Case II	Squashes	Turnips
Joan	20	30
Terry	100	50

For each case, determine who should specialize in producing squashes and then suggest an exchange rate for squashes and turnips that will benefit both Joan and Terry.

Appendix:
Graphic Analysis

Economists often use graphs to illustrate the relationships between and among economic variables. Graphs are pictorial representations of the presumed relationships between or among variables. Graphs can display a great deal of information in a small area; they show at a glance how two or more variables are related.

The Features of Graphs

The major features of a graph are shown in Figure 2.A1. In the lower left-hand corner is the *origin*, the point at which the value of both variables represented in the graph is zero. Extending out from the origin are the horizontal, or *X*, axis (also called the abscissa) and the vertical, or *Y*, axis (also called the ordinate). The relationship among variables is shown graphically by a series of points in the interior of the graph (between the vertical and horizontal axes). The points combine various values scaled along the two axes.

For example, suppose we scale the number of bushels of apples consumers will buy at different prices along the horizontal axis, and the various prices per bushel along the vertical axis. If consumers buy 50 bushels of apples a day when the price of apples is $5 a bushel, that price-quantity combination can be represented by point *a* on the graph. Other price-quantity combinations like *b* and *c* can be plotted and connected to form a line, or curve, like the one in color in the figure.

The Slope of Curves

The curves plotted on a graph can have almost any shape. One important characteristic of their shape is the slope. The *slope* is the ratio of the vertical movement up a curve (sometimes called the "rise") to the corresponding horizontal movement along the curve (also called the "run"). Mathematically, the slope can be expressed as follows:

$$\text{slope} = \frac{\text{rise}}{\text{run}} = \frac{\text{change in } y}{\text{change in } x}$$

Figure 2.A1. Features of a Graph.
The vertical axis of a graph is sometimes called the *Y* axis, or the ordinate. The horizontal axis is called the *X* axis, or the abscissa. The point of intersection of the two axes is called the origin. A series of points inside the graph portray assumed or deduced relationships between the variables on the *X* and *Y* axes, like the price and quantity of apples sold. The line that connects those points is called a curve. The curve shown here has a negative slope (moves downward from left to right).

That is, the slope is equal to the ratio of the change in the value on the vertical axis to the change in the value on the horizontal axis.

The slope can be either positive or negative, depending on which way the curve slants. It is said to be positive when the curve moves up toward the right and negative when it moves down toward the right. Figure 2.A1 shows a curve with a negative slope. As the price per bushel goes down (vertical axis), the number of bushels sold goes up (horizontal axis). This kind of relationship, called an inverse relationship, produces a negative slope. If the price of a bushel of apples falls from $5 to $3 while the quantity consumers purchase rises from 50 to 100 bushels, the slope of

the curve will be $\dfrac{-2}{50}$, or -0.04:

$$\text{slope} = \frac{\text{change in } y}{\text{change in } x} = \frac{P_1 - P_2}{Q_1 - Q_2} = \frac{(\$3 - \$5)}{(100 - 50)} = \frac{-2}{50} = -0.04$$

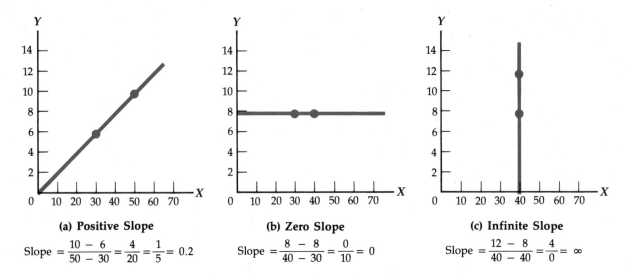

$$\text{Slope} = \frac{10 - 6}{50 - 30} = \frac{4}{20} = \frac{1}{5} = 0.2 \qquad \text{Slope} = \frac{8 - 8}{40 - 30} = \frac{0}{10} = 0 \qquad \text{Slope} = \frac{12 - 8}{40 - 40} = \frac{4}{0} = \infty$$

Figure 2.A2. Curves with Various Slopes.
Curves that move upward from the left to the right—panel (a)—are said to have a positive slope. Curves that are horizontal to the X axis—panel (b)—have a zero slope; curves that are vertical to the X axis—panel (c)—have an infinite slope.

When the change in both x and y is positive, the ratio, or slope, is positive, and the relationship between x and y is said to be direct. The curve slants up toward the right, as in Figure 2.A2(a).

A curve that runs parallel to the horizontal axis has a slope of zero—it has no vertical rise or fall (see Figure 2.A2(b)). When its zero numerator (the rise) is divided by a positive denominator, the result is zero. A curve that runs perpendicular to the horizontal axis has a slope of infinity—even with no horizontal movement, it continues upward indefinitely (see Figure 2.A2(c)). When its positive numerator is divided by a zero denominator, the result is infinity.

Curves with Changing Slopes

Straight curves (sometimes called linear curves) like the ones in Figures 2.A1 and 2.A2 have the same slope at all points. The rise is always the same for any given run, no matter where on the curve it is measured. Thus the ratio of the rise to the run is said to be constant. But not all curves are straight lines. The slope of the curve in Figure 2.A3, for example, is steeper near the origin than at the other end. Because the slope of a curve like this is constantly changing, it must be measured at specific points on the curve.

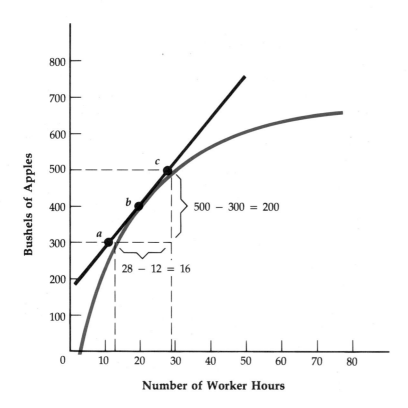

Figure 2.A3. Curves with a Changing Slope.
Because this curve bends downward as it moves from the left up to the right, it is said to have a decreasing positive slope. (Slope at $b = \dfrac{200}{16} = \dfrac{25}{2} = 12.5$)

To obtain the slope at any given point on such a curve, draw a straight line tangent to the curve, as in Figure 2.A3. Measure the rise and the run between any two points on that tangent straight line, and divide the rise by the run. In Figure 2.A3, the rise of the line tangent to point b, measured between points a and c, is 200; the run is 16 ($28 - 12$). Hence the slope is:

$$\frac{200}{16}, \text{ or } \frac{25}{2}.$$

The changing slope of a curve has practical implications. In Figure 2.A3, the rising curve shows the contribution made by additional worker hours to the total output of apples. As the curve rises past point b, its slope becomes progressively flatter. In other words, beyond a certain point, as the number of hours worked grows, each new hour adds less to total output.

The Uses and Misuses of Graphs

A comparison of Table 2.A1 and Figure 2.A4 demonstrates the efficiency of graphs in displaying economic variables. The table and the graph both show a measure of the nation's overall price level, the consumer price index, over time. By scrutinizing the figures in the table, you can determine that the price level rose and fell several times during the nineteenth century, before skyrocketing in the second half of this century. Figure 2.A4 shows the same trend at a glance, however. The dramatic upward surge in prices from 1940 on, visible immediately, shows that inflation is, to a significant extent, a modern phenomenon.

Graphs, like statistics, can be misused. The mere plotting of two variables on a graph does not establish a cause-and-effect relationship between them. For instance, the number of major-league home runs hit each season can be plotted against the annual snowfalls in Rochester, New York—but the resulting curve will make no sense, regardless of its shape and slope. A graph proves nothing about the way in which two variables are influenced by one another. Relationships are established by theory.

Table 2.A1. U.S. Price Level, 1800–1984

Year	CPI[a]	Year	CPI	Year	CPI
1800	51	1865	46	1930	50
1805	45	1870	38	1935	41
1810	47	1875	33	1940	42
1815	55	1880	29	1945	54
1820	42	1885	27	1950	72
1825	34	1890	27	1955	80
1830	32	1895	25	1960	89
1835	31	1900	25	1965	95
1840	30	1905	27	1970	116
1845	28	1910	28	1975	161
1850	25	1915	30	1980	247
1855	28	1920	60	1984	311
1860	27	1925	53		

[a] CPI stands for consumer price index; 1967 = 100.
Sources: U.S. Bureau of the Census, *Historical Statistics of the United States: Colonial Times to 1970* (Washington, D.C.: U.S. Government Printing Office, 1975), pp. 210, 211; *Economic Report of the President* (Washington, D.C.: U.S. Government Printing Office, 1985), p. 291.

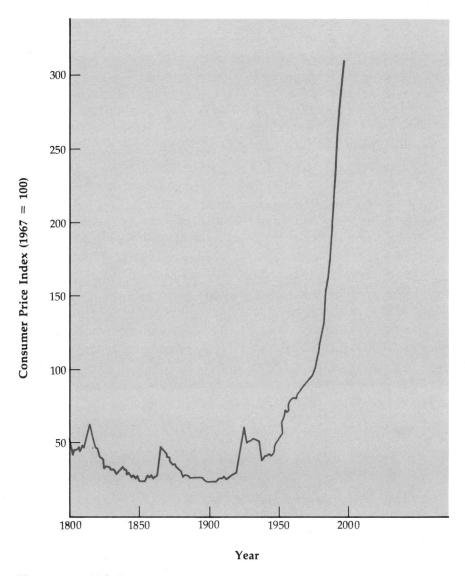

Figure 2.A4. U.S. Price Level, 1880–1984.
The general movement of prices over a long period of time can be shown graphically by plotting the consumer price index (vertical axis) for each year (horizontal axis). At a glance one can see that the price level moved up and down at relatively low levels between 1800 and 1940. Over recent decades, however, it has risen sharply.
Sources: U.S. Bureau of the Census, *Historical Statistics of the United States* (Washington, D.C.: U.S. Government Printing Office, 1975), pp. 210–211; *Economic Report of the President* (Washington, D.C.: U.S. Government Printing Office, 1985), p. 291.

Central Question

How does the competitive market work?

Key Terms

Competition

Perfect competition

Demand

Increase in demand

Decrease in demand

Supply

Increase in supply

Decrease in supply

Market surplus

Equilibrium price

Equilibrium quantity

Market shortage

Efficiency

Price ceiling

Price floor

Short-run equilibrium

Long-run equilibrium

Chapter 3

The Elements of Supply and Demand

Competition, if not prevented, tends to bring about a state of affairs in which: first, *everything will be produced which somebody knows how to produce and which he can sell profitably at a price at which buyers will prefer it to the available alternatives;* second, *everything that is being produced is produced by persons who can do so at least as cheaply as anybody else who in fact is not producing it; and* third, *that everything will be sold at prices lower than, or at least as low as, those at which it could be sold by anybody who in fact does not do so.*
Friedrich Hayek

*I*n the heart of New York City, Fred Lieberman's small grocery is dwarfed by the tall buildings that surround it. Yet it is remarkable for what it accomplishes. Lieberman's carries thousands of items, most of which are not produced locally, and some of which come thousands of miles from other parts of this country or abroad. A man of modest means, with little knowledge of production processes, Fred Lieberman has nevertheless been able to stock his store with many if not most of the foods and toiletries his customers need and want. Occasionally Lieberman's runs out of certain items, but most of the time the stock is ample. Its supply is so dependable that customers tend to take it for granted, forgetting that Lieberman's is one small strand in an extremely complex economic network.

How does Fred Lieberman get the goods he sells, and how does he know which ones to sell and at what price? The simplest answer is that the goods he offers and the prices at which they sell are determined through the market process, the interaction of many buyers and sellers trading what they have (their labor or other resources) for what they want. Lieberman stocks his store by appealing to the private interests of suppliers—by paying them competitive prices. His customers pay him extra for the convenience of purchasing goods in their neighborhood grocery—in the process appealing to his private interests. To determine what he should buy, Fred Lieberman considers his suppliers' prices. To determine what and how much they should buy, his customers consider the prices he charges. The Nobel Prize–winning economist Friedrich Hayek has suggested that the market process is manageable for people like Fred Lieberman precisely because prices condense into usable form a great deal of information, signaling quickly what people want, what goods cost, and what resources are readily available. Prices guide and coordinate the sellers' production decisions and consumers' purchases.

But how are prices determined? In competitive markets, as this chapter describes, prices are established by the forces of supply and demand.

The Competitive Market Process

So far, our discussion of markets and their consequences has been rather casual. In this section we will define precisely such terms as *market* and *competition*. In later sections we will examine the way markets work and learn why, in a limited sense, markets can be considered efficient systems for determining what and how much to produce.

The Market Setting

Most people tend to think of a market as a geographical location—a shopping center, an auction barn, a business district. From an economic perspective, however, it is more useful to think of a market as a process. You may recall from Chapter 1 that a market is defined as the process by which buyers and sellers determine what they are willing to buy and sell, on what terms. That is, it is the process by which buyers and sellers decide the prices and quantities of goods to be bought and sold.

In this process, individual market participants search for information relevant to their own interests. Buyers ask about the models, sizes, colors, and quantities available and the prices they must pay for them. Sellers inquire about the types of goods and services buyers want and the prices they are willing to pay.

This market process is self-correcting. Buyers and sellers routinely revise their plans on the basis of experience. As Israel Kirzner has written:

> The overambitious plans of one period will be replaced by more realistic ones; market opportunities overlooked in one period will be exploited in the next. In other words, even without changes in the basic data of the market (i.e., in consumer tastes, technological possibilities, and resource availabilities), the decisions made in one period of time generate systematic alterations in corresponding decisions for the succeeding period.[1]

The market is made up of people, consumers and entrepreneurs, attempting to buy and sell on the best terms possible. Through the groping process of give and take, they move from relative ignorance about others' wants and needs to a reasonably accurate understanding of how much can be bought and sold and at what price. The market functions as an ongoing information and exchange system.

Competition Among Buyers and Among Sellers

Part and parcel of the market process is the concept of competition. **Competition** is the process by which market participants, in pursuing their own interests, attempt to outdo, outprice, outproduce, and outmaneuver each other. By extension, competition is also the process by which market participants attempt to avoid being outdone, outpriced, outproduced, or outmaneuvered by others.

Competition does not occur between buyer and seller, but among buyers or among sellers. Buyers compete with other buyers for the limited number of goods on the market. To compete, they must discover what other buyers are bidding and offer the seller better terms—a higher price or the same price for a lower-quality product. Sellers compete with other sellers for the consumer's dollar. They must learn what their rivals are doing and attempt to do it better or differently—to lower the price or enhance the product's appeal.

This kind of competition stimulates the exchange of information, forcing competitors to reveal their plans to prospective buyers or sellers. The exchange of information can be seen clearly at auctions. Before the bidding begins, buyers look over the merchandise and the other buyers, attempting to determine how high others might be willing to bid for a particular piece. During the auction, this specific information is revealed as buyers call out their bids and others try to top them. Information exchange is less apparent

Competition: the process by which market participants, in pursuing their own interests, attempt to outdo, outprice, outproduce, and outmaneuver each other.

---

1. Israel Kirzner, *Competition and Entrepreneurship* (Chicago: University of Chicago Press, 1973), p. 10.

in department stores, where competition is often restricted. Even there, however, comparison shopping will often reveal some sellers who are offering lower prices in an attempt to attract consumers.

In competing with each other, sellers reveal information that is ultimately of use to buyers, and vice versa. From the consumer's point of view,

The function of competition is here precisely to teach us *who* will serve us well: which grocer or travel agent, which department store or hotel, which doctor or solicitor, we can expect to provide the most satisfactory solution for whatever particular personal problem we may have to face.[2]

From the seller's point of view—say the auctioneer's—competition among buyers brings the highest prices possible.

Competition among sellers takes many forms, including the price, quality, weight, volume, color, texture, power, durability, and smell of products, as well as the credit terms offered to buyers. Sellers also compete for consumers' attention by appealing to their hunger and sex drives or their fear of death, pain, and loud noises. All these forms of competition can be divided into two basic categories, price and nonprice competition. Price competition is of particular interest to economists, who see it as an important source of information for market participants, a coordinating force that brings the quantity produced into line with the quantity consumers are willing and able to buy. In the following sections, we will construct a model of the competitive market and use it to explore the process of price competition. Nonprice competition will be covered in a later section.

Supply and Demand: A Market Model

Perfect competition: a market composed of numerous sellers and buyers of an identical product, such that no one individual or buyer has the ability to affect the market price by changing the production level. Entry into and exit from a perfectly competitive market is unrestricted.

A fully competitive market is made up of many buyers and sellers searching for opportunities or ready to enter the market when opportunities arise. To be described as competitive, therefore, a market must include a significant number of actual or potential competitors. A fully competitive market offers freedom of entry: there are no legal or economic barriers to producing and selling goods in the market.

Our market model assumes perfect competition, an ideal situation that is seldom, if ever, achieved in real life but that will simplify our calculations. **Perfect competition** is a market composed of numerous sellers and buyers of an identical product, such that no one individual seller or buyer has the ability to affect the market price by changing the production level. Entry into and exit from a perfectly competitive market is unrestricted. Producers can start up or shut down production at will. Anyone can enter the market, duplicate the good, and compete for consumers' dollars. Since each competitor produces only a small share of the total output, the individual competitor cannot significantly influence the degree of competition or the market price by entering or leaving the market.

---

2. Friedrich H. Hayek, ''The Meaning of Competition,'' *Individualism and Economic Order* (Chicago: University of Chicago Press, 1948), p. 97.

This kind of market is well suited to graphic analysis. Our discussion will concentrate on how buyers and sellers interact to determine the price of tomatoes, a product Mr. Lieberman almost always carries. It will employ two curves. The first represents buyers' behavior, which is called their demand for the product.

The Elements of Demand

To the general public, demand is simply what people want. But to economists, demand has a much more technical meaning. **Demand** is the assumed inverse relationship between the price of a good or service and the quantity consumers are willing and able to buy during a given period, all other things held constant.

Demand as a Relationship

The relationship between price and quantity is normally assumed to be inverse. That is, when the price of a good rises, the quantity sold, *ceteris paribus* (Latin for "everything else held constant"), will go down. Conversely, when the price of a good falls, the quantity sold goes up. Demand is not a quantity, but a relationship. A given quantity sold at a particular price is properly called *quantity demanded.*

Both tables and graphs can be used to describe the assumed inverse relationship between price and quantity.

Demand as a Table or a Graph

Demand may be thought of as a schedule of the various quantities of a particular good consumers will buy at various prices. As the price goes down, the quantity purchased goes up, and vice versa. Table 3.1 contains a hypothetical schedule of the demand for tomatoes in the New York area during a typical week. The middle column shows prices that might be charged. The right-hand column shows the number of bushels consumers will buy at those prices. Note that as the price rises from zero to $11 a bushel, the number of bushels purchased drops from 110,000 to zero.

Demand may also be thought of as a curve. If price is scaled on a graph's vertical axis and quantity on the horizontal axis, the demand curve has a negative slope (downward and to the right), reflecting the assumed inverse relationship between price and quantity. The general shape of the demand curve is shown in Figure 3.1, which is based on the data from Table 3.1. Points *a* through *l* on the graph correspond to the price-quantity combinations A through L in the table. Note that as the price falls from P_2 ($8) to P_1 ($5), consumers move down their demand curve from a quantity of Q_1 (30) to the larger quantity Q_2 (60).[3]

---

3. Mathematically, the demand relationship may be stated as $Q_d = a - bP$, where Q_d is the quantity demanded at each and every price; *a* is the quantity consumers will buy when the price is zero; *b* is the slope of the demand curve; and *P* is the price of the good. Thus the demand for tomatoes described in Table 3.1 and Figure 3.1 may be written as $Q_d = 110,000 - 10,000\,P$.

Demand: the assumed inverse relationship between the price of a good or service and the quantity consumers are willing and able to buy during a given period, all other things held constant.

Table 3.1. Demand for Tomatoes

Price–Quantity Combinations	Price per Bushel	Number of Bushels
A	$ 0	110,000
B	1	100,000
C	2	90,000
D	3	80,000
E	4	70,000
F	5	60,000
G	6	50,000
H	7	40,000
I	8	30,000
J	9	20,000
K	10	10,000
L	11	0

The Slope and Determinants of Demand

Price and quantity are assumed to be inversely related for two reasons.

First, as the price of a good decreases (and the prices of all other goods stay the same—remember *ceteris paribus*), the purchasing power of consumer incomes rises. More consumers are able to buy the good, and many will buy more of most goods. (This response is called the income effect.)

In addition, as the price of a good decreases (and the prices of all other goods remain the same), the good becomes relatively cheaper, and consumers will substitute that good for others. (This response is called the substitution effect.)

In sum, when the price of tomatoes (or razorblades, or any other good) falls, more tomatoes will be purchased, because more people will be buying them for more purposes.

Although price is an important part of the definition of demand, it is not the only determinant of how much of a good people will want. It may not even be the most important. The major nonprice factors that affect demand are called determinants of demand. They are:

consumer tastes or preferences

the prices of other goods

consumer incomes

number of consumers

expectations concerning future prices and incomes

A host of other factors, like weather, may also influence the demand for particular goods—ice cream, for instance.

Figure 3.1. Demand for Tomatoes.
Demand, the assumed inverse relationship between price and quantity purchased, can be represented by a curve that slopes down toward the right. Here, as the price falls from $11 to zero, the number of bushels of tomatoes purchased per week rises from zero to 110,000.

A change in any of these determinants of demand will cause either an increase or a decrease in demand. An **increase in demand** is an increase in the quantity demanded at each and every price. It is represented graphically by a rightward, or outward, shift in the demand curve. A **decrease in demand** is a decrease in the quantity demanded at each and every price. It is represented graphically by a leftward, or inward, shift of the demand curve. Figure 3.2 illustrates the shifts in the demand curve that result from a change in one of the determinants of demand. The outward shift from D_1 to D_2 indicates an increase in demand: consumers now want more of a good at each and every price. For example, they want Q_3 instead of Q_2 tomatoes at price P_2. Consumers are also willing to pay a higher price now for any quantity. For example, they will pay P_3 instead of P_2 for Q_2 tomatoes. The inward shift from D_1 to D_3 indicates a decrease in demand: consumers want less of a good at each and every price—Q_1 instead of Q_2 tomatoes at price P_2. And they are willing to pay less than before for any quantity—P_1 instead of P_2 for Q_2 tomatoes.

A change in a determinant of demand may be translated into an increase or decrease in demand in numerous ways. An increase in demand can be caused by:

An increase in consumers' desire for the good. If people truly want the good more, they will buy more of the good at any given price, or pay a higher price for any given quantity.

Increase in demand: an increase in the quantity demanded at each and every price, represented graphically by a rightward, or outward, shift in the demand curve.

Decrease in demand: a decrease in the quantity demanded at each and every price, represented graphically by a leftward, or inward, shift of the demand curve.

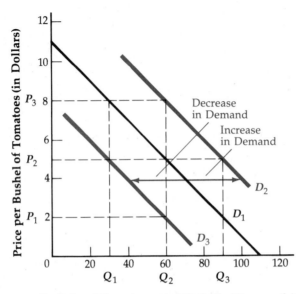

Figure 3.2. Shifts in the Demand Curve.
An increase in demand is represented by a rightward, or outward, shift in the demand curve, from D_1 to D_2. A decrease in demand is represented by a leftward, or inward, shift in the demand curve, from D_1 to D_3.

An increase in the number of buyers. If more people will buy the good at any given price, they will also pay a higher price for any given quantity.

An increase in the price of substitute goods (which can be used in place of the good in question). If the price of oranges increases, the demand for grapefruit will increase.

A decrease in the price of complement goods (which are used in conjunction with the good in question). If the price of records or tapes falls, the demand for stereo systems will rise.

Generally speaking (but not always), an increase in consumer incomes. An increase in people's incomes may increase the demand for luxury goods, such as new cars. But it may also decrease demand for low-quality goods (like hamburger) because people can now afford better-quality products (like steak).

An expected increase in the future price of the good in question. If people expect the price of cars to rise faster than the prices of other goods, then (depending on exactly when they expect the increase) they may buy more cars now, thus avoiding the expected additional cost in the future.

An expected decrease in the future price of a substitute good. If people expect the price of oranges to fall in the future, then (depending on exactly when they expect the price decrease) they may reduce their current demand for grapefruit, so they can buy more oranges in the future.

An expected increase in future incomes of buyers. College seniors' demand for cars tends to increase as graduation approaches and they anticipate a rise in income.

The determinants of a decrease in demand are just the opposite:

A decrease in consumers' desire or taste for the good.

A decrease in the number of buyers.

A decrease in the price of substitute goods.

An increase in the price of complement goods.

Generally speaking (but not always), a decrease in consumer incomes.

An expected decrease in the future price of the good in question.

An expected decrease in the future price of a substitute good.

An expected decrease in future incomes of buyers.

The Elements of Supply

On the other side of the market are producers of goods. The average person thinks of supply as the quantity of a good producers are willing to sell. But to economists, supply means something quite different. **Supply** is the assumed relationship between the quantity of a good producers are willing to offer during a given period and the price, all else being equal. Generally, because managerial costs tend to rise with expanded production, this relationship is presumed to be positive. Like demand, supply is not a given quantity—that is called quantity supplied. Rather it is a relationship between price and quantity. As the price of a good rises, producers are generally willing to offer a larger quantity. The reverse is equally true: as price decreases, so does quantity supplied. Like demand, supply can also be described in a table or a graph.

Supply: the assumed relationship between the quantity of a good producers are willing and able to offer during a given period and the price, everything else held constant.

Supply as a Table or a Graph

Supply may be described as a schedule of the quantities producers will offer at various prices during a given period of time. Table 3.2 shows such a supply schedule. As the price of tomatoes goes up from zero to $11 a bushel, the quantity offered rises from zero to 110,000, reflecting the assumed positive relationship between price and quantity.

Supply may also be thought of as a curve. If the quantity producers will offer is scaled on the horizontal axis of a graph and the price of the good is scaled on the vertical axis, the supply curve will slope upward to the right, reflecting the assumed positive relationship between price and

Table 3.2. Supply of Tomatoes

Price–Quantity Combination	Price per Bushel	Number of Bushels
A	0	0
B	1	10
C	2	20
D	3	30
E	4	40
F	5	50
G	6	60
H	7	70
I	8	80
J	9	90
K	10	100
L	11	110

quantity. In Figure 3.3, which was plotted from the data in Table 3.2, points *a* through *l* represent the price-quantity combinations *A* through *L*. Note how a change in the price causes a movement along the supply curve.[4]

The Slope and Determinants of Supply

The quantity producers will offer on the market depends on their production costs. Obviously the total cost of production will rise when more is produced, since more resources will be required to expand output. But the additional or marginal cost of each additional bushel produced also tends to rise as total output expands. In other words, it costs more to produce the second bushel of tomatoes than the first, and more to produce the third than the second. Firms will not expand their output unless they can cover their higher unit costs with a higher price. This is the reason the supply curve is thought to slope upward.

Anything that affects production costs will influence supply and the position of the supply curve. Such factors, which are called determinants of supply, include:

A change in productivity due to a change in technology.

A change in the profitability of producing other goods.

A change in the scarcity of various production resources.

---

4. Mathematically, the supply relationship may be stated as $Q_s = a + bP$, where Q_s is the quantity supplied; a is the quantity producers will supply when the price is zero; b is the slope; and P is the price. Thus the supply of tomatoes represented in Table 3.3 and Figure 3.3 may be written $Q_s = 0 + 10,000\,P$.

Figure 3.3. Supply of Tomatoes.
Supply, the assumed relationship between price and quantity produced, can be represented by a curve that slopes up toward the right. Here, as the price rises from zero to $11, the number of bushels of tomatoes offered for sale during the course of a week rises from zero to 110,000.

Many other factors, such as weather, can also affect production costs. A change in any of these determinants of supply can either increase or decrease supply. An **increase in supply** is an increase in the quantity producers are willing and able to offer at each and every price. It is represented graphically by a rightward, or outward, shift in the supply curve. A **decrease in supply** is a decrease in the quantity producers are willing and able to offer at each and every price. It is represented graphically by a leftward, or inward, shift of the supply curve.

In Figure 3.4, an increase in supply is represented by the shift from S_1 to S_2. Producers are willing to produce a larger quantity at each price—Q_3 instead of Q_2 at price P_2, for example. They will also accept a lower price for each quantity—P_1 instead of P_2 for quantity Q_2. Conversely, the decrease in supply represented by the shift from S_1 to S_3 means that producers will offer less at each price—Q_1 instead of Q_2 at price P_2. They must also have a higher price for each quantity—P_3 instead of P_2 for quantity Q_2.

A few examples will illustrate the impact of changes in the determinants of supply. If firms learn how to produce more goods with the same or fewer resources, the cost of producing any given quantity will fall. Because of the technological improvement, firms will be able to offer a larger quantity at any given price, or the same quantity at a lower price. The supply will increase, shifting the supply curve outward to the right.

Increase in supply: an increase in the quantity producers are willing and able to offer at each and every price, represented graphically by a rightward, or outward, shift in the supply curve.

Decrease in supply: a decrease in the quantity producers are willing and able to offer at each and every price, represented graphically by a leftward, or inward, shift of the supply curve.

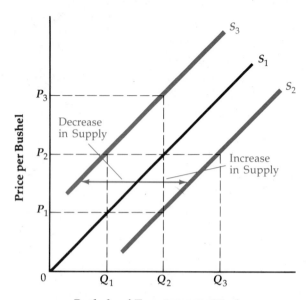

Figure 3.4. Shifts in the Supply Curve.
A rightward, or outward, shift in the supply curve, from S_1 to S_2, represents an increase in supply. A leftward, or inward, shift in the supply curve, from S_1 to S_3, represents a decrease in supply.

Similarly, if the profitability of producing oranges increases relative to grapefruit, grapefruit producers will shift their resources to oranges. The supply of oranges will increase, shifting the supply curve to the right. Finally, if lumber (or labor or equipment) becomes scarcer, its price will rise, increasing the cost of new housing and reducing the supply. The supply curve will shift inward to the left.

Market Equilibrium

Supply and demand represent the two sides of the market, sellers and buyers. By plotting the supply and demand curves together, as in Figure 3.5, we can predict how buyers and sellers will interact with one another. At any price other than the one at the intersection of the two curves, the desires of buyers and sellers will be inconsistent, and a market surplus or shortage of tomatoes will result.

Market Surpluses

Suppose that the price of a bushel of tomatoes is $9, or P_2 in Figure 3.5. At this price the quantity demanded by consumers is 20,000 bushels, much less than the quantity offered by producers, 90,000. There is a market surplus, or excess supply, of 70,000 bushels. A **market surplus** is the

Market surplus: the amount by which the quantity supplied exceeds the quantity demanded at a given price. Graphically, the excess supply that occurs at any price above the intersection of the supply and demand curves.

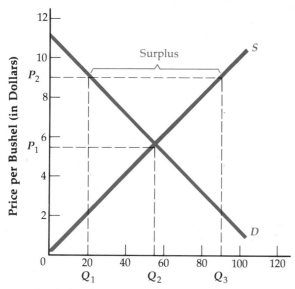

Bushels of Tomatoes per Week (in Thousands)

Figure 3.5. Market Surplus.
If a price is higher than the intersection of the supply and demand curves, a market surplus—a greater quantity supplied, Q_3, than demanded, Q_1—results. Competitive pressure will push the price down to the equilibrium price P_1, the price at which the quantity supplied equals the quantity demanded (Q_2).

amount by which the quantity supplied exceeds the quantity demanded at any given price. Graphically, it is the excess supply that occurs at any price above the intersection of the supply and demand curves.

What will happen in this situation? Producers who cannot sell their tomatoes will have to compete by offering to sell at a lower price, forcing other producers to follow suit. As the competitive process forces the price down, the quantity consumers are willing to buy will expand, while the quantity producers are willing to sell will decrease. The result will be a contraction of the surplus, until it is finally eliminated at a price of $5.50 or P_1 (at the intersection of the two curves). At that price, producers will be selling all they want to; they will see no reason to lower prices further. Similarly, consumers will see no reason to pay more; they will be buying all they want. This point, where the wants of buyers and sellers intersect, is called the equilibrium price. The **equilibrium price** is the price toward which a competitive market will move, and at which it will remain once there, everything else held constant. It is the price at which the market "clears"—that is, at which the quantity demanded by consumers is matched exactly by the quantity offered by producers. At the equilibrium price, the quantities desired by buyers and sellers are also equal. This is the equilibrium quantity. The **equilibrium quantity** is the output (or sales) level toward which the market will move, and at which it will remain once there, everything else held constant.

Equilibrium price: the price toward which a competitive market will move, and at which it will remain once there, everything else held constant. The price at which the market "clears"—that is, at which the quantity demanded by consumers is matched exactly by the quantity offered by producers.

Equilibrium quantity: the output (or sales) level toward which the market will move, and at which it will remain once there, everything else held constant. Reached when the quantity demanded equals the quantity supplied (at the equilibrium price).

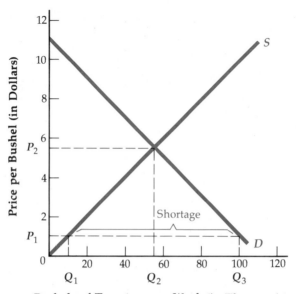

Bushels of Tomatoes per Week (in Thousands)

Figure 3.6. Market Shortage.
A price that is below the intersection of the supply and demand curves will create a shortage—a greater quantity demanded, Q_3, than supplied, Q_1. Competitive pressure will push the price up to the equilibrium price P_2, the price at which the quantity supplied equals the quantity demanded.

In sum, a surplus emerges when the price asked is above the equilibrium price. It will be eliminated, through competition among sellers, when the price drops to the equilibrium price.

Market Shortages

Market shortage: the amount by which the quantity demanded exceeds the quantity supplied at a given price. Graphically, the shortfall in supply that occurs at any price below the intersection of the supply and demand curves.

Suppose the price asked is below the equilibrium price, as in Figure 3.6. At the relatively low price of $1, or P_1, buyers want to purchase 100,000 bushels—substantially more than the 10,000 bushels producers are willing to offer. The result is a market shortage. A **market shortage** is the amount by which the quantity demanded exceeds the quantity supplied at any given price. Graphically, it is the shortfall that occurs at any price below the intersection of the supply and demand curves.

As with a market surplus, competition will correct the discrepancy between buyers' and sellers' plans. Buyers who want tomatoes but are unable to get them at a price of $1 will bid higher prices, as at an auction. As the price rises, a larger quantity will be supplied, because suppliers will be better able to cover their increasing production costs. At the same time the quantity demanded will contract as buyers seek substitutes that are now relatively less expensive compared with tomatoes. At the equilibrium price of $5.50, or P_2, the market shortage will be eliminated. Buyers will have no reason to bid prices up further, for they will be getting all the tomatoes they want at that price. Sellers will have no reason to expand production further; they will be selling all they want to at that price. The equilibrium price will remain the same until some force shifts the position of either the supply or the demand curve. If such a shift occurs, the price will move toward a new equilibrium at the new intersection of the supply and demand curves.

The Effect of Changes in Demand and Supply

Figure 3.7 shows the effects of shifts in demand and supply on the equilibrium price and quantity. In panel (a), an increase in demand from D_1 to D_2 raises the equilibrium price from P_1 to P_2 and quantity from Q_1 to Q_2. In panel (b), a decrease in demand from D_1 to D_2 has the opposite effect, lowering price from P_2 to P_1 and quantity from Q_2 to Q_1.

An increase in supply from S_1 to S_2—panel (c)—has a different effect. The equilibrium quantity rises from Q_1 to Q_2, but the equilibrium price falls from P_2 to P_1. A decrease in supply from S_1 to S_2—panel (d)—causes the opposite effect: the equilibrium quantity falls from Q_2 to Q_1, and the equilibrium price rises from P_1 to P_2.

The Efficiency of the Competitive Market Model

Early in this chapter we asked how Fred Lieberman knows what prices to charge for the goods he sells. The answer is now apparent: he adjusts his prices until his customers buy the quantities that he wants to sell. If he cannot sell all the fruits and vegetables he has, he lowers his price to attract customers and cuts back on his orders for those goods. If he runs short, he knows he can raise his prices and increase his orders. His customers then adjust their purchases accordingly. Similar actions by other producers and customers all over the city move the market for produce toward equilibrium. And the information provided by the orders, reorders, and cancellations from stores like Lieberman's eventually reach the suppliers of goods and then the suppliers of resources. Similarly wholesale prices give Fred Lieberman information on suppliers' costs of production and the relative scarcity and productivity of resources.

The use of the competitive market system to determine what and how much to produce has two advantages. First, it is tolerably accurate. Much of the time the amount produced in a competitive market system tends to equal the amount consumers want—no more, no less. Second, the market system maximizes output.

In Figure 3.8(a), note that all price-quantity combinations acceptable to consumers lie either on or below the market demand curve, in the shaded area. (If consumers are willing to pay P_2 for Q_1 then they should also be willing to pay less for that quantity—for example, P_1.) Furthermore, all price-quantity combinations acceptable to producers lie either on or above the supply curve, in the shaded area shown in Figure 3.7(b). (If producers are willing to accept P_1 for quantity Q_1, then they should also be willing to accept a higher price—for example, P_2). When supply and demand

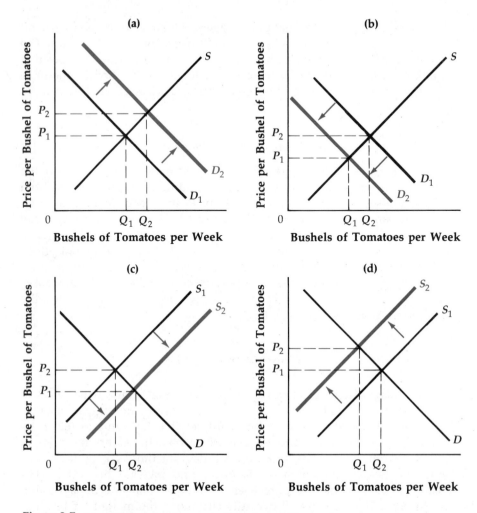

Figure 3.7. The Effects of Changes in Supply and Demand.
An increase in demand—panel (a)—raises both the equilibrium price and the equilibrium quantity. A decrease in demand—panel (b)—has the opposite effect: a decrease in the equilibrium price and quantity. An increase in supply—panel (c)—causes the equilibrium quantity to rise but the equilibrium price to fall. A decrease in supply—panel (d)—has the opposite effect: a rise in the equilibrium price and a fall in the equilibrium quantity.

Efficiency: the maximization of output through careful allocation of resources, given the constraints of supply (producers' costs) and demand (consumers' preferences).

curves are combined in Figure 3.8(c), we see that all price-quantity combinations acceptable to both consumers and producers lie in the darkest shaded triangular area. From all those acceptable output levels, the competitive market produces Q_1, the maximum output level that can be produced given what producers and consumers are willing and able to do. In this respect, the competitive market can be said to be efficient, or to allocate resources efficiently. **Efficiency** is the maximization of output through careful allocation of resources, given the constraints of supply

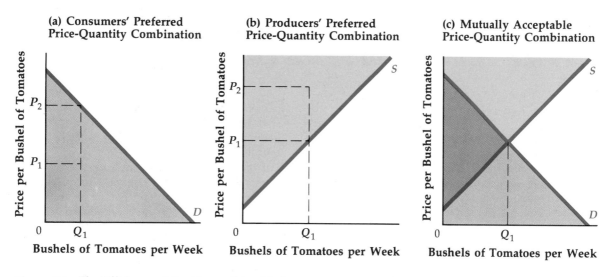

Figure 3.8. The Efficiency of the Competitive Market.
Only those price-quantity combinations on or below the demand curve—panel
(a)—are acceptable to buyers. But only those price-quantity combinations on or
above the supply curve—panel (b)—are acceptable to producers. Those price-
quantity combinations that are acceptable to both buyers and producers are shown
in the darkest shaded area of panel (c). The competitive market is efficient in the
sense that it results in output Q_1, the maximum output level acceptable to both
buyers and producers.

(producers' costs) and demand (consumers' preferences). The achievement
of efficiency means that consumers' or producers' welfare will be reduced
by an expansion or contraction of output.

The market system exploits all possible trades between buyers and
sellers. Up to the equilibrium quantity, buyers will pay more than suppliers
require (those points on the demand curve lie above the supply curve).
Beyond Q_1, buyers will not pay as much as suppliers need to produce
more (those points on the supply curve lie above the demand curve).
Again the market can be called efficient.

Nonprice Competition

Markets in which suppliers compete solely in terms of price are relatively
rare. Table salt is a relatively uniform commodity sold in a market in
which price is an important competitive tool. But even producers of salt
compete in terms of real or imagined quality differences and the reputation
and recognition of brand names. In most industries, competition is through
a wide range of product features, such as quality or the appearance of it,
design, and durability. In general, competitors can be expected to choose
the mix of features that gives them the greatest profit.

Perspectives in Economics: Price Floors and Price Ceilings

Political leaders have occasionally objected to the prices charged in open, competitive markets and have mandated the prices at which goods must be sold. That is, the government has enforced price ceilings and price floors. A **price ceiling** is a government-determined price above which a specified good cannot be sold. A **price floor** is a government-determined price below which a specified good cannot be sold. Supply and demand graphs can illustrate the consequences of price ceilings and floors. For example, some cities impose ceilings on the rents (or prices) for apartments. Such a ceiling must be below the equilibrium price—somewhere below P_1 in Figure 3.9(a). (If the ceiling were above equilibrium, it would be above the market price and would serve no purpose.) As the graph shows, such a price control creates a market shortage. The number of people wanting apartments, Q_2, is greater than the number of apartments available, Q_1. Because of the shortage, landlords will be less concerned about maintaining their units, for they will be able to rent them in any case.

If the government imposes a price *floor*—on a commodity like milk, for example—the price must be above the equilibrium price, P_1 in Figure 3.9(b). (A price floor below P_1 would be irrelevant, because the market would clear at a higher level on its own.) The result of such a price edict is a market surplus. Producers want to sell more milk, Q_2, than consumers are willing to buy, Q_1. Some producers—those caught holding the surplus $(Q_2 - Q_1)$—will be unable to sell all they want to sell. Eventually someone must bear the cost of destroying or storing the surplus—and in fact the government holds vast quantities of grain, cotton, and dairy products because of its past efforts to support an equilibrium price for those products.

In fact, price competition is not always the best method of competition, not only because price reductions mean lower average revenues, but because the reductions can be costly to communicate to consumers. Advertising is expensive, and consumers may not notice price reductions as readily as they do improvements in quality. Quality changes, furthermore, are not so easily duplicated as price changes. Consumers' preferences for quality over price should be reflected in the profitability of making such improvements. If consumers prefer a top-of-the-line calculator to a cheaper basic model, then producing the more sophisticated model could, depending on the cost of the extra features, be more profitable than producing the basic model and communicating its lower price to consumers.

If all consumers had exactly the same preferences—size, color, and so on—producers would presumably make uniform products and compete through price alone. But for most products, people's preferences differ. To keep the analysis manageable, we will explore nonprice competition in terms of just one feature, product size. Suppose that in the market for television sets, consumer preferences are distributed along the continuum shown in Figure 3.10. The curve is bell shaped, indicating that most

(a) Price Ceiling

(b) Price Floor

Figure 3.9. Price Ceilings and Floors.
A price ceiling P_c—panel (a)—will create a market shortage equal to $Q_2 - Q_1$. A price floor P_f—
panel (b)—will create a market surplus equal to
$Q_2 - Q_1$.

consumers are clustered in the middle of the distribution and want a
middle-sized television. Fewer consumers want a giant screen or a mini-
television.

Everything else being equal, the first producer to enter the market,
Terrific TV, will probably offer a product that falls somewhere in the
middle of the distribution—for example, at T in Figure 3.10. In this way,
Terrific TV offers a product that reflects the preferences of the largest
number of people. Furthermore, as long as there are no competitors, the
firm can expect to pick up customers to the left and right of center. (Terrific
TV's product may not come very close to satisfying the wants of consumers
who prefer a very large or very small television, but it is the only one
available.) The more Terrific TV can meet the preferences of the greatest
number of consumers, everything else being equal, the higher the price it
can charge and the greater the profit it can make. (Because consumers
value the product more highly, they will pay a higher price for it.)

The first few competitors that enter the market may also locate close to
the center—in fact, several may virtually duplicate Terrific TV's product.
These firms may conclude that they will enjoy a larger market by sharing

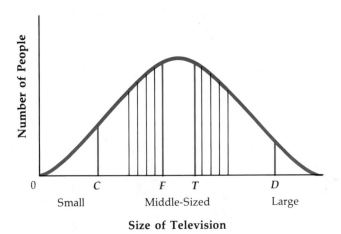

Figure 3.10. Consumer Preference in Television Size.
Consumers differ in their wants, but most desire a medium-sized television. Only a few want very small or large televisions.

the center with several competitors than by moving out into the wings of the distribution. And they are probably right. Though they may be able to charge more for a giant screen or a mini-television that closely reflects some consumers' preferences, there are fewer potential customers for those products.

To illustrate, assume that competitor Fabulous Focus locates at F, close to T. It can then appeal to consumers on the left side of the curve, because its product will reflect those consumers' preferences more closely than does Terrific TV's. Terrific TV can still appeal to consumers on the right half of the curve. If Fabulous Focus had located at C, however, it would have direct appeal only to consumers to the left of C, as well as to a few between C and T. Terrific TV would have appealed to more of the consumers on the left, between C and T, than in the first case. In short, Fabulous Focus has a larger potential market at F than at C.

However, as more competitors move into the market, the center will become so crowded that new competitors will find it advantageous to move away from the center, to C or D. At those points the market will not be as large as it is in the center, but competition will be less intense. If producers do not have to compete directly with as many competitors, they can charge higher prices. How far out into the wings they move will depend on the tradeoffs they must make between the number of customers they can appeal to and the price they can charge.

Like price reductions, the movement of competitors into the wings of the distribution benefits consumers whose tastes differ from those of the people in the middle. These atypical consumers now have a product that comes closer to or even directly reflects their preferences.

Our discussion has assumed free entry into the market. If entry is restricted by monopoly of a strategic resource or by government regulation, the variety of products offered will not be as great as in an open, competitive market. If there are only two or three competitors in a market, everything else being equal, we would expect them to cluster in the middle of a bell-shaped distribution. That tendency has been seen in the past in the broadcasting industry, when the number of television stations permitted in a given geographical area was strictly regulated by the Federal Communications Commission. Not surprisingly, stations carried programs that appealed predominantly to a mass audience—that is, to the middle of the distribution of television watchers. The Public Broadcasting System, PBS, was organized by the government partly to provide programs with less than mass appeal to satisfy viewers on the outer sections of the curve. When cable television companies were permitted to break into local television markets, television programs became more varied.

Even with free market entry, product variety depends on the cost of production and the prices people will pay for variations. Magazine and newsstand operators would behave very much like past television managers if they could carry only two or three magazines. They would choose *Newsweek* or some other magazine that appeals to the largest number of people. Most motel operators, for instance, have room for only a very small newsstand, and so they tend to carry the mass-circulation weeklies and monthlies.

For their own reasons, consumers may also prefer such a compromise. Though they may desire a product that perfectly reflects their tastes, they may buy a product that is not perfectly suitable if they can get it at a lower price. Producers can offer such a product at a lower price because of the economies of scale gained from selling to a large market. For example, most students take predesigned classes in large lecture halls instead of private tutorials. They do so largely because the mass lecture, although perhaps less effective, is substantially cheaper. In a market that is open to entry, producers will take advantage of such opportunities.

If producers in one part of a distribution attempt to charge a higher price than necessary, other producers can move into that segment of the market and push the price down; or consumers can switch to other products. In this way, an optimal variety of products will eventually emerge in a free, reasonably competitive market. Thus the argument for a free market is an argument for the optimal product mix. Without freedom of entry, we cannot tell whether it is possible to improve on the existing combination of products. A free, competitive market gives rival firms a chance to better that combination.

The case for the free market becomes even stronger when we recognize that market conditions—and therefore the optimal product mix—are constantly changing.

Competition in the Short Run and the Long Run

One of the best examples of the workings of both price and nonprice competition is the market for hand calculators. Since the first model was introduced in the United States in 1969, the growth in sales, advancement in technology and design, and decline in prices in this market have been spectacular. The early calculators were simple—some did not even have a division key—and bulky by today's standards. By 1976 they had shrunk from the size of a large paperback book to a tiny two by three-and-a-half inches for one model, and sales exceeded 16 million.

While quality improved, prices fell. The first calculator, which Hewlett-Packard sold for $395, had an eight-digit display and performed only four basic functions, addition, subtraction, division, and multiplication. By December 1971, Bowmar was offering an eight-digit, four-function model for $240. The next year, in an attempt to maintain its high prices, Hewlett-Packard introduced a sophisticated model that could perform many more functions, still for $395. But by the end of the year, Bowmar, Sears, and other firms had broken the $100 barrier, and firms were offering built-in memories, AC adapters, and 1,500-hour batteries to shore up prices. At the year's end, Casio announced a basic model for $59.95.

In 1973 prices continued to fall. By the end of the year, National Semiconductor was offering a six-digit, four-function model for $29.95, and Hewlett-Packard had lowered the price of its special model by $100 and added extra features. In 1974, six-digit, four-function models sold for as little as $16.95. Eight-digit models that would have sold for over $300 three or four years earlier carried price tags of $19.95. By 1976, consumers could buy a six-digit model for just $6.95. All this happened during a period when prices in general rose at a rate unprecedented in the United States during peacetime. Thus the relative prices of calculators fell by even more than their dramatic price reductions suggest.

Yet the drop in the price of calculators was to be expected. Although the high prices of the first calculators partly reflected high production costs, they also brought high profits and tempted many other firms into the industry. These new firms duplicated and then improved the existing technology and increased their productivity in order to beat the competition or avoid being beaten themselves. Firms unwilling to move with the competition quickly lost their share of the market.

The increase in competition in the calculator market can be represented visually with supply and demand curves. Such an analysis permits us to observe long-run changes in market equilibrium. Given the limited technology and the small number of firms producing calculators in 1969, as well as restricted demand for this new product, let us assume that the supply and demand curves were initially S_1 and D_1 in Figure 3.11. The initial equilibrium price would then be P_2, the quantity sold, Q_1. This is the short-run equilibrium. **Short-run equilibrium** is the price–quantity combination that will exist so long as producers do not have time to change their production facilities (or some other resource that is fixed in the short run).

Short-run equilibrium did not last long. In the years following 1969, firms expanded production, building new plants and converting facilities that had been producing other small electronic devices. Economies of scale resulted, and technological breakthroughs lowered the cost of production still further. Several $150 circuits were reduced to very small $2 chips. The increased supply shifted the supply curve to the right, from S_1 to S_2 (see

Short-run equilibrium: the price–quantity combination that will exist so long as producers do not have time to change their production facilities (or some other resource that is fixed in the short run).

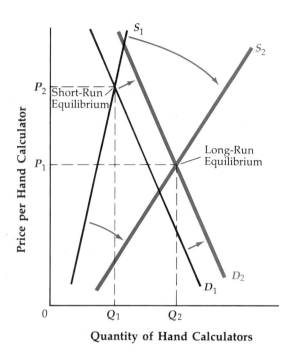

Figure 3.11. Long-Run Market for Calculators.
With supply and demand for calculators at D_1 and S_1, the short-run equilibrium price and quantity will be P_2 and Q_1. But as existing firms expand production and new firms enter the industry, the supply curve shifts to S_2. Simultaneously, an increase in consumer awareness of the product shifts the demand curve to D_2. The resulting long-run equilibrium price and quantity are P_1 and Q_2.

Figure 3.11). Meanwhile, because of advertising and word of mouth, people became familiar with the product and market demand increased, shifting the demand curve from D_1 to D_2. Because supply increased more than demand, the price fell from P_2 to P_1, and quantity rose from Q_1 to Q_2. The new equilibrium price and quantity, P_1 and Q_2, marked the new long-run market equilibrium. **Long-run equilibrium** is the price–quantity combination that will exist after firms have had time to change their production facilities (or some other resource that is fixed in the short run).

The market does not always move smoothly from the short run to the long run. Because firms do not know exactly what other firms are doing, or exactly what consumer demand will be, they may produce a product that cannot be sold at a price that will cover production costs. In fact, in the mid-1970s prices fell enough that several companies were losing money. Long-run improvements sometimes come at the expense of short-run losses.

In this example, a long-run market adjustment caused a drop in price (because supply increased more than demand). The opposite can occur: demand can increase more than supply, causing a rise in the price and

Long-run equilibrium: the price–quantity combination that will exist after firms have had time to change their production facilities (or some other resource that is fixed in the short run).

Figure 3.12. Prices in the Long Run.
If demand increases more than supply, the price will rise along with the quantity sold—panel (a). If supply keeps up with demand, however, the price will remain the same even though the quantity sold increases—panel (b).

the quantity produced. In Figure 3.12(a), when the supply curve shifts to S_2 and the demand curve shifts to D_2, price increases from P_1 to P_2 and quantity produced rises from Q_1 to Q_2. Supply and demand may also adjust so that price remains constant while quantity increases. (Figure 3.12(b).)

Shortcomings of Competitive Markets

Though the competitive market may promote long-run improvements in product prices, quality, and output levels, it has deficiencies, and we must note several before closing. (Market deficiencies will be discussed further in later chapters.)

First, the competitive market process can be quite efficient because production is maximized. Consumer demand, however, depends on the way income is distributed. If market forces or government programs distort income distribution, the demand for goods and resources will also be distorted. If, for example, income is concentrated in the hands of a few, the demand for luxury items will be high, but the demand for household appliances and new housing will be low. In such a situation, the results of competition may be efficient in a strict economic sense, but whether these results are socially desirable is a matter of values—of normative, rather than positive, economics.

Second, the outcome of competition will not be efficient to the extent that production costs are imposed on people who do not consume a product. People whose house paint peels because of industrial pollution bear a portion of the offending firm's production cost, whether or not they buy its product. At the same time, the price consumers pay for the product is lower than it would be if all costs, including pollution costs, were incurred by the producer. Because of the low price, consumers will buy more than the efficient quantity. In a sense, this is an example of overproduction. Because all the costs of production have not been included in the producer's cost calculations, the price is artificially low.

Third, in a free market, competition can promote socially undesirable products or services. A competitive market in an addictive drug like alcohol or heroin can lead to lower prices and greater quantities consumed—and thus increase in social problems associated with addiction. Competition can be desirable only when it promotes the production of things people consider beneficial. But what is beneficial is a matter of values.

Fourth, opponents of the market system contend that competition sometimes leads to "product proliferation"—too many versions of essentially the same product, such as aspirin—and to waste in production and advertisement. Because so many types of the same product are available, production of each takes place on a very small scale, and no plant is fully utilized. This may be true. But the validity of this objection hinges on whether the range of choice in products compensates for the inefficiencies in production. The question is whether firms should be forced to standardize their products and to compete solely in terms of price. What about people who want something different from the standard product?

Fifth, unscrupulous competitors can take advantage of customers' ignorance. A competitor may employ unethical techniques, such as circulating false information about rivals or using bait-and-switch promotional tactics (advertising very low-priced, low-quality products to attract customers, in hope of switching them to higher-priced products when they get into the store). Competition can control some of these abuses. For instance, competitors will generally let consumers know when their rivals are misrepresenting their products. Still, fraudulent sellers can move from one market to another, keeping one step ahead of their reputations.

Summary and Extensions

The market is a system that provides producers with incentives to deliver goods and services to others. To respond to those incentives, producers must meet the needs of society. They must compete with other producers to deliver their goods and services in the most cost-effective manner.

A market implies that sellers and buyers can freely respond to incentives, that they have options and can choose among them. It does not mean, however, that behavior is totally unconstrained, that producers can choose from unlimited options. What a competitor can do may be severely limited by what rival firms are willing to do.

The market system is not perfect. Producers may have difficulty acquiring enough information to make reliable production decisions. People take time to respond to incentives, and producers can make high profits while others are gathering their resources to respond to an opportunity. In the electronics industry, three or four years were required to reduce the price of a basic calculator from $300 to $40. Some consumers still may not be getting exactly the kind of calculator they want.

An uncontrolled market system also carries with it the very real prospect that one firm will acquire monopoly power, restricting the ability of others to respond to incentives, produce more, and push prices and profits down.

Major Conclusions

1. The competitive market can best be defined as a process through which buyers and sellers, pursuing their own interests, attempt to outwit, outdistance, or outmaneuver other buyers and sellers. In this process, market rivals are forced to reveal the limits of what they will accept in terms of price, quantity, quality, and so on.
2. Price competition among producers will push the price and quantity toward the intersection of the market supply and demand curves, called the equilibrium point.
3. Market shortages will occur if a market price is below the equilibrium price. Market surpluses will occur if a market price is above the equilibrium price.
4. When the market price and quantity move toward the equilibrium price and quantity, the market is said to be operating efficiently.
5. Nonprice competition leads to a greater variety of goods that meet the demands of different buyers.

1. Why does the demand curve have a negative slope and the supply curve a positive slope?
2. The mercantilists argued that a country's wealth consisted of its holdings of "gold bullion" (money). To keep gold in a country, they proposed tariffs and quotas to restrict imported goods and services. How do you react to that argument?
3. Suppose that supply and demand are represented by the following formulas:

$$Q_d = 110 - 10P$$

$$Q_s = 10 + 10P$$

   What is the equilibrium price and quantity?
4. In what sense can competition in the production of undesirable goods be bad?
5. List what you consider to be the deficiencies of the free market system. Do the deficiencies outweigh the benefits?
6. Why will the competitive market tend to move toward the price-quantity combination at the intersection of the supply and demand curves? What might keep the market from moving all the way to that equilibrium point?
7. Under what conditions could competition cause market prices to move away from equilibrium?
8. Suppose the demand for blue jeans suddenly increases. Discuss the possible short-run and long-run movements of the market.
9. If the government imposes a price ceiling on gasoline, what would be the result?
10. If the government imposes a price floor on whole milk and buys the resulting surplus, can it later sell what it has bought and recoup its expenditure? What else can the government do with the milk surplus?

Questions to Ponder

Central Question

From an economic perspective, what are the functions of government?

Key Terms

Private sector

Public sector

Budget deficit

Budget surplus

Property rights

Personal income taxes

Corporate income taxes

Excise taxes

General sales tax

Property tax

Progressive tax system

Regressive tax system

Proportional tax system

Marginal tax rate

Average tax rate

Externalities

External benefits

External costs

Common access resources

Monopoly

Macroeconomic policy

Fiscal policy

Monetary policy

Chapter 4

The Public Sector

The end of law is not to abolish or restrain but to preserve and enlarge freedom; for in all the states of created beings capable of laws, where there is no law, there is no freedom. For liberty is to be free from restraint and violence of others, which cannot be where there is no law; but freedom is not, as we are told: a liberty for every man to do what he lists—for who could be free, when every man's humor might domineer over him?—but a liberty to dispose and order as he lists his . . . actions, possessions, and his whole property, within the allowance of those laws under which he is.

John Locke

Our study of markets in the last chapter may have suggested that all economic decisions are made by individuals acting in their own self-interest, constrained by the forces of supply and demand. Nothing could be further from the truth. Many economic decisions are made by government, which allocates tax revenue for various public uses, such as national defense, retirement income, education, and garbage collection. Government decisions also influence the types of products we buy, the quality of the air we breathe and the water we drink, the safety of our workplaces, and the number of goods we can buy from foreign countries. In all these ways, government influences how scarce resources are allocated among competing public and private ends.

Because government is so powerful, it must be considered in any economics course. We need to ask why, from an economic perspective, government exists in the first place and how its policies affect private economic activity. After distinguishing the public and private sectors, we will briefly survey the extent of government taxation and expenditure. We will conclude by examining the economic justification for government's various roles.

An Overview of the Public Sector

In most Western nations, economic life from year to year depends critically on trillions of decisions by millions of individuals acting on their own and as members of social and business organizations. This complex private sector, from which most of us draw a substantial portion of our livelihood, is largely an unintended consequence of purposeful individual action. The **private sector** encompasses all the economic transactions undertaken voluntarily by individuals, either alone or in association with others. Some economists have characterized activity in the private sector as "ordered anarchy," (for its myriad individual actions tend somehow toward economic stability). Others have called it "spontaneous order" (because it occurs without direction) or "self-generating order" (because it emerges on its own and is self-perpetuating). Without some help from government, however, the private economy may not be very orderly, spontaneous, or self-generating.

Private sector: all the economic transactions undertaken voluntarily by individuals, either alone or in association with others.

Many crucial decisions are not made by individuals acting independently, but by people acting collectively through government. Government decisions are binding on all citizens, and government activities are paid for by forced taxation. The lack of individual control in the public sector is necessary partly because not everyone agrees with government decisions, and partly because the benefits of many government activities, such as highways and national defense, cannot be distributed selectively. Without taxation, those who benefit from government activities would be unlikely to pay for the services voluntarily, and the services might never be provided. (More will be said about this later.) The **public sector** includes the activities of federal, state, and local government. Government decisions are normally made collectively, either by voters in a referendum or by Congress, and are financed primarily by forced taxation.

Public sector: the activities of federal, state, and local government.

At all levels of government—federal, state, and local—government in the United States is big business. All told, it accounts for approximately one-third of the nation's total output. In its 1986 budget (see Table 4.1), which was proposed in early 1985, the federal government planned to spend approximately $974 billion in fiscal year 1986; $286 billion (or 29 percent) of this total was to be spent on national defense and $399 (or 41

Table 4.1. Federal Government Outlays and Receipts, 1986[a] (in millions of dollars)

Budget Receipts	793,729
Individual income taxes	358,889
Corporation income taxes	74,088
Social insurance taxes and contributions	289,436
Excise taxes	34,998
Estate and gift taxes	5,345
Customs duties	12,342
Miscellaneous receipts:	
Deposits of earnings by Federal Reserve System	16,932
All other	1,698
Budget Outlays	973,725
National defense	285,669
International affairs	18,349
General science, space, and technology	9,285
Energy	4,671
Natural resources and environment	11,884
Agriculture	12,629
Commerce and housing credit	2,206
Transportation	25,860
Community and regional development	7,323
Education, training, employment, and social services	29,288
Health	34,920
Social security and medicare	269,404
Social security	202,245
Medicare	67,158
Income security	115,769
Veterans benefits and services	26,769
Administration of justice	6,587
General government	4,845
General purpose fiscal assistance	2,797
Net interest	142,550
Allowances	399
Undistributed offsetting receipts	−37,478

[a] Estimates available in 1985.

Source: Executive Office of the President, Office of Management and Budget, *Budget of the United States Government, Fiscal Year 1986* (Washington, D.C.: U.S. Government Printing Office, 1985), pp. 9–12, 9–13.

Table 4.2. Federal Government Receipts, Selected Years, 1900–1985

Year	Billion Dollars	Year	Billion Dollars
1900	0.6	1950	39.5
1905	0.5	1955	65.5
1910	0.7	1960	92.5
1915	0.7	1965	116.8
1920	6.6	1970	193.7
1925	3.6	1975	279.1
1930	4.1	1980	517.1
1935	3.7	1985	736.9
1940	6.4	1986	793.7
1945	45.2		

Sources: U.S. Bureau of the Census, *Historical Statistics of the United States* (Washington, D.C.: U.S. Government Printing Office, 1975), pp. 1104–1105; *Economic Report of the President* (Washington, D.C.: U.S. Government Printing Office, 1985), pp. 316–317; Executive Office of the President, Office of Management and Budget, *Budget of the United States Government, Fiscal Year 1986* (Washington, D.C.: U.S. Government Printing Office, 1985), p. 9–10.

percent) was to be paid directly to individuals under a variety of programs. Social security and income security outlays, which include retirement benefits, payments to disabled workers, and medical care for a wide range of people, were budgeted at $485 billion (or 50 percent of total federal outlays). The federal government also planned to spend $29 billion on education and $13 billion on agriculture. Billions more were budgeted for energy, international affairs, transportation, and housing.

Of the $794 billion that were expected to be collected in revenues in 1986, most ($359 billion, or 45 percent) were expected to come from individual income taxes. Another $74 billion (or 9 percent) were to come from corporate income taxes, and Social Security taxes were expected to add $289 billion, or 36 percent. Significant revenues were expected to come from excise taxes on products like gasoline, tobacco, and alcohol, and on inheritance.

As Table 4.2 shows, federal receipts have grown substantially, rising from less than $600 million in 1900 to $794 billion in 1986. Most of this growth has occurred since the 1930s. Though inflation has played a large part—dollars are worth much less now than they were in the 1930s—much of the growth is due to an expansion in the federal government's activities. Growth in federal outlays has been even more dramatic than growth in receipts. As a consequence, the federal budget deficit has mushroomed. A **budget deficit** is the amount by which outlays exceed receipts during any given accounting period. It is the opposite of a **budget surplus,** the amount by which receipts exceed outlays during a given accounting period.

Figure 4.1 shows federal outlays and receipts since 1970. Between 1970 and 1984, outlays grew from 20 to over 23 percent of total domestic production. The growing reliance on deficit spending is indicated by the

Budget deficit: the amount by which outlays exceed receipts during any given accounting period.

Budget surplus: the amount by which receipts exceed outlays during a given accounting period.

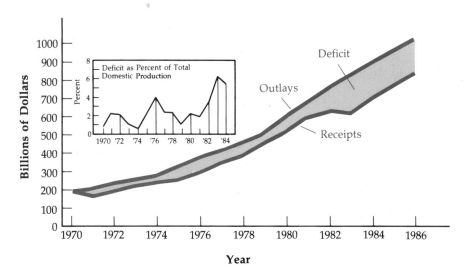

Figure 4.1. Federal Budget Receipts and Outlays, 1970–1986.
Federal outlays have risen substantially over the past fifteen years. Because they
have risen faster than receipts, the budget deficit (shaded area) has also grown.
Note: Estimated figures for 1985 and 1986.
Sources: U.S. Bureau of the Census, *Statistical Abstract of the United States* (Washington, D.C.:
U.S. Government Printing Office, 1985), p. 300; Executive Office of the President, Office of
Management and Budget, *Budget of the United States Government, Fiscal Year 1986* (Washington,
D.C.: U.S. Government Printing Office, 1985), p. 9–10.

shaded area. The federal deficit expanded from one to two percent of total
domestic production in the early 1970s to five to six percent of total
domestic production in the early 1980s (see the insert in Figure 4.1).

In 1981 the fifty state governments spent a total of $170 billion, most of
which went for roads, education, police protection, and local government.
They obtained their revenue largely from state income and sales taxes. To
their revenue from local property taxes and fees for services provided, the
eighty-five thousand local governments (counties, cities, and towns) added
$107 billion received from the state and the federal governments, to spend
a total of $254 billion. Most local expenditures went for services such as
police and fire protection, roads, sewers, and water systems. A relatively
small percentage went to welfare programs.

Besides making its own expenditures, government regulates private
production. According to one estimate, federal regulation of business
activities, including pollution, occupational safety, and product design,
costs the private sector over $100 billion annually in added production
expenses. State and local regulations increased the bill.

Governments also influence the use of resources through tax exemptions.
For example, individuals can deduct the interest paid on borrowed money
from their federally taxable incomes. Thus their taxes go down when they
take out loans and mortgages. The economic effect of such a deduction is
to reduce the after-tax price of many vacations, cars, and houses, and to

increase sales of those goods. Businesses can also reduce their federal tax bills, by up to 10 percent of the cost of new plant and equipment. The so-called Investment Tax Credit (which the Reagan administration proposed in 1984 to abolish) encourages the formation of capital and the updating or expansion of industrial equipment. Like government tax and spending decisions, these tax deductions and credits divert resources from private to public uses. Private expenditures made in order to take advantage of tax deductions and credits are called "tax expenditures."

Government decisions loom large in the overall economy, adding to and subtracting from individuals' incentives to work, save, and invest for the future. As government budgets increase, citizens must ask whether all governmental activities are necessary and justifiable.

Several functions traditionally belong to government:

to define and protect property rights;

to protect the public from crime and bring criminals to justice;

to provide for the national defense;

to educate the general public; and

to establish a stable monetary system.

In modern times, however, government responsibilities have expanded to include other functions:

to stabilize the economy—that is, moderate the swings in general economic activity and unemployment;

to control the use of the environment, regulate industry, and protect consumers from perceived abuses of the competitive market process; and

to provide income security and health insurance.

We will examine most of these governmental functions, starting with the traditional function of protecting property.

Minimal Government: Protection of Property

Although the last chapter's discussion of the market system rarely mentioned government, it was actually based on the existence of some collective authority. In the market system, what is really sold is not tomatoes or hand calculators, but the property rights to tomatoes and hand calculators—and property rights are generally established and protected by government. **Property rights** define the permissible uses of resources, goods, and services, both privately and collectively.

Property rights are a social phenomenon—a response to the problem of living peaceably in a world where few have everything they want. In places where people are separated from one another by natural barriers, or where resources are abundant, property rights have no meaning. To

Property rights: legally defined and permissible uses, both private and collective, of resources, goods, and services.

Robinson Crusoe, shipwrecked on a lonely island, property rights were inconsequential. His behavior was restricted only by the resources he found on the island, the tools he took from his wrecked ship, and his own ingenuity. Though he encountered problems in allocating his time efficiently—between food gathering, shelter building, and so on—the notion of property never restrained his behavior. He simply took from the ship, with impunity, whatever seemed most useful.[1]

With the arrival of Friday, it became necessary to establish some restrictions on behavior. The problem was particularly acute because Friday was a cannibal. Clearly each man had to establish property rights to his body. Then the two had to work out a system of ownership for the various possessions on the island.

The property rights traded in the market system are based ultimately on the need for social order. These rights bring obligations as well as privileges. A person who buys a house is actually buying the right to live in the house under certain conditions—for example, so long as he or she does not disturb others, or does not allow the property to deteriorate so much as to threaten the neighbors' safety. These rights and obligations of property owners draw their legitimacy, to a significant degree, from government enforcement of the law.

Just how much markets depend on government for the protection of private property rights is hard to determine. Markets existed in the Old West, which lacked formally instituted government. Even today, we cannot depend on government to arbitrate all questions of property rights. In college dormitories, disputes over property rights are usually settled before they reach the student council, to say nothing of the dean's office or the police station. In society at large, most conflicts over property are resolved personally, and many never arise because people conform to socially accepted standards of behavior.

Nevertheless government definition of property rights represents an important difference between the public and private sectors. When government defines or redefines property rights, it changes the economic circumstances—including the wealth—of individuals in the private sector. For instance, when the federal government imposes price ceilings, as it did in 1971, it restrains the freedom of buyers and sellers in the market system. One purpose of economics is to analyze the effects of a government-ordered realignment of property rights on the efficiency of production.

We are inclined to think of property rights as being natural, a part of our birthright. The Declaration of Independence speaks of "certain unalienable rights," and it is hard to imagine a world without rights to property. But, in addition, government enforcement of property rights has an economic basis.

---

1. The absence of other human beings affected Crusoe's idea of what was useful. Discovering a coffer of gold and silver coins on the ship, he exclaimed, "Thou art not worth to me, no, not the taking off of the ground; one of those knives is worth all this heap." On second thought, however—perhaps after considering the possibility of rescue—Crusoe took the coins.

Perspectives in Economics: Sources of Income in the Public Sector

Government at all levels—local, state, and federal—is a major user of the nation's resources, and a major buyer of its goods and services. It secures the funds for massive expenditures by borrowing money and by levying taxes on income, sales, and property.

At the national and state levels, most tax revenues come from personal and corporate income taxes. **Personal income taxes** are government revenues collected from individual earnings, after allowance for certain exemptions and deductions. Under federal tax law in 1985, individuals pay taxes on their gross earnings minus exemptions for dependents (taxpayer, spouse, and children) and deductions for certain expenses (interest payments on home mortgages and loans, charitable contributions, and business expenses, among others). **Corporate income taxes** are government revenues collected on a corporation's computed profits, as reported on its profit and loss statements. A corporation's taxable profits are computed by subtracting its business expenses from its sales revenues.

Because of exemptions and deductions many people, including high income earners, pay no federal income taxes. In 1983, 299 millionaires paid no federal taxes. Many other high income earners paid only a small percentage of their income in taxes. Most high income earners who paid little or no tax did so by purchasing municipal bonds, the interest on which is not taxed; or by investing in real estate and taking deductions for depreciation. Other ways of reducing taxes might include charitable contributions, deductions for legitimate business expenses (for example, office supplies and business travel), and personal expenses disguised as business expenses (lunches, home office expenses, and vacations).

Taxes on sales of various commodities also provide income for government. **Excise taxes** are taxes levied on specific products or services, for specific purposes. For instance, an excise tax on gasoline might be used to fund road construction and repair. Sometimes an excise tax is levied to discourage consumption of a product: many liquor taxes serve this purpose. Excise taxes are levied at all levels of government, primarily federal and state. They are normally a percentage of the purchase price. The **general sales tax,** a tax on most, but not necessarily all, consumer purchases, is another type of levy on sales. The tax is usually imposed by states, but in some areas local governments may share its revenues or raise the tax slightly. The amount of the sales tax varies from place to place, ranging from 2 to 8.5 cents on the dollar (1984) in states that have sales tax.

The third source of tax revenues, property, is a major source of revenue for local government, as well as a minor source of revenue for most states and the federal government. The **property tax** is a tax on specified assets, usually real estate, cars and boats, household goods, bank account balances, and stocks and bonds.

The economic effect of all these taxes varies according to the way they are administered. In general, tax systems may be described as progressive, regressive, or proportional. A **progressive tax system** is any means of collecting government

Recall the imaginary island world of only two people, Fred and Harry. Let's assume that initially, like Crusoe and Friday, they have neither rules nor natural barriers to divide their spheres of interest. Furthermore, each man wants more than he can produce by himself. Each has two fundamental options for increasing his welfare. He can use his labor and other resources to produce goods and services, or he can steal. Fred and Harry can be expected to allocate their time in the most productive way. With no social revenues in which the percentage of income that is paid in taxes rises with income. For example, a tax system in which the tax rate rises from 10 to 50 percent as income rises from $15,000 to $100,000 a year is progressive. Personal income taxes are generally progressive, as are corporate income taxes at the federal level. Property taxes are also progressive, since people with higher incomes tend to save and invest a higher percentage of their income in taxable property.

A **regressive tax system** is any means of collecting government revenues in which the percentage of income that is paid in taxes declines as income rises. Under a regressive tax system, as income rises from $15,000 to $100,000, the tax rate would fall—from 20 to 10 percent, for instance. The general sales tax is considered regressive, because lower income groups tend to spend a higher percentage of their incomes on consumer purchases than higher income groups. If a man earning $10,000 a year spends 98 percent of his income, a 5 percent general sales tax on those purchases constitutes 4.9 percent of his earned income. If a woman earning $100,000 a year spends 75 percent of her income, the same 5 percent sales tax works out to only 3.75 percent of her earned income.

A **proportional tax system** is any means of collecting government revenues in which all income earners pay the same tax rate. Under a proportional tax system, the tax rate might be 10 or 20 percent across the board. At the state level, corporate income taxes are often proportional. In South Carolina in 1985, the corporate income tax was a straight 7 percent.

The economic effect of a tax depends largely on the marginal (as opposed to average) tax rate. A **marginal tax rate** is the percentage of any additional income that is subject to taxation. An **average tax rate** is the percentage of total income that is paid in taxes. It is obtained by dividing total taxes paid by total taxable income. The federal income tax system is founded on progressive marginal tax rates. As income rises, additional earned income is taxed at higher and higher rates, up to a limit of 50 percent as of 1985. Thus the more income a person earns, the more tax he or she is forced to pay.

In all their forms, taxes tend to discourage the economic activity they are levied on. Income taxes, especially if they are progressive, can discourage people from earning a taxable income, or from seeking a higher income through education or job training. Generally speaking, the higher the income tax rate, the less the incentive to earn an income, and the more the incentive to avoid taxes. High corporate taxes can discourage investment in corporations, and retard the growth of industry. As already mentioned, excise taxes can—and are often intended to—reduce consumption of certain goods and services. General sales taxes can encourage consumer spending on the relatively few products and services—for example, food or clothing—that are not subject to the sales tax. And property taxes can discourage people from accumulating property and can encourage them to consume instead. In all of these ways, government tax policies can have a significant impact on general economic activity.

or ethical barriers restricting their behavior, each man will steal from the other as long as theft is more rewarding than the production of goods and services. Each will then have to divert some of his resources into protecting what he has produced (or stolen). Presumably this approach will eventually become counterproductive. And each will be investing so much in attacks and counterattacks that neither one of them will find further investment in the activity profitable.

In a limited economic sense, the resources Fred and Harry spend on stealing and preventing theft are wasted, for they are taken away from the production of new goods and services. If those resources were applied to production, total output would rise, and both Fred and Harry would be better off. The wastefulness of plunder is the economic principle that underlies the establishment of property rights. Through social contracts people restrict their behavior so as to avoid the heavier restraints associated with anarchy. The fear of being attacked on the streets at night can be far more confining than laws that restrict people from attacking one another. As John Locke wrote, "The end of law is not to abolish or restrain but to preserve and enlarge freedom."

Even when they recognize the benefits of a social contract, Fred and Harry may be tempted to chisel on the agreement. Fred may find that although he benefits from agreeing to property rights, he benefits even more if he then violates those rights (that is, as long as Harry does not retaliate). By stealing or otherwise ignoring Harry's rights, Fred can redistribute some of Harry's wealth to himself. Of course, if Harry retaliates, the two producers could end up back in a state of anarchy.

Thus the social contract can disintegrate because of individuals' offensive actions as they seek to improve their own positions. But defensive actions can also lead to a return to anarchy. Each citizen must consider what the other might do. Neither would want to be caught upholding an agreement while the other violates it. If Fred thinks Harry might violate his rights, he may violate Harry's rights first, or vice versa. Many wars and battles, both on the street and internationally, have been fought because one party was afraid the other would attack first.

To prevent violations both offensive and defensive, societies have developed police, court, and penal systems to protect the rights specified in the social contract. The costs of such systems may be high, but they are less than the costs of anarchy, in which resources would be diverted to predatory and defensive uses. The costs of making and enforcing the contract will determine just how extensive the contract is.

The social contract that defines property rights establishes only the limits of permissible behavior. Fred and Harry may not be satisfied with the property rights they have, even if they respect them. Both men will try to improve their individual well-being, most likely through socially approved trading arrangements. Suppose the only goods on their island are coconuts and papayas. The social contract specifies the division of fruits between Fred and Harry—whatever each can produce. Suppose also that the additional satisfaction each receives from the last coconut and papaya in his possession is as follows:

	Coconut	Papaya
Fred	10 utils	15 utils
Harry	90 utils	30 utils

Fred receives more satisfaction from his last papaya (15 utils) than from his last coconut (10 utils). He would be better off if he could trade a coconut (sacrificing 10 utils) for a papaya (gaining 15).[2] Harry, on the other hand, would receive more satisfaction from his last coconut; he would gladly trade a papaya for one more coconut. Thus Fred and Harry can be expected to exchange coconut and papaya rights until they can no longer gain from trade. We can also expect them to specialize in producing the fruit in which they have a comparative advantage (see Chapter 2 for a review of comparative advantage).

Government Production of Public Goods

The protection of property rights that undergirds Fred and Harry's system of specialization and trade requires certain services, such as police and court systems. These services, called public goods, are generally produced by government. They include goods and services that benefit all members of the community. By their nature, no one can be excluded from the benefits of public goods.

Unlike public goods, private goods benefit only those individuals who possess them. The benefits of a Snickers bar, for example, are received exclusively by the person who eats it. If someone else wants a Snickers bar, a new one will have to be produced and purchased; it cannot be consumed simultaneously by two people. Because only one person can eat a particular candy bar, the producer can withhold it until payment is made, just as Fred and Harry can withhold fruit from the market until a favorable rate of exchange has been established. That is why private firms are willing and able to sell private goods.

By their very nature, public goods are not suited to private production. National defense is one of the best examples. No citizen can be denied the benefits of national defense; all are protected by it, more or less simultaneously. Thus the benefits of defense cannot be withheld from consumers until payment is made, as is usual in a free market system. Most people would not pay for goods that they could get free. Instead, they would take the free benefits and assume their payment would be so small that it would not be missed. In other words, they would free-ride on the payments of others. Few private firms would be willing to produce under such conditions, for they could not sell enough even to recover their costs. Consequently government must undertake the production and payment for this public good.

National defense is a relatively pure public good, in the sense that almost everyone in the community can benefit from it. Many government services are only partially shared, however, and not necessarily by those who provide the good. Care of the environment, education, and poverty relief would fall into this category. The argument for government provision here is that market exchanges in certain goods and services affect people

---

2. A util is the economist's name for a unit of satisfaction. We have no idea what a unit of satisfaction is, but it provides a measure that we need to make our point.

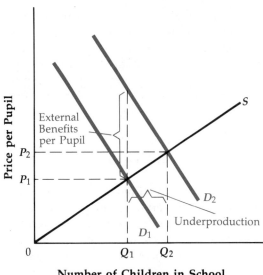

Figure 4.2. The External Benefits of Education.
Given market supply and demand curves D_1 and S, only Q_1 people will be educated. If the external benefits of education were recognized by the market, demand would be D_2, and the number of people educated would be Q_2. Without government intervention in this market, education will be underproduced. The misallocation of resources can be corrected by a per pupil subsidy equal to the vertical distance between D_1 and D_2.

Externalities: the positive (beneficial) or negative (harmful) effects that market exchanges have on people who do not participate directly in those exchanges. Third-party, or "spillover," effects.

other than the buyers and sellers. To use an economic term, the benefits (or costs) of such transactions are "externalized." Externalized costs are often referred to as externalities. **Externalities** are the positive (beneficial) or negative (harmful) effects that market exchanges have on people who do not participate directly in those exchanges. Externalities are third-party, or "spillover," effects.

External Benefits

External benefits: benefits of production and consumption that are received by people not directly involved in the production, consumption, or exchange of a good. Positive effects on some third party.

Beneficial externalities are called external benefits. **External benefits** are benefits of production and consumption that are received by people not directly involved in the production, consumption, or exchange of a good. They are positive effects on some third party. Education is a good example of a service that provides external benefits. It helps both students and others in the community. Education equips people for more productive jobs and prepares them for their civic responsibilities.

The effects of external benefits can be illustrated graphically. Suppose the demand curve D_1 in Figure 4.2 reflects parents' private benefit from and demand for their children's education. The supply curve S reflects the supply of places in school. Without government intervention in the education market, the number of children attending school would be Q_1. However, if the external benefits of an education were added to parents' demand, demand would be D_2 instead of D_1. The vertical distance between D_1 and D_2 indicates the external benefits that are not being captured by the market system. Education is being underproduced by $Q_2 - Q_1$ places.

The government could remedy the underproduction by using some of its tax receipts to provide subsidies to parents with children in school. This move would push the demand for education to D_2, thus increasing the number of children in school to Q_2. Such a scheme would spread the cost of the external benefits among the people in the community who receive them.

Notice that the government need not become directly involved in the production of education (that is, in running the schools) in order to correct the misallocation of resources. Education can be encouraged through subsidies to private schools or the pupils who attend them. Garbage collection, which captures external health benefits, is often procured through contracts with private firms. Fire, police, and even penal correction services can be secured through government contract rather than government production.

External Costs

Harmful externalities are called external costs. **External costs** are costs of production and consumption that are imposed on people not directly involved in the production, consumption, or exchange of a good. These are negative effects on some third party. Smoke pollution is an example of an external cost. It results from a process that benefits the producers of the pollution and consumers, but harms others in the area.

The external cost of pollution can be shown graphically. Suppose that in Figure 4.3, the demand curve D represents car owners' demand for gasoline, which depends on their demand for driving, and that S_1 represents the costs refineries incur in producing the gasoline. In the competitive market, the equilibrium price will be P_1 and the equilibrium quantity will be Q_2. But when car owners drive, they pollute the atmosphere, causing other people discomfort or even ill health. This cost of gasoline use is just as real as refiners' costs of hiring labor and buying crude oil, but *it is not paid by refiners or drivers* and so is not included in supply curve S_1. If it were, the supply curve would shift to S_2, and the equilibrium gasoline price and quantity would be P_2 and Q_1. In other words, consumers of gasoline would have to pay a higher price and would cut back on their use of the product.

Thus if producers and consumers are not required to pay for pollution costs, they will overuse gasoline by $Q_2 - Q_1$ gallons. In this sense, resources have been misallocated. Social welfare would be increased if less gasoline were used. The overuse might be corrected with a tax on gasoline production, equal to the vertical distance between S_1 and S_2. If producers have to pay such a tax, the supply curve will shift to S_2, the price will be bid up, and consumers will cut back on their consumption of gasoline.

External costs: costs of production and consumption that are imposed on people not directly involved in the production, consumption, or exchange of a good. Negative effects on some third party.

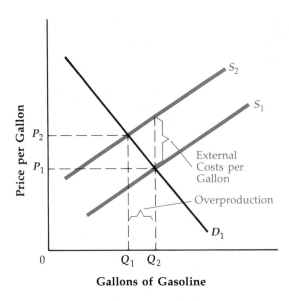

Figure 4.3. The External Costs of Pollution.
Given market supply and demand curves S_1 and D, the number of gallons of gasoline sold will be Q_2. If producers had to pay the external costs of pollution associated with gasoline use, however, the supply curve would be S_2 and the number of gallons sold would be Q_1. Without government intervention, gasoline will be overproduced. To correct the misallocation of resources, government can impose a tax on each gallon of gasoline sold, which will shift the supply curve to S_2 and reduce the quantity of gasoline sold to Q_1.

Government Protection of Common Access Resources

It may seem that in the ideal economy everyone would have the right to use all resources, goods, and services, and no one—not even the state—would have the right to exclude anyone from their use. In fact, the rights to many scarce resources are held "in common," or communally, with only minimal restrictions, if any, on their use. When access to resources is open to almost everyone, they are called common access resources. **Common access resources** are resources that are owned in common instead of privately by individuals. Thus individuals may not be excluded from their use. Rights to the use of a college or university's facilities are frequently held in common. So long as a student conforms to certain rules and regulations, he or she cannot be excluded from the use of the library, the parking lots, and other common facilities. The rights to city parks are also held communally. For several millennia before whites immigrated to this continent, Indian tribes held communal rights to hunting grounds. During the early part of the nineteenth century, whites living on the prairie held communal grazing rights. Anyone could let cattle loose on

Common access resources: resources owned in common instead of privately by individuals. Thus individuals may not be excluded from their use.

the plains. (The United States government claimed the right to exclude people from the plains, but did not exercise it.)

Communal property rights can be employed efficiently if (1) there is more than enough of the resource to go around—in other words, there is no cost to its use; or (2) the people who use the resource account fully for the effects of their use on others. Unless one of these two conditions is met, the resource will tend to be overused.

While a common access resource is being used, it is in effect the temporary private property of the user. Yet the users pay nothing for the privilege. Freeway drivers get a toll-free trip on a well-engineered road. If they are rational, they will use the road until the trip is not worth the cost to them in time and gas. One cost they may overlook, however, especially as it applies to themselves personally, is the alternative use to which their space might have been put by other drivers. (Environmentalists argue that many roads should never have been built. The alternative use in that case would have been scenery.) Increased highway congestion and the discomfort of other drivers are other hidden costs. These external costs, sometimes called social costs, of driving are just as important as other costs. But because drivers do not incur such costs themselves, they are effectively subsidized by others. Thus drivers will tend to overuse the road.

To lessen highway congestion the government could impose a tax on gasoline or a toll on road use. Drivers might then have to pay the true cost of their use of the road and would be encouraged to cut back on their driving. Or the government could turn the road into private property, giving the new owners the right to charge for its use. Such a solution would have essentially the same effect, reducing the use of the road. The main difference is that the revenues collected would go directly to individuals instead of to the government—a result that is either good or bad depending on one's personal values.

If the road is privately owned and no alternate mode of transportation is available, the owners may overcharge. In doing so they would be exploiting a monopoly on transportation. A **monopoly** is a sole seller of a good or service. Because a monopoly has no competitors, it can cut back on production (thus limiting the quantity supplied), charge higher prices, and reap greater profits than other firms. But for that matter, the state may also overcharge, acting like a monopolist. Though state agencies may not make a profit in the normal sense of the term, their revenues can be used to improve the salaries and working conditions of state employees. The question is whether the drawbacks of state or private use outweigh the drawbacks of communal use.

Some additional examples will help clarify the problems associated with communal ownership of common access resources.

Monopoly: a sole seller of a good or service. Because a monopoly has no competitors, it can cut back on production (thus limiting the quantity supplied), charge higher prices, and reap greater profits than other firms.

Air and Water

Though federal and state governments hold the rights to the nation's water and airways, until recently they have not asserted much control over the use of these communal resources. Pollution has been the unhappy result. In dumping waste into the air and rivers, polluters are using a common access resource as if it were their own. Owners of private property generally exact payments for its use. But when polluters draw a common access resource away from an alternative use, like unspoiled scenery, no one reimburses society for the loss. No one compensates the people who live next to a plant with billowing smokestacks for their eye irritation or the additional paint jobs their homes require.

Pollution is often seen as a product of antisocial behavior, as indeed it often may be. Many who pollute simply do not care about what they do to others. However, much pollution results from a failure to recognize that individual behavior has an affect on the environment. The person who drops a cigarette butt to the ground may believe that littering on that scale cannot materially affect anyone's sensibilities. If everyone follows the same line of reasoning, however, the cigarette butts will accumulate into an eyesore. Even then an individual may reason that his own behavior has little effect one way or the other. This type of reasoning, of course, is a powerful argument against communal rights.

Endangered Species

The hunting grounds of the Labrador Peninsula were originally held in common by Indian tribes. All Indians could hunt as they wished without fear of exclusion. Because of the difficulty of hunting and the limited demand for meat, skins, and bones, the area was not overhunted, and wildlife flourished. With the emergence of the European fur trade, however, the value of skins skyrocketed, encouraging the Indians to hunt beyond the area's natural capacity.

Once again communal rights were to blame. Hunters did not have to consider how their actions affected other hunters' ability to trap and hunt. Yet when one hunter killed a beaver, the task of hunting was made more difficult for others. Unlimited hunting imposed a social cost much like the cost imposed by unlimited driving. Moreover, hunters had little incentive to avoid excessive trapping. If one hunter did not kill a beaver, surely another would.

The Labrador Indians solved the problem of overkill by assigning private property rights to portions of their hunting grounds. Because he could exclude others, each hunter then had an incentive to control his take from the land.

Not all endangered species can be saved so easily. Whales have been hunted for centuries, but the threat of extinction is relatively recent. Until about two hundred years ago people did not have the technology to kill whales faster than the whales could reproduce. Theoretically, the problem could be solved in the same way as the beaver problem, through the establishment of private property rights. Some whales, however, migrate through six thousand miles of ocean annually. Establishing and enforcing private property rights over such a wide expanse, to say nothing of working out the international legal complications, would doubtless prove costly.

Whales will probably remain communal property, and the species' survival will continue to be threatened.

Communal property rights can also influence the methods of hunters. In the 1970s the Canadian government in effect declared the first fifty thousand baby seals killed annually to be a common access resource. Rights to the seals were allocated communally on a first-come, first-served basis, a rationing system that encouraged hunters to act quickly and ruthlessly.

The Canadian government permitted no more than 50,000 animals to be taken, so hunters worked with speed to make their kills before the legal maximum was reached. They swarmed over the ice floes and crushed the babies' skulls with heavy clubs. Government offices received many protests that the seals were unhumanly clubbed (by humans) and often skinned alive.[3]

Public Property

In a condominium development in Blacksburg, Virginia, most of the grounds are held communally by the owners' association. By contract, all owners must become dues-paying members of the association and contribute their share toward the cost of upkeep. Thus no one can free-ride on the groundskeeping efforts of others, and the grounds are reasonably well kept, even though communally owned.

Not all the land in the development is held communally, however. Each unit comes with its own small back yard, which is the unit owner's responsibility. To encourage the upkeep of these yards, the condominium association bought lawn mowers, garden tools, and grass seed and stored them in a communal shed. This communal property was abused. Within a few months the garden tools had mysteriously disappeared. After a year the lawn mowers fell apart from rough use and lack of maintenance. The grass seed too seemed to disappear rapidly, though enough had been purchased to cover the entire community several times.

The argument for the purchase of communally held tools and seed had been economies of scale. It seemed more efficient to have one lawn mower for all than one for each small back yard. The system never achieved the planned economies, however, because residents had no incentive to use communal property with care. Like the whale and seal hunters, the members of the association fell victim to the negative effects inherent in communal property rights.

Communal property rights do not always bring this type of problem. The family is an institution in which much property is owned communally and with tolerably efficient results. In many cases, however, government intervention of some kind is necessary to prevent overuse and abuse of common access resources.

---

3. Armen A. Alchian and Harold Demsetz, ''The Property Rights Paradigm,'' *Journal of Economic History*, 33 (March 1973), 20.

Economists in History: Thomas Malthus (1766–1834)

The Reverend Thomas Robert Malthus was born in England in 1766, ten years before the publication of Adam Smith's *Wealth of Nations*. Though Malthus was educated for the ministry, he devoted his life to teaching history and political economy (the original name for economics).

Malthus's most famous work, his *An Essay on the Principle of Population*, was published anonymously in 1798. The book depicts a bleak future for the human race. Malthus contended that the production of food tends to grow arithmetically (by the addition of a constant number), whereas population tends to grow geometrically (by the multiplication of a constant number). Sooner or later, he warned, people's capacity to reproduce themselves would outstrip their ability to feed and house themselves. The result would be war, famine, and pestilence.

Malthus also argued that the rapid growth of the population would ultimately lower workers' wages to subsistence level (no more than necessary to sustain life). New and better ways of producing

Government Provision of Income Security and Health Insurance

Government programs to guarantee incomes and provide health insurance are often justified on ethical grounds. If enough people feel that citizens are entitled to a minimum standard of living, income security can be viewed as a good for which there is a demand, like any other good. Government simply produces this good for the same reason a farmer produces apples.

In addition to helping recipients, some argue, income security increases the general social welfare. As income rises, the value of each additional dollar of income diminishes, for people generally satisfy their most pressing needs and wants first. Additional income is used to satisfy less pressing needs and wants. Hence if some income is taken from the well-off and given to the poor, the transferred money will be put to better use. Opponents of income redistribution would counter that the value of income is just as great for the well-off as for the poor. Therefore income redistribution would not improve societal welfare.

Suppose we accept that income security is a worthwhile service. Why should it be provided by government? The answer generally given is that externalities make private provision unworkable. If contributions to welfare programs were private and voluntary, many people might refrain from contributing, reasoning that they would not gain as much benefit from the program as others. Others might reason that they as individuals could abstain without jeopardizing the benefits to others. If enough people goods would be found, increasing profits and hence wages. But the higher wages would lead to more births and longer lives, and the growing supply of workers would eventually drive wages back down to subsistence level.

With Malthus's theory in mind, Thomas Carlyle described the new discipline of economics as the "dismal science," a name that persists to this day. Even so, Malthus's thinking influenced the two most powerful political ideologies of the twentieth century. His theory of population became a cor-

nerstone of Karl Marx's theory of the exploitation of labor and the inevitable demise of capitalism, first outlined in the *Communist Manifesto* (1848). And Malthus's suggestion that recessions (periods of high unemployment and low production) sprang from inadequate demand for goods and services predated John Maynard Keynes's thinking on the use of government expenditure and tax policy to lower unemployment. Keynes's theory has greatly influenced the macroeconomic policies of capitalist governments for the past half-century.

withheld support, contributions might not cover the benefits paid out under the program. From this perspective, income security programs can be seen as an effort to overcome the external benefit problem—that is, underproduction in the private sector.

Government Stabilization of the Economy

Throughout history, the general level of economic activity has fluctuated in business cycles. Sometimes overall economic activity rises, increasing the nation's output and employment. At other times it declines, decreasing production and throwing people out of work. Until recently the U.S. government has generally not attempted to interfere with these economic swings. But since the 1940s, the federal government has increasingly tried to use macroeconomic policy to control the overall level of economic activity, including prices, output, and employment and unemployment. **Macroeconomic policy** is the manipulation of taxes, federal expenditures, and the money supply to promote a high and stable level of employment and production, price level stability, and economic growth.

This change in attitude was spurred by the writings of John Maynard Keynes, a British economist whose theory of business cycles was published during the Great Depression. Keynes believed that swings in economic activity were caused by changes in the demand for goods and services by consumers, government, and business. Government could moderate those swings, he taught, by monitoring and if necessary stimulating or restraining demand for goods and services.

Macroeconomic policy: the manipulation of taxes, federal expenditures, and the money supply to promote a high and stable level of employment and production, price level stability, and economic growth.

Fiscal policy: the manipulation of federal expenditures and taxes to promote a high and stable level of employment and production, price level stability, and economic growth.

Monetary policy: the manipulation of the rate of growth of the nation's money supply to promote price level stability and a high and stable level of employment and production.

Just what the government should do to moderate swings in the economy remains a highly controversial question. Keynesians argue for the manipulation of fiscal policy, meaning taxes and expenditures. **Fiscal policy** (also called budgetary policy) is the manipulation of federal expenditures and taxes to promote a high and stable level of employment and production, price level stability, and economic growth. Monetarists, in contrast, maintain that business swings are caused largely by changes in the rate of growth of the nation's money stock. These economists recommend that the government moderate the swings through monetary policy. **Monetary policy** is the manipulation of the rate of growth of the nation's money supply to promote price stability and a high and stable level of employment and production. Much of our study of economics will involve the implications of these and other theories for government policy. Here we need only stress that stabilization of the nation's economic activity has come to be a major function of government.

The Shortcomings of Government Action

In this and the last chapter, we discussed some of the shortcomings of the market system: an inability to provide public goods; the existence of external costs and benefits; and distortion in the allocation of resources by monopolies. The free market system does not always use the economy's scarce resources efficiently. But it does not follow that government should always attempt to correct market failures. Government too has its shortcomings.

All government action requires the use of scarce resources—and they will not necessarily be used more efficiently than in the private sector. A private monopoly may distort the allocation of resources, but the distortion may be slight compared with the cost of an antitrust suit against the monopoly. Cigarette smokers may throw their butts on the ground, but the cost of their pollution may be less than that of an antilitter campaign.

Government is itself a kind of monopoly. Because it faces no competition in many of its activities, it can become quite inefficient, distorting the allocation of resources, reducing the quality of the goods and services produced, or increasing their price. The U.S. Postal Service can afford to charge monopoly prices for first-class mail service precisely because the law prohibits private firms from entering that market.

Summary and Extensions

Markets depend on property rights, which form the basis of trade. The private sector of our economy depends on the government to define and enforce property rights. In establishing the political and economic framework for trade, government performs an essential economic function.

Government has many other functions, some more essential than others. Government sometimes acts as a producer in order to correct for inefficiencies created by external costs and benefits, or to produce public goods that cannot be provided privately. It may also use its power to tax to provide goods and services not traditionally among its responsibilities, such as public welfare services. Though economists are certainly not opposed to the relief of economic distress, many of them are becoming more and more concerned with the inefficiencies of government attempts to promote the national well-being.

1. The economic functions of government include: defining and protecting property rights; providing public goods like national defense; reducing the inefficiencies associated with external costs and benefits; protecting common access resources; providing for the public's health and security; and stabilizing overall economic activity.
2. Government establishment and enforcement of property rights increases production by freeing producers from the need to engage in wasteful conflicts over property.
3. Where property rights are defined and protected, markets will emerge, and mutually beneficial trades will be made.
4. Failure to define property rights frequently results in overuse and abuse of resources. Common access resources are inefficiently used partly because no one has to pay for their use.
5. Economists disagree as to whether and how government should act to stabilize the economy. Some recommend the use of fiscal policy, others the use of monetary policy.
6. Like the free market system it sometimes attempts to correct, government is far from perfect in an economic sense. Its actions can be costly or even monopolistic.

Major Conclusions

1. What are property rights? Why do they exist?
2. In economic terms, describe the causes of the pollution of some portion of your environment.
3. How is the cost of enforcement related to the existence of property rights? What might be the effect of an increase in the cost of enforcement? A decrease?
4. "Government can correct for inefficiencies due to external benefits by subsidizing producers and/or consumers." Do you agree? Illustrate your answer with supply and demand curves.
5. "Government can correct for the external costs of pollution by imposing taxes on the pollutants firms emit or on the products they produce." Do you agree? Explain your answer with supply and demand curves.
6. Economists frequently refer to national defense as a public good. What does that term mean? If national defense benefits everyone, why do so many people demonstrate against it?
7. Name ten government-administered programs and give an economic justification for each. Which if any of those programs could be "privatized"—that is, turned over to private firms or produced by private firms with government subsidies?

Questions to Ponder

Part II

The Macroeconomy

Central Question

What are the major ways of measuring overall economic activity in the United States?

Key Terms

Gross national product (GNP)

Final goods and services

Intermediate goods and services

Real (constant dollar) gross national product

Net national product (NNP)

National income

Personal income

Disposable income

Unemployment rate

Labor force

Labor force participation rate

Inflation

Consumer price index

Chapter 5

Measurements of the Macroeconomy

"But 'glory' doesn't mean 'a nice knock-down argument,'" Alice objected.

"When I use a word," Humpty Dumpty said in a rather scornful tone, *"it means just what I choose it to mean—neither more nor less."*

"The question is," said Alice, *"whether you can make words mean so many different things."*

"The question is," said Humpty Dumpty, *"which is to be the master—that's all."*

Lewis Carroll

Our era is replete with macroeconomic problems. In newspaper headlines and news broadcasts, these problems are referred to as "recession," "unemployment," "inflation," "idle industrial capacity," "retarded economic growth," and "stagflation." In plainer language, they are lost production, lost income, rising prices, quiet factories, a stalled standard of living, and economic stagnation coupled with rising prices.

What can and should be done to correct these problems? That is the central question of the macroeconomic policy debates that greet us almost daily in the news media, and the central question of macroeconomics itself. Twenty years ago, economists generally agreed on the policies the government should follow to reach acceptable levels of national production, employment, and inflation. But years of high inflation and unemployment, both here and abroad, have shown how difficult it is for government, constrained by political reality, to achieve its stated policy objectives. In fact, many economists now suspect that government policy has increased unemployment and inflation—that the nation would have been better off without the government's attempts to alter overall economic performance. Others argue that to reduce unemployment and inflation, government must exercise even more powerful and direct control over the economy.

The following chapters attempt to develop an understanding of this issue. But first, to appreciate the magnitude and complexity of our macroeconomic problems, we must consider the problem of how to measure macroeconomic activity. This chapter covers macroeconomic measurement, and Chapter 6 outlines macroeconomic problems and policies. Then we must understand how the macroeconomy works, or how conditions in the various parts of the economy affect general economic activity— employment, production, incomes, and prices. Finally, we must appreciate the conflicts and tradeoffs that accompany policymakers' attempts to manipulate the macroeconomy. Macroeconomic theory and policy are treated in depth in Chapters 8 through 16.

Measurement is important in macroeconomics, for inaccurate or misleading measures can distort the statistics on which government policy decisions are based. Among the many ways of measuring macroeconomic activity, the most important are:

1. Gross national product, a measure of overall national production.
2. National personal and disposable income, measures of consumer buying power before and after taxes.
3. The unemployment rate, a measure of people's inability to find work.
4. The consumer price index, a measure of change in the general price level.

Gross National Product (GNP)

Measuring gross national product, or total production of goods and services, allows economists and policymakers to evaluate a nation's economic progress over a period of years and to monitor the impact of government policy on production and incomes. It also enables economists to test their theories of how the macroeconomy works against real-world data. And it allows government officials to develop policies that will increase the nation's production.

Business people use general economic data as they plan for future production. They understand that the sales of their product depend in part on the level of production in the economy as a whole. Automobile producers, for example, realize that the income and productivity of workers in other industries will influence the number of cars sold. If production is down elsewhere, people will earn less money and have less to spend on automobiles. With data on recent and current economic activity, business people can estimate roughly how much they should produce to meet future market demand, or how much to spend on raw materials and labor.

Thus any measurement of the nation's economic activity does more than record what has happened in the past; it also influences future policy. Figures showing that prices have been rising too fast can create public dissatisfaction, which may well influence future government policy. If figures show that production has dropped sharply in some sectors of the economy, businesses in other sectors of the economy may cut back on their production, thereby contributing to the slump. In short, economic measures like the GNP have an effect on the economy themselves. The methods used in calculating such data are therefore crucial to macroeconomic policy debates.

Definition of GNP

Though there are many ways of measuring the nation's general level of economic activity, the one used most often in developing government policy, and cited most often in the news media, is the gross national product (GNP). **Gross national product (GNP)** is the current market value in dollars of all final goods and services produced in the economy in a given period. Certain key words in this definition must be stressed. First, national production is measured in terms of current market value, which means current market prices. Market prices sometimes overstate, and sometimes understate, the intrinsic value of goods. To that extent, GNP may be distorted as a measure of general social welfare. GNP also includes the social "bads" that result from production, such as pollution and congestion, as well as goods designed to remedy them.

Second, only final goods and services are included in GNP. **Final goods and services** are those goods and services that are purchased for consumption rather than for further processing or resale. That is, GNP excludes the dollar value of intermediate goods used in the production process. **Intermediate goods and services** are goods and services that are purchased for further processing or resale. If intermediate goods were included in GNP, the total value of the nation's production would be vastly overstated. All intermediate goods would be counted at least twice—once when they are sold to be used in the production of final goods and again when the final products are sold.

Gross national product (GNP): the current market value in dollars of all final goods and services produced in the economy in a given period.

Final goods and services: those goods and services that are purchased for consumption rather than for further processing or resale.

Intermediate goods and services: goods and services that are purchased for further processing or resale.

Consider the intermediate good wheat, for instance. Wheat is used to make flour, an intermediate good used to make bread. The table below shows sales prices of given quantities of wheat, flour, and bread. If we add the value of all three transactions, our measure of total economic activity will be $600.

Wheat sold to the miller	$100
Flour sold to the baker	200
Bread sold to the consumer	300
	$600

But this procedure counts the value of the wheat three times: once by itself, once as part of the flour, and once as part of the bread. Because the value of the bread includes the value of the wheat and flour as well, total production can be measured by the market value of the final product alone—the bread.

Furthermore, if intermediate goods were included in GNP, that measure would change with changes in the structure of an industry. For example, if wheat production, flour milling, and baking were originally three separate businesses, but were later consolidated into one firm, our measure of total economic activity would fall from $600 to $300. Yet economic activity would not have changed. The farmer and miller would still be producing their products. But because they were now parts of a single firm, no market value would be attached to their activities.

Computation of GNP

Gross national product is normally stated in annual terms, though data are also compiled quarterly. Table 5.1 shows the gross national product for 1984, along with the figures used to calculate it. As in the example of bread production, the value of the nation's final products is stated as their dollar value at the time of sale. Of the $3,661 billion total, over $2,342 billion was consumer purchases ("personal consumption expenditures").

Table 5.1. Gross National Product, 1984[a]

	Billions of Dollars
Personal consumption expenditures	2,342.3
Gross private domestic investment	637.3
Government purchases of goods and services	748.0
Net exports (exports minus imports)	−66.3
Total	3,661.3

[a] Preliminary estimate.
Source: *Economic Report of the President* (Washington, D.C.: U.S. Government Printing Office, 1985), pp. 232–233.

Another $637 billion was purchased by businesses, in the form of plant and equipment and additions to inventory, and by households, in the form of new houses ("gross private domestic investment"). Federal, state, and local governments spent a little over $748 billion on goods and services ("government purchases of goods and services").

The negative figure in the last category of expenditures, "net exports," shows that exports from the United States totaled $66 billion less than imports into the nation. Since all exports are a part of U.S. production, you may wonder why only *net* exports are tabulated here. It is because other categories of expenditures include goods imported into the United States. For instance, when imported clothing is purchased by consumers, it is counted as a personal consumption expenditure. Yet imports are not part of U.S. production. They are the output of foreign countries, and should be subtracted from any measure of U.S. economic activity. By subtracting imports from exports, the net exports figure does just that.

Because the dollar amount buyers spend on goods and services must equal the dollar amount received by producers, total expenditures must equal the total value of goods produced. When added together, then, the four major categories of expenditures shown in Table 5.1 yield the gross national product.

Figure 5.1 shows GNP from 1929 to 1984. To a limited extent, this graph indicates the nation's economic progress over the long term. We can see, for example, that the Great Depression of the early 1930s was a substantial blow to the nation's economic activity. Furthermore we can see that production has grown irregularly, rising and then leveling out before rising again. By studying such data, economists can begin to draw some conclusions about the relationship between business and government policy and national production.

Shortcomings of the GNP

Though the gross national product is probably the best available measure of overall production in the United States, it is by no means perfect. One of its deficiencies, the fact that it omits entirely certain sectors of the economy, is of increasing concern to economists.

Nonmarket Production

With a few exceptions, the gross national product includes only final goods and services that are bought and sold in the market.[1] It excludes people's unpaid activities that benefit themselves, their families, and their friends. For instance, GNP includes the price paid for meat, potatoes, and lettuce,

1. The Department of Commerce assigns a value to the farm products that farmers grow and consume themselves. It also estimates the rental value of homes occupied by their owners. Both those figures are included in personal consumption expenditures.

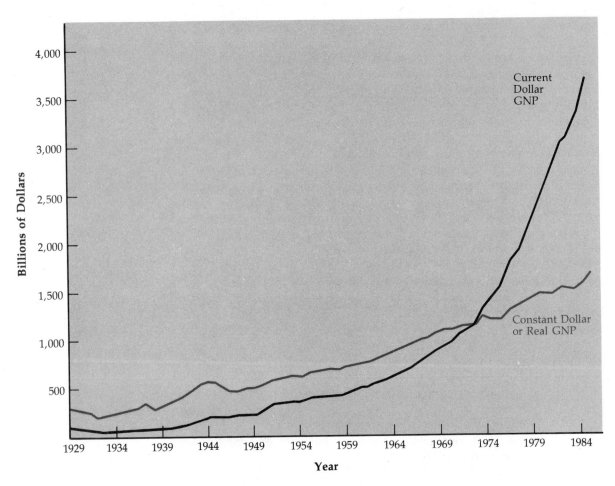

Figure 5.1. Gross National Product, 1929–1984.
The gross national product has increased significantly over the past five
or six decades.
Source: *Economic Report of the President* (Washington, D.C.: U.S. Government Printing Office,
1985), pp. 232, 234.

but not the value of the work done to prepare a meal. (It does include the
price of meals purchased at restaurants.) GNP includes the price paid for
landscaping, but not the value of yard work done by homeowners.

Two reasons have been given for excluding nonmarket activities from
GNP. First, it is extremely difficult to assign a value to the services people
provide for themselves, because the quality of those services varies greatly
from person to person. Second, economists have found it difficult to decide
which nonmarket activities should be included. Perhaps dishwashing,
clothes washing, and garbage removal should be included, but what about
tooth brushing? That service, when performed by a dentist, has a market
value—but few of us think we are adding to national production when
we brush our teeth.

Because nonmarket activities are excluded, trends in GNP may not accurately reflect changes in social welfare. For example, during the Great Depression, GNP fell from $103.1 billion in 1929 to $55.6 billion in 1933. Although people were much worse off in 1933 than in 1929, total production, including both market and nonmarket activity, had not fallen as much as GNP indicates. People who lost their jobs invested more time in maintaining their households. More people kept bigger gardens and did more repair work around the house than they had before the economic downturn. Although such activities could not compensate fully for lost income, people were able to offset their losses in part. But this increase in home-related productive activity was not included in GNP.

The Underground Economy

Many goods and services—hard drugs, moonshine liquor, and prostitution, for instance—are illegal in most areas of the United States. Nonetheless, they are part of the nation's total production—and because they are produced surreptitiously, they escape measurement. Other transactions are not counted because people are trying to evade taxation. To avoid taxes, many people trade rather than sell the goods they produce for the things they want. Others sell their goods and services for cash but do not report the income to the Internal Revenue Service. Waiters and waitresses, for example, often report only part of their tips; producers of firewood do not always declare the cash they receive; and many wealthy people store earnings from foreign assets in Swiss bank accounts closed to IRS inspection. Estimates of the size of the so-called underground economy vary. Some economists believe that the value of productive activity in this sector may be as high as a quarter of GNP.

Leisure Time

GNP makes no allowances for changes in the amount of time workers spend at their jobs. During this century the length of the work week (the average number of hours worked by each laborer each week) has gradually decreased, from about sixty hours in 1900 to just under forty hours in 1984. The value of today's workers' greater leisure time is not reflected in GNP. If people were still working as many hours as they once did, the total value of the nation's production would be much higher.

Production of "Bads"

In the course of producing goods and services, the economy also produces "bads"—things that detract from the quality of life. For example, steel mills often pollute the environment. Other industrial processes create solid wastes that are difficult to dispose of. The negative value of these by-products is not subtracted from the gross national product. Equipment purchased to clean up a pollution problem, however, is counted as part of GNP. Thus a snowfall in New York City or a flood in Lincoln, Nebraska, can lead to greater national production, but not greater national welfare.

Table 5.2. Gross National Product, 1929–1984

Year	GNP in Current Dollars (billions) (1)	GNP in Constant 1972 Dollars (billions) (2)	U.S. Population (millions) (3)	Per Capita GNP in Constant 1972 Dollars [(2) ÷ (3)] (4)
1929	$ 103.4	$ 315.7	121.8	$2,591
1933	55.8	222.1	125.6	1,768
1940	100.0	344.1	132.1	2,604
1950	286.5	534.8	152.3	3,511
1960	506.5	737.2	180.7	4,079
1970	992.7	1,085.6	205.1	5,293
1980	2,631.7	1,475.0	227.7	6,477
1984	3,661.3	1,639.0	236.6	6,927

Source: *Economic Report of the President* (Washington, D.C.: U.S. Government Printing Office, 1985), pp. 232–235, 265.

Prices of Goods and Services

Because GNP is computed in terms of current prices, comparisons over time are distorted by inflation. If prices rise, the GNP will reflect the inflation, exaggerating the increase in production of actual goods and services.

In Table 5.2, Column 1 shows the current-dollar value of the GNP for selected years from 1929 to 1984. At first glance, it appears that U.S. production was over 35 times greater in 1984 than in 1929. Output appears to have fallen by nearly 50 percent between 1929 and 1933, and to have risen by almost 270 percent between 1970 and 1984. Much of this apparent change in production is actually a change in prices, however. Prices fell significantly between 1929 and 1933, magnifying the underlying real drop in output. During the 1970s, prices rose at unprecedented peacetime rates, puffing the rather modest increases in total production out of proportion.

To eliminate distortions caused by price changes, the Department of Commerce adjusts GNP figures against various price indexes. These indexes measure changes in the price levels in particular sectors of the economy—such as lumber, agriculture, and energy—in relation to some base year, like 1972. For example, if the price of lumber rose 87 percent between 1972 and 1984, the price index for lumber would be 1.87 in 1984. To eliminate the influence of inflation, the Department of Commerce divides the 1984 production figure by 1.87. Similar adjustments are made for all sectors, and the resulting figures are then summed to obtain real, or constant dollar GNP. **Real (or constant dollar) gross national product** is the gross national product adjusted for price changes. Once such adjustments have been made for all years, changes in GNP over time will reflect changes in actual production, not changes in price.

Real (constant dollar) gross national product: the gross national product adjusted for price changes.

Table 5.3. Method of Computing Current Dollar Gross National Product and Real, or Constant Dollar, Gross National Product

Year	GNP in Current Prices (1)	GNP in Constant 1972 Prices (2)
1929	$P_{29} \times Q_{29}$	$P_{72} \times Q_{29}$
1933	$P_{33} \times Q_{33}$	$P_{72} \times Q_{33}$
1940	$P_{40} \times Q_{40}$	$P_{72} \times Q_{40}$
1950	$P_{50} \times Q_{50}$	$P_{72} \times Q_{50}$
1960	$P_{60} \times Q_{60}$	$P_{72} \times Q_{60}$
1970	$P_{70} \times Q_{70}$	$P_{72} \times Q_{70}$
1980	$P_{80} \times Q_{80}$	$P_{72} \times Q_{80}$
1984	$P_{84} \times Q_{84}$	$P_{72} \times Q_{84}$

Note: P = price; Q = quantity.

Table 5.3 shows the way real GNP is computed. The Ps and Qs stand for prices and quantities, respectively; the subscripts indicate the year. Notice that the values in column 1 vary with changes in both price and quantity, whereas the values in column 2 vary only with changes in quantity. If such adjustments are made for all the figures in column 1 of Table 5.2, we arrive at column 2 of Table 5.2, GNP in constant 1972 dollars. Constant dollar, or real, GNP figures for 1929 to 1984 are also plotted in Figure 5.1.

The absolute values of the figures represented in Figure 5.1 and in column 2 of Table 5.2 are less meaningful than their relative value. These constant dollar figures show that production in the United States was indeed greater in 1984 than in 1929—slightly more than 5 times greater. They also show that between 1929 and 1933, total production of goods and services fell less than current dollar figures would suggest—by approximately 30 percent rather than 50 percent. And between 1970 and 1984 output grew much less than the price-inflated figures in column 1 suggest. This can be illustrated by comparing the curves in Figure 5.1.

Note that in 1982 real GNP actually declined. Table 5.4 shows GNP for each quarter-year from 1981 to 1984. Real output fell by 3 percent between the third quarter (III) of 1981, when it was $1,525.8 billion, to the fourth quarter (IV) of 1982, when it was only $1,480.7 billion. Real GNP began to rise again in 1983; by the final quarter of 1984, it was nearly 12 percent above its 1982 low.

Population Growth

Real gross national product may increase over time, but if population grows faster, people will not be better off. To determine whether production

Table 5.4. Gross National Product by Quarter, 1981–1984

Year	Quarter	GNP in Current Dollars (billions) (1)	GNP in Constant 1972 Dollars (billions) (2)
1981	I	2,866.6	1,510.1
	II	2,912.5	1,512.5
	III	3,004.9	1,525.8
	IV	3,032.2	1,506.9
1982	I	3,021.4	1,485.8
	II	3,070.2	1,489.3
	III	3,090.7	1,485.7
	IV	3,109.2	1,480.7
1983	I	3,171.5	1,490.1
	II	3,272.0	1,525.1
	III	3,362.2	1,553.4
	IV	3,432.0	1,570.5
1984	I	3,553.3	1,610.9
	II	3,644.7	1,638.8
	III	3,694.6	1,645.2
	IV[a]	3,752.5	1,661.6

[a] Preliminary estimate.

Source: *Economic Report of the President* (Washington, D.C.: U.S. Government Printing Office, 1985), p. 232.

per capita (per person) is increasing, we must divide real GNP by yearly population figures. This procedure yields per capita real GNP, shown in column 4 of Table 5.2. On a per capita basis, U.S. production increased less than threefold between 1929 and 1984—less than the figures in columns 1 and 2 would suggest. Per capita figures offer no insight into how the national output is distributed among the population, however.

Quality of Goods and Services

GNP estimates the money value of goods and services. But prices do not necessarily reflect changes in the quality of goods, especially over a long period of time. As we have seen, the prices of calculators declined while their quality improved. Nor do prices reflect the division of output between consumer goods and government purchases. If a nation shifts production from consumer goods in peacetime to war equipment in wartime, the average citizen's standard of living may suffer, even though factories are operating night and day. Production increased dramatically during the Second World War, but many consumer goods, such as butter and hosiery, were so scarce they had to be rationed. And while some people may have

Table 5.5. Gross National Product, Net National Product, and Disposable Personal Income, 1929–1984 (in current dollars)

Year	Gross National Product (billions) (1)	Net National Product (billions) (2)	Disposable Personal Income (billions) (3)	Per Capita Disposable Personal Income (4)
1929	103.4	93.7	82.3	676
1933	55.8	48.3	45.5	363
1940	100.0	91.0	75.2	570
1950	286.5	262.3	205.5	1,362
1960	506.5	460.2	352.0	1,947
1970	992.7	904.7	695.3	3,390
1980	2,631.7	2,338.5	1,829.9	8,032
1981	3,073.0	2,713.8	2,176.5	8,874
1982	2,954.1	2,624.5	2,047.6	9,385
1983	3,304.8	2,927.7	2,340.1	9,977
1984[a]	3,661.3	3,258.4	2,578.1	10,893

[a] Preliminary estimate.

Source: *Economic Report of the President* (Washington, D.C.: U.S. Government Printing Office, 1985), pp. 254–261.

benefited because the demand for war materials increased the demand for and the price of their services, others—those who paid higher taxes to finance the war—may have been worse off.

Net National Product (NNP)

Gross national product includes the current value of all final goods and services, including plant and equipment (sometimes called capital goods) purchased by businesses to replace worn-out plant and equipment. Because replacement plant and equipment is included, GNP overstates the actual increase in total goods and services. To estimate the increase more accurately, the Department of Commerce subtracts the value of worn-out plant and equipment (called the capital consumption, or depreciation, allowance) from the gross national product. This adjusted measure is called net national product (NNP). **Net national product (NNP)** equals gross national product minus an allowance for replacement of worn-out plant and equipment (called the capital consumption allowance). Because replacement of old equipment has been subtracted, net national product is a better measure of the real growth of production than gross national product.

Net national product usually amounts to between 91 and 92 percent of gross national product (see Table 5.5, column 2). The two measures are equally good indicators of change in production over time.

Net national product (NNP): gross national product minus an allowance for replacement of worn-out plant and equipment (called the capital consumption allowance).

Net national product is a reasonably good indicator of national production over time, but it is not the best available measure of social welfare. It does not tell us how much of the rewards of production ends up in people's pockets. To see how much money people have to spend, and therefore how much of the gross national product they can buy, we must look at measures of national income.

National Income

National income is another way of measuring productive activity in the macroeconomy. When people produce goods and services, they generate wages and salaries that reflect their contribution to production. The rewards of production must ultimately be distributed to these people—employees, managers, or owners of capital assets. Thus total income received must equal the total value of goods and services produced. For instance, if $100 worth of goods is produced, the people who produce them must earn a total of $100 in income. The figure for national income is not obtained by summing individual incomes, however, but by making technical adjustments to net national product. **National income** is the total payment made to owners of productive resources for the use of those resources during a given period. It is equal to the total cost of producing the goods and services included in the net national product.

National income: the total payment made to owners of productive resources for the use of those resources during a given period.

Table 5.6 shows the method for computing national income from NNP. The most significant adjustment is the subtraction of indirect business taxes, like federal excise taxes on liquor and local property taxes, which are not considered to be payments to resource owners.

National income does not tell us how much money consumers earn. That figure is called personal income. **Personal income** is that part of national income which is paid to individuals as opposed to businesses.

Personal income: the part of national income that is paid to individuals as opposed to businesses.

Corporate profits, interest payments that do not go directly to individuals, and Social Security taxes must be subtracted from national income to obtain the figure for personal income. Then government transfer payments, interest income, corporate dividend payments, and business transfer payments received by individuals must be added (see Table 5.6). The method of accounting is somewhat arbitrary; Social Security taxes are deducted but personal income taxes are not. (No good reason has been given for the discrepancy.)

Personal income still does not tell us how much money people have to spend. Because of taxation, people's take-home pay is usually much less than their total income. A better measure of their welfare may be what they take home after taxes for use in the purchase of goods and services. This measure is called disposable (personal) income. **Disposable income** is personal income minus personal income tax payments.

Disposable income: personal income minus personal income tax payments.

Disposable income in the United States is shown in columns 3 and 4 of Table 5.5. In 1984, Americans received a total disposable income of $2,578 billion, or approximately 70 percent of the gross national product for that year. Of that amount, consumers spent $2,421 billion and about $157

Table 5.6. Relationship of Net National Product, National Income, Personal Income, and Disposable Income, 1984[a] (in billions of dollars)

Gross national product	3,661.1
Less: Capital consumption allowances	402.9
Equals: *Net national product*	3,258.4
Less: Indirect business taxes	304.3
Business transfers	17.3
Statistical discrepancy	−8.2
Plus: Subsidies less current surplus of government enterprises	14.4
Equals: *National income*	2,959.4
Less: Corporate profits	284.5
Net interest	285.0
Contributions for social insurance	305.9
Wage accruals less disbursement	.0
Plus: Government transfer payments to persons	399.5
Personal interest income	434.8
Personal dividend income	77.7
Business transfer payments	17.3
Equals: *Personal income*	3,013.2
Less: Personal tax and nontax payments	435.1
Equals: *Disposable personal income*	2,578.1
Composed of: Personal outlays	2,421.2
Personal saving	156.9

[a] Preliminary estimate.
Source: *Economic Report of the President* (Washington, D.C.: U.S. Government Printing Office, 1985), pp. 254–260.

billion (6.1 percent) was saved. In 1929, by contrast, Americans received approximately 80 percent of GNP as disposable income. The 10 percentage-point drop in personal income between 1929 and 1984 is mostly because taxes were higher in 1984 than in 1929.

Disposable income figures must be adjusted for price changes and population growth before they can accurately reflect changes in consumer purchasing power. (See column 4 of Table 5.5 for per capita disposable income in current dollar terms.)

The Unemployment Rate

Gross national product and national income are positive measures of the nation's economic activity. The unemployment rate, on the other hand, estimates economic activity that is not occurring. This negative measure indicates the portion of the nation's labor force that is out of work.

Unemployment data are compiled monthly by the Bureau of Labor Statistics. Table 5.7 shows the average monthly unemployment rate for selected years from 1950 to 1984. The 1950 unemployment rate of 5.3 percent was considered high at the time. Two decades later the rate had fallen slightly to 4.8. But in 1975, the rate hit an alarming 8.3 percent, and by the early 1980s it had almost doubled its 1970 level.

Like GNP, the unemployment rate is interpreted by the press, by the public, by government officials, and by business people as a sign of how successfully public policy goals are being met. Almost everyone thinks that an increase in the unemployment rate is a sign of worsening economic activity and increasing social hardship. Like a drop in GNP, a rise in unemployment could induce some businesses to curtail their production plans in anticipation of reduced consumer demand—perhaps causing even more workers to be laid off. Worsening unemployment can be a boon to opposition candidates in election years. In 1980 President Reagan scored political points with the unemployed, unions, and other worker groups by stressing the apparent failure of the Carter administration to control unemployment, then at 7 percent.

In evaluating the unemployment rate and the statements of politicians, it helps to remember Humpty Dumpty's remark in Lewis Carroll's *Through the Looking Glass.* "When I use a word, it means just what I choose it to mean—neither more nor less." When the Bureau of Labor Statistics uses the term "unemployment rate," the bureau chooses it to mean something very specific. The rate is computed using precise definitions of "employed" and "unemployed," which have a significant effect on its numerical value.

Computing the Unemployment Rate

Unemployment rate: the ratio of the number of people estimated to be unemployed to the number of people estimated to be in the labor force, stated as a percentage.

Stated rigorously, the **unemployment rate** is the ratio of the number of people estimated to be unemployed to the number of people estimated to be in the labor force, stated as a percentage, or

$$\text{unemployment rate} = \frac{\text{number unemployed}}{\text{labor force}}$$

Labor force: all persons sixteen years of age or older who are willing and able to work and who are counted as either unemployed or employed.

Labor force also has a very specific meaning: the **labor force** consists of all persons sixteen years of age or older who are willing and able to work and who are counted as either unemployed or employed,[2] or

$$\text{labor force} = \text{number unemployed} + \text{number employed}$$

Specifically, the only people who can be counted as employed or unemployed are those who are at least sixteen years old and who are not institutionalized—that is, do not reside in a penal or mental institution or

---

2. The civilian labor force equals the labor force minus the members of the armed forces of the United States. The civilian unemployment rate is the number unemployed divided by the civilian labor force.

Table 5.7. Number of People Employed and Unemployed, and the Unemployment Rate, 1950–1984

Year	Millions of People Employed (1)	Millions of People Unemployed (2)	Millions of People in the Labor Force [(1) + (2)] (3)	Unemployment Rate (percent) [(2) ÷ (1)] (4)	Labor Force Participation Rate[a] (percent) (5)
1950	58.9	3.3	62.2	5.9	59.2
1960	65.8	3.9	69.7	5.6	59.4
1970	78.7	4.1	82.8	5.0	60.4
1980	99.3	7.6	106.9	7.1	63.8
1981	100.4	8.3	108.7	7.6	63.9
1982	99.5	10.7	110.4	9.7	64.0
1983	100.8	10.7	111.5	9.6	64.0
1984	106.7	8.5	115.2	7.4	64.7

[a] Labor force participation rate = labor force ÷ noninstitutionalized population.
Source: *Economic Report of the President* (Washington, D.C.: U.S. Government Printing Office, 1985), p. 266.

a home for the aged, infirm, or needy. The Bureau of Labor Statistics excludes persons under sixteen years of age because child labor laws, compulsory education, and general social customs prevent most of them from working.

Subject to the restrictions indicated above, employed persons include:

1. All persons who, during the week in which the survey was taken, did any work at all for pay, or who worked at least fifteen hours without pay in a family-operated business.
2. All persons who were not working during the survey week, but who were temporarily absent from their jobs or businesses because of illness, bad weather, vacation, strikes, or a number of personal reasons.
3. Members of the military.

Unemployed persons include:

1. All persons who did not work at all during the week of the survey, but who were looking for work and were available for work.
2. All persons who had made some effort to find work in the past four weeks (such as filling out an application) and were waiting for the results.
3. All persons who (a) were waiting to be called back to a job from which they had been laid off, (b) were waiting to report to a new job within the next thirty days, or (c) would have been looking for work if they had not been sick.

Classified as "not in the labor force" are all those who are not considered either employed or unemployed, and who are not in the military. This group includes people who

are under 16 years of age, or are full-time students

are homemakers

are unable to work

are retired

work fewer than fifteen hours a week without pay for their family business

work without pay for a charitable or religious organization

do seasonal work and are idle because it is off season

are scheduled to report to a new job in more than thirty days

Columns 1 and 2 of Table 5.7 show the numbers of people employed and unemployed, from which the yearly unemployment rates in column 4 were computed.

Unemployment statistics are gathered from a survey of a representative sample of people in approximately fifty-five thousand housing units located in nearly one thousand counties and cities throughout the nation. They include data on over one hundred thousand people sixteen years of age or older. Each household is interviewed for four consecutive months, dropped for the next eight months, and then interviewed again for four more months. In gathering the data, the Bureau of Labor Statistics relies on the voluntary cooperation of those who are questioned.

Shortcomings of Employment and Unemployment Statistics

Like any data, employment and unemployment figures are no more reliable than the workers who administer the survey and those who are interviewed. If survey procedures are changed or if survey workers do not follow established procedures—that is, if they vary the wording or emphasis of the questions—the results of the survey will be distorted. If those who are interviewed conceal their true employment status, the results will be distorted further. Small changes in unemployment rates from month to month may reflect errors and procedural changes as much as true changes in the number of people employed and unemployed.

Unemployment statistics do not measure the hardship borne by the underemployed. Anyone who has worked for pay at all during the survey week is counted as employed—even those who have worked only five or ten hours. If production cuts in the automobile industry drastically reduce the number of days or hours its employees can work, unemployment figures for auto workers will not be affected.

Finally unemployment statistics are not adjusted for changes in the relative size of the labor force. One reason for the increase in the unemployment rate over the last three decades is that a growing percentage of the working-age population has been looking for jobs. For a more accurate picture of national employment, we must look at the labor force participation rate. The **labor force participation rate** is the number of people employed divided by the number of people in the labor force. Table 5.7 shows that the labor force participation rate increased almost 5 percentage points from 1950 to 1984, slightly more than the increase in the unemployment rate.

Labor force participation rate: the number of people employed divided by the number of people in the labor force.

Reducing the Unemployment Rate

For several reasons, the unemployment rate as defined by the Bureau of Labor Statistics, can never be reduced to zero. In a dynamic economy people will always be changing jobs. Among them will be some who expect to report to a new job within thirty days, but are classified as unemployed by the government. Others may decline a job that is offered in hope of finding a better one. Some who are willingly unemployed may claim they are still job hunting so that their unemployment pay will continue. Those who are employed in the illegal underground economy may not admit they are working. And finally, some people simply do not have the skills to earn the minimum wage rate for even the most menial jobs. In short, because of government procedures, voluntary unemployment, and unreported employment, the unemployment rate may exaggerate the extent of economic hardship in the nation.

For these reasons, it is doubtful that the unemployment rate, as currently defined, can be reduced much below 5 percent (some would say 6 percent). Others contend that unless some changes are made—like the elimination of the minimum wage law and of union barriers to entry into various labor markets—the unemployment rate will not fall much below 7 percent for very long.

The Consumer Price Index (CPI)

Another negative measure of the nation's economic well-being is the inflation rate. **Inflation** is a rise in the general level of prices over a period of time. If the prices of some goods rise but others fall, the general price level has not necessarily risen, although the relative prices of goods have changed. Inflation occurs when a rise in the prices of many goods and services is not offset by a decrease in the prices of other goods and services. In other words, during inflationary times, the price level, or weighted average of all prices, rises.

The measurement of price levels and ultimately inflation rates depends on what prices are averaged and how they are weighted. The consumer price index (CPI), computed by the Bureau of Labor Statistics, is the measure of price level most often cited. The **consumer price index (CPI)** is the ratio of the cost of specific consumer items in any one year to the cost of those items in the base year, 1967. Because the CPI includes things consumers buy regularly, it is frequently called the cost of living index. The index does not, however, represent everyone's cost of living. It is

Inflation: a rise in the general level of prices over a period of time.

Consumer price index (CPI): the ratio of the cost of specific consumer items in any one year to the cost of those items in the base year, 1967.

designed to represent the changes in the prices of specific goods that are bought in large quantities by people who work and shop in cities, like craftsmen, factory supervisors, carpenters, and salespeople.

The CPI provides a reasonably accurate estimate of the price level of thousands of items produced by twenty-four thousand businesses in eighty-five urban areas, however. The so-called market basket, or list of items covered by the survey, includes most goods and services urban consumers buy. Food, clothing, automobiles, homes, house furnishings, household supplies, fuel, drugs, and recreational goods; fees to doctors, lawyers, and beauty shops; rent, repair costs, transportation fares, public utility rates, and sales, property, and excise taxes are all included. Prices are weighted according to their importance in a typical family budget in the years 1971–1973.[3] Then the index figure is obtained by dividing the cost of the market basket for the year by its cost in 1967, the base year, and multiplying by 100. For example, the consumer price index for 1984 will be figured this way:

$$\text{consumer price index} = \frac{\text{cost of market basket in 1984}}{\text{cost of market basket in 1967}} \times 100$$

The index figure for 1967 is equal to 100 (that is, the cost of the market basket for 1967 divided by the cost of the same basket of goods, which equals 1, multiplied by 100). Because prices were lower in the years before 1967, the index figures for those years are less than 100. Since 1967 prices have been higher, and the index figures are greater than 100.

Table 5.8 gives the consumer price index for selected years from 1929 to 1984. Prices fell by around 24 percent between 1929 and 1933, the period of the Great Depression. They nearly tripled in the three decades between 1933 and 1967, and more than tripled again in the decade-and-a-half between 1967 and 1984. From a yearly rate of 1.6 percent in 1960, inflation jumped to 13.5 percent in 1980 before dropping to 4.0 percent in 1984.

Summary and Extensions

The gross national product, the unemployment rate, and the consumer price index measure the performance of the U.S. economy in terms of national production, the percentage of the work force without jobs, and the level of prices. These figures will always be rough approximations of the variables they measure. The method used for determining gross national product dictates that much productive activity will go unmeasured, for we lack a reasonable means of estimating the monetary value of the goods and services we produce for ourselves and for the underground economy. And the method used for calculating the unemployment and employment rates counts as employed some people who are hard hit by economic decline, whereas others who are working (in the underground exonomy) are considered unemployed.

---

3. The Bureau of Labor Statistics found that the average family of four allocated its budget as follows: 24.8 percent for food, 22.5 percent for housing, 8.4 percent for transportation, and 44.5 percent for medical care, services, and clothing.

Table 5.8. Consumer Price Index, 1929–1984 (base year 1967)

Year	Consumer Price Index (1)	Annual (year-to-year) Percentage Change in Consumer Price Index (2)
1929	51.3	0.0
1933	38.8	−5.1
1940	42.0	1.0
1950	72.1	1.0
1960	88.7	1.6
1967	100.0	2.9
1970	116.3	5.9
1980	246.8	13.5
1984	311.1	4.3

Sources: U.S. Bureau of the Census, *Historical Statistics of the United States* (Washington, D.C.: U.S. Government Printing Office, 1975), pp. 210–211; *Economic Report of the President* (Washington, D.C.: U.S. Government Printing Office, 1985), pp. 294, 296.

Slight inaccuracies like these are unavoidable. All-inclusive surveys of employment and price levels would be prohibitively costly. The Bureau of Labor Statistics cannot interview every potential worker in the United States every month. Nor can it hope to record the monthly prices of all the millions of goods and services produced by the economy. Thus the Bureau has adopted sampling procedures based on broad categories of employment status and a representative selection of consumer goods.

As rough as they are, macroeconomic statistics can influence the nation's economic performance. Changes in the gross national product and other indexes can cause businesses to alter their production plans and support or undermine the public's confidence in the economy. If the statistics look bad, politicians may feel compelled to do something to demonstrate their concern, even though their response may be inadequately planned, ill-timed, and perhaps unwarranted. Unless we understand the meaning of these statistics—their sample base, limitations, and deficiencies—they may become our masters, as Humpty Dumpty suggested. People unfamiliar with the definition of *unemployed* may ask why government does not try to reduce unemployment to zero, for instance. They may expect more of government than it can possibly deliver.

Major Conclusions

1. Gross national product is a measure of total production of final goods and services in the United States during a specified period of time— usually one calendar year. GNP is deficient in several respects: it values goods in terms of their market prices; does not include all production in the economy; does not allow for changes in the amount of time people spend at work; is not adjusted for the production of economic

"bads"; and does not reflect the impact of changes in the price level and in population.

2. The computation of real GNP corrects for price changes. The calculation of per capita GNP corrects for population changes.

3. Net national product is obtained by subtracting a capital consumption allowance for replacement of old equipment from gross national product. NNP measures real growth in production rather than maintenance of existing productive capacity.

4. National production can be computed by adding up either the total market value of the goods and services sold, or the total expenditures made on those goods and services. Because the market value of goods is determined by the amount of money people spend on goods and services, the two measures must be equal.

5. National income is a measure of the income received by all resources. Personal income is a measure of the income people receive before personal taxes. Disposable income is a measure of the amount of income people have available to spend after taxes.

6. The unemployment rate is an indicator of lost production as well as a measure of the economic hardship suffered by workers. The calculated unemployment rate is based on very precise definitions of who is and is not employed and unemployed. Because of the definition of unemployed used by the Bureau of Labor Statistics, the unemployment rate cannot be expected to fall to zero.

7. Because the unemployment rate does not recognize partial employment or underemployment, it does not capture the full extent of social hardship and forgone production. The unemployment rate also fails to reflect changes in the size of the labor force.

8. The consumer price index is a means of measuring inflation. Because it is based on a survey of goods and services that are not bought in the same proportions by everyone, the CPI does not give a true indication of changes in the cost of living for all consumers.

1. Are absolute current-dollar GNP figures meaningful?
2. Using the definitions of employed, unemployed, and not in the labor force, classify each of the following:
   a. A person who works twenty hours a week without pay in a family-owned drugstore.
   b. A person who works ten hours a week for a charitable organization.
   c. A person who works six hours a week for pay.
   d. A person who is on strike.
   e. A steel worker who has been laid off because of a strike in the automobile industry.
   f. A person who expects to report back to work within ten days.
   g. A person who is not working but who expects to report to a new job within sixty days.
   h. A person whose hours have been cut from forty to twenty per week.
   i. A person who is not working but who expects to report to a new job within fifteen days.
   j. A full-time college student.
   k. A person out of work because of sickness.
   l. A person fifteen years old who works thirty hours a week for pay.
   m. A person seventeen years old who works fourteen hours a week on his family's farm.
3. Presuming the data in question 2 cover the whole labor force, determine the unemployment rate.
4. Should much importance be attached to small month-to-month changes in the unemployment rate and consumer price index? Why? How may government interpret such changes? How may an opposition party interpret them?
5. Do people have sufficient incentive to learn about the limitations and deficiencies of economic statistics? Given your answer, how may these statistics be used by politicians?

Questions to Ponder

Central Question

What major macro-economic problems does our nation face, and what macro-economic policies have been designed to solve them?

Key Terms

Demand-pull inflation

Cost-push inflation

Structural inflation

Transitional (frictional) unemployment

Cyclical unemployment

Structural unemployment

Natural rate of unemployment

Phillips curve

Stagflation

Trend

Business cycle

Recession

Trough

Recovery

Peak

Leading indicator

Aggregate demand

Aggregate supply

Chapter 6

Macroeconomic Problems and Policies

*What can be done [about
inflation]? Before we look for
remedies, we must examine the
causes. Inflation is like cancer:
many substances are
carcinogenic, and many
activities generate inflation.
The sources of inflation can be
diagnosed at several levels. . . .
Inflation usually is the final
link in the chain of well-meant
actions. Inflation is the long-
run consequence of short-run
expediencies. Life, to be sure, is
a succession of short runs, but
every moment is also the long
run of some expedience of long
ago. We are now experiencing
the long-run consequences of
the short-run policies of the
past. These consequences are as
unacceptable as rain on
weekends, and just as easy to
change.*
Henry Wallich

*T*he last chapter described several ways economists measure macroeconomic activity—or the lack of it. In this chapter we will use those measures to explore the depth and breadth of the economic problems our nation faces, as well as various theories about the causes and cures of those problems.

A macroeconomic policy to improve the welfare of much or all of a nation's population must pursue goals that have achieved some general consent. Macroeconomic goals on which policymakers and the public generally agree include:

1. Full and stable employment
2. Price stability
3. High and rising incomes

Attaining these goals is no simple matter, however.

The opening chapters of this book noted that every economic endeavor has a cost. This is certainly the case with macroeconomic policy. The pursuit of stable prices may require that we forgo some jobs. Attempts to stabilize employment may reduce economic growth. The search for macroeconomic stability may also require that we sacrifice some individual freedoms, since no government policy ever enjoys the consent of all citizens. Therefore, in considering our macroeconomic problems and the policies available to us, we might ask:

How serious is the problem?

What can be done about it?

At what costs will the problem be resolved?

Macroeconomic Problems

In recent decades, the United States and most other nations have failed to reach their macroeconomic goals. In varying degrees, they have faced inflation, unemployment, or both of those problems simultaneously—a macroeconomic condition that has been called stagflation. Economic growth has been sluggish in many parts of the world. We will examine the effects and suspected causes of each of these problems in turn.

Inflation

The price level has been changing throughout U.S. history. Periods of increasing prices have alternated with periods of decreasing prices (see Figure 6.1). Most episodes of rapid inflation have occurred during wartime: the War of 1812, the Civil War, the two world wars, and the Korean and Vietnam wars (1950–1953 and 1961–1973).

Persistent growth in the peacetime inflation rate is a recent problem. Over the nineteenth century, prices drifted gradually downward. In 1800

Figure 6.1. The Consumer Price Index, 1800–1984.
Over the past two centuries the price level has moved both up and down. Many of the fluctuations occurred during times of major change in the nation's monetary institutions.
Sources: U.S. Bureau of the Census, *Historical Statistics of the United States* (Washington, D.C.: U.S. Government Printing Office, 1975), pp. 210–211; *Economic Report of the President* (Washington, D.C.: U.S. Government Printing Office, 1985), p. 291.

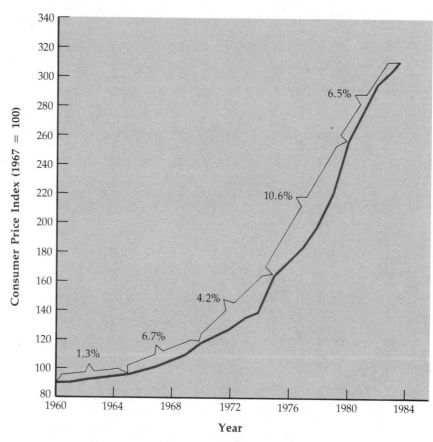

Figure 6.2. The Consumer Price Index, 1960–1984.
Over the past twenty-five years the consumer price index has moved sharply upward, reflecting rising rates of inflation. From an average of 1.3 percent in 1960–1964, inflation rose to an average of 8.9 percent in the last half of the 1970s. By 1984, however, the rate had fallen to an average of 6.5 percent.
Source: *Economic Report of the President* (Washington, D.C.: U.S. Government Printing Office, 1985), p. 291.

the consumer price index stood at less than 40; one hundred years later, after several periods of ups and downs, it was only 25.[1] Not until the 1920s did the index regain its 1800 level. But by 1950, the CPI stood at 72—44 percent higher than it had been just twenty years earlier. And in the next decade alone, the price level rose 23 percent.

The generally upward course of prices over the last twenty-five years is shown more clearly in Figure 6.2. During the first half of the 1960s, the inflation rate was a modest 1.3 percent. But in the second half of the

1. The index figures for the years before 1930, when data were not gathered regularly, are rough estimates only.

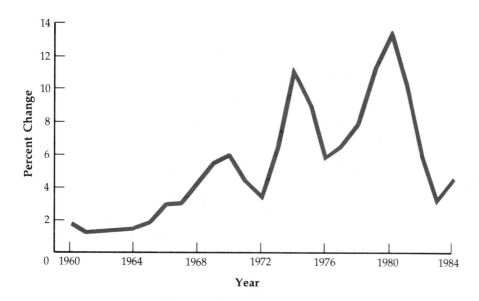

Figure 6.3. Percent Change in the Consumer Price Index, 1960–1984.
The inflation rate, as measured by the percentage change in the consumer price index, generally moved sharply upward during the 1960s and 1970s. However, the pace of price increases was very irregular, especially during the 1970s. On an annual basis, the inflation rate peaked at an average of 11 percent in 1974, only to fall to 5.8 percent in 1976. In 1980 it peaked again at an annual average of 13.5 percent. On a month-to-month basis, the inflation rate in 1980 was even more volatile: it fell from 18.2 percent in January to 1.2 percent in July, and then rose to 14 percent in November.
Source: *Economic Report of the President* (Washington, D.C.: U.S. Government Printing Office, 1985), p. 295.

decade, as the war in Vietnam escalated, prices began to move sharply upward. The average rate of inflation for the period 1965 to 1970 was 4.2 percent. For the early 1970s, despite government-imposed price controls, the rate was even higher, 6.7 percent. In 1974, it hit a shocking 11 percent, and for the rest of the decade inflation continued high, at an average of 10.6 percent. Not until the early 1980s—a decade after the end of the Vietnam War—did inflation return to the levels of the late 1960s.

The generally rising inflation rate was all the more difficult to deal with because it varied from year to year. It might reach 6 percent in one year and fall to 4 percent the next, and then rise to double-digit levels. At times during 1979 and 1980, the rate of inflation rose to 15 to 18 percent. Predicting future inflation rates became an exercise in crystal-ball gazing, and planning future purchases became a risky endeavor for both consumers and business people. The volatile annual U.S. inflation rates are shown in Figure 6.3.

U.S. inflation has been lower than that of many other nations (See Table 6.1). During the late 1950s and most of the 1960s, the United States had one of the world's lowest compound inflation rates, 2 percent. The

Table 6.1. Inflation Rates in Selected Countries, 1955–1982

Country	Compound Annual Rate of Change in Consumer Prices				
	1955–1968	1969–1974	1975–1978	1980–1981	1981–1982
Chile	28	225	180	20	10
Argentina	27	32	244	105	165
Brazil	38	21	36	106	98
Colombia	10	15	23	28	25
Ecuador	2	11	13	16	16
Peru	9	9	38	75	65
France	5	7	10	13	12
West Germany	2	6	4	6	5
Italy	3	8	15	18	17
Japan	4	10	7	5	3
Switzerland	2	7	7	7	6
United Kingdom	3	9	15	12	9
Canada	2	5	8	12	11
United States	2	6	7	10	6

Source: U.S. Congress, Joint Economic Committee, *Industrial Policy Movement in the United States: Is It the Answer?* 98th Congress, 2nd Session (Washington, D.C.: U.S. Government Printing Office, June 8, 1984), p. 24.

compound rate was higher in 1970, 7 percent, but still one of the world's lowest. Even the double-digit rate of 1980–1981 was below the rates of most other nations.

The record of the past two-and-a-half decades nevertheless raises some questions:

What causes inflation?

Why has inflation risen so dramatically in the last several decades?

How does inflation affect our ability to produce and earn a living?

What are the costs and benefits of inflation?

What role does government policy play in creating inflation?

What can government do to stop or at least moderate inflation?

These questions have no easy answers. If they did, inflation would surely not be such a persistent problem. As the Wallich quotation at the opening of this chapter suggests, part of the difficulty is that inflation has many causes.

Types of Inflation

There are three types of inflation: demand-pull, cost-push, and structural. Each has a different cause. **Demand-pull inflation** occurs when total planned expenditures increase faster than total production. That is, people

Demand-pull inflation: a general rise in prices that occurs when total planned expenditures increase faster than total production.

want to buy more than the economy is producing. In bidding for the limited number of goods and services available, they pull prices up. Demand-pull inflation may be stimulated by increases in the supply of money or in government expenditures—a subject to which we will return in later chapters.

Cost-push inflation occurs when restrictions are placed on the supply of one or more resources, or when the price of one or more resources is increased. For example, cost-push inflation may result from a cutoff in oil imports because of war or political disturbances. Competition for the restricted supply pushes oil prices up. Or it may arise from a curtailment of food supplies, like wheat or soy beans, because of poor weather. Cost-push inflation may also stem from wage increases that are not matched by productivity increases or from price fixing on the part of monopolies and oligopolies. In all these instances, output is restricted, either physically, or as in the last two cases, because a higher price reduces the demand for a resource. Competition among consumers for the limited output then forces the general price level up.

Structural inflation occurs when producers cannot readily shift production in response to changes in the structure of the economy. Changes in the demand for a product, in the technology of its production, and in the competition producers face can all cause structural inflation. Structural inflation may result when the overall composition of what consumers, businesses, and governments want to buy changes and producers cannot readily alter their employment of resources and their product mix. It may also be caused by the introduction of a major production innovation—for example, the advent of trains or the development of assembly-line robots. Changes in the structure of the economy create strategic shortages, or bottlenecks, in production supply lines. If a good like steel is caught in such a bottleneck, its price will rise, and that increase will then be transmitted to the prices of many other goods that use steel.

Reducing Inflation

There are two major problems in dealing with inflation. The first is identifying which type of inflation is at work, because each type needs a different response. Demand-pull inflation may be tackled by reducing total spending—for example, by cutting government expenditures or increasing income taxes (since higher taxes will reduce consumer spending). Programs to increase the supply of certain key products, such as oil, may relieve cost-push inflation. Structural inflation may be attacked by eliminating the problems workers encounter in moving among different industries.

The second problem is to overcome political objections to implementing the appropriate policies. If inflation is caused by increases in the amount of money in circulation or by excessive government spending, then the obvious solution is to control the money supply and the government's tendency to overspend. But such steps may be politically unpopular. As long as citizens believe in the existence of the free lunch, governmental belt tightening—especially when it hits one's favorite government program—is bound to be controversial.

Cost-push inflation: a general rise in prices that occurs when restrictions are placed on the supply of one or more resources, or when the price of one or more resources is increased.

Structural inflation: a general rise in prices that occurs when producers cannot shift production in response to changes in the structure of the economy.

Unemployment

During most of the years from 1959 to 1970, unemployment fluctuated between 3 and 7 percent. After 1970, however, the rate moved irregularly upward, peaking above 10 percent in 1982 (see Figure 6.4).

Unemployment means lost output as well as personal hardship for those who are out of work. Besides reducing output, unemployment triggers higher government expenditures on unemployment compensation and welfare programs. Eventually those expenditures are translated into higher taxes for the reduced working population—a problem in itself.

As in the case of inflation, the data on national production and unemployment raise many questions:

Why is the national production level not greater than it is? Why is it not smaller?

Why is the unemployment rate so high? Why has the rate not fallen below 4 percent more often? Why does the economy seem unable to operate with unemployment of less than 3 percent?

How has government policy affected the nation's unemployment and production levels?

Why has a growing percentage of the labor force sought employment outside the home? Why has the economy not provided all such people with jobs?

Types of Unemployment

Unemployment has various causes, each requiring its own remedy. Unemployment may be transitional (frictional), cyclical, or structural. **Transitional (frictional) unemployment** occurs when people move from one job to another requiring similar skills. Transitional unemployment is caused by normal shifts in the supply of and demand for products. It is generally temporary, lasting a few days to a few weeks. **Cyclical unemployment** is caused by downswings of the business cycle—that is, by a broad-based reduction in the overall level of spending in the economy. It generally lasts for a period of weeks or months, until an increase in business activity raises national output and increases demand for labor. **Structural unemployment** is caused by major changes in the skills needed by workers, because of technological innovation or changes in the relative competitiveness of an industry. Structural unemployment can last for years, until workers are retrained for new jobs.

Reducing Unemployment

The three types of unemployment require different solutions. Transitional unemployment may be shortened by providing information on jobs—for example, through Job Service offices. Manipulation of government spending and tax policies can moderate business cycles, thus reducing cyclical

Transitional (frictional) unemployment: unemployment that occurs when people move from one job to another requiring similar skills.

Cyclical unemployment: unemployment that is caused by downswings of the business cycle—that is, by a broad-based reduction in the overall level of spending in the economy.

Structural unemployment: unemployment that occurs with major changes in the skills needed by workers.

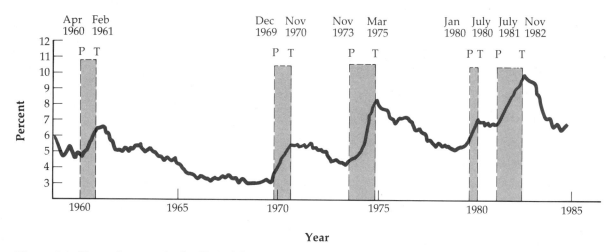

Figure 6.4. Unemployment in the United States.
Over the past twenty-five years, the unemployment rate has rarely dropped below 4 percent. Since the late 1960s, the rate has gradually increased, rising to unusually high levels during times of recession (the shaded areas). The *P*s correspond to peaks, the *T*s to troughs.
Source: U.S. Department of Commerce, Bureau of Economic Analysis, *Business Conditions Digest* (February 1985), p. 18.

unemployment. Relief of structural unemployment may require the introduction of special training programs or changes in the educational system.

Realistically, however, unemployment can never be completely eliminated. The natural rate of unemployment is always higher than zero. The **natural rate of unemployment** is that minimum percentage of the labor force that is unemployed because of structural problems in the economy and transitional movement among jobs. As we saw in the preceding chapter, the unemployment rate is really a snapshot of the economy at a given point in time. At any particular moment, some people will be caught changing jobs. Others will be counted as unemployed because of the way the Department of Commerce defines unemployed. In a dynamic economy, furthermore, some workers are bound to be out of work because of changes in the structure of the economy. That is, their skills are no longer easily employed where they live. Until they adjust their skills or location, they will be counted among the unemployed.

Economists generally agree that the natural rate of unemployment is several percentage points above zero. But they do not agree on exactly what the figure might be, and whether or not it has been rising over time. (See the box on the rise in the natural unemployment rate, pages 136–137.) In the 1960s, many economists felt that the natural unemployment rate might be as low as 3 or 4 percent. Nowadays, many believe it is at least 6 percent, if not 7 percent or more.

Natural rate of unemployment: the minimum percentage of the labor force that is unemployed because of structural problems in the economy and transitional movement among jobs.

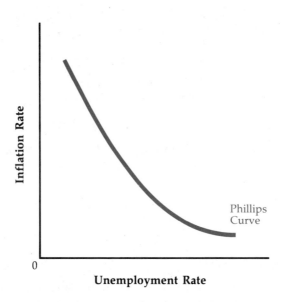

Figure 6.5. The Tradeoff Between Inflation and Unemployment.
The Phillips curve illustrates the presumed inverse relationship between unemployment and inflation. Theoretically, the inflation rate rises when the unemployment rate falls, and vice versa.

Stagflation

As recently as twenty years ago, most economists and government policymakers believed that high unemployment would be accompanied by low rates of inflation, and vice versa. During periods of high unemployment, they reasoned, workers would be competing for a restricted number of jobs and thus would lose much of their ability to drive up wages. (Wage increases would be passed on to consumers as higher prices.) High unemployment would also depress people's incomes, and thus the demand for goods and services. Lower demand would mean less upward pressure on prices.

This presumed relationship between unemployment and inflation is shown graphically by the Phillips curve, named for the British economist who first observed it (see Figure 6.5). The **Phillips curve** is a graphical representation of the presumed inverse relationship between unemployment and inflation. Since the 1960s, much of government policy has been based on the idea that a lower unemployment rate could be traded for a higher inflation rate, and vice versa. In other words, using government fiscal and monetary powers, policymakers could move the macroeconomy up or down the Phillips curve at will. The only question facing policymakers was which combination of unemployment and inflation they should seek.

Events of the 1970s and early 1980s disproved that line of thinking, however. As Figure 6.6 shows, inflation and unemployment were not inversely related in those years—at least not for more than a few months.

Phillips curve: a graphical representation of the presumed inverse relationship between unemployment and inflation.

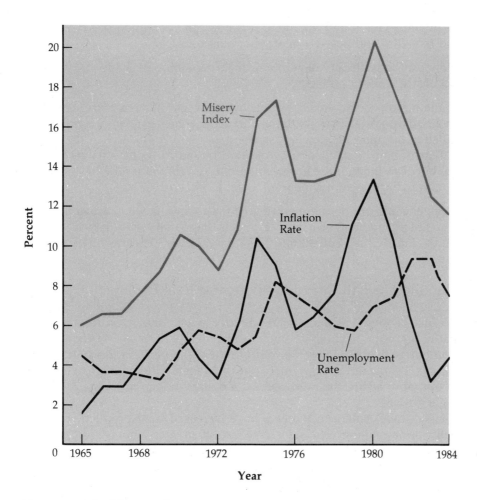

Figure 6.6. The Misery Index, 1965–1984.
Over the past twenty years both unemployment and inflation have tended to move upward. The misery index—the sum of the unemployment and inflation rates—has therefore moved upward as well. The experience of the last two decades suggests that unemployment and inflation may not be inversely related, as economists once thought.
Source: *Economic Report of the President* (Washington, D.C.: U.S. Government Printing Office, 1985), pp. 269, 291.

From 1965 to 1984, both unemployment and inflation followed a general upward trend. In fact, in the 1970s the overall relationship may well have been positive. That is, the higher the inflation rate, the higher the unemployment rate, and vice versa. The long-run positive tendency is particularly striking if the two rates are summed to obtain the so-called misery index (see Figure 6.6).

This twin problem of high unemployment and high inflation is often called stagflation. **Stagflation** is the combination of persistently high rates

Stagflation: the combination of persistently high rates of unemployment and inflation.

of unemployment and inflation. This economic condition has challenged old remedies and posed a new set of questions:

How can high unemployment and high inflation coexist? Is stagflation a peculiarly modern problem?

Is there a cause-and-effect relationship between inflation and unemployment? If so, what is it? Is there a tradeoff between unemployment and inflation disguised somewhere in the data for 1970–1984? Can the unemployment part of stagflation be reduced by reducing the inflation rate? If so, how can inflation be lowered, and how long will it take for the lower rate to reduce unemployment?

Have government policies contributed to the simultaneous rise of inflation and unemployment? To what extent is stagflation caused by economic forces outside the United States, like the oil price increases of 1974?

Lagging Growth in Productivity and Real Income

Because people's incomes are tied directly to what they produce, increases in the aggregate national income must be tied to increases in productivity. Without an increase in worker output, there can be no increase in worker income. People can be given more dollars to spend. But without an increase in output to spend them on, the extra dollars will go up in the smoke of higher prices.

Historically American workers have increased their productivity gradually through improved skills, the use of greater amounts of physical capital, and the discovery of new and less costly sources of energy. Between 1947 and 1970, for instance, output per man-hour in the private sector expanded at an average annual rate of 2.3 percent. After 1970, however, growth in worker productivity dipped below 2 percent per year and almost ground to a halt during the last three years of the 1970s. That slowdown in productivity growth diminished the growth of real purchasing power. Beginning in 1983, worker productivity turned upward again, along with the increase in general economic activity that began then.

Table 6.2 shows the rate of growth in real GNP in several industrialized nations from 1960 to 1983. In the 1960s, output grew more slowly in the United States than in most other nations. In the late 1970s, however, only Japan had a noticeably higher growth rate than the United States. The baby boom generation reached working age in the 1970s, and the labor force participation rate rose as more women took jobs outside the home. The result was a sharp increase in the size of the U.S. work force.

Still more questions suggest themselves:

What caused the slowdown in the growth of worker productivity during the 1970s?

Is worker productivity affected by the rate of inflation? By tax increases? By government policy? If so, how?

What can government do, if anything, to promote growth in productivity?

Table 6.2. Rate of Growth in Real Gross National Product, 1960–1983 (percent change)

Country	Annual Average				1981	1982	1983
	1961–1965	1966–1970	1971–1975	1976–1980			
United States	4.7%	3.2%	2.6%	3.7%	2.6%	−1.9%	3.4%
Canada	5.7	4.8	5.0	3.1	3.8	−5.0	3.8
Japan	10.0	11.2	4.6	5.0	3.2	2.5	2.0
France	5.8	5.4	4.0	3.3	0.2	1.5	0.5
West Germany	5.0	4.2	2.2	3.5	0.2	−1.2	1.2
Italy	5.2	6.2	2.4	3.8	−0.1	−0.3	−1.5
United Kingdom	3.1	2.5	2.1	1.6	−2.0	0.5	2.5

Source: U.S. Congress, Joint Economic Committee, *Industrial Policy Movement in the United States: Is It the Answer?* 98th Congress, 2nd Session (Washington, D.C.: U.S. Government Printing Office, June 8, 1984), p. 26.

How will policies to promote growth in productivity affect the inflation and unemployment rates?

Business Cycles

As Figures 6.3 and 6.4 show, recent economic activity has proceeded in fits and starts. In fact, the history of the U.S. economy has been one of ups and downs, booms and busts. Figure 6.7 shows the irregular path of the nation's annual rates of growth in real GNP from 1910 to 1984. The Great Depression of the 1930s, the rather large shaded area in the middle of the graph, stands out as this century's longest period of economic distress. In recent decades, business activity has been substantially higher than the overall trend. Much of that apparent surge in activity can be ascribed to inflation, however.

The long-run upward movement of economic activity seen in Figure 6.4 is called a trend. A **trend** is a long-run directional change, up or down, in some economic variable—for example, real GNP. Because they are long-run measures, trends may be obscured by the small irregularities, or ups and downs, in year-to-year business conditions. These smaller movements, which can last for several years, within the long-term trend are called business cycles. A **business cycle** is a recurring but irregular swing in general economic activity, a smaller pattern of ups and downs within a major long-term trend.

Business cycles have four phases: a recession, a trough, a recovery, and a peak (see Figure 6.8). The cycle begins with a downturn in activity, called a recession. A **recession** is a downward movement in general economic activity, especially in national production and employment. The Department of Commerce defines a recession as a downward movement in real GNP that lasts at least six months. An especially severe recession, with a substantial decline in real production and an unemployment rate of 15 percent or more, is called a depression.

Trend: a long-run directional change, up or down, in some economic variable—for example, real GNP.

Business cycle: a recurring swing in general economic activity, a smaller pattern of ups and downs within a major long-term trend.

Recession: a downward movement in general economic activity, especially in national production and employment.

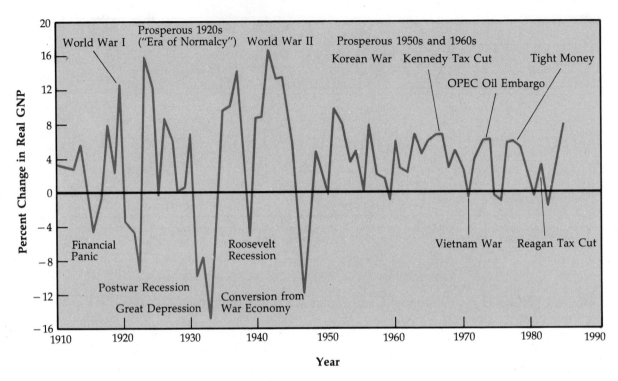

Figure 6.7. Business Cycles in the United States, 1910–1985.
Overall, economic activity in the United States has expanded over the last century. But the generally upward trend includes many boom-and-bust cycles, the most severe of which led to the Great Depression of the 1930s.
Sources: U.S. Bureau of the Census, *Historical Statistics of the United States* (Washington, D.C.: U.S. Government Printing Office, 1975), pp. 226–227; *Economic Report of the President* (Washington, D.C.: U.S. Government Printing Office, 1985), p. 234.

Trough: the bottom of the business cycle, the point at which general economic activity ceases to fall.

Recovery: an upward movement in general economic activity, especially in national production and employment.

Peak: the phase of the business cycle that occurs when general economic activity is no longer rising.

When real GNP stops falling and unemployment stops rising, the trough of the business cycle has been reached. The **trough** is the bottom of the business cycle, the point at which general economic activity ceases to fall. Once the economy hits bottom, it may shift upward almost immediately or languish there for several months. When real GNP begins to rise and unemployment to fall, the economy has entered the recovery phase. A **recovery** is an upward movement in general economic activity (real GNP and employment). A recovery may continue until full employment is approached or it may be aborted fairly quickly by another recession.

The business cycle ends when the recovery phase reaches its peak. A **peak** occurs when general economic activity is no longer rising. The peak is the top of the business cycle, the transition from the recovery phase of one cycle to the recession phase of another. Thus a peak cannot be identified until a new recession has been declared—at least six months after real GNP begins to fall.

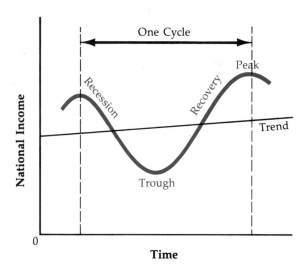

Figure 6.8. The Business Cycle.
A complete business cycle has four phases: recession, trough, recovery, and peak.

Table 6.3. Business Cycles in the United States, 1926–1982

Peak	Trough	Length of Cycle from Peak to Peak (in months)
October 1926	November 1927	41
August 1929	March 1933	34
May 1937	June 1938	93
February 1945	October 1945	93
November 1948	October 1949	45
July 1953	May 1954	56
August 1957	April 1958	49
April 1960	February 1961	32
December 1969	November 1970	116
November 1973	March 1975	47
January 1980	July 1980	62
July 1981	November 1982	18

Source: U.S. Department of Commerce, Bureau of Economic Analysis, *Business Conditions Digest* (February 1985 and earlier issues).

The length of a business cycle is measured from peak to peak. As Table 6.3 shows, recent U.S. business cycles have varied significantly in length, from one to several years. Look again at Figure 6.7. No two business cycles are exactly alike in depth or timing. These variations make predicting future business conditions an imperfect science at best.

Perspectives in Economics: Economic Instability in the Twentieth Century

Clark Nardinelli

During the twentieth century the real gross national product of the United States has grown at a modest rate of about 3 percent a year. But although the overall trend has been positive, annual growth rates have fluctuated widely (see Figure 6.7). Especially in the first half of the century, the economy swung back and forth between rapid growth and negative growth.

These swings were not random, but related to historical events. The first major downswing of the century, the recession of 1913 to 1914, was due partly to a financial panic that caused a run on the banks. Both the panic and the recession were short-lived. They were followed by a period of inflationary growth, caused by mobilization for the First World War. When the war ended in 1918 the price level fell, and the nation had to convert its factories back to peacetime production. The result was a new downturn, the recession of 1919 to 1921. But the gains made after that recession more than offset its losses.

The 1920s were years of rapid economic growth. But the postwar boom halted abruptly with the onset of the Great Depression of 1929 to 1933, the greatest peacetime cataclysm in American history.

In just four years the nominal gross national product fell from $104.6 billion to $56.1 billion. Even allowing for the simultaneous fall in prices, real GNP dropped at a precipitous rate.

Like earlier recessions, the Great Depression was followed by an economic expansion. This recovery, however, did not advance the economy past earlier highs. Its gains almost, but not quite, made up for depression losses. (The chart shows that the upswing following 1933 is of almost the same magnitude as the downswing preceding 1933.) In 1938, real GNP was almost the same as it had been in 1929.

The stagnation of the 1930s ended with mobilization for the Second World War (1939–1945), which brought another inflationary boom. Real GNP, the price level, and manufacturing output all rose rapidly after 1940. Once the United States became an active participant in the war (1941), unemployment virtually disappeared. As had happened after the First World War, the end of the hostilities was followed by deflation and problems of readjustment to peacetime production. The result was a short but severe recession from 1945 to 1947. Recovery was rapid, however, and growth

---

Leading indicator: an index of business activity that tends to move up or down several months before measures of general economic activity, like real GNP, do so.

Among the tools economists use in predicting business conditions are measures called leading indicators. A **leading indicator** is an index of business activity that tends to move up or down several months before measures of general economic activity, like real GNP, do so. The composite index of leading economic indicators for the 1964–1985 (first quarter) shown in Figure 6.9 combines information on stock prices, size of the money stock, unemployment, building permits, housing starts, commercial and industrial loans, and so forth, into a single measure of economic activity that tends to forecast changes in real GNP. By watching the index, as well as the individual indexes that go into the composite, economists and policymakers can get some clues as to what will happen in the future. If had resumed by the 1950s, aided somewhat by the expansion accompanying the Korean War (1950–1953). Growth remained positive throughout the decade, except for a brief recession in 1954 following the end of the Korean War.

The 1960s witnessed sustained economic growth, leading some economists to conclude that business cycles were a thing of the past. Indeed, the chart shows a moderation of the wide swings of the first half of the century. Though the Vietnam War brought the usual wartime inflation, it did not produce the rapid economic expansion associated with previous wartime eras.

The naive belief that the business cycle was obsolete collapsed in 1974–1975, when the Arab oil embargo plunged the United States and other industrial nations into the most severe recession since the 1940s. But though the ensuing recovery more than offset the losses of that recession, it was accompanied by the century's highest rate of peacetime inflation. In 1980 the consumer price index rose an alarming 13.5 percent. The recession that followed in 1981–1982 may have been caused in part by the adoption of anti-inflationary policies in the early 1980s.

Though events of the 1970s and 1980s have shown that the business cycle is not dead, the rate of change in real GNP has clearly been much steadier since 1950 than before. Why has the business cycle become less extreme? One possibility is that since 1950, the nation has experienced no events as catastrophic as the Great Depression or the Second World War. The U.S. economy may be more stable because the world as a whole is more stable. Another possibility is that the countercyclical policies the federal government has pursued in the last few decades have moderated the effects of business cycles. As government policymakers learn more about macroeconomics, their effectiveness may be increasing. Finally, the moderation of business cycles may stem from the increasing size of government itself. Government economic activity tends to be more stable than private economic activity, and the government's share of real GNP has been growing in the latter half of the century.

Whatever the reason, the U.S. economy has become more stable since 1950. Most economists believe that this greater stability will continue through the end of the century.

the composite index turns down for several months, economists can predict a recession with some confidence.

Our survey of business cycles raises still more questions about the macroeconomy.

What causes the ups and downs in general business activity? Why is the overall upward trend not a smooth one?

What can government do to make recessions less likely or less severe?

Do government policies contribute to the length and severity of business cycles?

Macroeconomic Policies

Economists differ widely on what should be done to remedy the macro-economic problems we have been discussing. In later chapters we will explain their views in considerable detail. Here we will simply outline them briefly.

The Classical School

Before the 1930s, most economists believed that the forces of supply and demand would eventually remedy problems of unemployment and low levels of production. According to classical theory, a rise in unemployment would depress wage rates, for more workers would be competing for fewer jobs. When the price of labor fell, employers would hire more workers, lowering the unemployment rate and boosting production. Classical economists blame persistent unemployment and underproduction on unions and laws that prevent wage rates from falling in response to falling demand. Their prescription is straightforward: eliminate all legal impediments to flexibility in prices and wages.

Lagging growth in productivity can also be solved by the free market system, according to classical economists. If people want more goods and services enough to pay for them, then businesses will invest more, and the newer, more efficient equipment will permit a rise in productivity and future output. In the view of classical economists, lagging productivity indicates that consumers are not willing to pay for greater future output by forgoing current consumption. (For more on the classical school of economics, see Chapter 10.)

The Keynesian School

Keynesian economists—followers of the British economist John Maynard Keynes—believe that the principal cause of low production and unemployment is inadequate total spending. Together, consumers, businesses, and government do not demand enough goods and services to employ the labor force fully. Keynesians would say that the fluctuations in macroeconomic activity reflect the fluctuations in demand, especially the demand for investment in capital goods. Their solution for unemployment is to increase total spending in any of several ways. One possibility is to reduce taxes, thereby increasing consumer and business purchasing power (and ultimately demand). Another is to increase government spending. A third is to lower interest rates by increasing the money stock, thereby encouraging businesses and consumers to obtain loans for new purchases. In fact, Keynesians believe any policy that stimulates the demand for investment will ultimately increase both production and the rate of growth in worker productivity.

Keynesians also tend to see inflation as primarily a demand problem. Consumers demand more in total than the economy can produce, putting

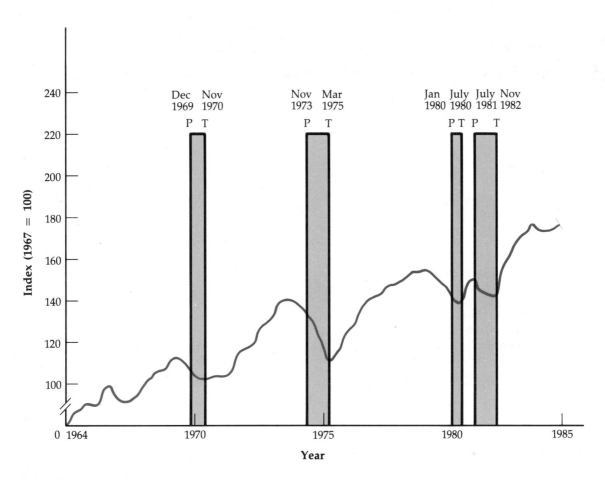

Figure 6.9. Composite Index of Leading Economic Indicators.
The composite index of leading economic indicators is compiled from indexes that economists find useful as predictors, including indexes of stock prices, size of the money stock, unemployment, building permits, housing starts, and commercial and industrial loans. The composite index tends to change direction several months before a change in general economic activity—for example, a change in real GNP. Thus it aids economists in forecasting future economic conditions.
Note: The shaded areas correspond to recessions, with *P* for the peaks and *T* for the troughs of the business cycles.
Source: U.S. Department of Commerce, Bureau of Economic Analysis, *Business Conditions Digest* (February 1985), p. 10.

upward pressure on prices. The solution: reduce total demand by reversing the policies prescribed to reduce unemployment. Raise taxes, dampening consumer and business spending; or reduce government spending; or raise interest rates, reducing business and consumer loans and purchases. Unfortunately, according to traditional Keynesian theory, policies designed to reduce inflation will tend to raise unemployment, and vice versa. (See Chapters 11–13 for more on the Keynesian model of the macroeconomy.)

Perspectives in Economics: The Rising Natural Rate of Unemployment

Henry F. Myers

Does the rise in unemployment to 7.4% of the civilian labor force last month [January 1985] indicate that we have already seen the lows in joblessness for the current business expansion? Do we face a rerun of the 1970s and early 1980s, when the low achieved in each succeeding business cycle was consistently higher than in the previous one?

Most economists don't expect much improvement in unemployment figures anytime soon. The latest consensus forecast by the four dozen analysts surveyed monthly by Blue Chip Economic Indicators, a Sedona, Arizona, newsletter, envisioned unemployment averaging 7.1% this year [1985] and next year [1986].

However, Audrey Freedman, a senior research associate at the Conference Board, notes that her own prediction that unemployment "will sit around 7.2% this year" isn't a prediction that nothing will be going on. Far from it. Just to keep unemployment from rising, she says, "you will have to create 1.5 million jobs" to match the growth in the labor force. She expects those jobs to be created, but not many more—not enough to reduce unemployment further—because "the recovery is aging and flattening out."

So far in this cycle, the unemployment rate hit its low, 7.1%, last June [1984] and again last November [1984]. That may well be as far down as it gets; unemployment tends to be a leading indicator at cyclical peaks. Moreover, that low substantially exceeds the highest monthly rate, 6.1%, during the 1969–70 recession.

Here is how the unemployment rate lows have been trending during the four previous business expansions:

Cycle Peak	Lowest Rate	Month
Dec. '69	3.4%	Jan.–May '69
Nov. '73	4.6	Oct. '73
Jan. '80	5.6	May '79
July '81	7.2	Apr. '81

Analyzing such trends, economists try to filter out cyclical joblessness from the unemployment lingering on even during booms—often called the natural rate of unemployment. That unemployment, which can't be reduced without unleashing steep inflation, is divided into frictional unemployment—the 3% or so of workers voluntarily between jobs—and structural unemployment—workers with inadequate skills.

During the 1970s, most economists believe, the natural rate of unemployment rose. Michael Wachter of the University of Pennsylvania cites three reasons:

—Unfavorable demographics. Baby boomers and women flooded into the labor force, and jobs couldn't be created fast enough. Moreover, youths and women tend to be less attached to the labor force, and as they float in and out of jobs, frictional unemployment rises.

—Rising government transfer payments. As unemployment compensation, welfare and Social Security benefits increased, the unemployed could be choosier about jobs.

—Inflationary shocks. Surges in oil and food prices hit when many labor and commodity markets were already tight, and the government felt forced to clamp down and fight inflation more quickly—at the cost of jobs—than it would in a slack economy.

Now, Professor Wachter estimates, the natural rate of unemployment probably has dropped to about 5¾% from perhaps 6¼% in the late 1970s. He notes that the surge of new job-seekers has slowed, and in the future "the demographics will continue to be favorable." So they will. According to the Bureau of Labor Statistics, the labor force aged 16 and over, which grew 1.3% a year in 1950–60, 1.7% in 1960–70 and 2.6% in 1970–80, is rising only 1.6% in 1980–90 and will increase just 1% annually in 1990–95.

Furthermore, President Reagan has halted the increase in inflation-adjusted transfer payments. And inflation is down, although Professor Wachter notes the danger posed by steep federal budget deficits.

Other factors may also be paring the natural rate of unemployment. Professor Wachter observes that the minimum wage, often said to inhibit hiring of low-skilled workers, has been eroded by inflation since its last increase, to $3.35 an hour, in January 1981. If the minimum had kept up with the 16.5% gain in nonsupervisory production workers' average pay since then, it "would now be $3.90," he adds.

Meanwhile, the youths and women who earlier swamped the labor market have acquired wider job skills and now presumably could, if laid off, find new jobs more quickly. And as actual unemployment drops, their increasing skills may reduce the natural rate.

Moreover, as Mrs. Freedman noted in a recent paper, "Union power to set industrywide wage rates has clearly decreased during the past four years." Unions thus have lost some of their ability to keep real wages from falling enough to enable employers to hire most of the jobless.

But tending to raise the natural rate of unemployment has been rapid technological change, which forces more job switching. In fact, a study by Michael Podgursky of the University of Massachusetts found that by the late 1970s, the primary source of structural unemployment had shifted from youths to prime-age males; unions couldn't halt surging imports, factory automation or the decline of smokestack industries. High-tech industry can't replace lost basic-industry jobs and, by lifting productivity, it enables output to rise faster than employment.

Economists figure that the economy must grow about 3% annually merely to provide jobs for new labor-force entrants, but the Blue Chip group, on the average, expects growth only slightly above that this year and below that next year. Without a new surge of growth, we may be stuck with 7%-plus unemployment for some time.

Henry F. Myers, "High Unemployment Is Likely to Linger On," *Wall Street Journal* (February 25, 1985), p. 1.

The Monetarist School

The monetarists tend to see inflation and economic instability as largely a monetary problem. They believe that inflation results when too many dollars are pumped into the economy by government authorities (in the United States, principally the Federal Reserve System, which controls the money stock). The monetarists' solution is to reduce the growth in the amount of money in the economy.

The monetarists also believe many irregularities in economic activity stem from the irregular growth of the money stock. They argue that the Great Depression was worsened by the Federal Reserve's contraction of the money stock by as much as a third during the early 1930s. Prices and wages simply could not adjust downward as rapidly as the money stock contracted; the result was severe unemployment.

Although they emphasize variations in the growth of the money stock, the monetarists share many of the views of the classical school of economics. Much of modern unemployment, they believe, is due to legal restrictions like minimum wage laws, which keep wage rates from falling and labor markets from reaching equilibrium. Monetarists also believe some unemployment must be expected, given people's attempts to find the best jobs available and the existence of unemployment compensation and welfare benefits. In fact, if unemployment benefits and the growth of the money stock increase simultaneously, the monetarists would predict a rise in both inflation and unemployment. (Details of the monetarist theory are founded on the principles of money creation and control developed in Chapters 7, 8, and 9, and on theoretical points presented in Chapter 14.)

The Supply-Side School

Rcently some analysts have begun to suspect that much of our unemployment and inflation is due to problems with supply (not demand, as the Keynesians would argue). These supply-side economists see high income tax rates as an important cause of low production and unemployment. Because government takes a relatively high percentage of what citizens earn, they reason, people have inadequate incentive to work, save, invest, and create jobs. Supply-side economists also see inflation as partly a supply problem. Price increases, they point out, can be moderated by an increase in production—in the supply of goods and services people want.

A supply-side solution to unemployment, inflation, and productivity problems is to reduce tax rates, increasing people's willingness to work, save, and invest. Reduced unemployment and greater national output should result; and if the number of dollars in circulation stays constant or rises less than output, the increase supply of goods and services should exert downward pressure on prices. Reducing the tax rate may also (but will not necessarily) increase government revenues, for the rise in disposable income may more than offset the lower tax rate. (See Chapter 15 for more information on supply-side economics).

The Rational Expectations School

Although people's expectations play a role in the Keynesian, monetarist, and supply-side models, they are a central element in the rational expectations model of the macroeconomy. Rational expectations theorists assume that people will acquire some rationally determined amount of information on the impact of government policies and will act on that information. For example, if people observe that government deficits and interest rates are positively related, they will try to borrow money when the government deficit goes up, expecting a rise in interest rates.

Unfortunately the increased demand for borrowed funds will drive interest rates up almost immediately, not some time in the future. So while Keynesian theory predicts that an increase in the government deficit will raise national production (because demand rises with greater government spending), rational expectations theorists would expect a higher deficit to lead to higher interest rates and an offsetting reduction in investment spending. Similarly government efforts to change the money stock will be offset by people's defensive reaction, based on their expectations of what will happen to interest rates, prices, and production costs. Pushed to its logical limits, rational expectations theory suggests that government is virtually incapable of affecting national production and employment levels, even in the short run, by varying taxes, expenditures, or the money stock. (More will be said about rational expectations theory in Chapter 16.)

Common Ground Among Theories

Our discussion of the various schools of macroeconomic thought has emphasized the differences among the Keynesian, monetarist, supply-side, and rational expectations theories. Those differences explain why economists often disagree about the policies government should adopt toward unemployment, inflation, and lagging growth. They disagree because they subscribe to different theories.

Discussing schools of thought separately has allowed us to highlight macroeconomic variables and their probable effects. Keynesian economics focuses on the impact of demand on production, income, and employment. Monetarism considers how growth in the money supply influences inflation. Supply-side economics stresses factors that affect aggregate supply, and rational expectations theory emphasizes the influence of people's expectations on interest rates, inflation, and unemployment.

Readers should not conclude, however, that Keynesians are unconcerned with prices and expectations; or that monetarists do not recognize government budgets' effect on prices; or that supply-side economists ignore the effect of demand on production; or that rational expectations theorists do not recognize influences other than people's expectations. Almost all macroeconomic theories allow for the interplay of a combination of economic forces. Those forces invariably include money, aggregate demand, aggregate suply, and expectations. Theories differ primarily in their relative emphasis on these forces.

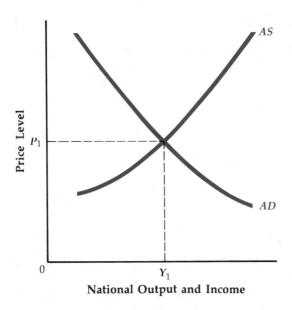

Figure 6.10. Aggregate Demand and Aggregate Supply.
Aggregate demand and supply relate the nation's price level to its output. Here the macroeconomy will be in equilibrium at a price level of P_1 and a national output level of Y_1. At any price level above P_1, the goods and services available will exceed the quantity demanded by households, firms, and government. Competitive pressure will force the price level back down to P_1. At any price level below P_1, the quantity of goods and services demanded will exceed the quantity supplied. Competitive pressure will force the price level back up to P_1.

Aggregate Demand and Supply: A Macroeconomic Model

Chapter 3 showed how the laws of supply and demand determine the prices and quantities of particular goods in a market economy. Similar concepts can be applied to macroeconomics. In future chapters, we will see how aggregate (total) demand and aggregate (total) supply determine the general price level, national output, and national income. The aggregate demand and supply model will prove a useful tool for analyzing the various schools of macroeconomic thought.

Aggregate Demand

Graphically, aggregate demand can be described as a downward sloping curve, like the curve labeled *AD* in Figure 6.10. It looks much like the demand curve for individual products. The market demand curve and the

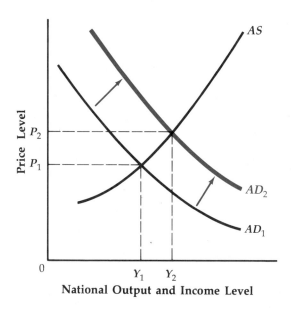

Figure 6.11. Effects of an Increase in Aggregate Demand.
If aggregate demand rises from AD_1 to AD_2, the equilibrium price level will rise
from P_1 to P_2, and the national output level will rise from Y_1 to Y_2.

aggregate demand curve are two different concepts, however. The market demand curve relates the price of a given good to its consumption level; the aggregate demand curve relates the general price level to total desired spending on national output. **Aggregate demand** is the presumed negative relationship between the general price level and the total quantity of goods and services consumers, business, and government want to buy.

The two curves slope downward for different reasons. The individual demand curve slopes downward because changes in price cause income and substitution effects. The aggregate demand curve slopes downward because changes in the general price level affect people's wealth (not because the market demands for individual products slope downward). When the price level falls, people can buy more with their cash, stocks and bonds, and other monetary assets; their aggregate real wealth rises, and they will buy more goods and services. Conversely, when the general price level goes up, aggregate purchases will decline along with aggregate real wealth.

Aggregate Supply

Aggregate supply relates national output to the general price level. **Aggregate supply** is the presumed positive relationship between the general price level and the total quantity of goods and services produced

Aggregate demand: the presumed negative relationship between the general price level and the total quantity of goods and services consumers, business, and government want to buy.

Aggregate supply: the presumed positive relationship between the general price level and the total quantity of goods and services produced in the economy during a given period of time.

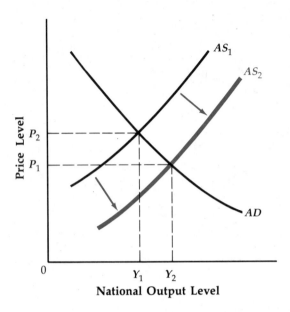

Figure 6.12. Effects of an Increase in Aggregate Supply.
If aggregate supply increases from AS_1 to AS_2, the price level will fall from P_2 to P_1, yet the national output level will rise from Y_1 to Y_2.

in the economy during a given period of time. The short-run aggregate supply curve slopes upward, like the curve labeled AS in Figure 6.10. In the short run, production may be expected to rise with an increase in the price level, because price increases may take time to be translated into cost increases. Until costs catch up, producers will expand production to reap extra profits. In the long run, cost increases usually do catch up with price increases, and supply contracts. •

Aggregate Demand and Supply

Analysis of aggregate demand and supply resembles analysis of market supply and demand in one important respect: equilibrium occurs at the intersection of the supply and demand curves. In Figure 6.10 the equilibrium national output level is Y_1, the equilibrium price level P_1. If the price level is higher than P_1, the aggregate quantity of goods and services demanded will not meet the quantity producers offer on the market. The price level will fall, increasing the quantity business, government, and consumers will buy and decreasing the quantity producers will offer. If the price level is lower than P_1, all sectors of the economy will demand more than producers offer. Total production will expand, and the total amount all sectors want to buy will contract.

The following chapters will discuss the details of how price and output levels adjust, and how changes in aggregate demand and supply affect production, employment, and the price level. Briefly, an increase in government demand for goods and services (unless offset by a reduction in consumer and business demand) can cause an expansion in national production and possibly an increase in the price level. The increase in government demand will shift the aggregate demand curve out, say from AD_1 to AD_2 in Figure 6.11. At the initial price level, total planned spending will be greater than total supply; the price level will rise, prompting producers to expand production. A decrease in taxes could cause the same result. If disposable income rises, increasing aggregate demand, price levels and national output will increase.

The price level may also fall, as a result of an increase in aggregate supply. If tax rates are reduced, increasing people's willingness to work and produce, the aggregate supply curve will shift outward to the right, say from AS_1 to AS_2 in Figure 6.12. A higher national output level, Y_2, but a lower price level, P_1, will result.

Just how and why aggregate demand and supply change is the subject of considerable dispute among economists. Many suspect that business cycles are caused by these shifts in aggregate demand and supply. When aggregate demand or supply shifts back and forth, everything else held constant, general economic activity will pick up or slow down. In fact macroeconomics is largely the study of how broad sectors of the economy affect one another through their effect on aggregate demand and supply. More will be said about aggregate demand and supply in Chapter 13.

Summary and Extensions

Inflation, unemployment, and lagging growth in productivity affect almost all of us to some extent. We must all cope with uncertainty about future prices. And to the extent that unemployment means lost output—that is, unsatisfied wants—it also affects everyone. Reductions in productivity growth will make us all less well off in the future than we might have been.

What should we do about these problems? Economists disagree not only on which theory should guide policy, but on what goals government should pursue. Some believe government should do virtually nothing aside from creating a stable monetary system. They contend that, despite good intentions, government action has left us worse off on balance.

Most economists believe government bears some responsibility for promoting full employment, high productivity, and price stability. They do not always agree on how those goals should be achieved, however, for they base their policies on different theories. We would all be happier if the solutions to macroeconomic problems could be presented in a few pages. Unfortunately, the policy debate is not yet resolved, and probably will not be for some time.

Major Conclusions

1. Persistent high peacetime inflation is a relatively recent phenomenon in the United States. Though the inflation rate has varied considerably from month to month and year to year, over the last two decades the overall trend has been upward.
2. Since the Second World War, the U.S. economy has operated below capacity much of the time. The gap between actual real GNP and potential real GNP reflects the unusually high rates of unemployment during this period.
3. In the last two decades, policymakers have confronted the problem of stagflation, or high inflation combined with high unemployment. Economists disagree on the causes of stagflation.
4. Economists differ on what should be done about inflation and unemployment. The classical, Keynesian, monetarist, supply-side, and rational expectations schools of thought stress different factors as the primary cause of economic difficulties.

Questions To Ponder

1. Can you think of a macroeconomic problem not mentioned in this chapter?
2. Look up aggregate business expenditures in the most recent issue of *The Statistical Abstract of the United States*, published by the Department of Commerce. Then graph investment expenditures over the last twenty years. Do the same for the prime interest rate. Do the two measures seem to be related?
3. Find several articles on macroeconomic problems in recent issues of the *Wall Street Journal*. Classify the statements of the economists quoted in those articles by school of thought. Do the articles represent a variety of theories?
4. What actions has the government taken recently to deal with inflation, unemployment, and low productivity? How are those actions supposed to affect the economy?
5. Are there tradeoffs in dealing with inflation, unemployment, and low productivity? If so, explain how the problems may be interrelated.

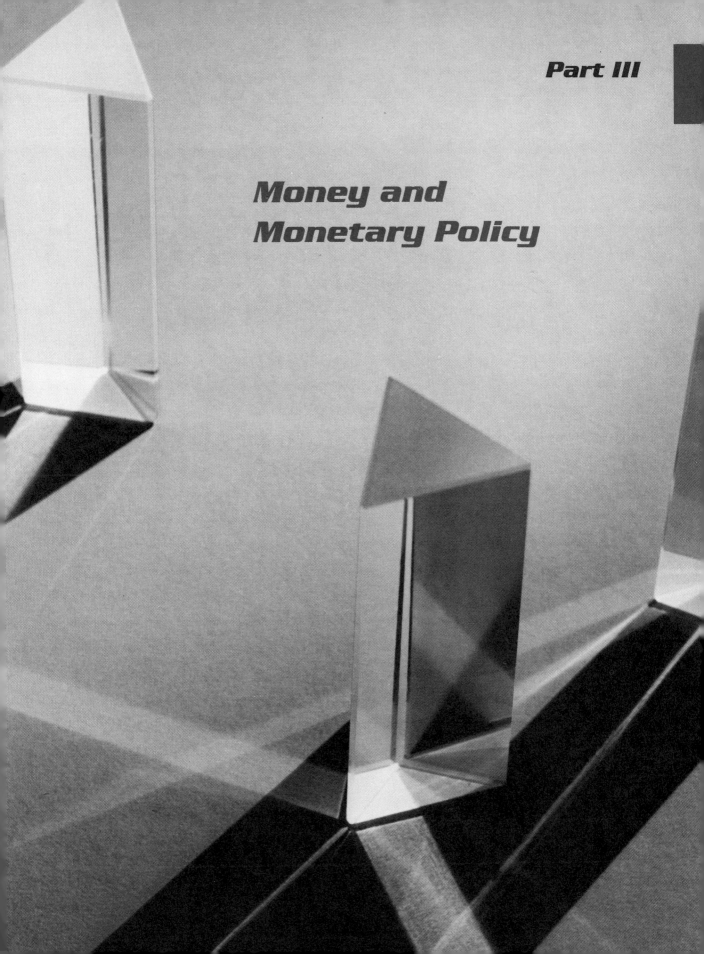

Part III

Money and
Monetary Policy

Central Question

What is money and how is it created?

Key Terms

Liquidity

Transactions demand for money

Precautionary demand for money

Speculative demand for money

Money stock

M1

M2

Full-bodied commodity money

Representative commodity money

Fiat money

Reserves

Reserve deposits

Reserve requirement

Excess reserves

Chapter 7

The Meaning and Creation of Money

Money is a contract—the
freest, most gorgeous contract
of them all. Money is
somebody else's promise to
pay, to give me what I want,
when I want it. What a
magnificent conception! . . .
Whatever else history may
ultimately record of the
Western Bourgeoisie, this
honor most certainly must be
accorded them: They perfected
modern money, which is a
contract with parties unknown
for the future delivery of
pleasures undecided upon.
David Bazelon

You may not think the dollar is very valuable, but you are likely to be more concerned about losing one than about losing a plain piece of paper. Have you ever wondered why dollars have value—why, for example, you are willing to buy a wallet to protect them? Do you know how they are created? What form does the money in your bank account take, and what are you actually giving when you hand someone a check? How can banks make loans to some people at the same time others are withdrawing their deposits?

Though superficially there is nothing baffling about money, its effects on the macroeconomy are sufficiently mysterious to occupy the time of a great many economists. (More will be said on that subject in Chapters 8 and 9.)

The Meaning of Money

Money is a social phenomenon that has taken different forms in different cultures. In the United States, we think of money in terms of dollars. In Great Britain, it is the pound sterling; in France, the franc. At other times and in other places, money has been anything from silver to cigarettes, beads, or seashells. Today in some parts of Tanzania, the monetary unit is the cow or bull, and cattle are used in exchange just as we use dollar bills.

Money can be traded to obtain the things we want or held until we decide we want to use it: that is its essence. Because it is used so widely, however, money also serves as a unit of account. It is, in other words, a kind of common denominator in which the relative values of most other goods and services can be expressed. In all its different forms, money is both a readily acceptable medium of exchange (means of making payment) and a financial asset—a form of savings that represents a store of readily usable purchasing power.

Money is so commonplace in our society that people take for granted the convenience it bestows. As we have stressed before, in a barter economy—one that uses no money—goods trade only for other goods, and people are paid for their labor with the goods they and others produce. In barter, the buyer must find a seller who not only offers the desired goods but also wants the goods the buyer has to trade. For instance, the person who has turkeys to sell and wants pigs must find someone who has pigs to sell and wants turkeys. The person who is paid in corn must trade it to people who are paid in the goods and services he or she wants. Needless to say, barter is a very complicated, time-consuming, and costly way to trade.

When money is used as a medium of exchange, it facilitates trade and contributes to national production. If money is readily accepted by others, people with money need only find the things they want to buy. Those who receive money for what they sell can in turn use money to buy the things they want. The cost (time and effort) of searching for mutually beneficial trades is reduced, and the time saved can be used to produce goods and services.

In this indirect way, money contributes to national production. If money is withdrawn from an economy for some reason, we would expect people to spend much more time consummating trades and much less time producing goods. That is what happened in Germany in the years after both world wars. National output fell dramatically, in part because of the destruction of plant and equipment, but also because the German currency lost its acceptability in trade. When output rose again, it was partially because the government instituted a new, more acceptable currency.

As a store of purchasing power, money gives its owner another kind of convenience, called liquidity. **Liquidity** is the ease with which any asset can be converted into another form, especially into money. The owner of money can quickly and inexpensively convert it into other assets, like furniture, a loaf of bread, or even stock in a corporation. At little or no cost, money can be traded for practically anything else. Other financial assets, such as corporate bonds, cannot be as easily converted. To exchange a bond for a car, the owner must typically sell the bond for money and then use the money to buy the car. The extra transaction takes time, and the seller may have to pay a fee to the agent or brokerage house that sells the bond. A house is even less liquid than a corporate bond; it may take weeks or months to sell.

For money to be a good means of storing purchasing power, its value—that is, how much it will buy—must be reasonably stable. If prices rise rapidly, the purchasing power of stored money will deteriorate rapidly. Instead of holding on to their money, people will use it to buy goods and services, like gold, jewels, and stocks, before its purchasing power deteriorates even further. Conversely if prices fall rapidly, people will want to hold on to more money than usual. They will delay their purchases, hoping to buy things at lower prices.

Liquidity: the ease with which any asset can be converted into another form, especially into money.

The Value of Money

Why does money have value, in the sense that people will accept it in exchange for goods and services? Obviously, dollar bills themselves have no intrinsic value. Dollars in bank accounts cannot have intrinsic value—they are just figures on paper. And though the paper used for dollar bills is tough and relatively expensive, the purchasing power of the dollar is far greater than the value of the paper used.

Furthermore, the dollar's value is not based on some kind of "gold backing"—there is no such thing. Contrary to popular belief, the government no longer holds gold in Fort Knox to back the dollar. Until 1971, the government was required to hold $0.25 in gold for every dollar outstanding. Even then, however, the gold did not determine the value of the money, since $0.25 in gold cannot give a dollar bill a dollar's worth of value.

From an individual standpoint, trading goods for dollars and vice versa is quite sensible. The dollars received can always be traded to someone else. Dollars are valuable simply because people have confidence that others will accept them. The same was true of gold and silver coins when they were used as money. Although silver and gold have always had intrinsic value, in the sense that they can be used for jewelry and dental fittings, they would have been worth much less if they had not been used as money. The reason that they were valued so highly was that people were willing to accept them readily in exchanges.

Although it may seem a little like magic, confidence in its general acceptability is the stuff money is made of. The message printed on a dollar bill—"This note is legal tender for all debts public and private"— gives a dollar some commercial value. But the value of money ultimately depends on an unwritten social agreement that it is valuable. And there are good reasons for demanding money.

The Demand for Money

Transactions demand for money: the desire to hold money balances in order to carry out anticipated purchases of goods and services.

Precautionary demand for money: the desire to hold money balances in order to finance unexpected or emergency purchases of goods and services.

Speculative demand for money: the desire to hold money balances in anticipation of a decrease in the price of other assets and in anticipation of future profits.

Because of the benefits of using and holding on to money, there is a demand for money, just as there is a demand for other goods. Holding money also involves an opportunity cost: the forgone benefits or return on some other asset not acquired—for example, the furniture one could have purchased or the profits one could have earned by investing in a business. Despite the costs, there are three good reasons for holding on to or demanding money. One is the need for money as a medium of exchange; this is called the transactions demand for money. The **transactions demand for money** is the desire to hold money balances in order to carry out anticipated purchases of goods and services. A second is the need for security; this is called the precautionary demand for money. The **precautionary demand for money** is the desire to hold money balances in order to finance unexpected or emergency purchases of goods and services. A third reason for demanding money is the desire to be able to take advantage of future opportunities; this is called the speculative demand for money. The **speculative demand for money** is the desire to hold money in anticipation of a decrease in the price of other assets and in anticipation of future profits.

The demand for money is influenced by personal income, interest rates, the general price level, and expectations about future prices, as well as other economic variables to be considered later. Specifically:

A rise in people's incomes will generally increase the transactions demand for money. Higher incomes mean more purchases, hence a greater need for money balances to finance those purchases.

A rise in interest rates will raise the opportunity cost of holding on to money, discouraging people from maintaining large money balances for any purpose. People will try to economize on their use of money.

An increase in the price level will increase the demand for money to finance transactions, which now require more dollars.

If people expect prices to rise, they will buy now to avoid higher prices in the future, reducing the money balances they individually seek to hold. If people expect prices to fall, they will hold on to money so as to take advantage of lower prices later.

The Money Stock

Aside from dollar bills and coins, several other financial assets serve as mediums of exchange and stores of purchasing power. Demand deposits, or money in checking accounts, are highly liquid. So are savings accounts and certificates of deposit, which are like government savings bonds but are issued by banks.

How do economists measure the amount of money that exists in the economy at any point in time? The answer depends on how one defines the money stock. A broad definition is easily given. The **money stock** is the sum of all identified forms of money held by the public (as opposed to the banks) at a given point in time. Actually measuring the money stock is a more complicated problem. How many dollars are there? Which dollars should be counted? These questions are still subject to much debate. Different groups of economists measure the money stock in different ways, and how one calculates the total amount of money in the economy changes with changes in the method of measurement.

Money stock: the sum of all identified forms of money held by the public (as opposed to the banks) at a given point in time.

Two measures of the money stock are used widely in economics journals and the financial sections of newspapers and magazines. The better known is M1, which includes cash and checking accounts. **M1** is the total of the public's (as opposed to the banks') holdings of currency (paper bills and coins), demand deposits at commercial banks (bank accounts against which withdrawals can be made on demand, or by check), traveler's checks, and other bank accounts against which checks can be written, such as NOW (negotiable order of withdrawal) and ATS (automatic transfer services) accounts. NOW accounts differ from regular demand deposits in that they earn interest. ATS accounts permit the automatic transfer of funds from savings accounts to checking accounts; this allows depositors to earn interest on the idle money in their checking accounts. If M1 is used as a measure of money, in December 1984 the money stock was $554.5 billion (see Table 7.1). Of that total, $158 billion (28 percent) was held in currency and $391.3 billion (71 percent) in demand deposits and other checkable deposits.

M1: the total of the public's (as opposed to the banks') holdings of currency (paper bills and coins), demand deposits at commercial banks, traveler's checks, and other bank accounts against which checks can be written, such as NOW (negotiable order of withdrawal) and ATS (automatic transfer services) accounts.

M2 includes savings as well as cash and checking accounts. **M2** is M1 plus savings accounts and small (less than $100,000) time deposits (bank accounts that generally are not subject to transfer by check, and sometimes not to withdrawal on demand) and certificates of deposit, plus money market accounts and other highly liquid assets. If M2 is used as a measure of money, in December 1984 the money stock was $2,376.3 billion—more than four times the size of M1 (see Table 7.1).

M2: M1 plus savings accounts and small (less than $100,000) time deposits and certificates of deposit, plus money market accounts and other highly liquid assets.

M1 and M2 reflect the two basic uses for money. M1 emphasizes the medium-of-exchange role. It consists of only those types of money that are used directly in trade—coin, paper bills, and demand deposits. M2 measures money as a store of purchasing power. When paper bills, coins, and demand deposits are not being actively used in exchange, they are being held as a store of purchasing power. Adding savings accounts, small certificates of deposit, and money market funds to M1 yields a measure of the nation's total store of purchasing power.

Perspectives in Economics: A Short History of Money

Dennis Placone

At various times in history, different forms of money have been used in trade. The very first monies were full-bodied commodity money. A **full-bodied commodity money** is a medium of exchange or store of value that has some intrinsic value as a consumer good or factor of production. In other words, it has some economic use apart from its monetary role. In parts of the ancient Roman Empire, rock salt was used as a form of money. Barley and silver served as monies three hundred years before the birth of Christ; seashells and tobacco, in colonial times in North America. Gold, cattle, woodpecker scalps, corn, and cigarettes have all been used as a medium of exchange.

All these goods were common to the communities or societies that used them. Therefore their market values were generally well known. People would accept such goods in trade, even if they did not have an immediate use for them, because they could always be sold at a known price. And if for some reason a commodity money lost part of its value as a money, it could always be used as a good instead. Barley could be ground into meal; cattle could be butchered; woodpecker scalps could be fashioned into ornaments; cigarettes could be smoked. Gold and silver monies, in particular, gradually became common around the world, because they were more useful, portable, divisible, durable, and recognizable in value than other commodity monies.

Full-bodied commodity monies were generally not created by government. Governments have sometimes attempted to influence or control the value of commodity monies, however. In 1791 the U.S. government sought to establish a bimetallic money standard by buying and selling gold and silver at official fixed prices. The task was not as simple as it had imagined, however. The price of gold was set at 15 times the price of silver, even though the market price of gold was 15.5 times the price of silver. As a result people bought gold from the federal treasury and sold it at a profit on the world market. Because silver was officially undervalued and gold officially overvalued, gold was driven out of circulation in the United States and sent abroad, where it was more highly valued.

Such an outcome was to be expected. People will always attempt to use money that is overvalued, because they expect that its relative market value may fall. They will tend to horde undervalued money, expecting that its value will rise. The U.S. government tried to halt the outflow of gold in 1834 by readjusting the official price to be 16 times the price of silver. But at the new official price, silver was undervalued and gold overvalued. Soon silver was driven out of circulation and replaced by gold.

As economic systems became more complex, new, more convenient forms of money emerged. The transactions costs of using gold and silver were high, because substantial resources had to be invested to mine and protect them. To cut those costs, banks developed representative commodity monies. **Representative commodity monies** are certificates or notes that can be converted into given quantities of a specific commodity, like gold or silver. Banks found that people would accept such notes in the belief that they could be redeemed for the gold banks held in their vaults. At first banks backed the notes fully, holding a dollar's worth of gold for every dollar note outstanding. But banks soon found they could issue notes for more than the value of the gold in their vaults. People would continue to circulate the notes in trade, confident they could be redeemed when desired.

So long as people felt secure in using notes as money, the representative commodity monetary system worked. But problems eventually emerged. From 1834 to 1860, over sixteen hundred state-chartered banks, most of them largely unregulated, issued notes. Many banks issued so many notes that they could not always redeem them at full face value. Runs on banks, in which panicked noteholders attempted to cash in their notes for gold, became common. Some banks collapsed when they could not redeem all the notes presented to them. Counterfeiting sometimes provoked a run on a bank. Because each of the sixteen hundred banks issued notes of its own design, the average trader could not always tell a counterfeit or worthless note from a genuine one. Counterfeit bills increased the information cost of using notes and reduced their general acceptance.

Because of these difficulties, governments began to issue paper money. In the United States, the federal treasury issued gold and silver certificates that could be redeemed for metal coin, and "greenbacks"—unbacked paper currency issued to finance the Civil War. The general acceptance of these monies was encouraged by the treasury's willingness to accept them in payment of taxes and by the requirement that creditors accept them in payment of debt. (If creditors refused to accept greenbacks and gold and silver certificates as payment, debtors were legally absolved of their obligations.)

When the Federal Reserve System was established in 1913, private bank notes became illegal and were replaced by Federal Reserve Notes, the paper money we use today. At first Fed notes were backed by a government pledge to redeem the notes in gold and silver. The number of notes in circulation was determined partly by the amount of gold held by the government. These notes were considered so sound by foreigners that they tended to be in short supply in the United States. To increase the money stock and raise prices, President Franklin Roosevelt took the United States off the gold standard in 1933. Roosevelt declared that dollars would no longer be redeemed in gold at the Treasury or the Federal Reserve. Indeed, he outlawed private hoarding of gold and required people who held it to sell it to the government for $22.50 an ounce. (Later the price of gold was set officially at $35 an ounce.) In 1968 Congress revoked the Fed's obligation to redeem silver certificates in silver.

The U.S. monetary system is now based entirely on inconvertible paper currency, or fiat money. **Fiat money** is a medium of exchange or store of value that cannot be redeemed for anything other than a replica of itself. A fiat dollar can be exchanged only for another dollar. The general acceptability of fiat money does not depend on either its intrinsic market value (as was the case with corn), or its redemption value (as was the case with silver certificates). It depends entirely on people's confidence in its continued usefulness in trade.

Table 7.1. Two Measures of the Money Stock, December 1984
(in billions of dollars)

	M1	M2
Currency (paper bills and coins)	$158.0	$ 158.0
Travelers checks	5.2	5.2
Demand deposits	248.3	248.3
Other checkable deposits	143.0	143.0
Overnight repurchase agreements net plus overnight Eurodollars		57.6
Money market mutual fund balances		168.1
Money market deposit accounts		410.0
Savings accounts		294.3
Small denomination time deposits		897.1
Totals	$554.5	$2,376.3

Source: *Economic Report of the President* (Washington, D.C.: U.S. Government Printing Office, 1985), p. 303.

Measurements of the money stock are extremely interesting to economists studying how the size of the money stock affects prices, national production, and unemployment. (In following chapters we will develop that subject in detail.) The particular measure an economist uses in statistical studies of these questions depends in part on his or her perception of money. Those who view money as something that is held, as opposed to something that is traded, will use M2 in their studies. Those who view money primarily as a medium of trade will use M1.

The Banking System

Demand deposits are an important part of M1 and time deposits an important part of M2. Both kinds of accounts are held at banks, which are an integral part of the monetary system. Broadly speaking, the U.S. banking system may be divided into depository institutions (local commercial banks and savings and loan associations) and the Federal Reserve System, a national institution.

Depository Institutions

Depository institutions are privately owned businesses. They hold deposits and checking and savings accounts for individuals and firms. They also make loans in return for interest payments on the amount of the loan.

Before 1981 banks could be categorized according to the types of deposits they received. Only commercial banks were permitted to accept demand deposits, funds that could be withdrawn "on demand," or without notice, by way of checks. Government regulation prohibited the payment of interest on demand deposits. Commercial banks also held some savings accounts, or time deposits, on which they paid a modest interest rate. Savings institutions (savings and loan associations, credit unions, and savings banks) concentrated on time deposits, on which they were allowed to pay a slightly higher interest rate than commercial banks.

These distinctions were obliterated by the Depository Institutions Deregulation and Monetary Control Act of 1980. Savings institutions can now carry what amount to checking accounts. All institutions can now pay interest on accounts with checking privileges. The act was intended to increase competition among banks by giving them greater flexibility.

Before 1981 banks came under the regulatory control of either a state banking commission or the Federal Reserve System, which is in effect the central bank of the United States. In 1980 only the largest banks, about 35 percent of the nation's thirteen thousand banks, belonged to the Federal Reserve System. Those member banks held about 80 percent of all demand deposits. As of 1981, however, all depository institutions—commercial banks, savings banks, savings and loan associations, and credit unions— became subject to partial control by the Federal Reserve System. To understand how banks operate, then, and how the money stock is controlled, we must examine the structure and powers of the Federal Reserve System.

The Federal Reserve System

The Federal Reserve System, created by an act of Congress in 1913, is made up of twelve Federal Reserve District Banks scattered throughout the nation. Figure 7.1 shows the geographical areas covered by the district banks. The Far West, for example, is served by the Federal Reserve Bank of San Francisco (district 12), which covers Alaska, Hawaii, Washington, Oregon, California, Idaho, Nevada, Utah, and most of Arizona. Each district bank has one or more branch offices.

The Federal Reserve System is headed by a seven-member Board of Governors. Each governor is nominated by the president of the United States and confirmed by the Senate for a term of fourteen years. The Chairman of the Board of Governors, like the chairperson of any collective organization, has limited powers, restricted to persuasion and administration. Nevertheless he is one of the most influential people in the nation when it comes to determining economic policy.

At the district level, each Reserve Bank has a president and is supervised by a board of directors made up of representatives from the district. Each district bank board submits nominations for president of its district bank to the Fed's Board of Governors. The Board of Governors then appoints the twelve district bank presidents.

The primary function of the Federal Reserve System is to establish and conduct the nation's monetary policy. As discussed in Chapter 4, monetary policy is the manipulation of the rate of growth of the nation's money stock to promote a high and stable level of employment and production. More specifically, monetary policy is the management of the growth rate

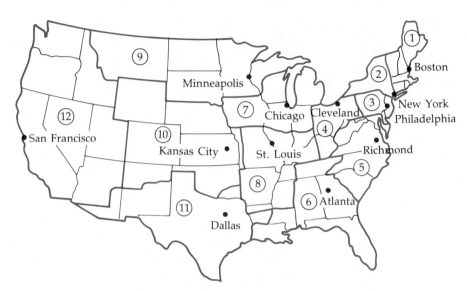

Figure 7.1. Federal Reserve District Banks.
The Federal Reserve System has twelve District Banks throughout the nation. Each Reserve Bank supervises the banks in its district. District Reserve Banks also hold reserve deposits for member banks, provide them with currency, and lend them money when necessary. The headquarters of the Federal Reserve System is in Washington, D.C.

of M1 or M2. Major monetary policy decisions are made by the Board of Governors and a group called the Federal Open Market Committee. The committee meets on the third Tuesday of every month to review the Fed's monetary policy. Members study the latest figures on GNP, unemployment, and consumer and wholesale prices before determining whether to increase or decrease the money stock, by how much, and by what action. Most decisions are implemented by ordering the purchase or sale of government bonds on the open bond market, actions that result in a change in the money stock.

The Federal Reserve System also serves as the central bank of the United States, a banker's bank that offers banks many of the same services that banks provide to their customers. When banks get deposits from their customers, they are entitled to claim an equal amount of reserves at the Fed. **Reserves** are the cash a bank has in its vault plus its deposits at the Federal Reserve Bank. As explained in detail on pages 157–158, reserves rise and fall with a bank's deposits. When banks gain customer deposits, their reserves rise, and vice versa. Reserves also change with loans to a bank's customers. They fall when the bank makes a loan, and they rise when the loan is repaid. The Federal Reserve System manages the reserve deposits for banks in its jurisdiction. **Reserve deposits** are the accounts that banks hold in Federal Reserve Banks. (A bank's reserve deposit balance plus its vault cash equals its total reserves.)

Reserves: the cash a bank has in its vault plus its deposits at the Federal Reserve Bank.

Reserve deposits: the accounts that banks hold in Federal Reserve Banks. (A bank's reserve deposit balance plus its vault cash equals its total reserves.)

Reserve Banks also make loans to all depository institutions and provide currency when needed. For instance, if a bank needs more currency to meet daily withdrawals, the manager can call the district Reserve Bank or one of its branch offices and order more. The bank pays for the currency with a reduction in its reserves. (The switch of funds from reserves to currency does not by itself reduce total bank reserves, since both currency and reserve deposits count as reserves. Bank reserves are reduced, however, when more cash is taken out of the bank than is deposited.) Like some large commercial banks, the Federal Reserve Banks also provide check-clearing services for banks. They collect, sort, and distribute checks to their banks of origin.

Checks and the Transfer of Money

When you write a check to your sister you know that eventually your bank balance will fall and hers will rise. But how does your money move from one bank to another? Actually nothing tangible ever moves. The figures on the banks' books are simply adjusted to account for your check.

To see how the process works, we must look at some simplified bank records called T accounts (so called because they look like a large T). Each side of the T represents one half of an accounting statement, or balance sheet, listing the bank's assets and liabilities (see Figure 7.2). The assets half includes all properties the bank owns. The liability half includes all claims that nonowners have against the bank. Assets are recorded on the left-hand side of the T, liabilities on the right-hand side. As the name balance sheet implies, the two sides of the T must balance. According to standard bookkeeping technique, an equal asset exists for every liability.[1]

Suppose you write a check for $10 to your university bookstore. Figure 7.2 shows the bookkeeping entries that will result. When the bookstore deposits your check, its demand deposits go up. Since the bookstore's checking account represents a legal claim that the bookstore has against its bank, First and Merchants National Bank, we classify the increase in the bookstore's deposits as a liability of First and Merchants. Thus we enter $10 in the name of the bookstore on the right-hand side of First and Merchants' balance sheet. This is entry *a*.

How does First and Merchants collect the money it has just received from your university's bookstore? The simplest is to send your check to the Federal Reserve. At the Fed, First and Merchants' reserve deposit rises (entry *b*), and the reserve deposit of your bank, Northwestern National, falls (entry *c*). But while First and Merchants' reserve deposit is a liability to the Fed, it is an asset to First and Merchants. Thus the check you wrote to the bookstore also results in a $10 increase in the assets column of First and Merchants' own bookkeeping records (entry *d*).

---

1. Actually, the balance sheet also includes an additional set of entries, called capital accounts, which represent the claims of the owners against the assets.

First and Merchants National Bank

Assets	Liabilities
Reserve deposits:	University bookstore's
+ $10	demand deposit
(entry *d*)	+ $10
	(entry *a*)

Federal Reserve Bank

Assets	Liabilities
	First and Merchants
	reserve deposit
	+ $10
	(entry *b*)
	Northwestern National
	reserve deposit
	− $10
	(entry *c*)

Northwestern National Bank

Assets	Liabilities
Reserve deposits:	Your demand deposit
− $10	− $10
(entry *f*)	(entry *e*)

Figure 7.2. Money Transfers in T Accounts.
If you write a check on your Northwestern National Bank account to your university bookstore, your demand deposit at Northwestern (bottom) will fall by the amount of the check. At the same time the bookstore's demand deposit at First and Merchants (top) will rise by the same amount. Northwestern's reserve deposit at the Federal Reserve will fall, while First and Merchants' reserve deposit will increase.

▬▬▬▬▬

Once the appropriate entries are made on the Fed's accounting records, your check is returned to your bank. Only when the check reaches your bank, perhaps three or four days after you wrote it, is your checking account balance reduced (entry *e* on Northwestern's balance sheet). Because your bank's reserve deposit with the Fed is down by $10 (entry *c*), Northwestern National must also deduct $10 from its own assets (entry *f*).

Several points should be made about these transactions.

1. The check causes your bank balance to fall and the bookstore's bank balance to rise (entries *e* and *a*).
2. The check causes an adjustment in the Fed's reserve deposits. Your bank's reserve deposit goes down; the other bank's reserve deposit goes up (entries *c* and *b*).

3. The Fed's reserve deposits are not the same as the deposits you and your bookstore maintain at your local banks. They are bookkeeping entries based on the demand deposits of member banks. Thus reserve deposits are not money. They are not used directly in trade, as demand deposits are.

4. Reserve deposits are assets to the member banks that maintain them (that point will become clearer in the next section). Thus any check you write causes your bank's assets at the Fed to fall, and the assets of another bank to rise (entries *f* and *d*). (This statement assumes that the person who writes the check and the person who receives it maintain accounts in different banks. If the two parties have accounts with the same bank, one person's deposit will go up and the other's down, but the bank's assets at the Fed will remain the same.)

5. Most important, when anyone writes a check, the nation's money stock does not change. Money is simply moved from one account to another.

The Creation of Money

When gold was used as a medium of exchange, the creation of money was much like the production of jewelry. Gold ore was mined from the ground and smelted, and the pure metal was molded into coins. How much money was created depended primarily on the amount of gold in the ground and the cost of getting it out. Today, in industrial nations like the United States, money is created principally through the commercial banking system. Banks create money; they create it every time they make a loan.

How is it done? Simply lending out someone else's money would amount to transferring money already in existence from one person to another. When banks create money it is by writing checks to, or increasing the deposits of, borrowers. Suppose you have negotiated a $5,000 car loan with Northwestern National Bank. You sign the necessary papers and the bank gives you a check to deliver to the car dealer. When the dealer deposits the check, money is created.

It is money's general acceptability in trade that enables your bank to create money out of thin air, as it were. So long as the car dealer is willing to accept the bank's check, and other people are willing to accept the checks the dealer writes, something has been created that has general acceptability: money.

The Reserve Requirement

Banks are not allowed to create unlimited amounts of money. Legally, the amount of money a bank can create depends on the level of its customer deposits. The more customer deposits it has, the more money it can lend and the more money it can create.

Reserve requirement: the portion of a bank's reserves that cannot be used to create money.

Excess reserves: the amount of a bank's reserves equal to the total reserves minus the required reserves.

The money-creating capability of banks is further restricted by the Federal Reserve. When a bank receives a customer's deposit, its reserve deposit with the Federal Reserve Bank increases. When you ask for a loan, your bank writes its check against this reserve account, and its reserve deposit decreases. The bank cannot write checks indefinitely against its reserve deposit, however. It must maintain a minimum deposit, called the reserve requirement. The **reserve requirement** is that portion of a bank's reserves which cannot be used to create money.

The reserve requirement is expressed as a percentage of the bank's total demand deposits. For example, if the reserve requirement is 15 percent, the bank must maintain a reserve deposit equal to at least 15 percent of its demand deposits. That is, through loans the bank can create money equal to 85 percent of its demand deposits. Thus the amount of money a bank can create depends on its excess reserves. **Excess reserves** are the amount over what the bank is required to hold, or:

$$\text{excess reserves} = \text{total reserves} - \text{required reserves}.$$

A bank's excess reserves depend on the reserve requirement, as shown in the table below. A decline in the reserve requirement increases a bank's excess reserves and money-creating capability. When the reserve requirement goes up, excess reserves and money-creating capabilities go down.

Reserve Requirement (percentage)	Loans Can Be Equal to: (percentage of demand deposits)
10	90
15	85
17	83
20	80

A bank with a total demand deposit of $10 million and a reserve requirement of 10 percent can make loans of up to $9 million (90 percent of $10 million). If the reserve requirement is 17 percent, the bank can make loans of only $8.3 million (83 percent of $10 million).

Many students have the impression that the reserve requirement is a means of ensuring that banks have some money on hand to meet the public's withdrawals. Actually, however, the reserve requirement is not intended to serve that purpose or to maintain the financial soundness of the banking system. The purpose of the reserve requirement is simply to restrict the amount of money that banks can create. If banks want security against customer withdrawals, they must maintain reserves above and beyond their required reserves, which are bookkeeping entries only. Banks do not really lend out other people's money when they make loans. Though reserve deposits are calculated on the basis of a bank's demand deposits, they are not the same thing. If they were, banks would not be able to create money. Loans would merely transfer money from depositor to borrower.

The Multiple Effects of Loans

So far we have considered only the immediate effects of creating money by loan. But the process extends beyond the addition of a specific amount of money to the economy in the form of a loan check. Assume Bank A has total customer deposits of $10 million and a reserve deposit of an equal amount. Its accounts and those of the Federal Reserve are shown in Step I of Figure 7.3. Assume also that the reserve requirement is 20 percent. Bank A can therefore lend against 80 percent of its $10 million in reserves, or as much as $8 million. Bank A decides to lend all $8 million to a local firm that needs new equipment. The firm buys the equipment, handing over Bank A's check to the supplier, who deposits it at Bank B.

Figure 7.3. The Creation of Money Through the Banking System.
In Step I, assuming a reserve requirement of 20 percent, Bank A has excess reserves equal to $8 million. In Step II, a loan of $8 million from Bank A ends up as a deposit in Bank B. Bank A's loan also shifts reserves from Bank A to Bank B at the Federal Reserve Bank. In Step III, Bank B can now make a loan for as much as $6.4 million (again, assuming a 20 percent reserve requirement). Bank B's loan ends up as a deposit in Bank C and shifts $6.4 million in reserves from Bank B to Bank C at the Fed. Bank C now has excess reserves equal to $5.1 million that it can loan. This money expansion process can continue as long as excess reserves exist. The maximum addition to the money stock from Bank A's initial $8 million loan would be $40 million.

Step I

Bank A		Federal Reserve Bank	
Assets	Liabilities	Assets	Liabilities
Reserve deposits: $10 million	Total deposits: $10 million		Reserve deposit of Bank A: $10 million

Step II

Bank A		Bank B	
Assets	Liabilities	Assets	Liabilities
Reserve deposits: $2 million (entry e)	Total deposits: $10 million	Reserve deposits: $8 million (entry f)	Total deposits: + $8 million (entry a)
Loans: $8 million (entry d)			

Federal Reserve Bank	
Assets	Liabilities
	Reserve deposit of Bank A: $2 million (entry c)
	Reserve deposit of Bank B: + $8 million (entry b)

Figure 7.3. *Continued*

Step III

Bank A	
Assets	*Liabilities*
Reserve deposits:	Total demand
$2 million	deposits:
Loans:	$10 million
$8 million	

Bank B	
Assets	*Liabilities*
Reserve deposits:	Total demand
$1.6 million	deposits:
(entry *h*)	− $8 million
Loans:	
$8.4 million	
(entry *j*)	

Bank C	
Assets	*Liabilities*
Reserve deposits:	Total demand
$8.4 million	deposits:
(entry *l*)	$8.4 million
	(entry *e*)

Federal Reserve Bank	
Assets	*Liabilities*
	Reserve deposit
	of Bank A:
	$2 million
	Reserve deposit
	of Bank B:
	$1.6 million
	(entry *i*)
	Reserve deposit
	of Bank C:
	$8.4 million
	(entry *k*)

Bank A's check increases Bank B's total customer deposits, a change shown on Bank B's balance sheet in Step II of Figure 7.3. Bank B's reserve deposit increases by $8 million, a change recorded in the Fed's liability column (entry *b*). At the same time, Bank A's reserve deposit falls from $10 million (Step I) to $2 million (Step II, entry *c*).

Bank A's assets are still worth $10 million, but they are rearranged because of the loan. Total loan assets increase by $8 million (entry *d*), and the reserve deposit decreases to $2 million (entry *e*). Bank B records in its own assets column the $8 million increase in its reserve deposit (entry *f*).

Total demand deposits rise from $10 million in Step I to $18 million in Step II ($10 million of demand deposits in Bank A plus $8 million in Bank B). In other words, the total money stock has increased. This is the reason we say that banks create money when they extend loans.

The money-creating process does not stop with the increases in Bank B's balance sheet. With its newly acquired reserves of $8 million, Bank B can also create money through a loan. It can lend against 80 percent of its additional reserves, or up to $6.4 million. Bank B's loan ends up as a deposit in Bank C, as shown in Step III (entry *g*). Bank B's reserve deposit decreases by $6.4 million to $1.6 million, both in its own records and in the Federal Reserve's (entries *h* and *i*). Bank B's loan account rises by $6.4 million (entry *j*). Finally, Bank C's reserve deposit increases by $6.4 million, both in its own records and in the Federal Reserve's (entries *k* and *l*). As a result of Bank B's loan, total demand deposits in the banking system rise to $24.4 million ($10 million in Bank A plus $8 million in Bank B plus $6.4 million in Bank C). Again the money stock has increased because of a bank loan.

Bank C can now extend loans based on its newly acquired demand and reserve deposits. Like Banks A and B, Bank C can lend against 80 percent of its reserve. As Bank C and successive banks extend new loans up to the legal maximum, the money stock continues to expand. It will not rise indefinitely, however. Each new loan is smaller than the one before it; each adds less to the money stock. Given the reserve requirement of 20 percent and initial excess reserves of $8 million, we can determine the maximum increase in the money stock through a simple formula:

$$= \text{Bank A's excess reserves} \times \frac{1}{\text{reserve requirement}}$$

$$= \$8 \text{ million} \times \frac{1}{0.20} = \$40 \text{ million}$$

Theoretically, once all banks have extended their loans to the legal maximum, the money stock cannot expand further without a change in total reserves or the reserve requirement. In Chapter 8 we will see how the Federal Reserve can change the total reserves and reserve requirement to increase or decrease the money stock.

Fluctuations in the Money Stock

The foregoing description of the creation of money was based on several assumptions made to simplify the analysis. Money creation does not actually proceed as smoothly as this theoretical model suggests. Day-to-day changes in business conditions cause temporary fluctuations in the money stock. For instance, banks are continually receiving payments on loans. Because they earn their income from such arrangements, they will attempt to relend the payments they receive as quickly as possible. (Banks often loan their excess reserves to other banks for periods as short as a day or less.) But a bank's loan payments do not always match its loan requests; at times they exceed requests. At such times, a bank will have excess reserves. Because it has not made as many loans as possible, it will not have created as much money as it can create. If all banks have problems of this kind, the total money stock will not be as great as it could be.

Moreover, not all bank loans end up as demand deposits in other banks. Part of the money created by banks may end up as currency held in the pockets of the public. Although currency is money, it is not the kind of money that permits banks to claim reserve deposits—not, therefore, the kind of money on which additional loans can be made. To the extent that bank loans end up as currency, the ability of banks to expand loans and increase the money stock is reduced.

For instance, suppose the firm that received the $8 million check from Bank A deposited only $7.5 million in Bank B, taking $500,000 in currency. Bank B would then have been able to lend only $6 million (80 percent of $7.5 million) instead of $6.4 million. Bank C would have received this smaller deposit and would have been able to lend less to Bank D. The total increase in the money supply would have been only $37.5 million instead of $40 million.

Finally, the public's willingness to hold money in the form of both currency and demand deposits will influence the overall level of the money stock. If the public reduces its demand deposits and increases its currency holdings, banks will have lower reserves and will not be able to make as many loans. Unless there are compensating changes (to be discussed in the next chapter), the money stock will fall. Similarly, if the public reduces its currency holdings by depositing currency in its demand accounts, bank reserves will rise. Banks will increase their loans, thereby increasing the money stock.

Summary and Extensions

Money is a medium of exchange that facilitates trade. In the form of currency and financial assets that can be stored or used to buy goods and services, money is productive. It reduces the time people must spend searching out mutually beneficial trades and increases the time they can spend producing goods and services. Currency, demand deposits, and savings deposits also provide liquidity, or ease of conversion into other assets.

Holding money involves costs as well as benefits. When people hold money, they forgo the goods and services that money could buy. People will not hold money unless the benefits of doing so are at least equal to the benefits of the goods and services it could buy.

Paper money and checks have value simply because they are used as money. People are willing to accept and hold them because they are confident that others will do so. For this reason, modern money is relatively easy to produce. The amount of money that can be created is not limited, for example, by the amount of gold beneath the earth's crust. It is figuratively created with the stroke of a pen, by governments, commercial banks, and the Federal Reserve System.

Government may be tempted to use its money-creating authority to produce money too fast. In recent history, many governments have succumbed to the impulse to inflate the money stock, and the result has been a continuing increase in price levels—that is, inflation—sometimes of runaway proportions. One of the most pressing problems of monetary economies is the question of how to control the money stock wisely. It is no simple problem, as we will see in the next two chapters.

Major Conclusions

1. Money is a medium of exchange and a store of purchasing power.
2. Money does not have value because of a backing in gold, but because of people's confidence in its general acceptability.
3. People hold money balances to finance transactions (the transactions

demand for money); to cover unexpected expenditures (the precautionary demand); and to take advantage of anticipated increases in interest rates (the speculative demand).

4. The two most widely used measures of the money stock in the United States are M1 and M2. M1 includes currency and demand deposits. M2 includes M1 plus savings account deposits at commercial banks and small certificates of deposit.

5. The Federal Reserve System is composed of twelve district banks and is headed by a Board of Governors, which is responsible primarily for the conduct of the nation's monetary policy.

6. When one person writes a check to another, the demand deposit of the person who receives the check increases, while the deposit of the person writing the check decreases. The bank that pays the check loses reserve deposits, and the bank that receives the check gains reserve deposits. The total stock of money remains the same, however.

7. When banks make loans, they create money.

8. A bank's ability to create money is restricted by its excess reserves and the reserve requirement.

9. The maximum amount of money that can be created equals the excess reserves in the system times the reciprocal of the reserve requirement (that is, one divided by the reserve requirement).

10. The money stock tends to fluctuate because of unevenness in the granting and repayment of bank loans and changes in the amount of currency held by the public.

Questions to Ponder

1. Suppose you head the government in a nation involved in an unpopular war. You can pay for the war by increasing taxes or by printing more money. Which option would you take? What would be the consequences of your action?

2. Dollar bills are elaborately engraved to prevent counterfeiting. Why? If dollar bills could be easily duplicated, what would happen to the money stock? To the nation's production and price levels? To the value of the dollar?

3. Do S&H Green Stamps qualify as money? Why?

4. Suppose you receive a $15 check from a friend who has an account at another bank. You deposit the check in your account. Using T accounts, sketch the entries that will be made on the books of your bank, your friend's bank, and the Federal Reserve Bank. What happens to the money stock because of the transaction? What happens to the ability of the two banks to make loans?

5. Suppose that your bank has total demand deposits of $20 million; that the reserve requirement is 10 percent; and that the bank has already made loans worth $5 million. How much more money can your bank lend to those who want to borrow?

6. If the reserve requirement is 100 percent, will banks be able to make loans? Will they be willing to handle the public's demand deposits?

Central Question

*How does the
Federal Reserve
control the
money stock?*

Key Terms

Discount rate

Open market operations

Equation of exchange

Velocity of money

Chapter 8

The Federal Reserve and the Money Stock

Do changes in the quantity of money matter? . . . There is massive historical evidence that they do. Every economic recession but one in the U.S. in the past century has been preceded by a decline in the rate of growth of the quantity of money. And the sharper the decline, the more serious the subsequent recession—though this tendency is far from uniform.
Milton Friedman

As the last chapter discussed, the amount of money banks can create depends on their reserves and the reserve requirement. This chapter describes how the Federal Reserve uses its powers to change the total reserves and the reserve requirement to control the money stock.

The Federal Reserve cannot control the money stock with precision. Its controls resemble the farmer's controls over crop size. The farmer who uses specific quantities of seed and fertilizer has a rough idea of how large his harvest will be. But because natural forces like the weather can change suddenly, the farmer can never be quite sure of the size of the harvest. Similarly, because of the many forces constantly interacting in the national economy, the governors of the Federal Reserve cannot always be sure exactly what will happen to the money stock when they employ one of the Fed's monetary controls. They know the approximate range within which change may occur, and the general direction the change should take, but no more.

Control of the Money Stock

The Federal Reserve exercises control over the money stock in three ways: (1) through the reserve requirement; (2) through loans to commercial banks; and (3) through the purchase or sale of government securities, mainly three-month bills and notes issued by the U.S. Treasury.

The Reserve Requirement

The reserve requirement is the portion of a bank's total reserves that cannot be used to create money through loans. It is expressed as a percentage of the bank's demand deposits (from which reserves are generated). That is, the bank's reserves, which include both its deposits at the Fed and the currency in its vault, can drop no lower than the specific percentage of its demand deposits.

Actually, the reserve requirement is not a single figure, but a set of figures that apply to different levels of demand deposits. Table 8.1 shows the reserve requirements on demand deposits as of March 1985. Banks were required to hold 7 percent of their first $2 million in demand deposits in required reserves; 9.5 percent of the next $8 million; and so on. Thus any bank with $350 million in demand deposits was required to hold minimum reserves of $43.35 million.[1] The average reserve requirement for such banks was 12.4 percent of demand deposits ($43.35 ÷ $350).

---

1. This figure is calculated by multiplying the first $2 million in demand deposits times 7%, the next $8 million by 9.5%, the next $90 million by 11.75%, and the next $250 million by 12.75%, and then adding the products.

Table 8.1. Reserve Requirement of Depository Institutions, March 1985[a]

Demand Deposits	Reserve Requirement (%)[b]
$0–$2 million	7.00
$2–$10 million	9.50
$10–$100 million	11.75
$100–$400 million	12.75
Over $400 million	16.25

[a] Depository institutions include commercial banks, mutual savings banks, savings and loan associations, credit unions, and agencies and branches of foreign banks.
[b] The reserve requirements became effective December 30, 1976.
Source: *Federal Reserve Bulletin* (March 1985), p. A7.

The general effect of a change in the reserve requirement is fairly simple. Suppose banks have loaned all the money they can, given the reserve requirement. If the requirement is reduced, they will be able to make more loans. As they do, the money stock will rise. The additional loans will end up as negotiable bank deposits or currency (see Chapter 7), which will supplement the existing money supply.

If the reserve requirement is increased, banks will have to increase their reserves. They will therefore make fewer loans. If banks cannot relend the money they gain when people repay their loans, the money stock must fall. Eventually the ratio of reserves to demand deposits will rise to the new required level.

Though we know that a decrease in the reserve requirement tends to increase the money stock, and vice versa, it is difficult to calculate when or how much the money stock will change. If the Fed lowers the reserve requirement, banks may not expand their loans immediately. Unfavorable business conditions may lead them to hold excess reserves. For instance, suppose banks expect interest rates to rise in the very near future. Instead of increasing their loans immediately, at relatively low interest rates, many banks may wait. Conversely, if the Fed increases the reserve requirement, some banks may not have to contract their loans immediately if they already have on hand all the reserves they need.

At different times, confronted with different market forces, the banking system will respond differently to a change in the reserve requirement. Sophisticated statistical procedures (called econometric model building) can increase the accuracy of the Fed's predictions. But even those methods are not always reliable. If a change in reserve requirements fails to produce the desired effect, the Fed may have to take corrective measures. Because a very small change in the reserve requirement can result in large changes in the money stock, and because banks have difficulty responding to changes in the reserve requirement, the Fed makes such changes infrequently—rarely more than once a year.

Northwestern National Bank		Federal Reserve Bank of San Francisco	
Assets	*Liabilities*	*Assets*	*Liabilities*
Reserve deposits:	Loan from	Loans to member	Reserve deposit
+ $1 million	Federal Reserve	bank	of Northwestern
(entry *c*)	+ $1 million	+ $1 million	+ $1 million
	(entry *a*)	(entry *b*)	(entry *d*)

Figure 8.1. Federal Reserve Loan to a Member Bank.
A Federal Reserve loan to Northwestern National Bank increases Northwestern's reserve deposit. Northwestern can use its new reserves to make loans to its customers, which will ultimately increase the money stock.

Loans to Member Banks

The Federal Reserve can increase or stabilize the money stock through loans to member banks. Just as individuals and business firms borrow from commercial banks, a commercial bank can borrow from the Federal Reserve Bank that serves its region. In return for its IOU, the bank receives an increase in its reserve deposit. This type of transaction is illustrated in Figure 8.1. Suppose Northwestern National Bank wants to borrow $1 million in reserves from the Federal Reserve Bank of San Francisco. Northwestern commits itself to paying the loan back and receives a $1 million increase in its reserves. The loan is listed as a liability on Northwestern's books (entry *a*) and, because interest is collected on it, as an asset on the Federal Reserve Bank's books (entry *b*). The $1 million reserve deposit that Northwestern acquires is an asset to it (entry *c*) and a liability to the Federal Reserve (entry *d*).

Northwestern can use its reserves either to make interest-bearing loans to the public or to ensure that it meets the reserve requirement. If it makes loans, they will increase the money stock. If it uses the new reserves to meet its reserve requirement, it will not have to reduce its outstanding loans, which would contract the money stock. For example, suppose Northwestern's demand deposits are $10 million and its reserves $1 million. If the reserve requirement is 20 percent, Northwestern has $1 million less than it needs to meet the requirement. It could get the extra reserves by reducing its outstanding loans, but that procedure would reduce the money stock. If it borrows $1 million in reserves from the Fed, Northwestern will not have to reduce its loans, and the money stock will not be reduced.

Banks borrow from the Fed for very short periods of time, usually a matter of days. When they pay back their loans, they reduce their reserves, and thus their ability to create money. Usually some banks are borrowing from the Fed while others are repaying their loans, so the total effect of such loans is to increase the money-creating potential of banks. Until late 1984, loans from the Fed hovered around $1 billion. For reasons that were not immediately clear, Fed loans shot up to $8 billion in early 1985. Even then, they amounted to less than 4 percent of total reserves.

Where does the Fed get the reserves that it loans to commercial banks? It creates them. The Fed simply accepts the bank's IOU and increases its reserve deposits, which are only bookkeeping entries.

The Fed can control the number and amount of the loans it grants in two ways. It can refuse to grant a loan (borrowing from the Fed is considered a privilege, not a right). It can also control the level of its lending by changing the interest rate it charges—the so-called discount rate. The **discount rate** is the interest rate the Federal Reserve charges on loans to member banks. A decrease in the discount rate will encourage banks to borrow, because it makes loans less costly. An increase in the discount rate will make loans more costly, discouraging borrowing.

In practice, changing the discount rate is not an important tool for controlling the money stock, for the number of loans the Fed makes to member banks is not an especially influential factor. But economists and financial analysts for major banks and brokerage firms often view changes in the discount rate as a signal that the Fed plans to take other actions that will significantly change bank reserves—open market operations, for example. In late 1984, two reductions in the discount rate were taken as signals that the Fed intended to increase the growth rate of the money stock.

Discount rate: the interest rate the Federal Reserve charges on loans to member banks.

Open Market Operations

By far the most important of the Fed's tools is its ability to sell government securities through its open market operations. **Open market operations** are the purchase and sale by the Federal Reserve of government securities, which can be bills, notes, or bonds. When the Fed buys government securities, it increases bank reserves and the money stock. When it sells government securities, bank reserves and the money stock decline.

Suppose the Fed buys a government bill from a private firm. The manager of the Fed's open market account, who works at the Federal Reserve Bank of New York, first asks dealers in the government securities market for the selling price on the bills they hold. Assume the Fed agrees to pay $1 million for the bill. It is delivered to the Federal Reserve, which issues a check for $1 million to the securities firm. The check ends up as a demand deposit in the firm's bank, increasing the money stock. The bank receiving the deposit can claim an increase in its reserves at the Fed.

Figure 8.2 shows the resulting entries on the books of Northwestern National Bank, which receives the deposit, and of the Federal Reserve. The Federal Reserve's bill holdings, an asset, increase (entry *a*), while the reserve deposit of Northwestern National, an offsetting liability, also increases (entry *b*). Similarly, Northwestern National records an increase in its demand deposits (entry *c*) and in its reserve deposit (entry *d*). Northwestern can now increase its loans up to the limit set by the reserve requirement. In short, it can start the process of money expansion described in Chapter 7 (see pages 161–163).

Open market operations: the purchase and sale by the Federal Reserve of U.S. government securities, which can be bills, notes, or bonds.

Northwestern National Bank		Federal Reserve Bank	
Assets	*Liabilities*	*Assets*	*Liabilities*
Reserve deposits:	Demand	Holdings of U.S.	Reserve deposit
+ $1 million	deposits:	government	of Northwestern
(entry *d*)	+ $1 million	securities	+ $1 million
	(entry *c*)	+ $1 million	(entry *b*)
		(entry *a*)	

Figure 8.2. Purchase of a Government Bill by the Federal Reserve.
The Fed's purchase of a government bill from a private firm increases the firm's deposit at Northwestern National Bank. It also increases Northwestern's reserve deposit at the Federal Reserve. By acquiring a government security, that is, the Fed increases Northwestern's ability to make loans and expand the money stock.

Where does the money to buy the bill come from? The Fed creates it. So long as people are willing to accept checks written by the Federal Reserve in exchange for their government securities, and so long as banks are willing to accept those checks as demand deposits, that which the Federal Reserve creates is money.

The Federal Reserve can just as easily reduce the money stock, by selling some of the government securities it holds. (In late 1984, the Fed held $162 billion worth of government securities.) When it sells a bill, the Fed receives a check drawn on someone's demand deposit, and the reserves of that person's bank fall. The Fed does not increase its accounts with the money represented by that check, however. It figuratively destroys the money by entering a zero on its books.

This transaction is shown in Figure 8.3. Assume that payment for the bill is made by a check written on an account with Northwestern National. Northwestern's demand deposits fall by the amount of the purchase price, $1 million (entry *a*). At the same time its reserve deposit falls by $1 million (entry *b*). The Federal Reserve loses an asset in the form of the government security (entry *c*) and dispenses with an equal liability in the form of a decrease in Northwestern's reserve deposit (entry *d*). One million dollars has disappeared from the money stock. But that is not all. Assuming that Northwestern has loaned up to its legal maximum before the sale of the bill, it must now reduce its loans in order to build its reserve deposit back up to the legal requirement. Thus the money stock decreases further.

Summary of Monetary Controls

The members of the Open Market Committee of the Fed have several ways of exerting control over the money stock. If they want to increase the money stock, they may:

Northwestern National Bank		Federal Reserve Bank	
Assets	*Liabilities*	*Assets*	*Liabilities*

Reserve deposits:
  − $1 million
  (entry *b*)
	Demand
	deposits:
	  − $1 million
	  (entry *a*)
		Holdings of U.S.
		government
		securities
		  − $1 million
		  (entry *c*)
			Reserve deposit
			of Northwestern
			  − $1 million
			  (entry *d*)

Figure 8.3. Sale of a Government Bill by the Federal Reserve.
The sale of a government bill by the Federal Reserve decreases the buyer's deposit at Northwestern National Bank. It also decreases Northwestern's reserve deposit at the Fed. Thus the sale of a security by the Fed reduces Northwestern's ability to make loans and create money.

1. Reduce the reserve requirement.
2. Increase the loans made to member banks.
3. Buy government securities on the open market.

If they want to decrease the money stock, they may:

4. Increase the reserve requirement.
5. Reduce the loans made to member banks.
6. Sell government securities held by the Fed.

If the committee takes any of the first three actions and the growth of the money stock accelerates, the Fed is said to be following an expansionary or loose monetary policy. If it takes any of the last three actions and the money stock decreases or slows its rate of growth, the Fed is said to be following a contractionary or tight monetary policy.

The Fed's controls over the money stock are powerful, but it is difficult to apply them precisely within narrow limits. Various forces may work against or in concert with monetary controls. For instance, banks may choose not to lend against all their excess reserves. Even if they do, the money expansion process takes time to work through the banking system. Furthermore, while the Fed is trying to increase reserves, the public may be increasing its currency holdings and reducing its demand deposits, thus reducing reserves and the potential to create money. Finally, the U.S. Treasury has demand deposits both at the Fed and in commercial banks around the nation. If it decides to move some of its deposits from commercial banks to the Federal Reserve, it will reduce reserves.

In short, the Fed's attempts to increase the money stock may simply offset opposing forces that tend to reduce the money stock. Indeed, the Fed often buys government securities (or reduces the reserve requirement, or increases loans to member banks) simply to keep the money stock from falling, rather than to increase it. Similar difficulties may frustrate attempts to contract the money supply.

A Monetary Explanation of Inflation and Deflation

The ultimate purpose of monetary policy is not simply to change the money stock, but to influence the nation's production, employment, and price levels. In recent years the Federal Reserve has been particularly concerned with the effect of its monetary policy on the rate of inflation.

Size of the Money Stock and the Value of Money

The value of anything is measured by what it can get in trade. Thus the value of money is what money will buy. If a dollar will buy a quarter-pound hamburger at the local McDonald's restaurant, the exchange value of the dollar is one quarter-pound hamburger. (Contrary to the opinion frequently quoted by the press, the value of the dollar is not about 32 cents. Very few people would trade a dollar for 32 cents.)

In general, the value of the dollar depends on the supply of dollars relative to the supply of goods and services people have to sell. If the supply of dollars people are willing to spend rises faster than the quantity of goods offered on the market, prices will rise. (Competition for the limited number of goods will drive prices up.) As prices rise, the dollar will buy fewer goods, and its value declines. That is why an increase in the money stock is normally associated with a decrease in the value of the dollar. People typically spend more when they have more money, driving prices up and deflating the dollar.

This relationship between the size of the money stock and the value of the dollar has been observed throughout history. When Alexander the Great conquered the Persian Empire and took its capital, Persepolis, he found an immense hoard of gold that the Persian emperors had been accumulating for generations. He spent the gold immediately, partly on his army and partly on himself. As a result, prices all over the Greek world rose sharply. When the supply of money suddenly increased in relation to the supply of goods and services, so many people wanted to spend their newly acquired gold pieces that the prices of goods and services rose, driving the value of the gold down.

There have been other instances of inflation in metallic currencies. Several centuries ago the Spanish discovery of gold and silver mines in the Americas increased the European supply of those metals, depressing their value. The California Gold Rush had much the same effect throughout the world. The most recent example of a gold-backed inflation occurred between 1890 and 1910, when the development of the cyanide flotation process of extracting gold from ore increased the supply of gold and decreased its value.

Modern monies are substantially different from the metallic currencies of the past, but the relationship between the money stock and the price level is the same. The German government financed the First World War largely by borrowing. After the war, instead of raising taxes to pay off its debt, the government printed new money in an effort to inflate it away. The sudden dramatic rise in the money stock caused prices to soar. By

1923, prices were a trillion times higher than their prewar levels. The value of German money diminished so rapidly that people ceased to accept it in trade or even to hold on to it. Germany became a moneyless economy, and economic activity virtually collapsed.

In recent years, governments in Italy, Great Britain, and several South American nations have also printed more money than their economies could absorb. At one point during the 1960s, the annual rate of inflation in Brazil was over 150 percent.

In the Untied States the story has been less dramatic. During the 1950s, both the money stock and the price level increased at an average annual rate of slightly less than 2 percent. In the first half of the 1960s, the average rate of growth of the money stock rose to 3 to 4 percent, and inflation followed at approximately the same rate. In the late 1960s and early 1970s, the average annual growth rate of money increased again to 6 percent, but inflation rose only to 5 percent, partly because of government price controls. In the mid-1970s, price controls were effectively discarded, the annual growth rate of money rose to 7 percent, and inflation accelerated to 9 percent.

Both the money stock and prices hit alarming double-digit rates late in the 1970s. In the early 1980s the Fed sharply reduced money growth to about 5 percent. This dramatic drop in the growth rate of money—indeed, the sudden reversal of policy from a rising to a decreasing rate of growth—was accompanied by two recessions. Real GNP dropped and unemployment increased sharply. When the Fed expanded money growth to nearly 13 percent between 1982 and 1983, however, price increases of the same magnitude did not follow. In fact, from 1982 to 1984, prices increased less than 4 percent, in part because production expanded along with prices. In mid-1983, the Fed again began to tighten up on money growth.

Although inflation has been the general rule throughout history, deflation—a general decrease in prices—has also occurred, usually after wars. Just as nations may be tempted to increase the money stock as a means of financing war-related expenditures, they often try to reduce war-inflated prices afterward by reducing the money stock. The result is deflation. England underwent a long period of mild deflation after the Napoleonic wars; so did the United States after the Civil War. Prices also dropped significantly in the United States in 1920–1921, following the First World War. In each case deflation was caused by a reduction in the money stock.

The Equation of Exchange

The relationship between the money stock and the price level is expressed by the formula $MV = PQ$, called the equation of exchange. The **equation of exchange** ($MV = PQ$) is a statement of mathematical equality between the product of the money stock (M) and the velocity of money (V) and the product of the price level (P) and the national output level (Q). That is, the money stock (M) multiplied by the **velocity of money** (V), or the average number of times each dollar is used during a given period, equals the prices of goods and services (P) multiplied by the quantity of goods

Equation of exchange ($MV = PQ$): a statement of mathematical equality between the product of the money stock (M) and the velocity of money (V) and the product of the price level (P) and the national output level (Q).

Velocity of money: the average number of times a dollar is used during a given period.

and services produced (*Q*). (Prices are normally measured in terms of some recognized index of the price level, like the Consumer Price Index.

On one level, the equation of exchange means simply that the dollar value of people's expenditures (*MV*) must equal the dollar value of what they buy (*PQ*). But the equation also relates changes in the money stock to changes in the price level. If *V* is held constant, an increase in the money stock, *M*, on the left-hand side of the equation must result in an increase in either *P* or *Q* on the right-hand side of the equation. If the economy is at full employment—producing all the goods and services (*Q*) it can—then an increase in *M* must be largely if not fully translated into an increase in the price level, *P*.

Effects of a Change in the Money Stock

The equation of exchange enables us to draw other conclusions about the relationship between production, the money stock, and the price level. Suppose that the nation's production level, *Q*, is continuously expanding as a result of increases in productivity. If the money stock and velocity remain constant, the price level, *P*, must fall. Otherwise *PQ* could not remain equal to *MV*. To keep the price level from falling when production is rising, either *M* or *V* (or both) must rise. In other words, during times of rising production, increases in the money stock can lead to price stability. Inflation will result only if the money stock, velocity, or both grow faster than the level of production. If production falls while the money stock rises (and velocity remains constant), too many dollars will be chasing too few goods, and prices will rise.

What will happen if the money stock decreases? If *V* is held constant, a drop in *M* on the left-hand side of the equation must be offset by a drop in either prices or production on the right-hand side. Generally prices will fall when the money stock falls, because fewer dollars will be competing for the nation's goods and services. The decrease in demand will cause producers to compete with each other through lower prices. Unless the costs of production fall along with prices, unemployment will result. If businesses must pay constant wages while receiving lower prices for their products, they cannot employ as many workers as before. Even if wages decline during times of deflation, they usually do not adjust rapidly enough to prevent unemployment from rising. The extent of the unemployment problem depends on how much and how fast the money stock is reduced and how rapidly wages and prices adjust downward.

Effects of a Change in Velocity

The equation of exchange also tells us that if *M* is held constant, a decrease in velocity will lead to a decrease in *P* or *Q*, with the same general result: unemployment. Conversely, an increase in velocity (*V*) can cause prices to rise. That is, assuming that *M* remains constant, an increase in *V* on the left-hand side of the equation must lead to an increase in *P* (the price level), in *Q* (output), or in both on the right-hand side of the equation.

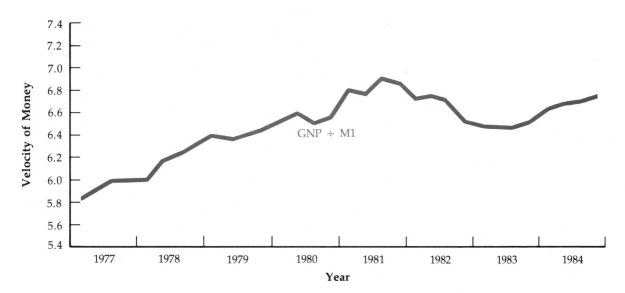

Figure 8.4. The Velocity of Money.
The velocity of money, defined as GNP divided by M1, rose gradually from 1976 to 1984. On a quarterly basis, however, it fluctuated considerably.
Source: Board of Governors of the Federal Reserve System, *Federal Reserve Chart Book* (February 1985), p. 8.

Increases in velocity, however, are not likely to cause long periods of continuous price increases. Velocity increases because people are using their money more rapidly, holding on to lower and lower money balances. But institutional constraints on velocity, such as regular pay periods, determine the minimum amount of money people must hold. Thus there are limits to how far and how fast velocity can increase—and to how much inflation it can cause.

Still, short-run changes in the velocity of money are possible. The rule is that the velocity of money varies inversely with the amount of money people want to hold. The more money people want to hold, the lower the rate of turnover. As we noted in the previous chapter, people want to hold money for three reasons: to cover expected and unexpected trans-actions, and in anticipation of higher interest rates. If economic conditions change—for example, if interest rates rise, changing the amount of money demanded—the velocity of money will change. Shifts in the velocity of money are readily seen in Figure 8.4, which shows the quarterly rate from 1976 to 1984.[2]

---

2. Figure 8.4 shows one measure of velocity, GNP divided by M1. Another measure, GNP divided by M2, showed no upward trend from 1976 to 1984. Both measures varied from quarter to quarter. (See the current issue of the *Federal Reserve Chart Book.*)

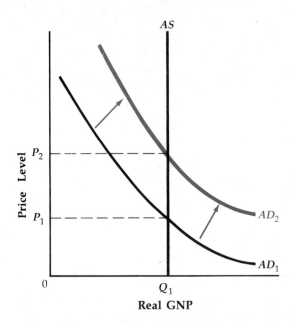

Figure 8.5. Effects of an Increase in the Money Stock on Aggregate Demand, Full Employment Assumed.
If the economy is at full employment—the aggregate supply curve is vertical—an increase in the money stock will shift the aggregate demand curve from AD_1 to AD_2. The price level will rise from P_1 to P_2, but output will remain the same: Q_1.

Inflation in Terms of Aggregate Demand and Supply

The effects of an increase in the money stock can also be analyzed in terms of aggregate demand and supply. If the economy is at full employment, additional output cannot be produced to compensate for a rise in M or V. In effect, the aggregate supply curve is vertical, as shown in Figure 8.5. Aggregate demand, however, will take on its normal downward sloping shape. With a given money stock, the price level will be P_1 and the output level Q_1 in Figure 8.5. If the money stock expands, people will have more money than they want to hold. As they try to use up their money balances, they will push aggregate demand up from AD_1 to AD_2. Because output cannot rise past Q, the price level will be pushed up to P_2. Though the output level stays at Q_1, the monetary measure of GNP rises with the increase in prices (GNP goes from $P_1 \times Q_1$ to $P_2 \times Q_1$).

If the economy is not at full employment, output can expand with the price level, and the aggregate supply curve will slope upward as in Figure

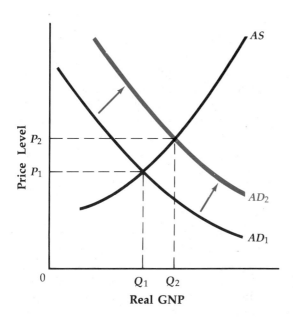

Figure 8.6. Effect of an Increase in the Money Stock on Aggregate Demand, Some Unemployment Assumed.
If the economy is not at full employment—the aggregate supply curve is positively sloped—an increase in the money stock will raise output. The aggregate demand curve will shift from AD_1 to AD_2, as it would under full employment. The resulting rise in prices from P_1 to P_2 encourages producers to raise output, from Q_1 to Q_2.

8.6. The increase in the money stock that is reflected in the shift in the aggregate demand curve from AD_1 to AD_2 will still push the price level up, from P_1 to P_2, reducing the velocity of money. But more important, output will expand in response to the change in the price level, from Q_1 to Q_2. In this case, the increase in the money stock increases both production and the price level.

The Politics of Monetary Policy

To the extent that increases in the money stock cause inflation, the Federal Reserve can be blamed for higher prices. It has sometimes increased the money stock more than was warranted by the nation's production level. But monetary policy is not created in a vacuum. The Fed operates in a system in which government fiscal policy often runs counter to monetary policy. It is subject to political pressure from government. And it must deal with competing economic objectives, such as the reduction of both inflation and unemployment.

Federal Government Deficits

One of the most troublesome influences on the Fed in recent decades has been the tendency of the government to overspend. Suppose that while the Federal Reserve is attempting to control inflation, the federal government is running up a budget deficit. To make up the difference between what it spends and what it collects in taxes, the government must borrow money by selling bonds in the bond market. This increases the demand for borrowed funds and perhaps the interest rates that businesses, individuals, and government at all levels have to pay. (The extent to which interest rates are raised by government deficit spending, if at all, is for many economists and policy makers an unsettled issue.)

In such situations, members of the House Banking Committee and the administration often accuse the Federal Reserve of adopting an unreasonably tight monetary policy. They will support their claim by citing rising interest rates on loans for everything from houses and cars to school construction and road improvements. Under political pressure, the Fed may then attempt to counteract heavy federal government borrowing by entering the market as a buyer of bonds, in effect increasing the money stock (see pages 171–172). The Fed's purpose is to keep interest rates down. But as we saw earlier, purchases of bonds by the Fed can raise prices. If inflation occurs, is the Fed responsible? In a sense it is. But Congress and the administration must also be held accountable for adopting inflationary spending policies.

Political Pressures on the Federal Reserve

Theoretically, the Federal Reserve is an independent agency. It is not required to seek the advice or consent of the administration or of Congress, but only to inform Congress of its immediate plans. Congress retains the power to change the Federal Reserve's charter, however, and thereby to curtail its independence—and members of Congress frequently threaten such an action. If it wishes to remain independent, then, the Fed cannot completely ignore administrative and congressional wishes. In the last decade the Federal Reserve has sometimes resisted political pressure from both parties with unusual vigor. (Its resistance was no doubt fortified by the unusually high rates of inflation of the 1970s.) At other times, however, it has expanded the money stock as if its primary purpose were to assure the president's reelection. The result has been an erratic monetary policy, with accompanying fluctuations in the inflation rate.

Cost-Push Inflation

Another problem for the Fed is the tendency of unions to seek wage settlements that cannot be supported by current market conditions. Such wage increases mean that employers cannot afford to hire as many workers as before. The result will be a rise in unemployment. Again, the Fed may be pressured by the administration and Congress to do something to alleviate the problem. Increasing the rate of growth of the money stock will enable businesses to hire more workers at the new wage rates. Such a policy will also contribute to inflation. Once again, the Open Market Committee of the Federal Reserve is only partially to blame, for it did not negotiate the inflationary wage settlements.

In fact, inflation has no one clearly defined cause. Rather the inflationary process is a set of interconnected causes, some related directly to technical control of the money stock and others related to political and market pressures. Asked what can be done about inflation, Henry Wallich, governor of the Federal Reserve, responded

The familiar debate about the sources of violence provides an analogy. Do guns kill people? Do people kill people? Does society kill people? Some assert that money, and nothing but money, causes inflation—the "guns kill people" proposition. Some assert that the entire gamut of government policies, from deficit spending to protectionism to minimum wage to farm supports to environmental safety regulations, causes inflation—the "people kill people" proposition. Some argue, finally, that it is social pressures, competition for national product, a revolution of aspirations, which are at the root—the "society kills people" proposition. The first view holds primarily responsible for the inflation the central bank, the second the government, and the third the people that elect and instruct the government.[3]

Summary and Extensions

The specific actions the Federal Reserve can take to expand or contract the money stock, and their impact on the price level, are technical matters. Its decisions, however, are very much influenced by the political setting in which it operates. The Fed is often pressured into taking actions contrary to its long-run policy objectives.

Occasionally the Fed's actions have been misguided. For instance, its attempts to keep interest rates low by buying government securities have increased the growth rate of the money stock, fueling inflation. As we will see in the chapters that follow, an increase in the inflation rate can also increase interest rates. Those who lend their money will require a higher interest rate to compensate for the depreciation of the dollar. Thus attempts to keep interest rates low can be self-defeating.

Major Conclusions

1. The Federal Reserve has three fundamental tools for controlling the money stock: (a) the reserve requirement, (b) loans to member banks, and (c) open market operations.
2. The Federal Reserve can increase the money stock by (a) reducing the

3. Henry C. Wallich, "Honest Money," *Macroeconomics 1979: Readings on Contemporary Issues* (Ithaca, N.Y.: Cornell University Press, 1979), p. 43.

reserve requirement, (b) increasing loans to member banks (which can be accomplished by lowering the discount rate), and (c) purchasing government securities.

3. The Federal Reserve can reduce the money stock by (a) increasing the reserve requirement, (b) decreasing loans to member banks (which can be accomplished by increasing the discount rate), and (c) selling government securities.

4. The Fed's open market operations are the most important and frequently used control over the money stock.

5. The equation of exchange, $MV = PQ$, states the relationship between the money stock and the price level. A change in either the money stock (M) or velocity (V) on the left-hand side of the equation will be reflected in an equal change in prices (P) or output (Q) or both on the right-hand side.

6. The extent to which prices or production levels are changed by an increase in the money stock depends on how close the economy is to full employment. Under conditions of effective full or nearly full employment (that is, when the aggregate supply curve is vertical), any action by the Fed that increases the money stock is likely to increase prices, with little or no effect on output. When unemployment exists, however (that is, when the aggregate supply curve slopes upward to the right), any action by the Fed that increases the money stock is likely to affect both price and production levels.

7. At times, the Fed uses its monetary controls to offset changes in velocity, which would otherwise affect prices and national output.

8. The velocity of money tends to vary significantly over the short run.

9. The Fed may increase the growth rate of the money stock in response to pressure from Congress or the White House to reduce interest rates and unemployment. In the long run, however, such increases in the growth rate of the money stock will probably lead to higher interest and inflation rates.

1. Suppose people decide to withdraw more money than usual from their demand deposits and convert it into currency. How would this shift affect banks' ability to make loans? What effect would it have on the money stock?

2. What can the Fed do to increase the money stock? What can it do to offset an increase in currency holdings? On the basis of your answers, does it follow that when the Fed buys bonds on the open market, it is always attempting to increase the money stock?

3. What is the relationship between people's willingness to hold money in currency and demand deposits and the velocity of money (the average number of times each dollar is used)? What is the relationship between the rate of interest and people's willingness to hold money? On the basis of your answers, what is the relationship between the interest rate and the velocity of money?

4. Suppose that we reestablish gold and silver coins as the medium of exchange in the United States. Under such a monetary system, would the nation still experience periods of inflation and deflation? Suppose that dimes are made of silver, and that the amount of silver in the dime varies from coin to coin. Which dimes would tend to be used in trade?

5. The Federal Reserve conducts monetary policy in part through the purchase and sale of government bills. If the Federal Reserve bought and sold private bills instead of government bills, would the effect be any different?

6. Suppose all the nation's power groups—large unions, corporations, and governmental units—pushed prices up and held them there, dramatically increasing the price of almost everything. Assume also that the money stock was held constant. What would be the effect on the economy? Explain your answer in terms of the equation of exchange.

7. If a nation's central bank increases the money stock too often and too much, causing high rates of inflation, what can be done to counteract the problem? Why might the central bank take such actions?

Who gains and who loses from inflation?

Variable-rate mortgage

Chapter 9

The Costs and Benefits of Inflation

In a full-employment situation money creation is strictly equivalent to taxation: Normal methods of taxation can be supplanted by the government's money creation, which . . . will cause inflation and a tax on people's average cash balances.

Roger Leroy Miller and
Raburn M. Williams

*T*he costs of inflation are widely recognized, and often exaggerated. When people think about inflation, they tend to consider only the reduction in the purchasing power of their dollar. They often fail to recognize that their wages rise along with prices during inflationary times. Many readers, then, may be puzzled by the reference to the benefits of inflation in the title of this chapter. But people both gain and lose from inflation. Indeed, if it benefited no one and hurt everyone, including government, the political opposition to inflation would probably be overwhelming.

Because government and some segments of the population benefit from rising prices, inflation is difficult to stop once started. Even if the rate of inflation is reduced, as it was between 1980 and 1984, government may find it difficult to hold down, as explained later in this chapter. But before discussing the benefits of inflation—including the incentives government has to inflate prices—we will review its more familiar costs.

The Costs of Inflation

The damage done by inflation depends primarily on two factors: (1) whether it is anticipated or unanticipated, and (2) what the rate of inflation is. We will begin by considering the effects of unanticipated inflation, a condition experienced in the United States in the mid-1960s and mid-1970s.

As noted in Chapter 8, inflation ran between 1 and 4 percent per year in the United States throughout the 1950s and early 1960s. Americans became accustomed to only moderate price increases. When prices started to rise at rates of 4 to 6 percent during the late 1960s, most people were caught off guard. Disgruntled grocery shoppers demonstrated against escalating prices. Richard Nixon railed against the "exorbitant" 5 percent rate of inflation in his campaign for the presidency in 1968. In August 1971, as public concern about inflation mounted, President Nixon froze the wages and prices of practically all goods and services.

At the time of the wage-price freeze the rate of inflation was 3.5 percent—relatively modest compared with the double-digit rates of 1974 and 1979 to 1980. But the unanticipated inflation of the late 1960s imposed costs that people were not prepared for. For that reason its consequences were perhaps more serious than the results of the later round of price increases. One of the most noticeable consequences, from the average citizen's point of view, was the decline in the relative value of cash savings.

Losses to Cash Holders

Unanticipated inflation hurts people with dollars in their pockets or in demand and savings accounts. The value of the dollars they are holding goes down, for the dollar buys less at today's prices than it did yesterday. The losses to cash holders are so clear that if people anticipate a high rate of inflation, they will convert their dollars into goods and services at present prices, before their purchasing power goes down. One might argue, then, that people who hold on to their dollars are wagering that the benefits of holding money will exceed the costs. Whether they should be expected to make such bets is an emotional issue. But from an economic perspective, the movement of financial resources into goods and services as the result of anticipated inflation reduces investment and ultimately lowers national production.

Losses to Institutional Creditors

Institutional creditors, like banks and insurance companies, also lose from unanticipated inflation. Assume that during noninflationary times a bank lends $30,000 to someone who agrees to repay the principal at the end of the year, with 6 percent interest. The bank expects $31,800 [$30,000 + (0.06 × $30,000)] on the termination date. But if prices rise unexpectedly by 10 percent, the *real* value of the dollars the bank receives (that is, what they will buy) will be less than the original value of the loan: $28,620 rather than $31,800. The creditor would have done better to invest the $30,000 in land or some other real good, whose price would have risen along with the prices of other goods and services. In that case, the asset purchased for $30,000 would now be worth $33,000 [$30,000 × (0.10 × $30,000)]. The *real* value, or purchasing power, of the $33,000 piece of property would be no greater than the original purchasing power of the $30,000—the bank would not have gained anything. But it would not have lost anything either.

If inflation is anticipated, banks and other creditors can demand a higher rate of interest on the money they lend, to compensate for the expected lost purchasing power of the dollars they receive in payment. That is why interest rates tend to rise with the inflation rate. High interest rates are generally a consequence rather than a cause of inflation.

Losses to Bond Buyers

Like banks that make loans, people who buy government and corporate bonds are creditors. When they buy bonds, they lend money to the bond issuer. In return they expect to be paid interest at regular intervals. They also expect to receive the principal (that is, the face value of the bond) on the date of maturity. Since both the interest payments and the principal are normally stated in terms of dollars, an unanticipated increase in the inflation rate can mean an unexpected drop in the purchasing power of the interest and principal.

Like banks, individuals can protect themselves against anticipated inflation by seeking an interest rate that compensates them for the expected loss of purchasing power. Unless they receive such a rate, they will tend to withhold their funds from the bond market, pushing interest rates up.

Losses to Businesses and Workers

Inflation means that prices in general are on the rise, not necessarily that all prices rise by the same amount. Some prices may not rise at all, and some may even fall.

Some prices tend to change rather rapidly and smoothly, reflecting changes in market forces, like the quantity and velocity of money. The prices of agricultural commodities like wheat and beef tend to mirror changes in their auction markets with reasonable rapidity. But the prices of many other goods take time to adjust upward. Price increases may be delayed when there are long time lags between the placement of an order and the delivery of the product, or when contracts specify the price at the time of delivery. Commercial airplanes, heavy electrical equipment, and many buildings are constructed and sold under these conditions. For the producers of these products, unanticipated inflation can mean cost increases and narrower-than-expected profit margins, or even losses, as well as payment in devalued dollars.

If the prices of products rise at different rates, then wages are likely to follow at different rates, for workers' wages depend in part on the prices charged for their products. In addition, some workers' wages are restrained by contracts that extend over a period of one or more years. In short, some workers' pay may keep pace with inflation; other workers' wages may lag behind price increases. The latter group will suffer a loss.

Not all reductions in the purchasing power of wages can be attributed to inflation, however. In any dynamic economy, there will always be groups of workers whose real wages decline because of the market forces affecting their industries. A decrease in the demand for a particular good, or an increase in the supply of workers in a particular industry, can cause such a decline in wages. Because more people are seeking college teaching positions, for instance, the real salaries of college professors have declined in recent years. The fairly high rate of inflation in the past decade only quickened the downward adjustment. In short, inflation can mean temporary losses in purchasing power for some groups, but not all.

Losses to Taxpayers

Because of the way income tax systems are structured, almost every income earner is hurt by inflation. Most tax systems are arranged so that they take a higher percentage of a person's money income as it rises. Thus if Ms. Jones's money income rises with inflation, the government will take a greater percentage of it in taxes—even if its real purchasing power merely remains constant. The purchasing power of Ms. Jones's after-tax income declines with inflation.

Suppose, for instance, that the marginal tax rate rises from 10 percent on the first $10,000 of taxable income to 20 percent on the next $20,000, and so on up to 50 percent on incomes over $75,000 (see Table 9.1). If Sue Jones earns $30,000 of taxable income, her tax bill for the year is $5,000 (10 percent of $10,000 plus 20 percent of $20,000). Her after-tax income is $25,000.

Table 9.1. Hypothetical Income Tax Schedule

Income	Marginal Tax Rate (percent)
$0 to $10,000	10%
$10,001 to $30,000	20
$30,001 to $50,000	30
$50,001 to $75,000	40
$75,001 and up	50

Over the following year prices rise by 10 percent, and Sue Jones receives a 10 percent increase in taxable income. While her dollar income rises to $33,000, her real income before taxes remains the same (since $33,000 will buy the same goods and services that $30,000 could buy a year earlier). But the extra $3,000 that permits her to keep pace with inflation puts Sue in a higher tax bracket. It is taxed at the higher marginal rate of 30 percent, increasing her tax bill to $5,900 (10 percent of $10,000 plus 20 percent of $20,000 plus 30 percent of $3,000). After taxes Sue has $27,100 ($33,000 − $5,900) to spend—$2,100 more than she had the previous year. But her purchasing power is only $24,390 ($27,100 × 0.90) after adjustment for the 10 percent inflation rate. In short, Sue loses $610 in purchasing power through what is called bracket creep. The government gains her lost purchasing power.

In 1981 the Reagan administration pushed through Congress an act requiring the Internal Revenue Service to adjust, or index, income tax rates for inflation. Tax indexing became effective in 1985. But in 1984, as the projected federal budget deficit reached $200 billion, some members of Congress began calling for the termination of indexing. It is not yet clear whether indexing will remain law, and what its long-term effects will be. Because indexing reduces the gains government can expect from inflation, it may reduce the government's incentive to inflate the money stock.

Losses to Pensioners

Retired people who depend on fixed monthly payments from their company pension plans are hurt by rising prices. Congress addressed the problem by providing for cost-of-living adjustments in Social Security checks.

General Losses from Inflation

During inflationary times, losses in the purchasing power of the dollar can encourage people to hold less money and more real assets, such as land, houses, gold, and collectibles (such as jewelry, artwork, and stamps).

Perspectives in Economics: Inflation and Inflated Demand for Housing

Dwight R. Lee

When the American economy went into a recession in the early 1980s, the housing industry experienced a full-fledged depression. In 1982, new housing starts were less than half the level of three years earlier. Construction and real estate firms went under in record numbers that year, and the future of the housing industry seemed questionable at best.

Most analysts attributed the slump to high interest rates. But the high and rising inflation rates of the previous two decades also played a role. During the 1970s, inflation combined with high interest rates to make investment in housing extremely profitable. Besides increasing the value of real estate, inflation increases the tax-deductible interest that is paid on mortgages. Thus it subsidizes the purchase of a house.

Suppose you are in the 40 percent tax bracket. Every dollar you pay in mortgage interest is deducted from your taxable income. In effect, you get a 40 percent subsidy on every dollar. If there were no inflation, the interest rate on your new

mortgage would be about 4 percent. But your after-tax interest rate would be only 2.4 percent (60 percent of 4 percent).

Now assume the inflation rate is 10 percent. The interest rate on your mortgage is now 14 percent (4 percent plus the 10 percent inflation rate), and the after-tax interest rate is 8.4 percent—much higher. But inflation is decreasing the value of the money you owe by 10 percent a year. In real terms, you are not paying interest of 8.4 percent, but negative 1.6 percent. This negative interest rate is in effect a subsidy on the purchase of a new home—a subsidy that increases with inflation.

This tax subsidy had a perverse effect on the type of new housing that was built during the 1970s. By any realistic standard, the size of newly constructed houses should have decreased. The average household size declined from 3.14 people in 1970 to 2.76 in 1980. The price of energy skyrocketed, dramatically increasing the cost of home heating and cooling. And median family income, after adjustment for inflation and federal

To the extent that reduced money holdings mean reduced business investment, inflation can lead to lower levels of production and lower incomes. Lower production levels mean fewer goods and services, hence ultimately even higher prices. These general losses will be spread throughout the economy.

Anticipated inflation can also lead to an overheating of the economy, or unrealistically high production levels. If business people expect higher rates of inflation in the future, they will build up their inventories now, to avoid paying higher prices later. At some point, having accumulated more inventory than necessary, business will cut back on orders for goods. Then production will fall, leading to unemployment and lost income for workers.

In periods of anticipated modest inflation, creditors can adjust their interest rates to compensate for the expected decrease in the value of the taxes, was $436 less in 1980 than in 1970. Nonetheless, during the 1970s the size of the average new house expanded from 1,510 to 1,760 square feet—an increase of nearly 17 percent. Rather than maintaining and expanding the nation's productive capital, Americans have been putting their savings into larger houses for smaller families.

Another factor that contributed to the inflation of housing demand during the 1970s was the increase in federal and state income tax rates. Higher tax rates increase the value of tax benefits, reducing the after-tax cost of housing still further. If your tax rate is 40 percent, the net after-tax cost of a dollar paid in interest is sixty cents. If your tax rate rises to 50 percent, the after-tax cost of your interest dollar falls to fifty cents.

In the early 1980s, critics of the Reagan administration pointed to the depressed housing industry as evidence that government policies, designed to reduce both tax rates and inflation, were not working. Of course the housing industry was suffering partly from the high unemployment of the early 1980s. But in any case, lower inflation and lower tax rates should be expected to deflate the demand for housing. Overall investment may be stimulated by falling inflation and tax rates, but some of these funds should be redistributed away from new housing and into other industries.

In sum, the housing industry benefits from inflation, especially when it is unanticipated. It is hurt by a reversal of the inflationary spiral—especially when a government policy reversal is unanticipated. If the federal government follows an anti-inflationary policy for the remainder of the 1980s, we should expect that smaller houses will be built. "Overbuilt" houses should be divided up or sold to larger families than are living in them at present.

At the same time, lower tax rates have a mixed influence on the housing industry. On the one hand, they increase the disposable income of home buyers, thus adding to the demand for housing. On the other hand, they reduce the tax benefits of a mortgage.

dollar. Similarly, workers can increase their wage demands. But during periods of very high inflation, sometimes called hyperinflation, the value of currency deteriorates so fast that people become reluctant to accept and hold dollars. To avoid significant economic losses, they tend to spend the dollars they receive as fast as they can. Hyperinflation can lead to a moneyless economy, a return to the barter system in which resources are devoted as much to searching out mutually beneficial trades as to production. In such circumstances production levels can fall significantly, as they did in Germany after the First World War.

In the early 1980s, economic growth slowed in Israel, Brazil, and some other Latin American countries, in part because of inflation rates that reached several hundred percent at year. Such economic downturns are felt not just in the nations where they occur, but in creditor nations like the United States, whose banks finance investments throughout the world.

The Benefits of Inflation

When one person loses from an unanticipated increase in prices, someone else usually gains. (The obvious exception is when inflation contributes to a downturn in total production, in which case almost everyone can lose.) Like the costs of inflation, benefits emerge largely because some people do not anticipate the rise in prices or cannot adjust readily to it. In such a situation, people who do foresee rising prices and move to counteract them will gain at the expense of others. They can buy early, at relatively low prices, and sell later at much higher prices. The possibility of reaping such gains is one factor that tends to draw resources away from production in inflationary times. People use their resources for speculation in the hope that they may be among the gainers from inflation.

Gains to Debtors

Probably the largest single group of people who gain from unanticipated inflation are debtors who owe money at the time inflation begins. The largest subgroup (not including the government) in this category is homeowners who are paying mortgages with fixed interest charges. They are a significant part of the population, since most single-family dwellings are financed this way. Homeowners benefit because the real value of their debts shrinks. Thus the person with a mortgage during an inflationary period is paying off the loan in dollars that are worth less than the dollars that were borrowed.

Consider a person who purchased a house for $30,000 in 1960, putting $1,000 down and taking out a mortgage for the remaining $29,000 at 6 percent interest. Today the dollar will purchase less than a third of what it could buy in 1960. Therefore the $29,000 mortgage is worth much less today to the bank that holds it than it was in 1960. But because the price of housing has risen slightly faster than other prices, the real or relative value of the house to the buyer has increased. Today the house could probably be sold for over $120,000. Thus while the dollar asset held by the mortgage company has shrunk, the debtor's real asset has appreciated.

The homeowner who has gained on his mortgage may not have gained overall from inflation, however. The homeowner may have some dollar assets, perhaps a government bond that pays 3 percent interest. The decline in the bond's real value because of inflation will partially if not entirely offset the decline in the value of the mortgage.

In periods of unstable prices, as we have seen, creditors charge higher interest rates to compensate for expected inflation. Because the rate of inflation tends to be variable and unpredictable, banks have moved away from fixed-rate mortgages to loans with variable rates. A **variable-rate mortgage** is one whose interest rate is adjusted periodically to agree with some market interest rate—for example, the rate on a specific type of government or corporate bond. If the designated market interest rate rises, the mortgage interest rate rises also, and vice versa. Market interest rates make good benchmarks for mortgage rates because they tend to move up

Variable-rate mortgage: a mortgage whose interest rate is adjusted periodically to agree with some market interest rate—for example, the rate on a specific type of government or corporate bond.

and down with the inflation rate, as lenders adjust their asking price to the expected rate of inflation.

The variable-rate mortgage does not eliminate the risks associated with inflation. It merely shifts them from the creditor to the debtor, whose mortgaged assets appreciate with inflation. Though debtors can still obtain fixed-rate mortgages, creditors are likely to charge a higher interest rate that incorporates a risk premium. This "risk cost" is another example of how inflation reduces the efficiency of the economy by increasing the cost of doing business.

Gains to Businesses and Workers

Not all prices adjust upward in times of inflation. Because of institutional barriers to the adjustment of wages and prices, such as lengthy production procedures and long-term labor contracts, some wages and prices rise less rapidly than others. Just as the people whose wages and prices adjust sluggishly are hurt by inflation, those whose wages and prices adjust quickly receive temporary benefits from unanticipated inflation. In particular, statistics show that business profits tend to rise in the early phases of a new and higher inflationary cycle, because product prices tend to rise faster than wages. In such a situation business owners gain at the expense of workers, who may not anticipate the increase in prices soon enough to incorporate it into their wage demands. In a minority of cases, workers are protected by special clauses in their contracts, called COLAs (cost-of-living adjustment clauses).

Gains to Politicians and Government Employees

Not surprisingly, those who are responsible for increasing the money stock and contributing to inflation tend to benefit from it. This observation holds true whether money is made of gold or paper, though the benefits tend to be smaller with metallic currencies. The discovery of gold in California in the nineteenth century benefited the gold miners who produced and sold it. The miners' benefits were limited to the difference between the cost of mining the gold and the price it commanded when sold, however. To the extent that mining increased the demand for equipment like shovels and pans, some product suppliers also benefited from the increase of the gold supply. The cost of the inflation was shared among everyone who was holding gold at the time, for the new discovery reduced the value of the existing gold.

Because paper money is much less difficult and expensive to produce than metallic currencies, the profits to the producers can be much greater. Modern governments often take advantage of inflation, particularly in wartime. Government can produce paper money in two ways. First, it can increase the money stock directly, either by printing new bills or by raising its bank balance at the central bank (in the United States, the Federal Reserve). The government then uses this newly created money to buy the new roads or military bases it needs. So long as people are willing to accept new dollar bills or checks drawn on the Federal Reserve account, the money stock will increase, and government will benefit from the increase. Politicians who promote government programs, workers who staff them, and people who benefit directly from them will all gain from the inflation. The losers will be those who hold dollar assets and those who must pay higher prices for goods and services because fewer resources are available for nongovernment uses.

The United States government does not increase the money stock in this direct manner, but often takes a more circuitous approach. The federal government runs a budgetary deficit, borrowing the difference between its tax receipts and its expenditures. First the U.S. Treasury sells bonds on the open market, which tends to decrease the price and increase interest rates. The Fed may then come under political pressure to keep interest rates from rising. In response, the Fed orders the Open Market Committee to buy bonds on the open market, which tends to increase the bonds' prices and decrease interest rates. Though the Fed is not bound by law to accommodate the Treasury's wishes, its directors sometimes feel a good deal of political pressure to keep interest rates from rising. If the pressure is great enough, the Fed will cooperate in inflating the money stock.

When the Fed accommodates the Treasury and buys federally issued bonds, the effect on prices is virtually the same as the effect of printing more dollars. The government gains at the expense of everyone holding financial assets valued in dollars, and at the expense of taxpayers, who must pay a higher percentage of their real income to the government as taxes.

Historically the Fed has made only sparing use of its powers to "monetize" the federal debt. Still, since the Second World War the government has benefited significantly as inflation eroded the value of the federal debt. Table 9.2 shows that the federal debt in current dollars (column 1) rose from about $271 billion in 1946 to $544 billion 1975 and $1.6 trillion in 1984. Because of inflation, however, the real value of the debt declined for most of the period. In constant 1967 dollars, the debt fell from $463 billion in 1946 to $338 billion in 1975, before rising again in the late 1970s. The federal government gained from inflation at the expense of holders of government securities.

From 1981 to 1984, inflation fell from double-digit levels to less than 4 percent. Yet market interest rates remained high by historical standards. In 1984, for example, home mortgage interest rates exceeded 15 percent in many parts of the nation. It is often argued that the expectation of continued high federal deficits (more than $200 billion annually) kept interest rates high. According to this theory, lenders feared the government would increase its credit demands, pushing up interest rates, and then repudiate the growing debt by monetizing it, as in the past. Creditors attempted to protect themselves from a new round of inflation by asking higher interest rates on their money.

Thus, by creating money, the government can redistribute resources from private to public use. Directly or indirectly, inflating the dollar increases the government's purchasing power. Because taxes also redistribute purchasing power from the public to the government, inflation can

Table 9.2. The Federal Debt in Current and Constant (1967) Dollars, 1945–1984

Year	Current Dollar Debt	Constant Dollar Debt[a]
1946	271.0	463.3
1950	256.9	356.3
1955	274.4	342.1
1960	290.9	328.0
1965	323.2	342.0
1970	382.6	329.0
1975	544.1	337.5
1976	631.9	370.6
1977	709.1	390.7
1978	780.4	399.4
1979	833.8	383.5
1980	914.6	370.6
1981	1,003.9	368.5
1982	1,147.0	396.8
1983	1,381.9	463.1
1984	1,576.7	506.8

[a] Computed with consumer price index.

Source: *Economic Report of the President* (Washington, D.C.: U.S. Government Printing Office, 1985), p. 318.

be considered taxation in disguise. Tax collected in this way is obscured by the complex mechanisms of money creation. However, inflation distributes the cost of government programs more haphazardly than normal taxation. And inflation is a kind of taxation without representation because it is never approved by Congress. For politicians who want to vote for public programs but not the taxes to pay for them, inflation may be the ideal tax system.

Should Inflation Be Stopped?

Many people are hurt by inflation, particularly long-term creditors who live on fixed incomes. Some benefit, particularly debtors and the government. Once inflation has been under way for a time, it becomes hard to stop without harming those who have made rational adjustments to the condition. If it appears that inflation will continue, home buyers will be willing to take on mortgages at a high rate of interest, on the assumption that the loans can be repaid with depreciated dollars. If the inflation rate is reduced, they will have to make high mortgage payments with dollars that do not depreciate as rapidly as expected. Mortgages can be refinanced, or paid off with funds from a new mortgage written at a lower rate. When long-term rates began to fall in 1984, many homeowners refinanced their mortgages. But refinancing often involves a penalty.

The predicament of farmers is more pressing. Many took out loans to buy land and machinery in the late 1970s and early 1980s. They anticipated that rising inflation rates would push up land and crop prices. They expected to cover their debt payments with devalued dollars. When the inflation rate dropped dramatically in the early 1980s, many farmers found themselves saddled with debts that had to be paid off with dollars that were more valuable than expected. The farmers' problems were compounded by falling land and crop prices, caused partly by the reduced profitability of farming and partly by the drop in demand for land as a hedge against inflation. Many farm bankruptcies were due at least in part to the unexpected reversal of the inflationary spiral.

The normative question raised by inflation is whether people should be expected to cope with such changes in the rate of price increase—changes that no individual can control. Monetary stability can be thought of as a public good, a benefit to the general population that the government can produce if the electorate demands it.

Summary and Extensions

Inflation causes problems mainly when the rate of price increase changes unexpectedly, and when the inflation rate is so high people will not accept dollars in trade. If inflation is anticipated, people can make adjustments in their financial and real assets and in the wages they demand for their labor. Creditors can require higher interest rates for the funds they lend. Laborers can incorporate expected price increases into their labor contracts. Even institutional barriers to price and wage adjustment—fixed salary schedules and contract periods, for example—can be changed to allow for regular adjustment for inflation. Inflation need not redistribute income from creditor to debtor, from employee to employer. As long as the rate of price increase is steady enough that people can expect a similar rate in the future, the costs of inflation will not be prohibitive.

Major Conclusions

1. Those who stand to lose from inflation include (a) holders of demand and savings deposits, (b) creditors, (c) bond buyers, (d) businesses and workers tied to long-term price and wage agreements, and (e) taxpayers.
2. Those who stand to gain from inflation include (a) debtors, (b) businesses and workers who are free to adjust their prices and wages faster than others, and (c) government.
3. It is primarily unexpected inflation that has redistributional effects.
4. Government creation of money can be interpreted as a hidden tax on the public. An increase in the rate of money creation can lead to an unanticipated increase in the rate of inflation, as well as to increased tax collections.

Questions to Ponder

1. How has inflation affected your real income, or your parents', during the last few years? List your gains and losses, and indicate the net effect.
2. Who gains and who loses from deflation?
3. Why do the effects of anticipated inflation differ from those of unanticipated inflation?
4. If everyone anticipated the rate of inflation perfectly, and could adjust his prices and wages freely to the new rate, would inflation do any harm?
5. The federal government currently increases the money stock through the sale of government bonds to the Fed. Would the effect on the economy be different if the government printed new dollar bills and dumped them out of airplanes?
6. Can inflation be stopped? Explain.

Part IV

National Income
and
Fiscal Policy

Central Question

What macroeconomic forces determine the national income and employment levels?

Key Terms

Real wage rate

Full employment

Say's law

Saving

Leakage

Injection

Investment

Planned investment

Unplanned investment

Equilibrium income level

Chapter 10

Unemployment and the Equilibrium Income Level: An Introduction

Revolutions occur infrequently in the United States. Or else, when these uprisings happen, there are few observers sufficiently alert to recognize them. Relative unobtrusiveness is only one reason that the "new" economics is so remarkable; with harldy a shot fired, it was named an "economic" revolution in its own time.

E. Ray Canterbery

*I*n this and the following three chapters we will cover macroeconomic theory, past and present. In particular, we will focus on the causes and cures of cyclical changes in national income and employment. To put the so-called Keynesian revolution into historical perspective, this chapter begins with a brief consideration of several earlier theories of unemployment. Then we will develop the basics of what has become known as the Keynesian macroeconomic model—not as John Maynard Keynes himself developed them, but as his followers have. Chapter 11 will extend and qualify that basic model. And Chapter 12 will show how the Keynesian model has been applied in government fiscal policy.

Unfortunately, economic theory—especially macroeconomic theory—does not always provide undisputed policy solutions to the macroeconomic problems of inflation, unemployment, and stagflation. Many of the policy recommendations drawn from Keynesian macroeconomic models are controversial. Alternative theories, discussed in the following section, offer conflicting policies. The debate will not be settled for many years, if ever; we certainly cannot offer conclusions here. Instead we will outline the framework economists use to think about unemployment and inflation, and in that way isolate the points of contention.

Before Keynes

John Maynard Keynes did not single-handedly bring about the Keynesian revolution. A number of economists who were studying unemployment during the Great Depression made many of the same recommendations as Keynes—including the suggestion that in times of heavy unemployment, the government should run a budgetary deficit to stimulate the economy and create jobs. Their theories may not have been as precisely developed as Keynes's, but their conclusions were identical. For instance, Jacob Viner wrote, "When business activity is declining, or is stagnant and at a low level, reduced taxation, and budget deficits are, from the point of view of the national economy as a whole, sound policy rather than unsound."[1] And Frank Knight wrote, "As far as I know, economists are completely agreed that the government should spend as much and tax as little as possible at a time like this—using the expenditure to do the most good in itself and also to point toward relieving the depression."[2]

To these and other economists, *The General Theory* was nothing new, and they may have been surprised when the book became the manifesto for the new economics. For an idea to become widely accepted, however, it must be effectively presented and promoted. Keynes's contribution probably lies more in the presentation of his theory—in a relatively simple, straightforward manner that attracted both professional and public attention—than in its originality.

---

1. As quoted in J. Ronnie Davis, *The New Economics and the Old Economists* (Ames: Iowa State University Press, 1971), p. 40.
2. Ibid., p. 16.

To appreciate the impact of the Keynesian revolution on people's thinking, we will look briefly at some theories that were in vogue before Keynes. The most influential was the classical explanation for unemployment.

The Classical Model of the Labor Market

Classical economists assumed that the number of workers employers will hire is inversely related to the wage rate, specifically the real or price-adjusted wage rate. The **real wage rate** is the nominal or money wage rate (the number of dollars a person earns per hour or day) adjusted for inflation or deflation. The real wage rate measures a worker's actual purchasing power. Because the general price level determines how much a given money wage will buy, the real wage rate can be expressed as the ratio W/P, where W is the money wage and P is an index (like the consumer price index) representing the general price level:

$$\text{real wage} = \frac{\text{money wage}}{\text{price index}} = \frac{W}{P}$$

Mathematically, the real wage rises with an increase in the money wage and falls with an increase in the price level.

If the real wage rate rises, then, the number of available jobs falls, and vice versa. Classical economists also assumed a direct relationship between the real wage rate and the number of laborers willing to work. That is, if the real wage rate rises, more workers will give up their leisure time and spend more time at work. Hence an increase in the real wage rate will cause the quantity of labor supplied to rise, and vice versa. The labor supply curve, like other supply curves, slopes upward.

The supply and demand curves for the classical model of the labor market are shown in Figure 10.1. As in other competitive markets, the equilibrium point falls at the intersection of the two curves. At the real wage rate $(W/P)_2$, everyone who is willing to work (Q_3) can find a job. In this limited sense, the competitive market process tends toward full employment. In classical theory, **full employment** occurs when the quantity of labor demanded equals the quantity of labor supplied at a market-determined real wage rate.

According to classical theory, if some workers are unemployed, it is because the going real wage is artificially high. In that case the market is not in equilibrium: the real wage is above the intersection of supply and demand. In Figure 10.1, any real wage rate above $(W/P)_2$ will produce unemployment. The number of workers supplied will be greater than the quantity demanded. Union wage rates, minimum wage laws, and other market restrictions can cause such an effect.

Even in a competitive market unhampered by a government- or union-fixed wage rate, unemployment can arise temporarily as a result of changes in supply and demand. Unemployment will persist until the real wage rate adjusts to a new equilibrium point. For instance, suppose the demand for labor in Figure 10.1 falls from D_1 to D_2 as the result of a change in

Real wage rate: the nominal or money wage rate (the number of dollars a person earns per hour or day) adjusted for inflation or deflation. The real wage rate measures a worker's actual purchasing power.

Full employment: the employment level that occurs when the quantity of labor demanded equals the quantity of labor supplied at a market-determined real wage rate.

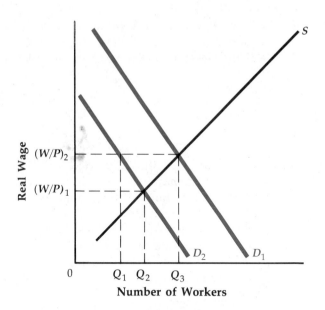

Figure 10.1. The Labor Market: The Classical Model.
With supply and demand for labor represented by curves S and D_1, full employment
will be achieved at a real wage rate of $(W/P)_2$. If the demand for labor in this
market falls to D_2, the number of workers willing to work (Q_3) will at first exceed
the number demanded (Q_1). Until the real wage rate adjusts downward to $(W/P)_1$,
some unemployment will persist.

consumer buying habits. The product made by the workers in this market
is now less desirable than some other product made by other workers.
This jarring change in demand will throw the market out of equilibrium.
The quantity of labor that employers demand at the initial real wage rate,
$(W/P)_2$, will fall to Q_1. But the number of people willing to work at that
rate will remain Q_3. Thus $Q_3 - Q_1$ people will be out of work. In a perfectly
competitive labor market, the real wage rate (along with the money wage)
may fall very quickly, eliminating this gap between the number of jobs
available and the number of people seeking them. In the real world,
however, markets never work that smoothly. Adjustment requires time—
months or even years—and during that period, some people will be
unemployed.

An increase in the supply of labor—that is, the number of people willing
to work at any given wage—can have a similar effect on unemployment,
again temporarily. The supply curve shifts outward, lowering the point
of intersection with the demand curve. If the real wage adjusts downward
in a competitive manner, the gap between the old real wage rate and the
new equilibrium wage will be closed. But as before, there will be unemployment during the transition.

If unemployment persists beyond a transitional period, classical economists would argue that it is because obstructions in the labor market are

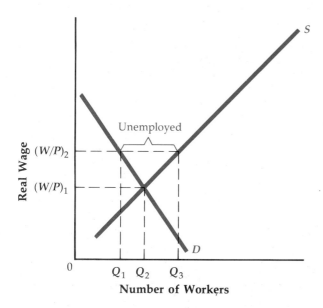

Figure 10.2. Obstruction in the Labor Market.
In a free competitive market, the real wage rate will settle at $(W/P)_1$. If the money wage is established at the artificially high level of $(W/P)_2$, however, it will push the real wage rate above equilibrium, causing unemployment equal to the difference between Q_1 and Q_3.

preventing the real wage rate from falling. Suppose the equilibrium real wage rate is $(W/P)_1$ (see Figure 10.2). If the money wage is raised by union contract to an artificially high rate while the price level remains unchanged [real wage $(W/P)_2$], unemployment equal to the difference between Q_3 and Q_1 will persist. As we saw in Chapter 8, the government can solve this unemployment problem by creating an increase in the money stock—and with it an increase in the general price level. With an increase in the price level [the denominator in $(W/P)_2$], the real wage rate will fall—assuming, of course, that the money wage rate remains constant. And if the real wage rate falls, the gap between the quantity of labor demanded (Q_1) and the quantity of labor supplied (Q_3) will evaporate. If unions are able to negotiate perpetual wage increases, however, a government intent on pushing the real wage rate down to the equilibrium point will have to inflate the price level continually. If money wages and prices rise together, the real wage will never reach equilibrium, and unemployment will never disappear.

Classical economists reasoned that an economy would never be completely free from unemployment. Continuing adjustments in the labor market, as well as restrictions that prevent the real wage from adjusting—minimum wage laws and union contracts—would keep unemployment from falling to zero.

Economists in History: John Maynard Keynes (1883–1946)

Probably no single individual has had a more profound influence on modern economic thought than John Maynard Keynes (1883–1946). An erudite British economist who accumulated a sizable fortune by speculating in foreign currencies, he wrote principally on monetary and international economics. His reputation rests primarily on a book published in 1936, *The General Theory of Employment, Interest, and Money*. In this work Keynes attacked the conventional, or "classical," explanation for unemployment, which focused on the supply and demand for labor. Classical economists tended to explain most unemployment in terms of obstacles that prevent wage rates from falling, and therefore from matching the number of people wanting to work with the number of jobs available in specific labor markets. Such obstacles to lower wages include union resistance to wage reductions, minimum wage laws, and unemployment compensation.

Unlike the classical theories, Keynes's theory of unemployment transcended specific labor markets and dealt instead with the economy as a whole. Rather than focusing on obstacles to a drop in the wage rate, he examined the effects of national income, saving, and investment levels on unem-

ployment. Thus while the narrower classical theories were and still are considered to be only partial models, Keynes truly devised a theory of the macroeconomy. His economic model combined the analysis of many different markets under the umbrella of a single general theory of unemployment.

Keynes wrote *The General Theory* during the depth of the Great Depression, a period of very low production, high unemployment, and falling wages and prices. He felt that the classical theories could not explain the persistence of high unemployment despite falling wages. In an effort to explain the events of his day, Keynes hit on the notion that unemployment results in part from the inability or unwillingness of consumers and businesses to buy enough goods and services to keep everyone employed. Because he integrated this model of insufficient aggregate demand with theories of the supply and demand for money and the determination of interest rates, Keynes's work was referred to as a "general theory." Recent events have shown that it is far from universal in its application, however.

Keynes was especially concerned with the welfare of the unemployed during the period when,

Early Theories of the Business Cycle

Modern economic history has seen a continuing series of business cycles, or alternating periods of recession and recovery. Before Keynes, economists explained these swings in national income and employment as the result of unfavorable growing conditions, excessive production of goods and services, or overexpansion and eventual contraction or collapse of the banking system.

Agricultural Theories

Economic life has always proceeded irregularly. There have always been good years and bad years, as measured, for example, by the gross national according to classical theory, the labor pricing system is readjusting. Falling wages and prices may eventually restore full employment, "but in the long run," Keynes reportedly observed, "we are all dead." Thus he sought solutions for short-term problems—extremely low production and high unemployment—like those of the Depression. During periods of heavy unemployment in the private sector, he argued, the government should stimulate economic activity by spending more or lowering taxes. In other words, the government should deliberately run a budgetary deficit.

Before Keynes, the prevailing philosophy was that government should balance its budget—that is, spend no more than it collects in taxes. Keynes's proposal—raise government spending or lower taxes—appeared to condone fiscal irresponsibility. Thus his recommendation was branded radical, and his analysis referred to as the "new economics" of unemployment. From the vantage point of the 1980s, however, Keynes's theory of the cause and cure of unemployment appears merely conventional. Over the past four decades, his theory has been interpreted, reinterpreted, refined, and extended. A plethora of doctoral dissertations and journal articles have asked not only "What did Keynes really say?" but "What do the interpreters of Keynes say that Keynes said?" By the 1960s, the Keynesian prescription for dealing with unemployment had become accepted doctrine among most economists and politicians. Only now, after the 1970s, a decade of high unemployment and inflation accompanied by large budgetary deficits, has the general faith in the Keynesian model been shaken.

Keynes tried to deal with the high unemployment and falling prices of the 1930s. But today's high unemployment and rising prices are a combination that Keynesian analysis was not designed to handle. Economists are now searching for an approach better fitted to the conditions of the 1970s and 1980s. Some believe the answer lies in a variation of the Keynesian model. Others have virtually abandoned Keynesianism for the newer monetarist, supply-side, or rational expectations models of the macroeconomy. In some respects, many have returned full circle to a more sophisticated version of classical theory. Keynesian theory is still important, however, for it helps to explain much of what has happened in the economy over the last fifty years, and the government policies that have been adopted as a consequence.

product. When a large proportion of the population was engaged in farming, economic ups and downs were caused by changes in the weather. Poor rainfall or an early frost altered farm production, and hence the level and distribution of income. These changes in turn would affect the demand for various goods and various types of labor. For instance, bad growing conditions hurt merchants who made their living by trading with farmers. And the new supply and demand conditions caused transitional unemployment while wage rates adjusted. During poor weather people moved out of the farm labor market, and unemployment increased among suppliers of agricultural equipment and household goods.

Because agriculture still dominated people's lives in the eighteenth and early nineteenth centuries, social scientists of that time looked to natural causes for an explanation of economic instability. One hundred years ago, for instance, the sunspot theory was a favorite explanation for changes in economic activity. Observers had noticed that sunspots were frequently followed by poor growing seasons. Today, of course, agriculture is much less important to national production, and causes other than sunspots must be sought for cyclical unemployment.

The Theory of General Glut

As commerce and industry developed, people realized that economic fluctuations are not necessarily connected to agriculture. Merchants observed that in some periods business was bad in all lines of merchandise, and they could not dispose of their goods at the usual prices in the usual volume. They reasoned that the problem was overproduction. Too much of all goods had been produced, leading to a general glut of merchandise. Resulting cutbacks in production caused unemployment.

This theory now seems unsophisticated, for the modern economy produces several times more than the level the early theorists considered excessive. In fact, the theory of general glut was attacked almost immediately by Jean Baptiste Say, a French economist of the late eighteenth and early nineteenth centuries. Say argued that in a barter economy, the production of one good for sale represented the demand for another, because its production was a means of gaining purchasing power. That is, we produce more than we want to consume so that we may trade with others to acquire what we want but do not produce. This proposition led to the formulation of Say's law. According to **Say's law**, supply creates its own demand—that is, the production of a supply of products creates an equal demand for goods and services.

In other words, an increase in the quantity of a good produced must mean that people are demanding more of other goods. Their motive for producing more is to be able to trade for more of something else. At times the wrong goods may be produced for sale, or the wrong quantities of goods. The result will be changes in the relative prices of goods and in the supply and demand for various types of labor, as well as transitional adjustments in employment. That does not mean, however, that a general glut exists, or that demand for all goods and services is insufficient.

Say's law: the macro-economic principle that supply creates its own demand—that is, that the production of a supply of products creates an equal demand for goods and services.

Monetary Theories of the Business Cycle

In a barter economy, Say's law is the correct answer to the theory of general glut. Say hinted, however, that his line of reasoning ran into difficulties when money was introduced into an economic system. If producers hold on to the money they receive from the sale of goods, rather than spending it immediately, the total supply of goods will be greater than the total demand. If a person sells the product of his labor for $100, for instance, but does not spend the money, $100 worth of other goods will be left on the market. Thus for the period of time people hold money, overproduction and a reduction in economic activity will result.

Most early monetary theorists blamed fluctuations in economic activity on the structure of the banking system, specifically contractions of the money supply that occurred during times of financial panic. In the eighteenth and nineteenth centuries, the money stock consisted of gold, silver coins, and paper money printed by banks, called bank notes. If a customer took a bank note to a bank and demanded payment, he would receive gold coins. Because banks made money by extending loans through the issuance of bank notes, there was always a risk of overextension—the banks might create too much money. From time to time, a bank would find itself unable to meet depositors' demands for gold and it would go "bankrupt." Bankruptcy might be the result of bad management or extraordinary circumstances, like poor weather, that made it impossible for people to repay loans. Because banks held deposits in other banks, one bank's financial problems could spread throughout the banking system.

The process of contaction proceeded as follows. A bank under pressure to pay off its customers would withdraw its deposits from other banks. Seeing the run on that bank, customers of other banks would lose confidence in the security of their deposits, and they too would attempt to withdraw their deposits. Banks did not (and still do not) hold sufficient reserves to meet their depositors' demands in times of widespread panic. As a result all banks within a city or perhaps even a nation would collapse at virtually the same time, causing a dramatic decrease in the money stock and in the prices of goods and services. (Remember that $MV = PQ$. With V held constant by institutional constraints, a decrease in M on the left-hand side of the equation must lead to a decrease in P and/or Q on the right-hand side—See Chapter 8. The classical economist argued that a decrease in M would have immediate impact on P.)

During widespread bank failure, businesses found that the real value of their financial obligations had risen. The price of their assets fell along with their incomes, yet their debts remained the same in dollar terms. Unable to cope with such financial pressures, many businesses also collapsed, further disrupting the flow of economic activity. At the same time, the dramatic decrease in prices increased real wages. (If the numerator of the real wage, W, remains constant while the denominator, P, falls, the real wage, W/P, increases.) The result was a decrease in the quantity of labor demanded and an increase in unemployment. Though in a competitive labor market, nominal and real wages will eventually move toward equilibrium, during a period of bank failure and contraction of the money stock, unemployment tends to persist. This periodic pattern—a collapse of the banking system followed by a rise in unemployment—prompted the classical economist Irving Fisher to suggest that depressions and booms were merely a consequence of "the dance of the dollar." Attempts were made to correct the instability of the early banking system. In the United States, the Federal Reserve System was created to ensure that banks could count on obtaining additional money when they needed it. In times of financial panic, banks can get all the currency necessary to satisfy depositors' demands from the Fed. By squelching bank runs and preventing the collapse of the banking system, the Fed prevents periods of deflation and their accompanying problems of recession and unemployment.

The Keynesian Perspective: The Essentials

The philosopher Thomas Kuhn has hypothesized that scientific knowledge is advanced in two distinct ways. New discoveries may be made gradually, in a relatively methodical and orderly procedure. Occasionally, however, there is a sudden radical change in the basic paradigm, or world view, held by scientists. Newton caused such a paradigm change in physics. Later Einstein and the quantum physicists brought about others.[3]

Keynes brought about such a paradigm change in economists' view of recessions and unemployment. Instead of taking the classical labor supply and labor demand curves as his frame of reference, Keynes focused on the interrelationship between the overall real national income level (and therefore employment, since the two are closely related) and the aggregate, or total, demand for goods and services. These two macroeconomic factors interact to form the basis of the circular flow of income.

The Circular Flow of Income

To see the connection between national income level and aggregate demand in the simplest terms possible, imagine an economy without government. (This assumption is highly unrealistic, but it allows us to develop the basic principles of Keynesianism. We will bring government into the analysis later.) This private economy is divided into two broad categories, households and firms, as in Figure 10.3. In this simplified macroeconomic model, households perform two roles. They supply resources such as labor and capital to firms, and they consume the goods and services produced by the firms. Similarly, firms perform two roles. They receive labor and capital from households and sell their products to them.

The two arrows shown in Figure 10.3 would be sufficient to describe a barter economy. Resources go from households to firms, which in turn supply goods to households in exchange for resources. In a monetary economy, however, the system is more complicated. Resources are supplied to firms in exchange for money or income in the form of wages, dividends, and interest. Households then use that money to buy goods and services from the firm. The flow of money is added to the flow of goods, services, and resources in Figure 10.4.

The money received by households (on the left-hand side of the outer flow) mirrors household earnings. It reflects the contribution of household members to the production of goods and services. If firms produce $100 worth of goods and services, households must earn an aggregate or national income of $100, simply because the full value of anything produced must ultimately be attributed to someone. On a conceptual level, income and the value of what is produced are equal (though in practice workers generally take home less than the full value of their earnings). In future discussions, the terms national output and national income will be used interchangeably.

---

3. Thomas S. Kuhn, *The Structure of Scientific Revolutions,* 2d ed. (Chicago: University of Chicago Press, 1970).

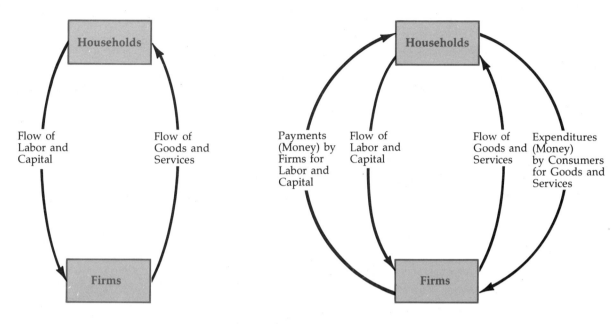

Figure 10.3. The Circular Flow of Income in a Barter Economy.
The macroeconomy can be divided into two sectors, households and firms. In a barter economy, resources like labor and capital flow from the households to the firms. Goods and services flow back from the firms to the households.

Figure 10.4. The Circular Flow of Income in a Money Economy.
In a money economy, firms make money payments to households for the resources they provide. Households then spend the money payments on goods and services produced by the firms.

   The circular flow model shows that the ability of firms to sell their products depends on the willingness of households to buy what is produced. And obviously the tendency of households to buy is influenced by the income they earn. Because they determine household income, firms' production plans influence how much households will buy, and thus how much firms will sell. If firms do not produce, households will not have the purchasing power to buy goods and services. Similarly, households' employment opportunities and income depend in part on their aggregate buying decisions. If households in the aggregate refuse to buy goods and services, there will be no basis for employment or paychecks.
   Since income and output are by definition equal in value, if households spend all their income on firms' output, all the output will be purchased. But what if firms fail to pay households all they have earned, or households fail to spend what they earn on the goods firms produce? Either households will not receive enough income to buy what has been produced, or firms will not be able to sell all they have produced. In either case, if firms keep producing at full-employment level—that is, at the point where everyone who wants a job can have one—and households continue to spend less than they earn, not all goods will be taken off the market. Unwanted

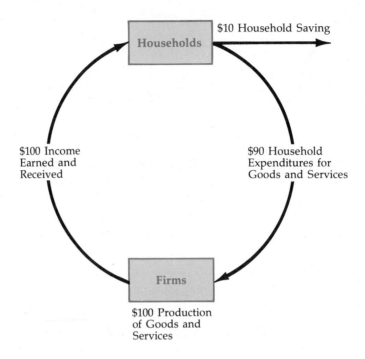

Figure 10.5. Leakage from the Circular Flow.
If households save $10 of each $100 they earn, they will buy only $90 of the $100 worth of goods and services produced. If firms then continue to produce at the level of $100, unwanted inventory will pile up. At some point firms will have to curtail production, and unemployment will rise.

inventory (unsold goods) will pile up. To stop the accumulation of unwanted inventory, firms will cut back on production, reducing household income (since fewer man-hours are needed to produce the lower output). To the extent that consumption depends on total income, consumers will reduce their expenditures. The result will be unemployment.

Saving: A Leakage from the Circular Flow

Saving: that portion of income not spent. Represents forgone expenditures on real goods and services.
Leakage (outflow): a withdrawal or outflow of income from the circular flow.

The process of income contraction we have been discussing is illustrated in Figure 10.5. Suppose firms pay households $100, but households choose to spend only $90 of their earnings and to save $10. **Saving** is that portion of income not spent; it represents forgone expenditures on real goods and services. Because saving does not go back to firms in the form of purchases, it represents a leakage from the circular flow of income. A **leakage** is a withdrawal or outflow of income from the circular flow. Saving, taxes, and imports are all leakages from the circular flow. As a result of the $10 saving leakage, firms will sell only $90 worth of what they have produced, and will be left with $10 worth of unwanted inventory. If they continue to produce $100 worth of goods and households continue to save $10, inventory will mount by $10 each time $100 worth of goods is produced.

Firms must eventually try to bring their production level into line with their sales. At that point they will reduce both employment and household income—depressing consumer expenditures as well as household saving. To take up this new slack, firms may have to reduce production still further. For example, if producers reduce production to $90 (because households have been spending only $90 out of $100), people may in turn reduce their saving from $10 to $7. But they will still be spending only $83 ($90 of income minus $7 of saving). Goods will continue to go unsold, and production will have to be reduced further.

At this point you may ask why prices do not fall in response to the surplus of goods and services. In practice they may very well fall. But in its most basic form, the Keynesian model of the macroeconomy assumes constant prices—a controversial assumption, as you can imagine. We will sidestep the difficulty for the moment by stating the rationale for the assumption of constant prices. First, the Keynesian model is intended to describe the short run, a period during which prices are more or less inflexible and adjustments in economic activity are expressed at least as much in output as in price. Income, in other words, is assumed to adjust faster than prices.

Second, as prices fall, wages and other payments to households must fall as well. Although a given number of dollars will now buy more, there are fewer dollars in income to buy with. Thus lower prices may not stimulate greater sales. Eventually, prices and wages may decline enough to induce consumers to buy more, if only because their savings are worth more after deflation. As prices fall, the purchasing power of bank account deposits rises, creating a "wealth effect." That is, because people feel wealthier at lower price levels, they tend to spend more. But again, the Keynesian model is designed for the short run. During the time it takes for wages and prices to fall, production and employment can also decline. As Keynes is supposed to have said, "In the long run we are all dead." Though economic problems may eventually work themselves out, that prospect provides small comfort to people who are unemployed during the weeks and months, or even years, of the adjustment process.

Investment: An Injection into the Circular Flow

The damaging effects of leakages from the circular flow can be partially offset by corresponding injections. An **injection** is an inflow of income into the circular flow. Investment, government expenditures, and exports are all injections. By investment we do not mean the purchase of stocks and bonds by individuals, but the purchase of investment goods by businesses. **Investment** is the purchase of capital goods—plant, equipment, and inventory—that can be used in the production of other goods and services.

Injection (inflow): an inflow of income into the circular flow.

Investment: the purchase of capital goods—plant, equipment, and inventory—that can be used in the production of other goods and services.

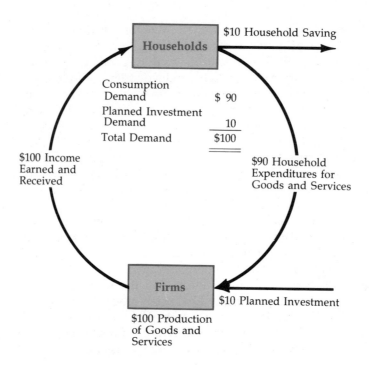

Figure 10.6. Injection into the Circular Flow.
When the saving outflow exactly equals the planned investment inflow, the macroeconomy is in equilibrium. The total demand for goods and services exactly equals the quantity of goods and services produced, and firms have no reason to expand or contract production.

Planned investment: anticipated, scheduled purchases of plant, equipment, and inventory.

Unplanned investment: unanticipated, unscheduled purchases of plant, equipment, and inventory.

Investment may be planned (and therefore desired) or unplanned (undesired). **Planned investment** includes anticipated, scheduled purchases of plant, equipment, and inventory. **Unplanned investment** includes unanticipated, unscheduled purchases of plant, equipment, and inventory. Unplanned investment is purchase by default. It represents goods that were produced to be sold, but ended up as inventory because no one bought them.

Figure 10.6 shows a planned investment expenditure of $10. If this inflow into the circular flow equals the saving outflow, all the goods the economy has produced will be purchased. Households will buy $90 and save $10. Firms will buy the remaining $10 worth of goods in the form of capital goods (plant and equipment) and perhaps some additions to inventory. Total planned expenditures by consumers and investors (TPE) will exactly equal the national income-output level (Y) at $100. The economy, in other words, will be in equilibrium. Firms will have no reason to produce more or less than they are already producing, for households and firms together will demand no more or less. Equilibrium is achieved when total planned spending equals national income or output. And that is precisely the case in Figure 10.6. Planned investment equals saving at $10, and national income and output do not change.

If an economic system is at full employment, it will tend to remain so as long as planned investment and saving remain constant. If discrepancies between saving and planned investment arise, however, aggregate income and employment will be affected. For instance, if saving rises to $15 while planned investment falls to $5, households and firms will spend a total of only $90 ($85 in consumption and $5 in planned investment). As a result $10 worth of goods will go unsold, ending up as unplanned investment. Firms will then seek to reduce their unplanned inventory by cutting back on production. The result will be a rise in unemployment.

Maintaining the Equilibrium Income Level

Keynes saw two problems in achieving and maintaining a full-employment national income level. The first had to do with getting wages and prices to adjust enough so that everyone who wanted to work would be employed. The second had to do with ensuring that demand would be sufficient to take off the market all the goods and services produced by the fully employed labor force. In terms of the circular flow model, saving must equal planned investment at the full-employment income level. Keynes questioned the classical theory that interest rates would adjust to bring saving in line with investment.

Equalizing Saving and Investment: The Classical Theory of Interest Rates

Is there a way to equalize saving and planned investment? Classical economists thought that a change in the market interest rate would bring saving into line with planned investment. That is, people will decide how much to save according to the interest rate. If the interest rate rises, they will save more, and vice versa. With higher interest rates, people will give up more goods and services today in anticipation of even greater quantities in the future.

Planned investment, on the other hand, decreases as the rate of interest increases—and vice versa. Obviously, firms will want each project to earn a rate of return at least as high as the cost of borrowing to finance it. At a 10 percent interest rate, for instance, firms will not wish to invest in any project that yields a return of less than 10 percent. Thus if interest rates are low, firms can afford to undertake a variety of projects, some of which may earn only a modest return. But at high interest rates, they can justify investing only in lucrative projects.

Figure 10.7 shows the relationship of investment and saving to interest rates. The investment curve slopes down, reflecting the inverse relationship between planned investment and interest rates. The saving curve slopes up, indicating the direct relationship between saving and interest rates. People save more (and invest less) as the interest rate rises.

Just how is the interest rate adjusted to bring saving and investment into line? Classical economists argued that in a competitive market, the interest rate will move automatically toward the intersection of the saving and investment curves—R_2 in Figure 10.7. If the interest rate is below that level—say R_1—the demand for funds to invest (I_3) will be greater than the amount of money made available for investment through saving (S_1). The interest rate will rise, causing investors to cut back on their planned investment and households to save more. At R_2, saving (S_2) will equal planned investment (I_2). Likewise, if the interest rate is above R_2, firms will want to borrow less (I_1) than people will want to save (S_3), and the interest rate will fall. Again, at R_2, the levels of saving and investment are equal. In terms of the circular flow of income, the economy will be in equilibrium. Then, classical theory indicates, unless obstacles in the labor market prevent adjustments in the wage rate and the prices of other resources, the economy will move toward full employment.

Keynesian Objections to the Classical Theory of Interest Rates

Keynes believed that interest rates cannot be expected to adjust quickly to close a gap between saving and investment. He emphasized that labor will resist wage reductions, which can keep the wage rate above equilibrium, creating temporary but major unemployment problems. Moreover, he argued, the interest rate depends on other forces besides the demand for investment and the supply of savings. People need to hold part of their incomes as cash or bank balances, both to carry out day-to-day transactions and to have some reserve for unexpected purchases or emergencies.

Some people also hold on to money in hopes that its value will rise in the future. This speculative motive for holding money requires additional explanation. If people expect interest rates to go up, they will want to maintain larger-than-usual money balances. For if they lend their money out now, they will be stuck with a low rate of interest in the future. But if they are correct in their expectations, they will be able to lend it at a higher rate later. While speculators wait for a better interest rate, they are neither spending their funds nor lending them to investors. Their speculation keeps the rate above the intersection of the investment and saving curves in Figure 10.7 and causes a leakage from the circular flow that is not offset by a corresponding injection.

Figure 10.8 shows the impact of this discrepancy on the national income level. Planned investment is only $5, while $15 is being saved. Consumers will buy $85 worth of goods and services ($100 in income minus $15 in saving) and investors will buy $5. Total planned spending will therefore be $90, $10 short of the value of the goods and services produced ($100). Because the planned investment inflow does not fully offset the saving outflow, producers will eventually cut back on production, to stop the accumulation of excess inventory. Production, income, and employment

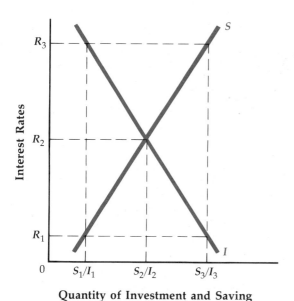

Quantity of Investment and Saving

Figure 10.7. The Relationship of Saving and Investment to Interest Rates: The Classical Theory.
Classical economists assumed that interest rates would adjust to maintain equality between saving (S) and investment (I). If saving falls short of the demand for investment, as at interest rate R_1, the rate will move up to R_2 to bring saving and investment into equilibrium. If saving exceeds investment demand, as at R_3, the rate will adjust down to R_2.

will spiral downward. With reduced production, fewer workers will be needed and household income will fall, reducing consumption and causing further cutbacks in production and employment.

This downward spiral, fortunately, will not continue indefinitely. Assuming (to simplify the analysis) that planned investment remains constant as saving and income fall, at some point saving and planned investment will become equal. This point is called the equilibrium income level. The **equilibrium income level** is the level at which producers have no reason to change their output level. It is reached when leakages equal injections. The process by which saving falls to meet planned investment is shown in Figure 10.9. As income decreases, the saving curve shifts to the left, reaching equality with planned investment at the higher interest rate of R_2. A new equilibrium income level is established—but at a lower national income and a higher unemployment rate.

We can now state the central difference between the classical and the Keynesian models. In the classical model, the theoretical focus is on how interest rates adjust to eliminate discrepancies between saving and investment. In the Keynesian model, the theoretical focus is mainly (but not exclusively) on how income adjusts to alleviate those discrepancies.

Equilibrium income level: the income level at which producers have no reason to change their output level. Reached when leakages equal injections.

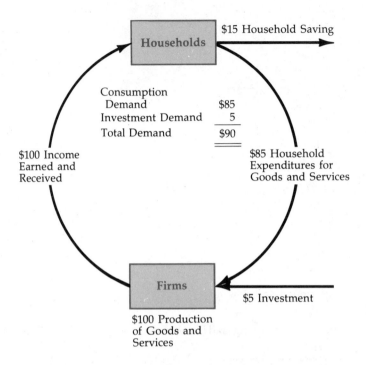

Figure 10.8. Disequilibrium in National Income.
When household saving ($15) is greater than investment expenditures ($5), aggregate demand ($90) falls short of the level of production ($100). Unwanted inventory will build up and eventually production will be cut back, reducing national income and raising the unemployment level.

Whereas the classical economists argued that the saving curve would not shift, because interest rates would adjust downward rapidly, Keynes insisted that speculation would slow down interest rate adjustments. Equilibrium would be reached only after production levels—and income—had fallen.

In the Keynesian model, the interest rate usually does adjust downward over the long run, as people alter their expectations about future interest rates. If workers believe that increasing unemployment and a falling national production level will cause interest rates to fall, for instance, they will lend their money at present interest rates rather than holding on to it. In doing so, they will reduce interest rates (because they will be increasing the supply of funds for hire). The lower interest rates will stimulate investment, production, and the demand for goods and services, increasing the need for labor. In the long run, a decline in wages and prices may cause a drop in the real wage rate and an increase in wealth held in dollars. It may bring additional increases in planned consumer and investment expenditures and additional reductions in unemployment. In the meantime, however, unemployment can be a significant social

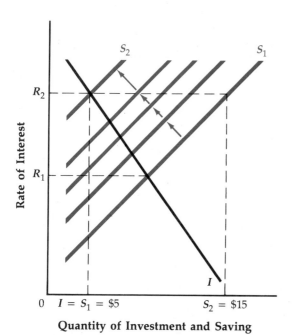

Quantity of Investment and Saving

Figure 10.9. The Relationship of Saving and Investment to Interest Rates: The Keynesian Theory.
According to Keynesian theory, the speculative demand for money may prevent interest rates from falling to bring saving into line with investment. If saving exceeds investment at interest rate R_1, aggregate demand will fall short of national production. Firms will cut back on production, causing further drops in income and saving (see Figure 10.8). As saving falls, the saving curve will shift inward from S_1 to S_2. Equilibrium will be restored at the higher interest rate R_2.

problem. The Keynesian prescription for government spending during a recession was directed at these short-run cyclical unemployment problems. Keynes was fully aware that his policy recommendations would not begin to solve long-run unemployment problems, which can last for decades.

Adding Government to the Circular Flow

So far we have seen that if households receive from firms an amount of income equal to their earnings, and spend all they receive on goods and services produced by firms, the income flow will remain constant and the macroeconomy will be at equilibrium. Saving, however, constitutes a leakage from the circular flow. And unless planned saving is offset by planned investment, the national income level will fall. If investment exceeds saving, the income level will rise—provided, of course, that unemployed resources can be used in production.

What can government do to modulate swings in economic activity that result from discrepancies between saving and investment? Like saving, government taxes are a diversion of consumer purchasing power away

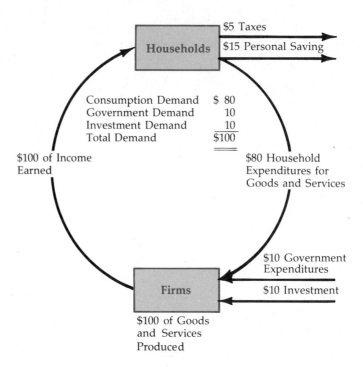

Figure 10.10. The Circular Flow of Income, Government Included.
If government is introduced into the circular flow model, equilibrium in national income occurs when total outflows—planned saving plus taxes—exactly equal total inflows—planned investment plus government expenditures. Here taxes at $5 plus saving at $15 equal government expenditures at $10 plus investment at $10.

from the circular flow.[4] Taxes may eventually reenter the circular flow in the form of planned government expenditures. But at the moment government extracts them from the flow, taxes have essentially the same effect as personal saving. For this reason, taxes are shown as an outflow in Figure 10.10. At the same time, government expenditures on goods and services (such as defense systems, buildings, and roads) are paid to firms, and constitute an inflow to the economy. Because they resemble business purchases of capital equipment (investment), planned government expenditures are also represented by an arrow pointing toward the circular flow.

Once government has been introduced into the analysis, we can see that equality in planned saving and investment is not enough to ensure that national income will be at equilibrium. National income equilibrium

---

4. Corporate income taxes, property taxes, and sales and excise taxes also divert funds from businesses and stockholders to the government. To keep the analysis as simple as possible, we shall ignore these forms of taxation. Their exclusion will not affect the general argument or the conclusions drawn.

occurs when total outflows (planned saving plus taxes) equal total inflows (planned investment plus government expenditures), as in Figure 10.10. Assume again that the economy produces $100 worth of goods and services. Households earn that amount in income, but they pay $5 in taxes and save $15. Planned government expenditures and planned business investment are each $10. The planned consumption demand of households is therefore $80 [$100 − ($5 + $15)]; business and government demand is $20 ($10 + $10). Total planned expenditure equals national income at $100. Since all the goods firms have produced are sold to investors, consumers, or the government, firms have no reason either to raise or to lower production.

Total planned expenditures (*TPE*) is now composed of three types of expenditure: planned consumption (*C*), planned investment (*I*), and planned government spending (*G*).

$$TPE = C + I + G$$

Similarly, people can do three things with the income they earn (*Y*); they can spend it (*C*), save it (*S*), or pay taxes with it (*T*).

$$Y = C + S + T$$

Since in equilibrium, total planned expenditure must equal national income (*TPE* = *Y*), the components of total planned expenditure must equal national income.

$$Y = C + I + G$$

In Figure 10.10, this condition is met. One hundred dollars of income is earned. Consumers in the aggregate spend $80 on goods and services; firms spend $10 on investment goods; and government spends $10.

$$TPE = \$80 + \$10 + \$10 = \$100 = Y$$

If total planned expenditures equal national income, the components of total planned expenditure must equal the components of national income.

$$C + I + G = C + S + T$$

This equation reduces to *I* + *G* = *S* + *T*, because the *C*s on either side of the equal sign cancel out. In terms of the circular flow model, *I* + *G* = *S* + *T* simply means that in equilibrium, planned inflows must equal planned outflows. That is the case in our example.

$$\$10 + \$10 = \$15 + \$5$$

The Function of Deficits

In the last example, planned saving is greater than planned investment. In our earlier model, when planned saving exceeded planned investment, the income level fell and unemployment rose. In this case, however, government expenditures offset the difference between saving and investment. Government planned expenditures exceed taxes by the same amount that saving exceeds investment, $5. The government runs a budgetary deficit in this example, borrowing $5 from savers to make up the difference between taxes and expenditures. In doing so, it keeps the national income level from falling.

According to Keynesian theory, budget deficits should not always be feared or avoided. The stable equilibrium income level achieved with a deficit exceeds the income level to which the economy might fall without a deficit. In our example, if taxes and government expenditures both equaled $10 (that is, if the budget were balanced), consumption demand would be only $75: $100 in income minus $10 in taxes and $15 in saving. Total demand would be $95: $75 in consumption plus $10 in government expenditures and $10 in investment. Five dollars worth of goods and services would not be sold, and firms would have to cut back on production. The national income level would decline in a spiraling process of lower consumption and lower income.

If some resources remain unemployed, government can raise the national income level by increasing outflows over inflows. It can reduce taxes or it can increase expenditures on roads, schools, and hospitals. Or it can reduce taxes and increase expenditures at the same time. Regardless, the Keynesian prescription for unemployment is to run a budgetary deficit— or if the government is enjoying a budgetary surplus, to run a smaller surplus. The overriding goal is to bolster total planned expenditures, which may or may not mean deficit spending.

Suppose, for instance, that the government increases expenditures from $10 to $15, as in Figure 10.11. Consumption demand is still $80, but with the increase in government spending, total planned expenditures rise to $105. Consumers, investors, and government are now demanding more than firms are producing, giving firms an incentive to raise their production levels. Increased production means a higher income level and increased consumption, which in turn induces firms to produce even more goods and services and generate more income. In this way, the national income level moves up.

As the economy moves upward toward the new, higher equilibrium income level, however, planned saving will rise in response. Taxes will also rise if income tax rates are tied to household income levels. For instance, if national income increases from $100 to $110, saving may rise from $15 to $16, and taxes may rise from $5 to $5.25. When the sum of planned saving and taxes equals the new, higher level of planned investment and government expenditure ($25), a new equilibrium income level will be achieved.

Reducing taxes can produce virtually the same increase in national income as increasing government expenditures. The main difference in this case is that people may put a portion of their tax reduction into saving. A $5 reduction in taxes may mean a $1 increase in saving, and as a result total outflows will fall by only $4 instead of $5. Therefore an increase in government expenditures will tend to have a slightly greater effect on the national income level than would an equal decrease in taxes.

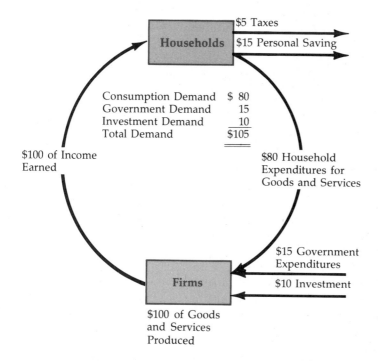

Consumption Demand $ 80
Government Demand   15
Investment Demand   10
Total Demand $105

Figure 10.11. Rising National Income.
When the total inflows exceed total outflows, total planned expenditures will exceed national income. If some resources, capital, and workers are still unemployed, the national income level will rise.

The Keynesian revolution must be seen in historical context. The classical approach to reducing unemployment is to speed up the flow of information to workers who are transitionally unemployed and reduce restrictions on wage and labor movements, such as minimum wage laws, union shops, and race and sex discrimination. But Keynes and his followers accepted such restrictions as a political reality, assuming little could be done about them in the short run. Instead they suggested another means of correcting unemployment—an increase in total demand for goods and services.

According to the Keynesian model of the circular flow of income, periods of low production and high unemployment result from a discrepancy between saving and planned investment. With everything else held equal, the national income level will fall and unemployment will rise when planned investment expenditures are less than the level of saving. (If planned investment expenditures exceed the level of saving, the national income level will rise and unemployment will fall.)

To restore national income and production to their former levels, government must somehow increase total demand, offsetting the gap

Summary and Extensions

between saving and investment. Government can boost total demand by increasing its expenditures while holding taxes constant. Or it can reduce taxes while holding government expenditures constant. A rise in government expenditures increases total demand directly. Reducing taxes achieves the same effect indirectly. If people take home more pay, they can be expected to spend more, increasing the level of total demand. In the next chapter we will explore these policies in more detail, as we examine a more complicated version of the Keynesian model.

Major Conclusions

1. John Maynard Keynes is remembered primarily for his *General Theory of Employment, Interest, and Money* (1936), a book that dealt with the high unemployment and low production levels that characterized much of the world economy during the Great Depression.

2. Before Keynes, economists attributed unemployment to normal shifts in the supply and demand for products, and to obstacles in the labor market that prevented wage rate adjustments. Unemployment was also thought to result from changes in the money stock, which affect the real wage rate paid to labor and therefore the quantity of labor supplied and demanded.

3. Keynes argued that unemployment could result from the failure of consumers and businesses to demand all the goods produced by the economy. If businesses and consumers do not plan to buy all that is produced, firms will accumulate excess inventory and will have to cut back on production, increasing the unemployment level.

4. In classical theory, the interest rate adjusts to equalize saving and investment. In the Keynesian model, the national income level adjusts to bring saving and investment into line.

5. In the Keynesian model of the circular flow of income, the conditions for macroeconomic equilibrium can be stated in two ways. First, the macroeconomy will be in equilibrium when total demand for goods and services exactly equals total output. Second, leaving government out of the analysis, the macroeconomy will be in equilibrium when the saving of households and firms exactly equals firms' planned investment expenditures (the purchase of plant and equipment). The equilibrium income level is not necessarily the full-employment level.

6. According to Keynesian theory, as long as some unemployment exists, government can expand national income and employment by increasing total spending. It can do so either by increasing its own expenditures on goods and services or by lowering taxes, thus increasing household and business expenditures.

7. According to the Keynesian model, government budgetary deficits are not necessarily bad. As long as some unemployment exists and saving

exceeds investment, government can raise the national income level by increasing its expenditures. Whether it must run a deficit to do so is not important.

1. According to the classical model of the labor market (see Figures 10.1 and 10.2), how will a rapid rise in the price level affect employment? What will happen to the money wage rate? To the real wage rate?
2. Suppose investment increases. What will happen to the equilibrium level of income, according to classical theory? According to Keynesian theory?
3. The graph below shows saving and investment as a function of the interest rate. Suppose the interest rate is held above equilibrium at R_2. If the equilibrium income level falls, as Keynesian theory suggests it should, what will happen to saving? Why?

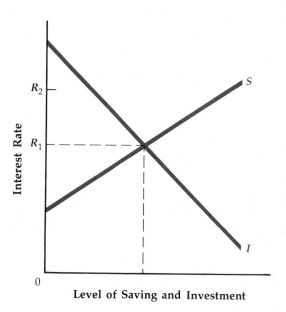

4. Given the information in the graph for question 3, assume that the interest rate declines slowly when saving exceeds investment. Will the equilibrium income level fall by as much as if the interest rate were held rigidly at R_2? Explain your answer using both a graph and a circular flow diagram like the one in Figure 10.6.
5. Suppose that saving and investment are equal and the government runs a budgetary deficit. What will happen to the national income level in the Keynesian model?

Central Question

*How are the equilibrium
national income
and employment
levels determined?*

Key Terms

Investment function

Marginal propensity to save

Saving function

Dissaving

Consumption function

Marginal propensity to
consume

Total expenditure function

Multiplier

Paradox of thrift

Chapter 11

Unemployment and the Equilibrium Income Level: A More Complicated Model

It is too early to say, but it does not now appear an extravagant statement, that Keynes may in the end rival Adam Smith in his influence on the economic thinking and governmental policy of his time and age. Both lived at profound turning points in the evolution of the economic order. Both were products of their times. Yet both were also powerful agents in giving direction to the unfolding process of institutional change.
Alvin Hansen

*T*he circular flow model developed in the preceding chapter provided a broad picture of the Keynesian macroeconomy. But the equilibrium national income level and its relationship to savings and consumer expenditures were only lightly sketched. And while the model demonstrated the direction in which national income will move when planned saving and investment are unequal, it did not indicate the extent of the change.

This chapter attempts to add precision to the Keynesian analysis of how the national income and employment levels are determined. First we will develop more fully the concepts of planned saving and investment and their role in determining the equilibrium national income level. Then we will examine national income from the perspective of total spending, using the concept of planned consumption. To keep the analysis simple, government will be excluded from the model. In the next chapter, however, we will reintroduce government in connection with the question of possible remedies for high unemployment and low production levels.

The Planned Investment and Saving Approach to Income Equilibrium

Chapter 10 presented three essential conclusions of Keynesian analysis. First, if the level of planned saving exceeds the level of planned investment during any given period, total spending on goods and services by households and firms will fall short of the national production level. Unable to sell all they have produced, firms will accumulate excess inventory and will eventually have to cut back on production. When production is curtailed, the national income level will fall. Because less is produced, total earnings (also called national income) must also be less.

Second, if planned investment expenditure exceeds planned saving, total spending for goods and services will exceed the quantity of goods and services produced. Production will fall short of sales, and inventory will dwindle to undesirably low levels. If some workers and other resources are unemployed, firms will hire them and expand production. The national income level will rise.

Third, when planned saving equals planned investment, the producing sector of the economy has no reason to expand or contract production. As long as planned saving and investment remain equal, the circular flow of income will remain constant and the macroeconomy will be at equilibrium.

We can now refine the Keynesian analysis, by adding detail to these fundamental conclusions.

The Investment Function

The planned investment expenditures of businesses on plant, equipment, and inventory are influenced by many variables, including the market interest rate; the national income level; expectations regarding the profitability of future production; government tax policies; the discovery of new ways of producing goods; and the development of new goods themselves.

As we saw in Chapter 10, planned investment expenditures are likely to be inversely related to market interest rates. That is, investment will rise as interest rates fall and decline as interest rates rise. There are at least two possible explanations for this inverse relationship. First, when interest rates are low, firms are better able to justify borrowing to expand their plant and equipment. A larger number of investment projects will meet their profitability criteria when the cost of borrowed funds is relatively low. Second, a rise in interest rates may persuade some firms to postpone investment until rates decline again.

The level of planned business investment tends to increase or decrease along with the level of national income and with the utilization of the nation's productive capacity. During prosperous periods, when national income is on the rise, businesses are more profitable and thus have more funds on hand to invest. Many businesses will expand their facilities to meet the rising demand for their products. Furthermore, entrepreneurs tend to project present business conditions into the future. Their confidence in future investments rises in prosperous times and falls during depressed periods. Planned investment can therefore be expected to rise and fall with current economic conditions, for it represents plant and equipment that can be used only in the future.

The introduction of new technology can significantly affect the general level of planned investment. The development of the automobile, for instance, stimulated considerable investment in roads, service stations, tourist facilities, and assembly lines. In the future, solar and wind technologies may have a similar effect on the level and distribution of planned investment expenditure. Government tax policies also influence the profitability of current investment. An increase in business taxes will generally reduce planned investment, for firms will have less after-tax income to devote to new plant and equipment.

National income is probably one of the most important factors affecting investment. Its relationship to investment is called the investment function. The **investment function** is the assumed relationship between national income and total planned expenditures on plant, equipment, and inventory. For the moment, however, we will assume that planned investment does not vary, not even with income. Later in our discussion we will discard this simplifying assumption and consider the effect of a change in interest rates or tax policy on investment and national income. For now, given our assumption, the investment function can be represented by a horizontal line, as in Figure 11.1(a), where planned investment is constant at I_1, or $400 billion.

Investment function: the assumed relationship between national income and total planned expenditures on plant, equipment, and inventory.

The Saving Function

The level of saving is influenced by many variables. They include current interest rates on bonds and savings accounts; personal income; income tax rates; job security; and current demand for goods and services (since saving is defined as the unspent portion of disposable income). High interest rates increase the relative price of current consumption, for a

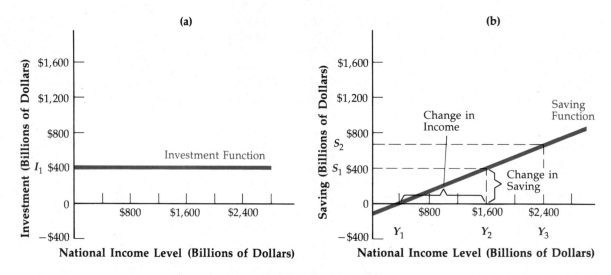

Figure 11.1. Planned Investment and Saving.
If it is assumed that planned investment is unaffected by the national income level, the investment function can be drawn as a horizontal line, as in part (a). Investment remains constant at I_1 at all income levels. If it is assumed that planned saving is directly related to national income, the saving function must be drawn as an upward-sloping curve, as in part (b). At an income level of Y_1, total saving is assumed to be zero. At income levels of Y_2 and Y_3, saving is S_1 and S_2, respectively.

failure to save means forgoing relatively more future income. During times of rising interest rates, then, people tend to reduce their consumption, save more of their incomes, and postpone some spending.

When personal income rises, people are encouraged to buy more security (among other goods and services). People purchase security by adding to their savings, thus increasing their financial reserves for less advantageous times. Because personal and corporate income taxes significantly affect workers' take-home pay and firms' after-tax profits, tax rates have an indirect influence on personal saving and corporate dividends and investment. Planned saving generally moves in the opposite direction from taxes. As taxes rise, saving falls, and vice versa.

Expectations about future inflation rates and income levels also influence current planned saving. If people expect prices to rise sharply in the future, they will tend to buy more and save less now, to avoid relatively high future prices. If they expect their future income to drop significantly, they are likely to save more now, to build up the cash reserves they will need.

To keep the discussion simple, we will assume that except for income, all variables that influence the level of saving are given. Like Keynes, we will assume that planned saving varies directly with the national income level. In the aggregate, people will save a portion of any increase in their income. This tendency, known as the marginal propensity to save, can be stated as a ratio. The **marginal propensity to save** (MPS) is the percentage of any change in total income that consumers are inclined to save.

$$MPS = \frac{\text{change in saving}}{\text{change in national income}}$$

To illustrate, if the marginal propensity to save is 10 percent (MPS = 1/10), people as a group will be inclined to change their level of planned saving by 10 percent of any increase or decrease in their income. If their incomes rise by $100, they will be inclined to save $10 more than before (10 percent of $100). Likewise a $100 decrease in total income will reduce planned saving by $10. The higher the marginal propensity to save, the greater the change in planned saving that results from any given change in national income.

The upward-sloping curve in Figure 11.1(b) represents this assumed direct relationship between saving and income, called the saving function. The **saving function** is the assumed direct relationship between national income and the amount of income saved (not spent on goods and services). As it is drawn, the saving function incorporates the assumption that there is some income level at which people save nothing—in Figure 11.1(b), level Y_1. The U.S. economy operated on the zero-saving income level for several years during the 1930s, when Americans as a group saved nothing. At income levels higher than Y_1, the planned saving level is positive— that is, people are adding to their financial assets. For instance, at an income level of Y_2, people plan to save a total of $400 billion ($S_1$). At an income level of Y_3, they plan to save $666 billion ($S_2$). When their income is less than Y_1, people engage in planned dissaving, also called negative saving. **Dissaving** is any net withdrawal from accumulated past savings, or any net increase in borrowing. That is, at levels below Y_1, people as a group are withdrawing funds from their savings accounts or borrowing to meet their financial obligations. Regardless of the particular income and planned saving levels, the upward-sloping curve reflects the fundamental assumption that income and saving are directly related.[1]

Marginal propensity to save: the percentage of any change in total income that consumers are inclined to save.

Saving function: the assumed direct relationship between national income and the amount of income saved (not spent on goods and services).

Dissaving: any net withdrawal from accumulated past savings, or any net increase in borrowing.

The Equilibrium National Income Level

Figure 11.2(a) shows both the saving and investment functions. Given the information summarized, we can determine that the economy will move toward an equilibrium national income level of Y_2, or $1,600 billion.

---

1. Geometrically, the slope of a curve like the planned saving function is equal to the opposite side of the triangle Y_1Y_2E divided by the adjacent side, or the change in S divided by the change in Y, which is also the marginal propensity to save:

$$\text{slope of saving function} = \frac{\text{change in saving}}{\text{change in national income}} = MPS$$

As the curve is drawn, the change in saving is substantially less than the change in income; the marginal propensity to save is much less than 1. In other words, people are assumed to save only a minor fraction of any change in income— an assumption supported by real-world experience.

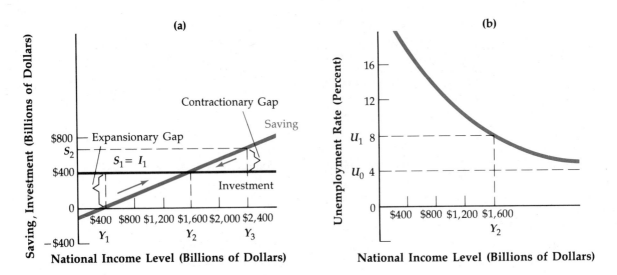

Figure 11.2. Determining the National Income Level: The Planned Investment and Saving Approach.
The equilibrium national income level is Y_2, or $1,600 billion, the point where saving equals investment. At national income levels above Y_2, saving will exceed investment and the national income level will fall. At national income levels lower than Y_2, investment will exceed saving and the national income level will rise.

The equilibrium income level may or may not be the full-employment income level. In part (b), the equilibrium income level corresponds to an unemployment rate of 8 percent.

Suppose the economy is generating an income of Y_3, or $2,400 billion. Planned investment will be at its assumed constant level of I_1, or $400 billion, but planned saving will be at the higher level of S_2. Rather than purchasing all Y_3 goods, that is, people will be saving part of their income, causing a gap between planned saving and investment. At an income level of Y_3, firms will produce more than they will sell. They will pile up unplanned additions to inventory, and at some point will have to cut back on production, thus reducing total income.

This reduction in total income will reduce planned saving. As Figure 11.2(a) shows, the movement back from Y_3 will eventually close the gap between planned saving and investment. At Y_2 the two will be equal. Once at Y_2, firms may try to expand production. If they do, planned saving will increase and unplanned investment (inventory) will again pile up, causing firms to move back toward Y_2 again.

If, on the other hand, the economy is operating below Y_2—say at Y_1—firms in the aggregate will have an incentive to expand production. At Y_1, planned saving is zero, but planned investment is at the higher level of I_1. Consumers are intentionally spending all they earn, but still firms want to buy additional capital goods. The total spending of households and investors is greater than the level of production. To satisfy the excess demand for goods and services, firms must produce more. In the process they will increase household income; and assuming a positive marginal propensity to save, the level of saving will rise with the increase in income. Eventually planned saving will reach the level of planned investment (assumed to remain constant). This will happen at the national income level of Y_2, or \$1,600 billion.

This example illustrates a basic point of Keynesian economics. There is some income level toward which the economy will gravitate, and at which it will tend to remain unless economic conditions change. This income level may or may not be the full-employment income level.

As more goods and services are produced, more resources, including workers, are needed for production. As national income rises, therefore, the unemployment rate falls. In Figure 11.2(b), the equilibrium national income level Y_2 corresponds to an unemployment rate of U_1 (8 percent). That rate is higher than the lowest possible unemployment rate, U_0, or 4 percent here.[2]

Here Keynesians depart from the classical notion that the economy will continue to move toward the minimum unemployment level. According to classical theory, if unemployment rises above that minimum rate, a reduction in wage rates will cause the national income level to rise and unemployment to fall. Keynesians, on the other hand, stress that the economy may fail to achieve full employment in the short run because households are saving too much and consuming too little—or because firms are not investing enough.

The Total Spending Approach to Income Equilibrium

Another way to arrive at the equilibrium-level national income is through the equation of national output with national income. In the preceding section we noted that when the equilibrium income level is achieved, planned saving (an outflow from the circular flow of income) is equal to planned investment (an inflow to the circular flow).

planned saving = planned investment

And Chapter 10 showed that when saving equals investment, total planned expenditures by households and firms exactly equal national output. That is, the equilibrium national income level is achieved when firms sell in the aggregate exactly what they have produced.

total planned expenditures = national output

With all firms selling exactly what they produce, business has no reason either to expand or to contract production.

These two different conditions for equilibrium are mathematically consistent. We know that national income (Y) is a mirror image of national

---

2. At any moment, some workers will be changing jobs. Therefore most economists do not believe that unemployment will ever fall below 4 percent. Many do not believe that an unemployment rate below 6 percent can be sustained.

output. National income is simply a reflection of what is produced in the economy, for without production there is no income. Furthermore, in our simple model, from which government has been excluded, households can do only two things with their income. They can use it for planned consumption (C) or for planned saving (S). Therefore income must equal consumption plus saving:

$$Y = C + S$$

If planned saving is equal to planned investment (S = I), we can rewrite this equation to read:

$$Y = C + I$$

Since national income and output measure the same thing, and since in our model consumption and saving make up total planned spending, the equations above mean that when planned saving and investment are equal, total national output equals total planned expenditure (TPE):

$$Y = C + I = C + S = TPE$$

In an economy at equilibrium, then, what is produced by firms is bought either by consumers (as consumer goods) or by businesses (as investment goods).

Thus the equilibrium national income level can be discussed in terms of the forces that determine total planned expenditures. That is the approach Keynes himself emphasized. His theory was built on two relatively simple propositions. First, he argued that the national income level (Y) depends on the level of total planned expenditures (TPE). That is, the amount of goods and services produced in the economy, and therefore the amount of income earned, depends on the amount of goods and services households and firms in the aggregate want to buy. Second, as we have just demonstrated, the equilibrium income level is the point at which total planned expenditures equal national income.

We now need to consider the forces that determine the levels of planned consumption (C) and planned investment (I).

The Consumption and Investment Functions

Like planned saving, households' planned consumption expenditures, or total demands, are influenced by a number of variables. Among them are the interest rates people receive on their savings; personal wealth; the expected rate of inflation; income taxes; and the national income level. Interest rates are likely to be inversely related to planned consumption expenditures. As interest rates rise, people will be inclined to save more and borrow less in order to buy things like furniture and cars. Expected inflation has the opposite effect. If people expect the inflation rate to increase, they are likely to buy more now, to avoid paying higher prices in the future. If income tax rates rise, on the other hand, people will reduce their planned consumption expenditures, for they will have less after-tax income to spend. Finally, an increase in the national income level is likely to increase planned consumption expenditures, simply because more income will enable people to satisfy more of their wants.

Among these variables, special attention must be paid to national income, whose relationship to consumption demand is called the consumption function. The **consumption function** is the assumed direct relationship between the national income level and the planned consumption expenditures of households. Keynesians make three intuitively plausible assumptions about the consumption function. First, as income rises, planned consumption expenditures will rise by a lesser amount. That is, people will not spend all of their extra income; they will save part of it. This inclination of consumers to spend only part of an increase in their income is called the marginal propensity to consume. The **marginal propensity to consume** (*MPC*) is the percentage of any change in income that consumers are inclined to spend. Like the marginal propensity to save, the marginal propensity to consume can be expressed as a ratio.

$$MPC = \frac{\text{change in consumption}}{\text{change in national income}}$$

If the marginal propensity to consume is 90 percent, for instance ($MPC = \%_{10}$), consumers will be inclined to spend 90 percent of any change in their income. If national income rises (or falls) by $100, planned consumption expenditures will rise (or fall) by $90. (The actual figure for *MPC* in the United States is about 92 to 94 percent.)

The marginal propensity to consume and the marginal propensity to save are complementary concepts. Indeed, in our simplified model, whatever portion of an increase in income consumers do not spend, they must save, for $Y = C + S$. If the marginal propensity to save is 0.10, therefore, the marginal propensity to consume must be 0.90. Together, $MPC + MPS = 1$.

Second, Keynesians assume that there is some national income level—a very low one—at which consumers will plan to spend all the income they earn. At that level, consumers may simply be unable to save; they may have to spend everything they earn for subsistence.

Third, at even lower national income levels, consumers will plan to spend more than they earn. If people's income levels are seriously depressed for a short period, they will withdraw funds from their savings accounts to meet their current obligations. If collectively people plan to spend more than they are earning, in effect they are planning to buy more goods than are currently being produced. (Income and output must always be equal.) For a while firms will be able to meet the excess demand by reducing their inventories. But consumption expenditures cannot exceed income indefinitely; firms will eventually run out of inventory.

Figure 11.3(a) shows the upward-sloping consumption function curve, which summarizes graphically the relationship between the national income level and household consumption expenditures. At a national income level of $400 billion ($Y_1$), the consumption level is also $400 billion ($C_1$). This is the income level at which people spend all they earn. At a

Consumption function: the assumed direct relationship between the national income level and the planned consumption expenditures of households.

Marginal propensity to consume: the percentage of any change in income that consumers are inclined to spend.

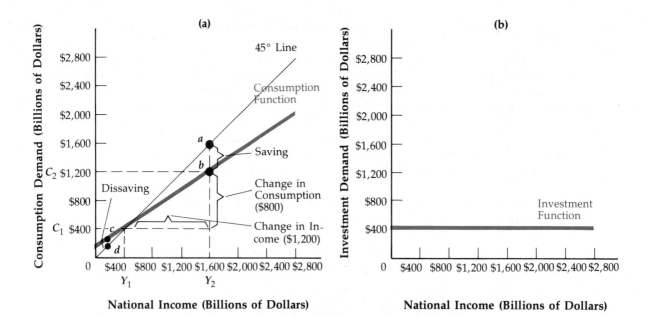

Figure 11.3. Planned Consumption and Investment.
Assuming that household consumption expenditures are directly related to national income, the consumption function may be drawn as an upward-sloping curve. At national income level Y_1, consumers are spending all they earn and saving nothing. At higher income levels consumption rises, but not as much as national income does. Consumers, in other words, are saving part of their income. For example, at a national income level of $1,600 billion, the consumption level is $1,200 billion; saving is $400 billion, or the distance between points a and b. Dissaving occurs at income levels below Y_1. Investment—part (b)—is assumed to be constant at $400 billion.

higher income level, $1,600 billion ($Y_2$), the consumption level is also higher, $1,200 billion. But the increase in consumption expenditures ($800 billion) is less than the increase in national income that caused it ($1,200 billion). As we saw above, the marginal propensity to consume is less than 1—in this case, ⅔.

$$MPC = \frac{\text{change in consumption}}{\text{change in national income}} = \frac{\$800}{\$1,200} = \frac{2}{3}$$

At all national income levels over $400 billion ($Y_1$), consumers in the aggregate will save some part of their income. The 45-degree line that extends out of the origin shows what the consumption function curve would look like if consumers spent all they earned. At a national income level of $1,600 billion, for instance, $1,600 billion would be spent. If consumers are spending only $1,200 billion at an income level of $1,600 billion, they must be saving the rest, namely $400 billion. This planned level of saving is represented in the figure by the vertical distance between points a and b. At higher national income levels, the vertical gap between the consumption function and the 45-degree line is larger, and the level of planned saving is greater. The growth of saving is consistent with our definition of the saving function, which specifies that the level of consumer saving is directly related to national income.

At national income levels below Y_1, the consumption function curve lies above the 45-degree line. Consumption exceeds the national income level. Consumers are spending more than they are earning, drawing down their savings accounts to meet current expenses. The amount of their dissaving is equal to the vertical distance between the 45-degree line and the consumption function. For example, at a national income level of $200 billion, the planned level of dissaving is $66 billion, or the vertical distance between points c and d in the graph. And if consumers are spending more than they earn at these low income levels, they must be buying more than is currently being produced. Businesses must also be drawing down their inventories to meet consumer demand.

In our simplified model of the macroeconomy, planned investment and consumption are the only components of total spending ($TPE = C + I$). We have already discussed investment demand (see pages 228–229); nothing more need be added here. For the moment, we continue to assume that planned investment does not vary with national income. We can therefore represent the investment function as a horizontal line, as in Figure 11.3(b).

The Equilibrium National Income Level

We have demonstrated that equilibrium in national income and employment is established where total planned expenditures equal national income (or output). In our model, total planned spending is composed of two variables, planned consumption and planned investment expenditures. To describe total planned spending graphically, therefore, we must add the investment function from Figure 11.3(b) to the consumption function of Figure 11.3(a). The resulting combined curve, shown in Figure 11.4(a), represents the total expenditure function. The **total expenditure function** is the relationship of total planned expenditures to national income. This is normally assumed to be a direct relationship.

In Figure 11.4(a), the line labeled $C + I$ is the total expenditure function. It is the graphical summation of the consumption function curve, C, which lies slightly below it, and the horizontal investment function curve. Investment demand is represented by the vertical difference between the consumption function curve, C, and the total expenditure function curve, $C + I$. The vertical space between the two curves, $400 billion, is equal to the value of the investment demand curve in Figure 11.3(b).

Given the total expenditures curve in Figure 11.4, we can deduce that the equilibrium national income level is $1,600 billion—the point where the $C + I$ curve crosses the 45-degree line. At that income level (Y_2), consumers will buy $1,200 billion worth of goods and services (that is,

Total expenditure function: the relationship of total planned expenditures to national income, normally assumed to be a direct relationship.

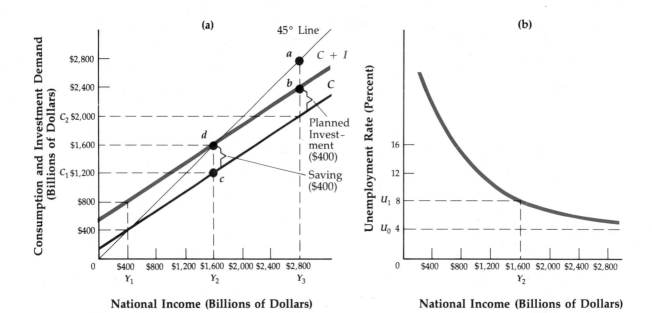

Figure 11.4. Determining the National Income Level: The Total Spending Approach.
The equilibrium national income level is Y_2, or $1,600 billion, the point where consumption plus investment equals national income. At income levels above Y_2, not all that is produced will be bought. At income levels below Y_2, consumers and businesses will want to buy more goods and services than are produced.
   In part (b), the equilibrium income level corresponds to the unemployment rate U_1 (8 percent).

their consumption demand will be C_1) and firms will buy $400 billion worth of plant, equipment, and inventory. Total expenditures will equal national income at $1,600 billion.

$$TPE = \$1,600 \text{ billion} = Y$$

Consumers and firms will be buying all that is produced.
   If the economy is producing either more or less, it will move toward a level of $1,600 billion. For instance, suppose the national income level is $2,800 billion ($Y_3$). Consumers in the aggregate plan to buy $2,000 billion worth of goods and services (C_2). Businesses plan to buy $400 billion worth. Total planned spending by consumers and firms will therefore equal only $2,400 billion, or $400 billion less than is being produced. So long as firms continue to produce $2,800 billion worth of output and to sell only $2,400 billion worth, unwanted inventory (unplanned investment) will accumulate. The vertical distance between points a and b represents this $400 billion of unwanted inventory.
   Instead of continually adding to their inventories, firms will at some point reduce their production levels. When they do, the national income level will fall, and planned consumer expenditures will fall with it, though

not by as much as national income. If national income initially exceeds total planned spending and falls faster than consumption demand, at some point it must become equal to total demand for goods and services $(C + I)$. This equality is achieved, as stated above, at a national income level of $1,600 billion (Y_2).

If the national income level is below Y_2, it will rise until it reaches that level. Suppose firms in the aggregate are generating only $400 billion worth of goods and services. At that income level, Y_1 in Figure 11.4(a), consumers are inclined to spend $400 billion and businesses are inclined to spend another $400 billion. Obviously total planned spending will exceed the quantity of goods and services produced.

$$TPE = C + I = \$400 \text{ billion} + \$400 \text{ billion} = \$800 \text{ billion}$$

To satisfy this high level of demand, firms must draw down their inventories and/or expand production. At some point they are likely to exhaust their inventories and will have to expand production. When they do, more national income will be generated, increasing planned consumption. If demand at first exceeds production, but production (national income) rises faster than planned consumer expenditures, at some point producers will be able to meet total demand. Again, the national income level at which they will be able to do this is Y_2, or $1,600 billion.

Note that Y_2 is the equilibrium income level arrived at by the saving-investment approach described in Figure 11.2. At Y_2, planned saving is equal to planned investment. That fact can be seen in Figure 11.4 as well. At Y_2, the vertical distance between the C and $C + I$ curves is the planned investment level ($400 billion). And the vertical distance between point c on the C curve and point d on the 45-degree line is the planned saving level ($400 billion). If both investment and saving are $400 billion, then planned saving is equal to planned investment. Figures 11.2(a) and 11.4(a) are both representations of the same Keynesian model, then, each emphasizing a different aspect of the model.

As Figure 11.4(b) shows, the equilibrium national income level (Y_2) is consistent with an unemployment rate of 8 percent (U_1). That is higher than the assumed minimum unemployment rate of 4 percent, which can be achieved at a higher production level. But before more is produced, firms and consumers must be inclined to buy more. Thus Keynesian analysis concludes that national income and employment depend on the level of total planned expenditures. In the classical model, unemployment results principally from shifts in the supply and demand for labor and from labor market obstructions to wage adjustments. In the Keynesian model, unemployment is caused by insufficient demand.

The information shown in Figure 11.4 can also be expressed in tabular form. Column 1 of Table 11.1 lists some possible national income levels, from $0 to $2,800 billion. Column 2 shows consumption, reflecting the three Keynesian assumptions described on page 225. At an income level of $0, planned consumption is $133 billion—more than income. At an income level of $400 billion, consumption equals income. Above $400 billion in income, consumption falls short of income. Thus, below $400 billion, consumers are dissaving; above it they are saving (column 3).

Table 11.1. National Income Equilibrium (in billions of dollars)

National Income (1)	Consumption (2)	Saving (+) or Dissaving (−) (3)	Investment Expenditures (4)	Total Planned Expenditures (5)
$ 0	$ 133	− $133	$400	$ 533
200	266	− 66	400	666
400	400	0	400	800
600	533	+ 67	400	933
800	667	+ 133	400	1,067
1,000	800	+ 200	400	1,200
1,200	933	+ 267	400	1,333
1,400	1,067	+ 333	400	1,467
1,600	1,200	+ 400	400	1,600
1,800	1,333	+ 467	400	1,733
2,000	1,467	+ 533	400	1,867
2,200	1,600	+ 600	400	2,000
2,400	1,733	+ 667	400	2,133
2,600	1,867	+ 733	400	2,267
2,800	2,000	+ 800	400	2,400

Under our simplifying assumption, planned investment is held constant at $400 billion for all income levels (column 4). Total planned expenditures is shown in column 5. By comparing it with column 1, we see that equilibrium with national income is achieved at an output of $1,600 billion. At income levels above $1,600 billion, total planned expenditures fall short of total output. Below $1,600 billion, expenditures exceed output.

Changes in Total Planned Expenditures

If the levels of planned investment and consumption determine the equilibrium national income level, then changes in the levels of planned investment and consumption will produce a different equilibrium income level. This section discusses the rather complicated effects that changes in planned investment and consumption can have on the equilibrium national income level.

Changes in Planned Investment

A change in any of the forces that influence investment decisions—interest rates, the national income level, expectations regarding the profitability of future production, and so forth—can change the planned level of investment and thus the national income level. Consider the assumed inverse relationship between the market interest rate and the planned level of investment, shown by the downward-sloping curve ID_1 in Figure 11.5. If the interest rate is initially R_3, planned investment will be I_1. And if this level of planned investment is constant, it can be represented by the planned investment curve I_1 in Figure 11.6(b). That level of investment corresponds to an equilibrium national income level of Y_2 (part (a) of Figure 11.6) and an unemployment rate of U_2 (part (c) of Figure 11.6).

If the interest rate falls to R_2 in Figure 11.5, the level of planned investment will rise to I_2 in Figure 11.6(b). And total planned expenditures will rise to $C + I_2$ in Figure 11.6(a). At the initial income level of Y_2, total planned expenditures $(C + I_2)$ will exceed output. In simple terms, firms will face a greater demand for goods and services than they can satisfy with current production schedules. Given this excess demand, firms will expand production, employing more workers and causing the unemployment rate to fall. Household incomes will rise, and people will save more. Eventually the economy will move toward the new equilibrium income level Y_3, where planned saving and investment are once again equal (Figure 11.6(b)). The new lower unemployment rate of U_1 is still above the minimum employment rate, however (Figure 11.6(c)).

If investment depends on the interest rate, and income and unemployment on investment, it follows that each interest rate in Figure 11.5 is related to a specific income and unemployment level in Figure 11.6. The minimum level of unemployment (U_0, the full-employment rate) will not be achieved until the equilibrium income reaches a much higher level than Y_3. Thus investment must rise higher than I_2, and the interest rate must fall lower than R_2, to achieve the full employment rate U_0.

An upward shift in the investment demand curve in Figure 11.5 can have an effect similar to a reduction in the interest rate. Such a shift might be caused by an increase in the expected profitability of an investment, perhaps because of an increase in the productivity of capital goods or a reduction in property taxes. If investment demand shifts from curve ID_1 to curve ID_2, for instance, and the interest rate remains constant at R_3, the level of planned investment will rise from I_1 to I_2. The equilibrium income level will rise from Y_2 to Y_3 in Figure 11.6(a), and unemployment will drop from U_2 to U_1 (Figure 11.6(c)).

A reduction in the level of planned investment expenditures, say from I_2 to I_1, will have exactly the opposite effect. The equilibrium income level will fall and the unemployment rate will rise. The level of planned investment can be reduced through either an increase in the interest rate or a downward shift in the investment demand curve in Figure 11.5.

As the economy moves toward a new equilibrium income level, a peculiar phenomenon occurs. In Figure 11.6, planned investment expenditures increase by the difference between I_2 and I_1, but the national income level increases a great deal more—by the difference between Y_3 and Y_2. In fact, the increase in national income is *three times* the increase in planned investment. The explanation of this phenomenon involves one of the most significant contributions of Keynesian analysis, the concept of the multiplier.

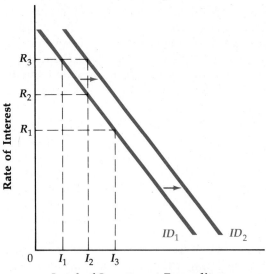

Figure 11.5. The Effect of Interest Rates on Planned Investment.
Planned investment is inversely related to the rate of interest firms have to pay on borrowed money. If the interest rate falls from R_3 to R_2, the level of planned investment will rise from I_1 to I_2. An outward shift in the investment demand curve has the same effect. If the interest rate remains constant at R_3 but the investment demand curve shifts from ID_1 to ID_2, the level of investment will rise from I_1 to I_2.

The Multiplier

Multiplier: the ratio of a change in national income to the change in total planned expenditures that stimulated it:

$$m = \frac{\text{change in } Y}{\text{change in } TPE}$$

Simply stated, the **multiplier** is the ratio of a change in national income to the change in total planned expenditures that stimulated it.

$$m = \frac{\text{change in } Y}{\text{change in } TPE}$$

In the example just given, the change in total planned expenditures is simply the change in planned investment. The concept of the multiplier is applicable to *any* change in total planned expenditures, however—to consumer and government spending as well as to planned investment. A multiplier of 3 means that the national income level will rise (or fall) by three times the increase (or decrease) in total planned spending—whether the change in *TPE* is due to a change in investment, in consumer demand for goods and services, or in government demand for goods and services. Rearranged slightly, the equation reads:

$$\text{change in } Y = m \times \text{change in } TPE$$

The formula for the multiplier is derived as follows. We know that at the initial equilibrium income level of Y_2, planned saving and investment are equal. We also know that planned saving and investment must again

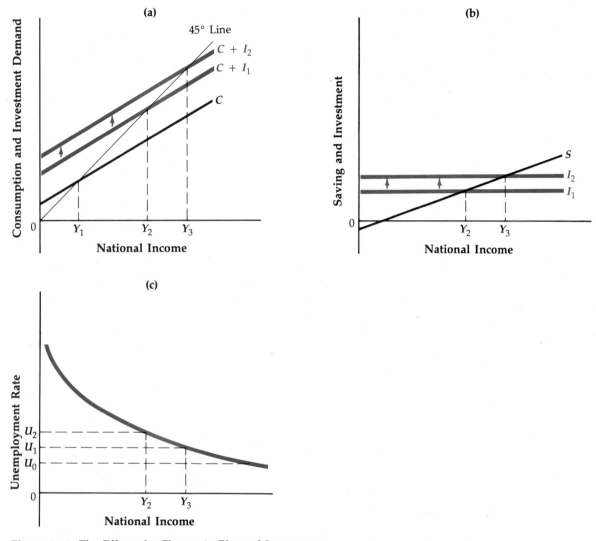

Figure 11.6. The Effect of a Change in Planned Investment.
If planned investment spending rises from a level of I_1 to I_2 in part (b), total
expenditures will rise from $C + I_1$ to $C + I_2$ in part (a). As a result the equilibrium
national income level rises from Y_2 to Y_3, and the unemployment rate falls from
U_2 to U_1 in part (c).

be equal at the new equilibrium income level of Y_3. Therefore any increase
in planned investment that causes firms to produce more must eventually
be matched by an equal increase in planned saving. If planned investment
goes up by $10 billion, for instance, causing a movement away from the
equilibrium income level, a new equilibrium level will not be reached until
planned saving has also risen by $10 billion.

   If we know the marginal propensity to save, we can figure the increase
in national income from the increase in saving. Suppose the marginal

Perspectives in Economics: A Keynesian Explanation of the Great Depression

In 1929, along with much of the rest of the world, the United States began to slide into the worst depression in its history. In that year the gross national product totaled $103 billion. By 1933, at the bottom of the Great Depression, GNP had fallen to $56 billion. During the intervening four years, practically all prices fell sharply. After adjustment for price reductions, the nation's measured output level fell by 31 percent. At the same time unemployment rose to 25 percent of the civilian labor force. Many more people who were underemployed as part-time workers were not counted in the unemployment statistics. The level of private business investment plummeted from $16 billion in 1929 to a little over $1 billion in 1933. The nation was wearing out its plant and equipment faster than it was replacing them. And the stock market crashed. At the peak of the boom in 1929, the total dollar value of stocks listed on the New York Stock Exchange was $90 billion. At the bottom of the market collapse three years later, it was $15 billion—83 percent less.

What caused it all? Keynesian economists point to the decrease in demand, particularly consumption and investment demand, that began in the late 1920s. In the first half of the decade, the demand for plant and equipment had been bolstered by several factors. The First World War had left much of Europe's industrial and agricultural plant and equipment in ruin. European nations looked to the United States for many of the capital goods and consumer products they could not supply themselves. Moreover there was a backlog of domestic demand for new and improved housing and consumer goods of all kinds, because during the war the United States had given priority to the production of war-related goods. Many industries had to expand and retool to meet this shift in domestic demand.

Third, during the 1920s the use of the automobile expanded considerably, and new products such as the radio, the electric stove, and the refrigerator became part of the American way of life. The demand for these new products created a demand for increased capital in the expanding industries that produced them. Finally, people were caught up in a wave of optimism. Some people believed the stock market would continue to rise indefinitely—and planned their expenditures accordingly. And businesses, ignoring a deterioration in underlying economic conditions, continued to base investment decisions on an assumption of sustained growth in demand and profit.

By the middle of the decade, however, most European industries had rebuilt and were able to satisfy their region's demand for many consumer products and capital goods. At the same time the productive capacity of many American industries had caught up with the backlog in consumer demand. In some industries, capacity had obviously been overextended. Table 11.2 shows the pattern in the housing industry. The construction

propensity to save is one-third (that is, people will save one-third of any change in their incomes). We can predict that income will rise by three times the change in saving. If planned saving must rise by $10 billion in order to equal planned investment, then national income must rise by $30 billion. At this point the *MPS* (1/3) times $30 billion equals $10 billion, the increase in saving that is necessary to reestablish equilibrium in national income.

Table 11.2. Urban Residential Construction in the United States, 1920–1929

Year	Dwelling Units	Year	Dwelling Units
1920	247,000	1925	937,000
1921	449,000	1926	849,000
1922	716,000	1927	810,000
1923	871,000	1928	753,000
1924	893,000	1929	509,000

Source: U.S. Bureau of the Census, *Historical Statistics of the United States* (Washington, D.C.: U.S. Government Printing Office, 1975), p. 393.

of new housing fell from its 1925 peak of 937,000 units to 509,000 units in 1929—a drop of 46 percent. Until 1928 this decline in residential construction was more than offset by the rise in nonresidential construction. But in 1929 total construction declined significantly, and purchases of automobiles and electrical appliances fell too.

All these downward trends in demand caused a significant drop in investment demand during the late 1920s. If productive capacity had caught up with consumer demand, there was no need for further investment, either in production or in new plant and equipment. According to Keynesian theory, such a reduction in planned investment will lead to a reduction in production, and thus to lower incomes and further reductions in consumer demand. Through the multiplier process, the economy headed downward into the Great Depression.

Thus the stock market collapse did not cause the Great Depression. The drastic fall in stock prices merely reflected investors' sudden recognition that the economic boom of the twenties was over. But the Great Crash, as it was called, worsened the problem. It dramatically shattered business confidence, causing a further decline in business investment. It also substantially reduced many people's personal wealth. To rebuild their lost security, Americans had to try to save more in times that were already hard. Even those with income resisted buying consumer goods out of fear that the Depression would eventually touch them. Consumers' reductions in planned expenditures also contributed to the downward spiral. Many banks collapsed, causing a sharp reduction in the money supply and the demand for goods based on credit. Finally, because of the growing riskiness of loaning money, interest rates rose to historically high levels, further suppressing investment. Given all these calamities, one might wonder why the Depression, which imposed considerable hardship on many Americans, was not even more severe.

Thus the size of the multiplier is related to the marginal propensity to save. Stated precisely, the multiplier is the reciprocal of the marginal propensity to save, or

$$m = \frac{1}{MPS}$$

Given a specific change in expenditures, the change in national income can be computed by multiplying the reciprocal of the marginal propensity to save[3] times the change in total planned expenditures, or

$$\text{change in } Y = \frac{1}{MPS} \times \text{change in } TPE$$

A concrete example may help explain why a change in planned investment (or consumer demand, or government demand) has a multiplying effect on national income. If businesses buy more plant and equipment— I_2 instead of I_1 in Figure 11.6—during a given period, their purchases result in higher output and greater income for the suppliers of those investment goods (construction workers and the owners of firms making heavy equipment). Suppliers will spend part of their increased incomes on personal consumption, including such goods as automobiles and refrigerators. The producers of automobiles and refrigerators will then have more income to spend on other items, such as groceries and clothes. In this way, an increase in expenditures for capital goods will affect incomes throughout the economy. But there is a limit to how much an increase in planned investment will raise the national income. As the income level rises, people tend to save more. Eventually the planned saving level will equal the new higher level of planned investment, at which point equilibrium will be attained.

Both the size of the multiplier and the potential change in the national income level are critically related to the value of the marginal propensity to save (or, geometrically, to the slope of the outflow curve). Compare the following sample values for the *MPS* with their associated multipliers.

$$MPS = 0.4 \qquad m = \frac{1}{0.4} = 2.5$$

$$MPS = 0.5 \qquad m = \frac{1}{0.5} = 2$$

$$MPS = 0.6 \qquad m = \frac{1}{0.6} = 1.66$$

Although these hypothetical values are much higher than the real-world *MPS*, they illustrate the inverse relationship between the *MPS* and the multiplier. As the marginal propensity to save rises, the value of the multiplier falls. Since the multiplier determines how much national income will rise with an increase in planned investment (change in $Y = m \times$ change in *TPE*), we can see the impact of *MPS*. The higher the *MPS*, the smaller the change in income with any change in investment—and vice versa. Thus if a nation's marginal propensity to save is very small—say

---

3. Since the marginal propensity to save and the marginal propensity to consume must add to 1, the multiplier can also be stated as

$$m = \frac{1}{(1 - MPC)}$$

(See the chapter Appendix for a more complete discussion of the multiplier.)

0.05—only a slight change in planned expenditures is required to cause a sharp change in the nation's income level. Finally, the multiplier operates on both increases and decreases in planned spending. A decrease has a negative multiplier effect. The national income level will fall by some multiple of any decline in planned investment. Unemployment will rise.

Changes in Planned Consumption and Saving

To many people, saving is a virtue. On an aggregate level, however, and within the confines of the Keynesian model of the macroeconomy, saving can have a detrimental short-run effect on income and employment. Suppose the economy is at equilibrium at a national income level of Y_2 and an unemployment rate of U_1 in Figure 11.7. Total expenditures are $C_1 + I$—part (a)—and saving is S_1—part (b). Now suppose people become more thrifty. Anticipating a recession, they decide to set aside more income. The saving curve shifts upward to S_2, reflecting this greater saving at each and every level of income. The level of planned saving now exceeds planned investment (I_1 in part (b)).

This shift in the saving curve is counterbalanced by a downward shift in the consumption curve in part (a). At the initial income level of Y_2, national production now exceeds total expenditure. Firms will not be able to sell all they produce. As their inventories pile up, they will reduce production, laying off workers in the process. Thus as national income falls, unemployment will rise (part (c)).

As income falls, however, saving will fall with it. At the lower national income level of Y_1, planned saving will again equal planned investment, and total planned expenditure will again equal national income. But in the process of lowering the nation's income level, the movement toward greater thrift has raised unemployment to U_2 (part (c)). Furthermore, at the new equilibrium income level, people can save no more than they could before, at the initial income level of Y_2. This perverse result is known as the paradox of thrift. According to the **paradox of thrift,** if people attempt to save more, they will end up earning less in the aggregate, and saving no more (and possibly less) than before. For this reason, Keynesian economists argue that efforts to save can be counterproductive, at least in the short run.

The national income level falls because people consume less when they try to save more. In fact, an increase in planned saving has the same negative multiplying effect on the income level as an equivalent drop in planned investment. In Figure 11.7, planned saving rises by the vertical distance between the two saving curves, S_1 and S_2. But the national income level falls by a much greater amount—three times as much, to be precise. As before, the marginal propensity to save (the slope of the saving curve) is 0.33, and the multiplier is 3.

Any *decrease* or any *increase* in planned consumption will have a multiplying effect on the economy. The important point is that the multiplier effect moves in the direction of the change in *total* planned expenditures.

Paradox of thrift: the theory that if people attempt to save more, they will end up earning less in the aggregate, and saving no more (and possibly less) than before.

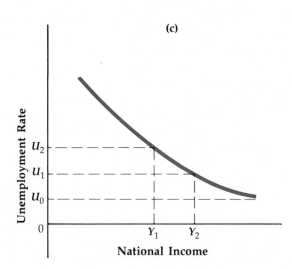

Figure 11.7. The Effect of a Change in Planned Saving.
An increase in the level of planned saving will cause the saving curve in part (b) to shift upward, from S_1 to S_2. This increase in planned saving causes downward shifts in the consumption curve—from C_1 to C_2 in part (a)—and in the total expenditure curve (from $C_1 + I$ to $C_2 + I$). The result is a decrease in the national income level, from Y_2 to Y_1, and an increase in the unemployment rate, from U_1 to U_2, in part (c).

Many policymakers use the Keynesian macroeconomic model developed in this chapter to explain the business cycle, or the intermittent swings between rising and falling levels of national income and employment. A decrease in planned investment or an increase in planned saving initiates a decrease in the national income level, which is magnified by the multiplier effect. A drop in planned investment, for instance, will lead to cumulative reductions in income and consumption and to further drops in production and income. An increase in planned investment and a decrease in planned saving will have a multiplicative effect in the opposite direction. The smaller the marginal propensity to save, the greater the value and effect of the multiplier.

Keynesian theory contradicts classical prescriptions for dealing with unemployment. To alleviate unemployment, classical economists recommended the elimination of labor market restrictions, such as minimum wage laws and union barriers to wage reductions. But the Keynesian model suggests that unemployment may be decreased by a reduction in the level of saving, and therefore increasing consumption. Through tax and expenditure policies, Keynesians believe that government can actively guide the economy toward the full-employment income level—a topic we will pursue in the next chapter.

Summary and Extensions

Major Conclusions

1. Using the planned investment and saving approach, one can show that equilibrium in national income and employment is established where the level of planned saving equals the level of planned investment.
2. Using the total planned spending approach, one can show that equilibrium in national income and employment is established where total planned expenditures for goods and services equals national income. (At this equilibrium income level, planned saving will equal planned investment.)
3. Planned investment is influenced by many factors, including the rate of interest firms pay on borrowed money. A decrease in the interest rate will cause an increase in the level of planned investment, and therefore in national income and employment; and vice versa. In the Keynesian model of the macroeconomy, each interest rate is associated with a specific national income level.
4. National income will increase or decrease by some multiple of any change in total planned expenditures. An increase in investment demand, for example, will cause an increase in the national income level greater than the increase in the investment demand.
5. In the Keynesian macroeconomic model, the multiplier is equal to the reciprocal of the marginal propensity to save.
6. According to the Keynesian macroeconomic model, the Great Depression was caused by decreases in planned consumption and investment.

Questions to Ponder

1. Suppose the nation's marginal propensity to save is 0.2; the level of consumption expenditures increases by $15 at each and every income level; and investment expenditures increase by $10. What will be the amount and direction of the resulting change in national income? What will happen to the unemployment rate?

2. Given the following values for the marginal propensity to save and for changes in investment, compute the multipliers and the resulting changes in national income:

MPS	Multiplier	Change in I	Change in Y
1/10	_____	+$10	_____
1/15	_____	−$20	_____
3/10	_____	+$5	_____

3. Suppose that saving rises by $10 at the same time that investment rises by $10. What will happen to the national income level?

4. The following graph reproduces the saving curve from the other figures in this chapter. The investment function, however, has been drawn as an upward-sloping curve instead of a horizontal line. The implied assumption is that investment is directly related to the national income level. That is, as national income increases, so does investment, and vice versa.

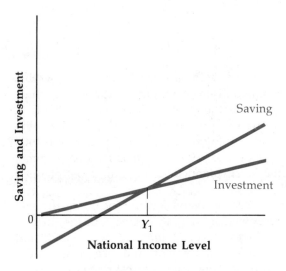

Given this information, suppose that the level of saving increases at each and every income level. (a) What will happen to the national income level and the unemployment rate? (b) What will happen to the actual level of saving? Explain the sequence of events on which your answers are based.

Appendix:
Derivation of the Multiplier

We noted on page 245 that the multiplier is related to the size of the marginal propensities to save and to consume. If investment expenditures rise by $10 billion, to use the example cited there, then planned saving must rise by an equal amount to reestablish equilibrium in national income. And if the marginal propensity to save is one-third, then the national income level must rise to $30 billion before planned saving again equals investment. The multiplier in this example is therefore 3 ($30 billion ÷ $10 billion = 3).

The formal derivation of the multiplier is as follows. To begin, we know that the change in national income will equal the multiplier times the change in total planned expenditures:

$$\text{change in } Y = m \times \text{change in } TPE$$

Furthermore, in the example on page 241, the change in total planned expenditures equals the change in investment. We can therefore substitute change in investment for change in total planned expenditures:

$$\text{change in } Y = m \times \text{change in } I$$

We also know that in an economy in equilibrium, planned saving must equal investment:

$$S = I$$

Before equilibrium in national income can be reestablished, then, any change in planned investment must be matched by an equal change in planned saving:

$$\text{change in } S = \text{change in } I$$

Again, we can substitute one variable for another—change in S for change in I—in the multiplier equation:

$$\text{change in } Y = m \times \text{change in } S$$

The equation change in $Y = m \times$ change in S can be rearranged as follows:

$$\frac{1}{m} = \frac{\text{change in } S}{\text{change in } Y}$$

Notice that the right-hand side of this equation is the formula for the marginal propensity to save. Thus:

$$\frac{1}{m} = MPS \quad \text{or} \quad m = \frac{1}{MPS}$$

Or stated verbally, the multiplier is the reciprocal of the marginal propensity to save.

If we know what the marginal propensity to save is, we can find the value of the multiplier. If the marginal propensity to save is one-third, as in our example, the multiplier must be 3:

$$m = \frac{1}{MPS} = \frac{1}{\frac{1}{3}} = 3$$

Since the marginal propensity to save is equal to 1 minus the marginal propensity to consume, the multiplier can also be stated as:

$$m = \frac{1}{1 - MPC}$$

Thus the value of the multiplier can also be computed from the marginal propensity to consume:

$$m = \frac{1}{(1 - MPC)} = \frac{1}{(1 - \frac{2}{3})} = \frac{1}{\frac{1}{3}} = 3$$

Central Question

Key Terms

What policy actions should the government take to influence national production, employment, and prices?

Automatic stabilizer

Chapter 12

Keynesian Fiscal Policy

*"Fiscal responsibility" is not
synonymous with "fiscal
restraint." Rather, it calls for
an intelligent fitting of tax and
spending positions to the needs
of the economy.*
Walter Heller

*T*he preceding chapter showed how, in the Keynesian model of the macroeconomy, changes in the demand for goods and services can affect national income and employment through the multiplier process. According to that model, the economy's equilibrium income level may not necessarily be its full-employment level. If changes in demand move the economy away from full employment, furthermore, the forces of supply and demand will not necessarily move the economy back toward full employment in the short run.

In this chapter we will consider how, theoretically at least, government fiscal policy can be used to counteract the negative effects of a change in demand. In Chapter 4, fiscal policy was defined as a government's use of tax and expenditure actions to achieve economic goals, such as full employment of the labor force or stable prices. Specifically, we will see how government can move the economy out of a recession by expanding aggregate demand (through a larger budgetary deficit or a smaller budgetary surplus). Conversely, it can reduce inflationary pressures by suppressing aggregate demand (through a larger budgetary surplus or a smaller budgetary deficit). Because such goals have shaped much of our government's economic policy over the past two decades, we will also be able to see the results of Keynesian theory in some real-world situations.

In macroeconomic theory, economic stability and full employment are considered public goods that can only be attained through collective government action. In the midst of a recession, for instance, the national income level can be increased only if firms as a group increase their planned expenditures on plant and equipment, or consumers as a group reduce their planned saving level. But individual households and firms have little incentive to contribute to the production of a public good like economic stability or full employment. A single household or firm is too small by itself to make a significant contribution to such an end, or to realize any substantial benefits from it. Firms and households do not operate in the common interest, but in their own private interest. All tend to become free riders. Thus government action is required for the production of economic stability as it is for the production of national defense.

Government as Economic Policymaker

To see how government attempts to produce economic stability, we will use graphs (like those in Chapter 11) that relate the various inflows and outflows to the national income level. In our model economy, tax payments and saving are directly influenced by the national income level. As income rises, people save more. Beyond some minimum level, people are required to pay taxes, and to pay more taxes the higher their income. This relationship between taxes, saving, and income is described in Figure 12.1(a). At income level Y_1, planned saving and taxes together are assumed to be zero. As income increases, however, planned saving and taxes rise. Any taxes that are collected inevitably reduce the saving outflow. The two outflows, in other words, are not independent. Still, this combined outflow curve has a steeper slope than the outflow curve in the last chapter, which included only saving.

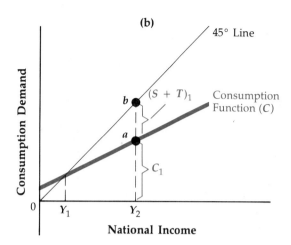

Figure 12.1. The Relationship of Planned Saving, Taxes, and Consumption to National Income.

Planned saving and taxes, shown by the upward-sloping curve in part (a), both increase with national income. The slope of this combined outflow curve is steeper than the slope of the outflow curve shown in the last chapter, which included only saving. After taxes, the consumption curve—part (b)—still slopes upward, but less than the consumption curve in the last chapter, for taxes reduce consumption. The vertical distance between the consumption function and the 45-degree line is equal to the combined total of planned saving and taxes shown in part (a).

The effect of taxation on consumption is illustrated in part (b) of Figure 12.1. There the consumption curve has a slightly lower slope than the one in Chapter 11, because taxes reduce consumer expenditures. People simply have less disposable income to spend after taxes. At a national income level of Y_2, total planned consumer expenditures are C_1, less than they would have been without the tax outflow. Planned saving and taxes are shown here by the vertical distance between the consumption curve and the 45-degree line (ab).

Government spending may well be influenced by the national income level. To keep the analysis simple, however, we will assume that neither planned government expenditures nor planned investment expenditures change with a change in national income. The planned government and investment expenditure curves are therefore horizontal, as in Figure 12.2(a) and (b). Combining these two curves yields a higher horizontal curve, like the one in part (c) of Figure 12.2.

Figure 12.3(a) combines the saving and taxes (outflow) curve from Figure 12.1 with the government spending and investment (inflow) curve from Figure 12.2. Figure 12.3(b) combines the consumption curve from Figure 12.1 and the government spending and investment curve from Figure 12.2 into a single total planned expenditure curve, $C + I + G$. With these two graphs we can see the equilibrium national income level.

National Income and Fiscal Policy

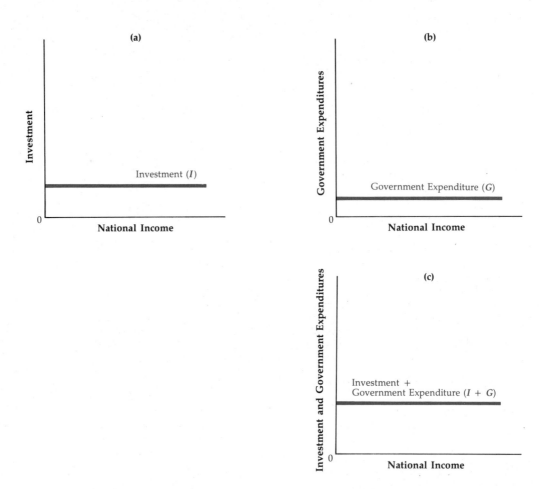

Figure 12.2. The Relationship of Investment and Government Spending to National Income.

Planned investment and government spending are assumed to be unaffected by the national income level. Therefore they are drawn as horizontal lines in parts (a) and (b). Planned investment and government spending combined can be represented by the horizontal curve shown in part (c).

From our discussion in the last chapter, we know that the equilibrium national income level will be reached where outflows equal inflows, or where total planned expenditures equal national income. These conditions are met at an income level of Y_2 in Figure 12.3(a) and (b). At any other income level, firms will want to cut back or expand production. For instance, at an income level of Y_3, outflows (saving plus taxes) are greater than inflows (planned investment plus government expenditures). This "contractionary gap" between outflows and inflows is indicated by the vertical distance between points a and b in Figure 12.3(a) and (b). Because firms will not sell all they have produced under such conditions, they will

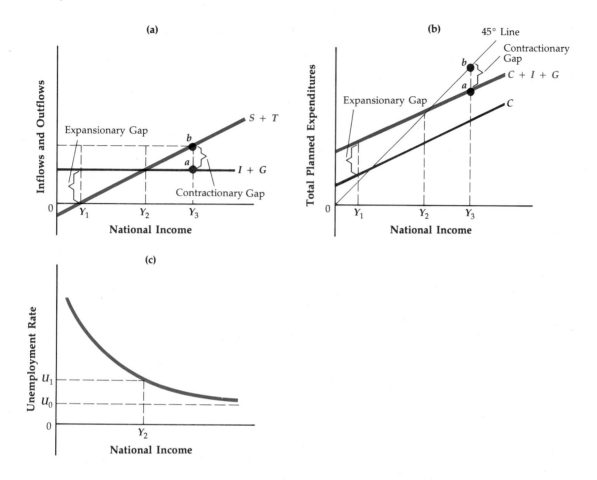

Figure 12.3. The Equilibrium National Income Level.
The equilibrium national income level is Y_2. At higher income levels, the planned saving and tax outflows exceed the planned investment and government spending inflows—part (a)—and national output exceeds total planned expenditures—part (b). The "contractionary gap" between what is produced and what is demanded by business, consumers, and government will move the economy back down toward Y_2. At income levels below Y_2, the investment and government spending inflows will exceed the planned saving and tax outflows—part (a)—and total planned expenditures will exceed national output—part (b). An "expansionary gap" between what is produced and what business, consumers, and government want will move the national income back up toward Y_2.

reduce production. As a result, the equilibrium national income level will contract toward Y_2, along with saving and taxes.

At income levels lower than Y_2, planned investment and government expenditure will be greater than planned saving and taxes, producing an "expansionary gap" between the inflow and outflow curves. Firms will be producing less than consumers want, and the excess demand will encourage them to increase production. As they do they will increase the national income level, as well as the outflows of saving and taxes. Eventually outflows will match inflows— at the equilibrium income level Y_2. At that level also, total planned expenditures will equal national income—Figure 12.3(b). Still, unemployment will be above the minimum rate of U_0, as indicated in Figure 12.3(c).

Changes in Planned Government Expenditures

We can now examine how government changes the national income level. Suppose the government's budget is balanced (taxes equal expenditures). If it then increases expenditures while holding taxes constant, the national income level will rise. Figure 12.4 illustrates the impact of such an increase in planned government expenditure, achieved in this case by running a budgetary deficit. With the increase in expenditures, the total planned expenditures curve $C + I + G_1$ shifts upward to $C + I + G_2$, in part (a). This shift is mirrored in part (b) by an upward shift of the inflow curve, from $I + G$ to $I + G_2$. An expansionary gap now exists between total planned inflows and total planned outflows. At income level Y_2, businesses are not producing enough to satisfy total demand. As they increase production, the national income level rises along with the saving and tax outflows. The economy reaches a new equilibrium income level at Y_3, where outflows again equal inflows and total expenditure equals national income. Significantly, unemployment has dropped in the process, from U_2 to U_1.

Notice that the change in national income ($Y_3 - Y_2$) is greater than the change in government expenditure that initiated it ($C + I + G_2 - C + I + G_1$, or $G_2 - G_1$). Here we see the influence of the multiplier effect (see pages 242–247). When the government spends more, production goes up and people's incomes increase. Consumers then spend more, causing another rise in production, incomes, and consumption. The upward spiral ends when saving and taxes increase enough to equal the increase in government expenditures.

In short, income will increase by some multiple (greater than 1) of the increase in government spending.[1] We know from Chapter 11 that the change in national income equals the multiplier times the change in total planned expenditures.

$$\text{change in } Y = m \times \text{change in } TPE$$

---

1. With the tax outflow added to the saving outflow, the multiplier is not quite as large as it was in the examples in Chapter 11. Like saving, taxes drain off consumers' purchasing power, limiting the effect of any change in government or investment spending. As we pointed out previously, the multiplier equals the reciprocal of the marginal propensity to save. In that analysis, the marginal propensity to save was the same as the slope of the outflow curve, since saving was the only outflow. With taxes added, the slope of the outflow curve is higher; hence the multiplier is lower. How much lower depends on how much the tax drain affects the saving outflow.

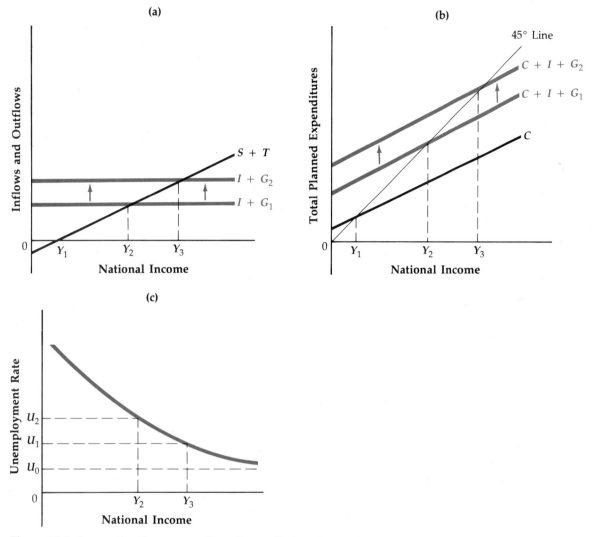

Figure 12.4. Increasing Government Spending to Reduce Unemployment.
An increase in government spending will shift the total planned expenditure curve
up from $C + I + G_1$ to $C + I + G_2$—part (a)—and the inflow curve up from
$I + G_1$ to $I + G_2$—part (b). The national income level will move from Y_2 to Y_3,
where total expenditures will again equal national output—part (a)—and inflows
will again equal outflows—part (b). Unemployment will drop from U_2 to U_1.

Since the change in total spending equals the change in government
spending, we can restate our equation to read:

$$\text{change in } Y = m \times \text{change in } G$$

Conversely, if the government decreases expenditures while holding
taxes constant, the national income level will fall. If the government spends

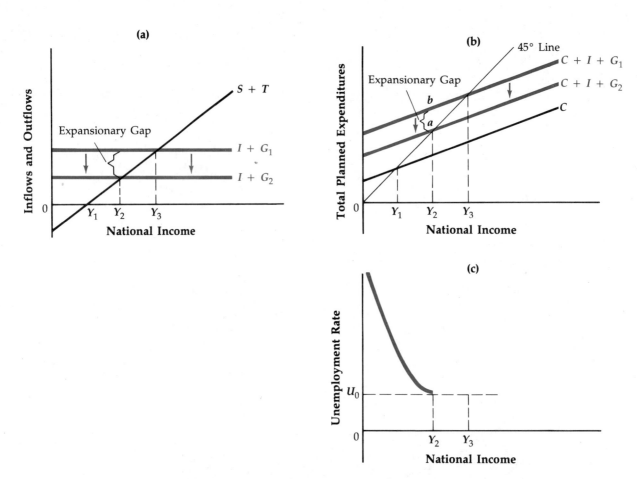

Figure 12.5. Decreasing Government Spending to Control Inflation.
If consumers, investors, and government together demand more goods than the economy can produce at full employment (Y_2), the gap between demand and output—points b and a in part (b)—will create inflationary pressure on prices. By reducing government expenditures, policymakers can reduce total planned expenditures to $C + I + G_2$, moving the economy away from the inflationary equilibrium income level of Y_3 to the noninflationary income level Y_2.

less, firms will produce less, workers will receive less income, consumers will consume less, and so forth. The national income level will decline by some multiple of the decrease in government expenditures, and unemployment will rise. In this case the government's fiscal policy causes or contributes to a recession.

Of course no government is likely to cause a recession intentionally. But government policymakers may very well reduce spending in an attempt to control the rate of inflation. In Figure 12.5, for instance, planned government expenditures and investment add up to $I + G_1$. The equilibrium income level is Y_3, where the outflow and inflow curves intersect (part (a)). But part (c) shows that the economy reaches the minimum unemployment rate, U_0, at a much lower national income level, Y_2.

In this case the nation simply does not have a labor force sufficient to produce at an output level of Y_3. Yet consumers are demanding that the economy produce at that level (part (b)). A gap exists between what consumers, investors, and government demand—point b in part (b)—and what the economy can produce (point a). This excess demand should produce inflation, since consumers will bid up the prices of goods that are in short supply. To eliminate the inflationary pressures, government policymakers may decide to reduce government expenditures, thereby reducing total planned expenditures to $C + I + G_2$. The equilibrium national income level will then be Y_2, the full-employment level for this economy.

Not all economists accept Keynesian doctrine on the effect of government spending. Some maintain that if the government has to create a deficit or increase its deficit in order to increase spending, the multiplier effect will be significantly weakened. When government borrows, it becomes a competitor in the money market, driving up interest rates and crowding private borrowers out of the market. (For a fuller explanation of crowding out, see pages 318–320.) If the government borrows funds that would otherwise be used elsewhere, these critics charge, any increase in government spending may be partially or totally offset by a decrease in private business ventures, or in state and local government spending.

If the government stimulates demand by spending more than it collects in taxes, it must either increase the money stock or borrow the difference between spending and taxes. The usual method is to borrow the money by selling bonds. Keynes argued that during a severe recession, the government would be borrowing funds that would otherwise remain idle. In a particularly serious recession, he felt, people tend to hold on to their money, fearing that loans to businesses are unsafe or anticipating that interest rates will rise. In that case government borrowing would not lead to a drop in private investment. Any increase in government spending would be fully reflected in the multiplier process.

But not all recessions are severe enough to scare lenders out of investing in private enterprise. What if private investment were to fall at the same time, and by the same amount, as government expenditures increase? Total planned expenditures would not change, and there would be no multiplier effect—no increase in the national income level. Even if private investment fell by less than the increase in government spending—say by $7 billion when government expenditures rose by $10 billion—the net change in total planned expenditures would be much reduced (in this example, to $3 billion). The multiplier effect would still occur, but it would be much smaller than predicted by our earlier analysis.

Especially since the late 1960s, this question has been the subject of considerable controversy. Keynesians cite statistical studies that support the strength of the muliplier effect. Economists of the monetarist, supply-side, and rational expectations schools disagree, as we will see in later chapters. A synthesis on the impact of fiscal policy has begun to emerge,

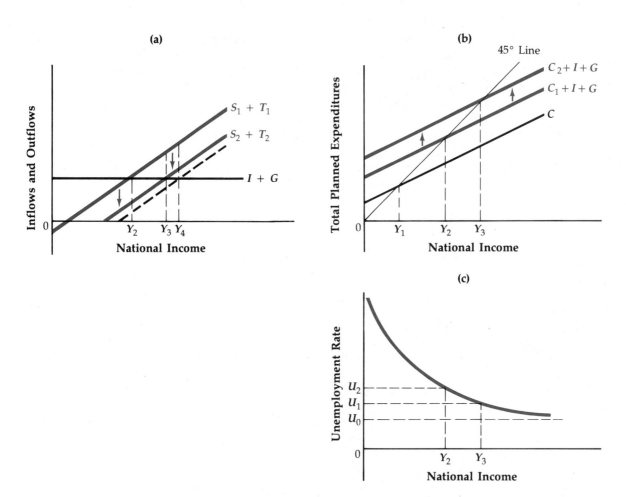

Figure 12.6. Decreasing Taxes to Reduce Unemployment.
A reduction in taxes shifts the combined outflow curve $S + T$ downward—part
(a)—though not by the full amount of the tax cut, as shown by the dotted line.
Some of the cut is saved, increasing the saving outflow at the same time the tax
outflow decreases. Total expenditures shift up, as shown in part (b). The equilibrium
national income level rises from Y_2 to Y_3, and the unemployment rate falls from
U_2 to U_1 (part (c)).

however. The economists who adhere to it acknowledge a modest short-
run multiplier effect. But they contend that after six months or possibly a
year, fiscal action is largely ineffective in influencing aggregate demand
and national income.

Changes in Planned Taxes

A change in tax rates can have similar effects on the equilibrium national
income level. If people's saving habits were not affected by the taxes they

pay, a reduction in taxes might cause a sizable downward shift in the outflow curve $(S_1 + T_1)$, to the dotted line in Figure 12.6(a). The equilibrium national income level would then climb all the way to Y_4. In fact, however, people tend to save some part of a tax reduction, particularly if it is a large one. The drop in the tax outflow is partially offset by the resulting increase in the saving outflow. The combined outflow curve shifts only part way, to $S_2 + T_2$. What is not saved is spent, for a reduction in taxes represents an increase in disposable income. Thus the total expenditures curve shifts up to $C_2 + I + G$, as shown in part (b). The national income level rises only to Y_3, and the unemployment level falls from U_2 to U_1.

How much of a tax cut taxpayers will spend can be estimated by multiplying the change in taxes by the marginal propensity to consume.

$$\text{change in } C = MPC \times -\text{change in } T$$

The minus sign is added in the right-hand side of the formula because consumption is expected to change in the opposite direction from taxes. If the marginal propensity to consume is nine-tenths and taxes are reduced by $30 billion, for example, consumption will rise by nine-tenths of $30 billion, or $27 billion. The remaining portion of the tax cut, $3 billion, will therefore be saved.

A planned tax increase will reduce people's disposable incomes, lowering both saving and consumption. Lower consumption will mean lower production, and eventually still lower incomes. Like a reduction in planned government expenditures, then, a tax increase is often (but not always) intended to reduce the inflationary pressures that arise when total planned expenditures exceed the economy's ability to produce. Lowering the demand for all goods and services dampens competition for scarce resources and slows price increases.

A comparison of this method of altering national income with the change-in-expenditure method discussed earlier leads us to two important conclusions. First, either a reduction in planned taxes or an increase in planned government expenditures will raise the national income level. A decrease in government expenditures or an increase in taxes will lower the national income level, exerting downward pressure on inflation.

Second, a change in planned government expenditures will have a greater effect on the national income level than an equal change in taxes. For instance, suppose the government increases its expenditures by $10 billion. If the multiplier is 3, the change in the national income level will be $30 billion (the multiplier times the change in total planned expenditures). If the government reduces taxes by $10 billion, on the other hand, not all of the reduction will be spent by consumers. If $3.33 billion ($MPS$ $\times$ $10 billion) of the cut goes into saving, consumption expenditures will rise by only $6.67 billion. Because the multiplier process is keyed to the increase in planned consumer expenditures, not to the tax reduction, the change in income will be only $20 billion (the multiplier times the change in total planned expenditures). Thus if government policymakers want to increase the national income level by reducing taxes, they will have to reduce them by an amount greater than the increase in expenditures needed to achieve the same effect.

The Balanced-Budget Multiplier

Assume the government's budget is balanced. Now suppose it increases both its expenditures and the taxes it collects by the same amount, thus keeping its budget balanced. Will such an action affect the national income and employment levels? On the surface, it may seem that the two increases will simply offset each other. The rise in expenditures would increase national income by the same amount as a tax increase would reduce it. But Keynesians argue that a simultaneous increase in government expenditures and taxes should have a small positive effect on national income.

To see why, assume that the marginal propensity to consume is ⅔. An increase of $10 billion in taxes will produce a $6.67 billion reduction in consumer expenditures.

$$\text{change in } C = MPC \times -\text{change in } T$$

$$= \tfrac{2}{3} \times -\$10 \text{ billion}$$

$$= -\$6.67 \text{ billion}$$

If the multiplier is 3, this increase in consumption demand will lead to a decrease in national income of $20 billion.

$$\text{change in } Y = m \times \text{change in } TPE$$

Or, in this case, since the change in total spending is equal to the change in consumption,

$$\text{change in } Y = m \times \text{change in } C$$

$$= 3 \times -\$6.67 \text{ billion}$$

$$= -\$20 \text{ billion}$$

But the increase of $10 billion in government spending will increase national income by $30 billion, for the same reason.

$$\text{change in } Y = m \times \text{change in } TPE$$

$$= m \times \text{change in } G$$
$$\text{(since change in } TPE = \text{change in } G)$$

$$= 3 \times \$10 \text{ billion}$$

$$= \$30 \text{ billion}$$

The net change in national income, then, will be $10 billion ($30 billion − $20 billion). This $10 billion rise in national income equals the increase in government expenditures and taxes that caused it. Thus when government expenditures and taxes are increased by the same amount, the combined multiplier, called the balanced-budget multiplier, is 1.

The Kennedy Tax Cut: A Real-World Case

When President John F. Kennedy took office in 1961, the economy was in a mild recession. He and his economic advisers concluded that the best way to fulfill his campaign promise to "get the economy moving again" was to reduce personal and business taxes, by approximately $12 billion.

Given that an equal increase in expenditures would have had a greater impact, why did Kennedy choose to reduce taxes? Political considerations probably played an important role in the decision. In either case the government would have to run a larger budgetary deficit, and no previous president had ever proposed to run a deficit or increase one simply to stimulate the economy. Indeed deficits had always been equated with fiscal irresponsibility. They were thought to impose a burden on future generations and to court national bankruptcy. In 1961, increasing government expenditures to stimulate the economy was too radical a move politically. Although the tax cut too was controversial, it was more acceptable to the public because it put extra money into the pockets of tax-payers.

There was a technical as well as a political reason for choosing a tax cut, however. Kennedy's economic advisers argued that tax rates were so high they would prevent the achievement of full employment. If the economy started to recover and national income to rise, tax revenues would become so high that people would lack the income necessary to raise consumption. The economy would stop moving upward at some point before reaching full employment. In short, the tax system would impose what the advisers called "fiscal drag" on the recovery. If a tax cut reduced this drain on personal purchasing power, Kennedy's economists argued, the extra money people had to spend would help to speed and extend the recovery.

Keynesian economists argue that the Reagan-backed tax package of 1981, which cut tax rates over the period 1981–1984, stimulated the economy in much the same way as Kennedy's tax cut. There is some debate over whether this most recent tax cut actually had the expected positive effect on national income, however. If the rise in Social Security tax rates and the impact of bracket creep are taken into account, the overall tax rate may not have been cut very much, if at all. Some economists have offered supply-side explanations for the recovery that began in late 1982—an issue that we will take up in Chapter 15. And others attribute the recovery to the rapid rate of increase in the money stock that began late in 1982, not the tax cut. We will consider this monetary explanation for the recovery in Chapter 14.

Fiscal Policy in the Context of the Business Cycle

We have seen how Keynesians use changes in government spending and taxes to counteract the negative effects of recession and inflation. Eventually, through the multiplier process, a small change in government spending or taxation will be translated into a much larger change in national income. This sort of corrective fiscal policy cannot be expected to eliminate all ups and downs in economic activity, however. Economic recovery takes time; and timing is one of the most crucial aspects of fiscal policymaking.

Difficulties in the Timing of Fiscal Actions

If policy changes could be put into effect as soon as they were needed, and if they worked almost immediately, fiscal action might be a relatively simple proposition. But almost inevitably the hoped-for increase in national income and employment, or decrease in prices, is slow in coming. Time is lost at several points along the way, starting with the lag in recognizing a problem.

Recognition Lag

Before fiscal action can be taken, government must recognize that a recession or a period of inflation is under way. This process may take several months, given the way some economic data are collected. In the beginning of a recession, signals are likely to be mixed. Some measures, like the number of housing starts per month, may indicate a decline in economic activity. Yet an upward trend may persist in others, like the number of new orders for heavy industrial equipment. Thus government policymakers may not begin to address an economic problem for some time—and then they may not be able to agree immediately on the appropriate fiscal actions.

Reaction Lag

After policymakers have concluded that the economy has changed direction, they will have to convince Congress that a change in taxes or expenditures is needed. Members of Congress may bargain for special benefits for their home districts. Thus policy action is further delayed by politicking. The Kennedy tax cut took sixteen months to go through Congress. The Reagan tax package took almost a year.

Impact Lag

If Congress approves an action, several more months will pass before its impact is felt. A tax cut will take effect as soon as people's take-home pay increases. An increase in government expenditures tends to work more slowly—new projects must be bid on, and contracts negotiated. All in all, the economy can be well on its way to the bottom or top of a cycle before the effects of a fiscal action become evident.

Unfortunately, if an action comes too late, it is likely to make the problem worse. If a fiscal stimulus is passed late in the recovery phase of a recession, it can add to the inflationary pressures that accompany the approach to the peak of a business cycle. Only in a world in which information is readily available and unambiguous can appropriate action be taken at the appropriate time. And because fiscal policies must be formulated in the political arena, appropriate timing is even more unlikely. If Congress uses Keynesian prescriptions to increase political support at home, a political business cycle—one that moves in accord with elections— may develop.

Use of Automatic Stabilizers

There is an alternative to the use of deliberate policy actions by government, one that does not involve the risk of poor timing. Some taxes and government expenditures vary automatically with changes in the national income level, and generally in the desired direction. These fiscal instruments are called automatic stabilizers. An **automatic stabilizer** is a tax or expenditure that increases total planned spending in times of recession and lowers it in times of economic expansion, without special action on the part of the administration and Congress. Among the more important automatic stabilizers are income taxes and unemployment and welfare benefits.

Automatic stabilizer: a tax or expenditure that increases total planned spending in times of recession and lowers it in times of economic expansion, without special action on the part of the administration and Congress.

Personal Income Taxes

Through the tax rate structure, personal income taxes are tied directly to the national income level. As their personal incomes rise, people are required to pay an increasing percentage of their taxable incomes to the government. When national income begins to fall, therefore, the government's tax collections decline as well. This drop in tax revenues partly offsets the drop in consumer purchasing power.

Corporate Income Taxes

Like individuals, corporations must pay a percentage of their profits in taxes to the government. And like personal income taxes, corporate income taxes vary with corporate income, or profits. This stabilizer has a particularly powerful effect on total spending, for corporate profits move dramatically in response to a change in national income. They fall considerably during recessions and rise steeply during economic expansions.

Unemployment Compensation and Welfare Benefits

When the national income level falls, the unemployment level rises. There is then an increase in unemployment compensation, as well as many welfare benefits—food stamps, rent subsidies, and aid to dependent children—increasing the level of government spending. Conversely, a rise in national income reduces unemployment, curtailing these social programs and lowering government spending.

The Pros and Cons of Deficit Spending

Before Keynes it was generally agreed that government should try to restrict its expenditures to the level of its tax receipts—in other words, balance its budget. Deficit spending during peacetime was equated with fiscal irresponsibility. An underlying assumption was that the federal government was like an individual household. It could not continually incur budgetary deficits without risking bankruptcy. Moreover, because individual debts must be paid back at some point, deficit spending was seen as a burden on future generations.

Perspectives in Economics: The Political Effects of Keynesian Economics

When Keynes wrote his *General Theory*, British economic policy was formulated by a small group of intellectuals. Keynes developed his arguments for government spending with such a system in mind. He assumed that given good policy recommendations, good men will do good things. He probably did not foresee that his ideas would be taken up by politicians in Washington, who keep one eye on the economy and the other on the opinion polls.

Those who follow the politics of economics have observed that politicians tend to vote for spending programs and against the taxes to pay for those programs.[1] Government expenditures benefit many. To the extent that they benefit a politician's constituency, they increase his or her political support. Taxes, on the other hand, impose costs on political constituencies. They tend to reduce a politician's support. If politicians accept the idea that government budgets must be balanced, some economists argue, they will vote for government expenditures only if the political support they generate exceeds the support lost by raising taxes to pay for the programs. But if politicians do not believe in the

Keynesian theory undermined the popularity of the balanced budget. Keynesians argued that during periods of slack demand and high unemployment, deficit spending creates no present or future costs. On the contrary, because of the implied increase in total spending, deficits allow more people to work, more income to be generated, and more products to be produced. These resources, both people and equipment, would otherwise remain idle. And since the real cost of any government action must be measured against what is forgone, it follows that the real cost of running a deficit during a recession is virtually zero.

Furthermore, to the extent that deficit spending is used to build roads, schools, and national parks, or to encourage private investment through government subsidies, future generations actually benefit from it. They have more capital assets to use in the production of new goods and services. And though they will have to meet the interest payments on the debt, they also have higher incomes with which to meet them. Besides, to the extent the interest is paid to U.S. citizens, such payments do not represent a loss of resources to the nation as a whole. Because we effectively owe the debt to ourselves, we pay the interest to ourselves—or so the argument goes.

During times of full employment, a government deficit does impose a cost on the private sector, because there are no idle resources to be taken up. Resources must be diverted from private to government use. At such times, the cost of a deficit can be measured by what must be given up in the private sector. Most Keynesians agree that deficit spending is generally balanced budget, they will court political support by voting consistently for government expenditures and against taxes. Given widespread acceptance of deficit spending, even politicians who are opposed to deficits may feel forced to accept them in order to survive politically.

In times of inflation, when the government should reduce total planned expenditures and run a budgetary surplus, the political appeal of a deficit becomes even more obvious. Politicians have an understandable aversion to budget surpluses, since they can be created only by raising taxes but not spending—or reducing spending but not taxes. For politicians, surpluses can spell a net loss in political support. Even during periods of excessive demand and inflation, politicians are more likely to vote for a lower surplus, or even a deficit, than for a higher surplus. Keynesian policy may be effective, but it cannot always be productively employed in the political arena.

1. James M. Buchanan and Richard E. Wagner, *Democracy in Deficit: The Destructive Legacy of Lord Keynes* (New York: Academic Press, 1977).

appropriate only during periods of relatively high unemployment.

Keynesians also question the analogy between government and household finances. They point out that even an individual household's debt can grow over time, as the family becomes better able to pay interest and to repay the principal. While a household is paying off some debts, it can incur new ones. People who are paying off a car loan, for instance, can still buy furniture on credit. As people's incomes grow over time, their ability to handle more debt increases.

This is just what has happened in the United States since the Second World War. In 1950 consumer debt (not including home mortgages) totaled $25 billion; by the end of 1984 it had risen to $575 billion. Even allowing for inflation, the increase in private debt had been substantial. Yet personal income has grown with it. Personal income increased from $227 billion to $3,013 billion between 1950 and 1984.[2] If members of households can increase their indebtedness over time, why not the government?

Furthermore, the idea that all debts will eventually come due cannot really be applied to government. Because people's lives are limited, members of an individual household must pay off all their debts—if necessary, through their estates, after death. But for all practical purposes the government can expect perpetual life. Granted, government bonds do

2. *Statistical Abstract of the United States* (Washington, D.C.: U.S. Government Printing Office, 1985), p. 501.

carry maturity dates, on which bondholders must be repaid the stated amounts. But government can refinance its debt by issuing new bonds and using the funds collected from them to pay off the old debt. Taken collectively, the debt of consumers is never paid off. So why should the government's debt be paid off?

The major constraint on the government's ability to expand its debt is citizens' willingness to buy bonds. The borrowing limit depends on both the stability of the government and people's propensity to save. If a government is in danger of being overthrown, people will of course be reluctant to lend it money. But so long as the government is stable and can pay the going market interest rate out of its tax collections, government bonds will be just as attractive as private bonds, if not more so. U.S. government bonds are generally considered to be safer investments than most corporate bonds, as evidenced by the higher interest rates borne by the latter. Finally, Keynesians would argue, if through deficit spending the government can raise the national income level, and therefore the nation's tax revenues, why worry about increasing the national debt?

We will return to this issue in following chapters, for economists from other schools of thought take issue with the Keynesians' benign view of government deficits.

Monetary Policy from the Keynesian Perspective

Though modern Keynesians advocate the use of both fiscal and monetary policy to relieve unemployment, Keynesian economics has historically been associated with the management of aggregate demand through fiscal policy. Keynes and his followers doubted that monetary policy could pull the economy out of a particularly severe recession like the Great Depression.

The Federal Reserve During the Depression

During the Great Depression banks were hit hard on both sides of their balance sheet. While borrowers became less capable of paying back their loans, depositors became skeptical of the solvency of banks and withdrew their deposits. Hundreds of banks failed, and many others came close to bankruptcy.

The banks' predicament was made more difficult by the Federal Reserve. The Fed was established to ensure that banks could borrow the reserves they needed whenever their customers made heavy withdrawals. Yet during the 1930s the Fed severely discouraged banks from borrowing at the discount window. Many banks failed simply because they could not obtain the necessary reserves from the Fed. Bank officers soon became extremely cautious about lending money, and worked to build up their reserve deposits with the Fed and other banks. When the Fed later attempted to increase the money stock, banks held on to part of the newly created reserves for their own protection.

To Keynesians, this buildup of excess reserves demonstrated that during a severe depression, people have a highly elastic demand for money. Even very small decreases in interest rates will cause banks to hold on to whatever reserves they can, and individuals to hold on to whatever money the Federal Reserve creates. The money simply will not be spent. And without an increase in spending, the economy will remain depressed.

Thus Keynes and his followers concluded that monetary policy could not alleviate a severe depression. The only way to stimulate the economy in such circumstances, they argued, was to increase spending or reduce taxes.

The Liquidity Trap

Keynesians deemphasize monetary policy not just because of its history during the Depression, but because of its role in Keynesian theory. Keynesians reject the classical theory that interest rates adjust to bring the demand for investment goods into line with the supply of savings (see pages 215–219). Instead they stress the demand for money versus the stock of money.

According to Keynesian theory, the demand for money is rooted primarily in the transactions demand and the speculative demand. (In Keynesian terms the transactions demand for money includes both the transactions and precautionary demands, as defined on page 150.) The transactions demand is determined primarily by the national income level. Money is needed to carry on trade, and the greater the national income level, the greater the need for trade. The direct relationship between the national income level and the transactions demand for money is illustrated in Figure 12.7(a).

The speculative demand for money is determined principally by expectations regarding future interest rates. If people think current interest rates are low, they will hold on to their money, waiting for rates to rise. If interest rates are falling, more and more people will begin to expect rates to rise in the future, and will hold on to their money for the present. The quantity of money demanded for speculative purposes will rise. This inverse relationship between interest rates and the speculative demand for money is illustrated in Figure 12.7(b).

Given an income level like Y_1 in Figure 12.7(a), the total demand for money will look something like the curve in Figure 12.7(c). Keynes argued that during severe depressions, the interest rate may fall so low that everyone will believe it is going to rise, and everyone will hold on to all the cash they can get. An economy in such circumstances has fallen into a "liquidity trap." The usual monetary policy remedy—expansion of the money stock—can offer no relief.

Suppose, for instance, that the demand for money looks like the downward-sloping curve in Figure 12.8(a), and that the money stock is fixed at MS_1. The equilibrium interest rate will be R_1, where the demand for money and money stock curves intersect. Notice that with this curve, an increase in the money stock, say from MS_1 to MS_2, will not lower the

Figure 12.7. The Demand for Money: The Keynesian View.
In the Keynesian model, the demand for money is composed of two major components: the transactions demand and the speculative demand. The amount of money demanded for making transactions—part (a)—is directly related to the national income level. The quantity of money demanded for speculation is inversely related to the interest rate (part (b)). The total demand for money—part (c)—is the summation of the transactions demand for money at a given income level—say Y_1—and the speculative demand for money.

interest rate any further, as it normally would be expected to do. If the interest rate remains at R_1, the investment level will stay at I_1 in Figure 12.8(b). With no increase in investment, the national income level must remain depressed.

Figure 12.8. The Liquidity Trap.
If the money demand curve flattens out at a low interest rate, as in panel (a), and the money stock curve intersects it in its horizontal range, the macroeconomy is said to be in a liquidity trap. An increase in the money stock from MS_1 to MS_2 will not result in a lower interest rate, and therefore will not increase the level of investment—panel (b).

The Effect of Changes in the Money Stock

Thus Keynesians explained the apparent ineffectiveness of monetary policy during the Great Depression. They concluded that in severe economic conditions, fiscal policy actions are the only means of stimulating the economy. But many Keynesians now recognize that monetary policy can be a useful means of fighting recession. In fact, the demand for money never flattens out completely, as it does in Figure 12.8(a). Rather, it slopes downward all the way, as in Figure 12.9(a). Hence an increase in the money stock, say from MS_1 to MS_2, will lead to a lower interest rate and an increase in investment spending, as in Figure 12.9(b). Through the multiplier process, this increase in investment will be translated into a much larger increase in national income, as in Figure 12.9(c).

Though economists now agree on the general effect of an increase in the money stock, debate continues over the magnitude of the effect. The size of the change in national income depends on several factors.

How far the interest rate will fall as the money stock rises depends on how people's demand for money responds to a change in the interest rate.

How much investment spending will increase as the interest rate declines depends on how investment demand responds to a change in the interest rate.

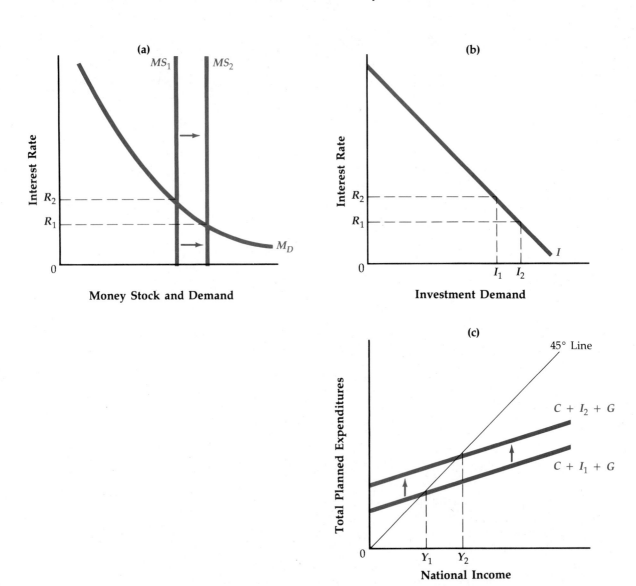

Figure 12.9. Effect of a Change in the Money Stock: A Modern View.
According to modern macroeconomic theory, the demand for money curve looks like the downward-sloping curve in panel (a). An increase in the money stock from MS_1 to MS_2 *will* lower the interest rate, from R_2 to R_1. Investment spending will increase from I_1 to I_2 (panel (b)), shifting the total spending curve from $C + I_1 + G$ to $C + I_2 + G$ (panel (c)). The national income level will increase through the multiplier process, from Y_1 to Y_2.

How much the national income level will change as a result of a change in investment spending depends on the size of the multiplier. And the size of the multiplier depends on the marginal propensity to consume and on income tax rates.

The Keynesian prescription for extremely high unemployment is to increase total planned expenditures, either by increasing government spending or by decreasing taxes. Both methods will increase national income. Either way, though, the government must be willing to create or increase a budgetary deficit or to reduce a budgetary surplus. In times of excessive demand and inflation, the Keynesian prescription is to increase taxes or reduce government expenditures, thus lowering the equilibrium national income level. Such action may require the government to run a budgetary surplus or a smaller deficit.

These same basic effects can be obtained by increasing or decreasing the money stock. An increase in the money stock will tend to lower interest rates, encouraging investment. A decrease in the money stock will do the opposite. Modern-day Keynesians feel that both monetary and fiscal actions can be used effectively, either separately or together, to relieve unemployment and inflation. As we will see in later chapters, however, there is considerable debate about the appropriateness of Keynesian policies. Part of that debate concerns the extent to which fiscal and monetary policy actions affect prices, which we have held constant in the foregoing analysis. That simplifying assumption will be dropped in the next chapter.

Summary and Extensions

Major Conclusions

1. Government can increase total planned expenditures, and thereby the national income level, by (a) increasing government spending while holding taxes constant; (b) reducing taxes while holding government spending constant; or (c) increasing government spending and decreasing taxes at the same time.
2. Government can reduce total planned expenditures, and thereby inflation, by (a) reducing government spending while holding taxes constant; (b) increasing taxes while holding government spending constant; or (c) reducing government spending while increasing taxes.
3. According to Keynesian theory, increases and decreases in government spending and/or taxes have a multiplier effect on the national income level. Thus the government should adjust its expenditures or its taxes by only a fraction of the desired change in national income.
4. An increase in government spending will have a greater effect on the national income level than a tax reduction of equal size. To increase the national income level through a tax cut, the government must reduce taxes by more than it would have to increase government spending to achieve the same effect.
5. When government borrows money to cover a deficit caused by an increase in its spending, the market interest rate may rise and businesses may reduce their investment spending. This reduction in planned business investment can partially (if not totally) offset the effect of higher government spending on the national income level.
6. Government budgetary deficits should not be incurred needlessly. But they may be acceptable if they emerge from a purposeful fiscal policy designed to stimulate the economy and raise the national income level.
7. Delays in the implementation of fiscal policy should be expected because of recognition lag (delay in recognizing the need for a change

in fiscal policy), action lag (delay in getting Congress to take the necessary action), and impact lag (delay in realizing the effects of the policy change).

8. Automatic stabilizers are fiscal changes triggered automatically by changes in the national income level, without special action on the part of the administration or Congress.

9. The national debt does not have to be paid off; it can be refinanced. When a portion of the national debt comes due, the government can issue new bonds to acquire the funds needed to pay it off.

10. Deficit spending benefits politicians seeking reelection, for their constituents receive more government goods and services without having to pay for them directly through higher taxes. Politicians can thus be expected to support larger deficits than may be necessary to achieve full employment and stable prices.

11. Monetary policy can also influence the national income level. An increase in the money stock will reduce the interest rate, increasing planned investment and total planned expenditures. Like fiscal actions, the increase in total planned expenditures will be translated, by the multiplier process, into an increase in the national income level.

1. Will an increase in government expenditures of $10 billion have the same effect on the national income level as a $10 billion decrease in taxes? Explain.
2. Will a decrease in the money stock reduce or increase the national income level? Explain your reasoning.
3. If a $10 billion increase in government expenditures causes a $10 billion decrease in investment expenditures, what will happen to the national income level?
4. In recent years, government has allowed a tax credit for investing in new plant and equipment. That is, businesses have been permitted to reduce their tax payments by a percentage of the value of new plant and equipment purchased during the year. Using the Keynesian model of income and employment, explain the possible effects of such an investment tax credit.
5. Does Keynesian theory promote unnecessarily high budgetary deficits? Explain your answer.

Questions to Ponder

Central Question

How do aggregate supply and demand interact to determine the national income and price levels?

Key Terms

Money illusion

Econometrics

Econometric model

Linear regression

Chapter 13

Aggregate Supply and Demand

Can the United States have high-unemployment prosperity without inflation? For some time, the American people have been asked to tune in tomorrow and find out; but the last episode of the serial has not yet been produced. In no period during the past forty years has the American economy been free of excessive **unemployment** *and inflationary tendencies simultaneously. Nor has any other industrial nation found the happier combination; hitting the dual target of high utilization and essential price stability remains the most serious unsolved problem of stabilization policy throughout the Western World.*

Arthur Okun

*S*o far we have focused almost exclusively on how changes in total spending affect the national income and employment levels. Little has been said about what happens to the price level when government fiscal or monetary policies change. We have ignored the price level for two reasons. First, Keynesian theory initially assumed that prices do not change very much or very rapidly with changes in total spending. A central point of Keynesian macroeconomics is that changes in total planned spending will be reflected in output and employment—a point that can be illustrated most clearly by holding prices constant. Second, the assumption of constant prices has helped us keep the analysis relatively simple.

This chapter will extend Keynesian macroeconomic theory in two ways. First, we will introduce prices. To explain how price changes can absorb some of the impact of a change in planned expenditures, we will return to the aggregate demand and supply model introduced in Chapter 6. Second, we will show how changes in the conditions of production can affect national income, employment, and prices.

Aggregate Demand

In Chapter 6 aggregate demand was defined as the presumed negative relationship between the price level and the total quantity of goods and services consumers, businesses, and government want to buy during a given period of time. Aggregate demand is not the same as the market demand for a given product or service. Market demand is the relationship between the price of a given product and the quantity consumers are willing and able to buy. Aggregate demand is the relationship between the general price level (an index of the prices of all products and services) and the total quantity of all goods and services demanded.

Aggregate demand also differs from the total planned expenditure function we discussed in Chapters 10 to 12. That function is the relationship between the national income level and total planned expenditures. Aggregate demand is the relationship between the price level and the total amount of goods and services, or national output, that people want. Aggregate demand permits us to monitor the influence of the price level on total planned expenditures.

Usually aggregate demand is drawn as a downward-sloping curve, like the one shown in Figure 13.1. Its downward slope reflects the negative relationship between prices in general and total product demanded. As the price level goes down, from P_2 to P_1, total real national income and product demanded rises, from Y_1 to Y_2. All market demand curves slope downward, but that is not why the aggregate demand curve does so. Its shape is a result of the effects of a change in the price level on interest rates and on people's real wealth.

The Effect of a Change in Price Level on Interest Rates

Recall our discussion of interest rates in Chapter 12 (see pages 272–276). In Keynesian theory, the interaction of the demand for money and the

Figure 13.1. Aggregate Demand.
Aggregate demand (*AD*) is the assumed inverse relationship between the price level and the total output demanded during a given period of time. If the price level falls from P_2 to P_1, for example, the total quantity of goods and services demanded by consumers, investors, and government rises from Y_1 to Y_2.

stock of money determines the interest rate. If the demand for money and the money stock are represented as MD and MS_1 in Figure 13.2(a), the interest rate will be R_2. Planned investment demand will be I_1 (part (b)), and the national income level will be Y_1 (part (c)).

A decline in the price level amounts to an increase in the purchasing power of the money stock. Because the amount of money in existence will now cover more transactions, the real money stock has expanded. A reduction in the price level therefore has the same effect as an increase in the money stock, say from MS_1 to MS_2 in Figure 13.2(a). The interest rate will drop from R_2 to R_1, increasing planned investment spending from I_1 to I_2. The increase in planned investment will then be translated, through the multiplier process, into a much greater increase in the national income level, from Y_1 to Y_2.

We have just deduced an important principle: a reduction in the price level causes an increase in the national income level. Conversely, an increase in the price level will reduce the real money stock, increasing the interest rate and decreasing planned investment and national income. Thus we can say that price level P_1 in Figure 13.1 is associated with a national income level of Y_2, and price level P_2 with a lower national income level, Y_1. That is, the price and national income levels are inversely (negatively) related.

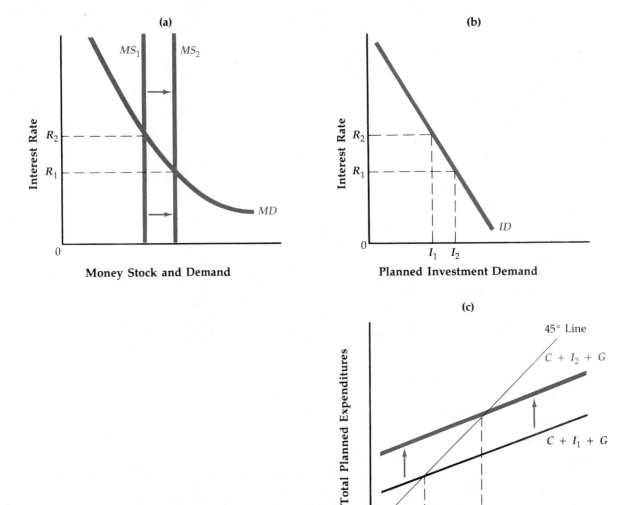

Figure 13.2. Effect of a Decrease in the Price Level on Interest Rates and Investment. When the price level falls, the real money stock curve (*MD*) shifts from MS_1 to MS_2, decreasing the interest rate from R_2 to R_1 (panel (a)). The drop in the interest rate increases planned investment spending (*ID*) from I_1 to I_2 (panel (b)). Through the multiplier process, the increase in planned investment spending from $C + I_1 + G$ to $C + I_2 + G$ will raise the national income level from Y_1 to Y_2 (panel (c)).

The Effect of a Change in Price Level on Real Wealth

A reduction in the price level can also make people who hold assets valued in dollars—bonds and bank accounts, for example—feel wealthier. With

Figure 13.3. Effect of a Decrease in the Price Level on Consumption.
When the price level falls, wealth valued in dollars rises, reducing the need for
saving and increasing total planned expenditures from $C_1 + I + G$ to $C_2 + I +$
G. The result is an increase in the national production and income level, from Y_1
to Y_2.

lower prices, people's dollar assets will purchase more goods and services.
As their real wealth increases, people may feel less need to save and more
freedom to spend their money. A reduction in the price level tends to
have a "wealth effect" on planned spending, as shown in Figure 13.3.
The total planned spending curve shifts up from $C_1 + I + G$ to $C_2 + I +$
G, and national income rises from Y_1 to Y_2. Here again we can deduce the
aggregate demand curve is downward sloping. As the price level goes
down, from P_2 to P_1 (Figure 13.1), the national income level goes up, from
Y_1 to Y_2. Conversely, an increase in the price level will make people feel
less wealthy, encouraging them to save more. The resulting drop in
consumption will shift the total planned spending curve down, reducing
the national income level.

The Size of the Effect of a Change in Price Level

While economists generally agree that the price and national income levels
are inversely related, the strength of the relationship remains in dispute.
Just how much of an increase in national income can be expected from a
decrease in the price level? In practice the size of any change in national
income is hard to predict. A reduction in the price level may have a

Figure 13.4. Size of the Effect of a Decrease in the Price Level.
A decrease in the price level from P_2 to P_1 may cause a large or a small increase in the total quantity of goods and services demanded and produced. If the aggregate demand curve looks like AD_1, the total quantity of goods and services demanded may rise from Y_1 to Y_3. But if the curve looks like AD_2, the quantity of goods and services demanded may rise only to Y_2. How much the quantity demanded will increase with any change in the price level depends on several factors, including how the interest rate responds to a change in the real money stock and how investment spending responds to a change in the interest rate.

substantial impact on national income, as in Figure 13.4. If aggregate demand is AD_1, a reduction in the price level from P_2 to P_1 will increase national income from Y_1 to Y_3. But much depends on the slope of the aggregate demand curve. If it is a much steeper slope—for instance, like AD_2 in Figure 13.4—the same reduction in price level will cause a much smaller increase in national income, from Y_1 to Y_2.

How much a given change in price level will change real national income depends on several factors, including:

how interest rates respond to a change in the real money stock

how investment expenditures respond to a change in interest rates

how consumption expenditures respond to a change in people's real wealth

how much the transactions demand for money changes with a change in the national income level.

The more interest rates respond to an increase in real wealth; the more investors respond to a drop in interest rates; and the more consumers

Figure 13.5. Effect of an Increase in the Transactions Demand for Money.
An increase in the real money stock from MS_1 to MS_2 (panel (a)) can decrease the
interest rate from R_3 toward R_1 and increase planned investment from I_1 toward
I_3. The resulting increase in national income, however, will increase the transactions
demand for money, shifting the total demand for money curve outward from MD_1
to MD_2. The shift in the demand for money curve (ID) will moderate the fall in
the interest rate, stopping it at R_2. As a result, the rise in investment spending
will stop short at I_2 (panel (b)), tempering the expansion in national income.

respond to a change in their real wealth, the greater will be the increase
in the real national income level. If interest rates do not fall very far when
the price level falls, and consumers do not increase their expenditures
very much when their real wealth increases, the aggregate demand curve
in Figure 13.4 may look more like AD_2 than AD_1. Although lower prices
increase the real wealth of consumers, they decrease the real wealth of
creditors, limiting the wealth effect of a drop in the price level. And a fall
in interest rates may be partially offset by an increase in the transactions
demand for money—the need to hold more money to finance the greater
quantity of goods and services produced and consumed.

Suppose, for example, that the price level falls and the real money stock
expands from MS_1 to MS_2, as in Figure 13.5 (part (a)). The interest rate,
R_3, will begin to fall toward R_1. The reduction in the interest rate will spur
investment spending (part (b)), increasing national income and with it
the transactions demand for money. The money demand curve will shift
outward from MD_1 to MD_2, reflecting this increase in the transactions
demand (from MD_{t1} to MD_{t2}). As a result, the interest rate falls only to R_2,
not R_3, and planned investment spending rises only to I_2 instead of I_3.
And of course the rise in the national income level is limited as well.

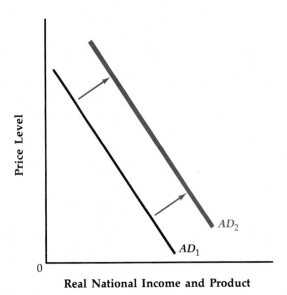

Figure 13.6. Change in Aggregate Demand.
An increase in aggregate demand, represented by an outward shift in the aggregate demand curve, can be caused by an expansionary fiscal or monetary policy. A contractionary fiscal or monetary policy will shift the aggregate demand curve inward.

While few economists dispute that the slope of the aggregate demand curve is negative, its exact slope is controversial. For the responsiveness of interest rates, investment, and consumption demand to a fall in the price level all influence the steepness of the curve. Most economists agree that the aggregate demand curve is flatter in the long run than in the short run. With more time, people are better able to respond to changes in the price level.

Changes in Aggregate Demand

The position of the aggregate demand curve in Figure 13.1 reflects a critical unstated assumption. We held constant all the economic factors that can affect the demand for goods and services—consumer and investment spending, fiscal and monetary policies. But if planned consumer and investment spending increase, they can shift the aggregate demand curve, say from AD_1 to AD_2 in Figure 13.6. An expansionary fiscal or monetary policy can have the same effect. Conversely, decreases in consumer and investment spending and contractionary fiscal and monetary policies will shift the aggregate demand curve inward.

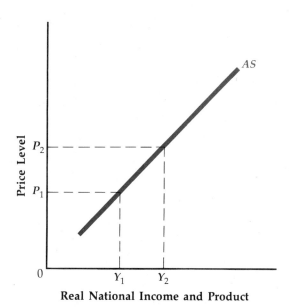

Figure 13.7. Short-Run Aggregate Supply.
Short-run aggregate supply is the assumed positive relationship between the price level and total production over a given period of time. If the price level rises from P_1 to P_2, total output rises from Y_1 to Y_2.

Economists disagree about the effectiveness of fiscal policy actions in shifting the aggregate demand curve. As we saw in Chapter 12, greater government spending may crowd out private investment and consumption, so that the net effect is a small shift in aggregate demand or none at all. Likewise the Federal Reserve's attempts to increase the money stock may be largely absorbed by increases in the public's money balances. Thus interest rates may not fall very much and investment spending may not rise very much in response to a calculated increase in the money stock.

Aggregate Supply

In Chapter 6 aggregate supply was defined as the presumed positive relationship between the general price level and the total quantity of goods and services that will be produced in the economy during a given period of time. Aggregate supply was shown graphically as an upward-sloping curve, like the one in Figure 13.7. If the price level rises from P_1 to P_2, the nation's output of goods and services rises from Y_1 to Y_2—and vice versa. To be more precise, we should say that the aggregate supply curve slopes upward in the short run. We will take up what happens in the long run later.

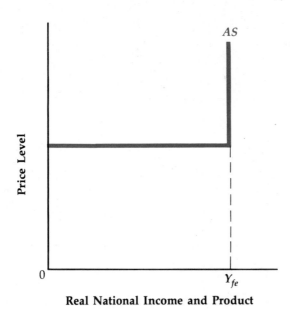

Figure 13.8. Early Keynesian Aggregate Supply Curve.
Early Keynesian theory assumed a constant price level up to the full-employment output level, Y_{fe}. As long as some workers remained unemployed, additional output could be achieved without raising prices. After full employment, any further increase in aggregate demand could be realized only at a higher price level.

Short-Run Aggregate Supply

Early Keynesians did not pay much attention to changes in the price level because they did not believe price increases were a major threat during times of severe recession. They thought the aggregate supply curve resembled the curve in Figure 13.8. Up to a full-employment national output level of Y_{fe}, no price increase was needed to induce greater production. At full employment, however, greater demand for output would be reflected in higher prices, as competitors bid up the price of the economy's limited labor resources.

Economists no longer think of the aggregate supply curve in this way. Modern aggregate supply theory assumes that output will increase only if people have some real or imagined incentive—like a price increase—to expand production. The short-run aggregate supply curve in Figure 13.7 illustrates this assumption.

In the short run, a phenomenon called money illusion provides the incentive needed to expand production. **Money illusion** is the mistaken belief that an increase in market price, stated in dollars, represents an increase in real price. When people find they can sell their labor or their products for a higher price, they initially believe they have received a real

Money illusion: the mistaken belief that an increase in market price, stated in dollars, represents an increase in real price.

increase in payment. Not recognizing that their wage increases are offset by an increase in the prices of the products they buy, workers may work harder and longer hours to take advantage of the apparent increase in real wages. Business owners may expand production. This burst of activity can raise national output, producing an upward-sloping aggregate supply curve like the one in Figure 13.7.

Some of these price increases may indeed be real. Many wage rates, for instance, are set by union contract and cannot be raised with the price level. In the short run, an employer may be able to raise the price of its finished product without having to pay more for labor. The employer will hire more workers, and production will go up. But such an arrangement will not be possible for all employers.

How much output will expand in response to an increase in the price level (how steep or flat the aggregate supply curve is) will depend on several factors:

the availability of unemployed resources

the ease with which unemployed resources can be put into use when prices rise

the extent of the money illusion

the extent to which labor contracts fix wages in current dollar terms

A short-run aggregate supply curve that reflects all these variables can have a slope that changes over the business cycle, as in Figure 13.9. During a recession or depression, the curve can be almost flat. Even a small increase in the price level will cause a significant expansion in national production. In normal times, when the economy is operating near full capacity, the slope is likely to be much steeper. A greater rise in prices will be needed to cover the high cost of drawing into the production process the last few unemployed (and possibly ill-suited) resources. Beyond full employment the aggregate supply curve will become practically vertical. When resources are, for all practical purposes, fully employed, little additional output can be produced, even if prices do rise.

When the recovery phase of the business cycle begins, expansion in output is likely to be relatively rapid and price increases modest. Such was the case with the recovery that began during the first term of the Reagan administration. In 1984 real GNP expanded at a rate of 6.8 percent, while the price level rose only 4 percent. Economists did not expect those favorable conditions to persist as the economy moved out of the recession.

Long-Run Aggregate Supply

The money illusion on which the short-run aggregate supply curve is founded will not persist indefinitely. With the passage of time, people come to realize that increases in their dollar wages are not necessarily real increases. They will cease to work extra hours to take advantage of those

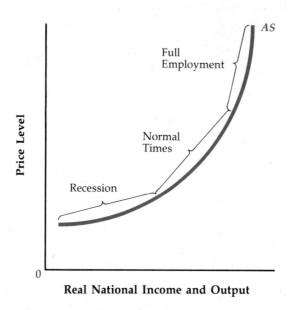

Figure 13.9. Short-Run Aggregate Supply in the Context of the Business Cycle. Producers' ability to respond to changing prices depends in part on the availability of unemployed resources. During a recession, when there is substantial unemployment of workers, plant, and equipment, a relatively small increase in the price level may bring a substantial rise in national output. During normal times, when the economy is operating near full employment, a much larger increase in the price level may be necessary to increase national production. When the economy is at or close to full employment, national production may respond very little to an increase in prices.

dollar increases. And as soon as they can, workers will adjust their labor contracts to reflect higher prices. In the process, the short-run aggregate supply curve—and the level of production—will shift backward.

It is not clear just how far back aggregate supply will shift. Many economists argue that the long-run aggregate supply curve is vertical— that an increase in the price level will not affect the long-run national output level. In Figure 13.10, suppose the price level rises from P_1 to P_2 because of an increase in aggregate demand following an expansion in the money stock. Production may expand for a while along the short-run aggregate supply curve AS_{sr1}, from Y_1 to Y_2. But people will eventually adjust to the change in the price level. At that point the aggregate supply curve will fall back toward AS_{sr4} and the original national output level of Y_1. The new price level will be P_3, however. So the long-term effect is the same as if the economy had moved straight up the vertical curve AS_{lr}. Prices have increased, but national output has not.

Figure 13.10. Long-Run Aggregate Supply Curve.
An increase in the price level from P_1 to P_2 may temporarily raise national output from Y_1 to Y_2. But in the long run, after people realize that their real wages have not risen, the supply of labor and other resources may contract, shifting the short-run aggregate supply curve upward from AS_{sr1} to AS_{sr4}. The end result may be a price level of P_3 and no long-run expansion in national production. In other words, the long-run aggregate supply curve (AS_{lr}) is vertical.

Changes in Aggregate Supply

The aggregate supply curve responds not only to price changes, but to anything that affects the availability of resources or people's incentive to work harder and produce more goods and services. For example, sudden cutbacks in oil production can cause energy shortages, crippling the production of a vast array of goods and services. Such "supply shocks" can shift the short-run aggregate supply curve backward, as in Figure 13.12, reducing national production from Y_3 to Y_1 and increasing the price level from P_1 to P_3.

The cutback in energy will not necessarily bring such a dramatic shift in the *long-run* aggregate supply curve, however. The higher price level, and the higher price of energy in particular, will encourage the discovery of alternative energy sources. The long-run aggregate supply curve may shift back only to AS_{lr2}, where the increase in price level (to P_2) and the decrease in national income (to Y_2) will be more moderate. We should not expect the national income level to return all the way to Y_3, however. New energy sources will probably be more costly to use, if only because resources will have been consumed just to make them available.

Perspectives in Economics: Econometrics

N. Keith Womer

The real economic world is highly complex. Every day millions of agents make billions of economic decisions. Goods are bought and sold, wages are paid, and investments are made in countless numbers. This daily market is so complicated that economists cannot study it directly. Instead, they must attempt to understand specific aspects of the market by developing and testing economic theories.

Economic theories are based on observations of the real world formalized into precisely stated assumptions. They are not conclusions, but tentative hypotheses whose predictive power must be tested scientifically.

Econometrics is the science of the statistical testing of economic theory and predictions. The *metric* in *econometrics* signifies measurement—the measurement of economic relationships. Using economic theory, relevant economic data, and statistical methods, econometricians construct and test econometric models. An **econometric model** is a statistical equation or set of equations that describes economic data.

The data econometricians use are sometimes collected directly, but are more often derived from data that have been collected for other purposes. From these data economic relationships must be carefully estimated through statistical analysis. Then the hypotheses about those relationships can be tested.

This approach can be used to reject or tentatively accept hypotheses. Rejected hypotheses form the basis for revisions of economic theory. Tentatively accepted hypotheses have not been proved. At best, they have been shown to be consistent with observed data. Much of the econometrician's work involves uneasy compromises among economic hypotheses, available data, and the requirements of statistical technique.

Consider the problem of estimating and testing the consumption function, for instance. Keynes stated, "The fundamental psychological law . . . is that men are disposed, as a rule and on the average, to increase their consumption as their income increases, but not by as much as the increase in income." The testable hypothesis derived from Keynes's theory is that the marginal propensity to consume (*MPC*) is positive but less than one.

Statistical technique requires that the relation between two variables be specified precisely. The relation between consumption and income is hypothesized to be linear. That is, if observations of consumption and income were plotted on a graph, the points would fall approximately on a straight line. If the consumption function is linear, the technique of linear regression can be used to estimate it. **Linear regression** is a statistical technique used to find the equation describing the straight line that comes closest to the plotted points of a curve.

Random samples of accurate data on individual consumption and income are difficult to obtain. Econometricians usually use yearly data on aggregate consumption and income together with population statistics to estimate per capita income and consumption. Then they often divide their data by a price index, to adjust for the effects of inflation. An aggregate consumption function derived from such constructed data is illustrated in Figure 13.11. Each point shows the level of consumption associated with a particular income level; the line shows the consumption function derived from the data. Mathematically, that line or function may be expressed as $C = 68.7 + 0.89\ Y$. C equals the consumption function. The estimated intercept (constant term) of the consumption function is $68.70, and 0.89 is the estimated marginal propensity to consume.

This estimate seems to support Keynes's theory. Our computed marginal propensity to consume, 0.89, is positive and less than one, just as he argued. Such a computation may have been generated by chance, however. To be confident that our computed *MPC* is a close approximation of the true *MPC*, we must run additional statistical tests.[1] If those tests yield the expected results, we can conclude with a high degree of confidence

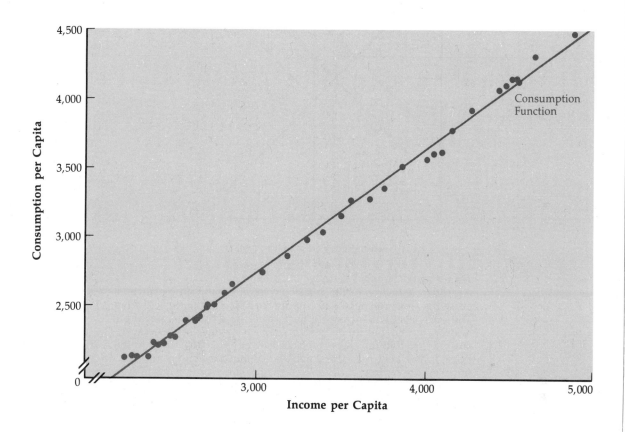

that the true *MPC* is not very different from our computed *MPC*. Though we have not *proved* Keynes's hypothesis, it has survived a challenge. If repeated tests yield the same findings, we will become even more confident that Keynes was correct.

1. To test the estimated marginal propensity to consume, an econometrician would first compare the errors around the consumption function (in the figure, the vertical distance between the data points and the straight line) with randomly selected data. If the errors appear to be random, then the econometrician will measure the precision of the estimate by computing a statistic called the standard deviation.

Figure 13.11. Estimated Consumption Function. The relation between consumption and income is linear. If data on consumption and income are plotted on a graph, the points will fall approximately on a straight line. Mathematically, the relation shown here may be expressed as $C = 68.7 + 0.89\ Y$.

Source: *Economic Report of the President* (Washington, D.C.: U.S. Government Printing Office, 1985), pp. 248 and 254.

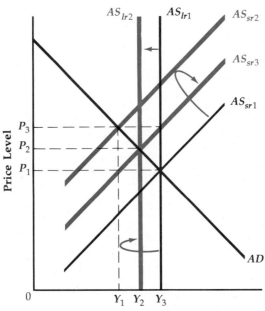

Figure 13.12. Supply Shock.
A sudden reduction in the availability of an important resource, such as oil, can cause the short-run aggregate supply curve to shift to the left, from AS_{sr1} to AS_{sr2}. The price level will increase from P_1 to P_3, and the national output level will fall from Y_3 to Y_1. Substitute resources may be developed because of the shock, however, so that the short-run aggregate supply curve shifts to the right again to AS_{sr3}. In the long run, then, national production may climb back to Y_2 and the price level may drop back to P_2. Thus the long-run aggregate supply curve does not shift as far to the left as the short-run curve.

The Equilibrium National Income and Price Levels

By putting the aggregate supply and aggregate demand curves in the same graph, as in Figure 13.13, we can see that in the short run the economy will gravitate toward the national income and price levels of Y_2 and P_1, respectively. At price levels above P_1—for example, P_2—the total quantity of goods and services producers want to offer (Y_3) will exceed the total quantity of goods and services consumers, businesses, and governments want to buy (Y_1). The price level will fall back toward P_1 as firms compete to get rid of their unwanted inventory. The price decline will stimulate spending by increasing the real money stock. Interest rates will fall, the level of planned investment will increase, and planned consumption expenditures will rise. Total planned expenditures will climb from Y_1 to Y_2. At the same time, recognizing that the rewards of their labor have shrunk, people will cut back on production. National output and income will drop from Y_3 to Y_2.

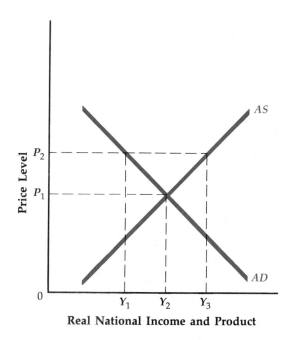

Figure 13.13. Short-Run Equilibrium in Real National Income and Prices.
Given these aggregate supply and aggregate demand curves, the macroeconomy
will move toward a price level of P_1 and a national production level of Y_2. At a
price level above P_1—for example, P_2—the total quantity of goods and services
produced will exceed the total quantity of goods and services demanded. The
price level will fall. As it falls, more goods and services will be demanded, while
fewer will be produced.

Similarly, at price levels below P_1, the total planned expenditures of
consumers, businesses, and government will exceed the total quantity of
goods and services produced. The prices of goods and services will be bid
up, reducing the real money stock and hence people's real wealth. Interest
rates will rise, reducing planned investment expenditures. Consumption
expenditures will fall as people attempt to rebuild their real wealth by
saving. And because of fixed wages and money illusion, production will
rise as producers and workers try to exploit the price increase.

The Real Effect of Expansionary Fiscal and Monetary Policies

What does the combined aggregate supply and demand model suggest
about the likely effect of Keynesian fiscal and monetary policies to increase
total planned expenditures? If government reduces taxes, increases its
expenditures, or expands the money stock—all steps that should cause
total planned spending to rise—the aggregate demand curve will shift

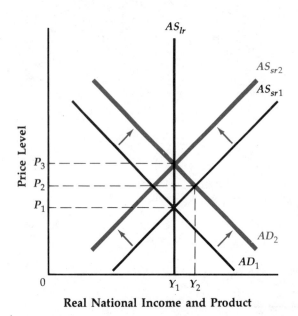

Figure 13.14. The Effect of an Expansionary Fiscal or Monetary Policy on Real National Income and Prices.
Expansionary fiscal and monetary policy can shift the aggregate demand curve upward, from AD_1 to AD_2. In the short run the shift in aggregate demand will cause an expansion in national production, from Y_1 to Y_2, and an increase in the price level, from P_1 to P_2. But in the long run the aggregate supply curve will shift up from AS_{sr1} to AS_{sr2}. Long-run equilibrium will be achieved at an even higher price level, P_3, and national production will return to its original level, Y_1.

outward. The result of the shift is shown in Figure 13.14. The national income level expands from Y_1 to Y_2. And the price level increases from P_1 to P_2.

In the long run, however, the aggregate supply curve will shift inward to AS_{sr2} as people adjust their work efforts to the price increase. If the long-run aggregate supply curve is vertical, the end result will be a return to the original equilibrium national income level of Y_1, but at a higher price level: P_3 instead of P_1. In fact, over a period of months or years, expansionary fiscal and monetary policies can produce a business cycle of their own. First a recovery period of expansion in production and employment is stimulated by monetary or fiscal policy. Then the resulting drop in short-run aggregate supply causes a new contraction in production and employment.[1]

1. In addition, over the long run the aggregate demand curve can shift back toward AD_1, reflecting the reduced investment demand caused by the increase in government spending. The effect of such a reduction in investment spending will be a price level lower than P_3.

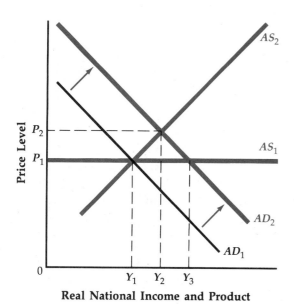

Figure 13.15 The Multiplier Effect on Real National Income and Prices.
With no change in price level—that is, with a horizontal aggregate supply curve
like AS_1—an increase in aggregate demand from AD_1 to AD_2 will cause national
production to rise from Y_1 to Y_3. But if prices rise with aggregate demand—that
is, if the aggregate supply curve slopes upward, as AS_2 does—the same increase
in aggregate demand will raise national production only to Y_2. The increase in the
price level absorbs part of the impact of the expansion of aggregate demand and
reduces the size of the multiplier.

The Real Size of the Multiplier

The Keynesian economic models used in Chapters 11 to 13 assumed that
prices would remain constant. Under that assumption, we can expect a
change in total planned expenditures to be fully reflected, through the
multiplier process, in a change in national income and production. In that
case, however, the aggregate supply curve would have to be horizontal,
like curve AS_1 in Figure 13.15. Given such a supply curve, an increase in
aggregate demand from AD_1 to AD_2 would cause national income and
production to rise from Y_1 to Y_3. But if prices must adjust upward to create
an incentive for increased production and income, as modern theorists
believe, then the aggregate supply curve will look like AS_2. In that case
the shift in aggregate demand from AD_1 to AD_2 will yield a smaller increase
in national income and production, from Y_1 to Y_2.

   If prices rise, then, the multiplier effect will be weaker, for the increase
in the price level will absorb part of the stimulus to demand. The higher
price level will reduce the real money stock, causing interest rates to rise
and planned investment spending to fall. And by reducing consumers'
real wealth, it will reduce consumption demand. In short, if prices adjust

to changes in demand, expansionary fiscal and monetary policies will not be as effective in relieving production and employment problems as early Keynesian theory would suggest. (Conversely, decreases in total planned expenditures will not depress the economy as much as early Keynesian theory would imply.)

Summary and Extensions

The aggregate demand and supply model offers a more realistic picture of the economy than the traditional Keynesian model because it includes the effect of price changes on the supply of goods as well as on the quantity demanded. Changes in the price level can lower the value of the multiplier, though the effect may not be dramatic. If the aggregate demand curve has a steep slope, the effect of price changes on total planned spending may be modest.

Changes in aggregate supply may also have a limited effect. The short-run aggregate supply curve slopes upward only to the extent that people mistake a nominal increase in the price of their labor or products for a real one. Money illusion can wear off fast, for workers and producers soon learn that an increase in the overall price level will raise the prices of things they buy as well as the prices of things they sell. They will adjust their contracts accordingly. The long-run aggregate supply curve, then, is likely to be steeper than the short-run aggregate supply curve. It may be practically vertical, so that output ultimately changes very little with changes in total planned spending.

Major Conclusions

1. The aggregate demand curve slopes downward because of the way prices affect interest rates and consumption. When the price level falls, the real money stock rises and the interest rate falls, increasing investment demand. Consumers' real wealth also increases, fueling consumer demand.
2. The slope of the aggregate demand curve depends on the extent to which a drop in the price level reduces the interest rate and increases planned investment spending, planned consumption, and the transactions demand for money.
3. Expansionary fiscal and monetary policies will shift the aggregate demand curve outward. Contractionary fiscal and monetary policies will shift the curve inward.
4. The short-run aggregate supply curve slopes upward partly because of money illusion and partly because resource owners cannot raise prices immediately when the general price level increases.

5. The long-run aggregate supply curve is steeper than the short-run aggregate supply curve. It may actually be vertical. Over time, people learn that a rise in the dollar price of resources does not necessarily represent a real increase in price. They adjust resource prices upward to match the increase in the price level.

6. Changes in tax rates can affect aggregate supply as well as aggregate demand, for they affect people's incentives to work, save, and invest. If both curves shift, the price level may go up or down, depending on the relative size of the shifts.

7. The equilibrium national income level is established by the intersection of the aggregate supply and demand curves. The price level adjusts upward or downward to bring supply and demand into balance.

8. A shift in the aggregate demand curve has a greater effect on national income in the short run than in the long run. Expansionary fiscal and monetary policies therefore have a greater impact in the short run than in the long run.

9. Changes in the price level will moderate the multiplier effect of a shift in total planned spending.

Questions to Ponder

1. Explain the difference between the market demand curve and the aggregate demand curve.

2. Explain the difference between the total planned spending function and the aggregate demand curve.

3. In each of the following cases, explain what will happen to the price and national income levels:
   a. Aggregate demand increases.
   b. Aggregate supply decreases.
   c. The expected profitability of investment rises.
   d. The money stock expands.
   e. Tax rates rise.

4. Why will an increase in aggregate demand have a greater effect on national income in the short run than in the long run?

5. Suppose a major new energy source is discovered. What will happen to the national income and price levels in the long run?

6. Explain how the size of the multiplier is affected by an adjustment in the price level.

7. How does the responsiveness of planned investment to a change in the interest rate affect the slope of the aggregate demand curve?

8. What can government do to shift the long-run aggregate supply curve outward?

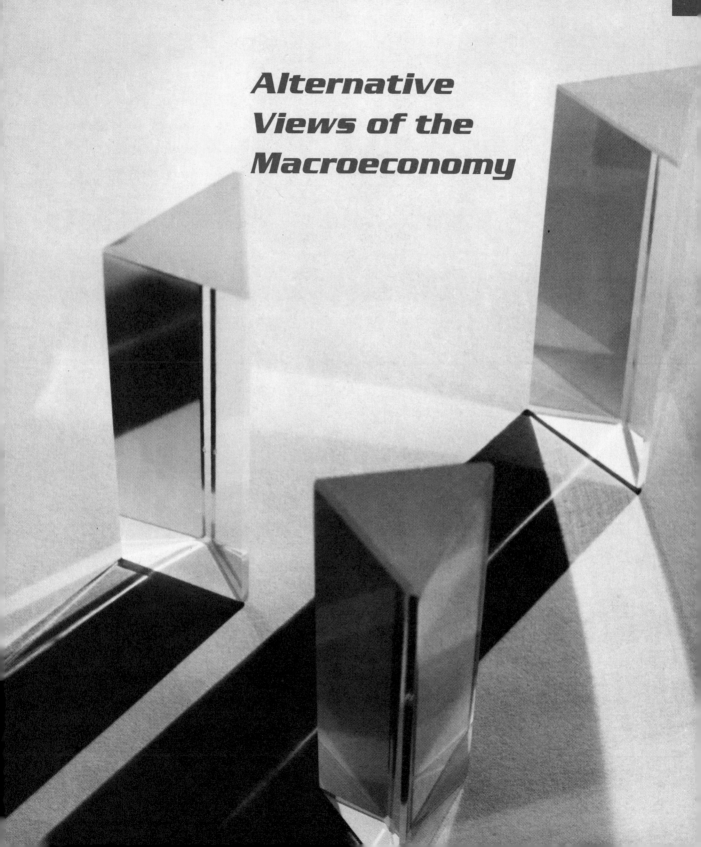

Part V

Alternative Views of the Macroeconomy

Central Question

*From the perspective
of the monetarists,
what are the causes
of unemployment and
inflation, and how
can they be remedied?*

Chapter 14

The Monetarist View of Unemployment and Inflation

My position regarding the cause of inflation and high market interest rates is that they both stem from the same source—an excessive trend rate of expansion of the nation's money stock. Monetary policy, therefore, can contribute to solving both of these problems over a period of a few years by fostering a noninflationary rate of growth of the money supply.
Darryl Francis

*W*e have stressed that Keynesian theory is controversial. Many of the objections to Keynesian theory come from economists of the monetarist school. This chapter will examine the monetarist interpretation of the macroeconomy, which is based largely on changes in the money stock.

Some caution is advisable in classifying economic thought as monetarist or Keynesian (or supply-side or rational expectations). Economists from different schools agree with each other on some points, which we will note when pertinent. And economists from the same school of thought often disagree. Keynesians have disputed the fine points of macroeconomic theory and policy among themselves, though they generally agree that macroeconomic problems can best be analyzed by focusing on total planned expenditures. Similarly monetarists do not always agree on particulars, though most agree that changes in the money stock explain many of our macroeconomic problems. This chapter outlines the broad theoretical framework that incorporates most monetarist thought.

The Rise of Monetarism

Keynes developed his *General Theory* during the Great Depression, when the industrialized nations of the West faced rapidly falling prices and high unemployment. Government spending then seemed a good tonic for an ailing economy, and Keynes's theories were widely adopted by legislators and government administrators. Over the past three decades, however, the United States has faced some problems for which Keynesian prescriptions are less suitable. We have had to contend with high and rising rates of inflation, accompanied by high rates of unemployment and growing federal expenditures. Events have apparently disproved the theory, accepted by many Keynesians, that unemployment and inflation are inversely related, and many economists, frustrated by the disparity between theory and reality, have begun to search for a better model of the macroeconomy.

To date, the most significant alternative to the Keynesian macroeconomic model is the monetarist model. The monetarists hold that the root cause of most cyclical swings in unemployment and inflation is abrupt changes in the rate of growth of the money stock. Without attention to the size of the money stock, they argue, fiscal policy will have only limited influence, if any, on the short-term problems of unemployment and inflation. Steady control of the monetary throttle will solve most problems of inflation, high interest rates, and cyclical unemployment.

The Monetarist View of Unemployment

In developing their theory of the macroeconomy, the monetarists (like Keynesians and others) have borrowed heavily from microeconomic theory. They begin with the basic classical propositions about the market. Long-term unemployment is seen as a consequence of obstacles in the labor market, which prevent real wage rates from falling enough to bring the number of workers demanded in line with the number of people willing

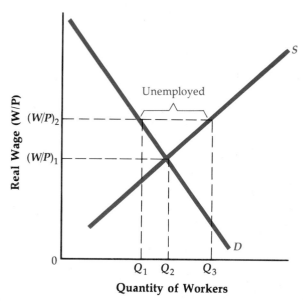

Figure 14.1. The Influence of the Price Level on Unemployment.
Assuming that the demand for labor slopes downward, the supply of labor slopes upward, and the real wage rate is fixed at $(W/P)_2$, $Q_3 - Q_1$ workers will be unemployed. As long as the money wage rate and the price level remain constant, unemployment will not fall.

to work. Minimum wage laws, union contracts, and restrictions on labor mobility (such as lack of information) all impede the achievement of an equilibrium wage level and full employment. Full employment may be promoted by wage concessions. Recently unions have been experimenting with this approach in declining industries like steel manufacture.

Consider Figure 14.1. There, as in classical theory, the demand for labor is inversely related to the real wage rate (the money wage rate divided by the price index), while the supply of labor is directly related to the real wage rate. If the real wage rate is prevented from falling below $(W/P)_2$, Q_3 workers will want to work, but only Q_1 workers will be hired. The difference between Q_3 and Q_1 is the number of people unemployed. According to monetarist theory, if the money wage rate and the price level remain constant or increase at the same rate, the real wage will not change and $Q_3 - Q_1$ unemployment will persist. If the price level rises while the money wage rate stays the same, the real wage rate will fall, reducing or eliminating unemployment.

The Phillips Curve

The relationship between unemployment and changes in the price level can be seen more clearly in Figure 14.2, which reproduces the Phillips curve from Chapter 6. The unemployment rate, shown on the horizontal

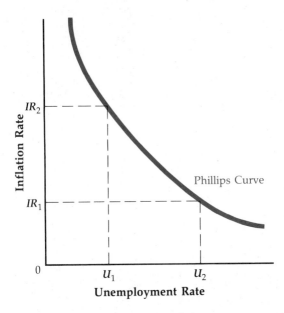

Figure 14.2. The Phillips Curve.
Keynesian economists have argued that the unemployment and inflation rates are inversely related. Thus an unemployment rate lower than U_2 can be achieved only at the cost of an inflation rate higher than IR_1. An unemployment rate of U_1, for example, could be obtained only at an inflation rate of IR_2.

axis, is obtained by dividing the number of unemployed workers by the total number of workers. Changes in the price level are indicated by the inflation rate, shown on the vertical axis. The graph shows that an inflation rate of IR_1 is consistent with an unemployment rate of U_2. To achieve a lower unemployment rate, U_1, the inflation rate must rise to IR_2. Early Keynesians argued that fiscal policy should be directed toward achieving some desired combination of unemployment and inflation rates as shown on the Phillips curve.

Monetarists have contended that the tradeoff between inflation and unemployment generally lasts only for the short run, however. When the inflation rate first accelerates, employers realize that prices are rising faster than wages. As the real wage falls, employers move down their labor demand curve, hiring more workers, and unemployment declines. But eventually workers become aware of the higher price level and see that their real wage rate has fallen. Unions will then bargain for higher wage increases. In competitive labor markets, where the demand for labor will rise because of the rising prices of final products, wages will be bid up. In the end, the economy will return to its original real wage and unemployment rates—but at a higher rate of inflation.

Figure 14.3 shows the sequence of events graphically. In the short run, higher inflation moves the economy up the Phillips curve to the lower unemployment rate of U_1. But as workers' expectations concerning prices

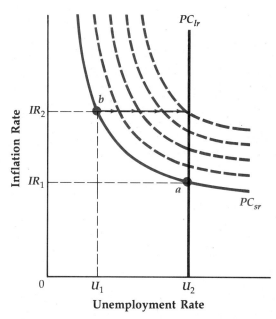

Figure 14.3. Short-Run and Long-Run Phillips Curves.
The rate of unemployment can be temporarily reduced by an unexpected increase in the price level. The economy will move up its short-run Phillips curve (PC_{sr}), from point a to point b. In the long run, however, money wages will catch up with the higher prices, and the short-run Phillips curve will shift outward. Unemployment will climb back to U_2, but at a higher rate of inflation. In the long run, the Phillips curve is vertical (PC_{lr}).

change, the Phillips curve will shift out to the right. While the inflation rate remains at IR_2, the unemployment rate will gradually rise back to U_2. In the long run, then, the Phillips curve is vertical. There is no tradeoff between unemployment and inflation. (This point is now accepted by many Keynesians.) If the unemployment rate is to remain below U_2, prices will have to be increased at progressively higher rates, forcing workers to play catch-up in their wage demands. Even then, though, workers may begin to anticipate the price spiral, and demand bigger and bigger wage increases as a matter of course.

A reduction in the rate of inflation will have the opposite effect. An unexpected slowing of the rise in prices will cause the real wage to rise. The gap between the number of workers wanting jobs and the number hired will widen (Figure 14.1). The economy will move down its short-term Phillips curve (Figure 14.3), from point b to point a, and unemployment will rise to U_2. In the long run, however, the increase in the number of unemployed will intensify competition for jobs, slowing the rate of increase in money wages. The real wage will fall back toward its original level, and employers will demand more workers. The short-term Phillips curve will shift inward, and the unemployment rate will move back toward U_1—but at a *lower* rate of inflation.

The crux of the monetarist position on unemployment is that there is no long-term tradeoff between unemployment and inflation. A higher rate of inflation may reduce unemployment temporarily. But in the long run the economy will return to its natural rate of unemployment. The natural rate of unemployment is the percentage of the labor force that is unemployed in the long run because of structural problems in the economy and frictional restrictions on employment. The way to reduce the natural rate of unemployment is to eliminate obstacles to wage adjustments and speed up the movement of the unemployed to expanding labor markets. It is *not*, as the Keynesians would claim, to increase total spending or expand the money stock.

The Historical Evidence

The past few decades have supplied considerable evidence in support of the monetarists' claim that the tradeoff between unemployment and inflation is only temporary. Figure 14.4 shows U.S. inflation and unemployment rates from 1953 to 1984. Instead of a neatly downward-sloping Phillips curve, the pattern looks more like a contrail left by a stunt plane. The unemployment rate moved up and down, averaging 5.6 percent per year. The inflation rate, until late in the period, moved higher and higher.

Monetarists argue that the relatively high unemployment rates of the last few decades resulted from obstacles to the adjustment of wages and to the movement of labor from one industry to another. They attribute short-term decreases in the unemployment rate to unexpected increases in the rate of inflation. And they believe the gradual increase in the unemployment rate seen in recent decades results from the growth in benefits to the unemployed and in government regulations that increase frictional and structural unemployment.

The Monetarist View of Inflation

The monetarists maintain that temporary changes in the level of inflation and unemployment (and resulting changes in national income) are linked directly to the rate of growth of the money stock. Their position can be summarized mathematically by referring to the equation of exchange developed in Chapter 8.

$$MV = PQ = Y$$

where M = the money supply, V = the velocity (or turnover rate) of money, P = an index of the price level, Q = quantity of goods and services, and Y = the national income level. This link between the growth rate of the money stock and the inflation rate is rooted in the individual's demand for and supply of money.

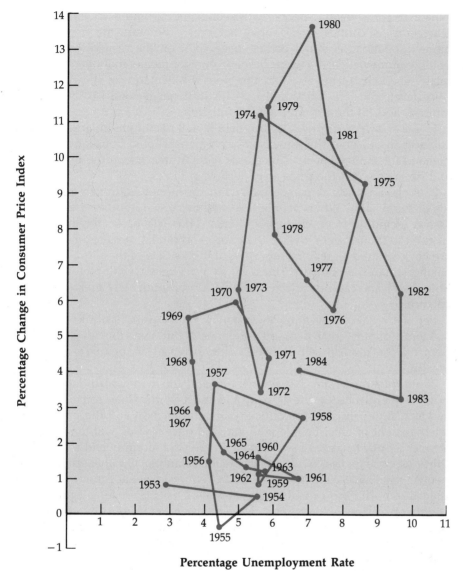

Figure 14.4. Inflation and Unemployment in the United States, 1953–1984. Between 1953 and 1984, the unemployment rate fluctuated between 3 and 9.5 percent, while inflation varied annually between practically zero and 14 percent. If a downward-sloping Phillips curve exists, it lasts only a few years. It appears to have shifted up and down over time.

The Demand for Money

To monetarists and many other economists, money is just one among many assets, such as goods and securities, that people hold for the services they provide. Television sets give people viewing pleasure. Securities yield income. Money enables people to carry out their day-to-day transactions.

Whatever their wealth, people will seek some optimum combination of real goods, securities, and money balances. Therefore the demand for money depends, as noted earlier (page 150), on the relative benefits of holding money and other assets. The five major factors that determine the relative benefits of money, and therefore the demand for it, are: (1) the price level, (2) personal wealth, (3) institutional factors, (4) the rate of interest, and (5) the expected rate of inflation.

1. *The price level.* If prices go up, people will need to hold larger money balances to carry out the same number of transactions. Consequently, the demand for money balances increases with an increase in the price level, and declines when the price level declines.

2. *Personal wealth.* A person's demand for money is directly related to his or her wealth. When people hold money, they forgo the use of other assets, including food, clothes, and cars. Thus it is easier for the rich to hold on to money than it is for the poor. And by the same token, the rich are likely to hold a greater proportion of their assets in the form of money balances than the poor do. Similarly, as a person's wealth increases over time, he or she can be expected to hold a proportionately greater money balance.

Because a nation's wealth grows slowly, total wealth has little short-run influence on the total demand for money. But over the long run, the demand for money will increase with increases in people's collective wealth.

3. *Institutional factors.* A person's demand for money also depends on how frequently he or she is paid and must in turn pay for goods and services. It depends on the difficulty of getting credit and the penalty for late payment of bills. People who are paid once a week will tend to hold smaller money balances than those who are paid monthly and must cover thirty days' expenses with their money balances. On the other hand, people who have easy access to credit require a smaller money balance than those who are considered to be credit risks. People categorized as creditworthy can borrow money to see themselves through any unforeseen financial emergencies. Because salary and bill payment patterns do not change very much or very rapidly, institutional factors have a steadying influence on the demand for money.

4. *The rate of interest.* Money that is held in checking accounts frequently does not earn interest. The forgone interest is the opportunity cost of holding money balances in the form of cash and demand deposits. As the interest rate rises, so does the opportunity cost of holding money. Thus people can be expected to vary their demand for money with changes in the interest rate. When the rate goes up, they will substitute bonds for money balances—theoretically, at least. Empirical studies suggest that interest rates have only a very slight effect on the demand for money.

5. *The expected rate of inflation.* If the rate of inflation increases and people expect it to continue to increase, the cost of holding money balances will go up. Because people will expect to pay more for goods and services in the future, they will prefer to use their wealth to buy goods and services at current prices. Their demand for money will decline.

The Effect of Changes in the Stock of Money

If the Federal Reserve increases the money stock, what will happen to prices as a result? People as a group will have more money than they need in relation to the price level, their wealth, institutional payment patterns, interest rates, and the expected rate of inflation. They will use their excess money to buy bonds or goods and services. An increased demand for bonds will cause a drop in the market interest rate, thereby increasing planned investment. And an increased demand for goods and services should cause an increase in the price level, as businesses and consumers bid against each other for the limited supply. This increase in the price level will lead in turn to greater employment and a higher national income level. Eventually, however, competition for labor will push wages up, which will return real wage rates to their normal levels and readjust the unemployment rate to its natural level—but at a higher price level.

In the real world the price level is generally on the rise, because the money stock is constantly growing. It must grow, if only because the labor force and production grow constantly. Only if the Federal Reserve increases the *rate* of growth of the money stock will the rate of inflation increase. The monetarists argue that if the rate of inflation rises continually, it will eventually exceed the rate of growth of the money stock. A 6 percent growth rate in the money stock might produce an inflation rate of 7 or 8 percent, for example.

The explanation of this phenomenon is reasonably straightforward. As the rate of inflation increases, the value of money held in currency or bank accounts falls at progressively faster rates. The cost of holding on to money rises. Consequently, people will hold fewer dollars in their bank accounts. Instead, they will buy more goods whose value has the potential to increase over time, such as real estate. As people increase their purchases, dollars will turn over faster (at a higher velocity). The price level will rise not only because more dollars are being used, but because the dollars in existence are being used more frequently. In terms of the equation of exchange ($MV = PQ$), both M and V will rise, forcing an equal rise in either P or Q or in the two together.

If the money stock *contracts* and people suddenly have fewer dollars to hold, depositors may find they have fewer dollars in their money balances than they want. To build up their money balances, some will convert (sell) a portion of their financial assets, such as bonds. Others will refrain from buying cars, furniture, and other consumer goods. With fewer dollars chasing after goods and services, manufacturers will have to lower their prices to sell their products. In this way a decrease in the money stock leads to a lower price level.

When the rate of growth in the money stock declines, fewer dollars will come onto the market. Upward pressure on prices will be diminished, and the rate of inflation will fall. Once the rise of prices has slowed, people's expectations about future inflation will adjust downward. The cost of holding money will drop, and people will again be able to justify keeping a larger portion of their assets in money balances. The velocity of money will fall, causing an equal fall in the PQ side of the equation of exchange.

In the monetarists' model, then, the short-run velocity of money is directly related to the rate of inflation. As the rate of inflation rises, so does the velocity of money, and vice versa. This stable relationship comes about because the rate of inflation determines how much money it is rational to hold.

From Monetary Growth to Unemployment

We are now ready to consider the sequence of events that follows an increase in the money stock, from the monetarists' perspective. The Federal Reserve begins the process, perhaps by buying government securities on the open market. Though more money has been put into circulation, people's need for money is relatively stable. Rather than holding the extra money that comes their way, they will use it to buy more real goods and securities, including bonds. The increased demand for bonds will lower interest rates, raising planned investment.

Together with increased consumer spending, the increase in investment will mean greater aggregate demand for goods and services—and higher prices. In terms of Figure 14.5, the aggregate demand curve shifts up from AD_1 to AD_2, and the price level begins to rise from its initial equilibrium level, P_1, toward P_2. As we saw in Figure 14.1, higher prices will temporarily reduce the real wages paid to labor. This short-run sequence of events thus reduces short-run unemployment and increases national production. The national income level moves up, from Y_1 to Y_2 in Figure 14.5.

In the long run, however, workers will demand higher wages in compensation for their higher cost of living. The real wage rate will return to its previous level, reducing employers' demand for labor and increasing unemployment. These adjustments in labor supply will be reflected by an inward shift in the short-run aggregate supply curve, from AS_{sr1} to AS_{sr2}. The price level will rise even further, to P_3, and the national income level will fall back to Y_1. Together these changes will reestablish equilibrium at the original output, but at a higher price level. The long-run aggregate supply curve, like the long-run Phillips curve, is vertical.

The sequence of events that follows a decrease in the money stock is exactly the opposite. Starting at the initial equilibrium point of P_3 and Y_1, the aggregate demand curve will shift down from AD_2 to AD_1. As price and output levels begin to fall, unemployment will temporarily increase. (When the real wage rises, employers demand fewer workers.) In the long run, however, higher unemployment will produce greater competition for jobs, lower money wages, and a drop in the real wage rate. Unemployment will return to its natural rate, and the aggregate supply curve will shift out, from AS_2 to AS_1. When national production returns to its initial level, Y_1, the price level will be lower.

This analysis can also be described in terms of change in the growth rate of the money stock. Assume an established rate of growth in the

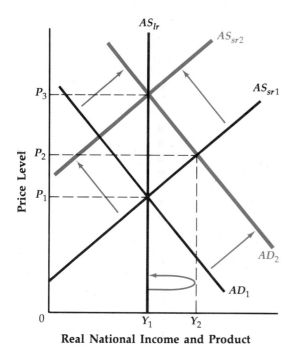

Figure 14.5. The Impact of an Increase in the Money Stock on Aggregate Supply and Demand.
An increase in the money stock will shift the aggregate demand curve up from AD_1 to AD_2, temporarily increasing the national income and price levels. When money wages adjust to the higher living cost, however, the aggregate supply curve will shift down from AS_{sr1} to AS_{sr2}. In the long run the national income level will return to Y_1, but at a higher price level, P_3. The opposite sequence of events will occur if the money stock declines.

money stock, which has produced an established rate of inflation to which workers have adjusted their wage demands. An increase in the growth rate of money will increase both demand and prices. Prices will rise faster than wages, the real wage will decrease, and employment and production will go up—temporarily, until workers can raise the rate of their wage increases. The process ends with a higher inflation rate, but a growth rate in national production that depends, in the long run, on the growth in technology and the availability of resources.

A decrease in the rate of growth in the money stock can cause money wages to rise faster than prices, at least temporarily. Unemployment will rise at first, but after long-run adjustments in the growth rate of money wages, it will return to its original level. For this reason the monetarists argue that the inflation rate can be lowered by reducing the rate of growth of the money stock—if people can endure a temporary increase in unemployment, lasting perhaps four years or more. Once the economy has reached its new equilibrium level, a steady rate of growth in the money stock of around 4 percent will moderate (but not eliminate) the

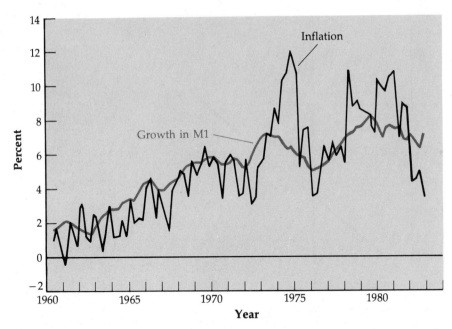

Figure 14.6. Inflation and the Rate of Growth of the Money Stock, 1960–1982.
The M1 growth line represents a twelve-quarter moving average of M1 growth.
The inflation line represents a quarter-to-quarter rate of change in the GNP deflator.
The vertical line between the third and fourth quarters of 1979 indicates a change
in the Federal Reserve operating procedures. In the short run the rate of inflation
has diverged from the rate of growth in the money stock. But over the long term,
swings in the rate of inflation have tended to follow swings in the rate of growth
in the money stock.
Source: Federal Reserve Bank of St. Louis *Review*, 65, May 1983, p. 11.

ups and downs of the business cycle. Steady growth of the money stock
should also steady the inflation and unemployment rates. In the monetarists' view, the unpredictable fluctuations in the growth rate of the
money stock are the primary cause of fluctuations in the unemployment
rate.

The Historical Evidence

To support their theory, the monetarists cite statistical studies of the
relationship between growth in the money stock and the rate of inflation.
One such study concluded that every major economic downturn in U.S.
history resulted from a contraction of the money stock. Likewise, every
period of rapid price increases has been accompanied by an equally rapid
increase in the size of the money stock.[1]

---

1. Milton Friedman and Anna J. Schwartz, *A Monetary History of the United States,
   1867–1960* (Princeton, N.J.: Princeton University Press, 1963).

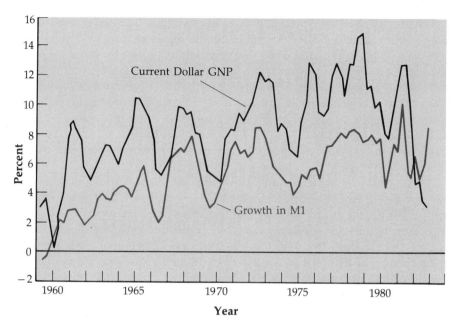

Figure 14.7. Growth Rates of the Gross National Product and the Money Stock, 1960–1982.

Each line represents a four-quarter growth rate. The vertical line between the third and fourth quarters of 1979 indicates a change in Federal Reserve operating procedures. Over the long run, the growth paths of the money stock and current dollar GNP have tended to move together. Short-run discrepancies have occurred, however.

Source: Federal Reserve Bank of St. Louis *Review*, 65, May 1983, p. 10.

Figures 14.6 and 14.7 plot the recent rate of growth of the money stock (M1) against the inflation rate and the rate of growth in current dollar gross national product. While the growth path of the money stock does not exactly match the patterns for inflation and GNP, swings in the growth of the money stock appear to be reflected in shifts in the inflation and GNP growth rates. Deviations among the three patterns can be attributed to time lags between growth in the money stock and its effects; to supply shocks such as OPEC's oil embargo of 1973 (see Figure 14.6); and to largely random changes in the velocity of money (see Figure 8.4 in Chapter 8).

The Monetarist View of High Interest Rates

According to early Keynesian theory, an increase in the rate of growth of the money stock will reduce interest rates. As the money stock grows, more funds become available for loans, lessening competition among borrowers. Monetarists agree, but argue that the decrease in rates will be temporary. In the long run, greater growth in the money stock will bring higher interest rates. (Many Keynesians also now accept this point.)

The monetarists' argument goes as follows. When the interest rate drops, many lenders will refuse to make loans, because the rate does not compensate them for the higher rate of inflation caused by the increase in the money stock. For example, if a lender can receive only 5 percent, but the inflation rate exceeds 6 percent, the money the borrower pays back will have less real purchasing power than the money that was loaned. But if the lender invests in real assets (like land) whose nominal value is rising at a rate of 7 percent, he can make a small profit. Unless interest rates rise, lenders will withhold their funds from the loan market and invest them in assets whose real value will not diminish.

Because of the higher rate of inflation, then, the supply of lendable funds will fall. At the same time households, businesses, and governments will speed up their purchases of goods and services, to avoid future price increases. Consumers will buy cars and appliances now, to avoid paying higher prices when the new models come out. Businesses will increase their current investment in plant and equipment. And governments will build schools and roads now to avoid higher construction costs in the future. To accomplish these goals, individuals, businesses, and governments will want to borrow more money.

This demand will increase at a time when lendable funds are in short supply because lenders are unwilling to make loans at the prevailing low interest rates. As a result market interest rates will increase. Together, faster growth in the money stock and a higher inflation rate should push rates up higher than they were initially. But the higher rates do not necessarily discourage investment—a point generally accepted in all schools of macroeconomic thought. Firms may pay higher interest rates for the money they borrow, but part of their interest payment is returned to them in price increases on the goods they sell. During a period of double-digit inflation, for example, a business may have to pay interest of 15 percent or more on the money it borrows to buy its raw materials. It can justify paying such a high rate because it knows that the price of the final goods it produces will rise over time, enabling it to meet the interest payments.

In short, the nominal, or market, rate of interest includes both the real rate of interest, which reflects the rate of return on capital goods, and the rate of inflation.

market interest rate = real interest rate + expected inflation rate

The way to reduce market interest rates, monetarists and others contend, is to reduce the rate of inflation. That means to control the growth of the money stock. As always, control of the money stock is a predominant issue in the monetarists' interpretation of macroeconomic problems.

The Monetarist View of Deficits

Monetarists have long argued that government fiscal policy is important because it determines the extent to which the nation's resources will be used for public rather than private purposes. That is, government expenditures impinge on the nation's limited resources, crowding individuals and firms out of the market. Monetarists attach little importance to the multiplier effect of government spending. In fact, many monetarists contend that an increase in government spending will have little if any effect on the nation's short-run income. For greater government spending necessarily means less spending by private firms and individuals. Increased government spending, in other words, does not translate into a significant and enduring increase in aggregate demand (unless it is accompanied by an increase in the money stock). Nor does it matter how the additional government expenditures are financed. If taxes are raised, consumption and business investment will fall, more or less offsetting the increase in government spending. If a deficit is incurred and the money stock is held constant, consumption and investment will still be reduced, because the government will absorb funds that would have been borrowed by consumers and businesses.

The monetarists' position on deficits can be expressed in terms of the equation of exchange, $MV = PQ = Y$. If deficit spending raises the national income level (Y), as the Keynesians suggest, it follows that MV must rise with it. If the money stock (M) is held constant, then velocity (V) must rise. Keynesians maintain that velocity does rise, because the government borrows and then puts into active use money that would otherwise have remained idle. But the monetarists contend that velocity remains more or less stable. Velocity, they say, is determined primarily by the expected rate of inflation, by institutional payment customs, and by personal wealth. Payment customs and personal wealth do not vary much in the short run, and velocity changes depend on changes in the rate of inflation—which in turn, according to the monetarists, depend on changes in the growth rate of the money stock. Therefore government deficits do not materially affect the national income level—or so the argument goes.

Monetarists recognize that the velocity of money depends to some extent on people's willingness to hold money balances. And their willingness to hold money balances is in turn inversely related to market interest rates. People can see that deficit spending puts upward pressure on interest rates, because more demand is chasing after the same amount of money. The higher interest rates go, the less money people will hold and the faster money will circulate. Theoretically, then, government deficits can induce people to hold less money, thereby increasing its velocity and boosting the national income level. But statistical studies apparently don't support this theory; they seem to show that interest rates have only a slight effect on the velocity of money.

How then do the monetarists explain the effects of the 1964 and 1981 tax cuts? In both cases the federal government ran a budget deficit and the national income level went up. Monetarists contend that increases in the rate of growth of the money stock, not deficit spending, sparked those increases in national income. Many (but not all) monetarists point out that after 1964, federal deficits led to greater borrowing by the Treasury, greater overall demand for lendable funds, and upward pressure on interest rates. In an attempt to keep interest rates down, the Federal Reserve expanded the money stock faster than in previous years. In other words, the government's fiscal policy had a significant short-run effect on unemployment, national income, and inflation only because it caused the Federal Reserve to increase the rate of growth in the money stock.

Similarly the recovery that began in late 1982 stemmed from a reversal of monetary policy. Beginning in 1979, the Fed had dramatically reduced the rate of growth in the money stock in order to fight double-digit inflation. Then, in late 1982, the Fed switched to a policy of rapid money growth. Because the economy was then in a serious recession, the change was not reflected in a higher rate of inflation.

The Importance of a Stable Rate of Monetary Growth

Because they believe money is crucial to the health of the macroeconomy, monetarists contend that government macroeconomic policy should be directed toward establishing a stable, predictable rate of growth of the money stock—say 4 percent a year. That is, the Federal Reserve should establish a policy of increasing the money stock at a given, more or less fixed rate. With the money stock growing at a fixed rate, a steady, largely predictable rate of inflation should result. For as we saw in Chapter 9, it is unanticipated inflation that redistributes the nation's income from creditors to debtors. Inflation would not be nearly as difficult a social problem if it were predictable.

Steady growth of the money stock and a predictable inflation rate would also reduce the risk of holding wealth in dollar assets. Lower risk would mean lower interest rates. And steady growth would eliminate many of the cyclical swings in economic activity that have resulted, according to the monetarists, from past shifts in monetary policy. The critical need, monetarists argue, is to establish a known and stable rate of increase in the money stock; its exact level is much less important. An annual growth rate of about 4 percent would allow for a modest annual rise in the production of goods and services (2 to 3 percent) because of increases in productivity and in the size of the labor force, as well as a relatively stable price level (inflation would be 1 to 2 percent or less). But other rates might serve just as well.

The money stock should increase rather than remain stable or contract. If the money stock remained fixed, prices would have to fall with an increase in output, since a growing quantity of goods and services would have to be purchased with a given quantity of money. Deflation—a drop in the money stock—can cause just as much redistribution of income as inflation. And it may give rise to special problems as well—especially since people have had little experience with deflation in recent history.

In addition, the monetarists argue that the time lags between recognizing macroeconomic problems and implementing monetary policies are often too long to make the policies effective. Moreover, monetarists frequently contend, monetary policymakers do not know enough about how changes in the growth rate of the money stock influence the economy to successfully "fine tune," or manipulate, macroeconomic activity. Monetary policy actions (for example, purchases of government securities) often have highly variable and largely unpredictable time lags, ranging from a few months up to two years. Therefore, Fed policy action taken today may affect prices and output six months from now, but they may not take effect for two years. Monetary actions may start to influence prices and output at a time when the actions will be counterproductive. Monetarists maintain that the Fed should try to control what it can best control (but still imperfectly)—the rate of growth of the money stock.

Critics of monetarist theory make several counterarguments. First, it is difficult to decide which measure of the money stock—M1 or M2 (or M3, not considered here)—should be controlled. Current measures of money are largely arbitrary, and new forms of money not included in the official money stock can be created. Suppose the Fed established a policy of increasing M1 at a rate of 4 percent. If people begin using money market accounts (not included in M1) as a store of purchasing power, the result could be an increase in the velocity of M1 and a higher-than-expected inflation rate.

Second, critics argue that the velocity of most money measures changes in response to a variety of economic factors. If those changes are not offset by changes in the growth rate of the money stock, the inflation rate could be affected.

Third, critics maintain that the growth of the money stock depends only in part on the growth of bank reserves and the reserve requirement, both variables that are directly controlled by the Fed (see Chapter 8). Many other variables—from interest rates to the public's demand for currency—can also affect the size of the money stock. As a consequence, the Fed may not be able to control the money stock precisely, or even within a certain range. As noted before, in 1979 the Fed made a serious effort to control money growth (or so it was thought). But over the next four years the money stock grew at monthly rates that ranged from more than 15 percent to less than −1 percent.

Critics of monetarism argue that if the Fed really wants to stabilize prices, it should worry about what is happening to prices, not to the money stock. That is, the rate of growth of the money stock should be adjusted from time to time to stabilize the rate of inflation. Monetarists counter that the Fed doesn't know enough about the link between money growth and inflation to stabilize prices in that way. Indeed, for most of this century the Fed has had the authority to control prices by controlling the money stock. Yet its record, especially in recent decades, is a blemished one.

Monetarists charge that the Fed has done a poor job of managing the growth rate in the money stock. They point out that between 1979 and 1982, the Fed slammed on the monetary brakes too hard. It permitted wide fluctuations in the rate of growth in the money stock, increasing the risk cost of holding money. Those wide swings, and the corresponding swings in real GNP, are evident in Figure 14.8.

Figure 14.8. Change in the U.S. Money Stock and Real GNP, 1979–1983.
During the early 1980s, the Fed permitted wide swings in the quarter-to-quarter
rate of change in the money stock (black line). Changes in the money stock were
accompanied by equally large swings in the quarter-to-quarter rate of change in
real GNP (color line).
Source: Oppenheimer Capital Corporation, *Manhattan Report*, 4, No. 3 (1984), 4.

In comparison, monetarists point to the success of monetarist policy
prescriptions in Japan, which began to stabilize its money stock in 1974.
The results of its policy change are shown in Figure 14.9. Before 1974,
wide swings in the money stock were accompanied by almost equally
wide swings in current dollar and real GNP. After 1974, swings in both
the money stock and GNP were moderated. Real and current dollar GNP
began to merge, indicating a reduction in the inflation rate.

Summary and Extensions

Money is not the only determinant of unemployment, inflation, and the
national income level in the monetarist model. Technological growth,
union power, personal wealth, and other factors also have long-term
effects. Money is an extremely important variable, however. The rate of
growth of the money stock is the prime determinant of the rate of inflation.
Changes in the rate of money growth will cause cyclical swings in both
unemployment and inflation. In the short run, then, monetary policy
matters a great deal and fiscal policy relatively little, except insofar as
government expenditures draw resources away from the private sector.
(Inefficient use of resources dampens economic growth.)

Whereas the Keynesian model of the macroeconomy provides a strong
argument for government intervention and control of the economy, the

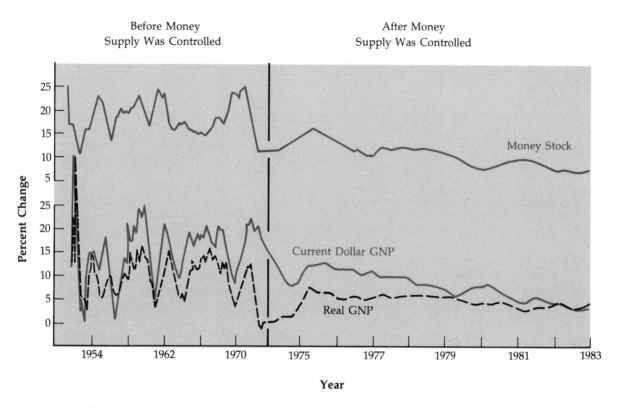

Before Money
Supply Was Controlled

After Money
Supply Was Controlled

Figure 14.9. Changes in the Japanese Money Stock and Real and Current Dollar GNP, 1954–1983.
Before 1974, when the money supply was not controlled, Japan experienced wide swings in the rate of change in the money stock. After 1974, the rate of change in both the money stock and GNP slowed and smoothed out. Current dollar and real GNP converged in the early 1980s, indicating a moderating of the inflation rate.
Source: G. T. Management (Asia) Ltd., *Manhattan Report*, 4, No. 3 (1984), 6.

monetarist model provides a strong argument against government involvement—except for control of the money stock. Keynesians argue that government manipulation of the budget and the money stock can foster economic stability and full employment. Monetarists, on the other hand, contend that, by itself, government manipulation of the budget will not lead to a lasting effect on the overall employment level. Furthermore, any increase in the rate of growth of the money stock will only temporarily reduce unemployment and increase inflation. In the long run, the unemployment rate will return to its natural level, which is determined by obstacles in the labor market. Thus the only lasting solution to unemployment, according to the monetarists, is to eliminate as many of those obstacles as possible.

Perspectives in Economics: Hitting the Money Growth Rate Targets

Monetarists argue that inflation can be contained by careful control of the growth rate of the money stock. The practical problem is which measure of money, M1 or M2, should be controlled. (Critics say monetarists sidestep this question too easily.) Changes in the velocity of money, and in the willingness of banks to make loans and of people to hold various forms of money—currency, demand deposits, and savings accounts—complicate the problem. Because people can shift their money from one form to another, attempts to limit the growth of one measure may simply provoke an explosion in the growth of another.

In the early 1970s, the Federal Reserve began to announce target ranges for the growth rates of M1 and M2.[1] Not until 1979, however, did the Fed become serious about keeping money growth rates within their announced target ranges. How well has the Fed met its goals? Figure 14.10 shows the growth of M1 and M2 from 1982 to 1984 (color lines). The black lines represent the upper and lower limits of the target ranges for the two measures, expressed in percentages. For example, beginning in November 1982, the Fed's target range for the growth rate of M1 was 4 to 8 percent. As you can see, the Fed missed its target by a wide margin. In early 1983 the Fed revised its target range to 5 to 9 percent and missed its target

again, at least for the next four months. In late 1983 the Fed refigured its goals on the basis of a larger money stock and lowered its target range to 4 to 8 percent. This time it managed to keep the money stock within announced limits.

The Fed was much more successful in controlling for the growth of M2. Only for two months during 1983 and 1984 did M2 stray from its target range. Perhaps the Fed was more serious about meeting its goals for M2 than for M1. Some monetarists, however, have questioned the Fed's dedication to controlling the size of the money stock. No one at the Fed was fired because M1 exceeded its target growth rates in 1982 and 1983.

Monetarist critics of the Fed believe that the Japanese government's success in meeting its money growth rate targets shows that control of the money stock is possible. Japanese money growth has been much more stable than U.S. money growth. The rate of growth has fallen gradually, and along with it, the inflation rate. The United States could achieve the same success, critics claim, if the Fed took monetarist policy prescriptions seriously.

1. The Federal Reserve is required to report to Congress twice a year, in February and July, to announce new target ranges for money growth and to explain the previous year's performance.

Major Conclusions

1. From the monetarist point of view, the primary cause of short-run swings in both the unemployment and inflation rates is abrupt changes in the rate of growth of the money stock.
2. Increases in the rate of growth of the money stock will produce unanticipated increases in the rate of inflation, a temporary reduction in the real wages paid to workers, and a temporary decrease in unemployment. In the long run, however, people will begin to anticipate a rise in inflation, and will work their expectations into their wage demands. Once money wages start to rise, unemployment will rise back to the level dictated by obstacles in the labor market, such as minimum wage laws.

(a)

(b)

Figure 14.10. Growth of the Money Stock and Federal Reserve Target Ranges, 1982–1984.
From late 1982 to late 1983, the growth of M1 (part (a)) exceeded the Fed's announced target ranges (black lines). Growth of M2 (part (b)) was much better contained.
Source: Federal Reserve Bank of Cleveland, *Economic Trends* (July 1984), pp. 16 and 17. Figures seasonally adjusted.

3. Decreases in the rate of growth of the money stock will produce an unanticipated reduction in the rate of inflation, a temporary increase in the real wages paid to workers, and a temporary increase in unemployment. In the long run, however, money wage rates will not rise as fast, real wage rates will fall, and unemployment will drop back to the level dictated by obstacles in the labor market.
4. There is no long-run tradeoff between unemployment and inflation, as suggested by the Phillips curve.
5. An increase in the anticipated rate of inflation will cause a simultaneous increase in the demand for, and a decrease in the supply of, lendable funds. The result will be a rise in the market interest rate. Conversely

a reduction in the anticipated rate of inflation will produce lower interest rates. In the monetarist model of the macroeconomy, high rates of inflation eventually raise the interest rate instead of lowering it, as in the Keynesian model.

6. In the monetarist model, government spending crowds out private (consumer and investment) spending. Indeed, the monetarists argue, a decrease in planned investment spending will virtually offset any increase in government spending intended to stimulate the economy. Deficit spending therefore has little or no effect on the national income and employment levels.

7. The monetarist prescription for a healthy economy is a stable, predictable rate of growth in the money stock.

Questions to Ponder

1. In the monetarist model of the macroeconomy, why will an increase in the rate of growth of the money stock not permanently reduce unemployment?

2. What actions would a monetarist president take to increase his or her chances of reelection in one year? In four years? If a president could be reelected more than once, would the options change?

3. "Given the equation of exchange, $MV = PQ = Y$, deficit spending alone can increase the national income. Deficit spending will increase the price level, which will lead in turn to an increase in V." According to the monetarist model, what is wrong with this statement?

4. Suppose the money stock begins to grow faster. What will happen to market interest rates in the short run? What will happen to them in the long run?

5. Suppose the Federal Reserve decreases the rate of growth in the money stock. What will happen to market interest rates in the short run? In the long run?

6. In the monetarist model, how does the Federal Reserve contribute to business cycles?

7. What policies would a monetarist recommend to solve the nation's long-run unemployment problem?

What are the basic tenets
of supply-side economics?

Chapter 15

Supply-Side Economics

The source of the gifts of capitalism is the supply side of the economy. In the capitalist economies of the West, this simple recognition is the core of all successful economic policy. It is a principle sometimes as obscure to conservatives, with their often excessive preoccupation with the statistics of money and deficit spending, as it is to liberals, with their obsession for aggregate demand and consumer spending. Wisdom on the subject can sometimes be found in strange places. Even Karl Marx knew enough not to stress, as the crux and keystone of capitalism, control over the means of consumption. Or even of the supply of money.
George Gilder

Keynesian economics was spawned during the Great Depression, when a substantial portion of the labor force was unemployed and prices were actually falling. It achieved academic and public prominence during the 1960s, when the inflation rate, at least for the first part of the decade, was a modest 2 to 3 percent, and the nagging social concern was unemployment. Keynesianism suggested that unemployment and inflation could be alleviated, if not eliminated, by government management of total spending. Unemployment could be reduced by an increase in total spending. Inflation could be reduced by a decrease in total spending (see Chapter 13).

If the goals of reduced inflation and reduced unemployment conflict, many Keynesians would say that policymakers should seek some socially acceptable short-run compromise. That is, they should aim for some combination of inflation and unemployment rates lying on the economy's Phillips curve. In the long run unemployment can be alleviated by education, on-the-job training, and poverty relief programs. And as improved labor skills and mobility increase production, the inflation rate will gradually go down. Monetarists would recommend controlling inflation by a gradual downward adjustment in the growth of the money stock.

Such was the general wisdom until the 1970s, when stagflation suddenly cast Keynesian theory into doubt. As one administration after another was foiled in its attempt to reduce inflation and unemployment simultaneously, many economists came to suspect that Keynesian theory was not the answer to all economic ills. The search began for new ways of analyzing and solving macroeconomic problems.

This chapter examines briefly one of the alternative schools of thought that arose from the crisis of the 1970s. Supply-side theorists see high tax rates as a major source of stagflation. Their overriding theme is that reductions in marginal tax rates will give people greater incentives to work, save, and invest. Their extra effort will raise productivity and national income, reducing unemployment and inflation. In short, supply-side economists offer microeconomic, or market, solutions to macroeconomic problems.

Tax Rates and Supply-Side Incentives

Much Keynesian economics implicitly assumes a positive relationship between tax rates and tax collections. Lower tax rates will produce lower tax revenues, allowing total spending to rise—thus stimulating production and employment by increasing demand. Supply-side economists, on the other hand, emphasize the effect of tax rates on the supply of goods and services produced. Tax rates affect people's willingness to earn a living and to report their income to the Internal Revenue Service. Thus many macroeconomic problems should be solved by reducing government impediments to production and increasing people's incentives to work, save, and invest in productive activities.

Three major propositions underlie supply-side theory. As you may surmise—and as supply-side economists freely admit—these propositions are based on the work of much earlier economists, including Adam Smith.

Basic Propositions of Supply-Side Theory

The first and most basic proposition of supply-side economics is that beyond some point, high marginal tax rates on personal income can reduce people's willingness to work. We have already defined the marginal tax rate as the percentage of any additional income that must be paid to the government. Marginal tax rate normally indicates the tax rate applied to the last increment of taxable income. The U.S. federal tax system is progressive, meaning that the marginal tax rate on additional income rises as earned income rises.[1] A taxpayer with a modest income may have a 25 percent marginal tax rate bracket; if he earns one more dollar, he must pay an additional twenty-five cents in taxes. A taxpayer with a very high income can face a marginal tax rate of 50 percent. Because of taxes, people's take-home pay is less than their earned income. Taxpayers must consider how much their additional earned income will be taxed in deciding whether to work more or harder.

Supply-side theorists propose that lower marginal tax rates on personal income should encourage people to enter the labor force and work longer hours. And lower marginal tax rates on business income should increase business demand for labor by increasing the after-tax return on labor. A reduction in marginal tax rates thus should increase both the supply of labor and the demand for it. Employment will expand in response to conventional microeconomic forces—that is, to a reduction in the after-tax price of labor. (The use of any other resource would also be expected to increase if its price declined.)

The second basic proposition of supply-side economics is that high marginal tax rates discourage people from investing in education and improving their work-related skills. They can also encourage businesses to invest abroad, where tax rates are lower, rather than in domestic operations. Again, high tax rates reduce the after-tax return on investments, lowering the nation's capital stock, both human and nonhuman. Growth in productivity will slow, depressing future national income levels. A reduction in marginal tax rates, therefore, should produce a more forward-looking, dynamic economy, in which more is invested in education, job training, and plant and equipment. The result will be a higher future national income level achieved through greater productivity.

The third basic proposition is that high marginal tax rates encourage people to work in the underground economy, where their incomes cannot be traced by the Internal Revenue Service. Barter and trade for cash, the clandestine sale of illegal goods and services such as drugs and prostitution, and the nonreporting of legitimate income all flourish under such conditions. High marginal tax rates also encourage people to spend considerable sums of money in search of tax loopholes. To the extent that efforts to

---

1. In 1985, the maximum marginal tax rate was 50 percent, and the Reagan administration was actively considering lowering it to 35 percent. At the same time, it was considering eliminating various deductions that high income earners use to lower their taxable incomes.

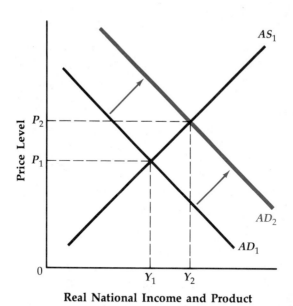

Figure 15.1. The Effect of a Cut in Tax Rates: The Keynesian Model.
According to Keynesian theory, a cut in tax rates will increase aggregate demand from AD_1 to AD_2. As a result, the price level will rise from P_1 to P_2, and the national income level will climb from Y_1 to Y_2.

avoid taxes use up otherwise productive resources, they reduce the efficiency of the economy. So a reduction in tax rates should increase not only the amount of income people report, but the nation's total income.

The Effects of a Reduction in Tax Rates

Because high marginal tax rates retard growth in the nation's productive capacity, supply-side economists contend they heighten the inflationary effect of an increase in the money stock. If $MV = PQ$ and Q is retarded, a rise in M must be matched mostly by a rise in P. If tax rates are reduced, then, and the supply of goods grows more rapidly in relation to the money stock, inflationary pressures should subside. As employment opportunities rise with the increase in production incentives, fewer people will find it desirable to work in the underground economy. Most people will be better off—earning more and able to keep a large share of their earnings.

Furthermore, a reduction in marginal tax rates need not reduce tax collections. Tax revenues are a function of two key variables, national income and tax rates. Stated mathematically, tax revenues equal the tax rate times the national income ($TR = rY$). If a given percentage decrease in tax rates is accompanied by a larger percentage increase in national income, the government's tax collections will rise. Suppose, for example,

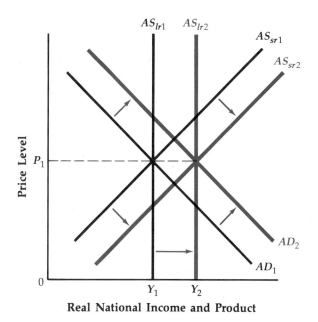

Figure 15.2. The Effect of a Cut in Tax Rates: The Supply-Side Model.
According to supply-side theory, a cut in tax rates shifts both the aggregate demand
curve and the short-run aggregate supply curve outward. At the new equilibrium
point (the intersection of AD_2 and AS_{sr2}), national income will be higher (Y_2 instead
of Y_1), but the price level will be the same. If the tax cut is perceived as permanent,
the long-run aggregate supply curve will also shift, from AS_{lr1} to AS_{lr2}. In that case
the increase in national income will be permanent.

that the national income is $3.5 trillion, and the average tax rate is 40
percent. Suppose further that if tax rates are reduced from 40 to 36 percent,
the national income will rise from $3.5 trillion to $4.2 trillion. Total tax
revenues rise from $1.4 trillion (40 percent of $3.5 trillion) to $1.51 trillion
(36 percent of $4.2 trillion). Under these circumstances, government
spending can actually be expanded—or so the argument goes.

The effect of supply-side proposals can also be described in terms of
aggregate demand and supply. As we have seen in previous chapters, a
reduction in tax rates will raise aggregate demand, shifting the aggregate
demand curve outward, from AD_1 to AD_2, in Figure 15.1. The price level
will rise from P_1 to P_2, and the national production level will climb from
Y_1 to Y_2. In the long run, however, national production will probably
return to Y_1, because the long-run aggregate supply curve is vertical.

Supply-side economists add that the aggregate supply curve will also
be affected by the tax rate reduction. In the short run, because people
have a greater incentive to work, save, and invest, the aggregate supply
curve will shift outward, from AS_{sr1} to AS_{sr2}, in Figure 15.2. This increase
in aggregate supply will tend to dampen, if not totally offset, the price
effect of the increase in aggregate demand. A tax rate reduction, in other
words, will not be as inflationary as Keynesian theory might suggest.

Perspectives in Economics:
The Impact of Tax Rates Across Countries

Alan Reynolds

Tax revenues are often expressed as a percentage of GNP, but governments cannot pay their bills with percentages. To finance real increases in spending, governments need real increases in tax revenues.

The table [Table 15.1] shows what happened to the growth of real revenues, from 1975 to 1982, among countries where taxes were a relatively high or low percentage of gross domestic product (GDP). The tax percentage is a static snapshot; the growth of real revenue over several years is a dynamic motion picture.

Without exception, countries with persistently high tax rates have sustained an actual loss of real tax revenues over the entire seven-year period. Those that attempted to counter this loss with even steeper tax rates, such as Belgium, had even larger revenue losses.

Countries in which taxes extracted the smallest share of GDP—Japan and Spain—have experienced by far the most rapid increase in real tax revenues. The reason, of course, is that real GDP (or GNP) is the tax base for real revenues, and production invariably grows most rapidly in low-tax countries, as Keith Marsden of the World Bank recently observed . . . last December 18 [1984].

The United Kingdom alone appears to have obtained sizable real revenue gains despite fairly high tax rates. But the seven-year average hides what really happened. British taxes dropped to 33.3% from 35.3% of GDP from 1976 to 1979, and real revenues increased 39%. The average tax rate then rose to 39.6% by 1982, with real revenues falling 20% from 1980 to 1982. Industrial production in the U.K. is now barely higher than it was in 1982 and unemployment is near 13%, so high tax rates undoubtedly continue to depress real revenue.

Revenues as a share of GNP or GDP measure an average tax rate, or "tax ratio," at any moment in time. But an increase in that tax rate implies an increase in the marginal tax rate on added output and income. When that happens, economic growth

Table 15.1. Rates and Revenues (1975–82; Percentage Change in 1972 Dollars)

	Average Tax Rate (% of GDP)	Change in Real Tax Revenues[a]
Sweden	49.2%	−12.4%
Netherlands	44.6	− 6.8
Belgium	44.6	−15.7
Denmark	43.4	−10.6
France	40.7	6.2
Austria	40.5	7.0
Germany	37.0	7.6
United Kingdom	35.7	29.1
Canada	32.8	6.7
Switzerland	30.9	5.4
United States	30.0	20.1
Portugal	27.9	12.1
Japan	24.3	54.1
Spain	22.7	59.8

[a] Adjusted by deflator for U.S. government purchases. Includes state and local government taxes.

stagnates or contracts. Inflation may nonetheless continue to raise nominal tax revenues, but it inflates government spending, too. Meanwhile, the tax suffocation of real output raises real government spending to alleviate the added poverty. With real spending up and real revenues flat or down, budget deficits become large and chronic. Deficits of 10% to 13% of GDP have become routine in places like Belgium and Sweden, and will remain that way until they cut marginal tax rates.

Japan also runs perpetual deficits, with a government debt nearly as large as that of Belgium and Sweden. Yet Japan is able to finance that debt at long-term interest rates that are half those of the overtaxed nations, including France (whose debt is only half as large as Japan's). Monetary stability in Japan is part of the explanation though

Belgium, too, is quite intolerant of inflation or deflation. Perhaps a better explanation of Japan's high credit rating is that its seemingly large deficits and debt are actually small relative to the rapid growth of real tax revenues. Just as a growing company can easily handle a growing debt, so can a growing national economy. Overtaxed nations, particularly the troubled developing countries, are an inherently bad credit risk, because the ultimate source of real revenues—added GNP—is limited by punitive tax rates.

Those who are proposing a tax increase for the U.S. do not seem to realize that the U.S. is already having an enormous tax increase. Since tax rates were reduced to 18.6% from 20.2% of GNP in 1983, federal tax collections rose almost 7% in real terms last year and are expected to rise an additional 6% to 7% this year. That is an increase in real revenues of almost Japanese proportions.

Such significant revenue effects from economic growth are typically delayed a year. In the first year of recovery, many companies have accumulated losses that initially reduce their taxes, and individual taxes, too, are often paid on the unexpected increases in the previous year's earnings.

A 6% to 7% increase in the U.S. government's real earnings can scarcely be the subject of great public sympathy. Most households and companies expect to get by with a much smaller increase in their own revenues. Attempts to improve the government's budget at the expense of the budgets of the private sector invariably fail, as the European welfare states are learning the hard way.

From 1963 to 1965, federal taxes in the U.S. dropped to 17.7% from 18.5% of gross national product, and real tax revenues soared (with the usual lag) by 19% in the following two years. That was better than we are doing in 1984–85, but the Kennedy tax cuts were more dramatic, and nobody in those days thought 7.2% unemployment constituted an argument for brutal monetary policy. From 1978 to 1981, by contrast, federal taxes rose to 20.8% from 19.1% of GNP, and real tax revenues

fell 12% in the following two years. It may be objected that the rising tax rates of 1979–81 just happened to be followed by stagnation and recession. But that was also true of the rising tax rates in 1974, 1969, 1958–59, 1953–54 and 1937–38. What we are missing is a single example of high or rising tax rates that were not followed by stagnation or recession, here or abroad.

When taxes rise as a percentage of GNP, it may simply mean that GNP slowed down even more than tax revenues. Indeed, this is what should be expected when taxes claim a rising share of added output. Robert Barro's revolutionary new text, "Macroeconomics," concludes that "an increase in the marginal tax rate . . . leads in the short run to less work, output and investment. Further, in the long run, there are reductions in the stock of capital, as well as in the levels of output and consumption."

With lower real GNP, we should expect much lower real tax revenues. Barro estimates that "a decline by 1% in real GNP causes real federal revenues to decrease by 1.8%." For any government to attempt to acquire a larger percentage of a smaller real GNP, it must move toward the top of the table, losing real revenue in the process. A 40% share of nothing is nothing.

In the back of every U.S. budget, federal spending is shown in real, inflation adjusted terms. But taxes are only shown in nominal terms, as a percentage of nominal GNP.

Those who demand a "tax increase" must make up their minds. If they want a big increase in real tax revenues, we already have that. If instead they want taxes to be a larger percentage of any remaining GNP, then that must be recognized as a well-tested plan to shrink real revenues, increase real transfer payments, and double the budget deficits.

Reprinted with permission from Alan Reynolds, "Less Will Get You More," *Wall Street Journal*, January 23, 1985, p. 32.

If the tax rate reduction is perceived as permanent, it can also shift the long-run aggregate supply curve outward, from AS_{lr1} to AS_{lr2}, in Figure 15.2. Again, the shift occurs because people have greater incentives to work and add to the nation's capital stock. The outward shift in the long-run aggregate supply curve means that some or all of the income effect of the tax rate cut can be permanent. It also means that the money stock can be expanded more than Keynesian theory might suggest. Whether the price level rises or falls, and by how much, depends on the relative impact of the cut on aggregate supply versus aggregate demand, and on the extent to which the money stock is increased when tax rates are lowered.

Does this scenario sound too good to be true? As you can imagine, many economists have serious reservations about some of the supply-side predictions. Nevertheless, the Reagan administration based its economic recovery strategy partly on such thinking. In 1981 it pushed through Congress a three-year, 25 percent cut in personal income tax rates.

A Critique of Supply-Side Theory

One of the more serious criticisms of supply-side theory has to do with the proposition that lower tax rates encourage people to work harder.

The Labor-Leisure Tradeoff

Critics of supply-side economics charge that high marginal tax rates do not necessarily reduce the number of hours people work. In fact, they can actually increase the amount of time spent at work. Thus a tax cut could reduce production.

Figure 15.3 shows the critics' view of the labor-leisure tradeoff. Assume the typical citizen-taxpayer has sixty hours to use for work or play each week. Time spent on work yields money income, as shown on the vertical axis. At an hourly wage rate of $10, a worker can earn a maximum of $600 per week. To earn money income, the worker must give up the direct benefits of leisure time, shown on the horizontal axis. In other words, the worker has a production possibilities curve that extends from a point somewhere on the horizontal axis to another point somewhere on the vertical axis.

The tax rate structure will affect the slope of the production possibilities curve. Without any income taxes, the worker's curve may look like Y_4T_1. Assume that the worker chooses point a on that curve. In doing so, she gives up thirty hours of leisure for $300 a week in income. She could move further up the curve and earn more money income. But presumably she values her leisure time more than the additional goods she could purchase with the additional money. In short, combination a maximizes the worker's utility.

Now suppose the government imposes a 30 percent tax on personal income. The worker will take home only $7 out of the $10 she earns for each hour of work. The relative cost of leisure, then, has gone down. Each

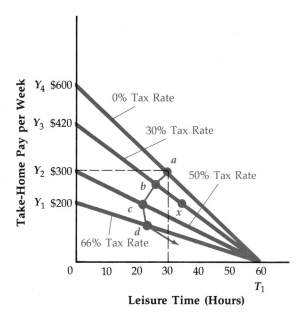

Figure 15.3. The Labor-Leisure Tradeoff.
At a tax rate of zero, a worker can consume along transformation curve Y_4T_1. A worker making $10 an hour might choose to consume at point *a*, earning $300 a week and taking thirty hours of leisure time. As the tax rate increases, however, the worker's transformation curve pivots downward. On curve Y_3T_1, the worker might choose point *x*, which offers less disposable income but more leisure time. Or she could move to point *b*, which minimizes the loss in income, but at the cost of less leisure time. The higher the tax rate, the lower the transformation curve, and the more leisure time the worker will have to give up to maintain her income.

hour now spent talking with friends means only $7 worth of goods forgone. At the same time the relative price of goods purchased with money has gone up. More leisure time must now be forgone for each good that is purchased. Thus a 30 percent tax rate pivots the production possibilities curve, from Y_4T_1 to Y_3T_1. The worker's maximum take-home pay is now $420 ($7 × 60 hours).

Supply-side economic theory suggests that when a 30 percent income tax is imposed, a worker will move from point *a* to a point like *x* on the new curve, choosing more leisure time and less work. But others argue that the worker may just as well move to point *b*, taking less leisure time and working more. Such a choice seems reasonable, at least for low tax rates. The person who has less take-home pay can be expected to buy less of most goods and services—including recreation. In short, lower tax rates do not necessarily mean greater national income. People may decide to work harder and longer to make up for the purchasing power lost because of a tax increase.

At very high tax rates a tax cut would probably increase the number of hours worked. Suppose the income tax rate is raised gradually, pivoting the transformation curve downward, from Y_4T_1 to Y_1T_1. At some point (in

Figure 15.3, when the tax rate is higher than 50 percent) the worker's tendency to work longer hours to make up for lost income is bound to halt. Consider the extreme case. If the income tax rate is 100 percent, the worker's consumption transformation curve will be perfectly flat, overlapping the horizontal axis. The rational individual can then be expected to work zero hours. (Would you work if all your income were taxed away?) At such an extreme rate, a tax cut could only encourage a worker to work more.

No government levies a 100 percent income tax, however. At lower rates, the effect of a tax cut is harder to predict. The outcome depends on both the actual level of the tax rate and the individual's personal preferences. A reduction in a very high tax rate may cause a worker to trade leisure for income, moving from point d to point c. Supply-side theory is based on this kind of response. But actual tax rates may be lower. If the taxpayer's choice lies in the c to b range, she may decide to take more leisure and work less.

From a strictly theoretical perspective, we cannot know whether a tax cut will cause people to work more. The question is an empirical one. A great deal of empirical evidence suggests that the labor supply curve slopes upward, and that workers respond positively to increased compensation. We might also agree that people will be better off if they are free to dispose of their own income—regardless of how many hours they work. But the actual effects of implementing supply-side policies cannot be predicted in the abstract.

Unfortunately, supply-side theorists' arguments about the impact of tax cuts on saving and investment are also inconclusive. Lower tax rates can encourage greater saving and investment, but they can also discourage it. Critics of supply-side economics point out that after the Reagan tax cut of 1981, the saving rate in the United States actually fell. Furthermore, even if a tax cut has a positive effect on saving and investment, it may not be very large.

Regardless of the actual outcome, many policymakers may continue to favor supply-side policy, reasoning that lower tax rates minimize government's distorting effects on the market process.

The Laffer Curve

Critics also take issue with the idea that tax cuts inevitably increase tax revenues. Tax revenues may go up or down, depending on the responsiveness of workers, savers, and investors to the tax cut.

At the bottom of this controversy is the so-called Laffer curve, named after the supply-side economist Arthur Laffer. The Laffer curve relates total tax revenues to tax rates, as in Figure 15.4. At low tax levels, an increase in tax rates produces an increase in tax revenues. For example, an increase in the tax rate from r_1 to r_2 would expand tax revenues from TR_1 to TR_2. Beyond some point, however, an increase in tax rates can be expected to reduce tax revenues. For example, an increase in the tax rate from r_3 to r_4 would reduce tax revenues from TR_3 to TR_2.

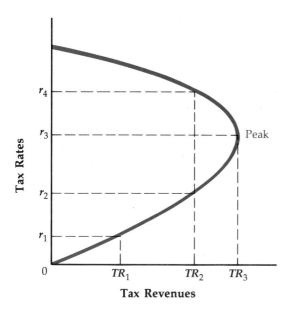

Figure 15.4. The Laffer Curve.
At low tax rates, represented by the lower half of the Laffer curve, an increase in tax rates, say from r_2 to r_3, can produce an increase in tax revenues (from TR_2 to TR_3). Beyond the peak of the Laffer curve, however, an increase in tax rates will lower tax revenues. For instance, an increase in the rate from r_3 to r_4 will decrease revenues from TR_3 to TR_2.

Why does the Laffer curve have the shape it does? At low tax rates, so the argument goes, people have little incentive to avoid taxes. Trading off income for leisure or saving and investment for consumption is not profitable. Finding ways to escape taxes or to move productive activity underground is not worth the trouble. At high tax rates it is costly not to avoid taxes, however. The result is that beyond some peak point, as shown in Figure 15.4, the reported tax base falls off enough that total tax collections go down.

The general shape of the Laffer curve can also be deduced from demand analysis. Because income buys goods, people have a demand for it. How much income they demand depends partly on its price, which is called the tax price in supply-side economics. The more taxes take out of earned income, the less income people will earn—a proposition that yields the downward-sloping income demand curve in Figure 15.5. At a tax rate of zero, citizens will earn a national income equal to Y_2. If the government raises its tax rate to r_1, tax revenues will rise from zero to r_1Y_1. This movement from zero to r_1 tax rate in Figure 15.5 is equivalent to a movement up the bottom half of the Laffer curve in Figure 15.4.

If the tax rate is raised indefinitely, at some point tax revenues will fall. If the tax price is raised all the way to r_2, people will earn nothing, and again the government will collect no taxes. In short, so long as the amount

Figure 15.5. Effect of the Tax Price on the Demand for Income.
At a tax price, or rate, of zero, the amount of earned income demanded by workers
is Y_2. The revenues collected by government are also zero. A tax rate of r_1 will
lower earned income to Y_1, but increase government revenues from zero to r_1Y_1.
Beyond some tax price, however, an increase in the tax rate with mean lower tax
revenues. At a tax price of r_2, workers will demand no earned income, and
government revenues will again be zero.

of income people demand varies inversely with the tax rate, the Laffer
curve must have a backward-bending portion.

Whether a particular tax cut will reduce tax revenues depends on three
factors: where the present tax rate places the nation on the Laffer curve;
how much people respond to a change in the tax rate; and the size of the
tax rate cut. If tax rates are above r_3 in Figure 15.4, for example, a tax rate
cut will expand tax revenues. At tax rates below r_3, the effect of a cut will
be just the opposite. A drop in tax rates all the way from r_4 to r_1 will also
lead, on balance, to a reduction in tax collections.

Most economists accept the general shape of the Laffer curve. But many
dispute the supply-side claim that marginal tax rates in the United States
are so high, at least for high-income groups, that the nation is on the
upper portion of the Laffer curve. There, of course, a tax rate cut would
increase tax revenues. Without more empirical evidence, many economists
will regard this claim with skepticism. Why indeed would politicians ever
have raised taxes to such a level? By reducing personal income so much
that total government spending (and benefits to their constituencies)
declined, they would surely have jeopardized their chances of reelection.
The critics contend that no one gains from being on the upper half of the
Laffer curve.

The Threat of Inflation

Finally, critics question the supply-side argument that, on balance, the nation is better off because of a tax rate cut. Cuts in marginal tax rates can increase deficit spending, which can eventually increase inflation.

Economists' response to this issue depends on whether they adhere to Keynesian or monetarist theory on matters of demand management. Keynesians tend to argue that in times of inflation, deficit spending will increase aggregate demand, thus adding to inflationary pressures. A cut in marginal tax rates may mean an immediate drop in tax collections and thus an increase in disposable income for consumers. Eventually it may stimulate an expansion of aggregate supply as well, but not until people have had a chance to respond to reduced tax rates by working, saving, and investing more. If spending increases rapidly but output increases slowly, the result will be a higher rate of inflation. (In terms of the equation of exchange, $MV = PQ$, deficit spending increases the velocity of money, V, necessitating an increase in P or Q on the other side of the equation. P will increase more rapidly than Q.)

Supply-side economists, on the other hand, tend to argue that the increase in the supply of goods and services stimulated by a tax cut will counteract any inflationary pressures from a deficit. Indeed they recommend that the Fed adopt an expansionary monetary policy when tax rates are reduced, to avoid deflation. Supply-side theorists criticized the Fed for adhering to monetarist theory from 1981 to 1984, the period of the Reagan tax cut. Growth of the money stock, they maintain, does not invariably lead to inflation. So long as monetary growth accommodates rapid growth in production, inflation should not be a problem. In 1984, they point out, the rate of inflation did not keep pace with the growth of the money stock, because output expanded unusually fast—at an annual rate of over 7 percent for much of that year.

Supply-side theorists generally agree with monetarists that government expenditures will crowd out private expenditures. Government expenditures, in their view, are the ultimate tax on the economy. But they are not particularly distressed by the prospect of deficit spending crowding out private investment through higher interest rates. Lower tax rates should mean more resources available for investment. First, people will save more, supply-side theorists believe. Their greater saving (or nonconsumption) will free resources for use by investors, shifting purchases from consumption to investment. Second, the greater national income generated in response to reduced tax rates will also mean more resources available for investment. And reduced tax rates should draw back home those investment resources previously employed outside the country.

Supply-side theorists argue too that deficits created by tax rate cuts are likely to be short-lived (just how short-lived is a matter of dispute). With the increased national income generated by lower tax rates, government revenues will rise, wiping out or reducing the deficit. Over a period of years, then, government should run fewer deficits, borrow less, and crowd out less private investment than if tax rates were never reduced. (Keynesians made similar arguments in support of the 1964 Kennedy tax cut, but

Perspectives in Economics: Soaking the Rich Through Tax Cuts

Richard Vedder and Lowell Gallaway

Almost a year ago [1984], the release of Internal Revenue Service data on 1982 income tax returns showed that higher-income Americans paid more in income taxes in 1982 than in 1981, whereas lower- and middle-income Americans paid less. The preliminary IRS data for 1983 tax returns are in, and repeat the pattern of the 1982 returns. Upper-income earners *are* paying a greater share of the tax burden after the Reagan tax-rate cuts.

A year ago, this interpretation was still open to question by critics and skeptics, while supply-siders proclaimed that since the top income-tax rate fell from 70% to 50% in 1982, the 1982 IRS data showed the tax cut was working just as they said it would. The incentives for higher-income Americans to engage in tax avoidance and even tax evasion were reduced and they responded accordingly. The fact that the number of returns from citizens with an adjusted gross income (AGI) of more than $1 million grew by nearly 60% amid the greatest recession in years was ample evidence that the tax cuts were working.

All of this, of course, was mildly embarrassing to Democratic presidential hopefuls who were spending most of last year trashing the Reagan administration for its tax policies that supposedly benefitted the rich and hurt the poor. However, a horde of commentators rose to their defense and attacked the supply-side view. They argued that the 1982 data were not typical. John Berry of the Washington Post suggested that the stock-market boom explained the rising affluence (and tax payments) of the rich, somehow assuming that the tax-rate reductions had no bearing on that boom. Joseph Minarik of the Urban Institute argued that because of inflationary "bracket creep," the payments from the rich typically rose and the 1982 results merely reflected a long-term trend.

Still others used different arguments. Donald Kiefer, a researcher for the Congressional Research Service, claimed that the wealthy, anticipating the tax-rate reductions, engaged in income-shifting tactics in late 1981 that swelled 1982 taxable income. Finally, some people maintained that because of rising nominal income, the definition of "rich" and "poor" was changing, meaning that a simple analysis of the data by constant-income classes led to distorted findings.

While supply-siders believe the bulk of these criticisms to be misdirected or exaggerated, the fact remains that conclusions were being drawn on the basis of a single year's observations. As Mr. Vedder said in a Joint Economic Committee study published last November ". . . the final word will be the 1983 data."

Well, the preliminary 1983 IRS data are in and they further support the contention that as after-tax rates of return rise the supply of labor and capital also increases. As the first table [Table 15.2] indicates, affluent Americans (say, those with an AGI of more than $100,000) paid substantially more than in 1981. Poor and middle-income Americans (those making under $50,000 AGI) paid less in 1983 than in 1982, and far less than in 1981. While tax payments rose 28% from 1981 to 1983 for the affluent group, they decreased nearly 12% for the low- and middle-income groups.

The increase in payments from the super rich was particularly dramatic—those with an AGI of $1 million or more paid 108% more in 1983 than in 1981, and the number of "tax millionaires" more than doubled in the greatest explosion of millionaires in U.S. history.

These results are not surprising. In the afore-

Table 15.2. Tax Payments By Income Groups, 1981 to 1983

Income Class[c]	Taxes Paid[a]			% of Total Taxes Paid[b]		
	1981	1982	1983	1981	1982	1983
$0–$15,000	$26,571	$23,949	$21,037	9.1%	8.4%	7.4%
$15,000–$30,000	80,475	74,196	67,000	27.6	26.0	23.6
$30,000–$50,000	88,322	86,363	84,736	30.3	30.2	29.8
$50,000–$100,000	52,156	51,732	55,179	17.9	18.1	19.4
Over $100,000	43,633	49,387	55,781	15.0	17.3	19.6
Over $1,000,000	4,901	6,955	10,231	1.7	2.4	3.6

[a] In millions of dollars; refers to total tax liability.
[b] These percentages do not add to 100 because of rounding.
[c] Adjusted gross income.

mentioned JEC study, an analysis of 29 years of tax data from 1954 to 1982 revealed that upper-income Americans have become highly sensitive to variations in marginal tax rates on both ordinary and capital-gains type income. The study revealed that some Americans were in the backward-bending portion of the Laffer Curve—where reductions in tax rates so stimulate growth in the tax base that total tax receipts from the group rise. Profs. James Gwartney of Florida State University, Richard Stroup of Montana State University and James Long of Auburn University have reached virtually identical conclusions using quite a different methodology and different data sources.

The rise in tax payments reflected mainly a boom in what might be termed "entrepreneurial" income—income from small businesses, partnerships, farms, etc., or from working. The second table [Table 15.3] indicates that passive or *rentier*

income, in the form of dividends, interest, royalties and the like, grew far less rapidly. It would appear that a big surge in entrepreneurial activity has occurred in response to the increase in the part of income that individuals keep after taxation.

The one argument of the critics that has not been addressed is the notion that rising nominal income normally pushes more Americans into higher tax brackets, increasing the pool of persons with incomes in excess of a given amount. One way to deal with this argument is to look at the relative income of Americans, that is, to examine, say the top 10% of income recipients, regardless of what their income may be. Analysis using this procedure indicates that the shift in tax payments toward the rich is somewhat less dramatic than shown in the first table, but it is occurring nonetheless. The share of total income taxes paid by the top 1% of income recipients grew from 17.44%

Continued

Perspectives in Economics: Soaking the Rich Through Tax Cuts

Continued

to 20.64% between 1981 and 1983, with the share of middle-income groups showing a noticeable decline.

A single index of progressivity is the "tax Gini coefficient." A value of 1 indicates perfect progressivity—one rich person pays all the taxes—while a value of 0 describes a situation in which everybody pays the same absolute tax, regardless of income. The tax Gini rose from .6488 to .6560 between 1981 and 1983, a move in the direction of greater progressivity. In other words, the 1981 tax cut seems to have been successful in promoting a key part of the liberal agenda of the past half-century, namely, "redistributive justice."

All of this, of course, speaks to the great tax debate beginning now in Washington. The Treasury, Kemp-Kasten and Bradley-Gephardt proposals all continue in the spirit of the 1981 legislation, further reducing marginal tax rates, raising the rate of return on investment in both human and physical capital, and stimulating growth, fairness and administrative simplicity in the tax system. The evidence from the period 1981 to 1983 indicates that these initiatives also hold the promise of making a welcome addition to the U.S.'s long-term economic vitality.

Reprinted with permission from Richard Vedder and Lowell Gallaway, "Soaking the Rich through Tax Cuts," *Wall Street Journal*, March 21, 1985, p. 30.

Table 15.3. Changing Income of the Very Rich, 1981 and 1983[a]

Income Source	AGI Reported (in millions of dollars)		% of Total AGI	
	1981	1983	1981	1983
Rentier income[b]	$ 4,509	$ 7,147	40.5	28.2
Entrepreneurial income[c]				
Business[d]	329	4,012	3.0	15.8
Financial[e]	4,105	8,718	36.9	43.4
Human capital[f]	2,186	5,452	19.6	21.5
Total entrepreneurial income	6,620	18,182	59.5	71.8
Total income	11,129	25,329		

[a] Very rich includes returns with an AGI of over $1,000,000.
[b] Dividends, interest, rent, royalty income, and estate and trust income.
[c] All income other than rentier income.
[d] Small business corporations, farms, partnerships, and business and professional income.
[e] Primarily capital gains.
[f] Wages and salaries.

they believed that the increase in national income would result from an increase in aggregate demand.)

To ensure that government does not crowd out private investment, supply-side economists often recommend eliminating "fat," "waste," and "counterproductive programs" from the federal budget. (Exactly what constitutes fat and waste varies, as you can imagine, from one economist or policymaker to another.) Budgetary deficits can also be avoided by authorizing tax rate cuts to take effect in the future, thus encouraging businesses to invest now to take advantage of lower tax rates on future income. Future productivity, production, and national income will rise, and when tax rates are actually lowered, government revenues will be no lower than they otherwise would have been.

In general, supply-side economists have opposed efforts to eliminate government deficits by increasing tax rates. Smaller deficits may mean reduced demand for lendable funds. But if tax revenues increase, the result will be a reduced supply of lendable funds. People will earn less and have less to save after taxes. Some supply-side theorists contend that a tax rate increase can only compound the deficit problem.

Economic Need Versus Political Reality

According to many of its supporters, supply-side policy is not a quick fix, but a long-term economic plan based principally on improving incentives for investment by lowering tax rates. Its advocates do not believe that government can fine-tune the economy. Instead, they assert, time is needed to turn incentives into real plant and equipment and improved human skills. To make the needed investment, businesses and individuals must be convinced that tax rates will not only be cut, but will be held down for some time to come.

Therein lies the Achilles' heel of Reaganomics, which was grounded in a three-year tax cut package. After the tax cut, taxpayers had little reason to believe the immediate future would be any different from the immediate past. Like the so-called tax cuts of the 1970s, the Reagan cuts seemed less likely to be permanent reductions than midcourse corrections in the generally upward movement of tax rates. Since long-term growth depends on expectations about future tax rates, many people remained cautious about investing, fearing that their earnings would go up in the smoke of higher taxes.

But the needs of political leaders, who must keep their eyes on the near term and the next election, may be inconsistent with the needs of investors, who look to the long term and the after-tax return on their investments. Politicians seeking the funds to provide benefits to their constituents may take advantage of people's short-run inability to respond to tax increases. Much of taxpayers' current income may depend on past investments in physical and human capital, which are not readily changed in the short run. People will not destroy their plant and equipment or cast off their work-related skills just because tax rates rise. Thus politicians may decide to maximize short-run revenues, positioning the nation at the peak of the

Perspectives in Economics: Flat Tax Proposals

Thomas M. Humbert

According to a January 1985 New York Times/CBS poll, the American public believes that the U.S. tax system is grossly unfair. An estimated half of all Americans believe they pay more than their fair share in taxes. Two out of three feel that income tax rates should be lowered and most deductions eliminated.

The current attack on the income tax system comes from throughout the political spectrum. Agreement appears widespread that loopholes in the current system, including numerous credits, deductions, exclusions, and exemptions, allow some Americans to escape paying what they should, while others face extremely high tax rates. The system may be considered unfair on two counts. First, loopholes, deductions, and credits violate the principle of horizontal equity—that taxpayers of similar income and circumstances should pay the same taxes. At the same time, they violate the principle of vertical equity—that persons of different circumstances should be taxed according to their differing ability to pay.

Supply-side economists believe that the current system is also inefficient and counterproductive. Because of all the special provisions in the tax code, marginal tax rates are much higher than they otherwise would have to be. These high marginal rates reduce the after-tax return on economic activity. They discourage work, saving, and investment and encourage taxpayers, especially those with high incomes, to seek out tax shelters and loopholes or participate in the underground economy. Business deductions, credits, and loopholes may also divert investment from heavily taxed to lightly taxed activities, distorting the flow of resources to their most productive uses. The end result is not only a less productive economy, but lower tax revenues than could be had under a more equitable tax system.

Most reformers seek a tax system that does not alter individual economic behavior. All activities would be taxed equally, so that the relative prices of leisure and labor or of savings and consumption would not change appreciably. In effect, the system would be neutral. A neutral tax system is a system that does not alter the relative prices of goods and services or of work and leisure.

Not everyone agrees on what constitutes a neutral income tax system, but many see it as a flat tax system. A flat income tax system is one in which the marginal income tax rate is constant, or the same for all income levels. It is a proportional tax system. A pure flat tax would eliminate all deductions, exemptions, and loopholes, and tax all income at the same low tax rate. Reformers estimate that a flat tax of 12 percent on all income would produce the same amount of revenue as the current system (1985), in which marginal tax rates range from 14 to 50 percent. Many supply-side theorists believe that such a tax would produce less distortion in the allocation of the nation's resources. It would also make the tax system substantially less complex and more equitable, and stimulate economic growth.

In January 1985, President Ronald Reagan responded to public criticism of the tax system by short-run Laffer curve. In the long run, of course, taxpayers will respond to higher tax rates by reducing their investments. Such a response would mean a long-run contraction in the nation's capital stock, income, and tax revenues.

If politicians do lower tax rates, however, the short-term result can be disastrous for them. Tax revenues will drop, at least in the short term, because people will not be able to expand their investments immediately announcing his support for a "modified flat" income tax system. The modified system he proposed significantly lowered marginal income tax rates, but did not equalize tax rates. It was a progressive tax system. By early 1985, two modified flat tax plans had been introduced in Congress, and one had been recommended by the Department of the Treasury. All three plans increased both the standard deduction and exemptions for dependents, to eliminate taxation of the poor. All three retained deductions that were politically popular or promoted activities considered socially desirable, like home ownership and charitable giving. And all three plans retained the graduated tax schedule characteristic of the old tax code.

The Bradley-Gephardt plan, introduced by Senator Bill Bradley (D.-N.J.) and Congressman Richard Gephardt (D.-Mo.), broadened the tax base by eliminating many loopholes and credits. But it retained deductions for charitable giving, a limited amount of home mortgage interest, state and local income and property taxes, payments to IRA and Keogh accounts (retirement plans), and business expenses. And it proposed three marginal tax brackets: 14, 26, and 30 percent.

The Kemp-Kasten plan, introduced by Representative Jack Kemp (R.-N.Y.) and Senator Robert Kasten (R.-Wisc.), eliminated most loopholes, except deductions for home ownership, charitable giving, savings and investment, and private health insurance. Unlike the Bradley-Gephardt plan, it levied a single 24 percent tax rate on all taxpayers. But it gave lower-income families a break by doubling the size of their personal exemptions, increasing their standard deduction, and excluding 20 percent of their wages and salaries from taxation. (This exclusion would gradually be phased out.)

Why did no one propose a pure flat tax, especially when supply-side economists believed that it would stimulate economic growth? First, legislators feared that the adoption of a pure flat tax would cause a massive redistribution of the tax burden, greatly favoring the wealthy at the expense of the poor and middle classes. Second, any attempt to eliminate deductions for mortgage payments or interest on tax-exempt municipal bonds would most assuredly have been politically unpopular. It would have inflicted considerable hardship on home buyers, who had incurred heavy mortgage payments on the assumption the interest would be tax-deductible. And it would have penalized buyers of municipal bonds, who had accepted lower-than-normal rates in return for the bonds' tax-exempt status.

Thus the various modified flat tax plans proposed so far represent compromises among the conflicting goals of efficiency, simplicity, and equity. Proponents of tax reform in Congress recognize that the ideal of the flat tax is both politically difficult and economically controversial. Many strongly believe that a modified flat tax would be a substantial improvement over the current system, as well as a stimulant to the nation's economic growth.

in response to the tax cut. If government expenditures are not reduced, the result can be a larger budget deficit. Politicians may then be accused of fiscal imprudence. When the federal budget deficit reached $200 billion in the mid-1980s, after passage of the Reagan tax package, supporters of the tax cut were frequently chided for their irresponsibility. Critics reminded supply-side theorists that some of them had predicted that the tax cut would bring a smaller deficit, not a larger one. Moreover, politicians who vote for tax cuts can be accused of neglecting current social needs, since lower tax revenues restrict the government's ability to provide social services. Thus the political benefits of a tax rate cut may be available only to future political leaders.

Because of the conflict between the needs of the economy and the realities of the political system, some supply-side theorists have suggested the establishment of constitutional checks on the government's spending and taxing powers.

Summary and Extensions

The debate between supply-side theorists and other economists hinges largely on empirical questions. How much more will people work, save, and invest in response to a specific tax rate cut for a specific number of years? Will government tax revenues go up or down in response to a tax rate cut? Will a tax rate cut raise or lower inflation in the short run and the long run? Economists have only recently begun to address these questions from the perspective of supply-side theory. Unfortunately the answers are not yet clear.

As evidence of the validity of their theory, supply-side economists point to the effect of the 1964 Kennedy tax cut package and to the rise in national income after 1982 and the Reagan tax cuts. But as we have seen, Keynesian theory attributes the rise in national income that followed those cuts to growth in aggregate demand. And monetarist theory attributes it to growth in the money stock. Because the forces of aggregate supply and demand interact, no one can be certain whether an increase in economic activity is a response to the pull of aggregate demand, as Keynesians and monetarists would contend, or to the push of aggregate supply.

Supply-side economists also point with pride to the very positive effects of state and local tax cuts in California and Puerto Rico during the 1970s. Both economies grew faster after property and income tax rates were reduced. But though many economists agree that a tax rate cut is likely to have some positive effect on growth, they differ as to how much of the growth in these economies was actually due to the tax cut. Other factors, such as changes in energy costs and in the comparative advantage of producing in those areas, may have been responsible for much of the economic growth in California and Puerto Rico.

Major Conclusions

1. One of the most important tenets of supply-side theory is that lowering tax rates gives people an incentive to work, save, and invest more than they would otherwise. Therefore a reduction in tax rates stimulates the economy through increased production rather than increased demand.

2. Another important tenet of supply-side theory is that a cut in tax rates can alleviate unemployment by increasing people's incentives to work and employers' incentives to create jobs. A tax rate cut can also lower the inflation rate by encouraging investment, thus stimulating the economy through greater productivity and expanded production.
3. Because tax collections depend on the national income level as well as on tax rates, a reduction in tax rates can (but will not necessarily) increase tax collections. Therefore a reduction in tax rates need not force cutbacks in government programs; it might actually allow an expansion. Similarly, an increasse in tax rates will not necessarily expand government revenues; it might reduce them instead.
4. In supply-side theory, a tax rate cut will shift the short-run aggregate supply curve outward, moderating the price effect of the outward shift in the aggregate demand curve. It will also shift the long-run aggregate supply curve outward.
5. The actual consequences of supply-side policy depend on three variables: (a) the responsiveness of workers, savers, and investors to a change in the tax rates; (b) the effect of a change in the tax rates on the total tax revenues collected; and (c) the relative impact of a change in the tax rates on aggregate supply and aggregate demand, and therefore on the rate of inflation.

Questions to Ponder

1. Keynesians contend that a reduction in tax rates will stimulate production by increasing consumption demand. Supply-side economists say that it will stimulate production by increasing the supply of labor. Is there any real difference between the two theories?
2. Why does the Laffer curve not slope continually upward toward the right, instead of eventually bending backward?
3. What happens if tax rates are lowered when an economy is on the upper half of the Laffer curve? When it is on the bottom half?
4. Suppose the nation is in a period of inflation, and you have been asked to formulate a remedy using the Keynesian model of the macroeconomy. Suppose further that the rich are taxed at very high rates, which place them on the upper portion of the Laffer curve, while the poor are taxed at very low rates, which place them on the bottom half of the Laffer curve. What would your solution be? Would your recommendations be politically acceptable?
5. List all the empirical issues involved in the Keynesian–supply-side controversy. What are the difficulties in resolving them?
6. List the current administration's tax and spending policies, and label them as monetarist, Keynesian, or supply-side.

Central Question

What are the basic propositions and conclusions of rational expectations theory?

Chapter 16

Rational Expectations

*You may fool all the people
some of the time; you can even
fool some of the people all the
time; but you can't fool all of
the people all the time.*
Abraham Lincoln

Keynesian theory suggests that unemployment can be alleviated by increasing government spending and/or expanding the money stock. Increased spending works directly on unemployment by increasing aggregate demand. Expansion of the money stock works indirectly by lowering interest rates, thus increasing investment demand.

Both government spending and the money stock virtually exploded during the late 1960s and early 1970s—but did not reduce unemployment as Keynesian theory would have predicted. Instead, unemployment and inflation both rose during the 1970s (see Chapter 14). That experience frustrated many economists, who believed that the validity of any science, physical or social, resided in the correctness of its predictions.

The last chapter described supply-side economists' attempts to reformulate and redirect macroeconomic theory and policy. This chapter examines rational expectations theory, another alternative to the traditional Keynesian model. To improve the predictive power of macroeconomic theory, this school emphasizes the role that expectations play in people's reactions to fiscal and monetary policy.

A cornerstone of the rational expectations theory is the assumption that people will behave rationally—an idea that underlies microeconomic theory as well. That is, people are assumed to be capable of ranking their options from most preferred to least preferred, and of acting on the basis of those priorities. They will develop expectations about the consequences of government fiscal and monetary policies, and will act on those expectations in the future. Rational expectations theorists contend that Keynesian predictions have been incorrect in the past because they did not recognize that government policies cause changes in people's expectations and behavior.

A central (and somewhat extreme) conclusion of many rational expectations models is that fiscal and monetary policy will have no effect on national income and employment, in either the short or the long run. That is, government cannot systematically control the ups and downs of the business cycle by altering its budget or the size of the money stock. People will inevitably learn to anticipate the consequences of such policies and will act to nullify them.

Before we can appreciate this theoretical innovation, we must first understand the role of expectations in traditional Keynesian thought.

Expectations in Keynesian Theory

The Keynesian model does not ignore expectations. They play a part in determining the investment, consumption, and money demand functions.

Investment

Expectations about the future profitability of business are critically important in determining the position and slope of the planned investment curve. In Keynesian theory, investment expenditures are inversely related

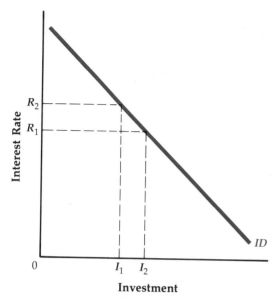

Figure 16.1. Investment Demand Curve.
The level of investment spending varies inversely with the interest rate. When the
interest rate falls from R_2 to R_1, investment spending rises from I_1 to I_2.

to the interest rate. When the interest rate falls—for example, from R_2 to
R_1 in Figure 16.1—investment spending increases, from I_1 to I_2. But the
actual position of the investment demand curve, *ID*, depends on business
people's assessment of the future profitability of their investment projects.
The anticipated rate of return on an investment project determines whether
a firm will borrow funds at prevailing interest rates.

An assumption implicit in Keynesian theory is that the investment
demand curve does not change much in response to fiscal policy. Therefore
when government demand rises, aggregate demand rises with it (see
Figure 16.2). Keynesians do not normally consider the possibility that if
government increases its deficit, business expectations may change, shifting
the investment demand curve down, in the opposite direction from
government demand. Investment may drop, but because of a rise in the
interest rate, not a shift in investment demand. On balance, Keynesians
believe, the increase in government spending will outweigh any decrease
in investment, shifting the aggregate demand curve up. The national
income and price levels will rise, from Y_1 and P_1 to Y_2 and P_2 in Figure
16.2.

Consumption

Expectations also play a role in determining consumption patterns. People's
consumption decisions are based not only on current income, but on
expected future income. The Keynesian analysis implicitly assumes that

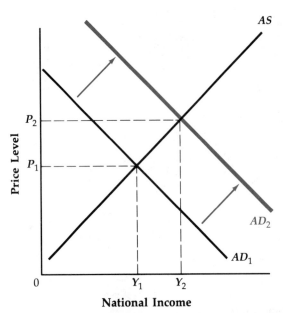

Figure 16.2. Fiscal Policy in the Keynesian Model.
In Keynesian theory, an increase in government spending is not fully offset by a reduction in investment and consumption spending. As a result, an increase in government spending can cause the aggregate demand curve to shift out, from AD_1 to AD_2. The national income level rises from Y_1 to Y_2, and the price level climbs from P_1 to P_2.

consumers' expectations, and therefore their consumption and saving patterns, remain more or less stable even if government fiscal and monetary policy change. In other words, when the government takes expansionary fiscal or monetary actions, the consumption function will not shift downward or upward, negating or reinforcing the effect of government policy. According to Keynesian theory, government expenditures affect consumption mainly through actual rather than anticipated changes in real income, prices, and interest rates.

Demand for Money

Finally, expectations play a role in the construction of the Keynesian demand for money curve. When interest rates fall, more and more people begin to expect them to rise again. They hold on to their money instead of lending it. The quantity of money demanded is therefore inversely related to the interest rate. The lower the rate, the higher the quantity of money demanded. And the demand for money can be represented by a downward sloping curve, as in Figure 16.3.

The actual market interest rate is established by the stock of, and demand for, money balances. (See Chapter 12 for a review of how interest rates

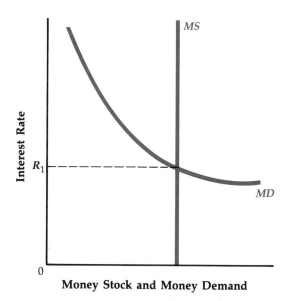

Figure 16.3. The Stock of and Demand for Money.
The money stock, *MS*, is controlled by the Federal Reserve and is more or less fixed, or vertical. The quantity of money demanded, *MD*, is inversely related to the interst rate—the higher the cost of money, the lower the demand. The market interest rate, R_1, is established by the intersection of the two curves.

are determined.) That is, the amount of money created by the Federal Reserve (which determines the stock or supply of money) interacts with people's expectations about future interest rates (which influence their demand for money) to determine the interest rate. In Figure 16.3, the equilibrium interest rate is R_1, the rate at which the money stock and demand curves intersect.

A change in expectations can change the demand for money and therefore the interest rate—which in turn can influence investment. Thus a change in expectations can be translated into a change in aggregate demand, national production, and employment. Keynesians have generally assumed, however, that the demand for money is relatively stable, at least in the short run. Hence they do not worry that government fiscal and monetary policy will be frustrated by changes in expectations that affect the demand for money.

Rational Expectations

Rational expectations theorists argue that Keynesian thinking does not account fully for changes in people's expectations about the consequences of fiscal and monetary policy. They contend that in pursuit of their own self-interest, people will gather a rationally determined amount of information on the past consequences of government policy. Then they will act accordingly. For instance, if expansionary fiscal policy has led to higher interest rates in the past (because of the government's increased demand for borrowed funds), people will come to expect higher interest rates as a result of increased government spending, and will take steps to protect themselves. Those who have bonds will attempt to sell them, driving bond prices down and interest rates up in the process. Thus the expectation of higher interest rates leads almost immediately to higher interest rates. (A contractionary fiscal policy can have the opposite effect. People will anticipate lower interest rates, and in the process of reacting to their expectations, they will drive interest rates down.) In Keynesian terms, the demand for money curve shifts up with an increase in government spending.

Suppose, for example, that the government increases its expenditures from G_1 to G_2 in Figure 16.4(a). Because experience has taught them that greater government spending is accompanied by greater budget deficits, people begin to expect interest rates to rise. This change in expectations will cause the demand for money curve to shift upward, as in Figure 16.4(b). People are now selling their bonds at high prices, so they can hold on to greater cash balances until bond prices drop and interest rates rise. So while the increase in government expenditures increases aggregate demand, the resulting upward shift in the demand for money curve boosts the interest rate from R_1 to R_2 (Figure 16.4(b) and (c)).

As the interest rate rises, the level of investment falls from I_2 to I_1 (see Figure 16.4(c)), counteracting the rise in government spending. In this instance the decrease in business investment, $I_2 - I_1$, just balances the expansion in government spending, $G_2 - G_1$. Aggregate demand remains constant (Figure 16.4(d)), and national income and employment are unaffected by the government's action.

Similarly, people may observe that prices rise faster when the Federal Reserve increases the rate of growth of the money stock. According to rational expectations theory, if there is such an acceleration in monetary growth, they will come to expect a higher rate of inflation. Business people will buy plant and equipment now, in anticipation of higher prices later. Wage earners will push for higher wages to protect their future purchasing power. Thus the very anticipation of price increases sets in motion forces that lead to higher prices. Any lag between the adoption of an expansionary monetary policy and the resulting increase in inflation is reduced (if not eliminated altogether) by the impact of people's expectations.

Various quite different models are used by theorists working in this relatively new area. In an effort to keep their models simple, many rational expectations theorists employ unrealistic assumptions about how expectations are formed. For example, some theorists base their models on these three extreme assumptions:

No cost is involved in gathering information about the nature and structure of the economy and the consequences of fiscal and monetary policies.

Prices and wages are perfectly flexible, both upward and downward.

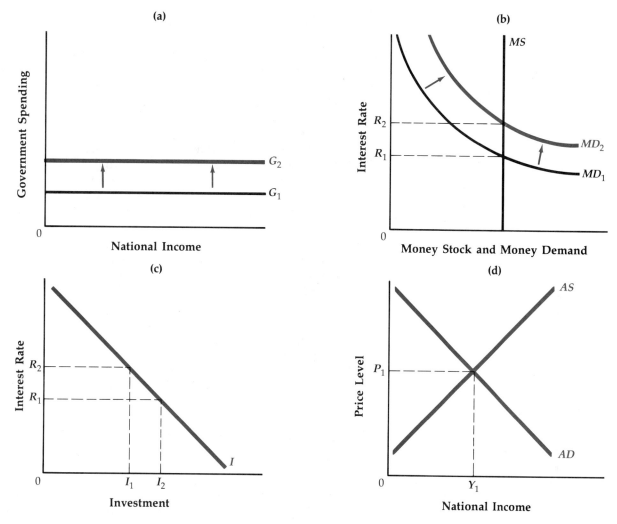

Figure 16.4. The Impact of Expectations on the Demand for Money.
Suppose that government increases its expenditures from G_1 to G_2 (part (a)) and
runs a larger deficit or a smaller surplus than people expect. According to rational
expectations theory, the demand for money curve will shift up from MD_1 to MD_2,
raising the market interest rate from R_1 to R_2 (part (b)). But the higher interest rate
will cause investment spending to fall from I_2 to I_1 (part (c)). The drop in investment
offsets the impact of increased government spending, so that aggregate demand
and supply do not change (part (d)). The nation's equilibrium price and income
levels remain the same (P_1 and Y_1).

Transactions based on expectations of government policy changes and
their consequences are costless.

Such assumptions make it relatively easy to conclude that people will fully
and accurately anticipate the consequences of government policy, eliminating any time lag between the government action and its consequences.

Of course, in the real world, markets and people do not work with the perfection implied in these assumptions. Recognizing that discrepancy, rational expectations theorists may conclude that on average, people will fairly quickly formulate reasonably correct expectations about the consequences of government policy. Although some time may elapse between the government's action and its consequences, the lag will be much shorter than is usually assumed.

Clearly people learn from experience. The Keynesian assumption that expectations are not changed by government policies may have been a useful working hypothesis during periods like the early 1960s, when people had had relatively little experience with such policies. But when expansionary policy is pursued year after year, people will eventually begin to anticipate its consequences. When that happens, economic predictions based on constant expectations will begin to miss their mark. Before we can predict what will happen in response to fiscal and monetary policy actions, rational expectation theorists contend, we must understand one principle. People develop certain expectations based on past experience. When the rules of the game are changed, people's experience and expectations will change. When government changes its fiscal and monetary policies, it changes the rules of the game. People's expectations will change accordingly. Their behavior will be different, and so will the consequences of government policies. Indeed, once people come to understand what government is doing (or thinking of doing) to the economy, government will lose its ability to do anything to change the nation's real output and employment levels.

Rational Expectations Theory from Other Perspectives

We have seen that rationally determined expectations can nullify the intended effect of government policy. To understand the principles of individual behavior that lie behind the phenomenon, we must return to monetarist theory.

In Chapter 14 we observed that the quantity of labor demanded and supplied is related to the real wage, W/P (see Figure 16.5). Assuming that the market clears at the intersection of the labor supply and demand curves, the equilibrium real wage rate will be $(W/P)_2$ and the equilibrium employment level will be Q_1. As we saw in Chapter 14 (pages 313–317), more rapid growth in the money stock will accelerate inflation. If prices rise faster than money wages, the real wage rate will fall, and employers will want to hire more workers. That is what happens in Figure 16.5. The real wage rate falls from $(W/P)_2$ to $(W/P)_1$, and employers increase employment from Q_1 to Q_2. As long as workers believe (incorrectly) that the increases in their money wages are increases in their real wages—that the real wage has gone *up*, to $(W/P)_3$—the quantity of labor supplied will expand from Q_1 to Q_2.

The resulting increase in employment will reduce the unemployment rate and increase real output. But once workers realize that their real wage

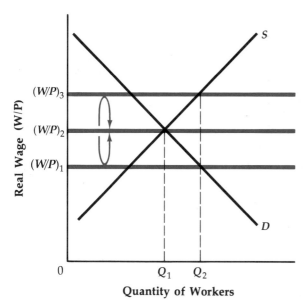

Figure 16.5. The Effect of Expansionary Monetary Policy on the Labor Market. Suppose an expansion in the money stock increases the price level. If employers interpret the increase as a reduction in the real wage, from $(W/P)_2$ to $(W/P)_1$, they will expand the quantity of labor they demand, from Q_1 to Q_2. As long as workers interpret the resulting rise in their money wage as an increase in real wages, from $(W/P)_2$ to $(W/P)_3$, the quantity of labor supplied will also rise, from Q_1 to Q_2. The national output and income levels will rise. But in rational expectations theory, workers and employers are not fooled by inflation. Almost immediately wages will adjust to account for price increases, so that the real wage remains at $(W/P)_2$. Thus the quantity of labor employed will remain Q_1, and national output and income will not expand.

has actually declined to $(W/P)_1$, they will demand higher money wages. The real wage will climb back up to $(W/P)_2$, negating the effects of the government-induced monetary expansion. Thus expansionary monetary policy can succeed only in the short run.

This process produces a long-run Phillips curve that is vertical rather than downward sloping (see Figure 16.6). When the inflation rate rises from IR_1 to IR_2, workers may at first be fooled into taking jobs at the lower real wage. Unemployment will drop from U_2 to U_1. But when workers realize that the real wage has fallen, they will begin to turn down jobs offered at that rate. The unemployment rate will return to its previous level, U_2. Once workers have learned to anticipate the effects of monetary expansion, the Phillips curve will be vertical even in the short run.

Thus monetarists draw essentially the same conclusion as rational expectations theorists. The main difference between the two schools of thought lies in the speed of the adjustment process. According to rational expectations theory, people will learn to react very quickly, if not immediately, anticipating higher prices and interest rates as a result of expansionary fiscal and monetary policy. Instead of moving back along the

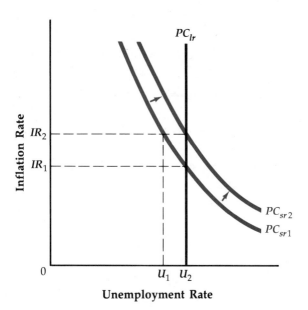

Figure 16.6. The Effect of Expansionary Monetary Policy on Unemployment.
In Keynesian and monetarist theory, an increase in the inflation rate can move the economy up along the short-run Phillips curve PC_{sr1}, reducing the unemployment rate from U_2 to U_1. But in rational expectations theory, wages adjust immediately or almost immediately to the increase, shifting the Phillips curve from PC_{sr1} to PC_{sr2}. The economy moves straight up along its vertical long-run Phillips curve, PC_{lr}, and the unemployment rate remains at U_2.

short-run Phillips curve PC_{sr1} in Figure 16.6, the economy will move straight up the vertical long-run Phillips curve almost immediately. In other words, the short-run Phillips curve is also vertical, or practically so. And instead of the gradual rise in interest rates and fall in investment spending predicted by the monetarists, rational expectations theorists forecast that the change in expectations underlying the money and investment demands will bring an almost immediate, if not instantaneous, rise in interest rates and fall in investment.

Rational expectations theory can also be seen in terms of aggregate supply and demand. So long as workers are deceived by an increase in the price level from P_1 to P_2 in Figure 16.7, employment will increase, shifting the aggregate demand curve from AD_1 to AD_2. National income will rise from Y_1 to Y_2. But as soon as workers wake up and demand higher wages, the aggregate supply curve will shift to the left, from AS_1 to AS_2. National income will return to Y_1 as producers cut back on production because of higher wages. Again, the monetarist and rational expectations views differ primarily as to the amount of time required for the adjustment. Monetarists tend to argue that people can be fooled for a short period of time. Rational expectations theorists argue that the downward adjustment of aggregate supply is immediate, or almost immediate.

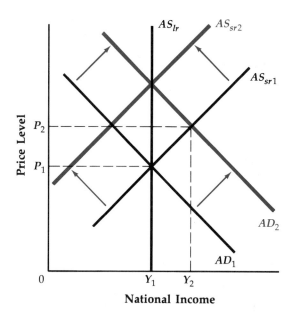

Figure 16.7. The Effect of Expansionary Monetary Policy on Aggregate Supply and Demand.

The increased consumption and investment spending caused by an expansionary monetary policy will shift aggregate demand from AD_1 to AD_2. The price level will rise from P_1 to P_2; and so long as workers are fooled into believing their real wages have risen, the national output level will rise from Y_1 to Y_2. Rational expectations theorists contend, however, that monetary policy will be ineffective once people have learned that an expansionary monetary policy leads to a higher price level. Workers will demand higher wages, shifting the aggregate supply curve in from AS_{sr1} to AS_{sr2} almost immediately. The result will be virtually no change in the national income level. In rational expectations theory, the short-run aggregate supply curve is almost vertical, like the long-run aggregate supply curve (AS_{lr}) in monetarist theory.

According to rational expectations theorists, the short-run aggregate supply curve is virtually vertical, just like the monetarists' long-run aggregate supply curve.

Thus the expansionary fiscal and monetary policy of the late 1960s and 1970s failed to reduce unemployment, because people anticipated and reacted to it, nullifying its effects. After only a few years of Keynesian fiscal policy, the government had played its hand too long. Some theorists argue that the same phenomenon explains the high real interest rates of the early and mid-1980s. People had learned to associate high federal deficits with high inflation and interest rates. Watching the deficit increase under President Reagan, they moved to protect themselves against another resurgence of inflation, in part by demanding high interest rates for their money. Like Lincoln, rational expectations theorists stress that you can't fool all of the people all the time.

Perspectives in Economics: Is the Federal Deficit a Burden?

Robert J. Barro

Everyone's talking about "large" recent budget deficits. In fact, the consensus is that the federal government's first priority should be to reduce the deficit. But be suspicious of this type of consensus: The last time I remember one this strong was in 1971 when every sensible person was supposed to believe that wage-price controls were a good idea. The current popular view on deficits falls into the same category—it is incorrect and is also likely to be discarded within a couple of years.

The appropriate first question is, how do today's deficits relate to history? Recent deficits—currently about 4%–5% of gross national product, or about $170 billion for fiscal 1984—are in line with what we would expect from experience, given the state of the economy. And they're in line with what we ought to be running. Under current conditions, I would be concerned if the deficit were either much larger or much smaller than it is.

Past U.S. deficits have had three main elements. The first is temporary federal expenditures, which arise primarily in wartime. In these cases a large budget deficit lessens the need to raise tax rates on a temporary basis. Since high tax rates blunt the incentives that help the economy deal with a war or other emergency, these kinds of deficits are a good idea. Wartime finance has, in fact, been the principal long-run source of the stock of public debt in the U.S. and other industrialized countries. But this factor has not been a consideration in recent years.

The second element is the business cycle. The federal deficit rises during recessions in order to avoid either large increases in tax rates or major cuts in government expenditures at these times. This process is well known and underlies the construction of a full-employment deficit (which attempts to filter out the part of the deficit or surplus that derives from the business cycle). This element was the most important source of the budget deficits during the recessions of 1975–76 and 1980–83. Despite the strong recovery since early 1983, the continuing effect of the last recession still matters for the current deficit. I estimate that the remaining shortage of output below the full-employment level accounted for about $60 billion out of the total deficit of $170 billion for fiscal 1984.

The third item is net federal interest payments, which totaled $111 billion for fiscal 1984. This element, which was of minor significance until the rise of inflation in the late 1960s, has become the key force behind current budget deficits. The question is, how much of interest payments should be financed by a deficit rather than by higher taxes?

One part that is reasonable to finance by a deficit is that corresponding to expected inflation. If the government pays for this part with new debt, then—on this count—it just plans for a constant real debt over time. Using an estimate for expected inflation of 6% for 1984 (somewhat above the actual rate), the resulting contribution to the deficit was 6% times a stock of debt of about $1.2 trillion, or $70 billion–$75 billion.

A second element of interest payments appropriate to finance by a deficit is that corresponding to temporarily high real interest rates. These payments are analogous to other types of temporarily high government expenditures—such as wartime spending—that call for a deficit rather than an increase in taxes. In this way the government avoids unnecessary fluctuations in tax rates over time. I estimate that this component accounted for about 2½% (excess of current real interest rates above normal) times $1.2 trillion of debt, or roughly $30 billion of the fiscal 1984 deficit.

Overall, it was reasonable to finance about $100 billion–$105 billion of interest payments by a deficit. Adding in the $60 billion contribution from the residual effects of the recession leads to a total of $160 billion–$165 billion, or almost all of the actual figure of $170 billion.

The historical view of deficits and the accounting for the present situation also tell us what to expect for the future. Basically, deficits will fall greatly in fiscal years 1985 and 1986 only if there is rapid economic growth or if there are substantial declines in interest rates. Typical forecasts of these variables lead to projections of budget deficits for both years of about $170 billion, the same as in 1984. The potential for economic growth to reduce deficits below this figure is limited to about $60 billion, which is the contribution of prior recessions to the 1984 deficit. Thus, the main element that could reduce the deficit further is lower interest rates, whether because of reduced inflationary expectations or decreased real interest rates.

My forecast of a budget deficit of $170 billion for fiscal 1986 contrasts with the Congressional Budget Office's estimate last summer of $200 billion–$210 billion (the figure has been revised upward, but new accounting procedures and growth projections make the old number more appropriate for this comparative analysis). Basically, the CBO projection is for given spending and tax programs, whereas my forecast factors in the likely congressional responses. In other words, I see some

combination of cuts in spending or increases in taxes that will total $30 billion–$40 billion for 1986.

It should be clear that there is a major interplay between recessions, interest rates and inflation on the one hand, and federal budget deficits on the other hand. But the channel that has been documented is from the economic variables to the deficit, and not the reverse. For example, recessions cause deficits (as is well known), but there is no evidence that shifts in the deficit have important effects on economic activity. Notably, the large deficits for 1983–84 did not prevent a strong investment-led economic recovery.

Similarly, an increase in interest rates (when it reflects either higher expected inflation or a temporary increase in real rates) can lead to a larger deficit. But, despite the efforts of many researchers to detect it, there is no evidence that shifts in deficits lead to higher interest rates, especially to the higher real rates that would deter investment.

The strongly held popular view is that large budget deficits—and the consequent rise in the real stock of public debt—tend to raise real interest rates and thereby crowd out private investment. Basically, this crowding-out view of deficits is a myth, which is reinforced mainly by repetition. It isn't supported by economic theory or empirical investigation.

In light of what has caused our recent deficits, and what they themselves are unlikely to cause, the national mania these days is rather hard to justify.

Robert J. Barro, "A Deficit Nearly on Target," *Wall Street Journal*, January 30, 1985, editorial page.

Problems with Rational Expectations Theory

Although it is supported by the monetarist and aggregate demand and supply models, rational expectations theory and its implications are disputed by many economists. Several criticisms must be noted. The first two concern the extreme nature of the assumptions underlying rational expectations theory.

The Cost of Acquiring Information

Critics point out that rational expectations theory expects too much of people. Economists spend years studying and modeling the macroeconomy and still cannot accurately predict the timing and impact of government policy, they observe. How then can ordinary people be expected to make such predictions, virtually without cost or delay? Though this criticism may reflect the wounded professional dignity of economists, it is also consistent with common sense. In an imperfect world, adjustment to government policy may not be as costless, accurate, and rational as rational expectations theorists assume.

Because of the cost of obtaining information on economic conditions, people do not become perfectly informed. As a result they sometimes over- or underestimate the consequences of government policy actions. Thus an expansion in the money stock could have a perverse effect: an increase in labor's wage demands, a reduction in employment, and a contraction in national income. Or the opposite could occur. That is, fiscal policy could have some temporary positive effect on employment and national income. Because of miscalculations and the time lags required to correct them, government fiscal and monetary policy can have at least some short-run effects on employment and national income. Policy need not be completely impotent, say critics of rational expectations theory.

Rational Ignorance

Rational expectations theory assumes that it is in people's self-interest to become aware of government policy. If government takes fiscal and monetary actions to influence citizens' welfare, people should have the necessary incentive to understand what government is doing. But critics stress that the macroeconomy is terribly complex, and that individuals have little incentive to keep abreast of government actions. One person can do little to influence the outcome of government policy. To varying degrees, people may be rationally ignorant about government policy—especially economic policy, a comparatively technical subject.

Rational expectations theorists counter that it is not necessary to assume that everyone keeps abreast of government policy. Just a few people may adjust their expectations in response to government actions. Their response will produce a change in pricing signals, which will lead others to adjust their behavior. But the criticism is still relevant. If prices must be adjusted and then readjusted, for a short period at least, people are effectively fooled. Government fiscal and monetary actions can therefore have some short-run effect.

Changes in the Composition of National Output

Many rational expectations theorists conclude that fiscal and monetary policy has neither short-run nor long-run effects. But critics protest that if government actions change the composition of demand and the relative prices of goods and services, they necessarily affect the composition of the nation's output. For instance, expansionary fiscal policy can produce more government goods and services and fewer private goods and services, including private investment. Expansionary monetary policy can lower interest rates (at least in the short run), thus increasing investment. Such changes in the composition of output necessarily have a long-run effect on the national output level. For example, a reduction in private investment because of greater government spending can mean a reduction in the nation's future capital stock, productivity, and income level.

Many rational expectations theorists accept this criticism. Their point is that, contrary to Keynesian analysis, government cannot systematically influence the employment and production levels by managing aggregate demand.

Contract and Wage Rigidities

Many rational expectations models assume that prices and wages are perfectly flexible. But there are many institutional rigidities in the real-world pricing system. Many producers, for instance, are bound by labor contracts that strictly prohibit wage and price adjustments for certain periods of time. As a result, wages cannot always be raised in response to a higher inflation rate. At least temporarily, real wages can fall while employment and national production expand.

To this criticism, rational expectations theorists may reply that experience will teach labor leaders to develop contracts that permit wage adjustments for inflation, including clauses for automatic cost-of-living increases.

Rational expectations theory is relatively new; only in the last several years has it received much attention. Because the theory is new, economists are still working to develop it and to test its usefulness in improving macroeconomic prediction. Many questions remain unsettled. For instance:

Summary and Extensions

Why would a government devise a macroeconomic policy if it would not (and people knew it would not) have any effect on the economy?

Do government policymakers overestimate their own power?

How is economic information transmitted in the macroeconomy?

Perspectives in Economics: Expectations and the Effects of Federal Deficits

William F. Shughart II

Almost two centuries ago the British economist David Ricardo (1772–1823) suggested that government expenditures will have the same effect on an economy whether the funds are raised through taxes or through deficit spending (borrowing). Ricardo's theorem is still debated among economists. It is especially controversial today, both because of the emergence of rational expectations theory and because the federal deficit is projected to run from $200 to $250 billion a year for the rest of the decade.

How do expectations influence the economy's response to a budget deficit? Deficit spending implies that the government will eventually have to raise taxes to pay off its creditors. Ricardo proposed that individuals will react to the expectation of higher future taxes just as they would to an increase in current taxes. Others have argued that individuals do not respond to deficits as they do to taxes. Instead, they see deficit spending as a way of shifting part of their tax liability to future generations. Whether or not one should be concerned about deficits depends, obviously, on which of these two views one subscribes to.

Suppose the government decides to increase spending this year by $1, but will return to its former level of spending next year, and each year thereafter. This year's extra spending could be financed by imposing a $1 tax surcharge this year. Taxpayers would then have $1 less to spend as they wished, but the government's budget would remain balanced.

Alternatively the government could pay for this year's extra spending by running a budget deficit. That is, the government would borrow $1 by issuing a bond on which the principal plus interest is due some time in the future. To keep the example simple, assume the loan would be repaid in one year. Although current taxes would not go up, next year's taxes would have to rise enough to cover the $1 of principal plus the interest on the bond, r. And the public would be aware of the impending increase.

Taxpayers could meet their increased future liability by buying a $1 bond that pays the same interest rate as the government's, r. By sellng the bond next year, they would have just enough money—$1 + r$—to pay their taxes. As in the first case, they would be one dollar poorer this year. Therefore the extra dollar's worth of public spending would have the same effect whether it is financed by raising taxes or by running a deficit.

Needless to say, these questions cannot be fully answered here. Refinements in theory can be expected with time, and tentative answers will be devised. For now, many see rational expectations as a rather sterile and unrealistic theory. It has made one important contribution to our understanding of government policy, however. That is the observation that the effectiveness of fiscal and monetary policy depend partly on the extent to which people correctly anticipate the impact of government policy and react accordingly. Insofar as government fiscal and monetary policy is effective, people have been fooled. The real value of rational expectations theory may lie in improved predictions and better understanding of the limits of government policy.

Of course, the government does not normally promise to repay the funds it borrows in one year. Government securities usually mature in four, ten, or even twenty years. In fact, the government can borrow money indefinitely, simply by issuing a new bond to pay off an old one when it comes due (a practice known as "rolling over" debt). In this way the government can delay repaying the principal, but it will still have to raise taxes enough to meet the interest payments on its debt.

Suppose, for instance, that a $1 increase in spending is financed by a bond that the government does not intend to retire when it matures. In that case, taxes in each future year must be higher by the amount of the interest, r. But again, taxpayers can meet their future tax liability by buying $1 worth of bonds this year. The r dollars in interest income they receive in each subsequent year will pay for their extra taxes. Ricardo's theorem still holds. The effect is the same whether the government raises taxes or borrows money to cover its extra spending.

But taxpayers do not live forever. Can they be expected to act as if they will? Some economists think that a concern for the welfare of their children would lead taxpayers to plan beyond their own lifetimes. They would make up for any tax burden the government imposed on their children by giving them larger inheritances. Otherwise part of their tax burden would be shifted to future generations.

Recent evidence suggests that the assumption that taxpayers would plan beyond their lifetimes may be wrong. An analysis of eighty-three federal budgets from 1900 through 1982 shows that holding other things constant (such as the size of government, interest payments on existing debt, and economic growth), increases in the average lifespan are associated with declines in deficit spending. In other words, individuals may prefer deficits to taxes if they do not expect to be living when the government's bonds mature. If so, deficit spending may well be the equivalent of a tax on future generations. As such, it will reduce the amount of capital future generations will inherit, benefiting the living at the expense of those yet to be born.

Adapted from W. F. Shughart II and R. D. Tollison, "A Contingent Liability Theory of Deficit Finance," manuscript, January 1985.

Major Conclusions

1. In Keynesian economics, expectations underlie the investment, consumption, and money demand curves. But Keynesians tend to assume that changes in people's expectations do not entirely offset the impact of fiscal and monetary policy on aggregate demand.
2. Rational expectations theory assumes that people will acquire information on the consequences of government fiscal and monetary policy, and will act on that information. The aquisition of information will change people's expectations for the future, altering the effectiveness of government policies.
3. In its strictest and most extreme form, rational expectations theory assumes that prices and wages are completely flexible; that the acqui-

sition of information on government policy is costless; and that adjust-ments based on changed expectations of the results of government policy are also costless. Given these assumptions, rational expectations theorists conclude that government fiscal and monetary policy will be completely ineffective, both in the short run and in the long run.

4. Both monetarists and rational expectations theorists conclude that fiscal and monetary policy will have no long-run effect on the national income level. Monetarists believe, however, that fiscal and monetary policy may have a short-run effect on the national income level. Rational expectations theorists argue that even the short-run effect is practically nil.

5. Criticism of rational expectations theory focuses on the assumptions that underlie it. Critics contend that information is costly to acquire and that citizens have an incentive to remain ignorant of government policy. Some delay between the initiation of government fiscal or monetary policy and its impact on prices and interest rates must therefore be expected. Critics charge too that fiscal and monetary policies alter the composition of the nation's output—between public and private goods, between investment and consumption goods—and thus affect produc-tion and national income in the long run. Finally, critics point out that

prices are not perfectly flexible. Labor contracts often fix wages, creating a time lag within which government policy can have some effect.

1. This chapter focused on the effects of expansionary fiscal and monetary policies. What should be the effects of contractionary fiscal and monetary policies (a) when they are not expected and (b) when they are expected?
2. Suppose the marginal cost of acquiring information increases as more information is obtained. How would the increasing cost of information affect the theory of rational expectations?
3. Suppose money wages cannot be adjusted downward and the real wage is consequently held above equilibrium. With the aid of a graph, explain how an expansionary fiscal policy would affect employment (a) if its consequences were expected and (b) if its consequences were not fully expected.
4. We have discussed four commonly cited objections to rational expectations theory. Can you think of any others?
5. How do expectations figure in Keynesian theory?
6. How do monetarism and rational expectations theory differ?

Part VI

*Principles
of Consumer
Behavior
and the
Theory
of Demand*

Central Question

What method of analysis do economists use?

Key Terms

Utility

Rational behavior

Money cost

Cost-benefit analysis

Present value

Irrational behavior

Chapter 17

Principles of Individual Behavior

*Man acts because he is
dissatisfied with the state of
affairs as it prevails in the
absence of his intervention.
Man acts because he lacks the
power to render conditions
fully satisfactory and must
resort to appropriate means in
order to render them less
unsatisfactory.*
Ludwig von Mises

With this chapter we begin a detailed examination of microeconomics, the study of how pricing and production decisions are made in individual markets. We have already seen how the forces of supply and demand determine prices (see Chapter 3 for a review). Now we will explore the determinants of the supply and demand for goods, services, and resources.

Microeconomics rests on certain assumptions about individual behavior. One is that people are capable of envisioning various ways of improving their position in life. This chapter reviews and extends the discussion begun in Chapter 2 of how people go about choosing among those alternatives. According to microeconomic theory, consumers and producers make choices rationally, so as to maximize their happiness.

Rationality: A Basis for Exploring Human Behavior

People's wants are ever expanding. We can never satisfy all our wants, because we will always conceive new ones. The best we can do is to maximize our satisfaction, or utility, in the face of scarcity. **Utility** is the satisfaction a person receives from the consumption of a good or service, or from participation in an activity.

The ultimate assumption behind this theory is that people act with a purpose. In the words of von Mises, they act because they are "dissatisfied with the state of affairs as it prevails."[1]

Utility: the satisfaction a person receives from the consumption of a good or service, or from participation in an activity.

The Acting Individual

If people act in order to satisfy their consciously perceived wants, their behavior must be inner-directed rather than externally controlled. However, there is no way to prove this assertion. Economists simply presume that actions are performed by individuals, as opposed to groups. It is the individual who has wants and desires, and looks for the means to fulfill them. It is the individual who attempts to render his or her state "less unsatisfactory."

Group action, when it occurs, results from the actions of the individuals in the group. Social values, for instance, draw their meaning from the values held collectively by individuals. Economists would even say that group action cannot be distinguished from individual action. Thus to understand group behavior, the economist looks to the individual.

Of course individuals in a group affect one another's behavior. In fact, the size and structure of a group can have a dramatic effect on individual behavior. When economists speak of a competitive market, they are actually talking about the influence that other competitors have on the individual consumer or firm.

---

1. Ludwig von Mises, *The Ultimate Foundations of Economic Science: An Essay on Method* (Princeton, N.J.: D. Van Nostrand, 1962), pp. 2–3.

Rational Behavior

When individuals act to satisfy their wants, they behave rationally. **Rational behavior** is consistent behavior that maximizes an individual's satisfaction. The notion of rational behavior rests on three assumptions.

First, the individual has a preference and can identify, within limits, what he or she wants.

Second, the individual is capable of ordering his or her wants consistently, from most preferred to least preferred.

Third, the individual will choose from these ordered preferences so as to maximize his or her satisfaction.

Even though the individual cannot fully satisfy all her wants, she will always choose more of what she wants rather than less. Furthermore, she will always choose less rather than more of what she does not want. In short, the rational individual always stands ready to further her own interests.

Some readers will find these assertions obvious and acceptable. To others they may seem narrow and uninspiring. Later in the chapter we will examine some possible objections to the concept of rational behavior. But first we must examine its logical consequences.

Rational behavior: consistent behavior that maximizes an individual's satisfaction.

Rational Decisions in a Constrained Environment

Several important conclusions flow from the economist's presumption of rational behavior. First, the individual makes choices from an array of alternatives. Second, in making each choice, a person must forgo one or more things for something else. All rational behavior involves a cost, which is the value of the most preferred alternative forgone. Third, in striving to maximize his or her welfare, the individual will take those actions whose benefits exceed their costs.

Choice

We assume that the individual can evaluate the available alternatives and select the alternative that maximizes his utility. But nothing in the economic definition of rational behavior suggests that the individual is completely free to do as he wishes. Whenever we talk about individual choices, we are actually talking about constrained choices—choices that are limited by external forces. For example, you as a student find yourself in a certain social and physical environment and have certain physical and mental abilities. These environmental and personal factors influence the options open to you. You may have neither the money, the time, nor the stomach to become a surgeon. Or your career goal may not allow you the luxury of taking many of the electives listed in your college catalog.

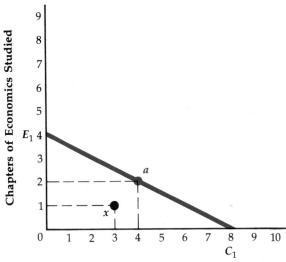

Figure 17.1. Constrained Choice.
With a given amount of time and other resources, you can produce any combination of study and conversation along the curve E_1C_1. The particular combination you choose will depend on your personal preferences for those two goods. You will not choose point x, because it represents less than you are capable of achieving— and as a rational person, you will maximize your utility. Because of constraints on your time and resources, you cannot achieve at a point above E_1C_1.

Yet though your range of choices may not be wide, choices do exist. At this moment you could be doing any number of things instead of reading this book. You could be studying some other subject, or going out on a date, or playing with your son or daughter. You could have chosen to go shopping, to engage in intramural sports, or to jog around the block. You may not be capable of playing varsity sports, but you have other choices. Although your options are limited, or constrained—you are not completely free to do as you please—you can still choose what you want to do. In fact, you must choose.

Assume that you have an exam tomorrow in economics and that there are exactly two things you can do within the next twelve hours. You can study economics, or you can converse with friends. These two options are represented in Figure 17.1. Suppose you spend the entire twelve hours studying economics. In our example, the most you can study is four chapters, or E_1. At the other extreme, you could do nothing but talk with your friends—but again, there is a limit: eight conversations, or C_1.

Neither extreme is likely to be acceptable. Assuming that you aim both to pass your exam and to maintain your friendships, what combination of conversation and study should you choose? The available options are represented by the straight line E_1C_1, the production possibilities curve for study and talk, and the area underneath it. If you want to maximize your production, you will choose some point on E_1C_1, such as a: two chapters

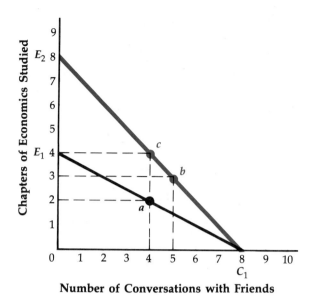

Number of Conversations with Friends

Figure 17.2. Change in Constraints.
If your study skills improve and your conversational ability remains constant, your production possibilities curve will shift from E_1C_1 to E_2C_1. Both the number of chapters you can study and the number of conversations you can hold will increase. On your old curve E_1C_1, you could study two chapters and have four conversations (point a). On your new curve, E_2C_1, you can study three chapters and have five conversations (point b).

of economics and four conversations. You might yearn for five conversations and the same amount of study, but that point is above the curve and beyond your capabilities. If you settle for less—say one chapter and three conversations, or point x—you will be doing less than you are capable of doing, and will not be maximizing your utility. The combination you actually choose will depend on your preferences.

Changes in your environment or your physical capabilities can affect your opportunities and consequently the choice you make. For example, if you improve your study skills, your production rate for chapters studied will rise. You might then be able to study eight units of economics in twelve hours—in which case your production possibilities curve would expand outward. Even if your ability to converse remained the same, your greater proficiency in studying would enable you to increase the number and length of your conversations. Your new set of production possibilities would be E_2C_1 in Figure 17.2.

Again, you can choose any point along this curve or in the area below it. You may decide against further conversations and opt instead for four chapters of economics (point c). Or you could move to point b, in which case you would still be learning more economics—three chapters instead of two—but would also be talking more with friends. The important point is that you are able to choose from a range of opportunities. The option you take is not predetermined.

Cost

The fact that choices exist implies that some alternative must be forgone when another is taken. If A and B represent two mutually exclusive opportunities and A is taken, then B is not—at least not at that moment. In the presence of choice—a situation in which no more than one alternative can be taken at a time—a cost must be incurred. Cost (or more precisely, opportunity cost) is the value of the most highly preferred alternative not taken. Put another way, it is the value the individual places on the most favored alternative not taken at the time the choice is made.

Notice that cost is not defined in terms of money. Money is a useful measure, because it reduces all costs to one common denominator. But money is only a means of measuring cost; it is not cost itself. The shoes you are wearing may have cost you $25 (a money cost), but the real cost (the opportunity cost) is the value of what you could have purchased instead. **Money cost** is a monetary measure of the benefits forgone when a choice is made. The real cost is the actual benefits given up from the most preferred alternative not taken when a choice is made. When economists use the term cost, they mean real, or opportunity, cost. You could have bought dozens of soft drinks or deposited the $25 in a savings account for future use. Either option would be a legitimate alternative to purchasing shoes. The point is that the cost of the shoes to you is the value of the most attractive option not taken, whether it be the soft drinks or the future use of the money.

So long as you have alternative uses for your time and other resources, there is no such thing as a free lunch. Nothing can be free if other opportunities are available. One goal of economics courses is to help you recognize this very simple principle, and to train you to search for hidden costs. There is a cost to writing a poem, to watching a sunset, to extending a common courtesy, if only to open a door for someone. Though money is not always involved in choices, the opportunity to do other things is. A cost is incurred in every choice.

Money cost: a monetary measure of the benefits forgone when a choice is made.

Maximizing Satisfaction: Cost-Benefit Analysis

An individual who behaves rationally will choose an option only when its benefits exceed its costs. Furthermore, individuals will try to maximize their satisfaction by choosing the most favorable option available. That is, they will produce or consume those goods and services whose benefits exceed the benefits of the most favored opportunity not taken.

This restatement of the maximizing principle, as it is called, explains individual choice in terms of cost. In Figure 17.1, the choices along curve E_1C_1 represent various cost-benefit tradeoffs. If you choose point a, we must assume that you prefer a to any other combination because it yields the most favorable ratio of benefits to costs.

A change in cost will produce a change in behavior. Suppose you and a friend set a date to play checkers, but at the last moment he receives a lucrative job offer for the day of the match. Most likely the contest will be rescheduled. The job offer will change your friend's opportunities in such a way that what otherwise would have been a rational act (playing checkers) becomes an irrational one. The cost of playing checkers will rise significantly, enough to exceed the benefits of most checkers games.

Economists see cost-benefit analysis as the basis of much (but certainly not all) of our behavior. **Cost-benefit analysis** is the careful calculation of all costs and benefits associated with a given course of action. Why do you attend classes, for example? The obvious answer is that at the time you decide to attend class, you expect the benefits of attending to exceed the costs. The principle applies even to classes you dislike. A particular course may have no intrinsic value, but you may fear that by cutting classes, you will miss information that would be useful on examinations. Thus the benefits of attending are a higher grade than you would otherwise expect. Besides, other options open to you on Tuesday morning at 10:00 a.m. may have so little appeal that the cost of going to class is very slight.

Or take another example. Americans are known for the amount of waste they pile up. Our gross national garbage is estimated to be more valuable than the gross national output of many other nations. We throw away many things that people in other parts of the world would be glad to have. However morally reprehensible, waste may be seen as the result of economically rational behavior. Wastefulness may be beneficial in a limited personal sense. The food wrappings people throw away are "wasted," but they do add convenience and freshness to the food. In the individual's narrow cost-benefit analysis, the benefits of the wrapping can exceed the costs.

Is life priceless? Though we like to think so, many of us are not willing to bear the cost that must be paid to preserve it. Several million animals— dogs, opossums, squirrels, and birds—are killed on the highways each year. Most of us make some effort to avoid killing these animals. We swerve to miss a doe that has strayed onto the road, and we put up warning signs at deer crossings. But there is some limit to our willingness to make an effort (to incur costs) to avoid animal highway deaths. If saving lives were all-important, we could drive less—but that would bring a significant cost. Even when human beings are involved, we sometimes refuse to bear the cost of preserving life. People avoid helping victims of violent crime, and doctors routinely pass by highway accidents although they might save lives by stopping to help. Indeed, revolutions are made through people's willingness to sacrifice lives—both others' and their own—to achieve political or economic goals.

The behavior of business people is not materially different from that of drivers or consumers. People in business are constantly concerned with such issues as whether the cost of improving the quality of a product is matched by the benefits of the improvement. Will consumers value the added benefits enough to pay for them? In assessing the safety of their products, business people must consider whether consumers are willing to pay the cost of any improvements.

Cost-benefit analysis: the careful calculation of all costs and benefits associated with a given course of action.

Perspectives in Economics: How Much Is a Life Worth?

Harry Schwartz

How much should society be willing to pay to save one individual's life or to prolong that life if the basic disease is incurable? Should the top limit on such expenditure be $10,000 or $100,000 or $1 million? Or perhaps there should be no limit.

Such questions used to be of purely theoretical interest. But they have become very practical and important in this era when society's agencies—the government or private insurance companies—pay most medical bills.

Just how topical these questions are was revealed last June 12 [1980] when the government announced that, with a few exceptions, Medicare will no longer pay for heart transplant operations. The average cost of such a procedure is about $100,000, and Health and Human Services Secretary Patricia Roberts Harris made no bones about the fact that cost had played a part in her decision.

"I don't like the idea of assessing the value of a human life. I don't think that can be done. At the same time we have to find out what the costs are. We have to ask, 'Will we buy this or will we buy something else?'", Mrs. Harris told an interviewer. Mrs. Harris is planning a two-year study of the medical, social, economic, and ethical aspects of heart transplants to serve as a basis for a future decision on whether such operations should be paid for by Medicare.

Hospital Draws the Line

The government is not the only participant in the health care field to be wondering about how much is enough. Last February the trustees of Massachusetts General Hospital turned down a request by their surgical staff to let heart transplants be done there—a decision based largely on cost considerations. And last May the *New England Journal of Medicine* ran an editorial titled, "Can We Afford to Treat Acute Leukemia?" The editorial answered the question affirmatively, but it showed clear uneasiness about the high cost of available treatment and asked pointblank: "Should these treatments be made available to all or even most of the patients in our country, not to mention the world, who have this disease?"

What these straws in the wind indicate is that this country is finally learning—as the British did long ago—that society cannot afford to pay all the medical bills would-be consumers of "free medical care" might generate. There is now no doubt that heart transplants are medically effective—half of Dr. Norman Shumway's patients at Stanford live five years or longer after their operations—and no one would stop the occasional millionaire who wants to pay for such an operation on himself. But should Medicare, Blue Shield, or private health insurers pay for everybody who can benefit from this procedure and whose doctor locates a transplantable heart?

Britain's National Health Service has long recognized that its finite resources cannot match the potential infinite demand for "free" medical care. Its solution in part is simply to deny some procedures to particular classes of people—for example, kidney dialysis or transplants to patients over 60 or 65, a policy that each year results in the death of 1,000 to 2,000 persons who might otherwise live longer. In greater part the NHS makes patients wait weeks or months to see a particular specialist and months or years for an operation—say, replacement of a hip destroyed by arthritis—that is not required to save a life.

The British government's approach to heart transplants also displays characteristic caution. Earlier this year two hospitals were authorized to perform the procedure and one actually was given almost $250,000 to improve its facilities. But the government has been more than content to have private contributions of about $750,000 to each of the two hospitals pay the bulk of the added cost.

Since only about 50 heart transplants a year are done in the U.S. and the supply of hearts for such procedures is very limited, it might be thought that Medicare's retreat from this type of surgery is not very significant in the national health picture.

That conclusion would be wrong. The same kind of reasoning is clearly going to be applied to other expensive new types of therapy that will emerge in the future.

Suppose interferon turns out to be effective against cancer, but continues to be extremely expensive to produce. Present estimates are that it will cost $30,000 to $50,000 to supply enough interferon for each case. Since about 750,000 Americans develop cancer each year (even ignoring the hundreds of thousands who develop skin cancer), that would pose a possible total for interferon costs well in excess of $20 billion annually.

Even more horrendous cost projections can be developed by considering either of the following two medical advances that might be made in the decade just ahead. [As already has been done on a highly experimental basis,] one might be an artificial heart that could successfully be put into a patient's chest to replace his old, defective natural heart. At one stroke this would eliminate the bottleneck of insufficient hearts that limits transplants and create overnight a demand from mil-

lions of heart disease sufferers who are, of course, also voters.

Or, alternatively, the biochemists and immunologists might come up with an ingenious new way to turn off the body's rejection mechanism that threatens every recipient of a transplanted heart or kidney. That would immediately smooth the way also for transplants of the lungs, liver, pancreas and other organs whose defective operation now often results in death. The pressure for vastly increasing the supply of organs for transplants and the number of transplant operations would be enormous, again threatening the health care system with fantastic new demands whose cost would run into double digit billions. . . .

The thought must occur that this medical populism is ultimately derived from vote considerations. The number of people who go to primary physicians or would like to go to them is a major fraction of the population. By comparison the number of people sick with life-threatening diseases is relatively small at any given time, and many of them are too sick to vote.

But America is aging, and every year the number of elderly victims of cancer, heart disease, stroke and other degenerative diseases rises steadily. A wise Health Secretary and a wise Congressman might well consider whether these swelling legions of the gray-haired will willingly acquiesce in policies aimed at denying them life-saving procedures, while trying to provide a full-fledged doctor for every sore throat and bellyache in every remote desert or mountain hamlet.

Reprinted from the *Wall Street Journal* (September 15, 1980), editorial page.

The Effects of Time and Risk on Costs and Benefits

When an individual acts, costs are not necessarily incurred immediately, and benefits are not necessarily received immediately. The decision to have a child is a good example. At 1984 prices, a college-educated couple's first child is estimated to cost the parents something over $175,000, from birth through college.[2] Fortunately this high cost is incurred over a relatively long period of time.

By stringing out their payments rather than making a single immediate lump-sum payment of $175,000, parents can keep some of that money in a savings account, where it will accumulate interest. Alternatively—for most new parents do not have $175,000 in the bank—they escape the necessity of borrowing the entire sum immediately and making interest payments on it. Either way, $175,000 spent over a period of twenty years is less costly than $175,000 spent now. To make rational choices, then, people must consider the period over which costs will be incurred.

Benefits received in the future must also be compared with present benefits. If you had a choice between receiving $10,000 now and $10,000 one year from now, you would take $10,000 today. You could, if nothing else, put the money in a bank, where it would earn interest. Or you could avoid the effects of future inflation by spending the money now. In other words, future benefits must be greater than present benefits to be more attractive than present benefits.

Present value: the value of future costs or benefits in terms of current dollars.

To compare future costs and benefits on an equal footing with costs and benefits realized today, we must adjust them to their present value. **Present value** is the value of future costs or benefits in terms of current dollars. The usual procedure for calculating present value—a process called discounting—involves an adjustment for the interest that could be earned (or would have to be paid) if the money were received (or due) today rather than in the future.[3]

If there is any uncertainty about whether future benefits or costs will actually be received or paid, further adjustments must be made. Without such adjustments, a perfectly rational act may appear to be quite irrational. For example, not all business ventures can be expected to succeed. Some will be less profitable than expected, or may collapse altogether. The average fast-food franchise may earn a yearly profit of $1 million, but only nine out of ten franchises may survive their first year. Thus the estimated profits for such a franchise must be discounted, or multiplied by 0.90. If 10 percent of such ventures can be expected to fail, on average each will earn $900,000 ($1 million × .90).

---

2. Thomas J. Espenshade, "The Value and Cost of Children" (Washington: Population Reference Bureau, 1980), as reported in the *Wall Street Journal* (October 2, 1980), p. 33. The reported cost of raising a child in 1980, $140,000, is adjusted here for price increases through 1984.

3. The mathematical formula for computing the present value of future costs or benefits received one year from now is $PV = 1/(1 + r) f$, where PV stands for present value, r for the rate of interest, and f for future costs or benefits.

The entrepreneur who starts a single business venture runs the risk that it may be the one out of ten that fails. In that case profit will be zero. To avoid putting all their eggs in one basket, many entrepreneurs prefer to initiate several new ventures, thereby spreading the risk of doing business. In the same way investors spread their risk by investing in several companies, and firms spread their risk by producing a number of products.

To give another example, criminal behavior may appear to be irrational if only the raw costs and benefits are considered. A burglar who nets $1,500 from the sale of stolen property may have to spend a year in jail if caught, prosecuted, and convicted. He could lose the annual income from his legitimate job, perhaps $10,000. That is a high cost to pay for a $1,500 profit on stolen property. But he pays that cost only if he is caught, prosecuted, convicted, and sentenced. The police cannot be everywhere at all times; prosecutors may be reluctant to prosecute; and suspended sentences are commonplace. All in all, even an inept burglar may have no more than a 10 percent chance of spending a year in jail.[4]

To estimate the actual cost faced by the burglar who is caught, sentenced, and sent to jail for a year, we might multiply the cost if caught, $10,000, by 0.10. That calculation indicates that to a burglar who is sent to jail for an average of one out of ten burglaries, the cost of any one burglary is only $1,000 ($10,000 × 0.10). Thus the actual cost of the burglary is less than the benefits received, $1,500. Although it may be morally reprehensible, the criminal act can conceivably be a rational one.

Surveys of criminal activities and their rewards tend to support such a conclusion. A study of burglary and grand larceny cases in Norfolk, Virginia, showed that for the unusual criminal who committed just one crime and was caught in the act, crime did not pay. But the typical criminal, convicted the average number of times and sentenced to the average number of years in prison, more than tripled the lifetime income he could have earned from a regular salaried job—even allowing for one or more years of unsalaried incarceration.[5] When this study was replicated in Minnesota, the results were not quite as dramatic, but the criminal's lifetime income still doubled.[6] For criminals who are never caught, crime pays even more handsomely.

The same logical process of discounting can be applied to your life as a student. When you sign up for courses, you usually have only a very rough idea of how difficult and time-consuming they will be, and what

4. This is not an unreasonably low figure. Gregory Krohm "concluded that the chance of an 'adult' (seventeen or older) burglar being sent to prison for *any single offense* is .0024 . . . For juveniles . . . the risk was much lower, .0015." "The Pecuniary Incentives of Property Crime," in *The Economics of Crime and Punishment,* ed. Simon Rottenberg (Washington: American Enterprise Institute for Public Research, 1973), p. 33.

5. William E. Cobb, "Theft and the Two Hypotheses," in *The Economics of Crime and Punishment,* ed. Simon Rottenberg (Washington: American Enterprise Institute for Public Policy Research, 1973), pp. 19–30.

6. David L. Johnson, "An Analysis of the Costs and Benefits for Criminals in Theft" (Economics Department, St. Cloud State College, St. Cloud, Minn., May 1974), mimeographed.

Economists in History: John Stuart Mill (1806—1873)

Delores T. Martin

John Stuart Mill, one of the greatest English philosophers, was the eldest son of the economist James Mill. Under his father's guidance Mill received a rigorous education, studying Greek at three, Latin at eight, and logic and political economy at twelve. At thirteen he took instruction from the famous economist David Ricardo. By the time he was fourteen, his formal education was complete.

Mill made many varied contributions to economic thought. He was the first economist to develop the concept of demand as a schedule, or function. He articulated the dynamics of supply and demand thoroughly and extended the theory of the mutual benefit of international exchange to include the role of cost and demand in determining the terms of trade. Finally, Mill extended Adam Smiths' work on wage differences by examining the economic effect of barriers to job mobility, such as the cost of education.

Mill was optimistic about the future of the human race. Like some other economists, he acknowledged that there were limits to investment and agricultural production, and hence to an economy's potential for growth. But unlike Malthus, Mill believed that society would learn to restrict population growth, thus tempering the demand for basics like food, clothing, and shelter. Slower population growth would mean more capital for investment and more development.

I confess I am not charmed with the ideal of life held out by those who think the normal state of human beings is that of struggling to get on; that the trampling, crushing, elbowing, and treading on each other's heels, which form the existing type of social life, are the most desirable lot of humankind, or anything but the disagreeable symptoms of one of the phases of industrial progress.[1]

Mill's work was highly influential. His *Principles of Political Economy*, published in 1848, was widely read and discussed, and served as the standard textbook on economics for over sixty years.

1. John Stuart Mill, *Principles of Political Economy*, edited by W. J. Ashley (New York: A. M. Kelley, 1965), pp. 747–48.

benefits you will receive from them. In other words, you are rarely certain of their costs and benefits. To make your decisions, you will have to discount the raw costs and benefits by the probability of their being realized. Risks are pervasive in human experience, and rational behavior accounts for them.

What Rational Behavior Does Not Mean

The concept of rational behavior often proves bothersome to the noneconomist. Most of the difficulties surrounding this concept arise from a misunderstanding of what rationality means. Common objections include the following.

1. People do many things that do not work out to their benefit. A driver speeds and ends up in the hospital. A student cheats, gets caught, and is expelled from school. Many other examples can be cited. To say that people behave rationally does not mean that they never make mistakes.

We can calculate our options with some probability, but we do not have perfect knowledge, nor can we fully control the future. Chances are that we will make a mistake at some point. But as individuals, we base our choices on what we expect to happen, not on what does happen. We speed because we expect not to crash, and we cheat because we expect not to be caught. Both can be rational behaviors.

2. Rational behavior implies that a person is totally self-centered, doing only things that are of direct personal benefit. Rational behavior need not be selfish. Altruism can be rational; a person can want to be of service to others, just as he can want to own a new car. Most of us get pleasure from seeing others happy—and particularly when their happiness is the result of our actions. Altruism may not always spring from rational cost-benefit calculations; however, it is not always inconsistent with economic rationality.

3. People's behavior is subject to psychological quirks, hang-ups, habits, and impulses. Surely such behavior cannot be considered rational. Human actions are governed by the constraints of our physical and mental make-up. Like our intelligence, our inclination toward aberrant or impulsive behavior is one of those constraints. It makes our choice process less precise and contributes to our mistakes, but it does not prevent our acting rationally.

Moreover, what looks like impulsive or habitual behavior may actually be the product of some prior rational choice. The human mind can handle only so much information and make only so many decisions in one day. Consequently we may attempt to economize on decision making by reducing some behaviors to habit. Smoking may appear to be totally impulsive, and the physical addiction that accompanies it may indeed restrict the smoker's range of choices. Why might a person pull a cigarette from the pack "without thinking"? Perhaps because she has reasoned earlier that contemplating the pros and cons of smoking each and every time she thinks of cigarettes is too costly. By allowing smoking to become more or less automatic, the smoker probably increases the number of cigarettes she smokes daily. But she saves the tedium of having to make the decision each and every time she smokes.

Some behavior is actually irrational, but the term needs careful definition. **Irrational behavior** is behavior that is inconsistent or clearly not in the individual's best interests, and that the individual recognizes as such at the time of the behavior. The existence of such behavior only adds an element of imprecision to economic theory. It does not contradict it.

4. Rational behavior implies that people know what they want, that they know which alternatives are available, and that they know how to act on that information. But people cannot assimilate all the information they need to make rational choices. People do lack information, and they could make better choices if information were easier to obtain. However, rational behavior does not require perfect information. People will make choices on the basis of the information they have or can rationally acquire. If they have less than perfect information, they may make mistakes in their choices. The success or failure of their choices must be judged within those constraints.

Irrational behavior: behavior that is inconsistent or clearly not in the individual's best interests, and that the individual recognizes as such at the time of the behavior.

5. People do not necessarily maximize their satisfaction. For instance, many people do not perform to the limit of their abilities. Satisfaction is a question of personal taste. To some individuals, lounging around is an economic good; by consuming it, they increase their welfare. Criticism of such behavior is tinged with normative value judgments. An observer who equates rational behavior with what he or she considers good will have no trouble demonstrating that much behavior is irrational. But to the economist, the values of the actor, not the observer or the social critic, determine the rationality of an act.

Summary and Extensions

The concept of rational behavior means that the individual has alternatives, can order those alternatives on the basis of preference, and can act consistently on that basis. The rational individual will also choose those alternatives whose expected benefits exceed their expected costs.

Traditionally economics has focused on the activities of business firms, and much of this book is devoted to exploring human behavior in a market setting. The concept of rational behavior can be applied to other activities, however, from politics and government to family life and leisure pursuits. No matter what the activity, we all tend to maximize our well-being. Any differences in our behavior can be ascribed to differences in our preferences and in the institutional settings, or constraints, within which we operate.

Institutional settings affect people's range of alternatives, and thus the choices they make. Thus it makes sense to examine the constraints of institutional settings. In this part of the book we will investigate the specific characteristics of the market system, the subject of microeconomic theory. Later we will look at the constraints of government. In both cases the range of choices open to individuals affects the ability of the system to produce the results expected of it.

1. The concept of rational behavior is a cornerstone of economic analysis. Rational behavior means that an individual knows, within limits, what he or she wants; is capable of ordering those wants from least to most preferred; and will choose alternatives that provide maximum satisfaction.
2. The individual is constantly faced with the need to choose. The choice of one alternative implies that another alternative must be forgone. In other words, there is a cost to choice. Cost is defined as the value of the most preferred alternative forgone.
3. The rational person will choose those alternatives whose expected benefits exceed their expected costs.
4. Rational behavior is also affected by the time at which benefits are received and costs incurred, and by the degree of uncertainty that benefits will be realized.

Major Conclusions

1. What are the costs of taking a course in economics? What are the benefits? (Obviously there is at least one, or you would not be taking the course.)
2. What are the costs and benefits of engaging someone in a conversation? Does rational behavior fully explain the length and types of conversations we engage in?
3. Some psychologists see behavior as determined by external, or environmental, forces. How would the concept of cost fit into that theory?
4. Cite some examples of irrational behavior.
5. Could the behavior of someone under the influence of drugs be considered irrational?
6. Under what circumstances could suicide be considered irrational behavior?

Questions to Ponder

Central Question

If consumers behave rationally, what predictions can we make about their demand for goods and services?

Key Terms

Marginal utility

Consumer equilibrium

Law of diminishing marginal utility

Law of demand

Price

Market demand

Price elasticity of demand

Elastic demand

Inelastic demand

Unitary elastic demand

Elasticity coefficient of demand

Perfectly elastic demand

Normal good or service

Luxury good or service

Inferior good or service

Indifference curve

Budget line

Chapter 18

Consumer Choice and Demand

*It is not the province of
economics to determine the
value of life in "hedonic units"
or any other units, but to work
out, on the basis of the general
principles of conduct and the
fundamental facts of social
situation, the laws which
determine prices of
commodities and the direction
of the social economic process.
It is therefore not quantities,
not even intensities, of
satisfaction with which we are
concerned . . . or any other
absolute magnitude whatever,
but the purely relative
judgment of comparative
significance of alternatives
open to choice.*
Frank Knight

*P*eople adjust to changes in some economic conditions with a reasonable degree of predictability. When department stores announce lower prices, customers will pour through the doors. The lower the prices go, the larger the crowd will be. When the price of gasoline goes up, drivers will make fewer and shorter trips. If the price stays up, drivers will buy smaller, more economical cars. Even the Defense Department will reduce its planned purchases when prices rise.

Behavior that is not measured in dollars and cents is also predictable in some respects. Students who stray from the sidewalks to dirt paths on sunny days stick to concrete when the weather is damp. Professors who raise their course requirements and grading standards find their classes are shrinking in size. Small children shy away from doing things for which they have recently been punished. And when lines for movie tickets become long, some people go elsewhere for entertainment.

On an intuitive level you will find these examples reasonable. Going one step beyond intuition, the economist would say that such responses are the predictable consequence of rational behavior. That is, people who desire to maximize their utility can be expected to respond in these ways. Their responses are governed by the law of demand, a concept we first introduced in Chapter 3 and now take up in greater detail.

Predicting Consumer Demand

The assumptions about rational behavior described in the last chapter provide a good general basis for explaining behavior. People will do those things whose expected benefits exceed their expected costs. They will avoid doing things for which the opposite is true. By themselves, however, such assumptions do not allow us to predict future behavior. The law of demand, which is a logical consequence of the assumption of rational behavior, does allow us to make predictions.

The alert reader may sense an inconsistency in logic. Rational behavior is based on the existence of choice. But a true choice must be free—it cannot be predetermined or predicted. If we can predict a person's behavior, can that individual be free to choose?

Choice is not completely free, nor is complete freedom required by the concept of rationality. As discussed in Chapter 17, the individual's choices are constrained by time and by physical and social factors that restrict his or her opportunities. There are limits to a person's range of choice.

Our ability to predict is also limited. We cannot specify with precision every choice the individual will make. For instance, we cannot say anything about what Judy Schwartz wants or how much she wants the things she does. Before we can employ the law of demand, we must be told what she wants. Even given that knowledge, we can only indicate the general direction of her behavior. Theory does not allow us to determine how fast or how much her behavior will change.

To see how consumer behavior can be predicted, we will derive the law of demand from the behavior of an individual consumer.

Rational Consumption: The Concept of Marginal Utility

The essence of the economist's notion of rational behavior can be summed up this way: more of these goods and services desired by the individual is preferable to less. This statement implies that the individual will use his entire income, in consumption or in saving or in some combination of the two, to maximize his satisfaction. It also implies that the individual will use some method of comparing the value of various goods.

Generally speaking, the value the individual places on any one unit of a good depends on the number of units already consumed. For example, you may be planning to consume two hot dogs and two Cokes for your next meal. Though you may pay the same price for each unit of both goods, there is no reason to assume that you will place the same value on each. The value of the second hot dog—its marginal utility—will depend on the fact that you have already eaten one. **Marginal utility** is the additional satisfaction received from consuming one additional unit of a good or service.

Marginal utility: the additional satisfaction received from consuming one additional unit of a good or service.

Achieving Consumer Equilibrium

Marginal utility determines the variety and quantity of goods and services you consume. The rule is simple. If the two goods, Coke and hot dogs, both have the same price, you will allocate your income so that the marginal utility of the last unit of each will be equal. Mathematically, the formula can be stated as

$$MU_c = MU_h$$

where MU_c equals the marginal utility of a Coke and MU_h equals the marginal utility of a hot dog.

If you are rational, and if the price of a Coke is the same as the price of a hot dog, the last Coke you drink will give you the same amount of enjoyment as the last hot dog you eat. When the marginal utilities of goods purchased by the consumer are equal, the resulting state is called consumer equilibrium. **Consumer equilibrium** is a state of stability in consumer purchasing patterns in which the individual has maximized his or her utility. Unless conditions—income, taste, or prices—change, the consumer's buying patterns will tend to remain the same.

Consumer equilibrium: a state of stability in consumer purchasing patterns in which the individual has maximized his or her utility.

An example will illustrate how equilibrium is reached. Suppose for the sake of simplicity that you can buy only two goods, Coke and hot dogs. Suppose further that each costs the same price, $1, and you are going to spend your whole income. (How much your total income is and how many units of Coke or hot dogs you will purchase are unimportant. We simply assume that you purchase some combination of those two goods.) Finally, suppose that the marginal utility of the last Coke you consume is equal to 20 utils, and the marginal utility of the last hot dog is 10 utils.

Obviously you have not maximized your utility, for the marginal utility of your last Coke is greater than (>) the marginal utility of your last hot dog:

$$MU_c > MU_h$$

You could have purchased one less hot dog and used the dollar saved to buy an additional Coke. In doing so, you would have given up 10 utils of satisfaction (the marginal utility of the last hot dog purchased), but you would have acquired an additional 20 utils from the new Coke. On balance, your total utility would have risen by 10 utils (20–10). If you are rational, you will continue to adjust your purchases of Coke and hot dogs until their marginal utilities are equal.

Even if you would prefer to spend your first dollar on a hot dog, after eating several you might wish to spend your next dollar on a Coke. Purchases can be adjusted until they reach equilibrium because as more of a good is purchased, its relative marginal utility decreases—a phenomenon known as the law of diminishing marginal utility. According to the **law of diminishing marginal utility**, as more of a good is consumed, its marginal utility or value relative to the marginal value of the good or goods given up diminishes. Thus, if $MU_h > MU_c$ to begin, and MU_h falls relative to MU_c as more hot dogs and fewer Cokes are consumed, sooner or later the result will be $MU_h = MU_c$.

Law of diminishing marginal utility: the rule that as more of a good is consumed, its marginal utility or value relative to the marginal value of the good or goods given up diminishes.

Adjusting for Differences in Price and Unit Size

Coke and hot dogs are not usually sold at exactly the same price. To that extent, our analysis has been unrealistic. If we drop the assumption of equal prices, the formula for maximization of utility becomes:

$$\frac{MU_c}{P_c} = \frac{MU_h}{P_h}$$

where MU_c equals the marginal utility of a Coke, MU_h the marginal utility of a hot dog, P_c the price of a Coke, and P_h the price of a hot dog. This is the same formula we used before, but because the prices of the goods were the same in that example, the denominators canceled out. When prices differ, the denominator must be retained. The consumer must allocate his or her money so that the last penny spent on each commodity yields the same amount of satisfaction.

Suppose a Coke costs $0.50 and the price of a hot dog is $1. If you eat hot dogs and Coke for lunch and the marginal utility of the last Coke and hot dog you eat are the same, say 15 utils, you will not be maximizing your satisfaction. In relation to price, you will value your Coke more than your hot dog. That is, MU_c/P_c (or 15 utils/$0.50) exceeds MU_h/P_h (or 15 utils/$1). You can improve your welfare by eating fewer hot dogs and drinking more Coke. By giving up a hot dog, you can save a dollar, which you can use to buy two Cokes. You will lose 15 utils by giving up the hot dog, something you would probably prefer not to do. But you will regain that loss with the next Coke purchased, and the one after that will permit you to go beyond your previous level of satisfaction.

Therefore, if you are rational, you will adjust your purchases until the utility-price ratios of the two goods are equal. As you consume more Coke, the relative value of each additional Coke will diminish. If you reach a point where the next Coke gives you 10 utils and the next hot dog yields 20 utils, you will no longer be able to increase your satisfaction by readjusting your purchases. By giving up the next hot dog, you save $1 and lose 20 utils of satisfaction. But now the most you can accomplish by using that $1 to buy two Cokes instead is to recoup your loss of 20 utils. In fact, the value of the second new Coke may be less than 10 utils, so you may actually lose by giving up the hot dog.

So far we have been talking in terms of buying whole units of Cokes and hot dogs. But the same principles apply to other kinds of choices as well. Marginal utility is involved when a consumer chooses a 12-ounce rather than a 16-ounce can of Coke, or a regular-size hot dog rather than a foot-long hot dog. The concept could also be applied to the decision whether to add cole slaw and chili to the hot dog. The pivotal question the consumer faces in all these situations is whether the marginal utility of the additional quantity consumed is greater or less than the marginal utility of other goods that can be purchased for the same price.

Most consumers do not think in terms of utils when they are buying their lunch. But in a casual way, they do weigh the alternatives. Suppose you walk into a snack bar. If your income is unlimited, you have no problem. But if you can only spend $3 for lunch, your first reaction may be to look at the menu and weigh the marginal values of the various things you can eat. If you have twenty cents to spare, do you not find yourself mentally asking whether the difference between a large Coke and a small one is worth more to you than lettuce and tomato on your hamburger? (If not, why do you choose a small Coke instead of a large one?) You are probably so accustomed to making decisions of this sort that you are almost unaware of the act of weighing the marginal values of the alternatives.

Consumers do not usually make choices with conscious precision. Nor can they achieve a perfect equilibrium—the prices, unit sizes, and values of the various products available may not permit it. But they are trying to come as close to equality as possible. The economist's assumption is that the individual will move toward equality, not that he will achieve it.

Changes in Price and the Law of Demand

Suppose your marginal utility for Coke and hot dogs is as shown in the table below.

Unit Consumed	Marginal Utility of Cokes (at $0.50)	Marginal Utility of Hot Dogs (at $1)
First	10 utils	30 utils
Second	9 utils	15 utils
Third	3 utils	12 utils

Economists in History: William Stanley Jevons (1835–1882)

Until the publication of William Stanley Jevons's *Theory of Political Economy* in 1871, economists had focused largely on questions of long-run economic growth. Jevons redirected economic analysis to the question of efficiency, or how to allocate resources for maximum utility. He posed the problem this way:

Given a certain population, with various needs and powers of production, in possession of certain lands and other sources of material; required, the mode of employing their labour which will maximize the utility of the produce.[1]

To Jevons, scarcity was the central problem of economics.

Jevons's major contribution was the development of marginal utility analysis. He demonstrated that the market price of a good is ultimately determined by its value to the consumer, rather than by the cost of its production. To illustrate the principle of diminishing marginal utility, he wrote:

Let us imagine the whole quantity of food which a person consumes on an average during twenty-four hours to be divided into ten equal parts. If his food is reduced by the last part, he will suffer but little; if a second tenth part be deficient, he will feel the want distinctly; the subtraction of a third part will be decidedly injurious; with every subsequent subtraction of a tenth part his sufferings will be more and more serious, until at length he will be upon the verge of starvation. Now, if we call each of the tenth parts an increment, the meaning of

these facts is, that each increment of food is less necessary, or possesses less utility, than the previous one.[2]

Using marginal utility analysis, Jevons solved a paradox that had perplexed Adam Smith. Water, which is necessary to life, sells for a low price, whereas diamonds, which are not at all important to life, command a high price. The key to the riddle, Jevons explained, was that prices are determined by the *marginal* values of goods. In most parts of the world, water is in far greater supply in relation to market demand than are diamonds.

Jevons's interests extended beyond economics to mathematics and the physical sciences, including chemistry, metallurgy, and biology. His research covered a wide variety of subjects, from a statistical study called *The Coal Question* (1865) to more theoretical works like *Pure Logic* (1863) and *The Principles of Science* (1874). At times Jevons combined his knowledge in several disciplines to produce a unique intellectual synthesis. His theory of business cycles, now discredited, was based on statistical correlations he found among general economic activity, agricultural production, and the occurrence of sunspots and rainfall.

1. William Stanley Jevons, *The Theory of Political Economy,* 5th ed. (New York: Kelly & Millman, 1957), p. 267.
2. Ibid.

If a Coke is priced at $0.50 and a hot dog at $1, $3 will buy you two hot dogs and two Cokes—the best you can do with $3 at those prices. Now suppose the price of Coke rises to $0.75 and the price of hot dogs falls to $0.75. With a budget of $3 you can still buy two hot dogs and two Cokes, but you will no longer be maximizing your utility. Instead you will be inclined to reduce your consumption of Coke and increase your consumption of hot dogs.

At the old prices, the original combination (two Cokes and two hot dogs) gave you a total utility of only 64 utils (45 from hot dogs and 19 from Coke). If you cut back to one Coke and three hot dogs now, your total utility will rise to 67 utils (57 from hot dogs and 10 from Coke). Your new utility-maximizing combination—the one that best satisfies your

Figure 18.1. The Law of Demand.
Price varies inversely with the quantity consumed, producing a downward-sloping curve like this one. If the price of Coke falls from $1 to $0.75, the consumer will buy three Cokes instead of two.

preferences—will therefore be one Coke and three hot dogs. No other combination of Coke and hot dogs will give you greater satisfaction. (Try to find one.)

To sum up, if the price of hot dogs goes down relative to the price of Coke, the rational person will buy more hot dogs. If the price of Coke rises relative to the price of hot dogs, the rational person will buy less Coke. This principle will hold true for any good or service, and is commonly known as the law of demand. The **law of demand** states the assumed inverse relationship between product price and quantity demanded, everything else held constant. If the relative price of a good falls, the individual will buy more of the good. If the price rises, the individual will buy less.

Figure 18.1 shows the demand curve for Coke—that is, the quantity of Coke purchased at different prices. The inverse relationship between price and quantity is reflected in the curve's downward slope. If the price falls from $1 to $0.75, the quantity the consumer will buy increases from two Cokes to three. The opposite will occur if the price goes up. (For a review of the law of demand as a schedule and an equation, see Chapter 3.)

Thus the assumption of rational behavior, coupled with the consumer's ability to substitute less costly goods when prices go up, leads to the law of demand. We cannot say how many Cokes and hot dogs a particular person will buy to maximize his or her satisfaction. That depends on the individual's income and preferences, which depend in turn on other factors

Law of demand: the assumed inverse relationship between product price and quantity demanded, everything else held constant. If the relative price of a good falls, the individual will buy more of the good, and vice versa.

Figure 18.2. Market Demand Curve.
The market demand curve for Coke, D_{A+B}, is obtained by summing the quantities that individuals A and B are willing to buy at each and every price (shown by the individual demand curves D_A and D_B).

(how much he likes hot dogs, whether he is on a diet, and how much he worries about the nutritional deficiencies of such a lunch). But we can predict the general response, whether positive or negative, to a change in prices.

Price: whatever a person must give up in exchange for a unit of goods or services purchased, obtained, or consumed. A rate of exchange, typically expressed in dollars per unit.

Price is whatever a person must give up in exchange for a unit of goods or services purchased, obtained, or consumed. It is a rate of exchange, and is typically expressed in dollars per unit. Note that price is not necessarily the same as cost. In an exchange between two people—a buyer and a seller—the price at which a good sells can be above or below the cost of producing the good. What the buyer gives up to obtain the good does not have to match what the seller-producer gives up in order to provide the good.

Nor is price always stated in dollars and cents. Some people have a desire to watch sunsets—a want characterized by the same downward-sloping demand curve as the one for Coke. The price of the sunset experience is not money. Instead it may be the lost opportunity to do something else, or the added cost and trouble of finding a home that will offer a view of the sunset. (In that case, price and cost are the same, because the buyer and the producer are one and the same.) But the law of demand will apply nevertheless. The individual will spend some optimum number of minutes per day watching the sunset, and will vary that number of minutes inversely with the price of watching.

Table 18.1. Market Demand for Coke

Price of Coke (1)	Quantity Demanded by A (D_A) (2)	Quantity Demanded by B (D_B) (3)	Market Demand: Quantity Demanded by Both A and B (D_{A+B}) (4)
$11	0	0	0
10	0	1	1.0
9	0	2	2.0
8	0.5	3	3.5
7	1.0	4	5.0
6	1.5	5	6.5
5	2.0	6	8.0
4	2.5	7	9.5
3	3.0	8	11.0
2	3.5	9	12.5
1	4.0	10	14.0

Note: The market demand curve, D_{A+B}, in Fig. 18.2 is obtained by plotting the quantities in column (4) against their respective prices in column (1).

From Individual Demand to Market Demand

Thus far we have discussed demand solely in terms of the individual's behavior. The concept is most useful, however, when applied to whole markets or segments of the population. **Market demand** is the summation of the quantities demanded by all consumers of a specific good or service at each and every price. To obtain the market demand for a product, we need to find some way of adding up the wants of the individuals who collectively make up the market.

The market demand can be shown graphically as the horizontal summation of the quantity of a product each individual will buy at each price. Assume that the market for Coke is composed of two individuals, A and B, who differ in their demand for Coke (see Figure 18.2). The demand of one person is D_A and the demand of the other is D_B. Then to determine the number of Cokes both of them will demand at any price, we simply add together the quantities each will purchase, at each price (see Table 18.1). At a price of $11, neither person is willing to buy any Coke; consequently, the market demand must begin below $11. At $9, A is still unwilling to buy any Coke, but B will buy two units. The market quantity demanded is therefore two. If the price falls to $5, A wants two Cokes and B, given her greater demand, wants much more, six. The two quantities combined equal eight. If we continue to drop the price and add the quantities bought at each new price, we will obtain a series of market quantities demanded. When plotted on a graph they will yield curve D_{A+B}, the market demand for Coke (see Figure 18.2).

Market demand: the summation of the quantities demanded by all consumers of a specific good or service at each and every price.

This is, of course, an extremely simple example, since only two individuals are involved. But the market demand curves for much larger groups of people are derived in essentially the same way. As more people demand more Coke, the market demand curve flattens out and extends further to the right.

Elasticity: Consumer Responsiveness to Price Change

In the media and in general conversation, we often hear claims that a price change will have no effect on purchases. Someone may predict that an increase in the price of prescription drugs will not affect people's use of them. The same remark is heard in connection with many other goods and services, from gasoline and public parks to medical services and salt. What people usually mean by such statements is that a price change will have only a slight effect on consumption. The law of demand states only that a price change will have an inverse effect on the quantity of a good purchased. It does not specify how much of an effect the price change will have.

In other words, we have established only that the market demand curve for a good will slope downward. The actual demand curve for a product may be relatively flat, like curve D_1 in Figure 18.3, or relatively steep, like curve D_2. Notice that at a price of P_1, the quantity of the good or service consumed is the same in both markets. If the price is raised to P_2, however, the response is substantially greater in market D_1 than in D_2. In D_1, consumers will reduce their purchases all the way to Q_1. In D_2, consumption will drop only to Q_2.

Economists refer to this relative responsiveness of demand curves as the price elasticity of demand. **Price elasticity of demand** is the responsiveness of consumers, in terms of the quantity purchased, to a change in price. Demand is relatively elastic or inelastic, depending on the degree of responsiveness to price change. **Elastic demand** is a relatively sensitive consumer response to price changes. If the price goes up or down, consumers will respond with a strong decrease or increase in the quantity demanded. Demand curve D_1 in Figure 18.3 may be characterized as relatively elastic. **Inelastic demand** is a relatively insensitive consumer response to price changes. If the price goes up or down, consumers will respond with only a slight decrease or increase in the quantity demanded. Demand curve D_2 in Figure 18.3 is relatively inelastic.

The elasticity of demand is a useful concept, but our definition is imprecise. What do we mean by "relatively sensitive" or "relatively insensitive"? Under what circumstances is consumer response sensitive or insensitive? There are two ways to add precision to our definition. One is to calculate the effect of a change in price on total consumer expenditures (which must equal producer revenues). The other is to develop mathematical values for various levels of elasticity. We will deal with each in turn.

Price elasticity of demand: the responsiveness of consumers, in terms of the quantity purchased, to a change in price.

Elastic demand: a relatively sensitive consumer response to price changes. If the price goes up or down, consumers will respond with a strong decrease or increase in the quantity demanded.

Inelastic demand: a relatively insensitive consumer response to price changes. If the price goes up or down, consumers will respond with only a slight decrease or increase in the quantity demanded.

Figure 18.3. Elastic and Inelastic Demand.
Demand curves differ in their relative elasticity. Curve D_1 is more elastic than
curve D_2, in the sense that consumers on curve D_1 are more responsive to a price
change than are consumers on curve D_2.

Analyzing Total Consumer Expenditures

An increase in the price of a particular product can cause consumers to
buy less. Whether total consumer expenditures rise, fall, or stay the same,
however, depends on the extent of the consumer response. Many people
assume that businesses will charge the highest price possible so as to
maximize profits. Although they sometimes do, high prices are not always
the best policy. For example, if a firm sells fifty units of a product for $1,
its total revenue (consumers' total expenditures) for the product will be
$50 (50 × $1). If it raises the price to $1.50 and consumers cut back to
forty units, its total revenue could rise to $60 (40 × $1.50). But if consumers
are highly sensitive to price changes for this particular good, the fifty-cent
increase may lower the quantity sold to thirty units. In that case total
consumer expenditures would fall to $45 ($1.50 × 30).

The opposite can also happen. If a firm establishes a price of $1.50 and
then lowers it to $1, the quantity sold may rise. But the change in total
consumer expenditures will depend on the degree of consumer response.
In other words, consumer responsiveness determines whether a firm
should raise or lower its price. (We will return to this point later.)

We can define a simple rule of thumb for using total consumer
expenditures to analyze the elasticity of demand. Demand is *elastic*:

if total consumer expenditures rise when the price falls, or

if total consumer expenditures fall when the price rises.

Unitary elastic demand: a consumer response to a price change in which the percentage change in price exactly matches the percentage change in quantity demanded. A change in price therefore does not alter consumer expenditures.

Elasticity coefficient of demand: the ratio of the percentage change in the quantity demanded to the percentage change in price.

Demand is *inelastic*:

if total consumer expenditures rise when the price rises or

if total consumer expenditures fall when the price falls.

Demand is said to be *unitary elastic* when total consumer expenditures do not change with either an increase or a decrease in price. **Unitary elastic demand** is a consumer response to a price change in which the percentage change in price exactly matches the percentage change in quantity demanded. A change in price therefore does not alter consumer expenditures. For example, if the price rises from $1 to $1.50 and the quantity purchased drops from 50 to 33.3 units, expenditures will still be $50. Demand is unitary elastic.

Determining Elasticity Coefficients

Although we have refined our definition of elasticity, it still does not allow us to distinguish degrees of elasticity or inelasticity. Elasticity coefficients do just that. The **elasticity coefficient of demand** (E_d) is the ratio of the percentage change in the quantity demanded to the percentage change in price. Expressed as a formula,

$$E_d = \frac{\text{percentage change in quantity}}{\text{percentage change in price}}$$

The elasticity coefficient will generally be different at different points on the demand curve. Consider the linear demand curve in Figure 18.4. At every point on the curve, a price reduction of $1 causes quantity demanded to rise by ten units. But a $1 decrease in price at the top of the curve is a much smaller percentage change than a $1 decrease at the bottom of the curve. Similarly, an increase of ten units in the quantity demanded is a much larger percentage change when the quantity is low than when it is high. Therefore the elasticity coefficient falls as consumers move down their demand curve. Generally, a linear demand curve has an inelastic range at the bottom, a unitary elastic point in the center, and an elastic range at the top.[1]

---

1. There are two formulas for elasticity, one for use at specific points on the curve and one for measuring average elasticity between two points, called arc elasticity. The formula for point elasticity, which is used for very small changes in price, is:

$$E_d = \frac{\text{change in quantity demanded}}{\text{initial quantity demanded}} \div \frac{\text{change in price}}{\text{initial price}} \text{ or } \frac{Q_1 - Q_2}{Q_1} \div \frac{P_1 - P_2}{P_1}$$

The formula for arc elasticity is:

$$E_d = \frac{Q_1 - Q_2}{1/2(Q_1 + Q_2)} \div \frac{P_1 - P_2}{1/2(P_1 + P_2)}$$

where the subscripts 1 and 2 represent two distinct points, or prices, on the demand curve.

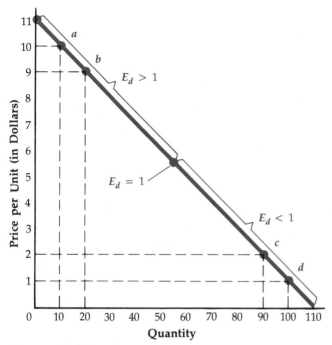

Figure 18.4. Change in the Elasticity Coefficient.
The elasticity coefficient decreases as a firm moves down the demand curve. The upper half of a linear demand curve is elastic, meaning that the elasticity coefficient is greater than one. The lower half is inelastic, meaning that the elasticity coefficient is less than one. At the midpoint of the linear demand curve, the elasticity coefficient is exactly one.

The change can be illustrated by computing the arc elasticity between two sets of points, *ab* and *cd*. Arc elasticity between points *a* and *b*:

$$E_d = \frac{10 - 20}{1/2(10 + 20)} \div \frac{10 - 9}{1/2(10 + 9)} = -\frac{10}{15} \div \frac{1}{9.5} = -\frac{90.5}{15} = -6.33$$

Arc elasticity between points *c* and *d*:

$$E_d = \frac{90 - 100}{1/2(90 + 100)} \div \frac{2 - 1}{1/2(2 + 1)} = -\frac{10}{95} \div \frac{15}{95} = -0.15$$

Elasticity coefficients can tell us much at a glance. When the percentage change in quantity is greater than the percentage change in price, an elasticity coefficient that is greater than 1.0 results. In these cases, demand is said to be elastic. When the percentage change in quantity is less than the percentage change in price, the elasticity coefficient will be less than 1.0. Demand is said to be inelastic. When the percentage change in the price is equal to the percentage change in quantity, the elasticity coefficient is 1.0, and demand is unitary elastic.[2] In short:

2. Actually all elasticity coefficients are negative and are preceded by a minus sign. (Remember that the demand curve has a negative slope.) Economists generally omit the minus sign.

Elastic demand: $E_d > 1$

Inelastic demand: $E_d < 1$

Unitary elastic demand: $E_d = 1$

Elasticity coefficients enable economists to make accurate comparisons. A demand with an elasticity coefficient of 1.75 is more elastic than one with an elasticity coefficient of 1.55. A demand with a coefficient of 0.25 is more inelastic than one with a coefficient of 0.78.

Although elasticity coefficients are useful for some purposes, their accuracy depends on data that are often less than precise. In the real world, there is constant change in the nonprice variables that influence how much of any product consumers want. It is extremely difficult for economists to separate the effects of a change in price from all the other forces operating in the marketplace. Small differences in elasticity coefficients may reflect the imperfections of statistical analysis rather than true differences in consumer responsiveness to price.

Elasticity Is Not the Same as Slope

Students often confuse the concept of elasticity of demand with the slope of the demand curve. A comparison of their mathematical formulas, however, shows they are quite different.

$$\text{slope} = \frac{\text{rise}}{\text{run}} = \frac{\text{change in price}}{\text{change in quantity}}$$

$$\text{elasticity} = \frac{\text{percentage change in quantity}}{\text{percentage change in price}}$$

The confusion is understandable. The slope of a demand curve does say something about consumer responsiveness: it shows how much the quantity consumed goes up when the price goes down by a given amount. But slope is an unreliable indicator of consumer responsiveness, because it varies with the units of measurement for price and quantity. For example, suppose that when the price rises from $10 to $20, quantity demanded decreases from 100 to 60. The slope is $-\frac{1}{4}$.

$$\text{slope} = \frac{-10}{40} = \frac{-1}{4}$$

If the price is measured in pennies instead of dollars, however, the slope comes out to -25.

$$\text{slope} = \frac{-1000}{40} = \frac{-25}{1}$$

No matter how the price is measured, the elasticity of demand remains -0.75.

Furthermore, two parallel demand curves of identical slope will not have the same elasticity coefficients. For example, consider the two curves

Figure 18.5. Two Parallel Curves Do Not Have the Same Elasticity.
Even two parallel demand curves of the same slope do not have the same elasticity.
Though a given change in price—for example, a $1 change—will produce the same
unit change in quantity demanded, the percentage change will differ. Here, a drop
in price from $5 to $4 produces a ten-unit gain in quantity demanded on both
curves D_1 and D_2. But a ten-unit increase in sales represents a lower percentage
change at an initial sales level of seventy (curve D_2) than at an initial sales level
of twenty-five (curve D_1).

The difference in the elasticity of the two curves can be illustrated by computing
the arc elasticity between two sets of points, ab on curve D_1 and cd on curve D_2.
Arc elasticity between points a and b:

$$E_d = \frac{25 - 35}{1/2(25 + 35)} \div \frac{5 - 4}{1/2(5 + 4)} = 1.50$$

Arc elasticity between points c and d:

$$E_d = \frac{70 - 80}{1/2(70 + 80)} \div \frac{5 - 4}{1/2(5 + 4)} = 0.60$$

in Figure 18.5. When the price falls from $5 to $4, the quantity demanded
rises by the same amount for each curve: ten units. Yet the percentage
change in quantity is substantially lower for D_2 than for D_1. (A rise from
seventy to eighty is not nearly as dramatic in percentage terms as a rise
from twenty-five to thirty-five.) Thus the elasticity coefficient is lower for
demand curve D_2.

Be careful not to judge the elasticity of demand by looking at a curve's
slope.

Applications of the Concept of Elasticity

Elasticity of demand is particularly important to producers. Together with the cost of production, it determines the prices firms can charge for their products. We have seen that an increase or decrease in price can cause total consumer expenditures to rise, fall, or remain the same, depending on the elasticity of demand. Thus if a firm lowers its price and incurs greater production costs (because it is producing and selling more units), it may still increase its profits. As long as the demand curve is elastic, revenues can (but will not necessarily) go up more than costs. Over the last three decades, the American Telephone and Telegraph Company has frequently lowered its prices on long-distance calls. To justify those decisions, AT&T had to reason that demand was sufficiently elastic to produce revenues that would more than cover the cost of servicing the extra calls. During the 1950s and 1960s, many electric power companies requested rate reductions, for the same reason.

Producers of concerts and dances estimate the elasticity of demand when they establish the price of admission. If admission costs $10, tickets may be left unsold. At a lower price, say $7, attendance and profits may be higher. Even if costs rise (for extra workers and more programs), revenues can still rise more.

Government too must consider elasticity of demand, for the consumer's demand for taxable items is not inexhaustible. If a government raises excise taxes on cars or jewelry too much, it may end up with lower tax revenues. The higher tax, added to the final price of the product, may cause a negative consumer response. It is no accident that the heaviest excise taxes are usually imposed on goods for which the demand tends to be inelastic, such as cigarettes and liquor.

The same reasoning applies to property taxes. Many large cities have tended to underestimate the elasticity of demand for living space. Indeed, a major reason for the recent migration from city to suburbs has been the desire to escape rising tax rates. By moving just outside a city's boundaries, people can retain many of the benefits a city provides without actually paying for them. This movement of city dwellers to the suburbs lowers the demand for property within the city, undermining property values and destroying the city's tax base. Thus if governments wish to maintain their revenues, they must be careful about their tax policies.

Determinants of the Elasticity of Demand

So far our analysis of elasticity has presumed that consumers are able to respond to a price change. However, consumers' ability to respond can be affected by various factors, including the number of substitutes; the number of competitors producing any given good; and the amount of time consumers have to respond to a change in price by shifting to other products or producers.

Substitutes

Substitutes allow consumers to respond to a price increase by switching to another good. If the price of orange juice goes up, you are not required to go on buying it. You can substitute a variety of other drinks, including water, wine, and soda pop.

The elasticity of demand for any good depends very much on what substitutes are available. The existence of a large number and variety of substitutes means that demand is likely to be elastic. That is, if people can switch easily to another product that will yield approximately the same value, many will do so when faced with a price increase. The similarity of substitutes—how well they can satisfy the same basic want—also affects elasticity. The closer a substitute is to a product, the more elastic demand for the product will be. If there are no close substitutes, demand will tend to be inelastic. What we call necessities are often things that lack close substitutes.

Few goods have no substitutes at all. Since there are many substitutes for orange juice—Coke, wine, prune juice, and so on—we would expect the demand for orange juice to be more elastic than the demand for salt, which has fewer viable alternatives. Yet even for salt there are synthetic substitutes. Furthermore, though human beings need a certain amount of salt to survive, most of us consume much more than the minimum and can easily cut back if the price of salt rises. The extra taste that salt adds is a benefit that can be partially recouped by buying other things.

Number of Competitors

When price rises, consumers can move not only to substitute goods, but to competing producers of the same good. Generally speaking, the more competitors, the more elastic the demand for a product. A competitor is, by definition, one among many producers selling more or less the same good. In other words, there are other sources for the goods a competitor sells, and consumers can easily switch to those sources if a producer raises prices.

In thinking about product demand, we must be careful to distinguish between the demand for a particular producer's product and the demand for a generic product, like orange juice. A particular producer of orange juice faces a demand curve that is generally more elastic than the demand for the generic good. If one producer raises prices, it may lose all or practically all its customers to other producers. But if all producers of orange juice raise their prices simultaneously, consumers must either pay the higher price or choose a substitute, like cranberry juice.

Some producers—those in perfectly competitive markets—face a perfectly elastic demand. The individual wheat farmer, for example, is only one among thousands of producers of essentially the same product. If the current market price is low, he can withhold his wheat from the market. That is all he can do, however. If a wheat farmer tries to charge more

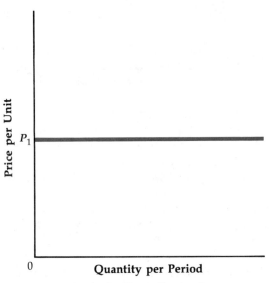

Figure 18.6. Perfectly Elastic Demand.
A firm that has many competitors may lose all its sales if it increases its price even slightly. Its customers can simply move to another producer. In that case its demand curve is horizontal, with an elasticity coefficient of infinity.

than the current market price, he probably will not sell any at all. Consumers will switch to other producers. In the perfectly competitive wheat market, the individual farmer is a price taker, reacting to the highly elastic demand for his product.

The demand curve facing the perfect competitor is horizontal, like the one in Figure 18.6. If the individual competitor raises his price even a minute percentage above the going market price, consumers will switch to other sellers. The elasticity coefficient of such a horizontal demand curve is infinite. Thus this demand curve is described as perfectly elastic. A **perfectly elastic demand** is a demand that has an elasticity coefficient of infinity. It is expressed graphically as a curve horizontal to the X axis.

Perfectly elastic demand: a demand that has an elasticity coefficient of infinity. Expressed graphically as a curve horizontal to the X axis.

Time

Consumption requires time. Accordingly, any demand curve must describe some particular time period. Over a very short period of time—say a day—the demand for a good may be quite inelastic. If a producer raises the price of a good, consumers may not react immediately. It takes time to find substitutes. With enough time, however, consumers will respond to a price increase. Thus a demand curve that covers a long period will be more elastic than one for a short period.

Oil provides a good example of how the elasticity of demand can change over time. In 1973, Arab oil producers raised the price of their crude oil and domestic producers of oil followed suit. For a time consumers were caught. Drivers were stuck with big, gas-guzzling cars and with suburban homes located far from their work places. Automakers were tooled up to produce big cars, not subcompacts. Over the longer term, however, alternative modes of transportation became available and alternative sources of energy were found. People altered their lifestyles, walking or riding bicycles to work. The long-term demand curve for oil is much more elastic than the short-term demand curve.

Changes in Demand

The determinants of the elasticity of demand are fewer and easier to identify than the determinants of demand itself. As we saw in Chapter 3, the demand for almost all goods is affected in one way or another by (1) consumer incomes; (2) the prices of other goods; (3) the number of consumers; (4) expectations concerning future prices and incomes; and (5) that catchall variable, consumer tastes and preferences. Additional variables apply in differing degrees to different goods. The amount of ice cream and the number of golf balls bought both depend on the weather (very few golf balls are sold at the North Pole). The number of cribs demanded depends on the birthrate. Together all these variables determine the position of the demand curve. If any variable changes, so will the position of the demand curve.

We saw in Chapter 3 that if consumer preference for a product—say blue jeans—increases, the change will be reflected in an outward movement of the demand curve (see Figure 18.7). That is what happened during the late 1960s, when college students' tastes changed and wearing faded blue jeans became chic. By definition, such a change in taste means that consumers are willing to buy more of the good at the going market price. If the price is P_1, the quantity demanded will increase from Q_2 to Q_3. But a change in tastes can also mean that people are willing to buy more jeans at each and every price. At P_2 they are now willing to buy Q_2 instead of Q_1 blue jeans. We can infer from this pattern that consumers are willing to pay a higher price for any given quantity. In Figure 18.7, the increase in demand means that consumers are willing to pay as much as P_2 for Q_2 pairs of jeans, whereas formerly they would pay only P_1. (If consumers' tastes change in the opposite direction, the demand curve moves downward to the left, as in Figure 18.8, and quantity demanded at a given price decreases.)

Whether demand increases or decreases, the demand curve will still slope downward. Everything else held constant, people will buy more of the good at a lower price than at a higher one. To assume that other variables will remain constant, of course, is unrealistic, since markets are generally in a state of flux. In the real world, all variables just do not stay put to allow the price of a good to change by itself. But even if conditions change at the same time that price changes, the law of demand tells us that a decrease in price will lead people to buy more than they would otherwise, and an increase in price will lead them to buy less.

Figure 18.7. Increase in Demand.
When consumer demand for blue jeans increases, the demand curve shifts from
D_1 to D_2. Consumers are now willing to buy a larger quantity of jeans at the same
price, or the same quantity at a higher price. At price P_1, for instance, they will
buy Q_3 jeans instead of Q_2. And they are now willing to pay P_2 for Q_2 jeans,
whereas before they would pay only P_1.

Normal good or service: any good or service for which demand rises with an increase in income, and falls with a decrease in income.

Luxury good or service: any good or service for which demand rises faster than income.

Inferior good or service: any good or service for which demand falls with an increase in income, and rises with a decrease in income.

For example, in Figure 18.8, the demand for blue jeans has decreased, because consumers are less willing to buy the product. A price reduction can partially offset the decline in demand. If producers lower their price from P_2 to P_1, quantity demanded will fall only to Q_2 instead of Q_1. Though consumers are buying fewer jeans than they once did (Q_2 as opposed to Q_3) because of changing tastes, the law of demand still holds. Because of the price change, consumers have increased their consumption over what it would otherwise have been.

A change in consumer incomes will affect demand in more complicated ways. The demand for most goods, called normal goods, increases with income. A **normal good or service** is any good or service for which demand rises with an increase in income, and falls with a decrease in income. The demand for a few, luxury goods actually outstrips increases in income. A **luxury good or service** is any good or service for which demand rises faster than income. And the demand for inferior goods goes down when income goes up. An **inferior good or service** is any good or service for which demand falls with an increase in income, and rises with a decrease in income. Beans are an example of a good many people would consider inferior. People who rely on beans as a staple or filler food when their incomes are low may substitute meat and other higher-priced foods when their incomes rise.

Figure 18.8. Decrease in Demand.
A downward shift in demand, from D_1 to D_2, represents a decrease in the quantity of blue jeans consumers are willing to buy at each and every price. It also indicates a decrease in the price they are willing to pay for each and every quantity of jeans. At price P_2, for instance, consumers will now buy only Q_1 jeans (not Q_3, as before). And they will now pay only P_2 for Q_1 jeans—not P_3, as before.

Thus though economists can confidently predict the directional movement of consumption when prices change, they cannot say what will happen to the demand for a particular good when income changes. That is because each individual determines for himself whether a particular good is a normal, inferior, or luxury good. Different people will tend to answer this question differently in different markets. Beans may be an inferior good to most low-income consumers and a normal good to most others.

For example, how do you think a change in income will affect the demand for low-, medium-, and high-quality liquor? You may have some intuitive notion about the effect, but you are probably not as confident about it as you are about the effect of a price decrease. In fact, during past recessions, the demand for both low- and high-quality liquor has increased. Some consumers may have switched to high-quality liquor to impress their friends, even if they could afford to buy less of it on their lower incomes. Others may have tried to maintain their old level of consumption by switching to a low-quality brand.

The effect of a change in the price of other goods is similarly complicated. Here the important factor is the relationship of one good, say ice cream, to other commodities. Are the goods in question substitutes for ice cream, like ice milk? Are they complements, like cones? Or are they used independently of ice cream? Demand for ice cream is unlikely to be affected by a drop in the price of baby rattles, but it may well decline if the price of ice milk drops.

Two products are generally considered substitutes if the demand for one goes up when the price of the other rises. The price of a product does not have to rise above the price of its substitute before the demand for the substitute is affected. Assume that the price of sirloin steak is $3 per pound and the price of hamburger is $1 per pound. The price difference reflects the fact that consumers believe the two meats are of different quality. If the price of hamburger rises to $2 per pound while the price of sirloin remains constant at $3, many buyers will increase their demand for steak. The perceived difference in quality now outweighs the difference in price.

Because complementary products—razors and razor blades, oil and oil filters, typewriters and typewriter ribbons—are consumed jointly, a change in the price of one will cause an increase or decrease in the demand for both products at once. An increase in the price of razor blades, for instance, will induce some people to switch to electric razors, causing a decrease in the quantity of razor blades demanded and a decrease in the demand for safety razors. Again, economists cannot predict how many people will decide the switch is worthwhile. They can merely predict from theory the direction in which demand for the product will move.

Irrationality and the Law of Demand

So far we have been discussing demand in terms of rational behavior. Even if some consumers behave irrationally, the law of demand will apply. So long as some people in the market respond rationally, demand will change with a change in price. For instance, many people buy cigarettes because they are addicted to them. At times habitual smokers may not consider price in making their purchases. Therefore we cannot expect the quantity they buy always to vary with price (except to the extent that it affects their total purchasing power). If occasional smokers take price into consideration when they buy, however, their demand for cigarettes will produce the normal downward sloping curve. If we add the quantity bought by smokers who are addicted to the quantity bought by those who are not, the total market demand curve will slope downward (see Figure 18.9). At a price of P_1, Q_1 cigarettes will be bought by addicted consumers, and $Q_3 - Q_1$ cigarettes by occasional consumers. If the price then rises to P_2, the total quantity bought will fall to Q_2, reflecting a predictable drop in the quantity purchased by occasional consumers.

This kind of reasoning can be extended to impulse buying. Some people respond more to the packaging and display of products than to their price. Their demand may not slope downward. As long as some people check prices and resist advertising, however, the total demand for any good will slope downward. Store managers must therefore assume that changes in

Figure 18.9. Demand Including Irrational Behavior.
If irrational consumers demand Q_1 cigarettes no matter what the price, but rational consumers take price into consideration, market demand will be D_1. The quantity purchased will still vary inversely with the price.

price will affect the quantity demanded. The fact that some people may behave irrationally reduces the elasticity of demand, but does not invalidate the concept of demand.[3]

Demand is not what people would like to have or are willing to pay for, nor is it the quantity that consumers are willing to buy at a given price. Rather it is the inverse relationship between price and quantity, a relationship described by a downward sloping curve.

Though economists do not have complete confidence in all applications of the law of demand, they consider the relationship between price and quantity to be so firmly established, both theoretically and empirically, that they call it a law. In the real world, when the price of a good goes down, the quantity purchased may fall rather than rise. In such cases, economists assume that some other variable has changed, offsetting the positive effects of the reduction in price.

Summary and Extensions

3. In fact, one economist has demonstrated rather convincingly that the assumption of rational behavior is unnecessary to the construction of a downward-sloping demand curve. The curve, he argues, can emerge from completely random behavior on the part of consumers. Gary S. Becker, *Economic Theory* (New York: Alfred A. Knopf, 1972), pp. 19–23.

Major Conclusions

1. Consumer equilibrium is reached when the individual has fully allocated his or her income and is getting the same marginal utility per penny (or dollar) for each good consumed.
2. The law of demand states that if everything else is held constant, quantity purchased will vary inversely with price.
3. The law of demand can be applied to anything consumers value, whether or not its price can be stated in dollars and cents.
4. The market demand curve is obtained by horizontally summing individual demand curves.
5. Consumer responsiveness, called the elasticity of demand, is different for different goods.
6. There are two ways of judging whether demand is elastic, inelastic, or unitary elastic: by analyzing total consumer expenditures, and by computing the elasticity coefficient of demand. The slope of a demand curve does not indicate its elasticity.
7. The major determinants of the elasticity of demand are the number of substitutes, the number of competitors, and the period of time in which consumers must react to a price change.
8. The location of the demand curve is determined by many factors. Different factors affect the demand for different goods, but three affect the demand for almost all goods: current and expected consumer incomes, current and expected prices of other goods (both substitutes and complements), and consumer preferences.

Questions to Ponder

1. What role does the law of demand play in economic analysis?
2. If the price of jeans rises and the quantity sold goes up, does the demand curve slope upward?
3. If the prices of most goods are rising by an average of 15 percent per year, but the price of gasoline rises just 10 percent per year, what is happening to the real, or relative, price of gasoline? How do you expect consumers will react?
4. Suppose that a producer raises the price of a good from $4 to $7, and the quantity sold drops from 250 to 200 units. Is the demand for the good elastic or inelastic?
5. Suppose the government freezes the price of gasoline, but people now find themselves waiting in line for gasoline. What has happened to the price of gasoline? What should happen to gasoline use?
6. If the campus police force is expanded and officers are instructed to increase the number of parking tickets they give out, what will happen to the number of parking violations? What may be necessary to eliminate all parking violations? (Why may that option be rejected?)
7. If the government subsidizes flood insurance, what will happen to the price of that insurance? What will happen to the value of the property that is lost during floods? Why?
8. If the price of ball-point pens falls, will the demand for ball-point pens change? What will happen to the demand for pencils? To the demand for paper?

Appendix:
Consumer Preferences and Possibilities—
Derivation of Demand from Indifference Curves and the Budget Line

Chapters 17 and 18 have been concerned with the problem of constrained choice. Much of the discussion has been founded on the notion of the rational pursuit of individual preferences. That is, we assume the individual knows what he or she wants and will seek to accomplish those goals. Preference, however, is a nebulous concept. To lend concreteness to the idea, economists have developed the indifference curve.

Individuals face limited production possibilities. That fact, together with the existence of indifference curves, can be used to derive an individual's demand for a product.

Derivation of the Indifference Curve

Consider a student whose wants include only two goods, pens and books. Figure 18.A1 shows all the possible combinations of pens and books she may choose. The student will prefer a combination far from the origin to one closer in. At point b, for instance, she will have more books and more pens than at point a. For the same reason, she will prefer a to c. In fact the student will prefer a to any point in the lower left-hand quadrant of the graph, and will prefer any point in the upper right-hand quadrant to a.

Figure 18.A1. Derivation of an Indifference Curve. Because the consumer prefers more of a good to less, point *a* is preferable to point *c*, and point *b* is preferable to point *a*. If *a* is preferable to *d* but *e* is preferable to *a*, then when we move from point *d* to *e*, we must move from a combination that is less preferred to one that is more preferred. And in doing so we must cross a point—for example, *f*—that is equal in value to *a*. Similarly, we may reason that point *i* is of equal value to *a*. Indifference curves are composed by connecting all those points—*a, f, i,* and so on—that are of equal value to the consumer.

Figure 18.A2. Indifference Curves for Pens and Books.
Any combination of pens and books that falls along curve I_1 will yield the same level of utility as any other combination on that curve. The consumer is indifferent among them. By extension, any combination on curve I_2 will be preferable to any combination on curve I_1.

We can also reason that the student would prefer *a* to *d*, where she gets the same number of pens but fewer books than at *a*. Likewise, she will prefer *e* to *a*, because it yields the same number of books and more pens than *a*. If *a* is preferred to *d* and *e* is preferred to *a*, then as the student moves from *d* to *e*, she must move from a less preferable to a more preferable position with respect to *a*. And at some point along that path, the student will reach a combination of books and pens that equals the value of point *a*. Assuming that combination is *f* (it can be any point between *d* and *e*), we can say that the individual is indifferent between *a* and *f*.

Using a similar line of logic, we can locate another point along the line *gih* that will be equal in value to *a* and therefore to *f*. In fact, any number of points in the lower right-hand and upper left-hand quadrants of the graph are of equal value to *a*. Taken together, these points form what is called an indifference curve (see curve I_1 in Figure 18.A2). An **indifference curve** shows the various combinations of two goods that yield the same level of utility.

Indifference curve: a curve that shows the various combinations of two goods that yield the same level of utility.

Using the same line of reasoning, we can construct a second indifference curve through point b. Because b is preferable to a, and all points on the new indifference curve will be equal in value to point b, we can conclude that any point along the new curve I_2 is preferable to any point on I_1. Using this same procedure, we can continue to derive any number of curves, each one higher than, and preferable to, the last.

From this line of reasoning, an economist can draw several conclusions about the student's preference structure (called an "indifference map").

1. The student's utility level rises as she moves up and to the right, from one indifference curve to the next.
2. Indifference curves slope downward to the right.
3. Indifference curves cannot intersect. (An intersection would imply that all points on all the intersecting curves are of equal value, contradicting the conclusion that higher indifference curves represent higher levels of utility).

The Budget Line and Consumer Equilibrium

From indifference curves we can derive the law of demand. First we need to construct the individual's budget line, a special form of the production possibilities curve. The **budget line** shows graphically all the combinations of two goods that a consumer can buy with a given amount of income. Assume that our student earns an income of $150, which she uses to buy books and pens. Books cost $3 each and pens cost $5 a package. The student can spend all $150 on fifty books or thirty pen packs. Or she can divide her expenditures in any number of ways to yield various combinations of books and pens. By plotting all the possible combinations, we obtain the student's budget line, B_1P_1 in Figure 18.A3.

Budget line: a curve that shows all the combinations of two goods a consumer can buy with a given amount of income.

All combinations on the budget line are possible for the student. She can choose point a, twenty-five books and fifteen pen packs, or point b, forty-five books and three pen packs. Either combination exhausts her $150 budget. The rational individual will choose that point where the budget line just touches (is tangent to) an indifference curve—point a in this case. Points farther up or down the budget line will put the student on a lower indifference curve and are therefore less preferable. (If, for instance, the student moves to c on the budget line, she will be on a lower indifference curve, I_2 instead of I_1.) At point a, the individual's wants are said to be in equilibrium. So long as her income and preferences and the prices of books and pens remain the same, she has no reason to move from that point.

What happens if prices change? Suppose the individual's wants are in equilibrium at point a in Figure 18.A4 when the price of pens falls from $5 a pack to $3 a pack. (The price of books stays the same.) The budget line will pivot to B_1P_2, reflecting the greater buying power of the student's income. (She can now buy fifty pen packs with $150.) The new budget line gives the student a chance to move to a higher indifference curve—for instance, to point c, twenty-two pen packs and twenty-eight books.

Figure 18.A3. The Budget Line and Consumer Equilibrium.
Constrained by her budget, the consumer will seek to maximize her utility by consuming at the point where her budget line is tangent to an indifference curve. Here the consumer chooses point a, where her budget line just touches indifference curve I_1. All other combinations on the consumer's budget line will fall on a lower indifference curve, providing less utility. Point c, for instance, falls on indifference curve I_2.

The Law of Demand

The result of the price reduction is that the student buys more pens. Thus we derive the law of demand, that quantity demanded is inversely related to price. The downward-sloping demand curve for pens shown in Figure 18.A5 is obtained by plotting the quantities of pen packs bought from Figure 18.A4 against the price paid per pack. When the price of pens falls from $5 to $3 a pack in Figure 18.A5, the consumer increases the quantity purchased from fifteen to twenty-two.

Figure 18.A4. Effect of a Change in Price on Consumer Equilibrium.
If the price of pens falls, the consumer's budget line will pivot outward, from
B_1P_1 to B_1P_2. As a result, the consumer can move to a higher indifference curve,
I_2 instead of I_1. At the new price the consumer buys more pens, twenty-two packs
as opposed to fifteen.

Figure 18.A5. Derivation of the Demand Curve
for Pens.
When the price of pens changes, shifting the
consumer's budget line from I_1 to I_2 in Figure
18.A4, the consumer equilibrium point changes
with it. The consumer's demand curve for pens is
obtained by plotting her equilibrium quantity of
pens at various prices. At $5 a pack, the consumer
buys fifteen packs of pens (point *a*). At $3 a pack,
she buys twenty-two packages (point *c*).

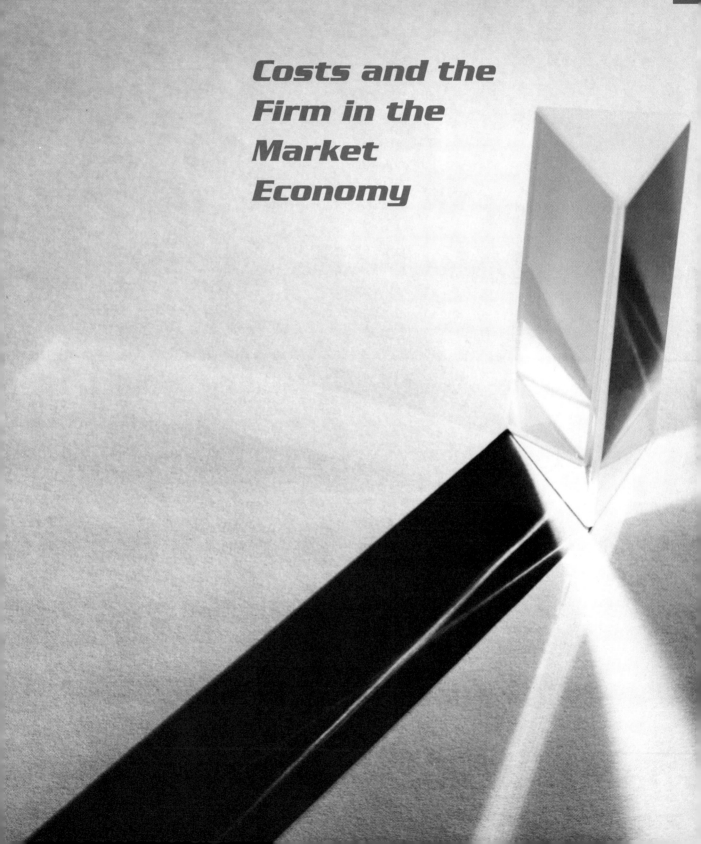

Part VII

Costs and the Firm in the Market Economy

Central Question

Key Terms

What are the major types of business organizations in the private sector, and how are they financed?

Proprietorship

Partnership

Corporation

Bond

Preferred stock

Common stock

Book profit

Economic profit

Opportunity cost of capital

Risk cost

Economic losses

Chapter 19

Business Organizations

The United States is the capitalist nation par excellence. That is to say, it is not merely the case that capitalism has flourished here more vigorously than, for instance, in the nations of Western Europe. The point is, rather, that the Founding Fathers intended *this nation to be capitalist and regarded it as the* only *set of economic arrangements consistent with the liberal democracy they had established. They did not use the term "capitalism," of course. . . . That invidious word, "capitalism," was invented . . . by anti-socialists . . . about a half-century later.*
Irving Kristol

*M*any goods and services, such as meals and entertainment, are produced in the home. But the vast majority of goods and services sold in the marketplace are produced by business firms. These firms vary in their organization; in their distribution of management responsibilities, ownership rights, and earnings; and in their sources of investment and operating funds. Most of them fall into one of the three major categories of business organization in the United States, the proprietorship, the partnership, and the corporation.

This chapter describes the characteristics of those three forms of organization. It explains why, though the majority of firms in the United States are proprietorships, most production occurs in corporations. And it describes how corporations raise the investment funds needed for production on a large scale.

Types of Business Organization

The producing sector of the U.S. economy is composed of millions of business organizations, which vary widely in their structure. The three principal types of organization, based on form of ownership, are single proprietorships, partnerships, and corporations. In 1980, 12.7 million firms in the United States were sole proprietorships, 1.4 million were partnerships, and 2.7 million were corporations. About 3 million of these firms, mostly proprietorships, were in agriculture, forestry, and fishing. Another 4 million, again mostly proprietorships, produced services, from catering and entertainment to dry cleaning. Two million were in finance, insurance, and real estate, and only 550,000 were in manufacturing. Slightly less than half of all manufacturers were corporations.

This tally alone does not adequately express the relative importance of the various forms of business, however. While the nation's 2.7 million corporations represented only 16 percent of all businesses, they accounted for over 88 percent of all nonfarm business receipts. The nearly 13 million proprietorships accounted for only about 8 percent of receipts, and partnerships for the remainder.

Why do corporations dominate the business world in the United States? The answer lies in the relative advantages and disadvantages of the three forms of organization. Though proprietorships are a popular form of ownership, certain limitations inherent in their structure prevent them from achieving success on a large scale.

Proprietorships

Proprietorship: any business venture owned and run by a single individual.

A sole **proprietorship** is any business venture owned and run by a single individual. Sole proprietorships are relatively simple to organize and administer. So long as a proprietor's business is legal and does not come under the regulatory authority of local, state, or federal government, it requires no government approval. Anyone who has an idea for a product or service can simply declare himself or herself in business and begin operation on any scale desired.

Nor does the sole proprietor have to worry about obtaining the approval of other investors, for there are none. The owner is in more or less complete control of what the firm produces, how the business is funded, and how the revenues and profits are dispersed. Within the bounds of law and the forces of competition, the proprietor can do as he or she wishes. Any profits earned in conducting the business are considered by the Internal Revenue Service (IRS) to be the income (the equivalent of wages) of the owner and are taxed as ordinary income.

The drawbacks of the sole proprietorship also stem directly from its ownership by a single individual.

The size of the firm and its scale of operation can grow no more than the owner's financial resources—savings and loans—will allow.

The owner does not benefit from the advice and encouragement of co-owners who have a personal interest in seeing the business succeed.

Although the owner reaps all the profits of the enterprise, he or she also assumes all the risks of failure. All losses are incurred solely and fully by one owner.

As far as the law is concerned, the business ceases to exist with the death of the proprietor.

Legally, the owner is fully liable for all the firm's debts. If a proprietor cannot meet financial obligations to creditors and employees and declares bankruptcy, the firm's assets can be sold by the courts to pay off outstanding debts. If the receipts from this liquidation of business assets are not sufficient to pay off all debts, the owner's personal property—home, car, boat, farm, savings accounts, and so forth—can also be sold.

Partnerships

A **partnership** is a business venture owned and managed by two or more persons. Partnerships vary greatly in terms of the number of partners involved and the division of responsibility among partners. Active partners participate directly in the management of the business. But other partners are silent: they provide financial capital but do not participate in the day-to-day operation of the business. The advantages of a partnership are:

With more than one owner, the company has greater access to financial capital, enabling it to grow and take advantage of economies of scale.

Profits and losses are shared in a manner prescribed by the articles of partnership, a legal agreement drawn up at the start of the business. A partnership spreads the risk of doing business.

Partnership: a business venture owned and managed by two or more persons.

As with proprietorships, company profits are treated as ordinary income by the Internal Revenue Service.

The relatively small number of partnerships in the United States can best be explained by the special legal handicaps partners bear. Legally, each partner is completely and fully responsible for all the partnership's debts. In the event of bankruptcy, each partner's personal property can be sold to pay off any remaining debts, no matter what the partner's share in the business or what the extent of the debts. The partners may agree in their articles of partnership to share the liability for any unpaid debts, but if one partner has few personal assets, the court can seize the others'— regardless of the terms of the articles. To be workable, partnerships require a great deal of personal trust, cooperation, and coordination. Because of the complexity of the legal relationship and the liability involved, this form of ownership tends to be limited to the legal and medical professions and to retail services—all businesses in which the partners' functions can be clearly defined.

A partnership ceases to exist with the withdrawal or death of a partner, which can make long-term operation of the business difficult. To continue the business, the remaining partners must devise another article of partnership among themselves and the deceased partners' heirs.

Corporations

John Marshall, chief justice of the United States Supreme Court from 1801 to 1835, once defined the corporation as "an artificial being, invisible, intangible, and existing only in the contemplation of the law." Marshall meant that under the law, the corporation is not a collection of individuals who have drawn together to conduct business. It is a legal entity, with the right to buy and sell, borrow and lend, sue and be sued, hire and fire in its own name. Strictly speaking, a **corporation** is a legal entity, created by government charter, with the right to conduct business in its own name, much as an individual does. The business of the corporation is not conducted in the name of its owners, but in the name of the corporation: Texas Instruments, Incorporated, for example.

This special legal status was created and is individually granted to corporations by states and the federal government, through the issuance of corporate charters. (The requirements for a corporation vary from state to state.) Under this special legal status, the corporation, not the individuals who manage and own it, is responsible for the company's business activities. The owners of the corporation bear only limited liability for the corporation's debts. In the event of bankruptcy, they can lose only the money they have invested, not their personal property. The limited liability of the owners reduces the risk investors must assume and increases the corporation's ability to raise capital. Such an arrangement is particularly appealing to people who do not care to become involved in a company's day-to-day operations.

Corporation: a legal entity, created by government charter, with the right to conduct business in its own name, much as an individual does.

From another perspective, the corporation can be viewed as a natural extension of the limited partnership, a form of organization in which one or more partners take an inactive role in the business. Such partnerships can achieve limited liability through an explicit contract with their creditors, stating that the owners' personal wealth cannot be used to pay off debts remaining after liquidation of the business. (Proprietorships can also enter into contracts that limit liability.) In this view the investors, not the state, create the corporation by mutual agreement on how to deal with outside interests. The state merely puts its stamp of approval on the investors' plans—and in fact most states approve corporate charters very routinely. The *Inc.* at the end of a corporate name is essentially an announcement—a warning—to prospective creditors that if the company's debts go bad, the owners' personal wealth cannot be claimed in repayment. To secure loans from creditors under such terms, the owners may have to pay a higher rate of interest than they would otherwise—though the company's enhanced ability to attract investors may offset the risk premium.

In addition to limited liability, the corporation offers investors several other notable advantages.

The life of the corporation is legally independent of the life of its owners. It is established in law by the corporate charter and continues indefinitely, until investors see fit to dismantle it. (Of course a corporation's profitability may sink with the death of an owner-manager. The corporation, like all businesses, depends for its success on the talents of its employees.)

Ownership rights can be transferred easily between buyer and seller through organized securities markets, such as the New York, American, Chicago, and Philadelphia stock exchanges.

Rights of ownership are clearly separated from the responsibilities of management. Owners need not devote time to the business in order to reap the rewards of ownership.

On the other hand, the corporation has several disadvantages as a form of ownership. The creation of a corporation requires state or federal approval, which generally means that some legal assistance is required. The fee for establishing even the simplest corporate charter is generally several hundred dollars. It can run into thousands of dollars, depending on the state and the legal complications involved. Furthermore, corporations must make financial reports to the state or federal chartering agency. If enough shares have been issued to the general public, they must also report to the Securities and Exchange Commission, which oversees the trading of stocks and bonds. Some business people do not believe the limited liability and other advantages of a corporation are worth the expense and red tape of securing a charter, especially since creditors can negate a corporation's limited liability by demanding higher interest rates or by asking owners to sign for loans in their own names.

Corporations are also at a disadvantage with respect to taxation. Some corporations are subject to special taxes. Small corporations that receive their revenue principally from rents and royalties (and, accordingly, are viewed as "personal holding companies" by the IRS) must pay a surtax of 70 percent of all profits not paid out as dividends to the owners. (The purpose of these special tax provisions is to prevent people from using the corporation as a tax shelter, or means of avoiding taxes.)

Corporate profits are taxed twice, first as the income of the corporation and then, if dividends are distributed to owners, as the personal income of the owners. (Small family-held corporations can avoid double taxation by increasing the wages of their manager-owners, thereby reducing the corporation's profits. Or they can organize under "subchapter S," which allows their profits to be taxed as personal income.)

All in all, however, the corporation's advantages can outweigh its disadvantages. Corporations are the dominant form of business organization in the United States today because they offer the best way to raise the financial capital necessary to expand and prosper.

Methods of Raising Financial Capital

In a modern economy, businesses use money to secure the materials and labor they need, to buy their plant and equipment, and to meet their marketing expenses. Firms can secure the capital they need from a number of sources:

Personal savings

Business savings (savings from after-tax profits, called retained earnings)

Loans from banks and credit unions or from friends and relatives

Trade credit, or credit extended when materials and supplies are purchased and immediate payment is not required

The sale of stocks and bonds—financial arrangements that are restricted to corporations.

The last source is sufficiently complicated to warrant special explanation.

Bonds

Bond: a long-term debt obligation of a corporation, generally traded on the open market.

A **bond** is a long-term debt obligation of a corporation that can generally be traded on the open market. When a company sells a bond, it is actually borrowing money. The company secures funds for the development of its business, either to purchase plant and equipment or to pay wages and rent. It commits itself to repay the money to the bondholder after a specific number of years (generally more than five and less than thirty) and to make periodic (usually quarterly) interest payments on the debt.

The interest payment that bondholders will receive from the corporation is usually stated on the face of the bond, either in dollars or as a percentage of the par value (face value) of the bond. If a bond is resold, the bond market (this is, the buyers and sellers of bonds) sets a price for the bond based on a comparison of the stated interest rate with the going rate at the time of the sale. If the market interest rate has risen since the bond was issued, the price of the bond will be lowered to compensate. If the rate has fallen, the price will be raised. After the price adjustment, the new bondholder receives an effective interest rate similar to the market rate.

$$\text{effective interest rate} = \frac{\text{stated interest payment}}{\text{market price of the bond}}$$

For example, a bond that pays interest of $10 annually (called its coupon rate) and sells for $98 carries an effective interest rate of 10.2 percent.

$$\text{effective rate} = \frac{\$10}{\$98} = 10.2 \text{ percent}$$

Because the market interest rate and the price of a bond are inversely related, an investor stands to lose part of his or her financial wealth during periods of rising interest rates. The new higher rates push down the price bondholders can get for their bonds, for no one wants to hold bonds that bear low interest rates when other financial assets of equal value offer higher interest rates. To attract buyers under such conditions, bondholders may have to sell at a loss. Conversely, a fall in the market interest rate will raise the prices of existing bonds. Needless to say, dealers attempt to make money by purchasing bonds when prices are low and selling them when prices are high. To do so, however, the investor must predict future interest rates accurately.

Because bonds guarantee the investor a fixed interest rate and repayment by a certain date, they are considered a relatively safe investment. The security they offer enables firms to obtain the financial capital they need at lower interest rates—a major advantage of bonds from the firm's point of view. At the same time, bonds permit the owners of the corporation to retain their claim to residual profits. No matter how profitable the firm becomes, bondholders never receive more than the stated interest and repayment of principal. The major disadvantage of bonds to the firm is that their fixed interest payments reduce the firm's discretion over how to use its revenues.

Preferred Stock

Companies can also raise capital by selling stock, or ownership rights to their businesses. Two kinds of stock, preferred and common, are generally offered. **Preferred stock** is a set of ownership rights in a corporation that entitles the investor to a fixed share of profits after taxes. To a certain extent, people who buy preferred stock are buying security. Preferred stockholders are guaranteed their fixed payment from after-tax profits, called fixed dividends, in dollars, so long as the corporation makes a profit. Of course, that security comes at a price. If the corporation does well and profits soar, preferred stockholders continue to receive their fixed

Preferred stock: a set of ownership rights in a corporation that entitles the investor to a fixed share of profits after taxes.

payments—nothing more. Preferred stockholders sometimes have the right to elect members of the board of directors, who oversee the management of the corporation.

Stockholders who buy cumulative preferred stock receive the right to deferred dividends in unprofitable years. Dividends missed because the company made no profit accumulate and must be paid up later when the company becomes profitable again. Convertible preferred stock gives owners the right to exchange (convert) their preferred stock for common stock. As we will see, holders of common stock stand to gain most if a company does well. Convertible preferred stock gives stockholders the security of a fixed dividend payment when a company is new and unstable in its earnings, and the profitability of common stock later, when the company is more successful.

Although preferred stock certificates may bear a nominal price, called the par value, they can be traded at whatever price they will command in the stock market. That price will depend on the stated dividend payment; the current interest rate on bonds (an alternative investment); the buyers' confidence in the firm's ability to meet its fixed dividends; and various rights, such as convertibility, that may go with the stock.

Unlike a bond, preferred stock does not entitle owners to repayment of funds invested in the corporation. Dividends are paid to stockholders only after the interest on the corporation's bonds has been paid to bondholders— as must be done even when the corporation is losing money. For this reason preferred stocks tend to be a riskier investment than bonds, and the dividends they bear are typically higher, as a percentage of funds invested, than the interest paid on bonds. Preferred stock is safer than common stock, however.

From the corporation's point of view, preferred stock offers a means of raising funds that need not be repaid. The firm does not have to pay dividends if it is unprofitable. But if it does make a profit, it has no control over the amount of the dividend. In other words, part of the firm's after-tax profits is committed to preferred stock dividends and cannot be reinvested instead.

Common Stock

Common stock: a set of ownership rights in a corporation that entitles the investor to a share of any profits remaining after all other obligations have been met.

Common stock is a set of ownership rights in a corporation that entitles the investor to a share of any profits remaining after all other obligations have been met. Common stockholders have what is called a residual claim to ownership. They are not entitled to any dividends until all expenses, including taxes, interest on bonds, and dividends on preferred stock, have been paid. Common stock dividends are not fixed. They can vary from nothing to a modest or a very high return, depending on the corporation's profitability and its plans for reinvestment of its profits. Though common stockholders assume the greatest risk of all stock- and bondholders, they also stand to gain the most. Their dividends, being unfixed, can rise with the company's profits.

Like preferred stock, common stock certificates may bear a par value, but their price is determined by people's willingness to buy and sell them.

Reinvestment of after-tax earnings often (but not always) improves a corporation's profitability.

Common stockholders can exercise control over the corporation through their right to elect all or most of the company's directors, who approve management policies, fix dividends, and set investment policies. Most stockholders do not exercise their voting power, however. If they are unhappy about the way the company is being run, they can sell their stock and invest in something else. In general, common stock appeals to investors who are willing to assume some risk in hopes of a high payoff, but do not want to be involved in managing a company.

From the firm's point of view, common stock affords maximum flexibility in the disposal of after-tax profits. No dividend payment is required, so leftover profits can be reinvested. As with bonds and preferred stock, the issuance of new common stock spreads the risk of ownership, but it can also dilute the original owners' claim on after-tax profits.

Calculating Business Profits and Losses

Businesses hope to make profits and avoid losses. Profits to firms are the amount by which sales revenues exceed costs. Losses are negative profits: the amount by which costs exceed sales revenues.

Costs, or expenses, vary greatly among businesses. They can include wages and salaries, utilities, rents, insurance, depreciation (computed, among other ways, by dividing the purchase price of plant and equipment by their expected useful life), interest on bonds and commercial loans, bad debts, office supplies, and materials used in production.

Consider the profit position of Widgets, Inc., a corporation with annual sales of $100 million and annual expenses of $35 million in wages and salaries, $20 million in materials, $5 million in office supplies, and $8 million in depreciation of equipment. The firm's profits can be computed as shown in the profit and loss statement below.

Widgets, Inc.

Profit and Loss Statement

Sales revenues		$100,000,000
Expenses:		
Wages and salaries	$35,000,000	
Materials	20,000,000	
Office supplies	5,000,000	
Depreciation	8,000,000	
Total expenses		68,000,000
Profits		32,000,000
Tax liability (46 percent of profits)[1]		14,720,000
After-tax profits		$ 17,280,000

---

1. For purposes of illustration. Actually, the corporate tax rate varies from a low of 16 percent on the first $25,000 of profits to a high of 46 percent on any profits over $100,000.

Perspectives in Economics: Reading the Stock Page

(1)	(2)	(3)	(4)	(5)	(6)	(7)	(8)	(9)	(10)	(11)

52 Weeks				Yld	P-E	Sales				Net
High	Low	Stock	Div.	%	Ratio	100s	High	Low	Close	Chg.
37	23¼	Dorsey	1.20	4.6	13	24	26⅜	26	26	– ¼
42½	31⅝	Dover	.82	2.3	13	337	35½	35⅜	35⅜	.....
33⅛	25¾	DowCh	1.80	6.3	10	2495	29¼	28¾	28¾	– ⅛
51⅜	35¾	DowJn	.78	1.7	22	435	45¼	44¾	45	+ ¼
14⅛	10⅞	Dravo	.50	3.9	.....	162	12¾	12⅛	12¾	+ ½
23⅛	15¼	Dresr	.80	3.9	15	720	20⅝	20¼	20⅜	.....
19	14¾	DrexB	2	11.	.....	23	18½	18¼	18⅜	+ ⅛
49⅝	23¾	Dreyfus	.50a	1.1	12	87	46⅛	45⅞	46	– ¼
54⅝	43¼	duPont	3	5.8	9	2277	52⅜	51½	51½	– ⅝
34¼	30⅝	duPnt	pf3.50	10.	.....	7	33¾	33¼	33¾	+ ¼
44¼	39	duPnt	pf4.50	10.	.....	27	44	44	44	+ ½
32⅝	22¾	DukeP	2.48	7.7	8	1261	u32¾	32⅜	32⅜	– ⅛
129	97	Duke	pf6.75	5.0	.....	1	u134	134	134	+5
77	64	Duke	pf8.70	11.	.....	z100	76	76	76	+1½
72¾	59½	Duke	pf8.20	12.	.....	z30	68	68	68	+ ¼
25⅞	21⅝	Duke	pf2.69	11.	.....	5	25½	25⅜	25½	.....
34	28	Duke	pf3.85	12.	.....	23	32⅜	32¼	32¼	.....
73	51¼	DunBrd	1.88	2.6	22	830	72¾	71¾	72¼	+ ⅜
16⅜	11½	DuqLt	2.06	13.	7	305	16	15⅞	15⅞	.....
58⅛	43⅛	Duq	pf7.20	13.	.....	z780	56¼	56¼	56¼	+ ¼
16½	8½	DycoP†	.60	4.7	10	19	13	12⅞	12⅞	+ ¼
25¼	17½	DynAm	.20	.8	12	5	24⅝	24⅝	24⅝	.....

The financial pages of the newspaper may look forbidding to the uninitiated. But as we will see, they provide investors with a great deal of useful information. The clipping shown here is an excerpt from the inside last page of the *Wall Street Journal*, which lists more than fifteen hundred stocks traded daily on the New York Stock Exchange.[1]

Suppose you want to buy stock in Dun and Bradstreet, a company whose primary business is investigating the credit worthiness of other firms. The stock page is an important source (but by no means the only one) of financial data on Dun & Bradstreet Corporation. Look at the clipping. The abbreviated name of the company, *DunBrd*, appears in the third column from the left. The headings at the top of each column indicate the type of information shown.

Column 1 lists the highest price at which the stock has sold during the preceding fifty-two weeks. At some time during the preceding year, Dun & Bradstreet sold for as much as $73 a share.

Column 2 lists the stock's lowest selling price during the preceding fifty-two weeks. At some point during the year, Dun & Bradstreet sold for $51.25 a share (stock prices are always quoted in eighths of a dollar).

Column 4 shows the dividends paid on the stock. When the clipping was published, Dun & Bradstreet was paying dividends at an annual rate of $1.88 per share of common stock. (The stocks

Several observations can be made about this profit and loss statement. First, company profits obviously vary directly with sales revenues and inversely with expenses. Second, a company can reduce its tax liability by increasing its expenses (and thereby reducing its profits). When the firm buys additional office supplies, the financial cost it incurs is less than the dollar amount it pays its supplier. Financial cost is the expense minus the reduction in taxes the company realizes because of the expenditure.

After-tax profits are more important to owners than before-tax profits. If taxes take too big a bite out of a firm's profits, the company may attempt to recoup some of the lost revenues by raising prices. Consumers then may pay part of the so-called corporate income tax through their purchases of goods and services. (How much of the tax the consumer will bear depends in part on the competitiveness of the firm's market. More will be said on that subject later.)

Depreciation of business plant and equipment can be calculated in several ways. One method is to divide the purchase price of a piece of with a *pf* following their names are preferred stocks yielding fixed dividends.)

Column 5 shows the yield on a share of common stock, or the dividends as a percentage of the stock's selling price. Owners of Dun & Bradstreet were earning an annual rate of 2.6 percent on their investment.

Column 6 contains the price-earnings ratio, or the price of the stock divided by the profits per share. At the time, Dun & Bradstreet had a price-earnings ratio of 22, meaning that the price of the stock was 22 times higher than the annual profits per share. Investors use the price-earnings ratio as a rough indicator of whether a stock is over- or underpriced. (Determining a stock's real value is a matter of judgment that depends, among other things, on the company's expected future profitability. Investors will buy a stock with even a relatively high price-earnings ratio if the company's future prospects are bright.)

Column 7 shows the number of shares sold in lots, groups of 100, in the trading day. On this day, 83,000 Dun & Bradstreet shares were traded.

Column 8 contains the highest price the stock brought on that day. Sometime during the day, Dun & Bradstreet sold for as much as $72.75 a share.

Column 9 gives the lowest price the stock commanded that day, $71.75 per share. In other words, Dun & Bradstreet's price fluctuated over a range of $1 during the day.

Column 10 lists the stock's closing price. The last time Dun & Bradstreet was traded that day, its selling price was $72.25 per share.

Column 11 shows the change in closing price from the day before. Dun & Bradstreet closed 37.5¢ above its closing price the day before. (The closing price on the preceding day was $71.85.)

The stock pages do not give investors all the information they need to make their investments, but they do give some indication of a stock's price over the past year, its present dividends, its profitability, and the immediate demand for it among investors.

1. "New York Stock Exchange Composite Transactions," *Wall Street Journal* (March 25, 1985), p. 56.

equipment by its expected usable life, in years. This is called the straight-line depreciation method. No matter how it is calculated, however, depreciation represents an expense on paper, not out of pocket. Thus legislation that reduces the number of years over which an asset can be depreciated raises the depreciation expense, reducing a firm's profits on paper but *increasing* the total funds (after-tax profits plus depreciation) available for reinvestment.

The $32 million pretax profit shown in Widgets's statement is more precisely referred to as a book profit. **Book profit** is the profit shown on a company's accounting books. Book profit must be distinguished from the true, or economic, profit of a business. **Economic profit** is the amount left after all costs, including the opportunity cost of capital and the risk of losing money, have been deducted from company revenues. The opportunity cost of capital and the risk cost of doing business are generally not included in the firm's profit and loss statement. Because they are not out-of-pocket expenses, and not tax deductible, they simply do not enter into

Book profit: the profit shown on a company's accounting books.

Economic profit: the amount left after all costs, including the opportunity cost of capital and the risk of losing money, have been deducted from company revenues.

Opportunity cost of capital: the return that might have been realized on the best alternative investment not undertaken.

Risk cost: the loss that can be anticipated because of the failure of a certain percentage of a firm's ventures.

Economic losses: the amount by which the accounting expenses, the opportunity cost of capital, and the risk cost of doing business exceed a company's revenues.

the calculation of book profit. The **opportunity cost of capital** is the return that might have been realized on the best alternative investment not undertaken. When an investment is made, some alternative investment is forgone. A real cost, though not a money cost, is incurred. To justify investing in a venture, a firm must be able to cover the opportunity cost of its capital. The **risk cost** of doing business is the loss that can be anticipated because of the failure of a certain percentage of a firm's ventures. Without perfect knowledge of the market, firms must expect some of their ventures to fail and reduce the firm's capital. To justify going into business, a firm must be able to cover the costs of its expected failures.

Since neither the opportunity cost of capital nor the risk cost has been deducted from the revenues of Widgets, Inc., the company's book profit exaggerates its true profitability. The government still levies taxes against the firm's book profits, however—not its economic profits. In effect, the firm must pay taxes on part of its cost of doing business. Thus its incentive to incur those costs is reduced. Indeed the corporation may actually be incurring economic losses while it is reporting a book profit to the Internal Revenue Service. **Economic losses** are the amount by which the accounting expenses, the opportunity cost of capital, and the risk cost of doing business exceed a company's revenues.

Inflation is another distorting influence on profits. Though inflation tends to raise both a firm's revenues and the cost of replacing its capital equipment, no allowance is made for rising prices of plant and equipment in the calculation of profits. Depreciation is typically calculated on the basis of the purchase price of existing capital equipment, not on the basis of today's higher replacement costs, the true economic cost of capital. Hence inflation tends to make companies appear more profitable than they really are. Both the reported rates of return on investments and the government's corporate income tax revenues tend to rise and fall with the rate of inflation.

The Bigness of Business

Today corporations dominate the U.S. economy, in terms of both sales and assets. In a number of industries—automobiles, cigarettes, cereal, light bulbs, and soap—the four largest firms control more than 50 percent of sales. (If imports are excluded, the four leading U.S. automakers control more than 90 percent of domestic sales.) Furthermore, a relatively small number of corporations—just a few hundred—dominates the entire corporate sector. Exxon Corporation, General Motors Corporation, and American Telephone and Telegraph Company reap annual revenues that exceed the gross domestic product of several nations. Some social observers complain that they wield enormous political influence as well.

But does "big" mean "bad" when it comes to business? Retired professor of economics John Kenneth Galbraith argues eloquently that corporations have become so big that stockholders are no longer in control. The relatively few but very large firms that dominate the economy enjoy considerable power over their markets, including the power to induce consumers to buy their products through advertising, and to set prices arbitrarily. These corporations make up what Galbraith calls "the new industrial state." Through price setting, he argues, they have in effect acquired the power to tax.[2] Ralph Nader's consumer protection group goes further:

In other words, our largest firms exercise extraordinary influence over the citizens of our country and other countries: they can spend decisive amounts in elections; market products that threaten the one ozone layer this planet has; determine which towns thrive and which gather cobwebs; stabilize or help overthrow foreign governments (Lockheed in Japan, ITT in Chile); develop technology that takes lives or saves lives.[3]

The proposed solution: democratize corporations by requiring them to include representatives from labor, environmental, consumer, and other public interest groups on their boards of directors.

Others have made the following counterarguments:

1. Large businesses do not actually have the market power attributed to them. They must compete not only with the several other firms in their industry, but with the many others that will move into the industry if the large firms raise prices or lower quality arbitrarily. For example, when American automakers failed to meet consumer demands for small, fuel-efficient cars in the 1970s, they lost sales to foreign producers. If large companies do not cater to consumers' demands, they will not remain large very long.

2. Though stockholders may not vote in corporate elections, they do vote with their investments. When a company does not make profits, many investors simply sell their interest in the company and move their money elsewhere. To the extent that a stock is considered undesirable, companies will have a difficult time acquiring capital. If corporations want to make money for their stockholders, they must produce the goods and services consumers—not managers—want.

3. Large corporations may exercise political influence, even to the extent of using their profits to bribe public officials. No bribe is effective, however, unless someone accepts it. Bribes are as much a problem of the political system as of the business system.

4. Whoever sits on the board of directors, a corporation is run by *individuals*—people who have their own opinions of what is right and wrong, what the company should and should not do. There is no reason to believe that a publicly appointed director would represent the public interest, however defined, better than a director elected by the stockholders. Because publicly appointed directors would not have a financial stake in the business, they would not be likely to take an active interest in producing the goods and services that consumers, and not board members, really want.

---

2. John Kenneth Galbraith, *The New Industrial State* (Boston: Houghton Mifflin, 1967).

3. Mark Green et al., *The Case for the Corporate Democracy Act of 1980* (Washington: Americans Concerned about Corporate Power, 1980), p. 2.

Summary and Extensions

The producing sector of the U.S. economy is composed of more than 18 million firms, most of which are small proprietorships. Though a substantial majority of sales is made by just a few hundred large corporations, that fact alone does not indicate that the economy is unhealthy. The big corporations can just as easily be seen as a sign of economic success.

Giant corporations affect the life and livelihood of nearly everyone. Many people work for one or invest in several, and almost everyone consumes the products of dozens or even hundreds of others. Combining the capital of millions of investors and the talents of millions of workers, giant corporations are a testament to the ability of free men, motivated by self-interest, to engage in sustained, large-scale, peaceful cooperation for their mutual benefit and enrichment.[4]

That is not to say that corporations should be left largely on their own, to do what they want. Some economists believe the structure of the corporation should be changed, to make it more responsive to the interests of the public. Before that can be done, however, we need to know more about how both the market and political systems operate. We need a firmer basis on which to judge whether democratizing corporate America (or politicizing it, depending on one's perspective) will enhance business efficiency.

Major Conclusions

1. The major types of business organization are proprietorships, partnerships, and corporations.
2. In terms of sales and assets, the corporation is the dominant form of organization in business today. Corporations' legal status permits them to raise the capital necessary to operate on the large scale required by modern technology.
3. Businesses raise capital primarily through personal saving and reinvestment of profits, trade credit, bank loans, and the sale of stocks and bonds.

---

4. Robert Hessen, *In Defense of the Corporation* (Stanford, Calif.: Hoover Institute Press, 1979), p. xi.

4. Corporations raise most of their capital by selling bonds, preferred stock, and common stock. Bonds are long-term debt obligations. Preferred stock is a form of ownership that entitles investors to a fixed dividend payment. Common stock carries a residual claim to ownership; dividends are paid only after all other claims on the firm's revenues have been met. From the investor's point of view, common stock carries the most risk of the three types of securities, but also the greatest potential for gain.

5. Although just a few hundred corporations dominate industrial production in the United States, the large size of those corporations does not necessarily mean that consumers must accept higher prices, lower-quality products, or restricted production. The impact of big corporations on the U.S. economy is a highly controversial issue.

1. List the reasons why an investor might choose to buy a bond rather than common stock.

Questions to Ponder

2. List the reasons why an investor might choose to buy common stock rather than preferred stock.

3. Why might members of a partnership choose not to incorporate?

4. Why are almost all large companies corporations?

5. What would be your objectives in buying common stock? What would you need to know about a company before you invested in it? Would you always want to invest in a "sure thing?" Explain.

6. Suppose a bondholder receives an interest payment of $13 a year and an effective interest rate on his or her investment of 13.6 percent. What is the market price of the bond? Suppose the interest rate rises to 14.5 percent; what would happen to the price of the bond?

7. Various investors hold bonds, preferred stock, and common stock in Ajax Corporation. Which security holders have first claim on the company's earnings? Second claim? A residual claim?

8. Why might an investor be interested in buying common stock in a profitable company that has never paid a dividend to common stockholders?

9. Why does a small family-held corporation have a tax incentive to provide its managers with fringe benefits in the form of insurance policies and company cars?

Central Question

How does cost affect and limit behavior?

Key Terms

Explicit cost

Implicit cost

Sunk cost

Marginal cost

Law of diminishing marginal returns

Marginal product

Marginal revenue

Chapter 20

Cost and Producer Choice

The economist's stock in trade—his tools—lies in his ability to and proclivity to think about all questions in terms of alternatives. The truth judgment of the moralist, which says that something is either wholly right or wholly wrong, is foreign to him. The win-lose, yes-no discussion of politics is not within his purview. He does not recognize the either-or, the all-or-nothing situation as his own. His is not the world of the mutually exclusive. Instead, his is the world of adjustment, of coordinated conflict, of mutual gain.
James M. Buchanan

*C*ost is pervasive in human action. We are constantly forced to make choices, to do one thing and not another. Cost, or more precisely opportunity cost, is the most highly valued opportunity not chosen. Though money is a frequently used measure of cost, it is not cost itself.

Although we may not recognize it, cost also pervades our everyday thought and conversation. When we say "that course is difficult" or "the sermon seemed endless," we are indicating the cost of activities. If the preacher's extended commentary delayed the church picnic, the sermon was costly. Although complaints about excessive costs sometimes indicate an absolute limitation, more often they merely mean that the benefits of the activity are too small to justify the cost. Many people who "can't afford" a vacation actually have the money, but do not wish to spend it on travel. And most students who find writing research papers "impossible" are simply not willing to put forth the necessary effort.

This chapter explores the meaning of cost in human behavior. We will begin by showing how seemingly irrational behavior can often be explained by the hidden costs of a choice. We will then develop the concept of marginal cost, which together with demand and the related concept of supply defines the limits of rational behavior, from personal activities like painting and fishing to business decisions like how much to produce.

Inevitably, points made earlier will be reviewed and extended in this chapter. There is a cost in this repetition, but there is also some benefit in a few varied reiterations.

Explicit and Implicit Cost

Explicit cost: the money expenditure required to obtain a resource, product, or service.

Not all costs are obvious. It is not difficult to recognize an out-of-pocket expenditure—the money price you pay for a product or service. This is called an explicit cost. **Explicit cost** is the money expenditure required to obtain a resource, product, or service. For example, the price of your book is an explicit cost of taking a course in economics. But other costs are less immediately apparent. Hidden costs of the course might include the time spent going to class and studying, the risk of receiving a failing grade, and the discomfort of being confronted with material that may challenge some of your beliefs. These are implicit costs; together they add up to the value of what you could have done instead. **Implicit cost** is the forgone opportunity to do or acquire something else, or to put one's resources to another use. Though implicit costs may not be recognized, they are often much larger than the more obvious explicit costs of an action.

Implicit cost: the forgone opportunity to do or acquire something else, or to put one's resources to another use.

The Cost of an Education

A good illustration of the magnitude of implicit costs is the cost of an education. Suppose a student takes a course, paying $200 for tuition and $20 for books. The money cost of the course is $220. But that figure does not include the implicit costs to the student. To take a course, the student must attend class for about 45 hours and may have to spend twice that much time traveling to and from class, completing class assignments, and studying for examinations. The total number of hours spent on any one course, then, might be 135 (45 hours in class plus 90 hours of traveling, studying, and so forth).

The student could have spent that time doing other things, including working for a money wage. If the student's time is valued at $4 per hour (the wage he or she might have received if working), the time cost of the course is $540 (135 hours × $4). Moreover, if the student experiences some anxiety because of taking the course, that psychic or risk cost must be added to the total as well. If the student would be willing to pay $10 to avoid the anxiety, the total cost of taking the course climbs to $770.

Explicit costs		
Tuition	$200	
Books	20	
Total explicit cost	$220	
Implicit costs		
Time	$540	
Anxiety	10	
Total implicit cost	$550	
Total cost of course	$770	

The opportunity cost of the student's time represents the largest component of the total cost of the course. The value of one's time varies from person to person. For students who are unable to find work, the time cost of taking a course may be quite small. That is why many young people go to college. Their time cost is generally lower than that of experienced workers, who must give up the opportunity to earn a good wage in order to attend classes full time.

The Cost of Bargains

Every Wednesday supermarkets run large newspaper ads listing their weekly specials. Generally only a few items are offered at especially low prices, for store managers know that most bargain seekers can be attracted to the store with just a few carefully selected specials. Once the customer has gone to the store offering a special on steak, he would have to incur a travel cost in order to buy other items in a different store. Even though peanut butter may be on sale elsewhere, the sum of the sale price and the travel cost exceed the regular price in the first store. Through attractive displays and packaging, customers can be persuaded to buy many other goods not on sale, particularly toiletries, which tend to bear high markups.

Supermarket chains do not necessarily make huge profits. The grocery industry is reasonably competitive, and supermarket chains as a group are not highly profitable compared to other corporations. But the stores manage to recoup some of the revenues lost on sale items by charging higher prices on other goods. In other words, the cost of a bargain on sirloin steak may be a high price for toothpaste.

Some shoppers make the rounds of the grocery stores when sales are announced. For such people, time and transportation are cheap. A person who values his or her time at $5 an hour is not going to spend an hour trying to save a dollar or two. The cost of gas alone can make it prohibitively expensive to visit several stores. And because of the costs of acquiring information, many shoppers do not even bother to look for sales. The expected benefits are simply not great enough to justify the information cost. These shoppers enter the market "rationally ignorant."

The Irrelevance of Sunk Costs

Sunk cost: a cost incurred in the past, which cannot be altered by current decisions.

In evaluating the implicit and explicit costs of a decision, the rational person considers only costs that will be incurred now or in the future. Sunk costs, which have already been incurred because of past choices, should be ignored. A **sunk cost** is a cost incurred in the past, which cannot be altered by current decisions. Because sunk costs cannot be changed, they are irrelevant to present choices. Unless they are ignored, they may misguide current choices.

Suppose a small airline company buys a plane for $1 million. The plane will last for ten years, after which it will have no scrap value. For purposes of discussion, suppose also that once purchased, the plane has no resale value. Though originally the owners thought the plane would be profitable, within the first few months of operation they determine that they will gross only $200,000 a year by operating the plane. Pilots' salaries, fuel bills, and repair expenses will cost them $160,000 a year. Should they fly the plane or ground it?

You might conclude that the plane should not be operated. Including $100,000 per year in depreciation, the total annual cost is $260,000— $60,000 more than the expected revenues of $200,000. A little reflection will show that the depreciation cost is irrelevant, however. The plane has already been purchased at a cost of $1 million. If it is not operated, the company will have lost $1 million at the end of ten years. If it is operated, the company will at least receive $40,000 per year in revenues after operating expenses. At the end of ten years, the net loss will be only $600,000. Obviously the decision to buy the plane was a bad one; if the buyers had that choice to make again, they certainly would not do it. But bygones are bygones. When the question of whether to operate the plane comes up, past mistakes and costs are no longer relevant.

If the plane could be resold, its resale value would affect the decision. In that case, the company could sell the plane and recoup part of its investment. If it operated the plane anyway, it would be deciding to forgo the opportunity to invest the funds earned from resale. In such a situation the relevant cost is the present resale price, not the price paid for the plane originally.

To give another example, many stores stay open at night even though they draw very few customers, and fewer sales, during those hours. If the store includes a prorated portion of rental payments, depreciation, and interest on loans made for equipment in calculating the cost of staying open late, evening operations will appear to be a losing proposition. But many of those expenses are irrelevant to the decision, for they are sunk costs. The firm will have to pay them whether or not it extends its hours. Thus the decision to stay open late must be based only on costs incurred directly because of the decision—additional wages, a higher electric bill, and perhaps some additional losses from shoplifting. Because those expenses can be quite modest, a store may well find nighttime operation profitable. Just a few sales are needed to cover the costs.

Marginal Cost

So far we have been considering cost as the determining factor in the decision to undertake a particular course of action. The rational person weighs the cost of an action against its benefits and comes to a decision: whether to invest in an education, to shop around for a bargain, or to operate an airplane. The question is, how much of a given good or service will an individual choose to produce or consume? How does cost limit a behavior once a person has decided to engage in it? The answer lies in the concept of marginal cost.

Rational Behavior and Marginal Cost

Marginal cost is the additional cost incurred by producing one additional unit of a good, activity, or service. Marginal cost is the cost incurred by reading one additional page, making one additional friend, giving one additional gift, or going one additional mile. Depending on the good, activity, or service in question, marginal cost may stay the same or vary as additional units are produced. For example, imagine that Jan Smith wants to give Halloween candy to ten of her friends. In a sense, Jan is producing gifts by procuring bags of candy. If she can buy as many bags as she wants at the unit price of fifty cents, the marginal cost of each additional unit she buys is the same, fifty cents. The marginal cost is constant over the range of production.

> **Marginal cost:** the additional cost incurred by producing one additional unit of a good, activity, or service.

Marginal cost can vary with the level of output, however, for two reasons. The first has to do with the opportunity cost of time. Suppose Jan wants to give each friend a miniature watercolor, which she will paint herself over the course of the day. To make time for painting, Jan can forgo any of the various activities that usually make up her day. She may choose to give up recreational activities, housekeeping chores, or work or study time. If she behaves rationally, she will give up the activities she values least. To do the first painting, she may forgo straightening up her room—an activity that is low on most people's lists of preferences. The marginal cost of her first watercolor is therefore a messy room. To paint the second watercolor, Jan will give up the next-to-last item on her list of favorite activities. As she produces more and more paintings, Jan will forgo more and more valuable alternatives. In other words, the marginal cost of her paintings will rise with her output.

Perspectives in Economics: Sunk Costs in the Railroad and Trucking Industries

Clinton H. Whitehurst, Jr.

Historically, a large part of a railroad's investment has been in assets with fixed costs—costs that do not vary with output in the short run. In the early 1900s, fixed costs were estimated to be as much as 75 percent of railroads' total costs. More recently they have been estimated at 40 to 50 percent.

A significant part of a railroad's fixed costs is the investment in its right of way—the 75- to 200-foot-wide corridors in which its tracks are laid. Most railroads purchased that land and paid for its grading many years ago, perhaps in the last century. Those costs are considered historical, or sunk.

To the degree that its costs are fixed, a railroad's average total cost decreases as its volume increases. The more tons it carries per mile, the lower the average total cost of moving a ton of freight. The railroad's fixed costs are simply spread out over more units of freight.

To use their hauling capacity fully and lower their average total cost, railroads have tended to set their rates low for long hauls. In the early days they often generated only enough revenues to cover their variable costs, not their total costs. But in many instances they compensated for low rates on long hauls by charging high rates on short hauls. In 1887, customer complaints about differences in rates prompted Congress to place railroad rates and routes under the regulation of the Interstate Commerce Commission (ICC). Throughout much of its history, the ICC considered rates that did not cover total costs to be unfair or predatory—designed, that is, to drive out competition. It insisted that railroads set their rates high enough to cover total costs.

After the Second World War, the rapidly growing trucking industry became the railroads' chief competitor. Fixed costs were much less significant in trucking than in railroads. As much as 90 percent of the total cost of trucking varied with the number of tons carried per mile. From the point of view of the trucking industry, then, the ICC's requirement that rates cover total costs made sense. But from the railroads' perspective, the requirement was disastrous. By keeping railroad rates high, the ICC enabled the trucking industry to compete for railroad business and expand its share of the transportation market.

In 1958, following an extensive lobbying effort by the railroads, Congress amended the Interstate Commerce Act. The amendment instructed the ICC that "Rates of a carrier shall not be held up to a particular level to protect the traffic of any other mode of transportation." Earlier Interstate Commerce Act provisions still barred "unfair or destructive competitive practices," however. Given the ambiguity of the legislation, the ICC continued to insist that rates cover total costs. In 1968 its interpretation was upheld by the Supreme Court.

Recently railroads have been given considerable freedom to set their own rates under the Railroad Revitalization and Regulatory Reform Act (1976) and especially the Staggers Rail Act (1980). Rates that cover only variable costs are no longer considered unfair and are not challenged by the Interstate Commerce Commission.

Meanwhile, the interstate highways—the right of way for trucks—are becoming more congested. Truck delivery, once much faster than railroad delivery, is slowing down. But railroad tracks remain underutilized. As circumstances change, railroads are putting their century-old investment in their rights of way to good use. By ignoring sunk costs and offering lower rates, they have recaptured much of the freight business they lost to trucks after the Second World War. Today, one often sees highway trailers riding on railroad flatcars, reflecting the new competitiveness of railroads. In fact, hauling trailers is now one of the fastest-growing railroad services.

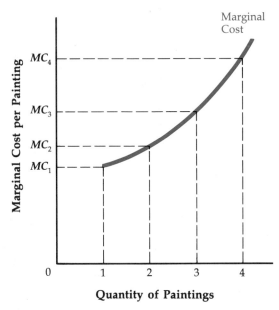

Figure 20.1. Rising Marginal Cost.
To produce each new watercolor, Jan must give up an opportunity more valuable than the last. Thus the marginal cost of her paintings rises with each new work.

If the marginal cost of each new painting is plotted against the quantity of paintings produced, a curve like the one in Figure 20.1 will result. Because the marginal cost of each additional painting is higher than the marginal cost of the last one, the curve slopes upward to the right.

Although the marginal cost curve is generally assumed to slope upward, as the one in Figure 20.1 does, that need not be the case. If Jan placed equal value on all the forgone activities, her marginal cost would be constant and the marginal cost curve would be horizontal.

The Law of Diminishing Returns

The second reason marginal cost may vary with output involves a technological relationship known as the law of diminishing marginal returns. According to the **law of diminishing marginal returns,** if successive units of one resource—labor, fertilizer, or any other resource—are applied to a fixed quantity of another resource—land, for instance—then at some point in the production process, the added output gained from each additional unit of the variable resource will begin to diminish. In other words, beyond some point less output is received for each added unit of a resource. That is, more of the resource will be required to produce the same amount of output as before. Beyond some point, the marginal cost of additional units of output rises.

Though the law of diminishing returns applies to any production process, its meaning is most easily grasped in the context of agricultural production.

Law of diminishing marginal returns: the law that if successive units of one resource are applied to a fixed quantity of another resource, then at some point in the production process, the added output gained from each additional unit of the variable resource will begin to diminish.

Assume you are producing tomatoes. You have a fixed amount of land—an acre—but can vary the quantity of labor you apply to it. If you try to do the planting all by yourself—dig the holes, pour the water, insert the plants, and cover them up—you will waste time changing tools. If a friend helps you, you can divide the tasks and specialize. Less time will be wasted in changing tools.

The time you would have spent changing tools can be spent planting more tomatoes, thus increasing the harvest. At first output may expand faster than the labor force. That is, one laborer may be able to plant 100 tomatoes an hour; two working together may be able to plant 250 an hour. Thus the marginal cost of planting the additional 150 plants is lower than the cost of the first 100. Up to a point, the more workers, the greater their efficiency, and the lower the marginal cost—all because of the economies of specialization. At some point, however, the addition of still more laborers will not contribute as much to production as in the past, if only because a large number of workers on a single acre of ground will start bumping into one another. Then the marginal cost of putting plants into the ground will begin to rise.

Diminishing returns are an inescapable fact of life. If returns did not diminish at some point, output would expand indefinitely, and the world's food supply could be grown on just one acre of land. (For that matter, it could be grown in a flower box.) The point at which output begins to diminish varies from one production process to the next, but eventually all marginal cost curves will slope upward to the right, as in Figure 20.1.

Table 20.1 shows the marginal cost of producing tomatoes with various numbers of workers, assuming that each employee is paid $5 and that production is limited to one acre. Working alone, one employee can produce a quarter of a bushel; two can produce a full bushel (columns 1 and 2). The third column shows the amount each additional employee adds to total production, called the marginal product. **Marginal product** is the increase in total output that results when one additional unit of a resource—for example, labor, fertilizer, land—is added to the production process. The first employee contributes 0.25 (one quarter) of a bushel; the second employee, an additional 0.75 of a bushel, and so on. These are the marginal products of successive units of labor.

Marginal product: the increase in total output that results when one additional unit of a resource is added to the production process.

The important information is shown in the last two columns of the table. Though two employees are needed to produce the first bushel (column 4), because of the efficiencies of specialization, only one additional employee is needed to produce the second. Beyond that point, however, returns diminish. Each additional employee contributes less, so that two more workers are needed to produce the third bushel and five more to produce the fourth. If the table were extended, each bushel beyond the fourth would require a progressively larger number of employees.

Column 5 shows that if all employees are paid the same wage, $5, the marginal cost of a bushel of tomatoes will decline from $10 for the first bushel to $5 for the second before rising to $10 again for the third bushel. That is, increasing marginal costs (or diminishing returns) emerge after the addition of the third employee.

Table 20.1. Marginal Cost of Producing Tomatoes

Number of Workers Employed (1)	Total Number of Bushels (2)	Contribution of Each Employee to Production (Marginal Product) (3)	Number of Employees Required to Produce Each Additional Bushel (4)	Marginal Cost of Each Bushel, Figured at $5 per Employee (5)
1	0.25	0.25 } (1st bushel)	2	$10
2	1.00	0.75		
3	2.00	1.00 (2nd bushel)	1	$ 5

Point at Which Diminishing Marginal Returns Emerge

4	2.60	0.60 } (3rd bushel)	2	$10
5	3.00	0.40		
6	3.30	0.30		
7	3.55	0.25		
8	3.75	0.20 } (4th bushel)	5	$25
9	3.90	0.15		
10	4.00	0.10		

If the marginal cost of each bushel (column 5) is plotted against the number of bushels harvested, a curve like the one in Figure 20.2 will result. Although the curve slopes downward at first, for most purposes the relevant segment of the curve is the upward-sloping portion above point *a*, which can also be thought of as the farm's supply curve. That is, it indicates the number of tomatoes the farm can produce at a given cost, everything else held constant. (This concept, and the relevance of point *a*, will be explained in detail in Chapter 21.)

The Cost-Benefit Tradeoff

Just as a producer's marginal cost schedule shows the increasing cost of supplying more goods, the demand curve, as explained earlier, shows the decreasing value or marginal benefit of those goods to the people consuming them. Together, marginal costs and benefits determine how many units will be produced and consumed. Up to the intersection of the marginal cost and demand (marginal benefit) curves, the marginal benefit of each additional unit exceeds its marginal cost. In other words, people can gain through production and consumption of those units. The intersection of the two curves represents the limit of production, or the point at which welfare is maximized.

To see this point, consider the costs and benefits of an activity like fishing.

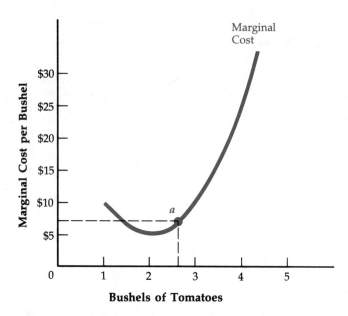

Figure 20.2. The Law of Diminishing Marginal Returns.
As production expands with the addition of new workers, efficiencies of specialization initially cause marginal cost to fall. At some point, however—here, just
beyond two bushels—marginal cost will begin to rise again. At that point, marginal
returns will begin to diminish.

The Costs and Benefits of Fishing

Gary Schmidt likes to fish. What he does with the fish he catches is of no
consequence to us; he can make them into trophies, give them away, or
store them in the freezer. Even if Gary places no value on the fish,
we can use dollars to illustrate the marginal costs and benefits of fishing
to Gary. (Money figures are not values, but a means of indicating relative
value.)

What is important is that Gary wants to fish. How many fish will he
catch? From our earlier analysis of Jan's desire to paint (page 441), we
know that the cost of catching each additional fish will be higher than the
cost of the one before. Gary will confront an upward-sloping marginal
cost curve like the one in Figure 20.3. Gary's demand curve for fishing
will slope downward, for as the cost of catching each additional fish rises,
Gary will be less and less inclined to spend more time in the activity (see
Figure 20.3).

From the positions of the two curves, we can see that Gary will catch
up to five fish before he packs up his rod and heads for home. He places
a relatively high value of $4.67 on the first fish (point *a* in the figure) and
pays the relatively low marginal cost of $1 in forgone opportunities for it
(point *b*). In other words, he gets $3.67 more value from using his time,
energy, and other resources to fish than he would receive from his best
alternative. The marginal benefit of the second fish also exceeds its marginal

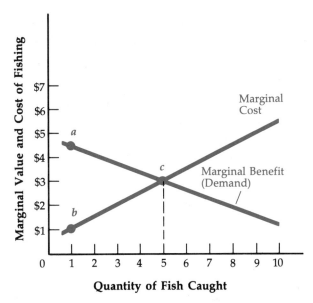

Figure 20.3. Costs and Benefits of Fishing.
For each fish up to the fifth, Gary receives more in benefits than he pays in costs. The first fish gives him $4.67 in benefits (point *a*) and costs him only $1 (point *b*). The fifth yields equal costs and benefits (point *c*), but the sixth costs more than it is worth. Therefore Gary will catch no more than five fish.

cost, although by a smaller amount—$2.75 ($4.25 − $1.50). Gary continues to gain with the third and fourth fishes. But the fifth fish is a matter of indifference to him. Its marginal value equals its marginal cost (point *c*). Though we cannot say that Gary will actually bother to catch a fifth fish, we do know that five is the limit toward which he will aim. He will not catch a sixth—at least during the period of time covered by the graph—because it would cost him more than he would receive in benefits.

The Costs and Benefits of Preventing Accidents

All of us would prefer to avoid accidents. In that sense we have a demand for accident prevention, whose curve should slope downward like all other demand curves. But preventing accidents also entails costs, whether in time, forgone opportunities, or money. Should we attempt to prevent all accidents? Not if the cost of preventing them exceeds the cost of the accident. Suppose the cost of ensuring that you will never stumble down the stairs is $100 (again, we are using dollars to indicate relative value). If the only injury you expect to suffer is a bruised knee, would you spend $100 to prevent the accident?

As with the question of how long to fish, marginal cost and benefit curves can help illustrate the point at which preventing accidents ceases to be cost effective. Suppose Al Rosa's experience indicates that he can

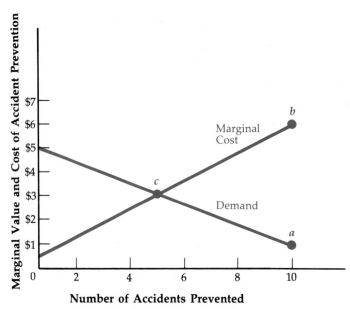

Figure 20.4. Costs and Benefits of Accident Prevention.
To prevent ten accidents Al Rosa would have to incur a marginal cost of $6.00
(point b). Yet the benefits of preventing that accident would be worth only $1.00
to him (point a). The rational person will choose to prevent accidents up to the
point where marginal cost equals marginal benefit—here, five accidents (point c).

expect to have ten accidents over the course of the year. If he tries to
prevent all of them, the value of preventing the last one, as indicated by
the demand curve in Figure 20.4, will be only $1 (point a). The marginal
cost of preventing it will be much greater: approximately $6.00 (point b).
If Al is rational, he will not try to prevent the last accident. As a matter
of fact, he will try to prevent only five accidents (point c). As with the
tenth accident, it will cost more than it is worth to Al to prevent the sixth
through ninth accidents. He would try to prevent all ten accidents only if
his demand for accident prevention were so great that his demand curve
intersected the marginal cost curve at point b.

Some accidents may be unavoidable. In that case, the marginal cost
curve will eventually become vertical. Other accidents may be avoidable
in the sense that it is physically possible to take measures to prevent
them—though the rational course may be to allow them to happen.

Price and Marginal Cost: Producing
to Maximize Profits

Many business people derive intrinsic rewards from their work. They may
value the satisfaction of producing a product that meets a human need
just as much as the profits they earn. Some business people may even

accept lower profits so their products can sell at lower prices and serve more people. But for most business people, the profit generated by sales is the major motivation for doing business.

How much will a profit-maximizing firm produce? Assume its marginal cost curve is like the one in Figure 20.5(a). Assume further that the owners can sell as many units as they want at a price of P_1. Because this firm is in business to make a profit, the price of its product can be thought of as the marginal benefit of each additional unit. P_1 is also the firm's marginal revenue. **Marginal revenue** is the additional revenue a firm acquires by selling an additional unit of output. Each time the firm sells one additional unit, its revenues rise by P_1.

Clearly, a profit-maximizing firm will produce and sell any unit for which the marginal revenue acquired *(MR)* exceeds the marginal cost *(MC)*. (Profits are the difference between total costs and total revenues. Therefore a firm's profits rise whenever an increase in revenues exceeds the increase in its costs.) At a price of P_1, then, this firm will produce up to, and no more than, Q_1 products. For every unit up to Q_1, price is greater than marginal cost.

The vertical distance between P_1 and the marginal cost of each unit, as shown by the marginal cost curve, is the additional profit obtained from each additional unit produced. By summing the vertical distance between P_1 and the marginal cost curve for all units up to Q_1, we can obtain the firm's total profits. (See the color-shaded area in Figure 20.5(a).) Total profits can also be represented as a curve, as in the line TP_1 in Figure 20.5(b). Notice that the curve peaks at Q_1, the point at which the firm chooses to stop producing. Beyond Q_1, marginal cost is greater than marginal revenue, and total profits fall, as shown by the downward slope of the total profits curve.

What will the firm do if the price of its product rises from P_1 to P_2? For the firm that can sell all it wants at a constant price, a rise in price means a rise in marginal revenue. Once the price rises to P_2, the marginal revenue of an additional $Q_2 - Q_1$ products exceeds their marginal cost. At the higher price, a larger number of units can be profitably produced and sold. The firm will seek to produce up to the point at which marginal cost equals the new, higher marginal revenue, P_2, or Q_2 in Figure 20.5(a). As before, profit is equal to the vertical distance between the price, P_2, and the marginal cost curve, or the color-shaded area plus the gray-shaded area in Figure 20.5(a). The total profit curve shifts to the position of the line TP_2 in Figure 20.5(b).

Marginal revenue: the additional revenue a firm acquires by selling an additional unit of output.

From Individual Supply to Market Supply

If a portion of the upward-sloping marginal cost curve is the firm's supply curve, and if market supply is the amount all producers are willing to produce at various prices, we can obtain the market supply curve by adding together the relevant portions of the individual firms' marginal cost curves. (This procedure resembles the one followed in determining the market demand curve in Chapter 18.)

Figure 20.5. Marginal Cost and Maximization of Profit.
At price P_1 (part (a)), this firm's marginal revenue, shown by the color-shaded area, exceeds its marginal cost up to an output level of Q_1. At that point total profit, shown in part (b), peaks (point a). At price P_2, marginal revenue exceeds marginal cost up to an output level of Q_2. (Marginal revenue equals both the color and gray shaded areas.) The increase in price shifts the profit curve upward, from TP_1 to TP_2, and profit peaks at point b.

Figure 20.6. Market Supply Curve.
The market supply curve (S_{A+B}) is obtained by adding together the amounts producers A and B are willing to offer at each and every price, as shown by the individual supply curves S_A and S_B. (The individual supply curves are obtained from the upward-sloping portions of the firms' marginal cost curves.)

Figure 20.6 shows the supply curves S_A and S_B, derived from the marginal cost curves of two producers, A and B. At a price of P_1, only producer B is willing to produce anything, and it is willing to offer only Q_1. The total quantity supplied to the market at P_1 is therefore Q_1. At the higher price of P_2, however, both producers are willing to compete. Producer A offers Q_1, while producer B offers more, Q_2. The total quantity supplied is therefore Q_3, the sum of Q_1 and Q_2.

The market supply curve, S_{A+B}, is obtained by adding the amounts A and B are willing to sell at each price and plotting the totals. Note that the market supply curve lies farther from the origin and is flatter than the individual producers' supply curves. The entry of more producers will shift the market supply curve farther outward and lower its slope even more. (More will be said about cost and supply in later chapters.)

Summary and Extensions

Cost plays a pivotal role in a producer's choices. Costs change with the quantity produced. The pattern of those changes determine the limit of a producer's activity, from the production of salable goods and services to the employment of leisure time. The individual will produce a good or service, or engage in an activity, until marginal cost equals marginal benefit (marginal revenue). Graphically, this is the point where the supply and demand curves for the individual's behavior intersect. At this point, though additional benefits might be obtained by producing additional units of the good, service, or activity, the additional costs that would be incurred discourage further production.

Costs will not affect an individual's behavior unless he or she perceives them as costs. For this reason the economist looks for hidden, implicit costs in all choices. Such costs, if uncovered, will affect choices that remain to be made. Implicit costs can also be helpful in explaining those choices that have already been made.

Major Conclusions

1. In our daily lives and in business, rational decisions are based on a consideration of total costs, including out-of-pocket expenditures (explicit costs) and forgone opportunities (implicit costs).
2. Sunk costs, or costs already incurred, are irrelevant to a producer's choice.
3. The marginal cost of producing additional units of a good will tend to rise as production is extended beyond the point of diminishing (marginal) returns.
4. A portion of the upward-sloping section of a producer's marginal cost curve may be thought of as the producer's supply curve.
5. So long as the marginal benefit (or marginal revenue) of producing an additional unit of a good or service exceeds the marginal cost, the producer will increase production.

Questions to Ponder

1. Evaluate the adages "haste makes waste" and "a stitch in time saves nine" from an economic point of view.
2. If executives' time is as valuable as they claim, why are they frequently found reading the advertisements in airline magazines en route to a business meeting?
3. Consider the information in the production schedule that follows. (a) At what output level do diminishing returns set in? (b) Assume that each worker receives $8. Fill in the marginal product column, and develop a marginal cost schedule and a marginal cost curve for the production process.

Number of Workers	Total Product of All Workers	Marginal Product of Each Worker
1	0.10	
2	0.30	
3	0.60	
4	1.00	
5	1.45	
6	2.00	
7	2.50	
8	2.80	
9	3.00	
10	3.19	
11	3.37	
12	3.54	
13	3.70	
14	3.85	
15	4.00	
16	3.90	
17	3.70	

4. In discussing accident prevention, we assumed an increasing marginal cost. Suppose instead that the marginal cost of preventing accidents remains constant. How will that assumption affect the analysis?
5. Using the analysis of accident prevention, develop an analysis of pollution control. Using demand and marginal cost curves for clean air, determine the efficient level of pollution control.
6. People take some measures to avoid becoming victims of crime. Why do they not take even greater precautions? How do the rational limits of crime prevention affect the ability of criminals to commit crimes?
7. If the money price of a good rises from $5 to $10, the economist can confidently predict that less will be purchased. One cannot be equally confident that denying a child a dessert will improve the child's behavior, however. Explain why.

Central Question

What is the structure of a firm's costs in the short run and the long run?

Key Terms

Short run

Fixed cost

Variable cost

Total cost

Cost structure

Average fixed cost

Average variable cost

Average total cost

Long run

Natural monopoly

Very long run

Isoquant curve

Isocost curve

Chapter 21

Cost in the Short Run and the Long Run

In economics, the cost of an event is the highest-valued opportunity necessarily forsaken. The usefulness of the concept of cost is a logical implication of choice among available options. Only if no alternatives were possible or if amounts of all resources were available beyond everyone's desires, so that all goods were free, would the concepts of cost and of choice be irrelevant.

Armen Alchian

*T*he individual firm plays a critical role both in theory and in the real world. It straddles two basic economic forces: the markets for resources—labor, capital, and land—and the markets for goods and services—everything from trucks to lollipops. The firm must be able both to identify what people want to buy, at what price, and to organize the great variety of available resources into an efficient production process. It must sell its product at a price that covers the cost of its resources, yet allows it to compete with other firms. And it must accomplish those objectives while competing firms are seeking to meet the same goals.

How does the firm do all this? Clearly, firms do not all operate in exactly the same way. They differ in organizational structure and in management style, in the resources they use and in the products they sell. This chapter cannot possibly cover the great diversity of business management techniques. Rather, our purpose is to develop the broad principles that guide the production decisions of most firms.

Like individuals, firms are beset by the necessity of choice, which as Armen Alchian reminds us, implies a cost. Costs are obstacles to choice; they restrict us in what we do. Thus a firm's cost structure (the way cost varies with production) determines the profitability of its production decisions, both in the short run and in the long run.

Fixed, Variable, and Total Cost in the Short Run

Time is required to produce any good or service. Therefore any output level must be founded on some recognized period of time. Even more important, the costs a firm incurs vary over time. In thinking about costs, then, we must identify clearly the period of time over which they apply. For reasons that will become apparent as we progress, economists speak of costs in terms of the extent to which they can be varied, rather than the number of months or years required to pay them off. While in the long run all costs can be varied, in the short run firms have less control.

Short run: the period during which one or more resources (and thus one or more costs of production) cannot be changed—either increased or decreased.

The **short run** is the period during which one or more resources (and thus one or more costs of production) cannot be changed—either increased or decreased. Short-run costs can be either fixed or variable. A **fixed cost** *(FC)* is any cost that does not vary with the level of output. Fixed costs include overhead expenditures that extend over a period of months or years: insurance premiums, leasing and rental payments, land and equipment purchases, and interest on loans. These costs remain the same whether the firm's factories are standing idle or producing at capacity. As long as the firm faces even one fixed cost, it is operating in the short run.

Fixed cost: any cost that does not vary with the level of output.

A **variable cost** *(VC)* is any cost that changes with the level of output. Variable costs include wages (workers can be hired or laid off on relatively short notice), materials, utilities, and office supplies. Variable costs increase with the level of output.

Variable cost: any cost that changes with the level of output.

Together, fixed and variable costs equal total cost. **Total cost** *(TC)* is the sum of fixed costs and variable costs at each output level.

Total cost: the sum of fixed costs and variable costs at each output level.

$$TC = FC + VC$$

Table 21.1. Total, Marginal, and Average Cost of Production

Production Level (number of widgets) (1)	Fixed Costs (2)	Variable Costs (3)	Total Costs (2) + (3) (4)	Marginal Cost (change in 3 or 4) (5)	Average Fixed Cost (2) ÷ (1) (6)	Average Variable Cost (3) ÷ (1) (7)	Average Total Cost (4) ÷ (1) or (6) + (7) (8)
1	$100	$ 30	$130	$30	$100.00	$30.00	$130.00
2	100	50	150	20	50.00	25.00	75.00
3	100	60	160	10	33.33	20.00	53.33
4	100	65	165	5	25.00	16.25	41.25
5	100	75	175	10	20.00	15.00	35.00
6	100	90	190	15	16.67	15.00	31.67
7	100	110	210	20	14.29	15.71	30.00
8	100	140	240	30	12.50	17.50	30.00
9	100	180	280	40	11.11	20.00	31.11
10	100	230	330	50	10.00	23.00	33.00
11	100	300	400	70	9.09	27.27	36.36
12	100	395	495	95	8.33	32.92	41.25

Columns 1 through 4 of Table 21.1 show fixed, variable, and total costs at various production levels. Fixed costs are constant at $100 for all output levels (see column 2). Variable costs increase gradually, from $30 to $395, as output expands from 1 to 12 widgets. Total cost, the sum of fixed and variable costs at each output level (obtained by adding columns 2 and 3 horizontally), increases gradually as well.

Graphically, fixed cost can be represented by a horizontal line, as in Figure 21.1. The total cost curve starts at the same point as the fixed cost curve, since total cost must at least equal fixed cost, and rises from that point. The vertical distance between the total and fixed cost curves shows the variable cost at each level of production.

Marginal and Average Cost in the Short Run

The central question of this and the following three chapters is how to determine the profit-maximizing production level. In other words, we want to know at what output level the firm that is interested in maximizing profits will choose to produce. Though fixed, variable, and total costs are important measures, they are not very useful in determining the firm's profit-maximizing (or loss-minimizing) output level. To arrive at that figure, as well as to estimate profits or losses, we need four additional measures of cost: (1) marginal, (2) average fixed, (3) average variable, and (4) average total. When graphed, those four measures represent the firm's

Figure 21.1. Fixed, Variable, and Total Cost in the Short Run.
Fixed cost does not vary with production; therefore it is drawn as a horizontal
line. Variable cost does rise with production. Here it is represented by the shaded
area between the total cost and fixed cost curves.

Cost structure: the
way various measures
of cost (total cost, variable cost, and so forth)
vary with the produc-
tion level.

cost structure. A **cost structure** is the way various measures of cost (total
cost, variable cost, and so forth) vary with the production level. These
four cost measures cover *all* costs associated with production, including
risk cost and opportunity cost.

Marginal Cost

In the preceding chapter, we defined marginal cost (*MC*) as the additional
cost of producing one additional unit. By extension, marginal cost can also
be defined as the change in total cost. And because the change in total
cost is due solely to the change in variable cost, marginal cost can also be
defined as the change in variable cost per unit.

$$MC = \frac{\text{change in } TC}{\text{change in quantity}} = \frac{\text{change in } VC}{\text{change in quantity}}$$

As you can see from Table 21.1, marginal cost declines as output expands
from one to four widgets, and then rises, as predicted by the law of
diminishing returns (see Chapter 20). This increasing marginal cost reflects
the diminishing marginal productivity of extra workers and other variable
resources the firm must employ to expand output beyond four widgets.

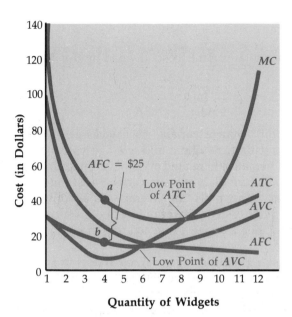

Figure 21.2. Marginal and Average Cost in the Short Run.
The average fixed cost curve (*AFC*) slopes downward and approaches, but never touches, the horizontal axis. The average variable cost curve (*AVC*) is mathematically related to the marginal cost curve, and intersects with the marginal cost curve (*MC*) at its lowest point. The vertical distance between the average total cost curve (*ATC*) and the average variable cost curve equals the average fixed cost at any given output level.

The marginal cost curve is shown in Figure 21.2. The bottom of the curve (four units) is the point at which marginal returns begin to diminish.

Average Fixed Cost

Average fixed cost (*AFC*) is total fixed costs divided by the number of units produced (*Q*).

$$AFC = \frac{FC}{Q}$$

In Table 21.1, total fixed costs are constant at $100. As output expands, therefore, the average fixed cost per unit must decline. (That is what business people mean when they talk about "spreading the overhead." As production expands, the average fixed cost declines.)

In Figure 21.2, the average fixed cost curve slopes downward to the right, approaching but never touching the horizontal axis. That is because average fixed cost is a ratio, *FC/Q*, and a ratio can never be reduced to zero, no matter how large the denominator (*Q*).

Average fixed cost: total fixed costs divided by the number of units produced.

Average Variable Cost

Average variable cost (*AVC*) is total variable costs divided by the number of units produced.

$$AVC = \frac{VC}{Q}$$

At an output level of one unit, average variable cost necessarily equals marginal cost. Beyond the first unit, marginal and average variable cost diverge, though they are mathematically related. Whenever marginal cost declines, as it does initially in Figure 21.2, average variable cost must also decline. The lower marginal value pulls the average value down. A basketball player who scores progressively fewer points in each successive game, for instance, will find her average score falling, though not as rapidly as her marginal score.

Beyond the point of diminishing returns, marginal cost rises, but average variable cost continues to fall for a time (see Figure 21.2). So long as marginal cost is below the average variable cost, average variable cost must continue to decline. The two curves meet at an output level of six widgets. Beyond that point, the average variable cost curve must rise, because the average value will be pulled up by the greater marginal value. (After a game in which she scores more points than her previous average, for instance, the basketball player's average score must rise.) The point at which the marginal cost and average variable cost curves intersect is therefore the low point of the average variable cost curve. Before that intersection, average variable cost must fall. After it, average variable cost must rise. For the same reason, the intersection of the marginal cost curve and the average total cost curve must be the low point of the average total cost curve (see Figure 21.2).

Average Total Cost

Average total cost (*ATC*) is the total of all fixed and variable costs divided by the number of units produced (*Q*).

$$ATC = \frac{FC + VC}{Q} = \frac{TC}{Q}$$

Average total cost can also be found by summing the average fixed and average variable costs, if they are known (*ATC = AFC + AVC*). Graphically, the average total cost curve is the vertical summation of the average fixed and average variable cost curves (see Figure 21.2).

Because average total cost is the sum of average fixed and variable costs, the average fixed cost can be obtained by subtracting average variable from average total cost: *AFC = ATC − AVC*. On a graph, average fixed cost is the vertical distance between the average total cost curve and the average variable cost curve. For instance, in Figure 21.2, at an output level of four widgets, the average fixed cost is the vertical distance *ab*, or $25 ($41.25 − $16.25, or column 8 minus column 7 in Table 21.1).

From this point on, the average fixed cost curve will not be shown on graphs, for it complicates the presentation without adding new information. Average fixed cost will be indicated by the vertical distance between the average total and average variable cost curves at any given output.

Marginal and Average Cost in the Long Run

So far our discussion has been restricted to time periods during which at least one resource, and therefore cost, is fixed. That assumption underlies the concept of fixed cost. Fortunately, over the long run all resources that are used in production can be changed. The **long run** is the period during which all resources (and thus costs of production) can be changed—either increased or decreased. By definition, there are no fixed costs in the long run. All long-run costs are variable.

The foregoing analysis is still useful in analyzing a firm's long-run cost structure. In the long run, the average total cost curve (ATC in Figure 21.2) represents one possible scale of operation, with one given quantity of plant and equipment (in Table 21.1, $100 worth). A change in plant and equipment, which are no longer fixed, will change the firm's cost structure, increasing or decreasing its productive capacity.

How do changes in long-run costs affect a profit-maximizing firm's production decisions? Generally, they can encourage firms to produce on a larger scale.

Long run: the period during which all resources (and thus costs of production) can be changed—either increased or decreased.

Economies of Scale

Figure 21.3 illustrates the long-run production choices facing a typical firm. The curve labeled ATC_1 is, in reduced form, the average total cost curve developed in Figure 21.2. Any additional plant and equipment will add to total fixed costs, and at low output levels (up to q_1) will lead to higher average total costs (curve ATC_2). On the new scale of operation, however, average total cost need not remain high. At higher output levels (q_1 to q_2), the firm may realize economies of scale, cost decreases that stem from an expanded use of resources (see page 27).

Economies of scale can occur for several reasons. Expanded operation generally permits greater specialization of labor. Technologically advanced equipment, like computers, can be used, and more highly skilled workers can be employed. Expansion may also permit improvements in organization, like assembly-line production. The important point is that by spreading the higher cost of additional plant and equipment over a larger output level, the firm can reduce the average cost of production.

Economies of scale cannot necessarily be realized in every kind of production. These are few or no economies of scale in the production of original works of art. But the principle will hold true for most production operations. Curve ATC_2 in Figure 21.3 cuts curve ATC_1 and then dips down to a lower minimum average total cost—at a higher output level. Curve ATC_3 does the same with respect to curve ATC_2.

Figure 21.3. Economies of Scale.
Economies of scale are cost savings associated with the expanded use of resources. To realize such savings, however, a firm must expand its output. Here the firm can lower its costs by expanding production from q_1 to q_2—a scale of operation that places it on a lower short-run average total cost curve (ATC_2 instead of ATC_1).

Diseconomies of Scale

Economies of scale do not last forever. That is to say, a firm cannot increase its use of resources indefinitely and expect its average total cost to continue to fall. At some point, a firm will confront diseconomies of scale, cost increases that stem from an expanded use of resources.[1] Diseconomies of scale are illustrated in Figure 21.4. Beyond curve ATC_4, an increase in the scale of operation leads to a higher minimum average cost.

What causes diseconomies of scale? Economists reason that beyond some scale of operation, the personal interrelationships of employees become complex and unwieldly, detracting from rather than contributing to productivity. People at the top of the organization may lose contact with or control of the people at the bottom. Business communications may lose their impact as they move from one section of the firm to another. More costs may need to be incurred just to keep the lines of communication open. Finally, in a large firm, each employee's individual contribution represents a smaller proportion of total output. When they feel they have

---

1. For a while, a firm may be able to avoid diseconomies of scale by increasing the number of its plants. Management's ability to supervise a growing number of plants is limited, however, and eventually diseconomies of scale will emerge at the level of the firm, if not the plant.

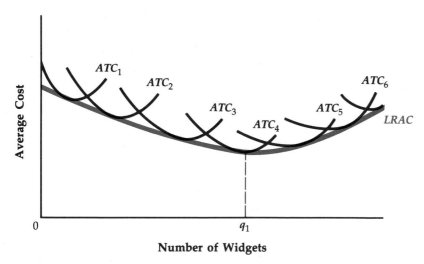

Figure 21.4. Diseconomies of Scale.
Diseconomies of scale may occur because of the communication problems of larger firms. Here the firm realizes economies of scale through its first four short-run average total cost curves. The long-run average cost curve begins to turn up at an output level of q_1, beyond which diseconomies of scale set in.

less effect on results, people may begin to shirk their responsibilities. As the firm expands, shirking becomes more difficult to detect and more costly to eliminate.

Average and Marginal Cost

When will a firm change its scale of operation? In markets filled with risk and uncertainty about actual costs and demand, that is a tough question. Ideally, the firm will change scale as soon as it becomes profitable—in Figure 21.3, at an output level of q_1. Before q_1 the average cost on scale ATC_1 is lower than the average cost on scale ATC_2. The fixed costs of additional plant and equipment simply cannot be spread over enough output to reduce the average total cost. Beyond q_1, however, the average cost on scale ATC_2 is lower than the average cost on scale ATC_1. Therefore the firm can minimize its overall cost of operation by expanding along the colored portion of the curve ATC_2. And it can push its average costs down even further by expanding its scale once again at output level q_2.

Assuming there are many more scales of operation than are represented in Figure 21.3, the firm's expansion path can be seen as a single overall curve that envelops all its short-run average cost curves. Such a curve is shown in Figure 21.4 and reproduced in Figure 21.5 as the long-run average cost curve ($LRAC$).

Like short-run average cost curves, the long-run average cost curve has an accompanying long-run marginal cost curve. If long-run average cost

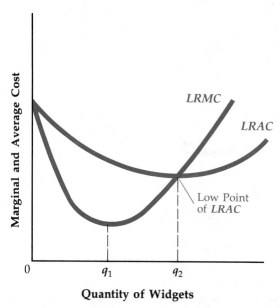

Figure 21.5. Marginal and Average Cost in the Long Run.
The long-run marginal and average cost curves are mathematically related. The long-run average cost curve slopes downward as long as it is above the long-run marginal cost curve. The two curves intersect at the low point of the long-run average cost curve.

is falling, as it does initially in Figure 21.5, it must be because long-run marginal cost is pulling it down. If long-run cost is rising, as it does eventually in Figure 21.5, then long-run marginal cost must be pulling it up. Hence at some point like q_1 long-run marginal cost must turn upward, intersecting the long-run average cost curve at its lowest point, q_2.

Individual Differences in Average Cost

Not all firms experience economies and diseconomies of scale to the same degree. Their long-run average cost curves, in other words, look very different. Figure 21.6 shows several possible shapes for long-run average cost curves. The curve in Figure 21.6(a) belongs to a firm in an industry with few economies of scale and significant diseconomies at relatively low output levels. (This curve might belong to a firm in a service industry, like shoe repair.) We would not expect profit-maximizing firms in this industry to be very large, for firms with an output level beyond q_1 can easily be underpriced by smaller, lower-cost firms.

Figure 21.6(b) shows the long-run average cost curve for a firm in an industry with modest economies of scale at low output levels and no diseconomies of scale until a fairly high output level. In such an industry—perhaps apparel manufacturing—we would expect to find firms of various

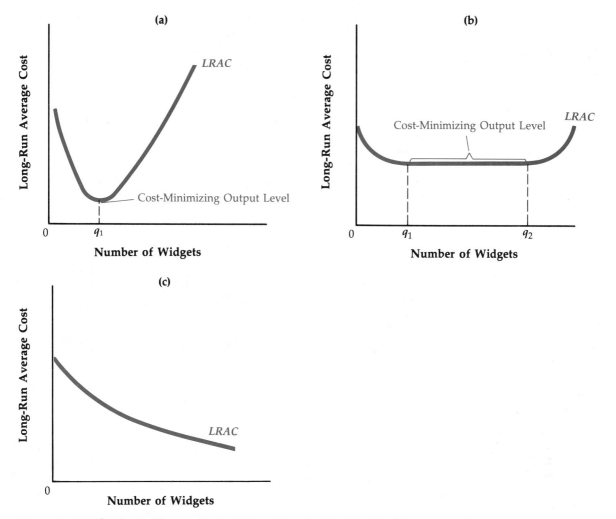

Figure 21.6. Individual Differences in Long-Run Average Cost Curves.
The shape of the long-run average cost curve varies according to the extent and persistence of economies and diseconomies of scale. Firms in industries with few economies of scale will have a long-run average cost curve like the one in part (a). Firms in industries with persistent economies of scale will have a long-run average cost curve like that in part (b). And firms in industries with extensive economies of scale may find that their long-run average cost curve slopes continually downward, as in part (c).

sizes, some small and some large. As long as firms are producing between q_1 and q_2, larger firms do not have a cost advantage over smaller firms.

Figure 21.6(c) illustrates the average costs for a firm in an industry that enjoys extensive economies of scale—for example, an electric power company. No matter how far this firm expands, the long-run average cost curve continues to fall. Diseconomies of scale may exist, but if so they occur at output levels beyond the effective market for the firm's product.

Perspectives in Economics: Dealing with the Very Long Run

Economic analysis tends to be restricted to either the short or the long run, for one major reason. For both periods, costs are known with reasonable precision. In the short run, firms know that beyond some point, increases in the use of a resource (for example, fertilizer) will bring diminishing marginal returns and rising marginal costs—unless offset by decreases in the use of another resource (for example, land). They also know that with increased use of all resources, certain economies and diseconomies of scale can be expected over the long run. Given what is known about the technology of production and the availability of resources, economists can draw certain conclusions about a firm's behavior and the consequences of its actions.

As economists look further and further into the future, however, they can predict less about a firm's behavior and its consequences in the marketplace. Less is known about the technology and resources of the distant future. In the very long

run, everything is subject to change—resources themselves, their availability, and the technology for using them. The **very long run** is the time period during which the technology of production and the availability of resources can change because of invention, innovation, and discovery of new technologies and resources.

By definition, the very long run is, to a significant degree, unpredictable. Firms cannot know today how to make use of unspecified future advances in technology. A hundred years ago firms had little idea how important lasers, satellites, airplanes, and computers would be to today's economy. Indeed, many products taken for granted today were invented or discovered quite by accident. Edison developed the phonograph while attempting to invent the light bulb. John Rock developed the birth control pill while studying sterility. Alexander Fleming's discovery of penicillin, Charles Goodyear's development of vulcan-

---

Natural monopoly: an industry in which long-run marginal and average costs decline with increases in production, so that a single firm dominates production.

This type of industry tends toward a single seller—what is called a natural monopoly. A **natural monopoly** is an industry in which long-run marginal and average costs decline with increases in production, so that a single firm dominates production. Given the industry's cost structure, that is, one firm can expand its scale, lower its cost of operation, and underprice other firms that attempt to produce on a lower, higher-cost scale. Electric utilities may be natural monopolies. (More will be said about natural monopolies in Chapter 25.)

Shifts in the Average and Marginal Cost Curves

The average cost curves we have just described all assumed that the prices for resources remain constant. This is a critical assumption. If those prices change, so will the average cost curves. The marginal cost curve may shift as well, depending on the type of average cost—variable or fixed—that changes.

Thus if a variable cost like wages rises, the firm's average total cost will rise along with its average variable cost ($AFC + AVC = ATC$), shifting ization, and Wilhelm Roentgen's invention of the x-ray—all were accidents. All had economic consequences that could not have been predicted.

Not all inventions or innovations are accidental, and we can know something about the very long run. Firms have some idea of the value of investments in research and development. Research on substitute resources can yield improvements in productivity that translate into cost reductions. Research on new product designs will yield more attractive and useful products. There will be failures as well—research projects that accomplish little or nothing. But over time, the rewards of research and development can exceed the costs.

Because of the risks involved in research and development, some firms may be expected to fail. In the very long run, they will not be able to keep up with the competition in product design and productivity. They will not adjust sufficiently to changes in the market and will suffer losses. The

computer industry provides many examples of firms that tried to build a better machine, but could not keep pace with the rapid technological advances of competitors.

Proponents of a planned economy see the uncertainty of the very long run as an argument for government direction of the nation's development. They stress that competitors often do not know what other firms are doing. Therefore they need guidance in the form of government subsidies and tax penalties to ensure that the nation's long-term goals are achieved. Proponents of the market system agree that it is difficult to look ahead to the very long run. But they see the uncertainties as an argument for keeping production decisions in the hands of firms. Private firms have the economic incentive of profit to stay alert to changes in market conditions. And they can respond quickly to changes in technology and resources. Government control might slow the adjustment process.

the average total cost curve. The firm's marginal cost curve will shift as well, for the additional cost of producing an additional unit must rise with the higher labor cost (see Figure 21.7(a)). If a fixed cost like insurance premiums rises, average total cost will also rise, shifting the average total cost curve, as in Figure 21.7(b). But the short-run marginal cost curve will not shift, because marginal cost is unaffected by fixed cost. The marginal cost curve is derived from variable costs only (see page 458).

Because changes in variable cost affect a firm's marginal cost, they influence its production decisions. As we saw in Chapter 20, a profit-maximizing firm selling at a constant price will produce up to the point where marginal cost equals price ($MC = P$). At a price of P_1 in Figure 21.7(a), then, the firm will produce q_2 widgets. After an increase in variable costs and an upward shift in the marginal cost curve, however, the firm will cut back to q_1 widgets. At q_1 widgets price again equals marginal cost. The cutback in output has occurred because the marginal cost of producing $q_2 - q_1$ widgets now exceeds the price. In other words, an increase in variable cost results in a reduction in a firm's output.

Because a shift in average fixed cost leaves marginal cost unaffected, the firm's profit-maximizing output level remains at q_1 (see Figure 21.7(b)).

Figure 21.7. Shifts in Average and Marginal Cost Curves.
An increase in a firm's variable cost (part (a)) will shift the firm's average total cost curve up, from ATC_1 to ATC_2. It will also shift the marginal cost curve, from MC_1 to MC_2. Production will fall because of the increase in marginal cost. By contrast, an increase in a firm's fixed cost (part (b)) will shift the average total cost curve upward, from ATC_1 to ATC_2, but will not affect the marginal cost curve. (Marginal cost is unaffected by fixed cost.) Thus the firm's production level will not change.

The firm may make lower profits because of its higher fixed cost, but it cannot increase profits by either expanding or reducing output.

This analysis applies to the short run only. In the long run all costs are variable, and changes in the price of any resource will affect a firm's production decisions. Long-run changes in the output levels of firms, of course, change the market price of the final product as well as consumer purchases. More will be said on those points later.

Summary and Extensions

Short- and long-run costs are important topics in the study of economics. In order to understand how competitive and monopolistic markets operate, we must first understand the firm's cost structure. In the next few chapters, we will combine the average and marginal cost curves described here with the demand curves described in earlier chapters. Within that theoretical framework, we will be able to compare the relative efficiency of competitive and monopolistic markets, and the role of profits in directing the production decisions of private firms.

1. The short run is distinguished from the long run by the relative ability of the firm to adjust the use of its resources. In the short run, the firm cannot change one or more of its resources; in the long run, it can vary all its resources.

2. The average fixed cost curve slopes downward to the right, approaching but never touching the horizontal axis. As fixed costs are spread over more and more units, average fixed cost will decline but will never disappear.

3. Reflecting the law of diminishing returns, the short-run marginal, average variable, and average total cost curves are U-shaped, first sloping downward to the right, then rising again at or after the point of diminishing returns.

4. The average variable cost curve is mathematically related to the marginal cost curve.

5. The intersection of the average variable and marginal cost curves is the point of minimum average variable cost.

6. The intersection of the average total cost and marginal cost curves is the point of minimum average total cost.

7. At any given output level, the vertical distance between the average variable cost curve and average total cost curve is the average fixed cost.

8. In the long run there are no fixed costs.

9. The long-run average cost curve envelops a series of short-run average total cost curves. Graphically its relationship to the long-run marginal cost curve is like that between the short-run average variable cost curve and the short-run marginal cost curve.

10. The downward-sloping portion of the long-run average cost curve reflects economies of scale. The upward-sloping portion reflects diseconomies of scale.

11. The shape of the long-run average cost curve varies from one industry to another, depending on economies and diseconomies of scale. Industries with extensive economies of scale tend to have only a few large firms, or sometimes even a single seller. Industries with few economies of scale will support many small producers. Industries with modest economies of scale at low output levels, and no diseconomies of scale except at very high output levels, will include firms of varying sizes.

12. An increase in a firm's short-run variable cost will shift its short-run marginal cost curve up and to the left, reducing the amount of output the firm can produce profitably at a constant price. An increase in the firm's short-run fixed cost will not affect either its short-run marginal cost or its short-run production level.

1. Complete the cost schedule given on the next page and develop a graph that shows marginal, average fixed, average variable, and average total cost curves.

Output Level	Fixed Cost	Variable Cost	Total Cost	Marginal Cost	Average Fixed Cost	Average Variable Cost	Average Total Cost
1	$200	$ 60					
2	200	110					
3	200	150					
4	200	180					
5	200	200					
6	200	230					
7	200	280					
8	200	350					
9	200	440					
10	200	550					

2. Explain why the intersection of the average variable cost curve and the marginal cost curve is the point of minimum average variable cost.

3. Suppose no economies or diseconomies of scale exist in a given industry. What will the firm's long-run average and marginal cost curves look like? Would you expect firms of different sizes to be able to compete successfully in such an industry?

4. Suppose the government imposes a $100 tax on all businesses, regardless of how much they produce. How will the tax affect a firm's short-run cost curves? Its short-run production?

5. Suppose the government imposes a $1 tax on every unit of a good sold. How will the tax affect a firm's short-run cost curves? Its short-run output?

Appendix:
Choosing the Most Efficient Resource Combination— Isoquants and Isocosts

The cost curves developed in this and previous chapters were based on the assumption that the producer had chosen the most technically efficient, cost-effective combination of resources possible at each output level. That is, resources were fully employed, were producing as much as possible, and were used in the lowest-cost combination. The short-run average total cost curve, for example, was as low as it could be, given the availability and prices of resources.

But how does the firm find the most efficient combination of resources? Most products and output levels can be produced with various combinations of resources. A given quantity of blue jeans can be produced with a lot of labor and little capital (equipment) or a lot of capital and little labor. In Figure 21.A1, a firm can produce 100 pairs of jeans a day with five different combinations of labor and machines. Combination *a* requires seven workers and ten machines; combination *b*, five workers and fifteen machines. (To keep output constant, the use of labor must be reduced when the use of machines is increased. If the use of both were increased, output would rise.)

Curves like the one in Figure 21.A1 are called isoquants. An **isoquant curve** (from the Greek words for "same quantity") is a curve that shows the various technically efficient combinations of resources that can be used to produce a given level of output. Different output levels have different isoquants. The higher the output level, the higher the isoquant curve, as shown in Figure 21.A2. For example, an output level of 100 pairs of jeans can be produced with the resource combinations shown on curve IQ_1. An output level of 150 pairs of jeans requires larger resource combinations, shown on curve IQ_2.

Isoquant curve: (from the Greek word *iso*, meaning "same") a curve that shows the various technically efficient combinations of resources that can be used to produce a given level of output.

Figure 21.A1. Isoquant.
A firm can produce one hundred pairs of jeans a day using any of the various combinations of labor and machinery shown on this curve. Because of diminishing marginal returns, more and more machines must be substituted for each worker who is dropped.

Figure 21.A2. Several Isoquants.
Different output levels will have different isoquants. The higher the output level, the higher the isoquant.

To understand how the firm determines its most efficient resource combination, we must remember that it operates under conditions of diminishing marginal returns. The firm will always produce in the upward-sloping range of its marginal cost curve; and marginal cost increases because marginal returns decline. Given a fixed quantity of one resource, therefore, as more of another resource is used, the additional output, or marginal product, of that resource must diminish.

Then as each additional worker is eliminated in Figure 21.A1, the number of machines added to keep output constant at 100 pairs of jeans must rise. And that is just what happens. Notice that as the firm moves down curve *abcde*, using fewer and fewer workers, the curve flattens out. At the same time that the marginal product of machines diminishes, the marginal product of the remaining workers rises.

We know, then, that the marginal product of resources differs with their level of use. But to determine exactly which combination of resources should be employed to produce any given output level, we need to know not only the marginal product, but the prices of labor and capital. The absolute prices of these resources will determine how much can be produced with any given expenditure. The relative prices will determine the most efficient combination.

Figure 21.A3. Finding the Most Efficient Combination of Resources.
Assuming the daily wage of each worker is $100, and the daily rental on each sewing machine is $20, an expenditure of $600 per day will buy any combination of resources on isocost curve IC_1. The most cost-effective combination of labor and capital is point a, three workers and fifteen machines. At that point, the isocost curve is just tangent to isoquant IQ_2, meaning that the firm can produce 150 pairs of jeans a day. If the firm chooses any other combination, it will move to a lower isoquant and a lower output level. At point b (on isoquant IQ_1), it will be able to produce only 100 pairs of jeans a day.

Suppose, for instance, that the daily wage of labor is $100, and the daily rental for a sewing machine is $20. With a daily budget of $600, a firm can employ six workers and no machines or thirty machines and no workers. Or it can combine labor and machinery in various ways. It can employ four workers at a total expenditure of $400 and add ten machines at a total expenditure of $200. Curve IC_1 in Figure 21.A3 shows the various combinations of workers and machines the firm could choose. This kind of curve is called an isocost curve. An **isocost** (meaning "same cost") **curve** is a curve that shows the various combinations of resources that can be employed at a given expenditure (cost) level and given resource prices.

There are different isocost curves for different output levels. The higher the output, the higher the isocost curve. So long as the prices of labor and capital stay the same, however, the various isocost curves for different output levels will be parallel to one another and will have the same downward slope.

Using both isoquant and isocost curves, we can determine the most efficient resource combination for a given expenditure level. Assuming a firm is on isocost curve IC_1 in Figure 21.A3 (which represents an expenditure

Isocost curve: (from the Greek word *iso*, meaning "same") a curve that shows the various combinations of resources that can be employed at a given expenditure (cost) level and given resource prices.

of \$600 per day), the most technically efficient and cost-effective combination of labor and capital will be point a, three workers and fifteen machines. At point a isocost curve IC_2 is tangent to isoquant curve IQ_2. The firm is producing as much as it can—150 pairs of jeans a day—with an expenditure of \$600. If it spent the same amount but used more labor or more capital, it would move to a lower isoquant and a lower output level. At point b on curve IC_1, for instance, the firm would lower its production level from 150 to 100 pairs of jeans per day.

Of course, with increased expenditures, the firm can move to a higher isocost curve. In Figure 21.A4, as the firm's budget expands, its isocost curve shifts outward from IC_1 to IC_2 to IC_3. At the same time, the firm's most efficient combination of resources increases from a to b and then to c. As expenditures on resources rise, we can anticipate that beyond some point the increase in output will not keep pace with the increase in expenditure; at that point the marginal cost of a pair of jeans will rise.

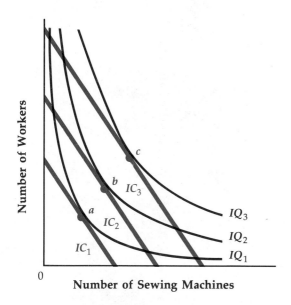

Figure 21.A4. The Effect of Increased Expenditures on Resources.
An increase in the level of expenditures on resources shifts the isocost curve outward from IC_1 to IC_3. The firm's most efficient combination of resources shifts from point a to point c.

Central Question

Given the market price and a firm's cost curves, how much will a firm produce in a perfectly competitive market?

Key Terms

Price taker

Price searcher

Pure monopoly

Monopolistic competition

Oligopoly

Chapter 22

Perfect Competition

Economists understand by the term **market,** *not any particular market place in which things are bought and sold, but the whole of any region in which buyers and sellers are in such free intercourse with one another that the prices of the same goods tend to equality easily and quickly.*

Augustin Cournot

*C*hapters 17 through 21 dealt with the two sides of markets, consumers and producers. We devised graphic means of representing consumer preferences (the demand curve) and producer costs (average and marginal cost curves). This chapter brings demand and cost analysis together in order to examine the way in which individual firms react to consumer demand in competitive markets. Our focus will be on a highly competitive market structure called perfect competition. We will investigate an intriguing question: at the limit, how much can competitive markets contribute to consumer welfare?

We will not attempt to give a full description of a real-world competitive market setting. Because markets are so diverse, such a description would probably not be very useful. Our aim is rather to devise a theoretical framework that will enable us to think about how markets work in general, as a constructive behavioral force. Though our model cannot tell us much that is specific about real-world markets, it will provide a basis for predicting the general direction of changes in market prices and output. Through its analysis, we should gain a deeper understanding of the meaning of market efficiency.

Perfect competition is only one of four basic market structures. The other three, and the detrimental effects of their restrictions on competition, are the subjects of Chapters 23 and 24.

The Four Market Structures

Markets can be divided into four basic categories, based on the degree of competition that prevails within them—that is, on how strenuously participants attempt to outdo, and avoid being outdone by, their rivals. The most competitive of the four market structures is perfect competition.

Perfect Competition

Price taker: a consumer or producer so small in relation to the entire market that its purchases and sales cannot affect the market price.

Price searcher: a consumer or producer large enough in relation to the entire market that its purchases and sales will affect the market price.

As we stressed in Chapter 3, perfect competition represents an ideal degree of competition. It has the following characteristics:

1. There are many producers in the market, no one of which is large enough to affect the going market price for the product. All producers are price takers, as opposed to price searchers or price makers. A **price taker** is a consumer or producer so small in relation to the entire market that its purchases and sales cannot affect the market price. The price taker must either accept or reject the market price, deciding how much to buy or sell on the assumption that the market price will not change. A **price searcher** (price maker) is a consumer or producer large enough in relation to the entire market that its purchases and sales will affect the market price. Through its consumption or production decisions, the price searcher helps to determine the market price. From the various price-quantity combinations available, it chooses that one combination that maximizes utility or profit.

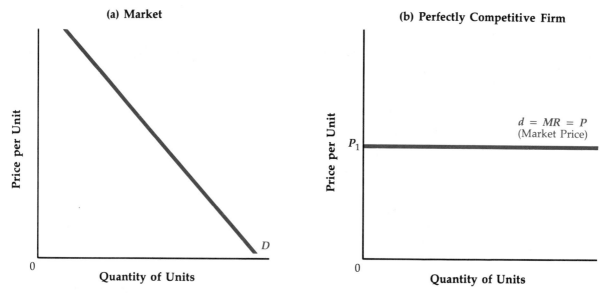

Figure 22.1. Demand Curve Faced by Perfect Competitors.
The market demand for a product (part (a)) is always downward sloping. But the perfect competitor faces a horizontal, or perfectly elastic, demand curve (part (b)). It cannot raise its price above the market price even slightly without losing its customers to other producers.

2. All producers sell a homogeneous product, meaning that the goods of one producer are indistinguishable from those of all others. Consumers are fully knowledgeable about the prices charged by different producers, and are totally indifferent as to which producer they buy from.

3. Producers enjoy complete freedom of entry into and exit from the market—that is, entry and exit costs are minimal, although not completely absent.

4. There are many consumers in the market, no one of whom is powerful enough to affect the market price of the product. Like producers, consumers are price takers.

As we have seen before (Chapter 18), the demand curve facing the individual perfect competitor is not the same as the demand curve faced by all producers. The market demand curve slopes downward, as shown in Figure 22.1(a). The demand curve facing an individual producer–price taker is horizontal, as in Figure 22.1(b). This horizontal demand curve is perfectly elastic. That is, the individual firm cannot raise its price even slightly above the going market price without losing all its customers to the numerous other producers in the market, or to other producers waiting for an opportunity to enter the market. On the other hand, the individual firm can sell all it wishes at the going market price. Hence it has no reason to offer its output at a lower price. The markets for wheat and for integrated computer circuits, or computer chips, are both good examples of real-world markets that come close to perfect competition.

Pure Monopoly

A **pure monopoly** is a single seller of a product for which there are no close substitutes. Pure monopolies are protected from competition by barriers to entry into the market. The barriers to entry into the monopolist's market will be described in Chapter 23. For now, we will simply note that because the monopolistic firm does not have to worry about competitors undercutting its price, it can raise its price without fear that customers will move to other producers of the same product or similar products. All the pure monopolist has to worry about is losing customers to producers of distantly related products.

Since the monopolist is the only producer of a particular good, the downward-sloping market demand curve (Figure 22.1(a)) is its individual demand curve. Unlike the perfect competitor, the monopolistic firm can raise its price and sell less, or lower its price and sell more. The critical task of the pure monopolist is to determine the one price-quantity combination of all price-quantity combinations on its demand curve that maximizes its profits. In this sense the pure monopolist is a price searcher. The best (but not perfect) real-world examples of a pure monopoly are regulated electric power companies, which dominate in given geographical areas, and the government's first-class postal system.

Monopolistic Competition

Monopolistic competition is a market composed of a number of producers whose products are differentiated and who face highly elastic, but not perfectly elastic, demand curves.

A monopolistically competitive market has the following characteristics:

1. There are a number of competitors, producing slightly differentiated products.
2. Advertising and other forms of nonprice competition are prevalent.
3. Entry into the market is not totally barred, but is restricted by modest entry costs, mainly overhead.
4. Because of the existence of close substitutes, customers can turn to other producers if a monopolistically competitive firm raises its price. Because of brand loyalty, the monopolistic competitor's demand curve still slopes downward, but it is fairly elastic (see Figure 22.2).

The market for textbooks is a good example of monopolistic competition. Most subjects are covered by two or three dozen textbooks, differing from one another in content, style of presentation, and design.

Oligopoly

An **oligopoly** is a market composed of only a handful of producers—as few as two and as many as twelve or more—whose pricing decisions are interdependent. Oligopolists may produce either an identical product (like

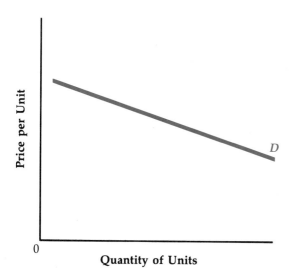

Figure 22.2. Demand Curve Faced by a Monopolistic Competitor.
Because the product sold by the monopolistically competitive firm is slightly different from the products sold by competing producers, the firm faces a highly elastic, but not perfectly elastic, demand curve.

steel) or highly differentiated products (like automobiles). Generally the barriers to entry into the market are considerable. But the critical characteristic of oligopolistic firms is that their pricing decisions are interdependent. That is, the pricing decisions of any one firm can substantially affect the sales of the others. Therefore each firm must monitor and respond to the pricing and production decisions of the other firms in the industry. The importance of this characteristic will become clear in Chapter 24.

Table 22.1 summarizes the characteristics of the four market structures.

The Perfect Competitor's Production Decision

As we learned in Chapter 3, the market price in a perfectly competitive market is determined by the interaction of the forces of supply and demand. If the price is above the equilibrium price level, a surplus will develop, forcing competitors to lower their prices. If the price is below equilibrium, a shortage will emerge, pushing the price upward (see Figure 22.3(a)). Given a market price over which it has no control, how much will the individual perfect competitor produce?

The Production Rule: $MC = MR$

Suppose the price in the perfectly competitive market for computer chips is \$5 (P_1 in Figure 22.3). For each individual competitor, the market price is a given that cannot be changed. It must be either accepted or rejected.

Table 22.1. Characteristics of the Four Market Structures

	Number of Firms	Freedom of Entry	Type of Product	Example
Perfect competition	Many	Very easy	Homogeneous	Wheat Computer chips Gold
Pure monopoly	One	Barred	Single product	Public utilities Postal service
Monopolistic competition	Many	Relatively easy	Differentiated	Pens Books Paper Clothing
Oligopoly	Few	Difficult	Either standardized or differentiated	Steel Light bulbs Cereal Autos

(If the firm rejects the price, however, it must shut down. If it raises its price even slightly above the market level, its customers will move to other competitors.) Demand, then, is horizontal at $5.

The firm's perfectly elastic horizontal demand curve is illustrated on the right-hand side of Figure 22.3. This horizontal demand curve is also the firm's marginal revenue curve, because marginal revenue is defined as the additional revenue acquired from selling one additional unit. Since each computer chip can be sold at a constant price of $5, the additional, or marginal, revenue acquired from selling an additional unit must be a constant $5.

Because profit equals total revenue minus total cost (profit $= TR - TC$), the profit-maximizing firm will produce any unit for which marginal revenue exceeds marginal cost. Thus the profit-maximizing firm in Figure 22.3(b) will produce and sell q_1 units, the quantity at which marginal revenue equals marginal cost ($MR = MC$). Up to q_1, marginal revenue is greater than marginal cost. Beyond q_1, all additional computer chips are unprofitable: the additional cost of producing them is greater than the additional revenue acquired.

Changes in Market Price

The perfectly competitive firm produces where $MC = MR$, both of which are equal to price. Thus the amount the firm produces depends on market price. So long as market demand remains constant, the individual firm's demand, and its price, will also remain constant. But if market demand

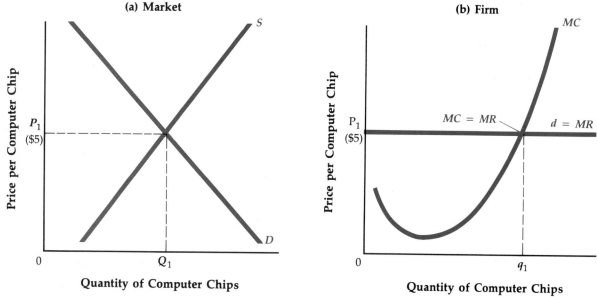

Figure 22.3. The Perfect Competitor's Production Decision.
The perfect competitor's price is determined by market supply and demand (part (a)). So long as marginal revenue (MR), which equals market price, exceeds marginal cost (MC), the perfect competitor will expand production (part (b)). The profit-maximizing production level is the point at which marginal cost equals marginal revenue (price).

and price increase, the individual firm's demand and price will also increase.

Figure 22.4 shows how the shift occurs. The original market demand of D_1 leads to a market price of P_1 (part (a)), which is translated into the individual firm's demand, d_1 (part (b)). The firm maximizes profit by equating marginal cost with marginal revenue, which is equal to d_1, at an output level of q_1.

An increase in market demand to D_2 leads to the higher price P_2 and a higher individual demand curve, d_2. At this higher price, which equals marginal revenue, the perfect competitor can support a higher marginal cost. The firm will expand production from q_1 to q_2. In the same way, an even greater market demand, D_3, will lead to even higher output, q_3, by the individual competitor.

Why does the market supply curve slope upward and to the right? The answer lies in the upward-sloping marginal cost curves confronted by individual firms. (The market supply curve is obtained by horizontally adding the supply curves of individual firms.) The individual firm's marginal cost curves slope upward because of diminishing (marginal) returns, a technological fact of the production process.

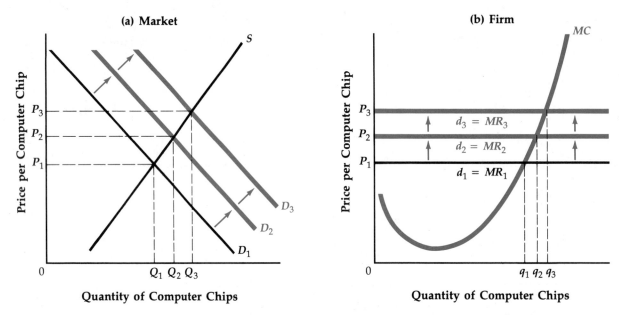

Figure 22.4. Change in the Perfect Competitor's Market Price.
If the market demand rises from D_1 to D_3 (part (a)), the price will rise with it, from P_1 to P_3. As a result, the perfectly competitive firm's demand curve will rise, from d_1 to d_3 (part (b)).

Maximizing Short-Run Profits

Can perfect competitors make an economic profit? The answer is yes, at least in the short run. To see this point, we must incorporate the average and marginal cost curves developed in the last chapter into our graph of the perfect competitor's demand curve, as in Figure 22.5(b). (Figure 22.5(a) shows the market supply and demand curves.) As before, the producer maximizes profits by equating marginal cost with price, rather than by looking at average cost. And that is exactly what the perfect competitor does. The firm produces q_2 computer chips because that is the point at which marginal revenue (which equals the firm's demand curve, which equals price) equals marginal cost. By producing anything less, the firm gives up more in revenue (as indicated by the firm's demand curve, d) than it saves in costs (as indicated by the marginal cost curve, which before q_2 is below the firm's demand curve). Similarly, by producing anything more than q_2, the firm incurs more additional costs (as indicated by the marginal cost curve) than it receives in additional revenue (as indicated by the demand curve, which beyond q_2 is below the MC curve).

At q_2 (and anywhere else), the firm's profit equals total revenue minus total cost ($TR - TC$). To find total revenue, we multiply the price, P_1 (which also equals average revenue) by the quantity produced, q_2 ($TR = P_1 q_2$). Graphically, total revenue is equal to the area of the rectangle bounded by the price and quantity, or $0P_1 a q_2$.

Economists in History: Alfred Marshall (1842–1924)

Alfred Marshall was born in England, just half a century after the death of Adam Smith. As a young man, Marshall turned down a theological scholarship to Oxford to take up mathematics at Cambridge. But his deep interest in philosophy and ethics eventually led him to economics. "I visited the poorest quarters of several cities and walked through one street after another, looking at the faces of the poorest people," Marshall recalled. "Next, I resolved to make as thorough a study as I could of Political Economy."[1]

Marshall originally saw his task as elaborating and modernizing classical economic thought. But he soon developed a new vision, which became the standard economic analysis. With the publication of his *Principles of Economics* in 1890, Marshall established the core of modern microeconomics.

Perhaps Marshall's most important contribution was his insight into the economic methodology and the problems of that methodology. He wrote:

Almost every scientific doctrine, whether carefully or formally stated, will be found to contain some proviso to the effect that other things are equal: the action of the causes in question is supposed to be isolated; certain effects are attributed to them, but only *on the hypothesis* that no cause is permitted to enter except those distinctly allowed for. It is true however that the condition that time must be allowed for causes to produce their effects is a source of great difficulty in economics. For meanwhile the material on which they work, and perhaps even the causes themselves, may have changed; and the tendencies which are being described will not have a sufficiently "long run" in which to work themselves out fully.[2]

During his twenty-three years as professor of political economy at Cambridge, Marshall influenced a great many of the next generation of economists. His *Principles*, which went through eight editions, became the standard economics textbook in England. If today's students find it relatively easy to comprehend such concepts as supply and demand, the consumer surplus, the importance of time in market adjustments, and the degree of producer and consumer responsiveness to price changes, it is because of the foundation laid by this great economist and teacher.

1. Quoted in J. M. Keynes, "Alfred Marshall, 1842–1924," *Memorials of Alfred Marshall*, ed. A. C. Pigou (New York: Kelly & Millman, 1956), p. 10.
2. Alfred Marshall, *Principles of Economics*, 9th ed. (London: Macmillan, 1961), p. 36.

Similarly, total cost can be found by multiplying the average total cost of production *(ATC)* by the quantity produced. The *ATC* curve shows us that the average total cost of producing q_2 computer chips is ATC_1. Therefore total cost is ATC_1q_2, or the rectangular area bounded by $0ATC_1bq_2$. The profits of the company are therefore $P_1q_2 - ATC_1q_2$, which is the same, mathematically, as $q_2(P_1 - ATC_1)$. This quantity corresponds to the area representing total revenue, $0P_1aq_2$, minus the area representing total cost, $0ATC_1bq_2$. Or, profit is the shaded rectangle bounded by ATC_1P_1ab.

The perfect competitor does not seek to produce the quantity that results in the lowest average total cost. That quantity, q_1, is defined by the intersection of the marginal cost curve and the average total cost curve. If it produced only q_1, the firm would lose out on some of its profits, shown by the darker shaded area *dca*. (Suppose the firm is producing at q_1. If it expands production to q_2, it will generate P_1 times $q_2 - q_1$ in extra revenue [price times the additional units sold], an amount represented graphically

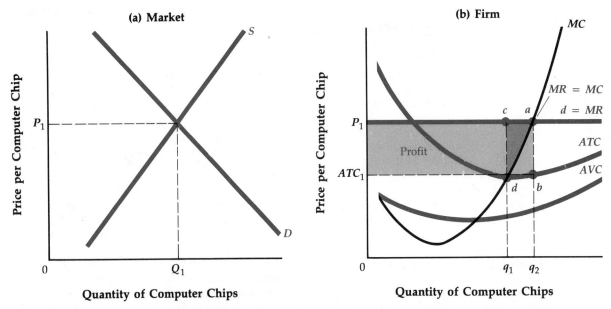

Figure 22.5. The Profit-Maximizing Perfect Competitor.
The perfect competitor's demand curve is established by the market clearing price (part (a)). The profit-maximizing perfect competitor will extend production up to the point where marginal cost equals marginal revenue (price), or point a in part (b). At that output level—q_2— the firm will earn a short-run economic profit equal to the shaded area ATC_1P_1ab. If the perfect competitor were to minimize average total cost, it would produce only q_1, losing profits equal to the darker shaded area dca in the process.

by the area q_1caq_2. The firm will incur additional costs as well, represented graphically by the area q_1daq_2. But by producing $q_2 - q_1$ additional units, the firm gains profits equal to the additional revenue, q_1caq_2, minus the additional cost, q_1daq_2.)

Naturally, profit-maximizing firms will attempt to minimize their costs of production. But that does not mean they will produce at the point of minimum average total cost. Instead, they will try to employ the most efficient technology available and to minimize their payments for resources. That is, they will attempt to keep their cost curves as low as possible. But given those curves, the firm will produce where $MC = MR$, not where ATC is at its lowest level. Managers who cannot distinguish between those two objectives will probably operate their businesses on a less profitable basis than they might—and will risk being run out of business.

Minimizing Short-Run Losses

In the foregoing analysis the market-determined price was higher than the firm's average total cost, allowing it to make a profit. But perfect

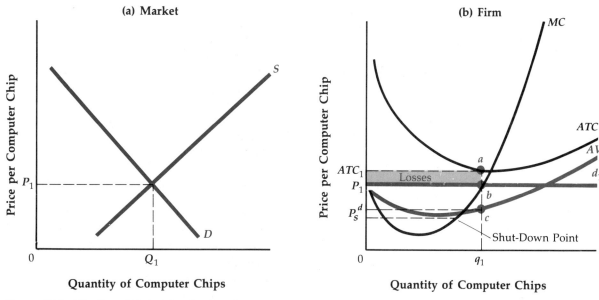

Figure 22.6. The Loss-Minimizing Perfect Competitor.
The market clearing price (part (a)) establishes the perfect competitor's demand curve (part (b)). Since the price is below the average total cost curve, this firm is losing money. So long as the price is above the low point of the average variable cost curve, however, the firm should minimize its short-run losses by continuing to produce where marginal cost equals marginal revenue (price), or point b in part (b). This perfect competitor should produce q_1 units, incurring losses equal to the shaded area P_1ATC_1ab. (The alternative would be to shut down, in which case the firm would lose all its fixed costs.)

competitors are not guaranteed profits. The market price may not be high enough for the firm to make a profit. Suppose, for example, that the market price is P_1, below the firm's average total cost curve (see Figure 22.6). Should the firm still produce where marginal cost equals marginal revenue (price)? The answer, for the short run, is yes. So long as the firm can cover its variable cost, it should produce q_1 computer chips.

It is true that the firm will lose money. Its total revenues are only P_1q_1, or the area bounded by $0P_1bq_1$, whereas its total costs are ATC_1q_1, or the area $0ATC_1aq_1$. On the graph its total losses equal the difference between those two rectangular areas, the shaded area bounded by P_1ATC_1ab. Whether the firm incurs losses is not the relevant question, however. The real issue is whether the firm loses more money by shutting down or by operating and producing q_1 chips.

In the short run, the firm will continue to incur fixed costs even if it shuts down. If it is not earning any revenues, its losses will equal its fixed costs. In the last chapter we saw that the average fixed cost of production is the vertical distance between the average variable and average total cost curves ($AFC = ATC - AVC$). At an output level of q_1, then, average fixed cost is equal to the vertical distance ac. Total fixed cost can be found by multiplying average fixed cost, ac, by the quantity produced, q_1. (If $AFC = FC/q$, then $FC = AFC\, q$.) In Figure 22.6, therefore, total fixed costs are represented by the rectangular area $dATC_1ac$. As you can see, $dATC_1ac$ is greater than P_1ATC_1ab—meaning that the firm will lose more money if it shuts down than if it produces at a level of q_1.

In short, as long as the price is higher than average variable cost—in other words, if the price more than covers the costs associated directly with production—the firm minimizes its short-run losses by producing where marginal cost equals marginal revenue. Only if the price dips below the low point of the average variable cost curve—where the marginal and average variable cost curves intersect—will the firm add to its losses by operating. The firm will shut down when price is at or below that point, P_s in Figure 22.6. At prices above that point, the firm simply follows its marginal cost curve to determine its production level. Above the average variable cost curve, then, the marginal cost curve is in effect the firm's supply curve. Therefore, if a perfect competitor produces at all, it produces in a range of increasing marginal cost—and diminishing marginal returns.

Our analysis has shown why, in the short run, fixed costs are sunk costs that should be ignored. The relevant question is whether a given productive activity will add more to the firm's revenues than to its costs. Understanding this principle, businesses may undertake activities that superficially appear to be quite unprofitable. Some grocery stores stay open all night, even though the owners know they will attract few customers. If all costs, including fixed costs, are considered, the decision to operate in the early morning hours may seem misguided. But the only relevant question facing the store manager is whether the additional sales generated are greater than the additional cost of lighting, goods sold, and labor. Similarly, many businesses that are obviously failing continue to operate, for by staying open they can at least cover a portion of their fixed costs—such as rent—that would still be due if they shut down. They stay open until their leases expire or until they can sell out.

Producing Over the Long Run

In the long run businesses have an opportunity to change their fixed costs. If the market price remains too low to permit profitable operation, a firm can eliminate its fixed costs—that is, sell its plant and equipment, or terminate its contracts for insurance and office space. If the market price is above average total cost, new firms can enter the market, and existing firms can expand their scale of operation. Such long-run adjustments in turn affect market supply, which affects price and short-run production decisions.

The Long-Run Effect of Short-Run Profits and Losses

When profits encourage new firms to enter an industry and existing firms to expand, the result is an increase in market supply, a decrease in market

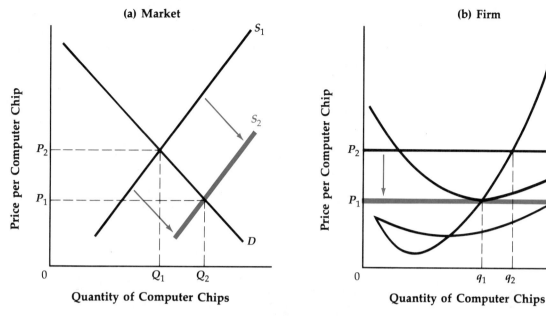

Figure 22.7. The Long-Run Effects of Short-Run Profits.
If perfect competitors are making short-run profits, other producers will enter the
market, increasing the market supply from S_1 to S_2 and lowering the market price,
from P_2 to P_1 (part (a)). The individual firm's demand curve, which is determined
by market price, will shift down, from d_1 to d_2 (part (b)). The firm will reduce its
output from q_2 to q_1, the new intersection of marginal revenue (price) and marginal
cost. Long-run equilibrium will be achieved when the price falls to the low point
of the firm's average total cost curve, eliminating economic profit (price P_1 in (b)).

price, and a decrease in the profitability of individual firms. For example,
in Figure 22.7(a), the existence of economic profits in the computer chip
market means that investors can earn more in that industry than in some
others. Some investors will move their resources to the computer chip
industry. Because the number of producers increases, the supply curve
shifts outward, expanding total production from Q_1 to Q_2 and depressing
the market price from P_2 to P_1.

The expansion of industry supply and the resulting reduction in market
price make the computer chip business less profitable for individual firms.
The lower market price is reflected in a downward shift of the firm's
horizontal demand curve, from d_1 to d_2 (see Figure 22.7(b)). The individual
firm reduces its output from q_2 to q_1, the intersection of the new marginal
revenue (price/demand) curve with the marginal cost curve. Note that q_1
is also the low point of the average total cost curve. Here price equals
average total cost, meaning that economic profit is zero. The firm is making
just enough to cover its opportunity and risk costs, no more.

Losses have the opposite effect on long-run industry supply. In the long
run, firms that are losing money will move out of the industry, because
their resources can be employed more profitably elsewhere. When firms

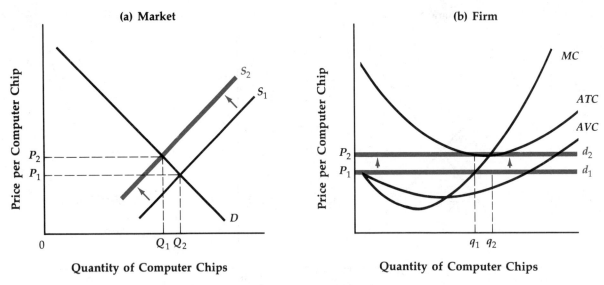

Figure 22.8. The Long-Run Effects of Short-Run Losses.
If perfect competitors are suffering short-run losses, some firms will leave the industry, causing the market supply to shift back from S_1 to S_2 and the price to rise, from P_1 to P_2 (part (a)). The individual firm's demand curve will shift up with price, from d_1 to d_2 (part (b)). Output will expand from q_1 to q_2, and equilibrium will be reached when price equals the low point of average total cost (P_2), eliminating the firm's short-run losses.

drop out of the industry, supply contracts and total production falls, from Q_2 to Q_1 in Figure 22.8(a). As a result the price of the product rises, permitting some firms to break even and stay in the business. Long-run equilibrium occurs when the price reaches P_2, where the individual firm's demand curve is just tangent to the low point of the average total cost curve (Figure 22.8(b)). The output of each remaining individual firm expands (from q_1 to q_2) to take up the slack left by the firms that have withdrawn. Again price and average total cost are equal, and economic profit is zero.

The Effect of Economies of Scale

In the long run, competition forces firms to take advantage of economies of scale, if they exist. If expanding the use of resources reduces costs, the perfect competitor must expand. Otherwise, other firms will expand their scale of operation, increasing market supply and forcing the market price down. Any firm that does not expand its scale will be caught with a cost structure that is higher than the market price. In addition to mere self-

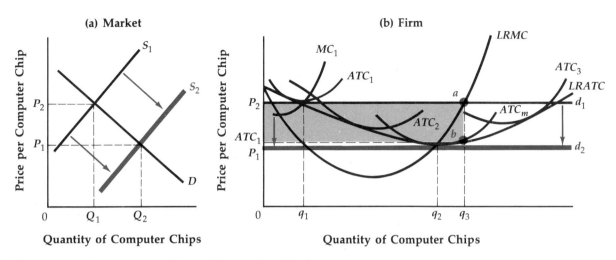

Figure 22.9. The Long-Run Effects of Economies of Scale.
If the market is in equilibrium at price P_2 (part (a)) and the individual firm is producing q_1 units on short-run average total cost curve ATC_1 (part (b)), firms will be just breaking even. Because of the profit potential represented by the shaded area ATC_1P_2ab, firms can be expected to expand production to q_3, where the long-run marginal cost curve intersects the demand curve (d_1). As they expand production to take advantage of economies of scale, however, supply will expand from S_1 to S_2 (part (a)), pushing the market price down toward P_1. Equilibrium will be achieved when the price has fallen to P_1, the low point of the long-run average total cost curve ($LRATC$). Economic profit will fall to zero. Because of rising diseconomies of scale, firms will not expand further.

preservation, the firm also has a profit incentive for expansion. If it expands before other firms, its lower average total cost will allow it to make greater profits for a short period of time.

Consider Figure 22.9, for instance. Initially the market is in short-run equilibrium at a price of P_2 (part (a)). The individual firm is on cost scale ATC_1, producing q_1 chips and breaking even (part (b)). If the firm expands its scale of operation and produces where its demand curve d_1 intersects the long-run marginal cost curve, it will make a profit equal graphically to the shaded area ATC_1P_2ab. That is the firm's incentive for expansion.

If the firm does not expand and take advantage of these economies, some other firm surely will. Then any firm still producing on scale ATC_1 will lose money. For when the market supply expands the price will tumble toward P_1, the point at which the long-run average total cost curve (and the short-run curve ATC_m) are at a minimum, and both industry and firm profits are zero. Because of rising diseconomies of scale, firms will not be able to expand further. Any firm that tries to produce on a smaller or larger scale—for example, ATC_2 or ATC_3—will incur average total costs higher than the market price and will lose money. Ultimately it will be driven out of the market or forced to expand or contract its scale.

The Efficiency of Perfect Competition: A Critique

Our discussion of perfect competition has been a highly theoretical one. In real life, the competitive market system is not so efficient as theory may suggest. Several aspects of the market deserve further comment from this perspective.

The Tendency Toward Equilibrium

Market forces are stabilizing: they tend to push the market toward one central point of equilibrium. To that extent the market is predictable, and to that extent it contributes to economic and social stability. However, price does not always move smoothly toward equilibrium, as it appears to do in supply and demand models. That may happen in markets where all participants, both buyers and sellers, know exactly what everyone else is doing. By definition, however, market participants have only imperfect knowledge of what others are going to do, for one function of the market is to generate the pricing and output information people need to interact with one another.

In a world of imperfect information, then, prices may not and probably will not move directly toward equilibrium. Those who compete in the market will continually grope for the "best" price, from their own individual perspectives. At times sellers will produce too little and reap unusually high profits.

This process of groping toward equilibrium can be represented graphically by a supply and demand "cobweb" (see Figure 22.10). Most producers must plan their production at least several months ahead on the basis of prices received today or during the past production period. Farmers, for instance, may plant for summer harvest on the basis of the previous summer's prices. Suppose farmers got price P_1 for a bushel of wheat last year. Their planning supply curve, S, will encourage them to work for a harvest of only Q_1 bushels this year. Given that limited output and the rather high demand at price P_1, however, the price farmers actually receive is P_4. The price of P_4 in turn induces farmers to plan for a much larger production level, Q_3, the following year. But the market will not clear for Q_3 bushels until the price falls to P_2. The next year farmers plan for a price of P_2 and reduce their production to Q_2—which causes the price to rise to P_3. As you can see from the graph, instead of moving in a straight line, the market moves toward the intersection of supply and demand in a web-like pattern.

Surpluses and Shortages

Some critics complain that the market system creates wasteful surpluses and shortages. But although all resources are limited in quantity, a true market shortage can exist only if the going price is below equilibrium.

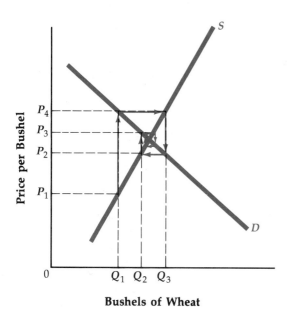

Bushels of Wheat

Figure 22.10. Supply and Demand Cobweb.
Markets do not always move smoothly toward equilibrium. If current production decisions are based on past prices, price may adjust to supply in the cobweb pattern shown here. Having received price P_1 in the past, farmers will plan to supply only Q_1 bushels of wheat. That amount will not meet market demand, so the price will rise to P_4—inducing farmers to plan for a harvest of Q_3 bushels. At price P_4, however, Q_3 bushels will not clear the market. The price will fall to P_2, encouraging farmers to cut production back to Q_2. Only after several tries may farmers find the equilibrium price-quantity combination.

Thus shortages can be eliminated by a price increase. How much of an increase, theory alone cannot say. But we do know that market forces, if allowed free play, will work to boost the price and eliminate the shortage. That means, of course, that people of limited financial resources will be eliminated from the market—an enduring concern that motivates many government efforts to legislate market conditions.

Similarly, all surpluses exist because the going price is above equilibrium. Competition will reduce the price, eliminating the surplus. In the process, of course, some firms will be driven out of the market and into other, more productive activities. Others will be unable to keep their employees working full-time. A frequent criticism of the market system is that when this happens, workers have difficulty finding employment in other lines of production. Part of the problem, however, is that labor contracts, community custom, or minimum wage laws prevent wages from adjusting downward. If prices are controlled by government—that is, if they are not permitted to respond to market conditions—surpluses and shortages will persist. (We will return to this subject in Chapter 31.)

Figure 22.11. The Efficiency of the Competitive Market.
Perfectly competitive markets are efficient in the sense that they equate marginal benefit (shown by the demand curve in part (a)) with marginal cost (shown by the supply curve). At the market output level, Q_1, the marginal benefit of the last unit produced equals the marginal cost of production. The gains generated by the production of Q_1 units—that is, the difference between cost and benefits—are shown by the shaded area in part (a).

The perfectly competitive market is also efficient in the sense that the marginal cost of production, P_1, is the same for all firms (parts (b) and (c)). If firm X were to produce fewer than its efficient number of units, q_x, firm Y would have to produce more than its efficient number, q_y, to meet market demand. Firm Y would be pushed up its marginal cost curve, to the point where the cost of the last unit exceeds its benefits. But competition forces the two firms to produce to exactly that point where marginal cost equals marginal benefit, thus minimizing the cost of production.

Marginal Benefit Versus Marginal Cost

Time lags, surpluses, and shortages notwithstanding, the competitive market can produce efficient results in one important sense. That is that the marginal benefit of the last unit produced equals its marginal cost (MB = MC). In Figure 22.11(a), for every computer chip up to Q_1, consumers are willing to pay a price (as indicated by the demand curve, D) greater than its marginal cost (as indicated by the industry supply curve, S). The difference between the price consumers are willing to pay—an objective indication of the product's marginal benefits—and the marginal cost of production is a kind of surplus value, or net gain received from the production of each unit. By producing Q_1 units, the industry exploits all potential gains from production, shown graphically by the shaded triangular area in the figure. That net gain is brought about by the price that is charged, P_1—a price that induces individual firms to produce where the marginal cost of production equals the price, which is also equal to consumers' marginal benefit.

The marginal cost of production for each individual firm is also P_1, a fact that results in the production of Q_1 units at the minimum total cost. Parts (b) and (c) show the cost curves of two firms, X and Y. In competitive equilibrium, firm X produces q_x units and firm Y produces q_y units. But suppose that the market output were distributed between the firms differently. Suppose, for example, that firm X produced one computer chip less than q_x. To maintain a constant market output of Q_1, firm Y (or some other firm) would then have to expand production by one unit. The additional chip would force firm Y up its marginal cost curve. To Y, the marginal cost of the additional chip is greater than P_1, greater than X's marginal cost to produce it. Competition forces firms to produce at a cost-effective output level, and therefore minimizes the cost of producing at any given level of output.

Perfectly competitive markets are attractive for another reason. In the long run, competition forces each firm to produce at the low point of its average total cost curve. Firms must either produce at that point, achieving whatever economies of scale are available, or get out of the market, leaving production to some other firm that will minimize average total cost.

Critics stress, however, that supply is based only on the costs firms bear privately. External costs like air, noise, and water pollution (see Chapter 4) are not counted as part of the cost of production. If the external costs of pollution were counted, the firm's supply curve would be lower, S_2 instead of S_1 in Figure 22.12. If producers and consumers had to pay all the costs of production, only Q_1 units would be bought. In this sense, competition leads to overproduction of $Q_2 - Q_1$ units. The cost of producing these $Q_2 - Q_1$ chips is the area under the supply curve between Q_1 and Q_2, Q_1abQ_2. The benefit to consumers is the area under the demand curve, or the area Q_1acQ_2. The extent to which the cost of overproduction exceeds the benefits to consumers is shown by the shaded triangular area abc.

Critics of the market system stress also that its cost efficiencies are achieved within a specific distribution of resources or wealth, one that

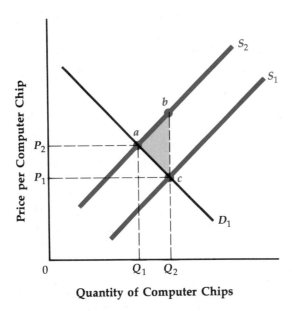

Figure 22.12. Inefficiency Caused by External Costs.
If external costs equal to the vertical distance bc are not counted as costs of production, supply will be artificially high at S_1, and firms will overproduce by $Q_2 - Q_1$ units. The inefficiency, or welfare loss, from such overproduction is shown by the shaded area abc, the amount by which the total cost of producing $Q_2 - Q_1$ units (shown by curve S_2) exceeds their total benefits (shown by the demand curve).

depends on the existing distribution of property rights. The distribution of economic power inherent in these property rights, they argue, has no particular ethical or moral significance.

Finally, critics of the market system argue that most real-world markets are not perfectly competitive. Actual markets are not inhabited by numerous firms producing standard commodities that can be easily duplicated by anyone who would like to enter the market. Indeed, many markets are inhabited by a few large, powerful firms that do not take price as a given. Many firms either are monopolies or possess a high degree of monopoly power. But the model of perfect competition was never meant to represent all or even most markets. It is merely one of several means economists use to think about markets and the consequences of changes in market conditions and government policy.

Summary and Extensions

Perfect competition is an idealized market structure that can never be fully attained in the real world. Nonetheless, the model helps to illuminate the influence of competition in the marketplace, just as the idealized concepts of the physical sciences help to illustrate the workings of the natural world.

Physicists, for example, deal with the concept of gravity by talking of the acceleration of a falling body in a vacuum. Vacuums do not exist naturally in the world as we know it, but as theoretical constructs they are useful in isolating and emphasizing the directional power of gravitational pull. In a similar fashion, the theoretical construct of perfect competition helps to highlight the directional influence and consequences of competition.

The model of perfect competition also provides a benchmark for comparing the relative efficiency of real-world markets. The perfectly competitive model clarifies the rules of efficient production and suggests that free movement of resources is essential to achieving efficient production levels. Without a free flow of resources, new firms cannot move into profitable production lines, increase market supply and push prices down, and force other firms to minimize their production costs. Competition requires mobility of resources.

Major Conclusions

1. The four market types—perfect competition, pure monopoly, monopolistic competition, and oligopoly—are distinguished by the number of firms in the market, the ease of entry into the market, and the nature of the product. Perfect competition is the most competitive market structure; pure monopoly is the least competitive.
2. In a perfectly competitive market, a profit-maximizing firm always produces at the level where marginal cost (MC) equals marginal revenue (MR).
3. In the short run, a profit-maximizing perfect competitor does not attempt to produce at the low point of its average total cost curve.
4. In the short run, a perfect competitor can make a profit so long as the price is above its average total cost.
5. A perfect competitor will continue to produce despite short-run losses so long as the price is above its average variable cost curve. If the price is below the low point of the average variable cost curve, the perfect competitor will shut down.
6. A perfect competitor's supply curve is the portion of its marginal cost curve that lies above its average variable cost curve.
7. In the long run, the perfect competitor is forced to produce at the low point of its average total cost curve, where price equals average total cost and economic profit is zero.
8. In the long run, the perfectly competitive firm will not accept continuing losses but will terminate its fixed costs and shut down.
9. In the long run, perfect competitors are forced to take advantage of any economies of scale that may exist and to produce at the low point of the long-run average cost curve.
10. Perfect competition is efficient in the sense that the marginal benefit of the last unit produced equals the marginal cost of its production. Perfect competition is also efficient in the sense that the marginal cost of production is the same for all producers, and that firms must produce at the low point of their average cost curves.

Questions to Ponder

1. In the graph below, identify the short-run production level for a profit-maximizing firm. Shade the area representing profits.

2. On the graph for question 1, indicate with a *Pm* the minimum price the firm requires to continue short-run operation.

3. On the graph for question 1, darken the firm's supply curve. Explain why that curve or portion of a curve is the firm's supply curve.

4. Why does a perfectly competitive firm seek to equate marginal cost with marginal revenue rather than to produce where average total cost is at a minimum?

5. If perfectly competitive firms are making a profit in the short run, what will happen to the industry's equilibrium price and quantity in the long run?

6. Suppose the market demand for a product rises. In the short run, how will a perfect competitor react to the higher market price? Draw a graph to illustrate your answer. What will happen to the market price in the long run? Why?

Central Question

What effect does monopoly have on market efficiency, and why and to what extent is that effect an argument for government control of the market?

Key Terms

Monopoly power
Price discrimination
Perfect price discrimination
Imperfect price discrimination

Chapter 23

Pure Monopoly

That competition is a virtue, at least as far as enterprises are concerned, has been a basic article of faith in the American tradition, and a vigorous antitrust policy has long been regarded as both beneficial and necessary, not only to extend competitive forces into new regions but also to preserve them where they may be flourishing at the moment.
G. Warren Nutter
Henry Adler Einhorn

At the bottom of almost all arguments against the free market is a deep-seated concern about the distorting (some would say corrupting) influence of monopolies. People who are suspicious of the free market fear that too many producers are not controlled by the forces of competition, but instead hold considerable monopoly power. Unless government intervenes, these firms are likely to exploit their power for their own selfish benefit. This theme has been fundamental to the writings of John Kenneth Galbraith.

The initiative in deciding what is produced comes not from the sovereign consumer who, through the market, issues instructions that bend the productive mechanism to his ultimate will. Rather it comes from the great producing organization which reaches forward to control the markets that it is presumed to serve and, beyond, to bend the customers to its needs.[1]

This chapter will examine the dynamics of monopoly power and attempt to place their consequences in proper perspective. We will also consider the usefulness of antitrust laws in controlling monopoly and promoting competition. In Chapter 24 we will apply the model of monopoly developed here to two forms of partial monopoly, monopolistic competition and oligopoly.

The Origins of Monopoly

We have defined the competitive market as the process by which market rivals, each pursuing its own private interests, strive to outdo one another. This competitive market process has many benefits. It enables producers to obtain information about what consumers and other producers are willing to do. It promotes higher production levels, lower prices, and a greater variety of goods and services than would be achieved otherwise.

Monopoly power:
the ability of a firm to raise the market price of its good or service by reducing production.

Monopoly power is the conceptual opposite of competition. **Monopoly power** is the ability of a firm to raise the market price of its good or service by reducing production. Whereas the demand curve of the competitive firm is horizontal (see page 406), a firm with monopoly power faces a downward-sloping demand curve. Thus by restricting production the monopoly can raise its market price. To maximize its profits (or minimize its losses), such a firm need only search through the various price-quantity combinations on its demand curve to discover the most advantageous combination. In very general terms, then, a firm with monopoly power is a price searcher. It can control price because other firms are to some extent unable or unwilling to compete. As a result, a monopolized market produces fewer benefits than perfect competition.

Businesses vary considerably in the extent of their monopoly power. The postal service and your local telephone company both have significant monopoly power. They confront few competitors, and entry into their markets is barred by law. IBM has less monopoly power. Though it can

---

1. John Kenneth Galbraith, *The New Industrial State* (Boston: Houghton Mifflin, 1967), p. 6.

affect the price it charges for its computers by expanding or contracting its sales, it is restrained by the possibility that other firms will enter its market. On a smaller scale, grocery stores face the same threat. They may have many competitors already, and they must be concerned about additional stores entering the market. Nevertheless, grocery stores still retain some power to restrict sales and raise their prices.

The exact opposite of perfect competition is pure monopoly. Since, by definition, the pure monopolist is the only producer of a product that has no close substitutes, the demand it confronts is the market demand for the product. Unlike the perfect competitor, which has no power over price, the pure monopolist can raise the price of its product without fear that customers will go elsewhere. With no other producers offering the same product, or even a close substitute, the consumer has nowhere to turn. As we will see, production levels are generally lower and prices higher under pure monopoly than under competition.

How does monopoly arise? To answer that question clearly, we must reflect once again on the basis for competition. Competition occurs because market rivals want to exploit profitable opportunities and can enter markets where such opportunities exist. In the extreme case of perfect competition, there are no barriers to entry, and competitors are numerous. Entrepreneurs are always on the lookout for any opportunity to enter such a market in pursuit of profit. Individual competitors cannot raise their price, for if they do, their rivals may move in, cut prices, and take away all their customers. If a wheat farmer asks more than the market price, for example, customers can move to others who will sell wheat at market price. For this reason perfect competitors are called price takers. They have no real control over the price they charge.

The essential condition for competition is freedom of market entry. In perfect competition entry is assumed to be completely free. Conversely the essential condition for monopoly is the presence of barriers to entry. Monopolists can manipulate price because such barriers protect them from being undercut by rivals.

Barriers to entry can arise from several sources. First, the monopolist may have sole ownership of a strategic resource, such as bauxite (from which aluminum is extracted). Second, the monopolist may have a patent or copyright on the product, which prevents other producers from duplicating it. For years, until Eastman Kodak developed an alternative process, Polaroid had a patent monopoly on the instant-photograph market. Third, the monopolist may have an exclusive franchise to sell a given product in a specific geographical area. Consider the exclusive franchise enjoyed by your local telephone company or your local electric utility. Fourth, the monopolist may own the rights to a well-known brand name with a highly loyal group of customers. In that case, the barrier to entry is the costly process of trying to get customers to try a new product. Finally, in a monopolized industry, production may be conducted on a very large scale, requiring huge plants and large amounts of equipment. The enormous financial resources needed to produce on such a scale can act as a barrier to entry, because a new entrant operating on a small scale would have costs too high to compete effectively with the dominant firm.

All in all, barriers to entry can be thought of as costs that must be borne by potential competitors before they can compete. Such barriers may be prohibitively high.

The Limits of Monopoly Power

Unlike the competitive seller, the monopolist has the power to withhold supplies from the market and to charge more than the competitive market price. But even the pure monopolist's market power is not completely unchecked. It is restricted in two important ways. First, without government assistance, the monopolist's control over the market for a product is never complete. Even if a producer has a true monopoly of a good, the consumer can still choose a substitute good whose production is not monopolized. For instance, in most parts of the nation, only one firm is permitted to provide local telephone service. Yet people can communicate in other ways. They can talk directly with one another; they can write letters or send telegrams; they can use their children as messengers. In a more general sense, consumers can use their income to buy rugs or bicycles instead of private lines. To the extent that the individual has alternatives, his consumption of any good must be considered voluntary. As the Nobel laureate Friedrich Hayek has written,

If, for instance, I would very much like to be painted by a famous artist (one who has monopoly power) and if he refuses to paint me for less than a very high price, it would clearly be absurd for me to say that I am coerced. The same is true of any other commodity or service that I can do without. So long as the services of a particular person are not crucial to my existence or the preservation of what I most value, the conditions he exacts for rendering these services cannot be called "coercion."[2]

That is not to say that the effects of monopoly are all positive. If monopoly means that one firm is garnering the assets and markets of all other competitors, it can be viewed as a force that reduces consumer choice. Although the monopolist's coercive power may not be complete, it nevertheless can restrict consumer freedom.

Monopoly power can develop for other reasons, however. A firm may gain monopoly power because it has built a better mousetrap or developed a good that was previously unavailable. In other words, a firm may be the only producer because it is the first producer, and no one has been able to figure out how to duplicate its product. In this instance, although monopolized, the new product results in an expansion of consumer choice. Furthermore, the monopoly may be only temporary, for other competitors are likely to break into the market eventually.

---

2. F. A. Hayek, *The Constitution of Liberty* (Chicago: University of Chicago Press, 1960), p. 136.

The monopolist is also restricted by market conditions—that is, by the costs of production and the downward-sloping demand curve for the good. If the monopolistic firm raises its price, it must be prepared to sell less. How much less depends on what substitutes are available. The monopolist must consider as well the costs of expanding production and of trying to prevent competitors from entering the market. The important point here is that there is a range of possible costs and prices at which the monopolistic firm can sell various quantities of a good. Its task is to search through the available price-quantity combinations for the one that maximizes profit.

In a free and open market, monopoly power can be dissolved in the long run. With time competitors can discover weakly protected avenues through which to invade the monopolist's domain. The Reynolds International Pen Company had a patent monopoly on the first ball-point pen, which it introduced in 1945. Two years later other pen companies had found ways of circumventing the patent and producing a similar but not identical product. The price of ball-point pens fell from an initial $12.50 to the low prices of today. Many other products that are freely produced today—calculators, video games, car telephones, and cellophane tape, to name a few—were first sold by companies that enjoyed short-run monopolies. Thus the imperfection of monopoly power is crucial. In the long run excessively high prices, restricted supply, and high profits give potential competitors the incentive to find and exploit imperfections in the monopolist's power. Like the proverbial hole in the dike, those imperfections can undermine even the strongest barrier.

One of the most effective ways for a monopoly to retain its market power is to enlist the coercive power of the state in protecting or extending its boundaries. This strategy has been used effectively for decades in the electric utilities industry and the cable television market. The insurance industry and the medical profession, both of which are protected from competition through licensing procedures, are also good examples. But even the power of the state may not be enough to shield an industry from competition forever. Consumer tastes and the technology of production and delivery can change dramatically over the very long run. The franchise monopoly of electric power companies, for example, is slowly being weakened by the introduction of home solar power. And the railroad industry's market, which was protected from price competition by the state for almost a century, has been gradually eroded by the emergence of new competitors, principally airlines, buses, and trucks. Even the first-class mail monopoly of the U.S. Postal Service is being eroded by Federal Express and other overnight delivery firms. And in the long run, government protection may be extended to the very competitors who arise to break a state-protected monopoly. (Such was the case, until recently, with the airline, bus, and trucking industries.)

Should government attempt to break up all monopolies? Since without state protection monopoly may eventually dissipate, the relevant public policy questions are how long the monopoly power is likely to persist if left alone, and how costly it will be while it lasts, in terms of lost efficiency and unequal distribution of income. The machinery of government needed to dissolve monopoly power is costly in itself. Thus the decision whether to prosecute antitrust violations depends in part on the costs and benefits of such an action. Often the rise of a monopoly does warrant government action, but in some cases the benefits of action cannot justify the costs. As described in Chapter 3, the first seller of hand calculators enjoyed a temporary monopoly of the U.S. market in 1969. Subsequently the industry developed very rapidly, however, and in retrospect it is clear that a long, drawn-out antitrust action would have been inappropriate.

To give another example, in 1969 the Justice Department found that IBM enjoyed an unwarranted monopoly of the domestic computer market, which was dominated by large mainframe computers. It concluded that an antitrust suit against IBM was justified. Prosecution of the case, which the Justice Department dropped in January 1982, took more than a decade. The accumulated documentation from the proceedings filled a warehouse, and the Justice Department and IBM devoted an untold number of lawyer-hours to the case. In the meantime, IBM's alleged monopoly was seriously eroded by new firms producing mini- and microcomputers. Thus the net benefits to society from the antitrust action against IBM are at best debatable, and probably negative. That is, the costs most likely exceeded the benefits.

Equating Marginal Cost with Marginal Revenue

In deciding how many times a week to play tennis, an athlete weighs the estimated benefits of each game against its costs. Producers of goods follow a similar procedure, although the benefits of production are measured in terms of revenue acquired rather than personal utility. A producer will produce another unit of a good if the additional (or marginal) revenue it brings is greater than the additional cost of its production—in other words, if it increases the firm's profits. The firm will therefore expand production to the point where marginal cost equals marginal revenue ($MC = MR$). This is a fundamental rule that all profit-maximizing firms follow, and monopolies are no exception.

Suppose you are in the yo-yo business. You have a patent on edible yo-yos, which come in three flavors—vanilla, chocolate, and strawberry. (We will assume there is a demand for these products.) The cost of producing the first yo-yo is $0.50, but you can sell it for $0.75. Your profit on that unit is therefore $0.25 ($0.75 − $0.50). If the second unit costs you $0.60 to make (assuming increasing marginal cost) and you can sell it for $0.75, your profit for two yo-yos is $0.40 ($0.25 profit on the first plus $0.15 profit on the second). If you intend to maximize your profits, you—like the perfect competitor—will continue to expand production until the gap between marginal revenue and marginal cost disappears. As a monopolist, however, you will find that your marginal revenue does not remain constant. Instead, it falls over the range of production.

The monopolist's marginal revenue declines as output rises because the price must be reduced to entice consumers to buy more. Consider the

Table 23.1. The Monopolist's Declining Marginal Revenue

Quantity Sold (1)	Price of Yo-yo (2)	Total Revenue (1 × 2) (3)	Marginal Revenue (change in 3) (4)
0	$11	$ 0	$ 0
1	10	10	10
2	9	18	8
3	8	24	6
4	7	28	4
5	6	30	2

price schedule in Table 23.1. Price and quantity are inversely related, reflecting the assumption that a monopolist faces a downward-sloping demand curve. (Because the monopolist is the only producer of a product, its demand curve is the market demand curve.) As the price falls from $10 to $6 (column 2), the number sold rises from one to five (column 1). If the firm wishes to sell only one yo-yo, it can charge as much as $10. Total revenue at that level of production is then $10. To sell more—say two yo-yos—the monopolist must reduce the price for each to $9. Total revenue then rises to $18 (column 3).

By multiplying columns 1 and 2, we can fill in the rest of column 3. As the price is lowered and the quantity sold rises, total revenue rises from $10 for one unit to $30 for five units. With each unit increase in quantity sold, however, total revenue does not rise by an equal amount. Instead, it rises in declining amounts—first by $10, then $8, $6, $4, and $2. These amounts are the *marginal revenue* from the sale of each unit (column 4), which the monopolist must compare with the marginal cost of each unit.

At an output level of one yo-yo, marginal revenue equals price, but at every other output level marginal revenue is less than price. Because of the monopolist's downward-sloping demand curve, the second yo-yo cannot be sold unless the price of both units 1 and 2 is reduced from $10 to $9. If we account for the $1 in revenue lost on the first yo-yo in order to sell the second, the net revenue from the second yo-yo is $8 (the selling price of $9 minus the $1 lost on the first yo-yo). For the third yo-yo to be sold, the price on the first two must be reduced by another dollar each. The loss in revenue on them is therefore $2. And the marginal revenue for the third yo-yo is its $8 selling price less the $2 loss on the first two units, or $6.

Figure 23.1. The Monopolist's Demand and Marginal Revenue Curves.
The demand curve facing a monopolist slopes downward, for it is the same as
market demand. The monopolist's marginal revenue curve is constructed from the
information contained in the demand curve (see Table 12.1).

Thus the monopolist's marginal revenue curve (columns 1 and 4) is
derived directly from the market demand curve (columns 1 and 2).
Graphically, the marginal revenue curve lies below the demand curve,
and its distance from the demand curve increases as the price falls (see
Figure 23.1).[3]

Figure 23.2 adds the monopolist's marginal cost curve to the demand
and marginal revenue curves from Figure 23.1. Because the profit-maximizing monopolist will produce to the point where marginal cost equals
marginal revenue, our yo-yo maker will produce Q_2 units. At that quantity,
the marginal cost and marginal revenue curves intersect. If the yo-yo
maker produces fewer than Q_2 yo-yos—say Q_1—profits are lost unnecessarily. The marginal revenue acquired from selling the last yo-yo up to

3. Prove this to yourself by plotting the figures in columns 1 and 2 versus the
   figures in columns 1 and 4, on a sheet of graph paper. (Another simple way of
   drawing the marginal revenue curve is to extend the demand curve until it
   intersects both the vertical and horizontal axes. Then draw the marginal revenue
   curve starting from the demand curve's point of intersection with the vertical
   axis to a point midway between the origin and the intersection of the demand
   curve with the horizontal axis.)

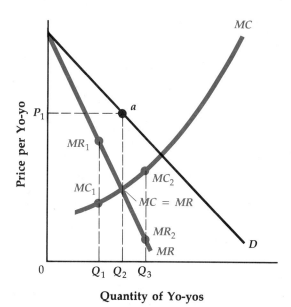

Figure 23.2. Equating Marginal Cost with Marginal Revenue.
The monopolist will move toward production level Q_2, the level at which marginal cost equals marginal revenue. At production levels below Q_2, marginal revenue will exceed marginal cost; the monopolist will miss the chance to increase profits. At production levels greater than Q_2, marginal cost will exceed marginal revenue; the monopolist will lose money on the extra units.

Q_1, MR_1, is greater than the marginal cost of producing it, MC_1. Furthermore, for all units between Q_1 and Q_2, marginal revenue exceeds marginal cost. In other words, by expanding production from Q_1 to Q_2, the monopolist can add more to total revenue than to total cost. Up to an output level of Q_2, the firm's profits will rise.

Why does the monopolist produce no more than Q_2? Because the marginal cost of all additional units beyond Q_2 is greater than the marginal revenue they bring. Beyond Q_2 units, profits will fall. If it produces Q_3 yo-yos, for instance, the firm may still make a profit, but not the greatest profit possible. The marginal cost of the last yo-yo up to Q_3 (MC_2) is greater than the marginal revenue received from its sale (MR_2). By producing Q_3 units, the monopolist adds more to cost than to revenues. The result is lower profits.

Once the monopolistic firm selects the output at which to produce, the market price of the good is determined. In this illustration, the price that can be charged for Q_2 yo-yos is P_1. (Remember, the demand curve indicates the price that can be charged for any quantity.) Of all the possible price-quantity combinations on the demand curve, therefore, the monopolist will choose combination a.

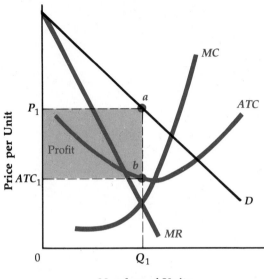

Figure 23.3. The Monopolist's Short-Run Profits.
The profit-maximizing monopoly will produce at the level defined by the intersection of the marginal cost and marginal revenue curves: Q_1. It will charge a price of P_1—as high as market demand will bear—for that quantity. Since the average total cost of producing Q_1 units is ATC_1, the firm's profit is the shaded area ATC_1P_1ab.

Short-Run Profits and Losses

How much profit will a monopolist make by producing where marginal cost equals marginal revenue? The answer can be found by adding the average total cost curve developed in the last chapter to the monopolist's demand and marginal revenue curves (see Figure 23.3). As we have seen, the monopolist will produce where the marginal cost and revenue curves intersect, at Q_1, and will charge what the market will bear for that quantity, P_1. We know also that profit equals total revenue minus total cost (Profit $= TR - TC$). Total revenue is P_1 times Q_1, or the rectangular area bounded by $0P_1aQ_1$. Total cost is the average total cost, ATC_1, times quantity, Q_1, or the rectangular area bounded by $0ATC_1bQ_1$. Subtracting total cost from total revenue, we find that the monopolist's profit is equal to the shaded rectangular area ATC_1P_1ab. (Mathematically, the expression profit $= P_1Q_1 - ATC_1Q_1$ can be converted to the simpler form, profit $= Q_1 (P_1 - ATC_1)$.)

Like perfectly competitive firms, monopolies are not guaranteed a profit. If market demand does not allow them to charge a price that covers the cost of production, they will lose money. Figure 23.4 shows the situation

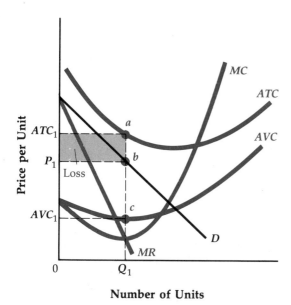

Figure 23.4. The Monopolist's Short-Run Losses.
Not all monopolists make a profit. With a demand curve that lies below its average total cost curve, this monopoly will minimize its short-run losses by continuing to produce where marginal cost equals marginal revenue (Q_1 units). It will charge P_1, a price that covers its fixed costs, and will sustain short-run losses equal to the shaded area P_1ATC_1ab.

of a monopoly that is losing money. Since losses are negative profits, the monopolist's losses are obtained in the same way as profits, by subtracting total cost from total revenue. The maximum price the monopolist can charge for its profit-maximizing (or in this case, loss-minimizing) output level is P_1, which yields total revenues of P_1Q_1 or $0P_1bQ_1$. Total cost is higher: ATC_1Q_1, or $0ATC_1aQ_1$. Thus the monopolist's loss is equal to the shaded rectangular area bounded by P_1ATC_1ab.

Why does the monopolist not shut down? Because it follows the same rule as the perfect competitor. Both will continue to produce so long as price exceeds average variable cost—that is, so long as production will help to defray fixed costs (see page 487). In Figure 23.4, average fixed cost is equal to the difference between average total cost, ATC_1, and average variable cost, AVC_1—or the vertical distance ac. Total fixed cost is therefore ac times Q_1, or the area bounded by AVC_1ATC_1ac. Since the firm will suffer a greater loss if it shuts down (AVC_1ATC_1ac) than if it operates (P_1ATC_1ab), it chooses to operate and minimize its losses.

Of course, in the long run, when the monopolistic firm is able to extricate itself from its fixed cost, it will shut down.

Perspectives in Economics: Taxing Monopoly Profits

Some people claim that the economic profits of monopoly can be taxed with no loss in economic efficiency. By definition, economic profit represents a reward to the resources in a monopolized industry that is greater than necessary to keep those resources employed where they are. It also represents a transfer of income, from consumers to the owners of the monopoly. Therefore a tax extracted solely from the economic profits of monopoly should not affect the distribution of resources, and should fall exclusively on monopoly owners. Or so the argument goes.

Figure 23.5 shows the reasoning behind this position. This monopoly produces Q_{m1}, charges P_{m1}, and makes an economic profit equal to the shaded area $ATC_1P_{m1}ab$. Since marginal cost and marginal revenue are equal at Q_{m1}, the firm is earning its maximum possible profit. Expansion or contraction of production will not increase its profit. Even if the government were to take away 25, 50, or 90 percent of its economic profit, then, the firm would not change its production plans or its price. Nor will it raise prices so as to pass the profits tax on to consumers. The monopolist price-quantity combination, P_{m1} and Q_{m1}, leaves the monopolist with the largest after-tax profit—regardless of the tax rate.

The economic profit shown on the graph is not the same as the firm's book profit, however. Book profit tends to exceed economic profit by the sum of the owners' opportunity cost and risk cost. And for practical reasons, government must impose its tax on book profit, not economic profit. As a result, the tax falls partly on the legitimate costs of doing business, shifting the firm's marginal cost curve upward, from MC_1 to MC_2 in Figure 23.5. The

Production Over the Long Run

In the long run the monopolistic firm follows the same production rule as in the short run: it equates marginal revenue with long-run marginal cost. In Figure 23.6(a), for instance, the firm produces quantity Q_a, and sells it for price P_a. (As always, profits are found by comparing the price with the long-run average cost. As an exercise, shade in the profits areas on the figure.) Unlike the perfect competitor, the monopolist does not attempt to produce at the lowest point on the long-run average cost curve. With no competition, the monopolistic firm has no need to minimize average total cost. By restricting output, it can charge a higher price and earn greater profits than it can by taking advantage of economies of scale.

Monopolists sometimes do produce at the low point of the long-run average cost curve. They do so only when the marginal revenue curve happens to intersect the long-run marginal and average cost curves at the exact same point, however (see Figure 23.6(b)). In this case the monopolist

monopolist, in turn, will reduce the quantity produced from Q_{m1} to Q_{m2}, and raise the price from P_{m1} to P_{m2}. Thus part of the government tax on profits is passed along to consumers as a price increase. Consumers are doubly penalized—first through the monopoly price, which exceeds the competitive price, and second through the surcharge added by the profits tax.

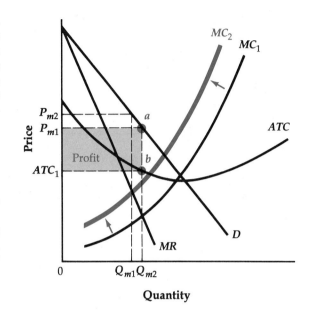

Figure 23.5. Taxing Monopoly Profits. Theoretically, a tax on the economic profit of monopoly will not be passed on to the consumer. But taxes are levied on book profit, not economic profit. As a result, a tax shifts the firm's marginal cost curve up, from MC_1 to MC_2, raising the price to the consumer and lowering the production level.

produces quantity Q_b and sells it at a price of P_b, earning substantial monopoly profits in the process.

If the demand is great enough, the monopolist will actually produce in the range of diseconomies of scale (see Figure 23.6(c)). How can the monopolist continue to exist when its price and costs of production are so high? Because barriers to entry protect it from competition. If barriers did not exist, other firms would certainly enter the market and force the monopolistic firm to lower its price. The net effect of competition would be to induce the monopolist to cut back on production, reducing average production costs in the process.

Monopolists cannot exist without barriers to market entry. If other firms had access to the market, the monopolist's profit would be its own undoing. For profit is what others want and will seek, if they can enter the market.

Figure 23.6. Monopolistic Production over the Long Run.
In the long run, the monopolist will produce at the intersection of the marginal
revenue and long-run marginal cost curves (part (a)). Unlike the perfect competitor,
the monopolist does not bother to minimize long-run average cost by expanding
its scale of operation. It can make more profit by restricting production to Q_a and
charging price P_a. In part (b), the monopolist produces at the low point of the
long-run average cost curve only because that happens to be the point where
marginal cost and marginal revenue curves intersect. And in part (c), the monopolist
produces on a scale beyond the low point of its long-run average cost curve,
because demand is high enough to justify the cost. In each case, the monopolist
charges a price higher than its long-run marginal cost.

Figure 23.7. The Comparative Efficiency of Monopoly and Competition.
Firms in a competitive market will tend to produce at point *b*, the intersection of
marginal cost and demand (marginal benefit). Monopolists will tend to produce
at point *c*, the intersection of marginal cost and marginal revenue, and to charge
the highest price the market will bear—P_m. In a competitive market, therefore, the
price will tend to be lower (P_c) and the quantity produced greater (Q_c) than in a
monopolistic market. The inefficiency of monopoly is shown by the shaded
triangular area *abc*, the amount by which the benefits of producing $Q_c - Q_m$ units
(shown by the demand curve) exceed their marginal cost of production.

The Comparative Inefficiency of Monopoly

The last chapter concluded that in a perfectly competitive market, firms
tend to produce at the intersection of the market supply and demand
curves. That point (*b* in Figure 23.7) is the most efficient production level,
in the sense that the marginal benefit to the consumer of the last unit
produced equals its marginal cost to the producer. All units whose marginal
benefits exceed their marginal costs are produced. All possible net benefits
to the consumer have been extracted from production.

When the supply and demand model is applied to a monopolized
market, the industry supply curve becomes the monopolist's marginal cost
curve (for the monopolist must run the plants that in a competitive industry
would belong to other producers).[4] Similarly, the industry's demand curve

---

4. The industry supply curve is not the monopolist's supply curve, however, for
   a firm's supply is its price-quantity relationship—and a monopolist's price will
   always exceed its marginal cost.

Perspectives in Economics: Monopolies of "Goods" and "Bads"

Because monopolies restrict output, raise prices, and misallocate resources, students and policymakers tend to view them as market failures that should be corrected by antitrust action. If a monopolized product or service represents an economic good—something that gives consumers positive utility—restricted sales will necessarily mean a loss in welfare.

Some products and services, however, may be viewed as "bads" by large portions of the citizenry. Drugs, prostitution, contract murder, and pornography may be goods to their buyers, but they represent negative utility to others in the community. Thus monopolies in the production of such goods may be socially desirable. If a drug monopoly attempts to increase its profits by holding the supply of drugs below competitive levels, the vast majority of citizens may consider themselves better off.

The question is not quite that simple, however. A heroin monopoly may restrict the sale of heroin in a given market. Yet because the demand for heroin is highly inelastic (because of drug addiction), higher prices may only increase buyers' expenditures, raising the number of crimes they must commit to support their habit. Paradoxically, then, reducing heroin sales could lead to more burglaries, muggings, and bank hold-ups.

Of course drugs and other underground services are not normally subject to antitrust action; they are completely illegal. But the analogy may be applied to legal goods and services, such as liquor. Given the negative consequences of drinking, as well as religious prohibitions, many people might consider alcoholic beverages an economic bad. In that case a state-run liquor monopoly could provide a social service. By restricting liquor sales through monopoly pricing, it would reduce drunk driving, thus limiting the external costs associated with drinking. (The same objective—fewer liquor sales and less drunk driving—could also be accomplished through higher taxes.)

becomes the monopolist's demand. But whereas individual competitors must produce at the intersection of supply and demand, the monopolistic firm can choose the price-quantity combination it prefers. By employing fewer resources from production, it can sell a smaller quantity at a higher price. And that is just what happens. In short, the monopolist produces less than the competitive level of production—Q_m instead of Q_c.

For each unit between Q_m and Q_c, the marginal benefits to the consumer, as illustrated by the heavy portion of the market demand curve, are greater than the marginal costs of production. These are net benefits that consumers would like to have, but that are not delivered by the monopolistic firm, which is interested in maximizing profits, not consumer welfare. The resources that are not used for their manufacture must either remain idle or be used in a less valuable line of production. (Remember, the cost of doing anything is the value of the next-best alternative forgone.) In this sense, economists say that resources are misallocated by monopoly. Too few resources are used in the monopolistic industry, and too many elsewhere.

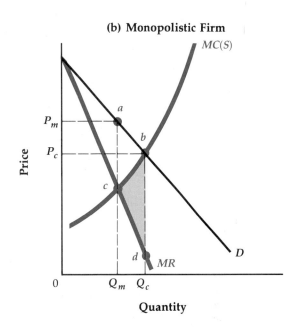

Figure 23.8. The Costs and Benefits of Expanded Production.
If the monopolist expands production from Q_m to Q_c in part (a), consumers will
receive additional benefits equal to the area bounded by $Q_m a b Q_c$. They will pay an
amount equal to the area $Q_m c d Q_c$ for those benefits, leaving a net benefit equal to
the vertically striped area *abcd*. To expand production, the monopoly must incur
additional production costs equal to the area $Q_m c b Q_c$ in part (b). It gains additional
revenues equal to the area $Q_m c d Q_c$, leaving a net loss equal to the shaded area *cbd*.
Thus expanded production helps the consumer but hurts the monopolist.

On balance, then, the inefficiency of monopoly is the benefits lost to
consumers when production is restricted. In Figure 23.7, the gross benefit
to consumers of $Q_c - Q_m$ units is equal to the area under the demand
curve, or $Q_m a b Q_c$. The cost of those additional units is equal to the area
under the marginal cost curve, or $Q_m c b Q_c$. Therefore the net benefit of the
units not produced is equal to the shaded triangular area *abc*. This area
represents the inefficiency of monopoly, sometimes called the dead-weight
welfare loss of monopoly. Or, to put it another way, area *abc* represents
the gain in consumer welfare that could be achieved by dissolving the
monopoly and expanding production from Q_m to Q_c.

A comparison of the net benefits and costs associated with expanding
production from Q_m to Q_c will clarify why consumers prefer Q_c and
producers prefer Q_m. Figure 23.8(a) shows the additional benefits consumers would receive from $Q_c - Q_m$ units, the area under the demand
curve, $Q_m a b Q_c$. The additional money consumers must pay producers for
$Q_c - Q_m$ units, shown by the area under the marginal revenue curve, is
a much smaller amount: only $Q_m c d Q_c$. That is, the additional benefits of

$Q_c - Q_m$ units exceed the cost to consumers by the shaded area *abcd*. Consumers obviously gain from an increase in production.

Yet for virtually the same reason, the monopolistic firm is not interested in providing $Q_c - Q_m$ units. It must incur an additional cost equal to the area Q_mcbQ_c (part (b)), while it can expect to receive only Q_mcdQ_c in additional revenues. The extra cost incurred by expanding production from Q_m to Q_c exceeds the additional revenue acquired by the horizontally striped area *cbd*. Thus an increase in production will reduce the monopolistic firm's profits (or increase its losses). Notice that consumers would gain more from an increase in production than the monopolist would lose. The shaded area in part (a) is larger than the shaded area in part (b). The difference is the triangular area *abc*.

Price Discrimination

A grocery store may advertise that it will sell one can of beans for $0.30, but two cans for $0.55. Is the store trying to give customers a break? Sometimes this kind of pricing may simply mean that the cost of producing additional cans decreases as more are sold. But at other times it may indicate that customers' demand curves for beans are downward sloping, and that the store can make more profits by offering customers a volume discount than by selling beans at a constant price. In other words, the store may be exploiting its limited monopoly power.

Consider Figure 23.9. Suppose the demand curve represents your demand for beans, and the supply curve represents the store's marginal cost of producing and offering the beans for sale. If the store charges the same price for each can of beans, it will have to offer them at $0.25 each to induce you to buy two. Its total revenues will be $0.50. As the graph shows, however, you are actually willing to pay more for the first can—$0.30—than for the second. If the store offers one can for $0.30 and two cans for $0.55, you will still buy two cans, but its revenues from the sale will be $0.55 instead of $0.50.[5] Similarly, to entice you to buy three cans, the store need only offer to sell one for $0.30, two for $0.55, and three for $0.75, and its profits will rise further.[6] The deal does not change the marginal cost of providing each can, which is below the selling price for the first two units and equal to the selling price for the third. The marginal cost of the first can is $0.09; the second, $0.14; and the third, $0.20. The total cost of the three cans to the store is $0.42, regardless of how the cans are priced.

A firm can discriminate in this way only so long as its customers do not resell what they buy for a higher price—and so long as other firms are unable to move into the market and challenge its monopoly power by

---

5. Notice that if the store had tried to sell all its beans at $0.30, you would have bought only one can, and the store would have forgone the opportunity to make a profit on the second can. Why?
6. Notice that if the cans had been priced at $0.25 apiece, you would have purchased only two cans. Can you explain the apparent contradiction?

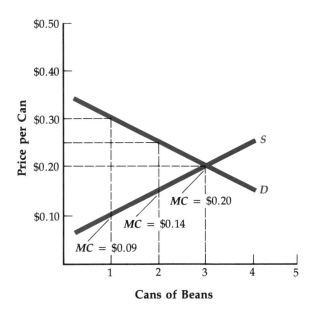

Figure 23.9. Price Discrimination.
By offering customers one can of beans for $0.30, two cans for $0.55, and three cans for $0.75, a grocery store collects more revenues than if it offers three cans for $0.20 each. In either case, the consumer buys three cans. But by making the special offer, the store earns $0.15 more in revenues per customer.

lowering the price. In the case of canned beans, resale is not very practical. The person who buys three cans has little incentive to seek out someone who is willing to pay $0.25 instead of $0.20 for one can. The profit potential—five cents—is just not great enough to bother with. But suppose a car dealer has two identical automobiles carrying a book price of $5,000 each. If the dealer offers one car for $5,000 and two cars for $9,000, many people would be willing to buy both cars and spend the time needed to find a buyer for one of them at $4,500. The $500 gain they stand to make would compensate them for their time and effort in searching out a resale.

Thus advertised price discrimination is much more frequently found in grocery stores than in car dealerships. **Price discrimination** is the practice of varying the price of a given good or service according to how much is bought and who buys it. Car dealers also discriminate with regard to price, however. The salesperson who in casual conversation asks a customer's age, income, place of work, and so forth is actually trying to figure out the customer's demand curve, so as to get as high a price as possible. Similarly, many doctors and lawyers quietly adjust their fees to fit their clients' incomes, using information they obtain from patient questionnaires. But whether price discrimination is unadvertised and based on income, as in the case of doctors and car dealers, or advertised and based on volume sold, as in the case of utilities and long-distance phone

Price discrimination: the practice of varying the price of a given good or service according to how much is bought and who buys it.

companies, the important point is that the products or services involved are typically difficult if not impossible to resell.

Some monopolies' products are not difficult to resell, and so they cannot engage in price discrimination. For example, copyright law gives the publishers of economics textbooks some monopoly power. But textbooks are easily resold, both through a network of used-book dealers and among students. Thus though textbook publishers can alter their sales by changing the price, they rarely engage in price discrimination. Nor do they encourage college bookstores to price-discriminate in their sales to students. The discounts publishers give bookstores on large sales reflect cost differences in handling large and small orders, not students' or professors' downward-sloping demand curves for books. The same can be said about a host of other products protected by patents and copyrights.

The monopolist whose production level was shown in Figure 23.7 could not discriminate among buyers or units bought by each buyer. A monopolist who has such power, however, can produce at a higher output level than Q_m and earn greater profits. Just how much greater depends on how free, or "perfect," the monopolist's power to discriminate is.

Perfect Price Discrimination

Perfect price discrimination: the practice of selling each unit of a given good or service for the maximum possible price.

The monopolist represented in Figure 23.10 can charge a different price for each and every unit sold. Theoretically, this firm has the power of perfect price discrimination. **Perfect price discrimination** is the practice of selling each unit of a given good or service for the maximum possible price. Under perfect price discrimination, the seller's marginal revenue curve is identical to the seller's demand curve. In Figure 23.10, for instance, the firm's marginal revenue curve is not separate and distinct from its demand curve, as in Figure 23.7. Its demand curve *is* its marginal revenue curve. If the first unit can be sold for a price of, say, $20, the marginal revenue from that unit is equal to the price, $20. If the next unit can be sold for $19.95, the marginal revenue from that unit is again the same as the price; and so on.

As in Figure 23.3, the perfectly price-discriminating monopolist equates marginal revenue with marginal cost. But equality occurs this time at point *a*, the intersection of the demand curve (also the marginal revenue curve) with the marginal cost curve (see Figure 23.10). Thus the perfectly price-discriminating monopolist achieves the same output level as does the perfect competitor. In this sense the perfect price discriminator is an efficient producer. As before, profit is found by subtracting total cost from total revenue. Total revenue here is the area under the demand curve up to the monopolist's output level, or the area bounded by $0P_1aQ_c$. Total cost is the area bounded by $0ATC_1bQ_c$ (found, you may recall, by multiplying average total cost times quantity). Profit is therefore the shaded area above the average total cost line and below the demand curve, bounded by ATC_1P_1ab.

Through price discrimination the monopolist increases profits (compare Figure 23.3). Consumers also get more of what they want, although not

Figure 23.10. Perfect Price Discrimination.
The perfect price-discriminating monopolist will produce where marginal cost and marginal revenue are equal (point *a*). Its output level, Q_c, is therefore the same as that achieved under perfect competition. But because the monopolist charges as much as the market will bear for each unit, its profits—the shaded area ATC_1P_1ab—are higher than the competitive firm's.

necessarily at the price they want. Thus in the strict economic sense, perfect price discrimination increases the efficiency of a monopolized industry. Consumers would be still better off if they could pay one constant price, P_c, for the quantity Q_c, as they would under perfect competition. But that is a choice the price-discriminating monopolist does not allow.

Discrimination by Market Segment

Charging a different price for each and every unit sold to each and every buyer is of course improbable, if not impossible. The best most producers can do is to engage in imperfect price discrimination—that is, to charge a few different prices, like the grocery store that sells beans at different rates. **Imperfect price discrimination** is the practice of charging a few different prices for different consumption levels or different market segments (based on location, age, income, or some other identifiable characteristic). The practice is fairly common. Electric power and telephone companies engage in imperfect price discrimination when they charge different rates for different levels of use, measured in watts or minutes. Universities attempt to do the same when they charge more for the first course taken than for any additional course. Both practices are examples

Imperfect price discrimination: the practice of charging a few different prices for different consumption levels or different market segments (based on location, age, income, or some other identifiable characteristic).

Figure 23.11. Imperfect Price Discrimination.
The monopolist that cannot perfectly price-discriminate may elect to charge a few different prices by segmenting its market. To do so, it divides its market by income, location, or some other factor and finds the demand and marginal revenue curves in each (part (a) and (b)). Then it adds those marginal revenue curves horizontally to obtain its combined marginal revenue curve for all market segments, MR_m (part (c)). By equating marginal revenue with marginal cost, it selects its output level, Q_m. Then it divides that quantity between the two market segments by equating the marginal cost of the last unit produced (part (c)) with marginal revenue in each market (parts (a) and (b)). It sells Q_a in market A and Q_b in market B, and charges as much as the market will bear in each segment. Generally, the price will be higher in market segments with a relatively inelastic demand (part (b)).

of discrimination based on consumption level. Drugstores price-discriminate when they give discounts to senior citizens and students, and theaters price-discriminate by charging children less than adults. In those cases, discrimination is based on market segment, namely age group. By treating different market segments as if they had distinctly different demand curves, the firm with monopoly power can charge different prices in each market.

Figure 23.11 shows how discrimination by market segment works. Two submarkets, each with its own demand curve, are represented in parts (a) and (b). Each also has its own marginal revenue curve. To price its product, the firm must first decide on its output level. To do so it adds its two marginal revenue curves horizontally. The combined marginal revenue curve it obtains is shown in part (c) of the figure. The firm must then equate this aggregate marginal revenue curve with its marginal cost of production, which is accomplished at the output level Q_m in part (c).

Finally, the firm must divide the resulting output, Q_m, between markets A and B. The division that maximizes the firm's profits is found by equating the marginal revenue in each market (shown in parts (a) and (b)) with the marginal cost of the last unit produced (part c). That is, the firm equates the marginal cost of producing the last unit of Q_m (part (c)) with the marginal revenue from the last unit sold in each market segment ($MC = MR_a = MR_b$). For maximum profits, then, output Q_m must be divided into Q_a for market A and Q_b for market B.

Why does selling where $MC = MR_a = MR_b$ result in maximum profit? Suppose MR_a were greater than MR_b. Then by selling one more unit in market A and one less unit in market B, the firm could increase its revenues. Thus the profit-maximizing firm can be expected to shift sales to market A from market B until the marginal revenue of the last unit sold in A exactly equals the marginal revenue of the last unit sold in B.

Having established the output level for each market segment, the firm will charge whatever price each segment will bear. In market A, quantity Q_a will bring a price of P_a. In market B, quantity Q_b will bring P_b. (Note that the price-discriminating monopolist charges a higher price in a market with an inelastic demand—market B.) To find total profit, add the revenue collected in each market segment (parts (a) and (b)) and subtract the total variable cost of production (the area under the marginal cost curve in part (c)) and the fixed cost.

The Total Cost of Monopoly

High prices and restricted production are not the only costs of monopoly. The total social cost of monopoly power is actually greater than is shown by the supply and demand model in Figure 23.7. Many firms attempt to achieve the benefits of monopoly power by erecting barriers to entry in their markets. The resources invested in building barriers are diverted from the production of other goods, which could benefit consumers. The total social cost of monopoly should also include the time and effort that the Antitrust Division of the Department of Justice devotes to thwarting such attempts to gain monopoly power, and to breaking it up when it is acquired.

Another, more subtle social cost of monopoly is its redistributional effect. Because of monopoly power, consumers pay higher prices than under perfect competition (P_m instead of P_c in Figure 23.7). The real purchasing power of consumer incomes is thus decreased, while the incomes of monopoly owners go up. To the extent that monopoly increases the price of a good to consumers and the profits to the producer, then, it may redistribute income from lower-income consumers to higher-income entrepreneurs. Many consider this redistributional effect a socially undesirable one.

In addition, when we measure the inefficiency of monopoly by the triangular area *abc* in Figure 23.7, we are assuming that demand for the monopolized product and all other goods is unaffected by the redistribution of income from consumers to monopoly owners. This may be a perfectly reasonable assumption when the monopolist is a maker of vegetable-slicing machines. It is less reasonable for other monopolies, such as the postal, local telephone, and electric power services. Those firms, which are quite large in relation to the entire economy, can shift the demand for a large number of products, causing further misallocation of resources.

Finally, our analysis has assumed that a monopoly will seek to minimize its cost structure, just as perfect competitors do. That may not be a realistic assumption, because the monopolist does not, by definition, face competitive pressure. If a monopoly relaxes it attentiveness to costs, the result can be the inefficient employment of resources.

Summary and Extensions

The consequences of monopoly are higher prices and lower production levels than are possible under perfect competition. Monopoly power can also result in inefficiency in production, for the monopolistic firm does not produce up to the point where its marginal cost equals the consumer's marginal benefit. Consumers might prefer that more resources be used in the production of a monopolized good, and might be willing to pay a price that exceeds the cost of production for additional units of the good. However, the profit-maximizing monopolist stops short of that point.

The next chapter examines the two remaining market structures, monopolistic competition and oligopoly. Much of the analysis in this chapter is applicable to those market structures, for each has a degree of monopoly power. But the power of the monopolistic competitor and the oligopolist is circumscribed by the existence of other firms in the industry, and by the fact that other firms may enter the market.

Major Conclusions

1. Monopoly is the antithesis of competition, the absence of the tendency of market rivals to try to outdo, and avoid being outdone by, others.
2. The primary source of persistent monopoly power is barriers to market entry. When a monopoly restricts output in order to raise its price and profits, however, it encourages other firms to surmount barriers to entry.
3. The monopolistic firm's demand curve is the same as the market demand curve for the good or service it produces.
4. A monopoly's market power is constrained by its cost structure and the market demand for its good.
5. A monopolist's power is never complete; consumers can always choose from substitute goods. Some monopolies—those that arise because of the invention of a new good or service—can actually contribute to consumer welfare.
6. The legal cost of an antitrust action may exceed the social costs of monopoly.
7. The monopolist, like all other profit-maximizing producers, will tend to produce where the marginal cost of the last unit produced equals the marginal revenue gained from its sale.

8. The monopoly's marginal revenue curve is derived from its demand curve. Like the demand curve, it is downward sloping.

9. A monopoly will not necessarily produce at the low point of its long-run average cost curve.

10. The monopolist will tend to charge a higher price and to produce less than firms in a perfectly competitive market.

11. Because it seeks to maximize profits, the monopolistic firm will not produce to the point where the marginal benefit to consumers equals the marginal cost of production. To that extent, monopoly is inefficient.

12. The inefficiency of monopoly stems from a misallocation of resources—too little to the monopolized product and too much to other goods and services.

13. Monopolies can increase their profits through price discrimination, the sale of goods and services at different prices according to how much is bought and who buys them.

14. To price-discriminate, a monopoly must be producing a good or service that cannot be readily resold.

15. A monopoly that can perfectly price-discriminate will produce at the perfectly competitive output level, because its demand curve is the same as its marginal revenue curve.

16. A monopoly can imperfectly price-discriminate according to consumption level or market segment.

17. A monopolist that price-discriminates by segmenting its market will equate the marginal cost of the last unit produced with the marginal revenue in each market segment. It will then charge a higher price in market segments with inelastic demand curves.

Questions to Ponder

1. Many magazines offer multiyear subscriptions at a lower rate than one-year subscriptions. Explain the logic of such a scheme. Why might it be considered evidence of monopoly power on the part of the magazines?

2. Explain why a monopolized industry will tend to produce less than a competitive industry.

3. "If a monopoly retains its market power over the long run, it must be protected by barriers to entry." Explain. List some restrictions on the mobility of resources that might help a firm retain monopoly power.

4. Why, from an economic point of view, should antitrust action not be taken against all monopolies?

5. Given the information on the following page, complete the monopolist's marginal cost and marginal revenue schedules. Graph the demand, marginal cost, and marginal revenue curves, and find the profit-maximizing point of production. Assuming this monopolistic firm faces fixed costs of $10, and must change the same price for all units sold, how much profit does it make?

Quantity Produced and Sold	Price	Total Variable Cost	Marginal Cost	Marginal Revenue
1	$12	$ 5		
2	11	9		
3	10	14		
4	9	20		
5	8	28		
6	7	38		

6. On the graph developed for question 5, identify the output and profits of a monopolist capable of perfect price discrimination.

7. Suppose a monopoly capable of imperfect price discrimination divides its market into two segments, as shown in graphs (a) and (b). In graph (c), draw the monopolist's combined marginal revenue curve. Then, using the monopolist's marginal cost curve, as shown in graph (c), determine the monopolist's profit-maximizing output level. Indicate the quantity and price of the product sold in each market segment.

(a) Market Segment A

(b) Market Segment B

(c) Monopolist

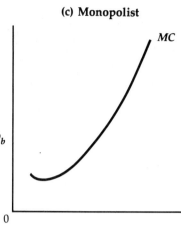

Central Question

In the real world of less than perfectly competitive markets, how are price and output levels determined?

Key Terms

Cartel

Duopoly

Tying contract

Exclusive dealership

Horizontal merger

Vertical merger

Conglomerate

Interlocking directorate

Chapter 24

Imperfect Competition

Difference in tastes, desires, incomes and locations of buyers, and differences in the use which they wish to make of commodities all indicate the need for variety and the necessity of substituting for the concept of a "competitive ideal," an ideal involving both monopoly and competition.

Edward Chamberlin

*W*e have so far considered two distinctly different market structures: perfect competition, characterized by producers that cannot influence price at all because of extreme competition; and pure monopoly, in which there is only one producer of a product with no close substitutes, whose market is protected by prohibitively high barriers to entry. Needless to say, most markets are not well described by either of those theoretical structures. Even in the short run, producers typically compete with several or many other producers of similar, if not identical, products. General Motors Corporation competes with Ford Motor Company, Chrysler Corporation, American Motors Corporation, and a large number of foreign producers. McDonald's Corporation competes with Burger King Corporation, Hardees, and a host of other burger franchises, as well as with Pizza Hut, Inc., Kentucky Fried Chicken, and Long John Silver's. Peoples Drug stores compete directly with other drug chains and locally owned drugstores, and indirectly with department and discount stores that sell the same nondrug products. And in the long run, all these firms must compete with new companies that surmount the imperfect barriers to entry into their markets. In short, most companies compete in the imperfect markets of monopolistic competition and oligopoly.

This chapter will show how the limited competition that exists in imperfect markets can cause producers to be more efficient in their use of resources than under pure monopoly—though less efficient than in perfect competition. One word of caution, however. The study of so-called real-world market structures can be frustrating. Though models may incorporate more or less realistic assumptions about the behavior of real-world firms, the theories developed from them are conjectural. At best, they allow economists to speculate on what may happen under certain conditions. Real-world markets are imperfect and complex phenomena that often do not lend themselves to hard-and-fast conclusions.

Monopolistic Competition

As we saw in Chapter 18, the greater the number and variety of substitutes for a good, the greater the elasticity of demand for that good—that is, the more consumers will respond to a change in price. By definition, a monopolistically competitive market like the fast-food industry produces a number of different products, most of which can substitute for each other. If Burger Bippy raises its prices, then, consumers can move to another restaurant that offers similar food and service. Because of consumer ignorance and loyalty to the Big Bippy, however, Burger Bippy is unlikely to lose all its customers by raising its prices. It has some monopoly power. Therefore it can charge slightly more than the ideal competitive price, determined by the intersection of the marginal cost and demand curves. But Burger Bippy cannot raise its prices too much without substantially reducing its sales.

The degree to which monopolistically competitive prices can stray from the competitive ideal depends on:

the number of other competitors

the ease with which competing firms can expand their businesses to accommodate new customers (the cost of expansion)

the ease with which new firms can enter the market (the cost of entry)

the ability of firms to differentiate their products, in either real or imagined characteristics (the cost of differentiation)

public awareness of price differences (the cost of gaining information on price differences)

Given even limited competition, a monopolist should face a relatively elastic demand curve—certainly more elastic than the oligopolist's.

Monopolistic Competition in the Short Run

In the short run, a monopolistically competitive firm may deviate little from the price-quantity combination produced under perfect competition. The demand curve for fast-food hamburgers in Figure 24.1 is highly, though not perfectly, elastic. Following the same rule as the perfect competitor and the pure monopolist, the monopolistically competitive burger maker produces where $MC = MR$. Since the firm's demand curve slopes downward, its marginal revenue curve slopes downward too, like the pure monopolist's. The firm maximizes profits at Q_{mc} and charges P_{mc}, a price only slightly higher than the price that would be achieved under perfect competition (P_c). (Remember, the perfect competitor faces a horizontal, or perfectly elastic, demand curve, which is also its marginal revenue curve. It produces at the intersection of the marginal cost and marginal revenue curves.) The quantity sold with monopolistic competition is also only slightly below the quantity that would be sold under perfect competition, Q_c. Market inefficiency, indicated by the shaded triangular area, is not excessive.

The firm's short-run profits may be slight or substantial, depending on the demand for its product and the number of producers in the market. In our example, profit is the area bounded by $ATC_1P_{mc}ab$, found by subtracting total cost ($0ATC_1bQ_{mc}$) from total revenues ($0P_{mc}aQ_{mc}$), as with monopolies.

Monopolistic Competition in the Long Run

Because the barriers to entry into monopolistic competition are not excessively costly to surmount, substantial short-run profits will attract other producers into the market. When the market is divided up among more competitors, the individual firm's demand curve will shift downward, reflecting each competitor's smaller market share. As a result, the marginal revenue curve will shift downward as well. The demand curve will also become more elastic, reflecting the greater number of potential substitutes

Figure 24.1. Monopolistic Competition in the Short Run.
Like all profit-maximizing firms, the monopolistic competitor will equate marginal
revenue with marginal cost. It will produce Q_{mc} units and charge price P_{mc}, only
slightly higher than the perfectly competitive price, P_c. (The perfect competitor's
combined demand and marginal revenue curve would be horizontal at price P_c.)
The monopolistic competitor makes a short-run economic profit equal to the area
$ATC_1P_{mc}ab$. The inefficiency of its slightly restricted production level is represented
by the shaded triangular area.

in the market. (These changes are shown in Figure 24.2.)   The results of
the increased competition are:

The quantity produced falls from Q_{mc2} to Q_{mc1}.

The price falls from P_{mc2} to P_{mc1}.

Profits are eliminated when the price no longer exceeds the firm's average
total cost. (As long as economic profit exists, new firms will continue to
enter the market. Eventually the price will fall enough to eliminate economic
profit.)[1]

Notice that the firm is not producing and pricing its product at the
minimum of its average total cost curve, as the perfect competitor would.[2]

1. The monopolistic competitor will still have an incentive to stay in business,
   however. It is economic profit, not book profit, that falls to zero. Book profit
   will still be large enough to cover the opportunity cost of capital plus the risk
   cost of doing business.
2. The perfect competitor produces at the minimum of the average total cost curve
   because its demand curve is horizontal—and therefore the demand curve's
   point of tangency with the average total cost curve is the low point of that
   curve.

Figure 24.2. Monopolistic Competition in the Long Run.
In the long run firms seeking profit will enter the monopolistically competitive market, shifting the monopolistic competitor's demand curve down from D_1 to D_2 and making it more elastic. Equilibrium will be achieved when the firm's demand curve becomes tangent to the downward-sloping portion of the firm's long-run average cost curve. At that point, price (shown by the demand curve) no longer exceeds average total cost; the firm is making zero economic profit. Unlike the perfect competitor, this firm is not producing at the minimum of the long-run average total cost curve. In that sense it is underproducing, by $Q_m - Q_{mc2}$ units.

(Nor did it in the short run.) In this sense the firm is producing below capacity, by $Q_m - Q_{mc2}$ units.

In terms of price and quantity produced, monopolistic competition can never be as efficient as perfect competition. But perfectly competitive firms obtain their results partly because all producers are producing the same product. Consumers can choose from a great many suppliers, but they have no product options. In a monopolistically competitive market, on the other hand, consumers must buy from a limited number of producers, but they can choose from a variety of slightly different products. For example, the pen market offers consumers a choice between felt-tipped, fountain, and ball-point pens of many different styles. This variety in goods comes at a price—the higher price illustrated in Figure 24.2.

Oligopoly

In a market dominated by a few producers, where entry is difficult—that is, in an oligopoly—the demand curve facing an individual competitor will be less elastic than the monopolistic competitor's demand curve (see Figure

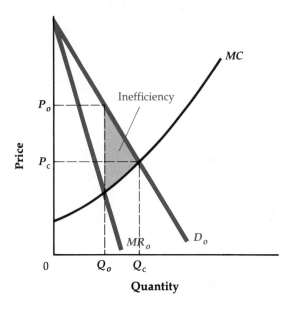

Figure 24.3. The Oligopolist as Monopolist.
With fewer competitors than the monopolistic competitor, the oligopolist faces a
less elastic demand curve, D_o. Each oligopolist can afford to produce significantly
less—Q_o—and to charge significantly more—P_o—than the perfect competitor, who
produces Q_c at a price of P_c. The shaded area representing inefficiency is larger
than that of a monopolistic competitor. (Compare Figure 24.1.)

24.3). If General Electric Company raises its price for light bulbs, consumers
will have few alternative sources of supply. A price increase is less likely
to drive away customers than it would under monopolistic competition,
and the price-quantity combination achieved by the company will probably
be further removed from the competitive ideal. In Figure 24.3, the
oligopolist produces only Q_o units for a relatively high price of P_o, compared
with the perfect competitor's price-quantity combination of $Q_c P_c$. The
shaded area representing inefficiency is fairly large.

Exactly how the oligopolist chooses a price is not completely clear. We
will examine a few of the major theories proposed.

Theories of Price Determination

Because each oligopolist is a major factor in the market, oligopolists'
pricing decisions are interdependent. The price one producer asks significantly affects the others' sales. Hence when one oligopolistic firm lowers
its price, all the others can be expected to lower theirs, to prevent erosion
of their market shares. The oligopolist may have to second-guess other

producers' pricing policies—how they will react to a change in price, and what that might mean for its own policy. In fact, oligopolistic pricing decisions resemble moves in a chess game. The thinking may be so complicated that no one can predict what will happen. Thus, theories of oligopolistic price determination tend to be confined almost exclusively to the short run. (In the long run, virtually anything can happen.)

The Oligopolist as Monopolist

Given the complexity of the pricing problem, the oligopolistic firm may simply decide to behave like a monopolist (since it does have some monopoly power). Like a monopolist, Burger Bippy may simply equate marginal cost with marginal revenue (see Figure 24.3) and produce Q_o units for price P_o. Here the oligopolist's price is significantly above the competitive price level, P_c, but not as high as the price charged by a pure monopolist. (If the oligopolist were a pure monopoly, it would not have to fear a loss of business to other producers because of a change in price.) Inefficiency in this market is slightly greater than in a monopolistically competitive market—see the shaded triangular area of Figure 24.3.

The Oligopolist as Price Leader

Alternatively, oligopolists may look to others for leadership in determining prices. One producer may assume price leadership because it has the lowest costs of production; the others will have to follow its lead or be under-priced and run out of the market. Or the producer that dominates industry sales may assume leadership. Figure 24.4 depicts a situation in which all the firms are relatively small and of equal size, except for one large producer. The small firms' collective marginal cost curve (minus the large producer's) is shown in part (a), along with the market demand curve, D_m. The dominant producer's marginal cost curve, MC_d, is shown in part (b).

The dominant producer can see from part (a) that at a price of P_1, the smaller producers will supply the entire market for steel. At P_1 the quantity demanded, Q_2, is exactly what the smaller producers are willing to offer. At P_1 or above, therefore, the dominant producer will sell nothing. At prices below P_1, however, the total quantity demanded exceeds the total quantity supplied by the smaller producers. For example, at a price of P_d the total quantity demanded in part (a) is Q_3, whereas the total quantity supplied is Q_1. Therefore the dominant producer will conclude that at price P_d, it can sell the difference, $Q_3 - Q_1$. For that matter, at every price below P_1, it can sell the difference between the quantity supplied by the smaller producers and the quantity demanded by the market.

As the price falls below P_1, the gap between supply and demand expands, so that the dominant producer can sell larger and larger quantities. If these quantities are plotted on another graph, they will form the dominant producer's demand curve, D_d (part (b)). Once it has devised its demand curve, the dominant producer can develop its accompanying

Figure 24.4. The Oligopolist as Price Leader.
The dominant producer who acts as a price leader will attempt to undercut the market price established by small producers (part (a)). At price P_1 the small producers will supply the demand of the entire market, Q_2. But at a lower price— P_d or P_c—the market will demand more than the small producers can supply. In part (b), the dominant firm determines its demand curve by plotting the quantities it can sell at each price in part (a). Then it determines its profit-maximizing output level, Q_d, by equating marginal cost with marginal revenue. It charges the highest price the market will bear for that quantity, P_d, forcing the market price down to P_d in part (a). The dominant producer sells $Q_3 - Q_1$ units, and the smaller producers supply the rest.

marginal revenue curve, MR_d, also shown in Figure 24.4(b). Using its marginal cost curve, MC_d, and its marginal revenue curve, it establishes its profit-maximizing output level and price, Q_d and P_d.

The dominant producer knows that it can charge price P_d for quantity Q_d, because that price-quantity combination (and all others on curve D_d) represents a shortage not supplied by small producers at a particular price in part (a). Q_d, as noted earlier, is the difference between the quantity demanded and the quantity supplied at price P_d. So the dominant producer picks its price, P_d, and the smaller producers must follow.[3] If they try to charge a higher price, they will not sell all they want to.

3. Consider market equilibrium with and without the dominant producer. In the absence of the dominant producer, the market price will be P_1, the equilibrium price for a market composed of only the smaller producers. The dominant producer adds quantity Q_d, which causes the price to fall, forcing the smaller producers to cut back production to Q_1 in part (a).

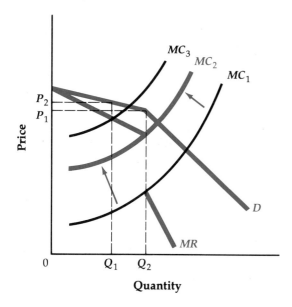

Figure 24.5. The Kinked Demand Curve.
The theory of the kinked demand curve is based on the questionable premise that an oligopolist's prices are relatively rigid, or unresponsive to cost increases. According to the theory, the individual oligopolist reasons that other oligopolists will match a price reduction in order to protect their market shares, but will not match a price increase. The individual oligopolist's demand curve is therefore kinked at the established price: the bottom part is less elastic than the top, where even a small increase in price will cause customers to go elsewhere. Given the kinked demand curve, the firm's marginal revenue curve will be discontinuous. Even if the oligopolist's marginal cost curve shifts upward from MC_1 to MC_2, the firm will not change its price-quantity combination, P_1Q_2.

Price Stability and the "Kinked" Demand Curve

Several decades ago, economists believed they had noticed something quite significant about oligopolies. For relatively long periods of time, prices in these industries seemed to remain more or less fixed. This observed "stickiness" of oligopolistic prices gave rise to the theory of the "kinked" demand curve—a theory that tries to explain not how prices are determined, but why they do not move very much.

Figure 24.5 shows the hypothetical kink in the oligopolist's demand curve that was thought to produce price stickiness. The notion was that the interdependent nature of oligopolistic pricing decisions gave rise to the kink. Suppose the price of steel is P_1. An oligopolistic firm can reason that if it lowers its price, other firms will follow suit to protect their shares of the market. Therefore the demand curve below that point is relatively inelastic. But if the firm raises its prices, it will lose customers to the other

Figure 24.6. The Kinked Demand Curve as Two Separate Curves.
The oligopolist's kinked demand curve can be viewed as the composite of two different demand curves. The portion above the kink comes from the top of a demand curve that is relatively elastic. The portion below the kink comes from the bottom of a demand curve that is fairly inelastic.

firms, which have no reason to follow a price increase. The demand curve above P_1 is therefore relatively elastic.

Because of the kink at P_1 the marginal revenue curve is discontinuous. At an output of Q_1, a gap develops between the upper and lower portions of the curve (see Figure 24.5). The existence of this gap is easier to understand if one thinks of the kinked demand curve as two separate curves intersecting at the kink. The curve's bottom half belongs to demand curve D_1 in Figure 24.6, and its top half to demand curve D_2. Seen that way, the two-part marginal revenue curve in Figure 24.5 is simply the composite of the relevant portions of the marginal revenue curves MR_1 and MR_2 in Figure 24.6.

Given this discontinuous composite marginal revenue curve, the oligopolist will maximize profits at Q_2, where the marginal cost and marginal revenue curves intersect (see Figure 24.5). At that output level, marginal cost can shift all the way up to MC_2 and the oligopolist will still maximize profits. And as long as output remains at Q_2, the price will remain P_1. A price increase would not benefit the firm unless its marginal cost curve rose higher than MC_2—say to MC_3. In that case the firm's profit-maximizing price would be only slightly higher, P_2.

Thus economists thought they had explained the rigidity of oligopolistic prices. The only problem is that further observation has cast doubt on the evidence that motivates the development of the theory. Research conducted over the last three decades suggests that prices in industries dominated by a few firms are no stickier than prices in monopolistically competitive industries. Because there is some disagreement on the interpretation of the data, the theory remains with us. But at best, it is a theory in search of reasonable confirmation.

The Oligopolist in the Long Run

In an oligopolistic market, significant barriers to entry face new competitors. Firms in oligopolistic industries can therefore retain their short-run positions much longer than can monopolistically competitive firms.

Oligopoly is normally associated with the automobile, cigarette, and steel markets, which include some extremely large corporations. There the financial resources required to establish production on a competitive scale may be a formidable barrier to entry. One cannot conclude that all new competition is blocked in an oligopoly, however. Many of the best examples of oligopolies are found in local markets—for instance, drugstores, stereo shops, and lumber stores—in which one, two, or at most a few competitors exist, even though the financial barriers to entry could easily be overcome. Even in the national market, where the financial requirements for entry may be substantial, some large firms have the financial capacity to overcome barriers to entry. If firms in the electric light bulb market exploit their short-run profit opportunities by restricting production and raising prices, outside firms like General Motors Corporation can move into the light bulb market and make a profit. In recent years General Motors has in fact moved into the market for electronics and robotics.

Oligopoly power remains a cause for concern. But the basis for competition is the relative ability of firms to enter a market where profits can be made—not the absolute size of the firms in the industry. The small regional markets of a century ago, isolated by lack of transportation and communication, were perhaps less competitive than today's markets, even if today's firms are larger in an absolute sense. In the nineteenth century the cost of moving into a faraway market may have effectively protected local businesses from the threat of new competition.

Cartels: Monopoly Through Collusion

In either a monopolistically competitive market or an oligopolistic market (or even sometimes in a competitive market), firms may attempt to improve their profits by restricting output and raising their market price. In other words, they may agree to behave as if they were a unified monopoly, an arrangement called a cartel. A **cartel** is an organization of independent producers intent on thwarting competition among themselves through the

Cartel: an organization of independent producers intent on thwarting competition among themselves through the joint regulation of market shares, production levels, and prices, in order to raise prices and profits above competitive levels.

joint regulation of market shares, production levels, and prices. The principal purpose of their anticompetitive efforts is to raise their prices and profits above competitive levels. In fact, however, a cartel is not a single unified monopoly, and cartel members would find it very costly to behave as if they were.

Incentives to Collude and to Chisel

The size of monopoly profits provides a real incentive for competitors to collude—to conspire secretly to fix prices, production levels, and market shares. Once they have reduced market supply and raised the price, however, each has an incentive to chisel on the agreement. The individual competitor will be tempted to cut prices in order to expand sales and profits. After all, if competitors are willing to collude for the purpose of improving their own welfare, they will probably also be willing to chisel on cartel rules to enhance their welfare further. The incentive to chisel can eventually cause the demise of the cartel. If a cartel works for long, it is usually because some form of external cost, such as the threat of violence, is imposed on chiselers.[4]

Though a small cartel is usually a more workable proposition than a large one, even small groups may not be able to maintain an effective cartel. Consider an oligopoly of only two producers, called a duopoly. A **duopoly** is an oligopolistic market shared by only two firms. To keep the analysis simple, we will assume that each duopolist has the same cost structure and demand curve. We will also assume a constant marginal cost, which means that marginal cost and average costs are equal and can be represented by one horizontal curve. Figure 24.7 shows the duopolists' combined marginal cost curve, MC, along with the market demand curve for the good, D.

The two producers can maximize monopoly profits if they restrict the total quantity they produce to Q_m and sell it for price P_m. Dividing the total quantity sold between them, each will sell Q_1 at the monopoly price $(2 \times Q_1 = Q_m)$. Each will receive an economic profit equal to the shaded area bounded by $ATC_1 P_m ab$, which is equal to total revenues $(P_m \times Q_1)$ minus total cost $(ATC_1 \times Q_1)$.

Once in that position, each firm may reason that by reducing the price slightly—say to P_1—and perhaps disguising the price cut through customer rebates or more attractive credit terms, it can capture the entire market and even raise production to Q_2. Each firm may imagine that its own profits can grow from the area bounded by $ATC_1 P_m ab$ to the much larger area bounded by $ATC_1 P_1 cd$. This tempting scenario presumes, of course, that the other firm does not follow suit and lower its price. Each firm must also worry that the other will chisel, cut the price, and steal its market.

Duopoly: an oligopolistic market shared by only two firms.

---

4. Or a cartel may provide members with some private benefit that can be denied nonmembers. For example, local medical associations can deny nonmembers the right to practice in local hospitals. In that case, the cost of chiseling is exclusion from membership in the group.

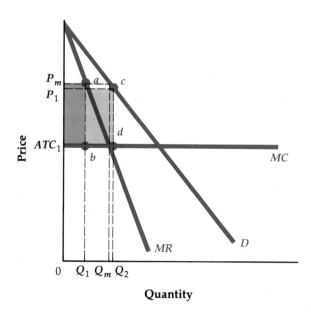

Figure 24.7. A Duopoly (Two-Member Cartel).
In an industry composed of two firms of equal size, firms may collude to restrict total output to Q_m and sell at a price of P_m. Having established that price-quantity combination, however, each has an incentive to chisel on the collusive agreement by lowering the price slightly. For example, if one firm charges P_1, it can take the entire market, increasing its sales from Q_1 to Q_2. If the other firm follows suit to protect its market share, each will get a lower price, and the cartel may collapse.

Thus each duopolist has two incentives to chisel on the cartel. The first is offensive, to garner a larger share of the market and more profits. The second is defensive, to avoid a loss of its market share and profits. Generally, firms that seek higher profits by forming a cartel will also have difficulty holding the cartel together, for much the same reason. As each firm responds to the incentive to chisel, the two undercut each other and the price falls back toward (but not necessarily to) the competitive equilibrium price, at the intersection of the marginal cost and demand curves. Just how far price will decline depends on the firms' ability to impose penalties on each other for chiseling.

The strength and viability of a cartel depend on the number of firms in an industry and the freedom with which other firms can enter. The larger the number of actual or potential competitors, the greater the cost of operating the cartel, of detecting chiselers, and of enforcing the rules. If firms differ in their production capabilities, the task of establishing each firm's share of the market is more difficult. If a cartel member believes it is receiving a smaller market share than it could achieve on its own, it has a greater incentive to chisel. Because of the built-in incentives first to collude and then to chisel, the history of cartels tends to be cyclical. Periods in which output and prices are successfully controlled are followed by periods of chiseling, which lead eventually to the destruction of the cartel.

Government Regulation of Cartels

Government can either encourage or discourage a cartel. Through regulatory agencies that fix prices, determine market shares, and impose penalties for violation of rules, government can keep competitors or cartel members from doing what comes naturally—chiseling. In doing so, government may be providing an important service to industry. Perhaps that is why, in most states, insurance companies oppose deregulation of their rate structures. In seeking or welcoming regulation, an industry may calculate that it is easier to control one regulatory agency than a whole group of firms plus potential competitors.

Thus in 1975, the airline industry opposed President Ford's proposal that Congress curtail the power of the Civil Aeronautics Board to set rates and determine airline routes. As the *Wall Street Journal* reported,

The administration bill quickly drew a sharp blast from the Air Transport Association, which was speaking for the airline industry. The proposed legislation "would tear apart a national transportation system recognized as the finest in the world," the trade group said, urging Congress to reject it because it would cause "a major reduction or elimination of scheduled air service to many communities and would lead inevitably to increased costs to consumers."[5]

The real reason the airlines opposed deregulation became clear in the early 1980s, when several airlines filed for bankruptcy. Partial deregulation, begun in 1979, had increased competition, depressing fares and profits. (Fares began to rise again in 1980, mainly because of rapidly escalating fuel costs.)

Government can suppress competition in many other ways that have nothing to do with price. Prohibiting the sale of hard liquor on Sunday, for example, can benefit liquor dealers, who might otherwise be forced to stay open on Sundays. In Florida, a state representative who managed to get a law through the legislature permitting Sunday liquor sales was denounced by liquor dealers. As one dealer commented, the legislator had "pulled the boner of the year."[6]

Antitrust Legislation

As we have seen, monopoly power leads to market inefficiencies, or a misallocation of resources. Reductions in monopoly power should therefore improve consumer welfare. Thus the U.S. government's antitrust policy

---

5. "Less Regulation of Airline Sector is Urged by Ford," *Wall Street Journal*, October 9, 1975, p. 3.
6. *St. Petersburg Times*, June 7, 1975, p. 1-B.

is designed, ostensibly, to improve market efficiency by reducing barriers to entry, breaking up monopolies, and reducing the monetary benefits of conspiring to restrict production or raise prices. It is based on three major laws, which have been amended and modified by court decisions: the Sherman, Clayton, and Federal Trade Commission acts.

The Sherman Act

The Sherman Act was passed in 1890, after a series of major corporate mergers. It contains two critical provisions. The first, Section 1, declares illegal "every contract, combination in the form of trust or otherwise, or conspiracy, in restraint of trade or commerce among several states or with foreign nations." The second, Section 2, declares that "every person who shall monopolize, or conspire with any other person or persons to monopolize any part of trade or commerce among the several states, or with foreign nations, shall be guilty of a misdemeanor. . . ." In short, the first section outlaws any form of monopoly; the second outlaws any attempt to acquire monopoly power.

The language seems clear enough, yet the courts were initially reluctant to rule against violations of the law, citing prosecutors' loose interpretation of the words "restraint of trade" and "conspire . . . to monopolize." But in 1911, the Supreme Court ruled that Standard Oil Company, which then controlled 90 percent of the nation's refinery capacity, should be broken up. By dividing the firm along geographical lines (which explains the names Standard Oil of Ohio and Standard Oil of California), the court effectively nullified the economic benefits of the breakup, however. In place of one large monopoly, the justices created smaller monopolies. Later, the court broke up the United States Steel Corporation and American Can Company on the grounds that they had followed "unfair and unethical" business practices.

The Clayton Act

Because the Sherman Act did not specify what constituted unfair and unethical business practice, and because the courts generally took a very narrow view of what constituted restraint of trade and commerce, Congress passed a new law in 1914. The Clayton Act listed four illegal practices in restraint of competition. It outlawed price discrimination, or the use of price differences not justified by cost differentials to lessen competition or create a monopoly. This provision was intended to prevent firms from cutting prices below cost in a particular geographical region in order to drive competitors out of the market. Railroads and department stores were allegedly involved in such "predatory competition."

The Clayton Act also forbade tying contracts and exclusive dealerships. A **tying contract** is an agreement between seller and buyer that requires the buyer of one good or service to purchase some other product or service.

Tying contract: an agreement between seller and buyer that requires the buyer of one good or service to purchase some other product or service.

Perspectives in Economics: Is OPEC an Effective Cartel?

The Organization of Petroleum Exporting Countries (OPEC), composed of thirteen countries,[1] most located in the Middle East, is widely believed to be a powerful and effective cartel. Since the 1970s, when OPEC agreed to reduce its oil exports, the price of crude oil has skyrocketed.

Yet can the dramatic rise in oil prices be fully attributed to OPEC agreements? Economists differ in their answers. Many are convinced that OPEC effectively controlled world oil prices until the early 1980s, by which time people had reduced their energy consumption and alternative energy sources had been found. Others, who doubt that a collection of rival countries could work effectively as a cartel, suggest that the price of oil would have risen rapidly during the 1970s even without OPEC.

Economists who take the latter view make three points. First, they question the baseline price to be used for comparison. During the 1950s and 1960s, they point out, private oil companies working in the OPEC countries realized that oil production would probably be nationalized in the late 1960s and early 1970s. Their incentive was thus to pump out all the oil they could, before nationalization made it the property of the host countries. In other words, before nationalization an oversupply of oil had artificially depressed the market price. The price increases that began in 1973 were the result of rational cutbacks in the market supply by countries that had an incentive to conserve their own reserves.

Second, a growing public fear that the world

Exclusive dealership: an agreement between a manufacturer and its dealers that forbids the dealers from handling other manufacturers' products.

Horizontal merger: the joining of two or more firms in the same market into a single firm.

Vertical merger: the joining of two or more firms that perform different stages of the production process into a single firm.

Conglomerate: a firm that results from the merging of several firms from different industries.

If IBM tried to force buyers of home computers to purchase only IBM software, for example, its purchase and sale agreement with customers might be considered a tying contract. An **exclusive dealership** is an agreement between a manufacturer and its dealers that forbids the dealers from handling other manufacturers' products. The Clayton Act is applicable only to exclusive dealerships that reduce competition "substantially," however. So long as other manufacturers' products are sold in the same area, manufacturers may organize exclusive dealerships covering designated territories, as is common in the automobile industry.

Section 7 of the Clayton Act forbids mergers, or the acquisition by a firm of its competitors' stock, if the effect of the merger is to reduce competition. The act applies only to horizontal mergers, however.

A **horizontal merger** is the joining of two or more firms in the same market—for example, two car companies—into a single firm. Vertical mergers were excluded from the act. A **vertical merger** is the joining of two or more firms that perform different stages of the production process into a single firm. For example, the merging of an oil drilling firm with a refining firm would be permitted by the Clayton Act. So would conglomerate mergers. A **conglomerate** is a firm that results from the merging of several firms from different industries. The combining of firms in two entirely different markets—washing machines and light bulbs, for instance—would be considered a conglomerate merger. These loopholes in the Clayton Act—vertical and conglomerate mergers—were closed in part by the Celler-Kefauver Antimerger Amendment, passed in 1952. But while would soon run out of oil encouraged owners of oil reserves to cut back on production. After all, if oil is running out, prices and profits should rise in the future. In other words, the opportunity cost of selling oil had risen, reducing current production.

Third, in the early 1970s Saudi Arabia, an important producer of oil, realized its market position and cut production so as to raise prices and profits. In terms of Figure 24.4, all oil producers taken together were producing a total output of Q_c in panel (a). Smaller producers were supplying Q_o, and Saudi Arabia was supplying $Q_c - Q_o$. When the Saudis cut production from Q_1 to Q_d in panel (b), they forced the market price up from P_c to P_d. From this perspective, the oil price hike was not the product of an effective working cartel, but the result of one or more dominant producers doing what comes naturally: exploiting their market power.

Still other economists contend that the U.S. government enhanced the market power of foreign oil producers by imposing price controls on energy in the United States. By restricting price increases for domestic oil, the federal government reduced the domestic supply, increasing the demand for foreign oil and the ability of foreign producers to charge a higher price.

1. Saudi Arabia, Algeria, United Arab Emirates, Ecuador, Gabon, Indonesia, Iran, Iraq, Qatar, Venezuela, Kuwait, Libya, and Nigeria.

---

the act has since been applied to vertical mergers, it has never been applied to conglomerates.

Finally, the Clayton Act declared interlocking directorates illegal. An **interlocking directorate** is the practice of having the same people serve as directors of two or more competing firms. If the same people direct competing firms and advise policies that effectively reduce industry output, they constitute a kind of de facto monopoly. Section 8 of the Clayton Act prohibits such arrangements if they "substantially reduced" competition.

Interlocking directorate: the practice of having the same people serve as directors of two or more competing firms.

The Federal Trade Commission Act

The original purpose of the Federal Trade Commission Act, passed in 1914, was to thwart "unfair methods of competition" among firms. The act empowered the Federal Trade Commission to investigate cases of industrial espionage, bribery for the purpose of obtaining trade secrets or gaining business, and boycotts.[7] Later the Wheeler-Lea Amendment expanded the commission's mandate to cover "unfair or deceptive acts or practices" that harmed customers, including the sale of shoddy merchandise and misleading or deceptive advertising.

---

7. Not all boycotts are prohibited, of course—only efforts designed to prevent goods from reaching their intended designation. That is, a union cannot prevent goods from crossing its picket lines, and firms cannot organize restrictions on the purchase of other firms' products.

Perspectives in Economics: Price Fixing—A Real-World Case

During the 1950s, General Electric Company, Westinghouse Electric Corporation, Allis-Chalmers, Southern States Equipment, and other firms and their executives were accused of conspiring to set prices and divide the market for electrical equipment.[1] Their conspiracy, which covered everything from two-dollar insulators to turbine generators, illustrates the incentives for competitors first to collude and then to chisel on their collusive agreement. As a result of a court case brought against them, which ended in 1961, fines of nearly $2 million were levied against the conspirators and the companies they represented. Six corporate executives were sent to prison, and twenty-four others were fined or given suspended sentences. It was the largest case brought to trial in the history of antitrust law, a classic example of the benefits and pitfalls of industrial conspiracy.

The seeds of the conspiracy were planted during the Second World War, when the prices of various types of electrical equipment were regulated by the Office of Price Administration (OPA). Under the auspices of the National Electrical Manufacturers Association, firms met on a regular basis to determine how they could supply the heavy wartime demand for electrical equipment. After their meetings, executives would regroup to talk about how they could get the OPA to raise prices.[2]

When the war was over and prices were no longer controlled, these manufacturers faced competition from a growing number of smaller companies. Increasingly, buyers were asking for sealed bids as a means of getting the lowest possible prices. The major manufacturers continued their meetings, this time to talk about price fixing and methods of dividing the market. They decided to agree on their bids ahead of time and to rotate the privilege of making the lowest bid. After learning what the lowest bid would be, the others would make higher bids. The business was divided on the basis of past sales volume. In the circuit-breaker market, for example, General Electric received 45 percent of the business, Westinghouse 35 percent, Allis-Chalmers 10 percent, and Federal Pacific 10 percent.[3]

The conspirators used code names and numbers, and kept in touch with one another by memoranda and telephone. They held working meetings every

The Purposes and Consequences of Antitrust Laws

The ostensible purpose of all these laws is to fight monopoly power by outlawing business practices that prevent or retard competition. By forcing firms to restrict production or fix prices surreptitiously, antitrust legislation makes collusion among competitors more costly. Violations of the law carry fines and penalties on conspiring firms and their employees.

Though many economists believe antitrust law has achieved some of these objectives, critics complain of its inefficiency. Detecting violators and bringing legal action against them takes time. Often market forces erode monopoly power before the government can prosecute. The result can be a huge waste of legal resources. As noted in the last chapter, the Department of Justice spent over twelve years prosecuting IBM for its dominance in the mainframe computer market, with questionable results.

In attempting to determine which firms possess monopoly power, the ten days to two weeks, to review the business each had gotten in recent weeks and decide on future bids. Executives were careful to keep their place of meeting secret. At times they held their conferences on the golf course.

Though the conspiracy had its benefits, the firms were no more reluctant to break their own rules than they were to violate the Sherman Act.

"Everyone accused the others of not living up to the agreement," Clarence Burke [general manager of the High Voltage Switchgear Department at General Electric] recalled, "and the ones they complained about tried to shift the blame onto someone else." The most constant source of irritation occurred in the sealed-bid business, where chiseling was difficult to detect. But breaks in book price to the utilities in the open-bid business also generated ill will and vituperation. Indeed, one of the many ironies of the whole affair is that the conspiracy couldn't entirely suppress the competitive instinct. Every so often some company would decide that cutthroat competition outside was preferable to the throat-cutting that went on in the cartel; they would break contact and sit out the conspiracy for a couple of years.[4]

In 1953, the cartel began to show signs of wear. Westinghouse, under pressure to increase its busi-

ness, cheated on a turbine deal in 1954. Soon others began to cheat, and price cuts came rapidly. By 1954–1955, prices quoted to switch-gear buyers had dropped to as much as 40 percent below book price. When prices fell as low as 60 percent below book in 1957–1958, the cartel collapsed temporarily. It resumed in the circuit-breaker market in 1959, but only after General Electric, Westinghouse, and Allis-Chalmers had conceded part of their market shares to Federal Pacific I-T-E. The Department of Justice broke the case when the Tennessee Valley Authority reported that it had been receiving identical bids from several firms.

1. For a more detailed account of this case, see Richard Austin Smith, "The Incredible Electrical Conspiracy," parts I and II, *Fortune,* April and May 1961, pp. 132 ff. (April) and pp. 161 ff. (May).
2. Ibid., April, p. 137.
3. Ibid., April, p. 136.
4. Ibid., April, p. 171. Clarence Burke said in 1953, "No one was living up to the agreement and we at G.E. were being made suckers. On every job someone would cut our throat." Ibid., p. 172.

Department of Justice and the Federal Trade Commission have relied on "concentration ratios," or estimates of the percentage of industry sales controlled by the largest domestic firms. But used arbitrarily, such ratios can be misleading. The top four firms in steel may have little monopoly power, for they must compete with producers of fiber glass, aluminum, and wood as well as each other. Nevertheless, to avoid the appearance of impropriety, firms may decide to operate on a smaller scale than competitive principles would normally dictate.

Finally, as amended, the Clayton Act gives private firms the power to initiate antitrust suits. If an antitrust violation is proven, prosecuting firms receive a reward equal to three times the computed damages. Critics charge that firms may use antitrust suits as a means of diverting their competitors' resources away from production. The mere threat of an antitrust suit may be enough to keep some large firms from competing actively through better product design and lower prices.

Summary and Extensions

Though the analysis of imperfect competition tells us something about the working of real-world markets, it does not answer all the questions economists have asked. The theories presented here have not done a good job of predicting the consequences of imperfect competition. Thus our conclusions regarding the pricing and production behavior of firms in monopolistically competitive and oligopolistic markets are tentative at best.

Economists interested in making firm, empirically verifiable predictions about market behavior rely almost exclusively on supply-and-demand and monopoly models. Though predictions based on those models may sometimes be wrong, they tend to be easier to use and may be more reliable than predictions based on models of imperfect competition.

Major Conclusions

1. Both monopolistically competitive and oligopolistic producers produce where marginal cost equals marginal revenue.
2. Monopolistically competitive firms tend to sell at a higher price, and to produce a lower quantity, than perfectly competitive firms.
3. The monopolistically competitive firm may make some short-run profits, but in the long run other competitors will enter the market and drive prices down, eroding the firm's profits.
4. In the long run, the monopolistically competitive firm will produce at a point on the downward-sloping portion of its average total cost curve.
5. Because of the complexity of oligopoly, economists are not certain how prices are established in that kind of market. Some oligopolists may determine prices as monopolists do. Others may act as price leaders in their markets.
6. The kinked demand curve is a graphic device for explaining the presumed stability of prices in oligopolistic industries. It is based on the argument that to protect their market shares, oligopolistic firms will match a price reduction but not a price increase. As a result the oligopolist's marginal revenue curve is discontinuous. An increase in marginal cost will not necessarily bring an increase in price.
7. Competing producers that collude to restrict output and raise prices have an incentive to chisel on any agreement they reach. Once the cartel has agreed on a price, members will be tempted to undersell each other to capture a larger share of the market. Thus cheating and the inability to prevent other producers from entering the market tend

to make cartels unstable. By restricting output and generating monopoly profits, cartels sow the seeds of their own destruction.

8. Generally speaking, the more competitors are involved in a cartel, the greater incentive each competitor has to chisel on the cartel agreement. The greater the cost the cartel must incur to thwart chiseling, the more likely it is to collapse.

9. Federal actions to thwart monopoly power and promote competition are founded on three principal laws. The Sherman Act outlaws any form of monopoly or any attempt to monopolize a market. The Clayton Act forbids certain forms of price discrimination, tying contracts and exclusive dealerships, horizontal mergers, and interlocking directorates. And the Federal Trade Commission Act empowers the Federal Trade Commission to investigate "unfair methods of competition." The ostensible concern of these laws is to prevent business practices that materially reduce competition. Antitrust laws have been employed to reduce competition, however.

10. Because government action against monopoly power is costly, not every instance of monopoly power warrants government action. The benefits of antitrust suits must exceed their costs.

Questions to Ponder

1. Under what circumstances could a monopolistic competitor earn an economic profit in the long run?
2. How is a monopolistic competitor like a monopolist? Like a competitor?
3. To achieve the efficiency of perfect competition, must a market consist of numerous producers? If not, what other conditions are required?
4. How does the number of producers in a market affect the chances of forming a workable cartel?
5. How do the costs of entering a market affect the chances of forming a workable cartel?
6. Are all oligopolies composed of very large firms like General Motors Corporation? Can you identify some likely oligopolists in your home town?
7. "The larger the number of colluders in a cartel, the greater the temptation for individual members to chisel on the cartel." Explain with the aid of a graph.
8. "In an economy in which resources can move among industries with relative ease, a cartel attempting to maximize short-term profits will sow the seeds of its own destruction." Explain.

Central Question

Why does government regulate business, and what are the economic consequences of government regulation?

Chapter 25

Business Regulation

The state—the machinery and power of the state—is a potential resource or threat to every industry in the society. With its power to prohibit or compel, to take or give money, the state can and does selectively help or hurt a vast number of industries.

George Stigler

*N*ame an industry that has not, in some way, been under the authority of a government regulatory agency at some time. At the start of the century such a task would have been relatively simple. Today, with government extending its activities in all directions, it is not. The list of federal regulatory agencies virtually spans the alphabet—ABC, FAA, FDA, FEA, FPC, FRS, FTC, ICC, NTHSA, OSHA, SEC—to say nothing of the various state utilities commissions, licensing boards, health departments, and consumer protection agencies. As a result, it is much easier to list regulated industries than to name an unregulated one. Air transport, telephone service, trucking, natural gas, electricity, stockbrokerage, health care, taxi service, massage parlors, pharmacies, postal services, television and radio broadcasting, toy manufacture, beauty shops, ocean transport, legal advice, slaughtering, medicine, embalming and funeral services, optometry, oyster fishing, banking, insurance—all are regulated. Regulation has become one of our nation's fastest-growing industries.

Beyond setting minimum and maximum prices, government regulations often control the entire rate structure of an industry. They may limit entry into the industry and stipulate what services and goods will be provided at what levels, to whom. In short, regulation can pervade all dimensions of production and distribution.

Explaining regulation—why and how it happens—is a major challenge to economists. Though several insightful theories have been proposed, statistical tests of those theories are incomplete and are at times based on crude data. Some instances of regulation or changes in regulatory policy cannot be explained by current theories. At best, we can only review what is known about regulation and project the economic results.

Today regulatory agencies are increasingly criticized by economists, business people, consumers, and consumer advocates. The major concern is the extent to which regulation is designed to benefit the regulated industry. Some critics want more regulation, others less, depending largely on how they view the process of regulation. Thus to understand the controversy surrounding regulatory policy, we must first understand the theory. This chapter begins with a brief description of several major federal regulatory agencies and then proceeds to the various theories.

Major Federal Regulatory Agencies

Federal regulatory agencies have existed for about a century. From their origins and functions we can learn much about the regulatory process.

The Interstate Commerce Commission (ICC)

The Interstate Commerce Commission (ICC) was established in 1887 to deal with unfair business practices in the railroad industry. By the latter half of the nineteenth century, railroad companies had overbuilt and were engaging in cutthroat competition through customer rebates and price discrimination. In self-defense several companies had formed a cartel to divide the market and set prices. The ICC was established to protect both consumers and small competitors, and was supported by both the railroads and their customers.

Since then the ICC's regulatory authority has been expanded to cover all motor carriers except airplanes engaged in interstate commerce—mainly trucks and boats. In the past, the commission has been authorized to set minimum and maximum rates. It is also responsible for ensuring adequate service. The seven members of the commission are nominated by the president and approved by the Senate for a term of seven years. No more than a simple majority of the commissioners may belong to the same political party, and a commissioner may be removed for "just cause," including conflict of interest. Nevertheless, regulation has tended to benefit those who are regulated, at the expense of consumers.

For decades now economists have advocated reducing the ICC's power. President John F. Kennedy made an unsuccessful attempt to do so during his administration. During the 1970s, the ICC came under attack by consumer advocates as well, for favoring transportation firms over consumers. Ralph Nader went so far as to recommend that the ICC in its present form be abolished.[1] Both Presidents Gerald Ford and Jimmy Carter asked Congress for sharp reductions in the ICC's jurisdiction over rates, routes, and entry into the market. Finally, in 1978, the trucking industry was partially deregulated. Though the ICC no longer sets truck rates and routes, it still controls market entry through its authority to issue licenses.

The Federal Trade Commission (FTC)

The five-member Federal Trade Commission (FTC) was established by Congress in 1914 to investigate tendencies toward greater industrial concentration and to advise the president and Congress on antitrust law. Commissioners are appointed and serve seven-year terms. To carry out their duties, they are given the power to probe through corporate records and summon corporate executives to hearings on antitrust practices. They can also issue formal complaints and order a company to cease its illegal acts. For example, state bar associations once restricted lawyers from advertising their services. The FTC ordered a halt to such restrictions on the grounds that they thwarted competition.

The Reagan administration has tried to reduce the regulatory power of the FTC by cutting its budget—a ploy resisted by Congress. In the early 1980s, however, FTC decisions began to reflect the free market views of its new chairman, James Miller, a Reagan appointee. (See the box on changes in antitrust policy at the FTC, page 566.)

1. Ralph Nader Study Group Report on the Interstate Commerce Commission and Transportation (Robert C. Fellmeth, project director), *The Interstate Commerce Commission* (New York: Grossman, 1970), p. 324.

The Federal Communications Commission (FCC)

The Federal Communications Commission (FCC), established by the Communication Act of 1934, regulates telephone, telegraph, and broadcasting companies. Its seven commissioners, who are appointed for seven-year terms, set rates for interstate telephone and telegraph services and issue licenses to radio and television stations. The FCC determines who can engage in broadcasting and it prescribes the nature of broadcast services, the location of radio and television stations, and the areas they serve. Licenses are issued for three years, after which the station's programming is reviewed for license renewal. To ensure renewal, a station must engage in some public-service broadcasting.

To the extent that some available frequencies have not been put into use for radio and television transmission, the FCC has restricted entry into the broadcast business. It has also held up the introduction of cable service, which would vastly increase television programming variety. Yet in other ways the agency has sought to increase competition. At one time the American Telephone and Telegraph Company (AT&T) had a virtual monopoly over the sale of telephones. Beginning in the late 1960s, however, the FCC moved to introduce competition into the sale of telephone equipment and the delivery of long-distance service. In 1984, AT&T was broken up into twenty-two companies. (See the box on the AT&T break-up, page 562–563 for a more detailed account.)

The Federal Power Commission (FPC)

The Federal Power Act of 1930 established the Federal Power Commission (FPC), whose authority was limited at first to the regulation of water power. In 1935, however, the FPC was authorized to regulate the rates, service, corporate practices, and security issues of interstate electric utilities. And beginning in 1938, it was empowered to fix rates for interstate natural gas service. The commission's five members serve five-year terms.

In the late 1960s and early 1970s, the FPC came under attack for its tight controls on the price of natural gas. In 1975, 1976, and 1977, several states experienced serious shortages of natural gas when the FPC-restricted price—only one-quarter of the going price in producer states like Texas—severely discouraged out-of-state sales. Natural gas was partially deregulated in early 1983, but was recontrolled in 1984 for two more years.

The Securities and Exchange Commission (SEC)

In response to many instances of stock fraud, as well as the plunge in stock prices during the Great Depression, Congress established the Securities and Exchange Commission (SEC) in 1934. The SEC licenses stock exchanges and polices their activities. It has, but no longer exercises, the authority to regulate fees charged by brokers for carrying out their customers' transactions. (In 1975, when the SEC decided to allow com-

petitive determination of stockbrokers' fees, those fees fell almost immediately by about 30 percent.) The SEC also supervises the issuance of new
securities by corporations and disclosure of information relating to those
issuances. The commission has five members, who are appointed by the
president for terms of five years.

The Food and Drug Administration (FDA)

Foods and drugs have been regulated to some degree since the turn of
the century. Not until 1931, however, was the Food and Drug Administration (FDA) established, as part of the Department of Health, Education,
and Welfare (now called the Department of Health and Human Services).
The FDA is responsible for ensuring the purity, safety, effectiveness, and
accurate labeling of certain foods and drugs. No drug can be sold on the
market before it has been judged safe and effective by the FDA. The
agency is also responsible for enforcing a wide variety of consumer
protection laws pertaining to the labeling, packaging, and advertising of
foods and drugs.

The Occupational Safety and Health Administration (OSHA)

Probably no government regulatory agency is currently more controversial
than the Occupational Safety and Health Administration (OSHA). Organized
in 1969, in response to numerous reports that worker safety and health
was not adequately protected, OSHA has formulated thousands of health
and safety standards. To meet its requirements businesses have had to
spend tens of billions of dollars. Those who believe government has an
important role in protecting workers have praised OSHA, suggesting that
if anything, the agency should conduct more inspections and impose
higher fines to induce businesses to meet established standards. But
businesses have condemned OSHA's expensive standards as ineffective
and wasteful.

The Public Interest Theory of Regulation

Regulation has often been justified on the grounds that it is in the public
interest, meaning that it helps to achieve commonly acknowledged national
goals. Some of the goals that may be pursued through regulation include:

a more democratic allocation of the nation's resources (and a reduction in
the importance of profit in such decisions);

an increase in market efficiency;

enhancement of the nation's ability to pursue certain essentially political
objectives—improvement of the national defense, redistribution of the
costs of economic decisions, and provision of certain public goods, such
as public safety.

Economists' theories of regulation tend to be based on the goal of increasing market efficiency. One of the sources of market inefficiency they cite most frequently is externalities, or third-party effects of market transactions.

Regulation to Capture Externalities

The market problems externalities can cause were discussed in Chapter 4. Regulation is often imposed to ensure public safety, an economic good that is sometimes, but not always, an externality. Product features that ensure the safety of the purchaser—for instance, shock-absorbing steering columns—can be handled with reasonable efficiency by the market. But safety devices that benefit other persons may not be provided by a market system.

For example, shock-absorbing bumpers benefit not only the person who buys a car but those who may be involved in a collision with the buyer. A driver who collides with a car protected by shock-absorbing bumpers may sustain less damage than she would have otherwise, without having paid for the protection received. She free-rides on the other driver's purchase. Because of the externality, the quantity of shock-absorbing bumpers purchased in an unregulated market will fall short of the economic optimum. Hence the need for regulation of safety equipment like shock-absorbing bumpers—as well as headlights, brakes, windshield wipers, and so on.

Regulation sometimes benefits all producers, particularly when it enhances their reputation for safety. If people believe that a given product is safe, unscrupulous competitors may take advantage of the public's faith by reducing the safety of their products and cutting their production costs. Bad experiences with a product can make consumers skeptical of all firms, thereby reducing the price they are willing to pay for goods that may not prove to be safe. Thus by restoring consumer confidence, consumer protection laws can actually benefit the food and drug industries and toy manufacturers. And to the extent that the SEC contributes to the securities industry's reputation for honesty, regulators can be seen as producers of public goods.

Regulation to Curb Monopoly

Monopoly is frequently cited as a source of market inefficiency. The first regulatory agencies were organized to deal with abuses of monopoly power. If ownership of an industry is concentrated in a few large corporations, they can form a cartel and behave as if they were a monopoly, dividing the market, restricting output, and raising prices. During the 1970s and 1980s, the fear of such monopoly power motivated proposals to regulate the oil and automobile industries, among others.

Figure 25.1 shows a cartelized industry producing at an output level of Q_m and selling at a price of P_m. That output level is inefficient in two

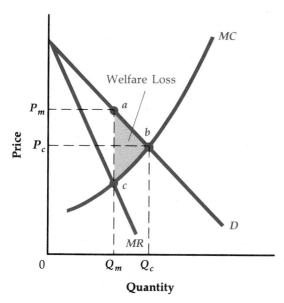

Figure 25.1. The Effect of Regulation on a Cartelized Industry.
The profit-maximizing cartel will produce only Q_m units and sell at a price of P_m. In the sense that consumers want Q_c units and are willing to pay more than the marginal cost of production for them, Q_m is an inefficient production level. Regulation can raise output and lower the price, ideally to Q_cP_c.

respects. First, it is less than the maximum, Q_c. Second, the marginal benefit of the last unit produced (equal to its price) is greater than its marginal cost. Though consumers are willing to pay more than the cost of producing additional units, they are not given the chance to buy those units. The cartel's price-quantity combination not only creates economic profit for the owners, which may be considered inequitable or unjust, but results in the loss of net benefits, or "deadweight welfare loss," equal to the shaded triangular area *abc*.

Regulation of this industry can force firms to sell at lower prices and to produce and sell larger quantities. Ideally, firms can be made to produce Q_c units and to sell them at price P_c, which is the same price-quantity combination that could be achieved under highly competitive conditions. At that output level, the marginal benefit of the last unit produced is equal to its marginal cost.

Government regulators need not demand that a company produce Q_c units. All they have to do is require it to charge no more than P_c. Once that order has been given, the portion of the demand curve above P_c, along with the accompanying segment of the marginal revenue curve, becomes irrelevant. The firm simply is not allowed to choose a price-quantity combination above point b on the demand curve. Then the profit-maximizing producer will choose to sell at P_c, the maximum legal price. With marginal revenue guaranteed at P_c, the firm will equate marginal revenue with marginal cost and produce at Q_c, the efficient output level.

Ideal results cannot be expected from the regulatory process, however. The cost of determining the ideal price-quantity combination can be extraordinarily high, if not prohibitive. Since regulators do not work for regulated industries, they will not know the details of a company's marginal cost calculations. The problem is particularly acute for regulators of monopolies, since there are no competitors from which alternative cost estimates can be obtained. Furthermore, if prices are adjusted upward to allow for a company's computed costs, a regulated firm may lose its incentive to control costs. But to the extent that regulators force prices below the level a regulated monopoly would otherwise charge, regulation serves the public interest by increasing market efficiency.

The cost of the regulatory process must be emphasized, however. If regulation is truly to serve the public interest, it must increase the efficiency of the entire social system. That is, its benefits must exceed its costs. Too often the net benefits of regulation are overestimated because of a failure to consider its costs, which were estimated to exceed $100 billion in the early 1980s.

The Special Case of the Natural Monopoly

So far our discussion of monopoly power has assumed rising marginal costs (see Figure 25.1). But one significant argument for regulation is based on the opposite assumption. Some believe that in industries like electric utilities, the marginal cost of producing additional units actually decreases over the long run. That is, within the relevant range of the market demand, the long-run marginal cost curve slopes downward. The argument is that such industries, called natural monopolies, naturally tend to be dominated by one firm, which will seek monopoly profits once it is established as the sole producer. Natural monopolies are seen as prime candidates for regulation, for their dominance in the market allows them to exert considerable monopoly power.

Assume, for example, that economies of scale lead to a long-run decline in the marginal cost of producing additional units of electricity. By producing on a larger scale, a firm can exploit the efficiencies of very large turbines to produce additional megawatts at a lower cost. Whether the size of generators can be increased indefinitely without producing diseconomies of scale is a matter of debate, as we will see later. Proponents of large electric plants believe that economies of scale are considerable—so extensive that in order to produce power at the lowest possible cost, only one extremely large electric company can operate in a specified geographical area. The fear is that once that firm emerges from the competitive struggle as the sole producer, it may be tempted to restrict production, charge a higher price, and reap monopoly profits.

The theory of natural monopoly is more fully explored in the appendix to this chapter. Here we will simply note that it is unconvincing to many economists, because it does not account for the presence of potential competitors. New firms, not currently competing in the market, may enter if the sole producer begins to extract economic profits through monopoly pricing. The possibility becomes more obvious if we think of a natural monopoly as the only hardware store in a small town, or the only amusement park within several counties, rather than as a large electric company. While such producers are technically natural monopolies, they must fear the entry of competition enough to restrain their monopolistic tendencies.

Regulation of Destructive Competition

Another argument for government regulation of electric utilities is based on the existence of competition. A firm must have transmission lines. Competition could mean several sets of power lines running down city streets, creating an environmental mess. This may be an argument for a government-protected and regulated monopoly on the transmission of electricity, but it has no bearing on the need for regulation of the generation of electricity. The interstate pipelines for gasoline products are regulated, but there is competition on the production and refining end of those lines. Even if there were only one refiner, it would have to base its pricing decisions on what other firms might do if it tried to extract monopoly profits. The generation of electric power can be organized in a similar way.[2] Duke Power, which serves parts of North and South Carolina, has proposed such a reorganization. As one of the nation's lowest-cost producers of electricity, Duke stands to expand its market share under a competitive system.

Regulation of prices is sometimes advocated as a safety measure. Some firms—for example, airlines and nuclear power companies—under competitive pressure to control costs may cut corners on safety. Regulation that keeps prices above competitive levels can induce such firms to compete in other ways—in terms of food quality, size of seats, or flight safety, for instance. Thus regulation can be seen as a means of correcting an underproduction of safety. (If this argument is correct, the deregulation of airline rates in 1978 should have lowered the airline safety ratings.)

Critics of this theory suggest that a desire to avoid higher insurance premiums gives unregulated firms an incentive to maintain their safety precautions. But safety costs may not be completely internalized by insurance premiums, as illustrated by the 1984 accident at the Union Carbide plant in Bhopal, India, which killed over twenty-five hundred people and injured thousands of others. Given continued population growth and industrial concentration, regulation in the interest of public safety may be expected to increase.

---

2. For an insightful discussion of the competitive potential among electric utilities, see Robert M. Spann, "Restructuring the Electric Utility Industry: A Framework for Evaluating Public Policy Options in Electric Utilities," in *Electric Power Reform: The Alternative for Michigan,* ed. William H. Shaker and Wilbert Steffy (Ann Arbor, Mich.: Institute of Science and Technology, University of Michigan, 1976).

The Evidence on Regulation

The public interest theory is not applicable to all forms of government regulation. Clearly, environmental, traffic, and other safety rules promote public goals. Nevertheless, economists worry that such regulations can be used to thwart competition. Most environmental laws impose more stringent pollution standards on new sources of pollution than on old ones. The ostensible reason for this double standard is that new sources can meet the requirements at lower cost than old ones can. But such provisions can also be used as barriers to entry into competition.

Research has raised especially serious doubt about the usefulness to the public of economic regulation—regulation designed to restrict entry, pricing, and production decisions in specific industries like trucking, airline, bus, stockbrokerage, taxi, cable, and shipping services. In such industries, which were heavily regulated in the past, neither the prices charged nor the difficulty of entry can be justified on the grounds of efficiency. Much research, for example, suggests that the regulation of electric power companies has tended to prop up electric rates and to favor industrial and commercial users over residential users.[3] Even in areas, such as legal services and drugs, where the need for regulation has seldom been challenged, its value to the consumer is now being questioned.

Does regulation affect the competitive performance of an industry? The evidence is mixed, and open to differing interpretations. Many health, environmental, and safety regulations have clearly imposed substantial costs on businesses, consumers, and workers. Both the profits and the competitiveness of U.S. steel firms and the wages of steelworkers appear to have been seriously damaged by environmental legislation, for instance.

In the late 1960s and 1970s, regulation may have depressed the returns earned by electric utilities. Regulated industries have always had to wait for an upward adjustment of rates after a rise in costs. Apparently the unusually high rates of inflation during that period increased the strain on regulated industries. The story was different in the airline industry, however. As one researcher wrote, "Paradoxically the [Civil Aeronautics] Board's policies, on the whole, have probably had little effect on the rate of profit earned by the industry; but, without the Civil Aeronautic Act and the Board, these profits would have resulted from quite a different sort of operation."[4] It was such arguments that led to the deregulation of the airline industry in the late 1970s. Other scholars have complained that FCC restrictions on entry into the broadcasting industry have enabled established broadcasting firms to make substantial profits.

3. For reviews of empirical studies and conceptual arguments, see Paul W. MacAvoy, ed., *The Crisis of the Regulatory Commissions: An Introduction to a Current Issue of Public Policy* (New York: W. W. Norton, 1970); James Miller III and Bruce Yandle, eds., *Benefit/Cost Analysis of Social Regulation* (Washington: American Enterprise Institute, 1979); and George C. Eads and Michael Fix, eds., *The Reagan Regulatory Strategy: An Assessment* (Washington: Urban Institute, 1984).

4. Richard W. Caves, "Performance, Structure, and the Goals of Civil Aeronautics Board Regulation," in *The Crisis of the Regulatory Commissions*, p. 134.

In the trucking industry, regulation had particularly poor results. Until the industry was partially deregulated in the 1970s, the ICC turned down hundreds of applications a year to enter the trucking business or extend existing service. In fact, from the late 1930s through the 1960s, the number of licensed carriers actually decreased because of regulation by the ICC. Regulations designed to ensure a "stable trucking industry" frequently took trucks miles out of their way, increasing the cost of hauling cargo and the rates charged. After taking a load to one destination, carriers were forbidden to pick up cargo for the return trip.

Overall, the weight of the evidence is against much economic regulation. It is true that regulatory agencies have sometimes denied rate increases and required firms—railroads and airlines, for example—to maintain services they would otherwise have eliminated. But many economists question whether regulatory agencies as a group have been pursuing the public interest in any systematic way.

The Economic Theory of Regulation

Why has regulation so often had little if any effect in reducing the profitability of regulated industries? Perhaps regulators have been inept at carrying out their responsibilities. Or regulation may be too difficult a task for any agency to handle properly. Regulated firms have an incentive to deceive regulators by juggling their books to inflate their costs. As we have seen, gathering accurate information on a company's true costs and profits can be prohibitively expensive.

A second explanation might be that while regulators are concentrating on prices and barriers to entry, firms may maintain profits by reducing the quality (and therefore the cost) of their products and services.

The intent of regulation may also be circumvented in another, more subtle way. Regulators sometimes determine prices on the basis of a so-called fair rate of return or profitability on investment. Such a standard encourages firms, particularly utilities, to substitute plant and equipment for other resources, such as labor, which do not count as investment. For example, suppose a regulatory agency establishes that 7 percent is a fair return on investment. Firms will then be allowed to make profits equal to 7 percent of the value of their plant and equipment. Suppose further that the same amount of additional electricity can be generated by spending $1 million on plant and equipment or $1 million on labor. If a firm invests in plant and equipment, it can ask the regulatory agency to raise its rates to allow for an additional $70,000 in profit (7 percent of $1 million). If it uses labor instead, it will have no increase in investment on which to base a request for a price increase. By making production capital intensive, firms can circumvent the intent of regulation.

Finally, although regulation may be instituted with good intentions, regulators may become the pawns of regulated firms. If regulatory agencies are staffed by men and women who made their careers in the industries they are regulating, regulated firms may gain undue influence over regulatory policy.

Perspectives in Economics: The Break-Up of AT&T

William F. Shughart II

Before 1983, the U.S. telephone industry was a textbook example of a regulated natural monopoly. Once the basic switching equipment, trunk lines, and satellites are in place, the average cost of providing telephone service falls with increased output. Thus the industry came to be dominated by a single firm. Government regulation was justified as a way of controlling the monopolist's tendency to charge more than the marginal cost of service.

Although telephone service was regulated in the public interest, not all groups fared equally well under Federal Communications Commission (FCC) control. For example, the rate structure benefited local customers at the expense of long-distance customers. This cross-subsidy generally worked against commercial callers, whose demand for long-distance service was greatest during normal business hours, when rates were highest. Of course, AT&T benefited from barriers to the entry of new firms. But in the 1970s, the tables were turned, and AT&T itself became the victim of regulation.

Judge Harold Greene's historic decision ordering the breakup of AT&T followed a series of events

that had been auguring change for over a decade. Most important was the development of microwave and satellite transmission technologies, which freed communications signals from earthbound telephone lines. In addition, since 1968 the FCC had been allowing customers to connect non-AT&T equipment to the Bell network. Throughout the 1970s it permitted new firms to compete with AT&T for long-distance service. AT&T was particularly hurt by the advent of competition in the long-distance market, which had long been among the most profitable of its operations. Discount carriers could charge less for the use of their long-distance transmission facilities mainly because they did not need to pay for switching equipment and local lines, which were owned by AT&T. In effect, MCI Communications Corporation and others were skimming the cream from AT&T's business.

By the late 1970s, then, the telephone industry was partly monopolistic (local service) and partly competitive (long-distance service)—an unworkable situation, from AT&T's perspective. One solution would have been to include the new carriers under the FCC's regulatory umbrella. The alternative was to break up Ma Bell, and this was the

For all these reasons, many economists have begun to discard the public interest theory of regulation in favor of an industry-centered view. Instead of seeing regulation as something thrust on firms, they have begun to view it as a service frequently sought by those who are regulated.[5]

The Supply and Demand for Regulation

In the new economic theory of regulation, government is seen as a supplier of regulatory services to industry. Such services can include price fixing, restrictions on market entry, subsidies, and even suppression of substitute goods (or promotion of complementary goods). For example, regulation

5. See George J. Stigler, "The Theory of Economic Regulation," in *The Citizen and the State* (Chicago: University of Chicago Press, 1975).

course advocated by the Department of Justice in its antitrust suit against AT&T, filed in 1974. In 1982 AT&T reached an agreement with the Department of Justice, approved by Judge Greene, which allowed it to retain its long-distance business. Its local business was divided among twenty-two local service companies. In return, AT&T was released from regulations that had prevented it from entering the computer business.

The history of AT&T shows clearly that regulation is not uniformly beneficial. Under deregulation increased competition has led to a proliferation of new telephone equipment and a decline in long-distance rates. Yet higher local rates and monthly access charges for long-distance service may wipe out those short-run gains.

Those who predict that local rates will eventually rise are assuming that before the breakup, AT&T was exploiting its monopoly power only in the long-distance market. In other words, long-distance rates were set above marginal cost to make up for the revenue lost on local service, whose rates were at or below marginal cost. Yet AT&T may well have enjoyed monopoly pricing for both local and long-distance service. Differences in the profitability of the two markets may have stemmed from differences in the levels and elasticities of demand. If this latter view is correct, prices for local service may not rise.

The FCC apparently continues to view local telephone service as a natural monopoly. Local service companies retain the exclusive right to provide local service. They remain subject to regulation by a variety of federal, state, and local agencies. Yet increasingly, business customers have bypassed local companies by establishing their own in-house communication services. The fact that these arrangements are viable on a much smaller scale than that of a local telephone monopoly suggests that the natural monopoly argument may no longer be valid. In any case, the availability of alternative arrangements for telephone services will restrain the local monopoly's ability to raise prices.

In sum, the telephone industry is now in a period of transition characterized by rapid changes in both structure and technology. The future development of AT&T should provide some interesting examples of the effects of regulation and deregulation.

enables milk producers to suppress the sale of margarine in Wisconsin. Through the FCC, commercial television stations have been able to delay the introduction of cable TV.

These regulatory services are not free; they are offered to industries willing to pay for them. In the political world, the price of regulatory services may be campaign contributions or lucrative consulting jobs, or votes and volunteer work for political campaigns.

Firms demand regulation for their own reasons. As we have seen, forming a cartel in a free market can be difficult, both because new firms may enter the market and because colluders tend to cheat on cartel agreements. The cost of reaching and enforcing a collusive agreement can be so high that government regulation is attractive in comparison.

The view that certain forms of regulation emerge from the interaction of government suppliers and industry demanders seems to square with much historical evidence. As Richard Posner has observed,

The railroads supported the enactment of the first Interstate Commerce Act, which was designed to prevent railroads from price discrimination, because discrimination was undermining the railroad's cartels. American Telephone and Telegraph pressed for state regulation of telephone service because it wanted to end competition among telephone companies. Truckers and airlines supported extension of common carrier regulation to their industries because they considered unregulated competition excessive.[6]

Barbers, beauticians, lawyers, and other specialists have all sought government licensing, which is a form of regulation. Farmers have backed moves to regulate the supply of the commodities they produce. And whenever deregulation is proposed, the industry in question almost always opposes the proposal.

Regulation as a Public Good for Industry

To the extent that regulation benefits all regulated firms, whether or not they contributed to the cost of procuring it, industries may consider regulation a kind of public good. Some firms will try to free-ride on others' efforts to secure regulation. But if all firms free-ride, the collective benefits of regulation will be lost.

The free-rider phenomenon is particularly noticeable in large groups, whose cost of organizing for collective action can be substantial. Someone must bear the initial cost of organization. Yet because the benefits of organization are spread more or less evenly over the group, the party that initiates the organization may incur costs greater than the benefits it receives. Thus collective action may not be taken. Free-riding may explain why some large groups, such as secretaries, have not yet secured government protection. Everyone may be waiting for everyone else to act. Small groups may have much greater success because of their proportionally smaller organizational costs and larger individual benefits. Perhaps it was because only a few railroad companies existed in the 1880s that they were able to lobby successfully for the formation of the ICC.

There are some exceptions to this rule. Several reasonably large groups, including truckers and farmers, have secured a high degree of government regulation, while many highly concentrated groups, such as the electrical appliance industry, have not. In highly concentrated industries, it may be less costly to develop private cartels than to organize to secure government regulation. In industries composed of many firms, on the other hand, any one firm's cost of securing regulation may be smaller than the costs of a cartel. Large groups also control more sizable voting blocks than small groups. They may have the advantage of established trade associations, whose help can be enlisted in pushing for protective legislation.[7]

---

6. Richard A. Posner, "Theories of Economic Regulation," *Bell Journal of Economics and Management* (Autumn 1974), p. 337.

7. See Chapters 1 and 2 of: Mancur Olson, *The Logic of Collective Action* (Cambridge, Mass.: Harvard University Press, 1971).

In broad terms, the economic theory of regulation explains much about government policy—but that is one of its weaknesses. It is so broad as to limit its usefulness as a predictor. It does not enable economists to forecast which industries are likely to seek or achieve government regulation. Nor does it explain the current movement to deregulate the trucking and banking industries, or to regulate the environment. Neither of these trends appears to meet the demand of any particular business interest group.

Regulation as Taxation

According to a third theory, much of today's regulation can be explained as an indirect form of taxation—in the sense that taxation is the government's means of extracting money to pay for what are viewed as public goods and services. For example, until 1978, airlines were permitted to charge fares that exceeded their operations costs for long-haul flights. The extra revenues helped subsidize the below-cost pricing of short-haul flights and compensated airlines for their losses on unprofitable routes they were required to serve. In effect, some airline passengers were taxed to subsidize the fares of others.

In the postal service, another closely regulated industry, revenues from first-class postage have for years offset losses on magazines and bulk mail. Again, through regulation, one group of customers is taxed for the benefit of another. Seen this way, regulation appears to be a rather clumsy way of administering national tax policy—one that raises serious questions of equity in the distribution of the tax burden.

The Deregulation Movement

Recent years have seen a plethora of proposals to deregulate American industry. Airline, trucking, and railroad rates and routes have been deregulated. Unless new legislation is passed, the price of natural gas will be decontrolled in 1986, and the elaborate price controls on oil will be more or less dismantled. Banks are now permitted to pay interest on checking accounts and soon will be almost completely free to fix interest rates on all their accounts.

Because economists have not extensively investigated the impetus for and results of deregulation, any assessment of the trend to deregulate must be considered tentative. In some cases, deregulation may have been a straightforward response to the inefficiencies of regulation. This seems a reasonable explanation for the deregulation of natural gas. The restricted supplies and shortages that characterized the industry under regulation were clearly not in the public interest.

The period of unusually rapid inflation in the late 1970s may also have encouraged the movement toward deregulation. In many industries, the process of seeking approval for price increases was cumbersome and time consuming, so that regulated prices lagged far behind the current rate of inflation. Under the circumstances, industry may have preferred the more

Perspectives in Economics: Changes in Regulatory Policy at the Federal Trade Commission

Bruce Yandle

The election of Ronald Reagan to the presidency in 1980 raised expectations of regulatory reform. At the Federal Trade Commission (FTC), Reagan's campaign commitment to deregulate U.S. business was taken seriously, especially after the appointment of economist James C. Miller III as chairman. And indeed Miller has engineered a major shift in FTC policy.

Before Miller's appointment, enforcement of FTC regulations was guided largely by the conventional wisdom of the consumer protection movement: that markets were seen as so imperfect that consumers were always at a disadvantage. On the whole, competition was not viewed as a viable force for discouraging unfair business practices. And bigness was equated with badness almost by definition. According to critics of the FTC—a number of whom have since been appointed to its staff—the commission had become overzealous in developing industrywide regulations and initiating industrywide antitrust investigations.

In the late 1970s, for example, the FTC was investigating the automobile industry for monopolistic control of domestic auto sales. At the time, competition from foreign imports had cut deeply into domestic producers' sales, forcing layoffs and plant closings. Yet the FTC saw the Big Three simply as big firms. Their share of the domestic auto market, not counting imports, was high and growing. Following their Big Is Bad logic, the FTC staff and commissioners were considering breaking the industry up into smaller pieces.

As chairman, Miller made several important changes in policy and practice. First, he appointed lawyer-economists—trained in both law and economics, especially cost-benefit analysis—to head the FTC's various bureaus. And he increased the influence of the Bureau of Economics, which is responsible primarily for cost-benefit and market competition studies, in the policymaking process.

Second, Miller developed a cost-benefit test for determining which antitrust actions the FTC should consider. The social benefits of any proposed action had to outweigh its cost to consumers. That cost included the potential disruption of markets, the chilling effect on innovation and on flows of information, and the elimination of competition that might occur as a result of an FTC decision. This cost-benefit approach to enforcement led the commission to review a different type of case. Wide-ranging industry studies were replaced by case-by-case investigations, which lend themselves to careful legal and economic analysis and to individually tailored remedies.

The FTC also began to use cost-benefit analysis more extensively to identify the sectors of the economy most afflicted by collusion or fraud. By that standard, the rapidly growing service industry seemed to need special attention. The agency also began to monitor medical and bar associations and other professional groups more closely. (These groups had been largely self-regulated in the past.) It stepped up its actions against professional groups for restricting advertising and market entry. And finally, it began to attack mail-order firms for fraud in mail and television advertisements.

Miller's third major change was to shift attention from the concentration of domestic industries to the degree of competition in the domestic marketplace, considering both foreign and domestic producers. Mergers would be allowed even among large firms, so long as they left the market reasonably competitive. General Motors, for example, was permitted to pool resources with Toyota to produce a compact car. Previous FTC commissioners probably would not have allowed a joint venture between two such large companies.

competitive and flexible market system to the comparatively rigid regulatory system. This seems a reasonable explanation for the deregulation of truck rates and railroad routes in 1979. It may also explain why, beginning in 1980, banks were allowed to pay interest on checking accounts. Bankers may not have wanted to pay interest, but they had little choice given the high returns depositors could earn on corporate and government bonds.

Another possibility is that regulated industries may simply have been outmaneuvered politically be consumer groups like Common Cause and Ralph Nader's Public Interest Research Group. The votes of group members may have wielded more influence with Congress than industry's campaign contributions, especially after the size of political contributions was restricted. This may be the explanation for the deregulation of the airline industry in 1979, despite industry opposition.

It is possible, however, that regulation has not decreased overall. In the late 1970s, government was extending its regulatory arm into such new areas as the environment and worker health and safety. These new regulations increased the effective tax on business, and thus the prices businesses charged consumers. Without doubt, the government's capacity to tax—that is, to impose costs on the private sector—is limited. Perhaps by deregulating some industries, the government was reducing the effective tax in one area so as to increase it in others.

Economic theory suggests that whenever an industry is deregulated, someone will be hurt by the action. When the price of oil was decontrolled, for example, some consumers found their purchasing power reduced by higher prices. Unless those who are hurt by deregulation are somehow compensated for their loss, they can create strong opposition to the change. One way to head off such opposition is to tax the gainers and subsidize the losers from deregulation. The windfall profits tax may be an example of such a scheme. When oil prices were deregulated in 1980, Congress imposed a heavy tax on profits in the domestic oil industry. The revenue from the tax was to be used for research on alternative energy sources like gasohol, and for low-income fuel subsidies.

Summary and Extensions

Treating the public interest and economic theories of regulation separately may have suggested that one or the other must be the correct theory of regulation. In the real world, however, the sources of regulation are complex. For instance, a combination of forces probably motivated the regulation of the airline industry. Some people were pursuing the public interest, as they saw it. Others, especially those connected with the airlines, saw an opportunity to protect their markets. The precise nature of any particular regulation probably reflects the relative strengths of these two forces, as well as the extent to which government allows them to be expressed.

Probably the most important lesson from the study of regulation is that while the public interest—especially as it relates to the improvement of market efficiency—is a valid basis for regulation, it can be easily exploited. Pretending to pursue the public interest, promoters of regulation can realize their own interest instead. The statistical studies cited in this chapter indicate a considerable tendency to abuse the intent of regulation. How then can government serve the public interest without allowing free rein to special-interest regulation? How can government regulate the regulators, and do so efficiently? These are the questions that must be addressed by any movement for regulatory reform.

Major Conclusions

1. Most industries in the U.S. economy are subject to some form of regulation at either the local, state, or federal levels.
2. The public interest theory of regulation is founded partly on the need to capture the externalities, like safety, associated with many products, and partly on the theory that some industries tend naturally toward monopoly, because substantial economies of scale allow only one producer to survive.
3. To induce a monopoly to produce at the efficient output level, regulators can require it to charge what they believe is the perfectly competitive price.
4. A natural monopoly is a monopoly whose marginal costs decrease over the long run. Regulation of natural monopolies is based on the theory that they are protected by formidable barriers to entry—an idea disputed by many economists.
5. Empirical evidence raises questions about whether many regulatory agencies actually serve the public interest, as opposed to the interests of the firms they regulate.
6. The economic theory of regulation is based on the proposition that if firms in an industry do not wish to compete, they will demand protective regulation. For a price, government will supply protection in the form of price fixing and barriers to entry.
7. In the United States, the political process tends to serve the interests of small groups, such as the firms in a regulated industry, at the expense of the general public.
8. Regulation can be seen as a method of taxation. Government forces some consumers to pay higher-than-market prices for certain products or services, like first-class mail, so prices can be lowered on other items, like bulk mail. In other words, government taxes one group of consumers for the benefit of others.

1. The economic theory of regulation suggests that firms have an incentive to support protective regulation. Do workers have a similar incentive? Under what conditions would they support protective regulation, and under what conditions would they oppose it?

2. Aircraft producers once supported government efforts to hold air fares above competitive levels. Explain their position.

3. Develop a public interest case for the regulation of barbers and beauticians.

4. If a regulatory agency determines electric prices on the basis of a fair rate of return on investment, how might its price-setting standard affect the use of fuels in producing electricity? Would fuel oil producers favor the fair-rate-of-return method for regulating electric utilities?

5. In the 1970s, regulatory agencies allowed electric companies to pass on to customers any increases in the cost of their fuel—a scheme that reduces companies' incentives to reduce fuel consumption and costs. Considered in the overall context of regulation, however, are such fuel adjustments necessarily inefficient? What might be the alternative to automatic increases based on the cost of fuel?

6. Which theory of regulation seems more persuasive to you, the public interest or the economic theory? Why?

7. Economists argue that if utilities charge higher prices for electricity during periods of peak demand, consumers will use less electricity then, reducing the strain on generators. Assume again that electric rates are based on the fair-return method of regulation. Will electric utility companies favor the institution of peak-load pricing? Why or why not?

8. From the data in the following table, plot this natural monopoly's marginal cost, average cost, and demand curves on a graph. Label the efficient output level. Will the firm actually produce at that level? Why or why not?

Quantity	Marginal Cost	Price Consumers Will Pay
1	$21	$45
2	18	36
3	15	27
4	12	18
5	9	9
6	6	0

Appendix:
A Graphic Analysis of Natural Monopoly

To expand on our earlier discussion of the behavior of natural monopolies (page 558), this appendix uses graphs to examine the arguments for and against regulation.

A Model of a Natural Monopoly

As Chapter 21 described, as the long-run marginal cost of production diminishes, the long-run average cost decreases as well, but at a slower rate. In Table 25.A1, the marginal cost of producing each additional megawatt, shown in column 2, decreases from $50 for the first megawatt to $10 for the fifth. Though the average cost of the first unit is equal to its marginal cost, the average cost of subsequent units falls less rapidly than their marginal cost.[8] If we plot the marginal and average cost curves from the table on a graph, they will look like the curves in Figure 25.A1.

Table 25.A1. Long-Run Marginal and Average Costs of Producing Electricity

Megawatts (1)	Long-Run Marginal Cost (2)	Long-Run Total Cost (3)	Long-Run Average Cost [(3) ÷ (1)] (4)
1	$50	$ 50	$50
2	40	90	45
3	30	120	40
4	20	140	35
5	10	150	30

---

8. Remember, average cost is the total cost divided by the number of units produced. If the total cost of two megawatts is $90 ($50 for the first megawatt plus $40 for the second), the average cost of each megawatt is $45 ($90 divided by two units).

Figure 25.A1. Long-Run Marginal and Average Costs in a Natural Monopoly. In a natural monopoly, long-run marginal and average costs decline continuously, over the relevant range of production, because of economies of scale. Though the long-run marginal and average cost curves may eventually turn upward because of diseconomies of scale, the firm's market is not large enough to support production in that cost range.

Figure 25.A2 shows these same curves along with the electric company's market demand and marginal revenue curves. According to traditional theory, a firm with decreasing costs will tend to expand production and lower its costs until it becomes large enough to influence price by its production decisions—that is, until it achieves monopoly power. Then it will choose to produce where all monopolists produce, at the point where marginal cost equals marginal revenue. Thus the monopolistic firm in Figure 25.A2 will sell Q_m megawatts at an average price of P_m, generating monopoly profits in the process. In other words, firms in decreasing-cost industries tend naturally toward monopoly.

But although a firm with decreasing costs can expand until it is the major producer in an industry, if not the only one, it will not necessarily be able to manipulate price as a result. Suppose a natural monopoly flexes its market muscle and charges P_m for Q_m units. Another firm, seeing the first firm's economic profits, may enter the industry, expand production, and charge a lower price, luring away customers. To protect its interests, the firm that has been behaving like a monopoly will have to cut its price and expand production to lower its costs. It is difficult to say how far the price will fall and output will rise. But only one firm is likely to survive such a battle, selling to the entire market at a price that competitors cannot undercut. That price will approximate P_1 in Figure 25.A2.

If the price does fall to P_1 and only one firm survives, its total revenue will be its price times the quantity produced, Q_1 (or $P_1 \times Q_1$). Notice that

Figure 25.A2. Creation of a Natural Monopoly.
Even with declining marginal costs, the firm with monopoly power will produce where marginal cost equals marginal revenue, making Q_m units. Unless barriers to entry exist, however, other firms may enter the market, causing the price to fall toward P_1 and the quantity produced to rise toward Q_1. At that price-quantity combination, only one firm can survive—but without barriers to entry, that firm cannot afford to charge monopoly prices. At a price of P_1, its total revenues just cover its total costs. Economic profit is zero.

at that level, the firm's average cost is equal to P_1. Therefore the total cost of production (the average cost times the quantity sold) is equal to the firm's revenue. The firm is just covering its costs of production, including the owners' risk cost. Now alone in the market, the firm may think it can restrict output, raise its price, and reap an economic profit. But still it faces the ever-present threat of some other company entering the market and underpricing its product.

Arguments for the Regulation of Natural Monopolies

From a purely theoretical perspective, then, the existence of a natural monopoly is insufficient justification for regulation. Unless there are significant barriers to entry to an industry, natural monopolies should not be able to charge monopoly prices. But proponents of regulation reply that some industries, like the electrical utilities, require such huge amounts of capital that no competitor could be expected to enter the market to challenge the natural monopoly. That argument presumes, however, that the generation of electric power must take place on an extremely large

Figure 25.A3. Underproduction by a Natural Monopoly.
A natural monopolist that cannot price-discriminate will produce only Q_1 mega-watts, less than Q_2, the efficient output level. If the firm trys to produce Q_2, it will make losses equal to the shaded area, for its price will not cover its average cost.

scale. Such is not necessarily the case. And the capital needed to produce electricity on a profitable scale can be raised by many large corporations, if economic profits exist.

Yet another argument for regulation—one more often voiced by the firms themselves than by consumers—is that production by natural monopolies generally requires large quantities of fixed capital assets, which become a sunk cost once purchased, to be ignored in short-run production and pricing decisions. If industries with long-run decreasing costs are vulnerable to destructive price wars, then firms that ignore massive fixed costs in the short run will eventually destroy themselves. But this argument presumes that entrepreneurs will enter an industry in which self-destruction is a likely outcome—a questionable presumption. In actuality, many industries—oil and automobile production, for instance—support a sig-nificant amount of competition despite extensive capital needs. Neither oil nor automobile producers seem likely to destroy themselves in the near future.

Proponents of the regulation of natural monopolies point also to insufficient output and revenues. Even if an unregulated industry produces Q_1 units and prices that output at P_2 (see Figure 25.A3), it has not reached the efficient output level. That would be the level at which marginal cost equals marginal benefit—the point at which the marginal cost curve intersects the demand curve. That level is Q_2 in Figure 25.A3. Why does output fall short?

Given the market demand curve, the firm could sell an output of Q_2 for only P_1, earning total revenues of P_1 times Q_2. Since the average cost of producing at that output level—AC_1 on the vertical axis—would be greater than the price, total costs, at $AC_1 \times Q_2$, would be greater than total revenues. The loss to a firm that tried to produce at the efficient output level is shown by the shaded area on the graph. To produce at the efficient output level, a company would require a subsidy to offset that loss. Or it would have to price-discriminate, charging progressively lower prices for additional units sold.

Once a firm is given a subsidy, its pricing and production decisions must be closely monitored, for its incentive to control costs will be weakened. If the firm allows its cost curves to drift upward, the price it can charge will also rise. In Figure 25.A4, the firm's long-run marginal and average cost curves shift up from $LRMC_1$ and $LRAC_1$ to $LRMC_2$ and $LRAC_2$. Following the rule that price should be set at the intersection of the long-run marginal cost and demand curves, regulators permit the price to rise from P_1 to P_2. The firm's subsidized losses shrink from the shaded area P_1abATC_1 to P_2cdATC_2. But the quantity produced drops also, from Q_2 to Q_1. Consumers are now getting fewer units at a higher price.

Thus production may be just as inefficient with regulation as without it. Critics point to the U.S. Postal Service as an example of an industry that is closely regulated and subsidized, yet highly inefficient. Yet if the postal industry were truly a natural monopoly, it would be a low-cost producer and would not need protection from competition. Proponents of regulation see the inefficiencies we have just demonstrated as an argument for even more careful scrutiny of a regulated firm's costs—or for government control of production costs through nationalization.

Not all natural monopolies need subsidies to operate at an efficient output level. For all megawatts up to Q_1 in Figure 25.A3, the unregulated firm can charge up to P_2, a price that just covers its costs on those units. If its product cannot be easily resold, the firm can price-discriminate, charging slightly lower prices for the additional units beyond Q_1. So long as its marginal prices are on or below the demand curve and above the marginal cost curve, the firm will cover its costs while moving toward the efficient output level. And it can do so without giving other firms an incentive to move into its market. If its product can be resold, however,

Figure 25.A4. Regulations and Increasing Costs.
If a natural monopoly is compensated for the losses it incurs in operating at the efficient output level (shaded area P_1ATC_1ba), it may monitor its costs less carefully. Its cost curves may shift up, from $LRMC_1$ to $LRMC_2$ and from $LRAC_1$ to $LRAC_2$. Regulators will then have to raise the price from P_1 to P_2, and production will fall from Q_2 to Q_1. The firm will still have to be subsidized (by an amount equal to shaded area P_2ATC_2dc), and the consumer will be paying more for less.

some people will buy at the lower marginal prices and resell to those who are paying P_2, cutting off the firm's profits.

Of course, the objectives and results of regulation cannot be evaluated solely in economic terms. Regulation may be intended to give citizens more influence on critically important decisions, such as the production of power, transportation, or defense readiness. Such objectives are essentially political, rather than economic, in nature.

Part VIII

Resource Markets

Central Question

How are wage rates determined, and why do they differ among different groups of workers?

Key Terms

Demand for labor

Supply of labor

Full wage rate

Human capital

Chapter 26

The Competitive Labor Market

*Labour, like all other things
which are purchased and sold,
and which may be increased or
diminished in quantity, has its
. . . market price.*
David Ricardo

*P*rofessional football players earn more than ministers or nurses. Social workers with college degrees generally earn less than truck drivers, who may not have completed high school. And professors of accounting typically earn more than professors of history with equivalent educational background and teaching experience. Even if your history professor is an outstanding teacher, capable of communicating effectively and concerned about students' problems, she probably earns less than a mediocre teacher of accounting.

Why do different occupations offer different salaries? Obviously not because of their relative worth to us as individuals. But just as there is a market for final goods and services—calculators, automobiles, dry cleaning—there is a market for labor as a resource in the production process. In this competitive labor market, the forces of supply and demand determine the wage rate workers receive.

By concentrating on the economic determinants of employment—those that relate most directly to production and promotion of a product—we do not mean to suggest that other factors are unimportant. Many noneconomic forces influence who is employed at what wage, including social status, appearance, sex, race, and personal acquaintances. Our purpose is simply to show how economic forces affect the wages paid and the number of employees hired. Such a model can show not only how labor markets work, but how attempts to legislate wages, like minimum wage laws, affect the labor market.

The general principles that govern the labor market also apply to the markets for other resources, principally land and capital. For the use of land and capital has a price, called rent or interest, which is determined by supply and demand. Furthermore, land, capital, and labor are all subject to the law of diminishing returns. Beyond a certain point and given a fixed quantity of at least one resource, more land, labor, or capital will produce less and less additional output.

The markets for land and capital will be covered in Chapter 28. This chapter deals with competitive labor markets, and Chapter 27 will cover the special case of markets dominated by unions or sole employers.

The Demand for and Supply of Labor

Labor is a special kind of commodity, one in which most people have a personal stake. The employer buys this commodity at a price: the wage rate the laborer receives in exchange for his or her efforts. In a competitive market, the price, or wage rate, of labor is determined just as other prices are, by the interaction of supply and demand. To understand why a person earns what he does, then, we must first consider the determinants of the demand and supply for labor.

The Demand for Labor

Demand for labor: the assumed inverse relationship between the real wage rate and the quantity of labor employed during a given period, everything else held constant.

The **demand for labor** is the assumed inverse relationship between the real wage rate and the quantity of labor employed during a given period, everything else held constant. The demand curve for labor generally slopes downward. At higher wage rates, employers will hire fewer workers than at lower wage rates.

The demand for labor is derived partly from the demand for the product produced. If there were no demand for mousetraps, there would be no need—no demand—for mousetrap makers. This general principle applies to all kinds of labor in an open market. Plumbers, textile workers, and writers can earn a living because there is a demand for the products and services they offer. The greater the demand for a product or service, the greater its market price and the greater the demand for the labor needed to supply it. And the greater the demand for a given kind of labor, everything else held equal, the higher the wage rate.

The productivity of labor—that is, the quantity of work a laborer can produce in a given unit of time—is another critically important determinant of the demand for labor. The price of the final product puts a value on a laborer's output, but her productivity determines how much she can produce. Together, labor productivity and the market price of what is produced determine the market value of labor to employers, and ultimately the employers' demand for labor.

We can predict that the demand for labor will rise and fall with increases and decreases in both productivity and product price. Suppose, for example, that mousetraps are sold in a competitive market, where their price is set by the interaction of supply and demand. Assume also that mousetrap production is subject to diminishing marginal returns. As more units of labor are added to a fixed quantity of plant and equipment, output expands by diminishing increments.

Column 2 of Table 26.1 illustrates diminishing returns. The first laborer contributes a marginal product—or additional output—of six mousetraps per hour. From that point on, the marginal product of each additional laborer diminishes. It drops from five mousetraps to four to three and so on, until an extra laborer adds only one mousetrap to total hourly production.

Table 26.1. Computing the Value of the Marginal Product of Labor

Units of Labor (1)	Marginal Product of Each Laborer (per Hour) (2)	Price of Mousetraps in Product Market (3)	Value of Each Laborer to Employer (Value of the Marginal Product) [(2) × (3)] (4)
First laborer	6	$2	$12
Second laborer	5	2	10
Third laborer	4	2	8
Fourth laborer	3	2	6
Fifth laborer	2	2	4
Sixth laborer	1	2	2

The employer's problem, once production has reached the range of diminishing returns, is to determine how many laborers to employ. She does so by considering the value of the marginal product of labor. Column 3 shows the market price of each mousetrap, which we will assume remains constant at $2. By multiplying that dollar price by the marginal product of each laborer (column 2) the employer arrives at the value of each laborer's marginal product (column 4). This is the highest amount that she will pay each laborer. If she pays workers less than the value of their marginal product, she earns a profit.

If the wage rate is slightly below $12 an hour, the employer will hire only one worker. She cannot justify hiring the second worker if she has to pay him $12 for an hour's work and receives only $10 worth of product in return. But if the wage rate is slightly lower than $10, the employer can justify hiring two laborers. If the wage rate is lower still—say slightly below $4—the employer can hire as many as five workers.

Following this line of reasoning, we can conclude that the demand curve for mousetrap makers, like the demand curves for other goods, slopes downward. That is, the lower the wage rate, everything else held constant, the greater the quantity of labor demanded. And theoretically, what is true of one employer must be true of all. That is, the market demand curve for a given type of labor must also slope downward (see Figure 26.1).[1] Thus profit-maximizing employers will not employ workers if they have to pay them more, in wages and fringe benefits, than they are worth. What they are worth depends on their productivity and the market value of what they produce. (Though this deduction may seem obvious, the inverse relationship between wages and employment is often overlooked in discussions of minimum wages and working conditions.)

If the price of the product, mousetraps in this example, increases, the employer's demand for mousetrap makers will shift, say from D_1 to D_2 in Figure 26.1. Because the market value of the laborers' marginal product has risen, producers now want to sell more mousetraps and will hire more workers to produce them. Look back again at Table 26.1. If the price of mousetraps rises from $2 to $4, the value of each worker's marginal product doubles. At a wage rate of $10 an hour, an employer can now hire as many as four workers. (Similarly, if the price of the final product falls below $2, the demand for workers will also fall.)

When technological change improves worker productivity, the demand for workers may increase. If workers produce more, the value of their marginal product may rise, and employers may then be able to hire more of them. Such is not always the case, however. Sometimes an increase in worker productivity decreases the demand for labor. For instance, if worker productivity increases throughout the industry, rather than in just one or two firms, more mousetraps may be offered on the market, depressing

1. The reader may get the impression that the market demand curve for labor is derived by horizontally summing the demand curves of individual firms, which are derived directly from tables like Table 26.1. Strictly speaking, that is not the case. See Chapter 28, pages 626–629, for an explanation of how the market demand for a resource is derived.

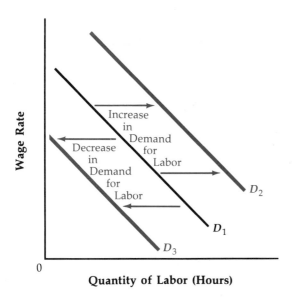

Figure 26.1. Shift in Demand for Labor.
The demand curve for labor, like all other demand curves, slopes downward. An increase in the demand for labor will cause a rightward shift in the demand curve, from D_1 to D_2. A decrease will cause a leftward shift, to D_3.

the equilibrium price. The drop in price reduces the value of the worker's marginal product, and may outweigh the favorable effect of the increase in productivity. In such cases the demand for labor will fall. Consumers will pay less, but employees in the mousetrap industry will have fewer employment opportunities and earn lower wages. Fortunately, this seemingly perverse result is not a certainty. The opposite can happen just as easily.

The Supply of Labor

The **supply of labor** is the assumed positive relationship between the real wage rate and the number of workers (or worker-hours) offered for employment during a given period, everything else held constant. The supply curve for labor generally slopes upward. At higher wage rates, more workers will be willing to work longer hours than at lower wage rates (see Figure 26.2). If you survey your classmates, for example, you will probably find that more of them would be willing to work at a part-time job that paid $7 an hour than would work for $4 an hour.

The supply of labor depends on the opportunity cost of a worker's time. Workers can do many different things with their time. They can use it to construct mousetraps, to do other jobs, to go fishing, and so on. Weighing the opportunity cost of each activity, the worker will allocate his time so

Supply of labor: the assumed positive relationship between the real wage rate and the number of workers (or worker-hours) offered for employment during a given period, everything else held constant.

Figure 26.2. Shift in the Supply of Labor.
The supply curve for labor slopes upward. An increase in the supply of labor will cause a rightward shift in the supply curve, from S_1 to S_2. A decrease in the supply of labor will cause a leftward shift in the supply curve, from S_1 to S_3.

that the marginal benefit of an hour spent doing one thing will equal the marginal benefit of time that could be used elsewhere (see pages 378–379). Because some kinds of work are unpleasant, workers will require a wage to make up for time lost from leisure activities like fishing. To earn a given wage, a rational worker will give up the activities he values least. To allocate even more time to a job (and give up more valuable leisure-time activities), a worker will require a higher wage.

Given this cost-benefit tradeoff, employers who want to increase production have two options. They can hire additional workers or ask the same workers to work longer hours. In either case they will have to pay a higher wage. Those who are currently working for $4 an hour must value time spent elsewhere at less than $4 per hour. To attract others, people who value their time spent elsewhere at more than $4 per hour, employers will have to raise wages, perhaps to $5 per hour. To convince current workers to put in longer hours—to give up more attractive alternative activities—employers will also have to raise wages. In either case, the labor supply curve slopes upward. More labor is supplied at higher wages.

The supply curve for labor will shift if the value of employees' alternatives changes. For example, if the wage that mousetrap makers can earn in toy production goes up, the value of their time will increase. The supply of labor to the mousetrap industry should then decrease, shifting upward and to the left from S_1 to S_3 in Figure 26.2. This shift in the labor supply

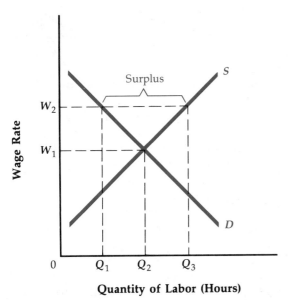

Figure 26.3. Equilibrium in the Labor Market.
Given the supply and demand curves for labor S and D, the equilibrium wage will be W_1, and the equilibrium quantity of labor hired, Q_2. If the wage rate rises to W_2, a surplus of labor will develop, equal to the difference between Q_3 and Q_1.

curve means that less labor will be offered at any given wage rate, in a particular labor market. To hire the same quantity of labor—to keep mousetrap makers from going over to the toy industry—the employer must increase the wage rate.

The same general effect will occur if workers' valuation of their leisure time changes. Because most people attach a high value to time spent with their families on holidays, employers who want to maintain operations then generally have to pay a premium for workers' time. The supply curve for labor on holidays lies above and to the left of the regular supply curve. Conversely, if for any reason the value of workers' alternatives decreases, the supply curve for labor will shift down to the right. If wages in the toy industry fall, for instance, more workers will want to move into the mousetrap business, increasing the labor supply in the mousetrap market.

Equilibrium in the Labor Market

A competitive market is one in which neither the individual employer nor the individual employee has the power to influence the wage rate. Such a market is shown in Figure 26.3. Given the supply curve S and the demand curve D, the wage rate will settle at W_1, and the quantity of labor employed will be Q_2. At that combination, defined by the intersection of the supply and demand curves, those who are willing to work for wage W_1 can find jobs.

The equilibrium wage rate is determined much as the prices of goods and services are established. At a wage rate of W_2, the quantity of labor employers will hire is Q_1, whereas the quantity of workers willing to work is Q_3. In other words, at that wage rate a surplus of labor exists. Note that all the workers in this surplus except the last one are willing to work for less than W_2. That is, up to Q_3, the supply curve lies below W_2. The opportunity cost of these workers' time is less than W_2. They can be expected to accept a lower wage, and over time they will begin to offer to work for less than W_2. Other unemployed and employed workers must then compete by accepting still lower wages. In this manner the wage rate will fall toward W_1. In the process, the quantity of labor that employers can afford to hire will expand from Q_1 toward Q_2.

Meanwhile, the falling wage rate will convince some workers to take another opportunity, such as going fishing or getting another job. As they withdraw from the market, the quantity of labor supplied will decline from Q_3 toward Q_2. The quantity supplied will meet the quantity demanded—and eliminate the surplus—at a wage rate of W_1.

In practice, the money wage rate—the number of dollars earned per hour—may not fall. Instead, the general price level may increase while the money wage rate remains constant. But the real wage rate—that is, what the money wage rate will buy—still falls, producing the same general effects: fewer laborers willing to work, and more workers demanded by employers. When economists talk about wage increases or decreases, they mean changes in the real wage rate, or in the purchasing power of a worker's paycheck.

Conversely, if the wage rate falls below W_1, the quantity of labor demanded by employers will exceed the quantity supplied, creating a shortage. Employers, eager to hire more workers at the new cheap wage, will compete for the scarce labor by offering slightly higher wages. The quantity of labor offered on the market will increase, but at the same time these slightly higher wages will cause some employers to cut back on their hiring. In short, in a competitive market, the wage rate will rise toward W_1, the equilibrium wage rate.

Why Wage Rates Differ

Some workers earn higher wages than others, sometimes much higher. A worker's wages may differ from the norm for his job or location because of differences in the secondary benefits of employment, called nonmonetary benefits. Differences in the competitiveness of various labor markets and personal differences in skills and productivity may also account for wage differentials.

Differences in Nonmonetary Benefits

So far we have been speaking as if the wage rate were the key determinant of employment. But what about job satisfaction and the way employers

Figure 26.4. The Effect of Nonmonetary Rewards on Wage Rates.
The supply of labor is greater for jobs offering nonmonetary benefits—S_2 rather than S_1. Given a constant demand for labor, the wage rate will be W_2 for workers who do not receive nonmonetary benefits and W_1 for workers who do. Even though wages are lower when nonmonetary benefits are offered, workers are still better off; they earn a total wage equal, according to their own values, to W_3.

treat their employees—are these issues not important? Some people accept lower wages in order to live in the Appalachians or the Rockies; college professors forgo more lucrative work to be able to teach, write, and set their own work schedules. The congeniality of their colleagues is another significant nonmonetary benefit that influences where and how much people work. Power, status, and public attention also figure in career decisions.

The tradeoffs between the monetary and nonmonetary rewards of work will affect the wage rates for specific jobs. The more people who desire the nonmonetary benefits of a given job, the greater the labor supply. Added to wages, nonmonetary benefits could shift the labor supply curve from S_1 to S_2 in Figure 26.4, lowering the wage rate from W_2 to W_1. But even though the money wage rate is lower, workers are better off according to their own values. At a wage rate of W_1, their nonmonetary benefits equal the vertical distance between points a and b, making their full wage equal to W_3. The **full wage rate** is the sum of the money wage rate and the monetary equivalent of the nonmonetary benefits of a job.

Workers who complain they are paid less than workers in other occupations often fail to consider their full wages (money wage plus nonmonetary benefits). The worker with a lower monetary wage may be receiving more nonmonetary rewards, including freedom from intense pressure, comfortable surroundings, and so on. The worker with the

Full wage rate: the sum of the money wage rate and the monetary equivalent of the nonmonetary benefits of a job.

higher money wage may actually be earning a lower full wage than the worker with nonmonetary income. Certainly many executives must wonder whether their high salaries compensate them for their lost home life and leisure time. And teachers who envy the higher salaries of coaches should recognize that a somewhat higher wage rate is necessary to offset the increased risk of being fired that goes with coaching.

Employers can benefit from providing employees with nonwage benefits. A favorable working climate attracts more workers at lower wages. Though benefits can be costly, they are worthwhile as long as they lower wages more than they raise other labor costs. Some nonwage benefits, like air conditioning and low noise levels, also raise worker productivity. Needless to say, an employer cannot justify unlimited nonwage benefits. Employers will not pay more in wages, monetary or nonmonetary, than a worker is worth. And in a competitive labor market they will tend to pay all employees a wage rate equal to the marginal value of the last employee hired.

Differences Among Markets

Differences in nonmonetary benefits do not entirely explain observed differences in wage rates. Supply and demand conditions may differ between labor markets. As Figure 26.5 shows, given a constant supply of labor, S, a greater demand for labor will mean a higher wage rate. Conversely, given a constant demand for labor, a higher supply of labor will mean a lower wage rate. Depending on the relative conditions in different markets, wages may—or may not—differ significantly.

People in different lines of work may also earn different wages because consumers value the products they produce differently. Automobile workers may earn more than textile workers because people are willing to pay more for automobiles than for clothing. Consumer preferences contribute to differences in the value of the marginal product of labor and ultimately in the demand for labor.

But by themselves, relative product values cannot explain long-run differences in wages. Unless textile work offers compensating nonmonetary benefits, laborers in that industry will be attracted by higher wages elsewhere, perhaps in the automobile industry. The supply of labor in the automobile industry will rise, and the wage rate will fall. In the long run, the wage differential will decrease or even disappear.

Certain factors may perpetuate the money wage differential in spite of competitive market pressures. Textile workers who enjoy living in North or South Carolina may resist moving to Michigan, where automobiles are manufactured. In that case, the nonmonetary benefits associated with textile work offset the difference in money wages. In addition, the cost of acquiring the skills needed for automobile work may act as a barrier to movement between industries—a problem we will address shortly. Finally, as explained in the next chapter, union power may hold the wages of automobile workers above the free market rate, while a kind of employment monopoly common in textile towns may hold textile workers' wages below the competitive level.

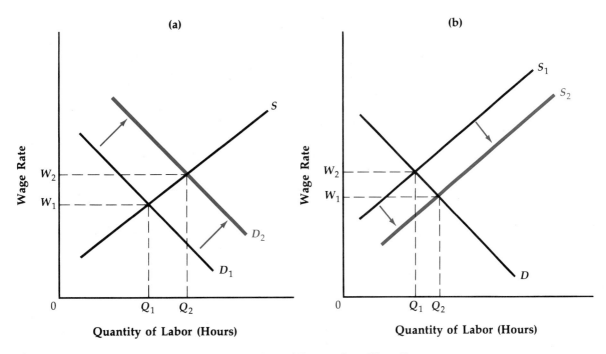

Figure 26.5. The Effect of Differences in Supply and Demand on Wage Rates. In competitive labor markets, higher demand for labor (D_2 in part (a)) will bring a higher wage rate. A higher supply of labor (S_2 in part (b)) will bring a lower rate.

Differences Among Workers

Differences in labor markets do not explain wage differences among people in the same line of work. Differences among workers must be responsible for that disparity. Some people are more productive than others, and thus more attractive to employers. Employers must pay such workers more because their services are eagerly sought after. But they can afford to pay them more, because their marginal product is greater.

Reggie Jackson earns an extremely high salary. The California Angels are willing to pay him so well both because of his popularity among fans—when Reggie plays, ballpark crowds are bigger—and because he is a successful hitter. Because a winning team generally attracts more support than a losing one, Reggie's presence indirectly boosts the team's earnings. In other words, Reggie Jackson is in a labor submarket like the one shown by curve D_2 in Figure 26.5(a). Other players are in submarket D_1.

Differences in skill may also account for differences in wages. Most wages are paid not just for a worker's effort but for the use of what economists call human capital. **Human capital** is the acquired skills and productive capacity of workers. We usually think of capital as plant and equipment—for instance, a factory building and the machines it contains. But a capital good is most fundamentally defined as something produced

Human capital: the acquired skills and productive capacity of workers.

or developed for use in the production of something else. In this sense capital goods include the education or skill a person acquires for use in the production process. The educated worker, whether a top-notch mechanic or a registered nurse, holds within herself capital assets that earn a specific rate of return. In pursuing professional skills, the worker, much like the business entrepreneur, takes the risk that the acquired assets will become outmoded before they are fully used. In the 1970s and early 1980s, students who majored in history expecting to teach found that their investment in human capital did not pay off. Many were unable to get jobs in their chosen field.

Finally, wage differences can result from social discrimination, whether sexual, racial, religious, ethnic, or political. Potential employees are often grouped according to some easily identifiable characteristic, such as sex or skin color. Employment decisions are then made primarily on the basis of the group to which the individual belongs, rather than on individual merit. Thus a qualified woman may not be considered for an executive job because women as a group are excluded. To the extent that employers prefer to work with certain groups, like whites or men, the labor market will be segmented. Employees in different submarkets, with different demand curves and wage differentials, will be unable to move easily from one market to another.

Competition among producers in the market for final goods can weaken (but not necessarily eliminate) discriminatory practices. Suppose employers harbor a deep-seated prejudice against women, which depresses the market demand and wage rates for female workers. If there is no rational reason for preferring men—if women are just as productive as men—an enterprising producer can hire women, pay them less, undersell the other suppliers, and take away part of their markets. Under competitive pressure, employers will start to hire women in order to keep their market shares. As a result the demand for women workers will rise, while the demand for men will fall. Such competition may not eliminate the wage differential between men and women, but it can reduce it. In industries where employers exercise market power, social discrimination may persist.[2]

Legislating Wage Rates: The Minimum Wage

Congress enacted the first federal minimum wage law in 1938, setting the rate at $0.25 an hour. By January 1981, the minimum wage had risen to $3.35 an hour. Though minimum wage laws enjoy considerable public support—in some quarters, opposition to the minimum wage is about as popular as opposition to motherhood—from an economic point of view they are an inefficient form of welfare legislation. Such laws have negative effects on both employment and social conditions.

2. For more on sex discrimination, see Richard B. McKenzie and Gordon Tullock, "Equal Pay for Equal Work," in *The New World of Economics*, 3d ed. (Homewood, Ill.: Richard D. Irwin, 1981).

The Effect of Minimum Wage Laws on Employment

Look once more at Figure 26.3. If the market is competitive and free of government intervention, the wage rate will settle at W_1. Suppose, however, that politicians consider that market wage too low to provide a decent living. They pass a law requiring employers to pay no less than W_2. The effect of the law will be to reduce employment. Employers will not be able to afford to employ as many people, and the quantity of labor demanded will fall from Q_2 to Q_1. Those who manage to keep their jobs at the minimum wage can be better off; their take-home pay will increase. But other workers will no longer have a job. They will either become permanently unemployed or settle for work in a different, less desirable labor market. If the minimum wage displaces them from their preferred employment to their next-best alternative, their full wage rate—that is, their money wage plus the nonmonetary benefits of their job—will have been reduced. If they become permanently unemployed, their money wage will have been reduced from a level judged politically unacceptable to zero.

To make matters worse, the introduction of a minimum wage increases the number of laborers willing to work (see Figure 26.3). Thus the workers who would have had a job at W_1, and who have fewer employment opportunities at W_2, must now compete with a larger number of workers.

Though there are some theoretical objections to the model just presented (to be discussed in Chapter 27), almost all the empirical studies done over the last three decades support its gloomy results. In 1969, two scholars concluded:

The impression created in most government studies that federal minimum wage policy has produced no adverse effects is erroneous. . . . Minimum wage rates produce gains for some groups of workers at the expense of those that are the least favored in terms of marketable skills or location.[3]

Other researchers observed that minimum wage laws tend to destabilize employment among workers covered by the law, particularly nonwhites and the young.[4] When demand for goods and services falls, employers cannot lower prices to boost sales, for wages cannot drop below the minimum. Instead, they adjust to changing market conditions by reducing employment.

A more recent study corroborates these findings. Minimum wage legislation was found to hurt teenagers particularly—especially nonwhite males. Specifically, the boost in the minimum wage from $1.25 in 1966 to $1.60 in 1972 increased unemployment among teenagers by 3.8 percent.[5]

---

3. John M. Peterson and Charles T. Stewart, *Employment Effects of Minimum Wage Rates* (Washington, D.C.: American Enterprise Institute for Public Policy Research, 1969), pp. 151–55.
4. Marvin Kosters and Finis Welch, "The Effects of Minimum Wages on the Distribution of Changes in Aggregate Employment," *American Economic Review*, 62 (June 1972), 323–31.
5. James F. Ragan, "Minimum Wages and the Youth Labor Market," *Review of Economics and Statistics*, 59 (May 1977), 129–36.

Perspectives in Economics: Sex Discrimination—A Market Information Problem

Adele Ernst Wick

Discrimination against women means different things to different people. Economists tend to look at what they have been trained to examine: discrimination in the job market. With their penchant for scientific objectivity, they concentrate on concrete signs of discrimination, like lower wages and barriers to entry, and try to measure those signs.

If society is sex-blind, a woman's wage should be the same as a man's, after adjustments for varying degrees of job congeniality, productivity, and the like. If a woman's wage is still lower than a man's after such adjustments, the difference may be attributed to discrimination. That is, the personal tastes of employers, other employees, or customers are assumed to act as a nonmonetary cost, reducing the overall return from hiring women. Unfortunately, because discrimination is residual—a leftover discrepancy that is unexplained by other variables—its measurement can be a yardstick of our ignorance as well. Discrimination may point to intangible but important characteristics of productivity that we have failed to identify.

Competition among firms ensures that in the long run, producers will behave as if they are trying to maximize profits. If they can minimize their costs by hiring cheaper but equally productive women instead of men, in the process they will bid up women's wages to the level of men's. Employee and customer bias may hamper this process, but as satisfying biased tastes becomes increasingly expensive to producers, the quantity of discrimination demanded should fall.

Not all markets are competitive, however. Labor markets in particular are riddled with barriers to entry and other controls, like unions and work rules. Moreover, if industries like steel and automobile manufacturing try to shore up their profits by restricting imports, we must take seriously the possibility that men, who still command impressive majorities in our legislatures and board rooms, will try to reduce competition for their jobs from the female half of the population. They need not do so consciously; they need only act as if their intent is to protect their own jobs. The earliest legislation on working conditions for women may well have read as if it was meant to protect women from themselves and from jobs considered too strenuous for them. But the effect of such restrictions is best determined by translating the legalese not into English, but into economics. Women's wages may be approaching or even surpassing men's wages in certain occupations, but in general, they are far from equal to men's. And though women may be paid more than men in certain occupational categories, men of equal talent may occupy jobs in superior fields, at much higher wages altogether.

In addition, the lessons of the competitive model are statements about tendencies toward equilibrium in the long run. But by then we will all be dead, as Lord Keynes reportedly said. As a description of the short run in which we live, competitive market theory may be dangerously deceptive. Indeed, the more dynamic the situation, the less compelling is any statement about equilibrium.

Significantly, the London *Economist* called the changing role of women the most important development of its time—more so than Freudianism,

Darwinism, fascism, the *Communist Manifesto,* and the Soviet revolution. Today, at the most basic level of socialization—the family—perceptions of the proper roles for girls are in flux. As parents encourage their daughters to be more career-ambitious, young women enroll and excel in courses like mathematics and engineering, once considered the exclusive province of males. Accordingly, women's training, both at home and school, enhances their future productivity. At the same time, demographic and economic shifts from the rust belt to the sun belt, and from smokestack to high tech industry, have rendered many gender-based distinctions obsolete.

In this context of rapid social change, another frequent assumption of the competitive model—perfect or even good information—can be highly inappropriate. Indeed, the residual wage differential we have called discrimination may be due less to bias against women than to the consequences of what economists call signaling. To be perfectly informed about all a prospective employee's characteristics would cost an employer more than it was worth, even if it were possible. Accordingly, employers tend to economize on their information-gathering by judging individuals as a group. If in the past women have been less stable or productive employees than men, women today may be judged by past standards. "Female," then, is a signal of productivity as well as of nonmonetary costs like employee or customer tastes.

Moreover, some women may choose to be less career-productive than men on the basis of imperfect or incorrect information. A cheap way for a woman to discover her career opportunities may be to look for female role models. If women find few female judges or engineers to emulate, they may not invest in the skills needed for a career in law or engineering. Rational ignorance can thus act as a barrier to entry. Like discouraged workers who do not look for jobs because they do not believe they will find them, women may not even try to enter male-dominated fields. Thus in times of rapid change, poor information can be especially costly. The word "female" may signal past characteristics that ill accord with the present and impede the future.

Among the many reasons for discrimination against women, which might justify governmental remedies? If discrimination results from employer or employee preferences, or from socialization, perhaps it should be shrugged off. But if it results from costly or outdated information in a time of change—and if government can provide information more quickly and cheaply than the private sector—perhaps government action is justified. If labor markets are not competitive because of barriers to entry, perhaps the government has a role there too.

In final analysis, however, the government is composed of men and women just as the private sector is. Indeed, it employs substantially more men than women. Can the government be trusted to remove the barriers to women's entry into the labor market? Or must women trust only their own efforts? "Women, signal harder!" is the advice one professor of economics gave to female graduate students.

Perspectives in Economics: Sex Discrimination—A Free Market View

Catherine England

It would be naïve to suggest that discrimination in hiring does not exist. Those who make employment decisions respond to their personal likes and dislikes just as consumers do in the purchase of goods and services. A personnel manager who graduated from Texas A & M may favor another Aggie over a University of Texas alumnus. A single man may be passed over because an equally well-qualified married man has applied.

The government does not concern itself with these forms of discrimination. A disgruntled employee cannot sue in federal court because his boss made a promotion decision on the basis of old school ties. The denial of one job or promotion because of personal prejudice will not seriously damage a person's long-term career. To be socially harmful, discrimination must be systematic.

Why then does public policy allow women to sue an employer or potential employer on the grounds of sex discrimination? The argument is that women are systematically discriminated against. That is, most people who hire and promote have outmoded attitudes about the proper role of women. Left to themselves, they refuse to allow women to advance, regardless of their qualifications.

There is some truth in this analysis. Many men holding middle and upper management positions are uncomfortable with the idea of working with women as equals or superiors. They may fear the additional competition represented by a highly motivated, well-qualified woman. Or they may feel the presence of women would force a change in the social mores of the boardroom. But the existence of sexist attitudes does not prove that discrimination is systematic. It does not prove that the long-run career opportunities of qualified women are seriously endangered, or that government action is the only way to promote equal opportunity for women.

In a freely competitive market economy, systematic discrimination against any qualified group cannot survive for long. It creates too many opportunities for profit. Suppose there is a large pool of qualified but underemployed and underpaid women. Why would not some enterprising entrepreneur hire them for less than the going wage for men and undercut the competing firms' prices? Any businessperson who insists on hiring only men at wages above those paid to equally qualified women is raising his cost of doing business unnecessarily. If he is not eventually driven out of business, he will at least have to accept lower profits than his unbiased competitors.

Why, then, do women as a group earn less than

Social and Nonmonetary Effects of Minimum Wage Laws

Strictly from an economic point of view, minimum wage laws can be said to have several social effects. By increasing unemployment, minimum wage laws increase the number of people on welfare and unemployment compensation. They may also increase the level of criminal activity, for crime is one alternative to employment in the legitimate labor market. And because a minimum wage increases the competition for jobs, it is likely to increase discrimination on the basis of sex, race, religion, or other such grounds.

men? There are a number of reasons, many of them rooted in the nation's social structure. First, many women in today's workforce grew up not expecting to be employed as adults. Until a generation ago, most young women believed they would spend most of their adult lives working at home as wives and mothers, rather than in factories and offices as wage earners. Their schooling and the skills they acquired reflected that belief.

Even among young women who acquire skills in anticipation of working, social expectations and biological factors affect career development. Women must interrupt their careers, however briefly, in order to have children. Most bear heavy responsibilities at home as well as at work, and many place their families ahead of their careers. These realities cause women to make different educational and career choices from those of men. Women tend to invest in skills that will allow them to drop in and out of the work force, to schedule their working hours around their family lives, and to move from one area to another with their husbands. In many cases, such skills pay less than those required in the more demanding, less flexible jobs traditionally held by men.

Despite these social factors, statistics show that younger women are rapidly closing the earnings gap with men. Indeed, young single women now earn slightly more than young single men. Even married women are moving into nontraditional fields. In 1984, the nation learned it was possible to be a mother and an astronaut.

The market is working. As attitudes change, as chores at home become less time consuming, as economic necessity forces women into the work force, they are acquiring more marketable skills. And the number of women holding traditionally male jobs is increasing. Like any new group entering a previously closed, homogeneous environment, however, women have had to struggle to gain access to and recognition in fields previously dominated by men. But like all new entrants before them, women are gradually becoming integrated into the managerial and professional ranks.

No one should be allowed systematically to deny women—or any other group—the opportunity to pursue a career. U.S. law protects that right. But the fact that many women choose not to pursue managerial or professional careers should not be interpreted as a sign of discrimination. As long as men and women choose to play different roles at home, they will necessarily play slightly different roles in the workplace. Equality of opportunity should not be confused with equality of results.

Another seldom recognized effect of the minimum wage is the reduction of the full wage rate. Employers usually pay their employees partly in money wages and partly in nontaxable fringe benefits. Assuming that the total of monetary and nonmonetary benefits is as high as the employees' productivity will allow, an increase in the minimum money wage will force employers to reduce their nonmonetary payments. They may turn down the air conditioning or raise production quotas. The full wage rate, then, will not rise by as much as the money wage that must be paid, and may even fall. And because the minimum wage creates a surplus of labor, employees can do little to prevent reductions in their nonmonetary wages.

Perspectives in Economics: Better Housing for Migrant Workers— Legislating Nonmonetary Benefits

Since the 1960s, television news documentaries have publicized the substandard, even squalid housing commonly provided to migrant farm workers. Most housing for migrants lacked plumbing and running water. Sleeping arrangements consisted of a few mattresses thrown on the floor.

To many, the obvious solution to the problem was to impose stricter housing standards on employers of migrant workers. Yet one consequence of such legislation has been reduced employment opportunities for migrant workers.[1] Figure 26.6 shows how the increased nonmonetary benefits lowered the demand for migrant labor. In a completely free market, employers are willing to pay a money wage of W_2 for migrant labor. If they are forced to pay workers more by meeting higher housing standards, their demand curve for migrant labor will fall from D_1 to D_2. The equilibrium money wage rate will fall to W_1, and employment opportunities will be reduced from Q_3 to Q_2. Again,

as in the case of minimum wages, those who keep their jobs will be better off. Their *full* wage rate will rise from W_2 to W_3 (W_1 in money wages plus $W_3 - W_1$ in nonmoney benefits). But the workers who are not hired will suffer a loss in income.

The farmers who employ migrant workers are caught in a competitive bind. Consumers want to buy their food at the lowest possible price. As producers, farmers must be able to sell their produce at a competitive price. That means minimizing the cost of production, including the full wage rate paid to employees. If farmers are forced to provide better housing for their laborers, they must reduce costs in other ways, including the substitution of machinery for labor.

This is precisely what has happened in many farm areas since the imposition of stricter housing standards. A federal law establishing migrant housing standards was passed in the late 1960s. In 1969 the farm labor service of the Michigan

The Political Support for Minimum Wage Laws

Why do minimum wage laws attract so much political support? Part of the reason may be that the general public is largely unaware of their negative effects. So many forces operate on the labor market that it is almost impossible for the average person to single out the effects of one law. Many people do not even realize that increasing the wage rate will affect employment opportunities. Those on whom the burden of these laws falls hardest—young, relatively unproductive workers, many of whom cannot vote—are least likely to understand the negative effects.

Another reason, just as important, is that many people benefit from minimum wage laws—those who retain their jobs and receive higher

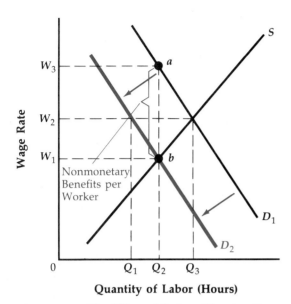

Figure 26.6. The Effect of Stricter Housing Standards on Employment.
Higher housing standards for migrant workers will reduce employers' demand for migrant labor from D_1 to D_2. The money wage rate will fall from W_2 to W_1, but the nonmonetary benefits of improved housing will increase by the vertical distance between points a and b. Though workers will be earning a full wage of W_3, fewer of them—Q_2 instead of Q_3—will be hired.

Employment Security Commission arranged jobs and housing for 27,163 migrants. But in the summer of 1970 it estimated that it would be able to place only 7,000 to 8,000 workers. State and local officials forecast that on balance, the new housing standards would eliminate 6,000 to 10,000 jobs. Meanwhile many growers, stung by the bad publicity surrounding migrant housing, closed their camps and switched to mechanical harvesting. As one grower put it, "It might be cheaper for me to continue using migrant help for a few more years, but mechanization is the trend of the future. And no matter what kind of housing I provide I'm going to be criticized for mistreating migrants. So I might as well switch now."[2]

1. Milton Friedman, "Migrant Workers," *Newsweek*, July 27, 1970, p. 60.
2. "Housing Dispute Spurs Migrant Farmers to Switch to Machines from Migrant Help," *Wall Street Journal*, June 29, 1970, p. 18.

paychecks. Many college students favor the minimum wage, perhaps because they are more productive than less educated members of their generation, and therefore less likely to lose their jobs as a result of the legislation. Labor unions also have an incentive to support minimum wage laws. When the government raises wages in nonunion sectors of the economy, it puts unions in a better bargaining position. Under such circumstances, it becomes less likely that union wage demands will prompt employers to move to nonunion sectors of the economy. In fact, the first minimum wage legislation was passed at a time when many companies were moving from the unionized North to the nonunionized South. The introduction of the minimum wage reduced the net benefit of moving south, retarding the exodus.

Summary and Extensions

In a competitive labor market, wage rates are determined by the interaction of willing suppliers of labor (employees) and demanders of labor (employers). Suppliers are influenced significantly by the nonmonetary benefits of employment, as well as by the value they place on their next-best alternative employment. Thus differences in money wage rates may not reflect true differences in full wage rates. Demand is influenced by the laborer's productivity and the price of the laborer's product.

In a competitive labor market, any attempt to change workers' incomes through minimum standards for wages or working conditions can benefit some workers only at the expense of others. As the economist Milton Friedman complains, "The old saying is that Quakers went to the New World to do good and ended up doing well. Today, well-meaning reformers go to Washington to do good and end up doing harm."[6] Can the mixed results of minimum wage legislation be construed as a clear-cut improvement in social welfare? Economic analysis cannot address that highly subjective question. But economists can urge that legislators attempt to find ways to increase rather than reduce the employment opportunities of those they seek to help.

Major Conclusions

1. The demand for labor depends on the productivity of workers, as measured by their marginal product, and the price of the product they produce. The supply of labor depends on the full benefits of employment and the value workers place on alternative uses for their time.
2. The demand for labor slopes downward, like the demand for all other goods and services. The supply of labor slopes upward, like the supply of other goods and services.

---

6. Milton Friedman, "Migrant Workers," *Newsweek*, July 27, 1970, p. 60.

3. In a competitive labor market, the wage rate and number of people hired are determined by the interaction of the supply of and demand for labor.
4. Nonmonetary benefits of employment tend to increase the supply of labor in a market, reducing the money wage rate and increasing the number of people hired.
5. Minimum wage laws increase the wage rates paid to some workers, but reduce employment opportunities for others.
6. Minimum standards for nonmonetary benefits tend to reduce both the money wage and the demand for labor. Such standards improve the full wage rate paid to some workers but reduce employment opportunities for others.

Questions to Ponder

1. In what ways can market-determined wages be considered just or unjust? Explain.
2. The government requires employers to pay time-and-a-half for labor in excess of forty hours a week. What effect should such a law have on the quantity of labor demanded? Why?
3. Does union support of laws outlawing child labor square with the private interests of union members? Should society protect some of its members from some kinds of employment regardless of monetary considerations? Why?
4. How could the minimum wage rate and migrant housing standards be expected to affect the prices of consumer goods? Explain, using supply and demand graphs.
5. Suppose government requires employers to pay a minimum wage of $10 per hour to workers over twenty-two years of age. What effect should such a law have on the employment opportunities of people over twenty-two? On the employment opportunities and wage rates of persons under twenty-two?

Central Question

How do employer cartels and unions affect wage rates and employment opportunities?

Key Terms

Monopsony

Monopsony power

Marginal cost of labor

Employer cartel

Right-to-work law

Union shop

Chapter 27

Monopsonies and Unions

*Labor associations can do
nothing to raise wages but by
force; it may be force applied
passively or force applied
actively, or force held in
reserve, but it must be force . . .
Those who tell you of labor
unions bent on raising wages
by moral suasion alone are like
those who tell you of tigers
who live on oranges.*
Henry George

*C*ompetition is bad for those who have to compete. Not only as producers but as employers, firms would rather control competitive forces than be controlled by them. They would like to pay employees less than the market wage—but competition does not give them that choice.

Similarly, workers find that competition for jobs prevents them from earning more than the market wage. Thus doctors, truck drivers, and barbers have an interest in restricting competition in their labor markets. Acting as a group, they can acquire some control over their employment opportunities and wages.

Such power is difficult to maintain without the support of the law or the threat of violence, whether real or imagined. And it comes at the expense of the consumer, who will have fewer goods and services to choose from at higher prices. As always, the exercise of power by one group leads not only to market inefficiencies but to attempts by other groups to counteract it. The end result can be a reduction in the general welfare of the community.

This chapter examines both employer and employee power in the labor market; the conditions that allow it to persist; its influence on the allocation of resources; and its effects on the real incomes of workers, consumers, and entrepreneurs.

The Monopsonistic Employer

Power is never complete. It is always circumscribed by limitations of knowledge and the forces of law, custom, and the market. Within limits, employers can hire and fire, and can decide what products to produce and what type of labor to employ. But laws restrict the conditions of employment (working hours, working environment) they may offer, as well as their ability to discriminate among employees on the basis of sex, race, age, or religious affiliation. Competition imposes additional constraints. In a highly competitive labor market, an employer who offers very low wages will be outbid by others who want to hire workers. Competition for labor pushes wages up to a certain level, forcing some employers to withdraw from the market but permitting others to hire at the going wage rate.[1]

For the individual employer, then, the freedom of the competitive market is a highly constrained freedom. Not so, however, for those lucky employers who enjoy the power of a monopsony. A **monopsony** is the sole *buyer* of any good, service, or resource. (Monopsony should not be confused with monopoly, the single *seller* of a good or service.) The term is most frequently used to indicate the sole or dominant employer of labor in a given market. A good example of a monopsony would be a large coal-mining company in a small town with no other industry. A firm that is not a sole employer

Monopsony: the sole buyer of any good, service, or resource.

---

1. Competitors who do not hire influence the wage rate just as much as those who do; their presence on the sidelines keeps the price from falling. If a firm lowers its wages, other employers may move into the market and hire away part of the work force.

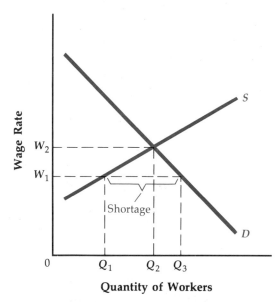

Figure 27.1. The Competitive Labor Market.
In a competitive market, the equilibrium wage rate will be W_2. Lower wage rates, such as W_1, would create a shortage of labor, and employers would compete for the available laborers by offering a higher wage. In pushing up the wage rate to the equilibrium level, employers impose costs on one another. They must pay higher wages not only to new employees, but to all current employees, in order to keep them.

but that dominates the market for a certain type of labor is said to have monopsony power. **Monopsony power** is the ability of a producer to alter the price of a resource like labor by changing the quantity employed. By reducing competition for workers' services, monopsony power allows employers to suppress the wage rate.

Monopsony power:
the ability of a producer to alter the price of a resource like labor by changing the quantity employed.

The Cost of Labor

Monopsony power reduces the costs of competitive hiring. Assume that the downward-sloping demand curve D in Figure 27.1 shows the market demand for workers, and the upward-sloping supply curve S shows the number of workers willing to work at various wage rates. If all firms act independently—that is, if they compete with one another—the market wage rate will settle at W_2, and the number of workers hired will be Q_2. At lower wage rates, such as W_1, shortages will develop. As indicated by the market demand curve, employers will be willing to pay more than W_1. If a shortage exists, the market wage will be bid up to W_2.

An increase in the wage rate will encourage more workers to seek jobs. But as long as there is a shortage, the competitive bidding imposes costs

Table 27.1. The Marginal Cost of Labor

Number of Workers Willing to Work (1)	Annual Wage of Each Worker (2)	Total Wage Bill [(1) × (2)] (3)	Marginal Cost of Additional Worker [Change in (3)] (4)
1	$20,000	$ 20,000	$20,000
2	22,000	44,000	24,000
3	24,000	72,000	28,000
4	26,000	104,000	32,000
5	28,000	140,000	36,000
6	30,000	180,000	40,000

on employers. The firm that offers a wage higher than W_1 forces other firms to offer a comparable wage to retain their current employees. If those firms want to acquire additional workers, they may have to offer an even higher wage. As they bid the wage up, firms impose reciprocal costs on one another, as at an auction.

Because any increase in wages paid to one worker must be extended to all, the total cost to all employers of hiring even one worker at a higher wage can be staggering. If the wage rises from W_1 to W_2 in Figure 27.1, the total wage bill for the first Q_1 workers rises by the wage increase $W_2 - W_1$ times Q_1 workers, or by the area W_2abW_1. Table 27.1 shows how the effect of a wage increase is multiplied when it must be extended to other workers. The first two columns reflect the assumption that as the wage rate rises, more workers will accept jobs. If only one worker is demanded, he can be hired for $20,000. The firm's total wage bill will also be $20,000 (column 3). If two workers are demanded, and the second worker will not work for less than $22,000, the salary of the first worker must also be raised to $22,000. The cost of the second worker is therefore $24,000 (column 4): $22,000 for his services plus the $2,000 raise that must be given to the first worker.

The cost of additional workers can be similarly derived. When the sixth worker is added, she must be offered $30,000 and the other five workers must each be given a $2,000 raise. The cost of adding this new worker, called the marginal cost of labor, has risen to $40,000. The **marginal cost of labor** is the additional cost to the firm of expanding employment by one additional worker. Note that as the number of workers hired increases, the gap between the marginal cost of labor and the going wage rate expands. When two workers are hired, the gap is $2,000 ($24,000 − $22,000). When six are employed, it is $10,000 ($40,000 − $30,000).

Figure 27.2, based on columns 1 and 4 of Table 27.1, shows the marginal cost of labor graphically. The marginal cost curve lies above the supply curve, for the cost of each new worker hired (beyond the first worker) is greater than the worker's salary.

Marginal cost of labor: the additional cost to the firm of expanding employment by one additional worker.

Figure 27.2. The Marginal Cost of Labor.
The marginal cost of hiring additional workers is greater than the wages that must be paid to the new workers. Therefore the marginal cost of labor curve lies above the labor supply curve.

The Monopsonistic Hiring Decision

The monopsonistic employer does not get caught in the competitive bind. By definition it is the only or dominant employer. Like a monopolist, the monopsonist can afford to search through the various wage-quantity combinations on the labor supply curve for the one that maximizes profits. The monopsonist will keep hiring more workers so long as their contribution to revenues is greater than their additional cost, as shown by the marginal cost of labor curve MC in Figure 27.3. To maximize profits, in other words, the monopsonist will hire until the marginal cost of the last worker hired (MC) equals his marginal value, as shown by the market demand curve for labor. Given the demand for labor D, the monopsonist's optimal employment level will be Q_2, where the marginal cost and demand for labor curves intersect. Note that that level is lower than the competitive employment level, Q_3.

Why hire where marginal cost equals marginal value? Suppose the monopsonist employed fewer workers—say Q_1. The marginal value of worker Q_1 would be quite high (point a), while her marginal cost would be low (point b). The monopsonist would be forgoing profits by hiring only Q_1 workers. Beyond Q_2 workers, the reverse would be true. The marginal cost of each new worker would be greater than his marginal value. Hiring more than Q_2 workers would reduce profits.

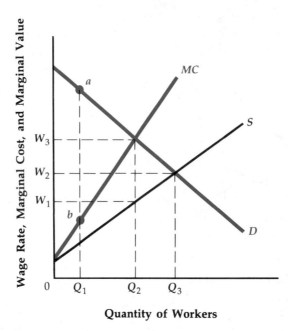

Figure 27.3. The Monopsonist.
The monopsonist will hire up to the point where the marginal value of the last worker, shown by the demand curve for labor, equals his or her marginal cost. For this monopsonistic employer, the optimum number of workers is Q_2. The monopsonist must pay only W_1 for that number of workers—less than the competitive wage level, W_2.

Once the monopsonist has chosen the employment level Q_2, it pays workers no more than is required by the labor supply curve, S. In Figure 27.3, the monopsonist must pay only W_1—much less than the wage that would be paid in a competitive labor market, W_2. In other words, the monopsonist hires fewer workers and pays them less than an employer in a competitive labor market.

It is the monopsonistic firm's power to reduce the number of workers hired that enables it to hold wages below the competitive level. In a competitive labor market, if one firm attempts to cut employment and reduce wages, it will not be able to keep its business going, for workers will depart to other employers willing to pay the going market wage. The individual firm is not large enough, in relation to the entire labor market, to exercise monopsony power. It reluctantly accepts the market wage, W_2, as a given.

Employer cartel: any organization of employers that seeks to restrict the number of workers hired in order to lower wages and increase profits.

Employer Cartels: Monopsony Power Through Collusion

Envying the power of the monopsonist, competitive employers may attempt to organize a cartel. An **employer cartel** is any organization of

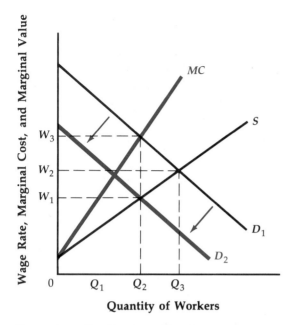

Figure 27.4. The Employer Cartel.
To achieve the same results as a monopsonist, the employer cartel will devise restrictive employment rules that artificially reduce market demand to D_2. The reduced demand allows cartel members to hire only Q_2 workers at wage W_1—significantly less than the competitive wage, W_2.

employers that seeks to restrict the number of workers hired in order to lower wages and increase profits.

The usual way of lowering employment is to establish restrictive employment rules that limit the movement of workers from one job to another. Such rules tend to reduce the demand for labor. In Figure 27.4, demand falls from D_1 to D_2. As a result, the wage rate drops, from W_2 to W_1, and employment falls, from Q_3 to Q_2. Although the method of limiting employment is different from that used in monopsony, the effect is the same. Whether the monopsonistic firm equates marginal cost with marginal value (shown by curve D_1) or the employer cartel reduces the demand for labor (to D_2), employment still drops to Q_2. In both cases workers earn a wage rate of W_1—less than the competitive wage.

One industry in which employers have tried to cartelize the labor market is professional sports. Owners of teams have developed complex rules governing the hiring of athletes. In the National Football League (NFL), for example, teams acquire rights to negotiate with promising college players through an annual draft. Once a player has been drafted by one team, no other team in the league can negotiate with him. Teams can buy and sell draft rights as well as rights to players already drafted, but within leagues they are prohibited from competing directly with one another for players' services. Violations of these rules carry stiff penalties, including revocation of a team's franchise.

In the National Collegiate Athletic Association (NCAA), similar rules govern the recruitment and retention of college and university athletes. The NCAA restricts the number of athletic scholarships schools may award and the stipends and fringe benefits athletes may receive. Once enrolled in a four-year college or university, an athlete cannot change schools without losing a year of eligibility.

School hiring is often cartelized. For example, the University of North Carolina system is a major employer in its region. Like most other state universities, North Carolina prohibits competition for faculty among its sixteen campuses. East Carolina University cannot consider hiring a professor from another campus—say Chapel Hill—unless the professor first applies for the position, with the permission of the Chapel Hill chancellor.

To give another example, the Civil Service Administration has developed a salary schedule for federal workers. The effect of this schedule is to reduce interdepartmental competition for workers—along with the salaries they are paid. The same practice is common in large companies that represent a significant force in their particular labor markets. To the extent that such rules are obeyed, firms gain the benefits of a monopsonistic market position.

The Inefficiency of Monopsony

Economically, a monopsony is inefficient because it misallocates employment opportunities. Too few people are employed by a monopsony or cartelized labor market; too many are employed elsewhere. Note that the marginal value of all jobs between Q_2 and Q_3 in Figure 27.5, as indicated by the demand curve, is greater than the workers' opportunity cost, as indicated by the supply curve. The additional market value of the product that could be created by employing an extra $Q_3 - Q_2$ workers is shown by the area under the demand curve, Q_2abQ_3. The opportunity cost of those workers' employment (the market value of their output from employment elsewhere) is shown by the smaller area under the supply curve, Q_2cbQ_3. If the monopsony increased its employment from Q_2 to Q_3, then, the additional workers would create more value than they currently create in their employment elsewhere. The net value gained from raising employment from Q_2 to Q_3 would be the shaded triangular area abc (the additional value Q_2abQ_3 minus the additional cost Q_2cbQ_3). By not extending production to Q_3, the monopsony sacrifices that net value.

Actually, the inefficiency of a monopsony may be even greater than the triangular area abc. For the only way a monopsony can continue to pay the below-market wage rate of W_1 is to erect and maintain costly barriers to entry and exit from its labor market. Otherwise other employers would try to move into the monopsonist's market, and workers would try to move out. Textile companies in the Carolinas, for example, have attempted to retain their monopsony position by limiting the availability of roads

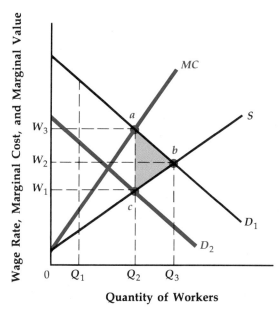

Figure 27.5. The Inefficiency of Monopsony.
Monopsonistic hiring is less efficient than competitive hiring, which is determined by the intersection of the supply and demand curves. In a competitive market, Q_3 workers would be employed. In a monopsony or cartelized labor market, only Q_2 workers are hired. The inefficiency of monopsony is therefore equal to the shaded triangular area below curve D_1.

and utilities, including water and sewer lines, to incoming employers. Limitation of educational expenditures is another means of maintaining monopsony, for education not only improves workers' skills, but encourages their mobility. Both strategies require the monopsonist to spend considerable time and effort in lobbying and other political activities.

For the employer cartel, the difficulties of maintaining market control are likely to be still greater. It must pay the costs of collusion as well as the other costs just mentioned. If the cartel includes many employers, each hiring only a small fraction of the total labor force, collusive agreements will be especially hard to enforce. For instance, if owners of hot dog and hamburger stands in large metropolitan areas tried to collude on their hiring, reducing their demand for labor, the wage rate might fall temporarily. But each firm would then have an incentive to take advantage of the lower wage by hiring more workers. If individual firms are small, an increase in employment will affect the market wage rate only slightly. But in a free market, new firms can enter to take advantage of the artificially low wage rate. If too many employers expand hiring, their competition for labor will bid up the market wage.

Given the incentives to chisel, the costs of enforcing cartel rules can be prohibitively high. Only in labor markets dominated by a small number of employers—a minority of markets—are cartels likely to survive. Professional sports cartels work because the number of teams is relatively small and, more important, because the league can revoke the franchises of teams that violate cartel rules. (Even so, entrepreneurs were able to organize the United States Football League (USFL) in 1982, circumventing cartel franchise rules.) And government employment rules work because the federal government controls departmental budgets. Positions simply are not funded for more than the salary limits.

The Employee's Market Power

In a highly competitive labor market, an individual worker is by definition powerless to raise the wage rate or improve conditions of employment. A worker who demands a higher wage may be turned down in favor of other workers willing to accept less. When a textile worker applies for a job, she must accept the personnel manager's offer; little or no bargaining is involved. Similarly, the textile worker cannot negotiate on her annual raise, which generally reflects conditions in the labor market for textile workers.

In short, competition means that the welfare of individual workers is controlled by what others do, acting independently. One worker's willingness to accept the market wage imposes a cost on those who would like to see the wage increased. Individual workers can surmount these forces in two ways: by differentiating their skills and by forming unions.

The individual worker can differentiate her labor from that of others by making use of her natural mental and physical talents or by developing new ones through education. She may move into an entirely different labor market, one with few competitors, who will not be inclined to accept low wages or poor working conditions. In any case, this skilled worker's terms of employment will depend less on what other workers are willing to do and more on what consumers are willing to pay.

Over the decades skill differentiation has probably been the single most important means by which workers have acquired some control over their own employment. High school students take jobs as menial workers to gain work experience that will make them more attractive to employers in other labor markets. Students go to college not only for the social life or the job of learning, but to improve their skills and become more employable. And some go on to professional school to differentiate themselves from the mass of college graduates. Musical groups work to develop a style that will distinguish them from other groups. Beauticians try to be the first to introduce a new hairstyle; authors try to improve their writing skills; basketball players spend long hours on the court; legal secretaries train to become paralegals. All these efforts and many more are attempts to override the forces of competition.

If all workers follow the course of skill differentiation, its benefits will be reduced and wages will be depressed. But those who reach a different market first can make gains. And although the benefits may be temporary,

Perspectives in Economics: Wage Determination in the National Football League

Employer cartels rarely acknowledge that their objective is to increase their profits at workers' expense. The National Football League, for example, contends that without the draft system and the so-called reserve clause, which commits players to particular clubs, financially strong teams would be able to raid financially weak teams for their good players, destroying the excitement of the sport. This may be true. But the league's rules have other results as well—including the suppression of competition for athletes, and thus of athletes' salaries.

Professional athletes can hardly be viewed as an oppressed class. Most players earn several times the average family income in the United States. One reason players do so well is that the NFL is an imperfect employer cartel: to some degree teams compete among themselves. And player contracts generally last only a few years, after which players can become free agents, to be hired competitively by the highest bidder.

But more important, players, especially the better ones, have a degree of market power of their own. They are the sole sellers of their football talents, monopolists of a rare degree of skill. There is only one Dan Marino, quarterback for the Miami Dolphins. His passing ability gives him significant monopoly power over the sale of his services. When a monopsonist like a football team faces a monopolist like Marino, the final negotiated wage depends largely on the relative market strengths and bargaining skills of the two parties.

Another consideration is that a player's attitude influences his performance on the field. A player who is seriously disgruntled because he considers his salary too low may not play up to his ability. A superior player who is not paid in proportion to his skills may reduce his efforts until his performance is no better than others making his wage. To be able to demand more from its better players, then, a team may agree to pay them more than their opportunity wage.

If a superstar's salary demands are not met, he may decide to withhold his labor. While the star is missing from the line-up, attendance may fall off, causing a significant drop in the team's gate receipts. It may well be willing to pay a premium in the form of a higher salary to avoid such a risk.

Then too, the league must always consider the possibility that its below-market wages will attract new entrants into its sports market. The United States Football League was formed not just because demand for football games was high in the early 1980s, but because USFL owners believed they could compete favorably with the NFL's monopsonistic salaries and monopoly prices for television rights.

Still, professional football teams have a built-in incentive to keep their wages below market value because they can sell and trade the rights to specific players. If a player signs a contract for less than his true market value, other teams will want to buy the rights to that player. That is, there will be a market demand for player rights. Competition among owners will establish market prices for those rights. The price will roughly approximate the difference between the present value of a player's assessed market value and his contracted salary. Suppose, for instance, that the value of a player's salary over the course of his career is $1 million, but he will bring his team benefits worth $1.5 million. The rights to that player should sell for roughly $500,000—a substantial bonus to the team that owns them.

they can be sufficient to cover the cost of acquiring the skills. Workers' new skills may also enable producers to make better final products, so that consumers benefit too. Skill differentiation means variety and choice.

Unions

Historically unions have been viewed as an important means of increasing workers' economic power, but their effectiveness may have been overrated. We will analyze union power in terms of supply, demand, and marginal cost of labor. But first, a brief look at the history of union membership.

Union Strength in the United States

Unions are an important force in the U.S. economy. But over the last three decades, union membership has grown more slowly than the labor force. Consequently, union membership as a percentage of the labor force has been slipping (see Table 27.2). In the mid-1950s unions accounted for more than one-quarter of the labor force; by 1980 they spoke for roughly one-fifth. And by 1984 membership had fallen back to the 1950s' level, covering about 15 percent of the labor force.

The decline in unions' share of the work force reflects several factors. First, product and service markets have become more competitive world-wide. In such markets, unions have considerable difficulty securing higher wages and fringe benefits for their members. If unions strike for higher benefits in competitive markets, product and service prices will rise and buyers will turn to other, nonunion producers, both in the United States and abroad. Workers may feel the benefits of union membership fall short of the cost of union dues.

Table 27.2. Union Membership in the United States, 1950–1980

Year	Union Membership (in millions)	Percentage of Labor Force
1950	15,000	23.7
1955	17,749	26.4
1960	18,117	25.3
1965	18,519	24.2
1970	21,852	24.4
1974	23,408	22.5
1980	22,811	21.0
1984 (Sept.)	17,417	15.1

Sources: 1950–1965, U.S. Bureau of the Census, *Historical Statistics of the United States* (1975), p. 176; 1970–1980, U.S. Bureau of the Census, *Statistical Abstract of the United States* (1985), p. 424; September 1984, Larry T. Adams, "Changing Employment Patterns of Organized Workers," *Monthly Labor Review* (February 1985), p. 26.

Second, most of the recent growth in U.S. employment has come in the new service and high-technology industries, where unions have not been established. Traditional smokestack industries, such as automobiles and steel, have cut back on employees and have grown at a slower pace, partly because of high union wages. When the nation's product mix changes rapidly, unions are at a disadvantage, for it takes time and money to organize workers. At the same time, the composition of the labor force has shifted from predominantly blue-collar to white-collar. Perhaps because they identify with management, white-collar workers have been particularly difficult to organize.

Demographic trends have also hurt unions. Over the past few decades, the labor force has been moving from the union-dominated states of the Northeast and Midwest to the southern and western states, which have right-to-work laws. A **right-to-work law** is a state statute that allows unionized firms to hire nonunion workers, and to continue to employ them whether or not they join the existing union. Right-to-work states permit nonunion workers to retain their jobs even if a majority of workers in a company votes to unionize. Thus nonunion workers who work in unionized plants can acquire many if not all the benefits of union workers. In such states, there is little incentive for workers to join a union and pay union dues.

Finally, management has learned from experience that if workers are not offered reasonable wages, fringe benefits, and working conditions, they will organize. Accordingly, managers of nonunion firms have reduced workers' incentives to organize by boosting benefits. Even in nonunion plants, many workers now enjoy the benefits of unionization without the obligations or problems it brings.

Right-to-work law: a state statute that allows unionized firms to hire nonunion workers, and to continue to employ them whether or not they join the existing union.

Using Union Power to Raise Wages

In a large and competitive labor market, the individual worker is an insignificant part of the total labor supply, with no power to influence his wage. His withdrawal from the labor market imposes no cost on employers, who can easily replace him at the competitive wage rate. But if a large group of workers acts collectively, it can impose substantial costs on employers. Through strikes and picketing, a group can reduce the available supply of workers significantly, forcing employers to cut back production and thereby restricting sales. Thus employers have an incentive to pay attention to union demands.

Figure 27.6 shows how unions use their collective power to restrict the labor supply in bargaining for higher wages. In a competitive labor market without unions the supply of labor will be S_1, the market wage rate W_1, and the number of workers hired Q_2. But in a unionized labor market, where some workers cannot work because they are not union members, the supply of labor will be restricted to S_2. The shift in the labor supply curve will push the wage rate up to W_2 and reduce the number of workers hired to Q_1. Beyond Q_1, each additional unionized worker costs more than he is worth to the employer.

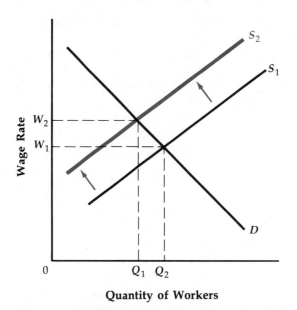

Figure 27.6. The Effect of Union Labor Restrictions on Wages.
By artificially reducing the supply of laborers from S_1 to S_2, unions can increase the wage rate from W_1 to W_2. The number of workers hired will be Q_1, less than the equilibrium employment level in a competitive market.

If the labor market is controlled by a single employer or employer cartel, as in professional sports, a union can raise the wage without affecting the number of workers hired. As shown in Figure 27.7, the monopsonistic firm will tend to hire Q_1 workers at a wage of W_1, even though it could justify paying as much as W_3 on economic grounds. Thus through strikes or the threat of a strike, unions can raise the wage rate up to W_3 without reducing employment. Only if the wage rate rises above W_3 will the number of workers hired fall.

If the wage rate settles somewhere below W_3—say at W_2—the number of workers hired will actually increase, to Q_2 in Figure 27.7. In such cases the union wage rate becomes the firm's marginal cost of labor. No longer does the marginal cost of labor curve slope upward. Rather, it is horizontal at wage rate W_2. As in a nonunionized market, the monopsonist will hire up to the point where the marginal cost of labor, now constant at W_2, equals its marginal value, as shown by the demand curve. That point is Q_2.[2] Minimum wage laws will have the same effect when imposed on monopsonistic labor markets. So long as the minimum wage is fixed below

---

2. If the union wage rate were set at the intersection of the supply and demand curves, the competitive employment level would be achieved. Can you explain why?

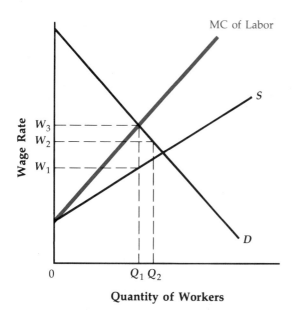

Figure 27.7. The Effect of Union Labor Restrictions in a Cartelized Labor Market. In a market where labor demand and wage rates have been artificially lowered by employer restrictions, a union can raise the wage rate, in this case from W_1 to W_2, without decreasing the number of workers hired. Employment will actually increase, from Q_1 to Q_2.

W_3 in the figure, employment will expand. Once the new employment equilibrium of W_2Q_2 has been reached, however, further increases in the wage rate will reduce the employment level, unless they are accompanied by an increase in labor demand. For instance, if the wage rate were raised again from W_2 to W_3, employment would fall back from Q_2 to Q_1.

Because of these effects, the economic argument for unions and minimum wage laws is most powerful when employers enjoy significant market power. Indeed, we should expect to find the most successful unions in monopsonistic labor markets. In competitive markets, where union wage demands are restricted by their adverse effects on total employment, unions will be less powerful. Unfortunately, government applies minimum wage laws to all markets, monopsonistic or not. Thus the net effect of such laws will depend on the extent of competition versus monopsony in the nation's labor markets. As we saw in the last chapter, studies conducted over the past thirty years have found that the overall effect of minimum wage laws is negative: they have reduced employment.

A second way unions can improve their members' employment opportunities is to promote union-made products and services. If they can increase demand for their products through advertising or lobbying, product prices will go up, and so will the demand for labor. In Figure 27.8, an increase in the demand for labor from D_1 to D_2 boosts the wage rate from W_1 to W_2 and the number of workers hired from Q_1 to Q_2. Thus

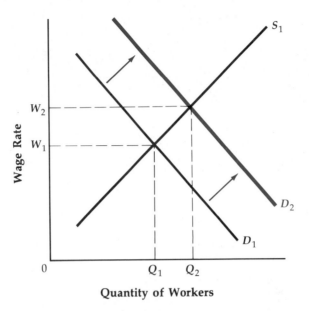

Figure 27.8. A Union-Inspired Increase in the Demand for Labor.
If unions can promote the purchase of union-made products and services, the demand for labor will rise from D_1 to D_2, increasing union employment from Q_1 to Q_2 and raising union wages from W_1 to W_2.

unionized garment workers promote union-made clothing, and automobile workers' unions lobby for increased government spending on highways.

Union efforts do not necessarily increase employment for all workers. An increase in government expenditures on aircraft, for instance, can mean less spent on educational programs and hence fewer teachers hired. Or the expenditure could be funded through a tax increase, which would reduce spending on consumer items like furniture and houses, depressing employment in those industries. All in all, union efforts to increase employment probably distort employment opportunities more than they improve them.

The Efficiency of Unions

Our analysis of union power presumes that unions are sufficiently large and well organized to affect the labor supply by striking. In a free and open market, however, taking collective action can be difficult, particularly when the labor market is large and the use of force is prohibited by law. Nonunion workers will tend to free-ride on unions' efforts to improve wages. If the union restricts the labor supply, it provides benefits (a public good) to all of the workers in that labor market. However, only union workers bear the cost of establishing those restrictions through organizing, paying dues, and striking.

Like cartelization, collective action is much more likely to succeed in small groups than in large ones. In a small union, where each worker is a significant part of the total labor supply, individual members can make significant contributions to the group's welfare, and can see direct benefits from them. In small groups, ties of friendship strengthen bonds based on economic need, discouraging free-riding. Workers in such settings are therefore more likely to be willing to bear the costs of union membership. In fact, unions first emerged in small-group settings, where employer and employee worked together closely.[3] Later small unions were organized into federations that could offer members special benefits, such as insurance policies, and recreational facilities.

Large unions developed last, doubtless because a worker in a large group represents only a small fraction of the total labor supply. Just as an individual worker's withdrawal from the market would have no detectable effect on the labor supply or wage rate, his contribution to a strike that secures a wage increase will never be noticed. The result would be the same with or without his participation in the movement. Thus workers in a large labor market may not have enough incentive to take on the costs involved in participating in a union movement.

For this reason the threat of force is common in many large union movements. Workers who cross a picket line may suffer personal injury or social ostracism. Individual workers must weigh the cost of not participating in the union (bodily injury or property damage) against the cost of participating (union dues, lost wages during strikes). The cost of not participating can be so great that membership even in a large union becomes a rational act. Of course, employers have used the same tactics to discourage union membership. The history of the labor movement has been rocky at best, replete with criminal acts by both owners and labor organizers. (See the box on the development of labor law.)

Federal and state laws also support union organizing efforts. Under the Wagner Act, if a simple majority of workers votes for unionization, their plant or firm can be organized as a union shop. A **union shop** is a place of employment where a worker, once employed, must join the recognized union as a condition of continued employment. If a new worker refuses to join the union, she is simply denied employment in that firm. Thus the government imposes a substantial cost on workers who do not participate in union activities. Before the Wagner Act, it was much more difficult to organize a union. By crossing the picket line, a few dissenting workers or strikebreakers (workers who move into a labor market to claim the jobs of striking workers) could undermine union organizing efforts.

While the institution of democratic elections has greatly reduced the potential for violence in such situations, it has also reduced the cost of organizing a union. Unions argue that compulsory membership through democratic elections (the union shop) is necessary to overcome the free-rider problem—in which nonmembers acquire the benefits of union

Union shop: a place of employment where a worker, once employed, must join the recognized union as a condition of continued employment.

---

3. Mancur Olson, "The Labor Union and Economic Freedom," in *The Logic of Collective Action: Public Goods and the Theory of Groups* (Cambridge, Mass.: Harvard University Press, 1971), pp. 66–97.

Perspectives in Economics:
The Development of U.S. Labor Law

John Warner

The growth of union membership in the United States and the development of labor law have closely paralleled changes in public opinion of unions. The earliest unions were craft unions, composed of highly skilled workers. Originating at the end of the eighteenth century, they were local in nature and tended to concentrate in the large eastern cities. Until the 1930s, the general public attitude toward unions was negative—and so were the laws that regulated them. At first unions were regarded simply as illegal conspiracies. In 1842 a Massachusetts court ruled that unions were not illegal per se (*Commonwealth* v. *Hunt*); nevertheless union growth remained slow until the 1880s.

In 1886, several craft unions joined together to form the American Federation of Labor (AFL). Samuel Gompers of the Cigar Workers Union became the first president of this nationwide organization of skilled workers. By emphasizing "bread and butter unionism," Gompers did much to persuade the American public that unions were more interested in economic issues than in the sweeping political and social change advocated by European unions. In so doing, he helped improve the public image of unions.

Unions still faced significant legal barriers, however. Following a strike of railway workers against the Pullman Company in 1894, the courts used the Sherman Antitrust Act of 1890 to rule that a strike was an illegal restraint of trade. They also upheld the legality of certain strikebreaking techniques, including the yellow-dog contract (which required employees not to join a union), the lockout, and the blacklist.

Not until the 1930s did economic and political forces bring fundamental changes in the legal attitude toward unions. Until then most unions had been craft unions and did not represent the interests of unskilled workers. During the 1920s, however, the most rapid employment gains came in the automobile, steel, and rubber industries, which employed primarily unskilled and semiskilled labor. Recognizing the potential political power of the working class, Franklin Roosevelt ran for president in 1932 on a platform that addressed the needs of the blue-collar worker.

Against the backdrop of the Great Depression, Roosevelt's platform had broad public appeal. Soon court rulings began to reflect the change in social attitudes. And in 1932, Congress passed the Norris-LaGuardia Act, which established the right

membership without paying for them. But critics maintain that the union shop merely substitutes a forced-rider problem for the free-rider problem.

The Davis-Bacon Act requires contractors on federally funded construction projects to pay the prevailing wage, which the Department of Labor usually interprets to mean the prevailing union wage in that area. Because nonunion contractors would have to raise their usual wage rates to work on federal projects, they rarely bid on them. Obviously, the Davis-Bacon Act increases the demand for union labor.

Though unions may be seen as a welcome counterforce to the market power of large, successful employer cartels, they can have negative effects as well. Just as union members have an interest in keeping each other of unions to bargain collectively. The act greatly restricted the conditions under which courts could issue injunctions against striking unions, and declared the yellow-dog contract illegal.

The National Labor Relations Act, commonly known as the Wagner Act, was passed in 1935. Often called labor's Magna Carta, the Wagner Act broadened the collective bargaining rights first set forth in the Norris-LaGuardia Act. It gave workers the right to form and join unions without interference from employers and required employers to bargain "in good faith" with any union certified by the newly established National Labor Relations Board. And it forbade employers to discriminate against union members in hiring or tenure of employment.

Under the Wagner Act, many new unions were formed, especially in industries that employed predominantly unskilled workers. Between 1933 and 1945 the unionized proportion of the labor force grew from 5.2 to 22.8 percent. But with the end of World War II, a series of long strikes coupled with rapid inflation brought a public clamor for the regulation of unions. The change in the public's attitude was followed by passage of the restrictive Taft-Hartley Act of 1947.

The Taft-Hartley Act outlawed certain labor practices as unfair, including "featherbedding," or the practice of requiring firms to hire more workers than needed for a job. It prohibited the closed shop, an arrangement that required employers to hire only union members. The act also provided for the regulation of unions' internal affairs and established guidelines for collective bargaining. And it empowered the president to declare a sixty-day injunction—called a cooling-off period—against strikes that "imperil the health and safety of the nation." The Taft-Hartley Act did permit the union shop (whose rules allow an employer to hire nonunion workers but require them to join the union after employment). But the act also allowed state right-to-work laws to supersede federal law. Currently nineteen states, most of them in the South, have right-to-work laws.

In 1959 the Landrum-Griffin Act reduced the influence of union officials over the rank-and-file membership by requiring secret balloting in union elections and restricting the conditions under which a union may fire or suspend a member. The act also clarified the responsibilities of union officers to their membership and required them to file reports with the federal government.

from accepting a lower wage (because the result of ensuing competition will be lower wages for all), they also have an interest in keeping any individual from improving his skills. If some workers compete by improving their productivity, all may have to follow suit. To reduce such competition among workers, unions typically seek wage schedules that are not based on job performance. In most unions, wages are based on seniority, and wage increases are distributed equally across the board. To the extent that hard work and improved skills are not rewarded in a union shop, unions contribute to production inefficiencies. (Union leaders counter that unions increase productivity by fostering workers' self-esteem and sense of control over their economic well-being.)

Perspectives in Economics: Employment at Will

Stephanie Saul

In 14 years with the Korvettes retail chain, Morton Savodnik received glowing evaluations, eventually working his way up to store manager. Then, 10 weeks short of being vested in the company pension plan, Savodnik was fired. "It was done very ungraciously," said Savodnik, now 61, who lives in New York state. "I was called to the home office at 2 p.m. and told that was it, I was to leave at 4 p.m. Six months prior to that I had gotten an increase in pay."

Savodnik fought the company in court and won the right to his $85.50-a-month pension. A federal judge ruled Savodnik's 1977 firing was an unconscionable attempt by Korvettes to avoid paying his retirement benefits.

About 3 million American workers are fired annually by their employers, and many of them are left outraged and financially strapped. But traditionally, when the boss has yelled, "You're fired," workers have had little recourse. The United States is the only industrial democracy that has not specifically protected its workers from unfair firing; instead, courts here have adhered to a doctrine called "employment at will," which gives employers the right to fire workers whenever they want, with or without justification.

As the Savodnik case shows, however, employment at will is under fire in some parts of the country. Courts are slowly eroding the doctrine, establishing exceptions to the idea that employers can fire employees without justification. And a growing number of legislatures and scholars have begun questioning the doctrine's fairness. But it still is an uphill struggle. . . . Most other industrial countries provide . . . [a] grievance systems or require employers to make expensive severance payments to employees fired unjustly. Even in feudal times, European civilizations recognized a worker's right to keep his job for one year. The English Statute of Laborers, enacted in 1562, required "reasonable cause" to dismiss an employee before a one-year employment period expired.

The idea of employment at will evolved in the United States during the Industrial Revolution. It remained entrenched in American attitudes toward employment well into the 20th century and has begun changing only recently. A major exception came with the rise of union membership and collective bargaining agreements, which now cover about 20 percent of all American workers. But the vast majority of workers in this country still remain subject to employment at will.

The watershed was the 1964 Civil Rights Act, according to New York labor lawyer Frank Carling, who represents employers. "The Civil Rights Act started to change people's thinking," he said. "You had a statutory exception to employment at will. The Civil Rights Act said that an employer may still discharge an employee, but the reasons cannot be because of race or sex." According to Carling, the Civil Rights Act raised the consciousness of both employers and workers, who began to question the legitimacy of their dismissals. White male workers under age 40, who did not fall into age, sex, or race discrimination categories, began taking their employers to court on other grounds, claiming, for instance, that their firings violated implied contracts or the dictates of public policy.

Today, the trend clearly is away from the concept of employment at will. . . Case law and statutes in half of the 50 states have established various exceptions to the idea of employment at will. Legislatures in three states—California, New York, and Michigan—have considered general laws prohibiting unjust dismissal, but none of the general laws has yet been passed. Some states have laws that prohibit firing for certain reasons, such as New York's recently passed statute that regulates the firing of "whistle blowers," employees who report violations of law by their employers.

Most exceptions to the old doctrine have been granted through court decisions. In some states, courts have held that firing is unjust only when an employer is guilty of some egregious conduct, such as asking his employee to commit a crime.

A landmark court decision involved Peter Petermann, who was employed as a Teamsters business agent. When Petermann was subpoenaed to testify before the California Legislature, his supervisor allegedly instructed him to lie. Petermann refused and was fired by the union the next day. The California Supreme Court said Petermann had grounds for a lawsuit because an employee's discharge for refusing to commit perjury would be "obnoxious to the interests of the state and contrary to public policy."

In California, the most proworker state in this area of law, the courts recognize all employment relationships as implied contracts that employers cannot terminate without just cause. And in 1982, the New York State Court of Appeals held that Walton L. Weiner could sue his employer, Mc-Graw-Hill, for firing him. The court said a statement in a McGraw-Hill personnel manual, as well as a superior's assurance that employees could be fired only for "just cause," constituted an implied contract.

Courts in many states have recognized language in personnel manuals as binding. . . . A side effect of the increasing litigation is that law firms are establishing entire departments to advise employers on the issues of employment at will. Through employment manuals, as well as through verbal assurances to workers, companies may unwittingly guarantee lifetime employment . . . One way that companies are avoiding lawsuits is by placing language in job applications and employee manuals advising employees that they can be fired for any reason at any time.

Blue Cross & Blue Shield of Michigan placed the warning in employee handbooks that employees "can be terminated with or without reason" after a landmark 1980 decision by the Michigan Supreme Court. The case involved Charles Toussaint, a middle-level manager for Blue Cross who was fired in 1974. When he was hired, Toussaint received assurances that he would not be discharged as long as he did his job, and a company employment manual stated that the company would not dismiss employees except for cause. The court ruled that those assurances were enforceable by Toussaint, who was awarded more than $100,000 in damages. . . .

Stephanie Saul, "Employment at Will," *Newsday* as reprinted in the Greenville, S.C., *News/Piedmont*, January 13, 1985, p. D1.

Summary and Extensions

The power of the employer to control the demand for labor, and the power of the employee to control the supply of labor, can produce inefficiencies in the allocation of resources. But in a free market, neither employer nor employee can ever have complete power. Employer cartels must compete with employers outside the cartel for the available supply of labor. Other employers can move into their labor markets if the wage is held down by collusion, and employees can move to other labor markets or employers. Because limited competition will always exist, the distortion of market forces may not be very great. As illustrated by the rivalry that developed during the early 1980s between the National Football League and the United States Football League, competition can become intense even among a limited number of employers.

Likewise for unions and union power. If workers organize and push wage rates up, employers may eventually move to nonunionized markets or areas. And as union power continues to expand, it will eventually be resisted by those who do not wish to see their job opportunities constricted.

To the extent that laws reduce the costs of organizing cartels and unions, they will promote concentration of market power in the hands of a few. Because of the benefits involved, groups are likely to take advantage of whatever power they can develop. The result will be reduced efficiency in production, as more and more resources are devoted to group organizing and the exercise of group power. Fewer resources will be available for production, or resources will be inefficiently allocated among alternative uses. Consumers will earn lower real incomes and will have less to choose from in the market-place. For this reason economists tend either to favor competition or to oppose government promotion of monopsony. The economist's argument for competition is an argument for the dispersion of power, so that no individual or firm will be able to control the market or be controlled by others.

Major Conclusions

1. The marginal cost of labor curve is derived from, and lies above, the firm's labor supply curve.
2. A monopsony will hire where the marginal cost of labor equals its marginal value. Therefore the monopsonistic employer hires fewer workers, and pays them less, than an employer in a competitive labor market.
3. An employer cartel reduces the demand for labor through restrictive hiring policies. The effect is the same as that of a monopsony: lower wages and employment levels than in a competitive market.
4. Monopsonists and employer cartels are inefficient in the sense that the value of the product that could be produced by additional workers is greater than the opportunity cost of their employment.
5. To maintain its market power, a monopsonist must be able to prevent other employers from moving into its labor market, and workers from moving out.
6. To maintain its market power, an employer cartel must prevent its members from cheating on the cartel's restrictive employment rules.

7. Union membership as a percentage of the U.S. labor force has been declining over the past decades. The decrease can be attributed to the decline of blue-collar industries, where union organizing has been strongest; to the increased benefits now enjoyed by nonunion workers; and to the gradual shift in population from the union states of the North and Midwest to the right-to-work states of the South and West.
8. Unions can raise their members' wage rate by (a) restricting the supply of labor in a given market through control of union membership; (b) negotiating for a higher wage rate through strikes or the threat of strikes; and (c) increasing the demand for union-made products.
9. Except in monopsonistic or cartelized labor markets, unions tend to reduce employment opportunities by raising wages above the competitive level. In cartelized markets, unions can raise both wages and employment.
10. To the extent that unions restrict employment, they cause market inefficiency, just as the monopsonist does.

1. Using the supply of labor schedule below, find the marginal cost of labor and plot both the supply curve and the marginal cost curve.

Questions to Ponder

Number of Workers	Weekly Wage of Each Worker	Weekly Wage Bill	Marginal Cost of Labor
1	$100		
2	125		
3	160		
4	200		
5	250		
6	310		

2. If a competitive labor market is cartelized, what will happen to employment and wages in that labor market? To employment and wages elsewhere?
3. If the government forces a monopsony to pay the competitive wage rate, what will happen to employment?
4. Under what conditions will an employer cartel fail to hold together?
5. If employers have to pay union workers more than the competitive market wage rate, some will move their firms to areas where they can hire nonunionized workers. What effect would such a shift have on union wage rates? On nonunion wage rates? On employment in both areas? On the efficiency of resource use?
6. If unions raise wages in the unionized sector of the economy, what will happen to the supply of labor in the nonunionized sector?
7. Why do unions sometimes threaten violence to enlist the cooperation of nonunionized workers in their strikes? Can employers use violence with the same effectiveness? Explain in economic terms.

Central Question

How are rents, interest, and profits established in a competitive market economy?

Key Terms

Economic rent

Quasi-rent

Interest

Interest rate

Market (nominal) interest rate

Pure interest rate

Rate of return on investment

Marginal rate of return on investment

Usury laws

Chapter 28

Rent, Interest, and Profit

Alertness toward new opportunities is stimulated by the heady scent of profits. . . . The lure of profits and fear of losses can be counted upon, in some measure, to attract at least some entrepreneurs. . . . The essence of the "profit incentive" . . . is thus not to be seen as motivation to work harder or to allocate resources more efficiently. The profit incentive (including, of course, the disincentive of loss) operates most significantly by sparking the alertness of entrepreneurs—by encouraging them to keep their eyes open for new information that will lead to new plans.

Israel Kirzner

Most people earn their living by working—by using the raw effort or labor power at their command. Their incomes are related directly to the number of hours they work and the wage rate they are paid for those hours. Yet many people also earn some income from other sources. Some rent their property—houses, commercial establishments, or equipment. Others lend money. And some make profits on the businesses they own.

What gives rise to these types of income? Many of the principles developed in the last two chapters are useful in answering this question. In competitive markets, the long-term return on resources like land and capital tends to reflect their marginal productivity. We will begin by explaining in greater depth how the demand for a resource is obtained, with special attention to resources whose supply is fixed, like land. Then we will consider how interest rates on lendable funds are determined. The chapter will conclude with an evaluation of various explanations for the existence of business profits. In most respects, we will see, the demand for these nonhuman resources is similar to the demand for labor resources.

The Demand for Nonhuman Resources

By definition, resources are productive. The marginal productivity of all resources, human or nonhuman, is reflected in expanded output. Given fixed quantities of labor and capital equipment, for instance, the addition of more land can increase total output. Thus the marginal product of land (or capital, or any other resource) is the additional output generated from the addition of one more unit of land (or capital, or any other resource) to a fixed quantity of one or more other resources.

The law of diminishing returns applies to nonhuman resources just as it applies to labor. In our study of competitive markets we noted that the competitive firm's upward-sloping marginal cost curve is its supply curve, and that marginal cost increases because of diminishing returns. In our analysis of diminishing returns we assumed that capital was held constant while the use of labor was expanded. But we could just as easily have held labor constant while expanding the use of land. Given a fixed quantity of labor, the addition of more land would eventually lead to diminishing returns and an increasing marginal cost of production. The same number of workers would be spread more thinly over a larger amount of land. They would have to spend more time getting from one place to another—and time spent in travel is time diverted from production.

The Firm's Demand

Just as with labor, we can derive a demand for land based on its marginal productivity and the price of the final product. Table 28.1 shows a marginal productivity schedule for a hypothetical piece of land. The price of the final product, tomatoes, is $8 a bushel. The value of each additional acre of land, called the value of the marginal product of land, is expressed in the last column. Given the amount of labor in use, the first acre is worth

Table 28.1. An Individual Firm's Demand for Land

Acres of Land (1)	Total Product (2)	Marginal Product (3)	Product Price (4)	Value of Marginal Product (3) × (4)
1	20	20	$8	$160
2	36	16	8	128
3	48	12	8	96
4	58	10	8	80
5	66	8	8	64
6	72	6	8	48

quite a lot, $160. The second acre is worth less—$128—because of its lower marginal product, shown in column 3. As the marginal product falls, the value of each new acre decreases.

What will be the firm's demand for land, given the information in Table 28.1? Suppose the price of using the land (not its purchase price) is slightly less than $160 an acre. At that price the firm will want to employ only one acre, for only the first acre yields a marginal product as valuable as its price. If the use price were $79, the firm would demand four acres, for beyond that point, additional acres will not produce a high enough return.

By considering additional use price–acreage combinations, we can establish a basic principle of resource use. A firm will employ a resource up to the point where its price (P_r) equals the value of its marginal product ($P_r = VMP$). We can see also that a firm has a downward-sloping demand for land, just as in the case of labor. The lower the price of land, the greater the quantity the firm will demand. That proposition will hold for all resources. As the use price of land (or capital equipment, or any other resource) falls, a firm will demand more of that resource. Its demand will be the same as the value of its marginal product schedule and the demand curve will look like the downward sloping VMP curve in Figure 28.1.

Market Demand

The market demand for a resource like land or labor is not, as one might suppose, equal to the horizontal summation of various firms' value of marginal product curves. Why not? If the price of land decreases for all land users, more acres will be demanded and more goods will be produced. The increased supply of goods will cause the market price of the final product to fall. And the lower product price in turn will cause the value of the marginal product to fall. As the value of the marginal product drops, firms will reduce the quantity of land they demand. Overall, the quantity of the resource the market demands goes up, but not by as much as the sum of individual demands.

Figure 28.1. The Individual Firm's Demand for a Resource.
A firm will employ a resource up to the point where its price equals the value of its marginal product. The lower the price of a resource, the lower the value of the marginal product a firm can accept. Thus the firm has a downward-sloping demand for a resource. As the price falls from P_2 to P_1, the firm's value of the marginal product (shown by curve VMP) drops with it. The firm increases the quantity of the resource it demands, from Q_1 to Q_2.

Consider Figure 28.2. Suppose that a firm's value of marginal product curve is initially VMP_1, and the price of land is P_3. Because a firm will employ a resource up to the point where $P_r = VMP$, this firm will demand Q_1 acres of land. Now suppose the price of land falls to P_2, causing the final product price, and with it the firm's value of marginal product curve, to fall—from VMP_1 to VMP_2. At the new, lower land price, P_2, the firm now demands Q_2 acres. A further decrease in the price of land to P_1 will have the same effect, shifting the value of marginal product curve to VMP_3 and increasing land use to Q_3. By imagining further decreases in the use price of all land, we can deduce that the firm's actual demand for land will be shown by the downward-sloping demand curve labeled D.

The market demand for land is obtained by horizontally summing individual firms' demand curves, as in Figure 28.2(b). The more firms in the market, the more curves that must be summed.[1] As with other

---

1. The firms do not have to be producing the same product or service; they simply use the same resource. The market for skilled carpenters or drill presses includes both housing contractors and toy manufacturers, for example.

Figure 28.2. Obtaining the Market Demand for a Resource.

If the market price of a resource falls from P_3 to P_2, more of the resource can be employed by all firms in an industry. If all firms use more of the resource, the supply of the final product will increase, lowering the product price. Because the value of the marginal product (*VMP*) is found by multiplying the marginal product by the product price, a reduction in product price will cause the *VMP* curve to fall, from VMP_1 to VMP_2 in panel (a). At the lower resource price P_2, the firm will increase its use of the resource from Q_1 to Q_2. But had the price of the final product not fallen—had the *VMP* curve not shifted down, the lower resource price would have meant a still greater increase in the firm's demand for the resource, to Q_3. By extending this line of reasoning, we obtain the demand curve for the individual firm in the context of the market, labeled *D*.

The market demand for the resource (panel (b)) is obtained by horizontally summing all firms' resource demand curves. In a market with two firms, A and B, demand for a resource will be D_{a+b}.

commodities, the market demand for a resource, D_{a+b} in Figure 28.2(b), slopes downward. The lower the price, the more of the resource will be demanded.

Economic Rent

In common use, the term rent means a payment made for the use of property—for example, an apartment. To an economist, however, rent (or more precisely, economic rent) has a special meaning. **Economic rent** is any payment received for the use of a resource or factor of production that exceeds its opportunity cost.

Economic rent: any payment received for the use of a resource or factor of production that exceeds its opportunity cost.

Figure 28.3. Economic Rent.
A resource that has only one use will have a vertical, or perfectly inelastic, supply curve (S). Because the opportunity cost of using the resource for its one and only purpose is zero, the revenues it earns are considered pure profit, or economic rent. If demand for the resource is D_1, the price of the resource in a competitive market will be P_1. The owner will receive revenues equal to the shaded area $0P_1aQ_1$. If the demand for the resource rises from D_1 to D_2, the price of the resource will rise from P_1 to P_2, and the owner's economic rent will expand to the area $0P_2bQ_1$. Note that the increase in price does not affect the quantity of the resource supplied; it remains at Q_1.

Theoretically, resources that earn a pure economic rent cannot be employed in any other line of production. Rent therefore does not affect the allocation of a resource—either the quantity that is available in the market or the way it is employed. Technically speaking, the supply of such factors of production is fixed; their supply curves are vertical, or perfectly inelastic. Figure 28.3 shows a vertical supply curve for a very special piece of land that has only one use—say tomato production. Still, the land can be productive, as indicated by the downward-sloping market demand curve D_1.

The use price of the land in Figure 28.3 is P_1 per acre per time period (per month or per year). Since the land has no other use, the opportunity cost of planting it in tomatoes is zero. Therefore the revenue received each time period for its use, found by multiplying its use price, P_1, times the quantity of land used, Q_1, is pure economic rent. (See the shaded area in Figure 28.3.) If the demand were higher—D_2 instead of D_1—the price would be higher, P_2 instead of P_1. The quantity of land demanded would remain the same, but the payment for its use—its economic rent—would be higher: $0P_2bQ_1$ instead of $0P_1aQ_1$.

Perspectives in Economics: Henry George and the Land Tax

Economists generally see taxes as distorting the allocation of resources. A tax on a good raises its price, reducing its consumption and encouraging the consumption of other goods. In the late nineteenth century, an economist turned politician named Henry George (1839–97) proposed that the distorting influence of taxes could be remedied or at least minimized by the imposition of a single tax on land.

George believed that poverty was due largely to the monopolization of land by the few. Reasoning that land is more or less fixed in supply, he saw the return on land as more or less pure economic rent. George assumed that competition among landholders would prevent them from passing a tax on land along to consumers in the form of higher prices. That is, any increase over the market price (P_1 in Figure 28.3) because of a tax on land would produce a market surplus, which would move prices back toward equilibrium. So the tax would be borne exclusively by landowners, paid out of their pure economic rent. Though the landlords' after-tax rents would be reduced, the allocation of resources would not be distorted, for fixed resources like land would continue to be used as they always had been.

The problem with George's proposal, which played an important part in his campaign for mayor of New York in 1886, was that it presumed land was fixed in supply. It is true that the world contains only so many acres of land. But the number of usable or productive acres is not fixed. That number depends critically on the economic reward for developing land into the kind of acreage people need and want. If the supply of usable acres slopes upward, a tax on land will affect how that resource is used. In other words, land taxes will distort the allocation of land.

Because the increase in rent does not affect the availability of the land, it may be viewed as an unearned profit. It reflects only the competitive bidding among those who want to use the land, not the efforts of the landowner to improve his property. The pricing of land still serves a useful economic purpose, however, for it determines who will use the land.

The selling price of the land, as opposed to the price of using the land during a given time period, will reflect the present value of its future economic rent. A rise in the demand for use of the land would cause the selling price of the land to increase. Thus when land is sold, its economic rent is captured by the original owner, not the buyer. The selling price is high enough that the original owner will receive most if not all of the economic rent the land will earn over time.

Quasi-Rents

Some people would require higher wages than others to work at the same job. One reason for such observed differences in wages is the difference in people's opportunity costs. Before an engineer would work as a bartender, he or she would generally require a higher wage than a

Figure 28.4. Quasi-Rent.
A resource that has more than one use will have an upward-sloping supply curve, reflecting differences in the opportunity costs of various units of the resource. Any revenue the resource earns above and beyond its opportunity cost can be considered pure profit, or quasi-rent. At a wage rate of W_2, the number of workers available for employment will be Q_2. Those who would be willing to work for less will receive quasi-rents equal to the difference between the going wage rate, W_2, and their opportunity costs, shown by the supply curve. For instance, a laborer willing to work for W_1 will receive a quasi-rent of $W_2 - W_1$. The total quasi-rent received by all workers at a wage rate of W_2 equals the shaded area above the supply curve, $W_1 W_2 a$.

maintenance worker would. The engineer's skills make his time worth more than the maintenance worker's.

The upward-sloping supply curve for labor implies such differences in the opportunity cost of workers' time. For example, the supply curve in Figure 28.4 indicates that a few people are willing to work for a wage of W_1. Further up the supply curve, people are unwilling to work except at a higher wage. If employers raise the wage rate to attract additional workers, those who are already employed will earn more than their opportunity cost of labor. At a wage rate of W_2, for instance, the number of workers willing to work is Q_2. The worker who was willing to work at W_1 now receives W_2, more than his minimum required wage. The difference between what that worker is willing to accept and what he gets, $W_2 - W_1$, is a form of economic rent—not a pure economic rent, since the supply of workers is not vertical, but a quasi-rent. A **quasi-rent** is the difference between the price of a resource and its opportunity cost, when the opportunity cost is not zero.

Quasi-rent: the difference between the price of a resource and its opportunity cost, when the opportunity cost is not zero.

In Figure 28.4, total compensation paid to workers at a wage rate of W_2 is shown by the rectangular area $0W_2aQ_2$ (or W_2Q_2). The part of that compensation that lies under the supply curve reflects workers' opportunity cost of labor. The rest—the shaded area above the supply curve—is their quasi-rent.

Any or all of the following conditions may account for differences in the opportunity cost of resources:

Differences in the quality of various units of a resource. Not all workers (or acres of land) that can be employed for a given use are equally productive elsewhere. Therefore not all have the same opportunity cost. At a low wage like W_1 in Figure 28.4, the ones employed will tend to be workers with low productivity elsewhere, and consequently a low opportunity cost. As the wage rate rises, workers with a higher opportunity cost will be attracted into the market. Those workers—the ones who are more productive elsewhere—will receive lower rents than workers with a low opportunity cost.

Differences in location. Some land is closer to where people want to be. Land in remote areas generally will not be used until more accessible land has been fully employed, or until the price of goods rises enough to compensate businesses for the higher costs associated with remote production and sales facilities. Therefore land that is close at hand will bring a higher price (quasi-rent) than remote land.

Differences in mineral deposits. Land varies considerably in the mineral deposits it contains. Land with the biggest, most accessible mineral deposits will tend to be used first. When less accessible deposits are employed, the more accessible ones will earn a quasi-rent. For example, production of oil is very cheap in OPEC countries, where oil is easy to drill. But because of the very strong worldwide demand for oil, wells are also drilled and operated at great expense in less accessible fields. Oil that is cheap to produce commands the same price as oil that is expensive to produce. The difference between the Saudis' low production cost and the price they receive is a form of quasi-rent.

Rent Seeking

In our study of monopoly (Chapter 23), we noted that monopolistic firms may be protected from competition, government regulation and tariffs, which give rise to economic profits. Such a profit is a form of economic rent. If economic rents can be gained through such means, should we not expect entrepreneurs and profit-maximizing firms to seek government protection?

Much has been written in economics in recent years about rent seeking, or the use of resources for lobbying and other activities directed at securing protective legislation.[2] One conclusion of those studies is that economic

---

2. See Richard B. McKenzie and Gordon Tullock, "Rent Seeking," *The New World of Economics: Explorations Into the Human Experience,* 3d ed. (Homewood, Ill.: Richard D. Irwin, 1981), chap. 15.

rents are not necessarily received by the people who appear to get them. For example, though tariffs on foreign textiles improve the market position and profits (rents) of domestic textile manufacturers, their net economic rent may not actually increase. The extra revenues may have already been spent on the effort to secure the tariffs. Similarly, some of the rents gained from restrictions on entry into the television market may go to the people who lobbied for them and the politicians who provided them.

Interest

Interest: a payment for deferred consumption, which in a competitive lendable funds market tends to reflect the productivity of capital.

Interest rate: the annual payment for deferred consumption, expressed as a percentage of the dollar amount loaned (which is equal to the deferred consumption).

Market (nominal) interest rate: the total payment that can be expected on a loan, expressed as a percentage of the loan.

Pure interest rate: the return one can expect from an investment in the absence of risk and inflation.

There is a cost to everything—that rule has been with us since the beginning of this book. The cost of a business investment can be measured in terms of the value of the goods and services that must be forgone by those who lend the capital to finance a project. In a market economy, people are willing to forgo current consumption—that is, to save—because they are paid interest on their money. **Interest** (normally expressed as a percentage or rate, as in *interest rate*) is a payment for deferred consumption, which in a competitive lendable funds market tends to reflect the productivity of capital. The **interest rate** is the annual payment for deferred consumption, expressed as a percentage of the dollar amount loaned (which is equal to the deferred consumption). Interest compensates lenders for releasing the resources needed in the production of capital goods.

In loan contracts, those who want to borrow funds for investment agree to repay the amount of the loan plus a specified interest rate. In effect, the lender is promised more goods in the future than could be had with the borrowed money today. (The offer of an equal amount of goods would not be attractive, because goods received in the future are typically worth less today than goods received immediately.)

The 7, 10, or 15 percent rate of interest that a saver receives on a bank account or bond is called the market, or nominal, interest rate. The **market interest** rate (sometimes called the nominal, or money, interest rate) is the total payment that can be expected on a loan, expressed as a percentage of the loan. The market interest rate has three components: a pure interest rate; a risk cost; and the estimated future inflation rate. The **pure interest rate** is the return one can expect from an investment in the absence of risk and inflation.

To understand how the market interest rate is determined, we must first understand how the pure interest rate is determined. That is, we must start with the simplifying assumption that the investment involves no risk and no inflation is expected. Since loans are the primary means by which consumption is deferred, we will use the lendable funds market as an example of how supply and demand determines the pure interest rate.

The Supply of Lendable Funds

Generally speaking, the higher the interest rate, the more funds will be made available for loans (see Figure 28.5). There are two reasons for this

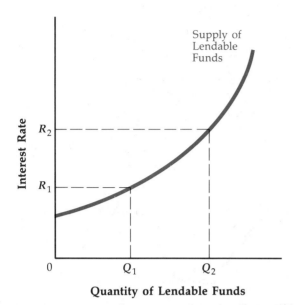

Figure 28.5. The Supply of Lendable Funds.
The supply of lendable funds curve slopes upward to the right because dollars received in the future are not worth as much as dollars received today. At higher interest rates, more funds are available for loans because lenders are compensated better for sacrificing current consumption for future repayment. Here, an increase in the interest rate from R_1 to R_2 brings an increase in the quantity of funds offered for investment, from Q_1 to Q_2.

relationship. First, as the interest rate goes up, more and more people are persuaded to forgo current consumption. Second, when people first lend funds, they forgo the goods and services they value least. To make additional loans, they will have to forgo more valuable goods and services. Thus the interest rate must rise to compensate lenders for their greater sacrifice.

The Demand for Lendable Funds

Just as interest rates determine the supply of lendable funds, the need for capital stock—new plant and equipment—determines the demand. Like other resources, capital is productive. It can be used along with labor, or in place of labor, to enhance a company's output. And capital too is subject to the law of diminishing returns. Additional units of capital add progressively less to a firm's total output. Hence, as capital stock is expanded, its marginal value diminishes.

Because capital is meant to last for some years, the return on capital is not readily stated in current dollar terms. Again, because dollars received in the future represent postponed consumption, they are not as valuable

Figure 28.6. The Demand for Lendable Funds.
The demand for lendable funds curve slopes downward because of the declining marginal rate of return on investment. The more capital is employed, the more the marginal rate of return declines. An increase in the interest rate from R_1 to R_2 will therefore reduce the quantity of funds demanded, from Q_2 to Q_1. At the higher interest rate, some firms will no longer be able to justify borrowing; the rate of return on their investment will not cover the increased cost of capital.

Rate of return on investment: the income earned from the purchase of capital, expressed as a percentage of the purchase price.

as current dollars. They must be discounted by some figure—say 10 percent—that translates their value into the value of dollars spent today. That percentage discount is called the rate of return on investment. The **rate of return on investment** is the income earned from the purchase of capital, expressed as a percentage of the purchase price.

As a firm's capital stock expands and returns diminish, the rate of return on investment also diminishes—and with it the value of added capital to the firm. The rule is that a firm's demand for capital goods is inversely related to the rate of interest on borrowed funds. A company will obviously not borrow funds at an interest rate higher than its rate of return on investment. It will, however, borrow funds for projects whose returns exceed the interest cost of borrowing. Technically speaking, a company will borrow up to the point where the interest rate equals the rate of return on investment.

Marginal rate of return on investment: the additional income earned from an additional purchase of capital goods.

Figure 28.6 shows how the marginal rate of return on investment falls as investment in capital goods increases. The **marginal rate of return on investment** is the additional income earned from an additional purchase of capital goods. The curve slopes downward both because of the diminishing marginal returns on capital and because investment opportunities differ in their profitability. If the market interest rate is R_2, or 10 percent, the firm will borrow Q_1. Up to that point, all investment projects offer a rate of return greater than the market interest rate; several, in fact, offer more than 15 percent. Beyond Q_1, however, the rate of return dips below the interest rate. A firm would reduce its profits if it borrowed money at 10 percent to secure a 7 percent return.

Note that if the interest rate fell to R_1, all the investment projects between Q_1 and Q_2 would suddenly become profitable. The quantity of funds demanded by the firm would increase to Q_2. In effect, then, the marginal rate of return on investment curve is the firm's demand curve for investable funds. The interest rate is the price paid for the use of lenders' funds. The lower the interest rate (price), the greater the quantity of funds demanded.

The Equilibrium Interest Rate

The market interest rate, or the price of lendable funds, is determined just as any other price is determined: by the interaction of supply and demand. In Figure 28.7, the competitive interest rate is established by the intersection of the supply and demand curves. At R_2, the funds supplied to investors exactly equal the funds demanded. If the interest rate were held above or below R_2, a shortage or surplus of funds would develop. (Can you explain the process using the figure?)

The market interest rate depends significantly on the productivity of capital (because the demand curve for lendable funds is the firm's marginal rate of return on investment curve). It also depends on inflation, because the rate of inflation affects the relative value of present and future goods and services.

The Effects of Risk Cost and Inflation

As we noted earlier, the market, or nominal, rate of interest includes the risk cost of investment and the estimated future inflation rate as well as the pure interest rate. Most investment opportunities involve some risk of failure. There is some chance that the goods produced with the invested capital will not be sold at the anticipated price. In the event of failure, the borrower may not be able to meet the interest payments promised in the loan agreement, or even to repay the principal. Lenders must therefore be compensated for the risk they assume. They will demand a market interest rate that not only allows them to consume more goods in the future, but covers their expected losses.

Graphically, the addition of a risk cost of investment to the pure interest rate shifts the supply of lendable funds curve inward, from S_1 to S_2 in Figure 28.8. The shift forces the market, or nominal, interest rate up from R_1 to R_2, causing a reduction in the level of investment from Q_2 to Q_1.

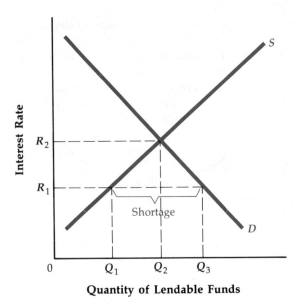

Figure 28.7. The Equilibrium Interest Rate.
In a competitive market, the interest rate for lendable funds is established by the interaction of supply and demand. Here the equilibrium interest rate will be R_2, the rate at which the quantity of funds demanded matches the quantity of funds made available for loans. A legal ceiling on the interest rate will create a market shortage. At R_1, for instance, Q_3 funds will be demanded for investment, but only Q_1 funds will be supplied.

The market interest rate is a good indicator of the risk involved in an investment. Interest rates are generally higher on investments in politically unstable countries, for instance, because doing business in those areas is relatively risky. Lenders realize that the capital their money is used to buy might be destroyed or confiscated as the result of a coup—an extraordinarily remote possibility in the United States. Interest rates also tend to be higher, and investment lower, in high-crime areas, where the risk cost of doing business is greater than elsewhere.

Expected inflation, or an anticipated decline in the purchasing power of the dollar, can also boost interest rates. If investors anticipate a rise in prices, they will want to borrow funds today, to be repaid tomorrow with devalued dollars. The demand for lendable funds will increase. In Figure 28.9, D_1 is the demand for lendable funds when the expected inflation rate is zero. An expected inflation rate of 5 or 10 percent will shift the demand for lendable funds curve up, to D_2.

At the same time, lenders will demand a higher interest rate to compensate for the expected lower value of the dollar payments on the loan. If S_1 is the supply of lendable funds when the expected inflation rate is zero, an expected inflation rate of 5 or 10 percent will shift the supply of lendable funds curve inward, to S_2. The simultaneous increase in

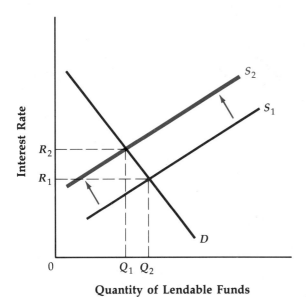

Figure 28.8. The Effect of Risk Cost on Interest Rates.
The addition of a risk cost to the pure interest rate will decrease the supply of lendable funds, from S_1 to S_2. As a result the market interest rate will rise, from R_1 to R_2, and the level of investment will fall, from Q_2 to Q_1.

demand and decrease in supply will raise the market interest rate from R_1 to R_2. The increase in the interest rate, $R_2 - R_1$, should approximate the rate of expected inflation. That is, if the pure interest rate is 3 percent and the expected inflation rate is 6 percent, the market interest rate will be 9 percent, excluding risk cost. (With risk cost, the interest rate would be even higher.)

Note that the quantity of funds invested, Q_1, remains the same. Because of inflation, investors are now paying a higher interest rate for the same number of dollars as before.

Economic Profit

In the realm of economics, profit is a highly controversial concept. How may businesses in a competitive market earn an economic profit?

Profit can arise in several ways. First, a firm may actually have been innovative. It may have produced something consumers really want and are willing to pay dearly for, like a computer, a hand calculator, or a quartz watch. (In that case, its success will attract other firms into the market, and competition will push its prices and profits down.) Or a company may have managed to keep its costs below its competitors'. In the case of

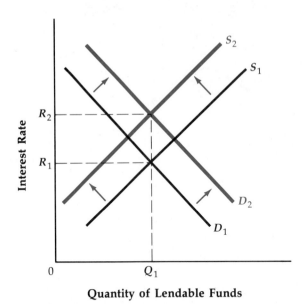

Figure 28.9. The Effect of Expected Inflation on Interest Rates.
Anticipated inflation will increase the demand for lendable funds from D_1 to D_2.
At the same time lenders will become less willing to forgo current consumption
and the supply of lendable funds will decrease, from S_1 to S_2. As a result the
market interest rate will rise, from R_1 to R_2. The quantity of funds offered for
investment will remain at Q_1, however.

product innovation, consumers clearly benefit; they get what they want.
Similarly, cost savings benefit society in general. Fewer resources are used
in the production of the good in question, leaving more resources available
for the production of other goods and services.

Second, profits sometimes emerge because of market accidents—totally
unexpected occurrences. In the 1970s, OPEC restrictions on the supply of
oil led to increased profits for bicycle manufacturers, who just happened
to be producing bicycles at a time when many people were attempting to
escape high gas prices.

Third, profits may emerge because of what is called entrepreneurship,
or the ability to recognize profitable opportunities and take advantage of
them. For decades real estate firms have traded previously owned homes.
Only in the last decade or so, however, have warranties covering structural
defects been made available to buyers of such homes. Firms that supply
the warranties have made a handsome profit on them. But in order to
make that profit, someone had to recognize that there was a market for
warranties.

Fourth, profits sometimes proceed from monopoly power. Barriers to
entry, such as exclusive ownership of resources, a patent, or government
regulation, may protect firms from competition. Or profits may emerge
from the exploitation of labor or other resources. Karl Marx argued that

Perspectives in Economics: Usury Laws

For centuries, religious groups and governments have viewed interest income as "unjust," "inequitable," or "unearned"—an exploitation of the borrower, especially the nonbusiness borrower. Accordingly, governments have attempted to control interest rates by passing usury laws, which fix the maximum interest rate—for example, 18 percent—that can be legally charged. **Usury laws** are legislated upper limits on the interest rates that lending institutions may charge to borrowers.

What are the economic consequences of such laws? Presumably the interest ceiling is set below the equilibrium interest rate—in Figure 28.7, R_2. (There would be no point in defining a ceiling higher than the equilibrium rate because market forces would tend to bring interest rates back down to equilibrium in any case.) Suppose that the ceiling is R_1. The quantity of funds demanded, Q_3, will exceed the quantity of funds supplied, Q_1.

Thus the law creates a shortage of funds equal to $Q_3 - Q_1$.

Usury laws are most often conceived as a means of protecting the poor from unscrupulous lenders. But the poor are the most likely to suffer from the laws. For if the interest rate cannot rise, lenders must find some other means of rationing their limited funds. They will tend to lend only to higher-income groups, who are best able to pay the loans back, thus reducing their risk of loss on unpaid debts. The poor, who exist on limited and unstable incomes, are less likely to get loans when interest rates are controlled.

Some economists have suggested that usury laws were really meant to help the well-to-do. Their effect is to allow the rich to borrow at legally restricted rates, while crowding the poor out of the legal money market and into the underground market.

firms paid laborers a subsistence wage and forced them to work longer than necessary for it. Marx called the difference between what workers earned and what they were paid "surplus value"; he could just as well have called it economic profit.

Summary and Extensions

The last three chapters have considered the market forces that determine incomes, specifically wages, rent, interest, and profits. We have stressed that in competitive markets, income is determined by supply and demand. The demand for a resource like labor is derived from its marginal productivity and the price people are willing to pay for the good or service it produces. In short, people with high incomes earn them by providing employers with a sought-after service.

Economic rent accounts for part of some incomes. Because rent does little or nothing to affect the quantity of resources available, some people view economic rent as unearned income. But rent is ultimately useful, because it ensures that resources will be employed in their most highly valued uses.

Not everyone considers economic profit equitable. Some see profit as a kind of surplus value, an unearned windfall that benefits some people at the expense of others. But others regard profit as a reward for entrepreneurship or innovation—an incentive that drives producers to find out what consumers want and to produce it efficiently. From that point of view, profit is a force for the efficient allocation of resources.

In evaluating the causes of differences in income, we should not overlook the effect of largely noneconomic forces, such as sexual and racial discrimination. More will be said about the actual distribution of income in the United States, and about government efforts to change it, in the next chapter.

Major Conclusions

1. The demand for any resource—land, capital, labor—slopes downward, because of diminishing (marginal) returns from the resource.
2. The individual firm's demand curve for a resource is the same as its value of the marginal product curve. The market demand curve for a resource is not the same as the horizontal summation of the individual firms' *VMP* curves, however. It is the horizontal summation of steeper individual demand curves, obtained by allowing for a fall in the value of the marginal product as more goods are produced at lower prices.
3. Pure economic rent—payment for a resource whose supply is fixed—arises because a resource has only one use. Quasi-rents, or the difference between the price of a resource and its opportunity cost, arise because of differences in the quality and location of resources.
4. Although the price of a resource whose supply is fixed does not affect the availability of the resource, it does determine which of the competing producers will actually use the resource.
5. The demand for lendable funds is derived from the marginal rate of return on investment. The supply of lendable funds depends on the relative values of present goods and future goods. The interest rate is the market's way of compensating lenders for doing without current goods and services in order to finance investment goods.

6. The market, or nominal, interest rate has three components: a pure interest rate, a risk cost, and an expected inflation rate. The higher the risk cost of investment and the expected inflation rate, the higher the market interest rate.

7. Usury laws, which hold interest rates below their market clearing level, tend to create shortages of lendable funds, especially among low-income people who are credit risks.

8. Economic profits may emerge in a competitive market system for any of several reasons—innovation, accident, entrepreneurship, monopoly power, or exploitation of resources.

Questions to Ponder

1. Suppose that the supply of a certain resource is fixed: its supply curve is vertical. Suppose further that the government taxes its use. What will happen to the price of the final good? To the price of the resource? To the after-tax income received by the resource owner?

2. If beginning professors in a given discipline would be willing to work for different salaries, why is it that their salaries tend to be equal in practice? Under what conditions will their wages be unequal, reflecting differences in their opportunity costs? Which professors will earn quasi-rents? What might cause those quasi-rents to rise?

3. How will an increase in the expected inflation rate affect interest rates? Explain, using supply and demand curves.

4. Evaluate the following statement: "Profit is the amount by which a firm's revenues exceed all its costs, including risk cost and the opportunity cost of the resources it employs. Therefore profit is unearned and unjustified."

5. What effect would a corporate income tax levied against book profits (not just economic profit) have on the allocation of resources? On the demand for investment goods? On the demand for labor and other resources?

6. Who will tend to pay higher interest rates, high- or low-income earners? The young or the middle-aged? Students or faculty? Why?

Central Question

What is the extent of poverty in the United States, and what are the problems government faces in relieving poverty?

Key Terms

Median family income

Mean family income

Poverty income threshold

In-kind transfer

Break-even income level

Cash transfer

Negative income tax

Guaranteed income level

Implicit marginal income tax

Implicit marginal income tax rate

Chapter 29

Poverty and Poverty Relief

What is poverty? Is it an income so low that it does not purchase enough food to allay hunger, as it was before 1800 and as it is in seven-tenths of the world today? . . . Or, is poverty eating hamburger when many others are eating steak? Is poverty having a cloth coat when others have fur coats, or having one bathroom when some have two or even three? . . . Is poverty always related to economic means? . . . In the absence of any scientific standards, is there any substitute for the judgment of the person setting the standard?

Rose Friedman

*E*arlier chapters have explored how markets determine wages, interest, rents, and profits. Using models of competitive and monopsonistic resource markets, we saw how the nation's income is allocated. Little was said about the justice or fairness of the resulting distribution of income, and even less about the poverty that inevitably accompanies a market economy.

This chapter is concerned with the social problem of poverty—how it is defined, how prevalent it is, and how and to what extent government can be expected to relieve it. Poverty is an important public issue, if only because in 1983, government at all levels spent more than $107 billion on poverty relief (including, but not limited to, Aid to Families with Dependent Children, general assistance, Medicaid, food stamps, and housing assistance). That amount represents $3,048 for each person officially defined as impoverished. If distributed evenly, it would have been enough to raise every poor family of four substantially above the income level at which a household is classified as poor. But though one of every five American citizens (42 million people) received some form of poverty relief in 1983, 40 percent of those defined as poor received no government aid at all. The nation has not only a poverty problem, but a problem providing relief to the many who are in need.

Before we can understand the difficulties government faces in relieving poverty, we need to know something about the distribution of the national income and the criteria used in determining who should receive relief.

Distribution of Income in the United States: Some Facts

Median family income: the midpoint of the family income distribution, above and below which an equal number of families fall.

Mean family income: the average family income level, or the total income of all families divided by the total number of families.

Table 29.1 describes the distribution of income among families in the United States. Of the nation's nearly 63 million families, 5 percent had an income of less than $5,000 in 1984, and another 9.4 percent earned incomes between $5,000 and $10,000. At the same time, 15.8 percent of all families had incomes of $50,000 or more. The median family income was $26,433, and the mean family income was $31,052. The **median family income** is the midpoint of the family income distribution. An equal number of families fall above and below the median level. The **mean family income** is the average family income level, or the total income of all families divided by the total number of families. The mean family income for 1984 was higher than the median family income because some families in the upper half of the distribution had very high incomes.

In fact, our national income is concentrated heavily at the upper end of the distribution (see Table 29.2). In 1984, the 20 percent of U.S. families with the lowest incomes received only 4.7 percent of the nation's total income. The next 20 percent of the nation's families received only 11.0 percent. The top fifth, by contrast, earned a disproportionate 42.9 percent of the nation's family income. Indeed, just 5 percent of the population— the families with the very highest incomes—received slightly more income (16.0 percent) than the bottom 40 percent of the population (15.7 percent).

The distribution of family income has not changed much over the last few decades (see Table 29.2). In 1952 the lowest fifth of U.S. families

Table 29.1. Distribution of Family Income in the United States, 1984

Income Bracket[a]	Percentage of Families[b]
Under $5,000	5.0%
$ 5,000– 9,999	9.4
10,000–14,999	10.8
15,000–19,999	10.8
20,000–24,999	10.7
25,000–34,999	19.0
35,000–49,999	18.4
50,000 and up	15.8
Median income	$26,433
Mean income	31,052

[a] Note that above $25,000, income brackets increase in size.
[b] Because of rounding, percentages do not add up to 100 percent.
Source: U.S. Bureau of the Census, *Current Population Reports*, P-60, no. 149 (Washington, D.C.: U.S. Government Printing Office, March 1985, advance data), p. 9.

Table 29.2. Percentage of National Income Received by Each Fifth of U.S. Families, Selected Years, 1952–1984

	Lowest Fifth	Second Fifth	Middle Fifth	Fourth Fifth	Highest Fifth
1952	4.9%	12.9%	17.1%	23.5%	42.0%
1962	5.0	12.1	17.6	24.0	41.3
1972	5.4	11.9	17.5	23.9	41.4
1982	4.7	11.2	17.1	24.3	42.7
1984	4.7	11.0	17.0	24.4	42.9

Source: U.S. Bureau of the Census, *Statistical Abstract of the United States* (1972, 1982, 1984 data); *Current Population Reports*, P-60, no. 149 (Washington, D.C.: U.S. Government Printing Office, March 1985, advance data), p. 11.

received 4.9 percent of the nation's income. By 1972 their share had risen slightly to 5.4 percent, but it fell back to 4.7 percent in 1982, where it remained in 1984. Although this group's share of the national income declined, it was not necessarily worse off in 1984 than in 1972. The absolute value of its income could still have risen. To determine whether this group's real income decreased, we would have to compare its earned income in 1972 and 1984, adjusted for inflation.

Table 29.3 shows the median family income in the United States for the years 1970–1984. As column 1 shows, median family income rose dramatically in those years, from $9,867 to $26,433 in current dollars. Much of that increase, however, was eaten up by lost purchasing power, for prices were higher in 1984 than in 1970. Column 2 shows the same figures adjusted for inflation. In constant dollar terms, the median family income in the United States was lower in 1981–1984 than at any time since 1971.

Table 29.3. Median Family Income, 1970–1984

Year	Current Dollars	Constant 1983 Dollars
1970	$ 9,867	$25,317
1971	10,285	25,301
1972	11,116	26,473
1973	12,051	27,017
1974	12,902	26,066
1975	13,719	25,395
1976	14,958	26,179
1977	16,009	26,320
1978	17,640	26,938
1979	19,587	26,885
1980	21,023	25,418
1981	22,388	24,525
1982	23,433	24,187
1983	24,580	24,580
1984	26,433	25,413

Source: U.S. Bureau of the Census, *Current Population Reports,* P-60, no. 149 (Washington, D.C.: U.S. Government Printing Office, March 1985, advance data), p. 9.

Taken by themselves, these figures do not tell us much about the extent of poverty in the United States. In order to arrive at a meaningful understanding of the problem, we must define what we mean by poverty, and by what criteria we will measure it.

Determining the Poverty Level

In 1984 the Bureau of the Census counted over 33 million Americans as poor. As Table 29.4 shows, that number is lower than it was in 1960, when nearly 40 million people were below the poverty level. But since the early 1970s, the poverty count has been steadily rising. In 1975 only 12.3 percent of the total American population was classified as poor; by 1983 the percentage had risen to 15.2 percent, only to fall to 14.4 percent in 1984.

The Official Definition

Poverty income threshold: the income level below which people are classified as being poor.

How are those numbers obtained? They are based on an official government definition of the poverty income threshold. The **poverty income threshold** is the income level below which people are classified as being poor. It is the minimum income believed necessary for basic subsistence. This measure was developed in 1964 by the Social Security Administration. It is based primarily on the cost of a nutritionally adequate but economically thrifty food plan, as defined by the Department of Agriculture. The cost

Table 29.4. Persons Below the Poverty Level, Selected Years, 1960–1984

Year	Number Below Poverty Level (Millions)	Percentage Below Poverty Level
1960	39.9	22.2%
1965	33.2	17.3
1970	25.4	12.6
1975	25.9	12.3
1980	29.3	13.0
1981	31.8	14.0
1982	34.4	15.0
1983	35.3	15.2
1984	33.7	14.4

Source: U.S. Bureau of the Census, *Current Population Reports*, P-60, no. 149 (Washington, D.C.: U.S. Government Printing Office, March 1985, advance data), p. 9.

of that food budget is multiplied by three, because a 1955 Department of Agriculture study found that across all income levels, people in families of three or more persons spent about one-third of their income on food. Then the threshold figure is adjusted for family size and age. In 1983 the poverty threshold for a single person averaged $5,278—$5,400 for a person between the ages of 15 and 64, and $4,978 for a person over 65. Finally, the threshold is adjusted each year to account for changes in the cost of living, as measured by the consumer price index. In 1984, the threshold for a family of four was $10,609, up from $10,178 in 1983.

The data in Table 29.4 seem to show that poverty is growing in the United States. But there are several problems with the government figures in that table, which tend to overstate the number of poor people and the growth of poverty over the last decade.

Shortcomings of the Official Statistics

First, government poverty figures are based solely on money income received as earnings or government grants. They do not include welfare benefits received in the form of food, housing, medical care, and education. Thus a family of four that earns $10,000 and receives food and housing benefits worth $3,000 is counted as poor, even though its buying power exceeds the poverty income threshold.

Second, the government does not consider the fact that some people defined as poor have access to additional income in times of emergency or need. A college student who lives alone and receives less than $5,180 in scholarships and grants would be counted as poor, even if she could fall back on her parents' income if necessary. Nor do government figures account for people's accumulated wealth—lump-sum payments from insurance policies or the sale of property, for example. Thus an elderly person who owns his own house may be counted as poor even though he does not have to make mortgage payments. Poverty statistics are not adjusted for unreported illegal income or for underreported legal income. Underreporting may distort income figures by as much as 23 percent.[1]

Poverty statistics are not adjusted for regional differences in the cost of living. (This oversight leads to both over- and underestimates.) And the consumer price index, which the Bureau of the Census uses to adjust the poverty threshold for changes in the cost of living, is thought to overstate the actual increase in the cost of living by as much as 25 percent. In other words, the real purchasing power represented by the poverty income threshold has changed over time. Especially in times of rapid inflation (such as the 1970s), the poverty threshold becomes distorted.

The method used to define the poverty income threshold also is flawed. The threshold is determined by multiplying an economical food budget by a factor of three, on the theory that families spend about one-third of their income on food. But the poor typically spend more than one-third of their income on food. Hence the poverty income threshold overstates the minimum income required to escape poverty.

Finally, government statistics do not allow for the fact that most poverty is temporary. According to some studies, between one-half and two-thirds of those who are officially defined as poor in any one year are not counted as poor the next year.[2] Many people with temporary incomes below the poverty level have savings on which they could draw.

In three important ways, however, poverty statistics probably *understate* the extent of poverty. First, many poor people, especially illegal aliens and the homeless, are probably unseen and uncounted. Second, children under the age of fifteen who live alone are simply excluded from the poverty count. And finally, poverty statistics do not account for sudden and substantial drains on people's incomes—for example, when they have accidents or become sick.

Poverty statistics are founded on a very precise definition of poverty, one that may be out of date. Though they indicate that a sizable and growing proportion of the nation's citizens is poor, they are only rough estimates, and controversial ones at that.

The Causes of Poverty

The causes of poverty are at least as complicated as the question of how to define it. Current thinking emphasizes four factors: low productivity, sexual and racial discrimination, low aggregate demand, and choice of life style.

---

1. For a list of relevant studies, see Bureau of the Census, *Money Income and Poverty Status of Families and Persons in the United States: 1983* (Current Population Reports, Series P-60, no. 145), p. 37.
2. See Greg J. Dunca, *Years of Poverty, Years of Plenty* (Ann Arbor, Mich.: University of Michigan, Institute for Social Research, 1984). This study suggests that less than 3 percent of the population is more or less permanently poor.

Low Productivity

At least some people are poor because of their low productivity. In their time on the job they do not produce much, and are therefore paid very little. Low productivity is often attributed to illiteracy, and indeed most poor families are headed by a person with only a grade-school education. Physical and mental handicaps also prevent some poor people from achieving high productivity rates.

Some believe that the poor are unproductive because they are trapped in a "cycle of poverty." Because they are poor they are unable to stay in school long or to move to a better school district. As children they have few books and toys to learn from at home; poor diets may keep them from being attentive in school. Some experts suspect that poor children lack the motivation to learn because their parents have little regard for formal education. Others suggest that because teachers expect disadvantaged children to learn very little, they demand little from them, creating a self-fulfilling prophecy of failure.

Sexual and Racial Discrimination

Another explanation for poverty focuses on racial and sexual discrimination. That is, many capable women and members of minority groups are not given the same opportunities as others. Their race or sex determines the jobs open to them, rather than their productivity. In the United States in 1984, 35 percent of all poor families were headed by women. In 1984 only 11.5 percent of the nation's white population was below the poverty line, compared with 33.8 percent of the black and 28.4 percent of the Hispanic population.

Table 29.5 shows family income figures by race for 1984. At the bottom of the income distribution, only 3.8 percent of white families received incomes of less than $5,000, while 13.1 percent of nonwhites fell into that category. At the top, the proportion of white families that earned incomes of $50,000 or more was more than twice as great as the proportion of nonwhite—16.9 percent as opposed to 6.2 percent. In 1984, the median income of white families was nearly two-thirds higher than the median income of nonwhite families. The gap between mean family incomes was almost as stark.

Low Aggregate Demand

A third explanation for poverty has to do with fluctuations in the nation's overall level of economic activity. If consumers, government, and business as a whole reduce their demand for goods and services, many people will lose their jobs. Others will have to accept part-time employment or settle for lower wages than usual. Such hardships can push people's incomes below the poverty line. During the recessions of the early 1980s, the number of poor people rose significantly for this reason.

Table 29.5. Distribution of Family Income in the United States by Race, 1984

Income Bracket[a]	All Families[b]	White Families[b]	Nonwhite Families[b]
Under $5,000	5.0%	3.8%	13.1%
$ 5,000– 9,999	9.4	8.1	17.6
10,000–14,999	10.8	10.3	14.2
15,000–19,999	10.8	10.7	11.8
20,000–24,999	10.7	11.0	9.2
25,000–34,999	19.0	19.8	13.8
35,000–49,999	18.4	19.4	12.1
50,000 and up	15.8	16.9	6.2
Median income	$26,433	$27,686	$17,098
Mean income	$31,052	$32,422	$22,076

Notes: [a]Note that above $25,000, brackets increase in size.
[b]Because of rounding, percentages do not add up to 100 percent.
Source: U.S. Bureau of the Census, *Current Population Reports*, P-60, no. 149 (Washington, D.C.: U.S. Government Printing Office, March 1985, advance data), p. 9.

Researchers have found that minorities and women tend to suffer more than others from economic slumps. In many companies, employment rules dictate that the last workers hired—who tend to be women and minorities—will be the first laid off or fired.

Choice of Life Style

Finally, poverty sometimes stems from a person's choice of lifestyle. Many people included in poverty statistics have chosen to work at low-paying jobs because they are personally rewarding in other ways. For instance, many farmers choose to stay on their farms although they could earn higher wages at industrial jobs. Others, from artists and musicians to entrepreneurs launching highly speculative business ventures, pursue careers that offer substantial income in the event of success, but continuing struggle otherwise. Anyone who puts job satisfaction above monetary reward pays a money price for the opportunity to spend his time as he wishes. At some time in their lives, such people are likely to be counted in the poverty statistics.

The Basis for Government Relief Programs

At the beginning of this century, government made little effort to relieve poverty by providing supplemental income, food, and housing. The task of aiding the poor was left largely to charity. Today government relief is extensive, involving large sums of money and affecting millions of people. On what grounds is government poverty relief justified? Though not all government relief programs are explained by economic logic alone, an analysis of the external costs and benefits of poverty underlies some of them.

Poverty Relief as a Public Good

Dilapidated housing, ill-fed children, sickness, and early death are all associated with poverty. The very presence of such conditions in a community is a depressing reality for almost everyone. No wonder that many citizens support aid to the poor, whether motivated by genuine concern or by guilt. Few of us enjoy the thought that others are suffering while we live in relative splendor.

The rich may help the poor for other, less benevolent reasons, however. The presence of poor people can impose heavy external costs on a community. Property values are depressed by the unpleasant sights of poverty, and home owners may have to protect their property from the criminal assaults of the poor. One way to avoid the unpleasant sights and high crime rates associated with poverty is to move to an area where the poor cannot live, because of either physical or social barriers. Zoning laws and housing restrictions that fix minimum lot and house sizes help the rich insulate themselves from the poor, who can never pay for luxury housing. But the rich pay a price for their escape. Government aid to the poor can reduce the costs they must incur to avoid contact with people who do not live as they do.

Thus aid to the poor can benefit everyone in a community, much as national defense and police protection do. Almost everyone receives some satisfaction from knowing that those around them have something to eat and a place to sleep. Aid that enables the poor to buy better housing and clothing improves the general appearance of the community and increases property values. But that does not mean that everyone will be willing to pay for it. As Milton Friedman, a widely recognized supporter of the market system, has written:

I am distressed by the sight of poverty; I am benefited by its alleviation; but I am benefited equally whether I or someone else pays for its alleviation; the benefits of other people's charity therefore partly accrue to me. To put it differently we might all of us be willing to contribute to the relief of poverty, *provided* everyone else did. We might not be willing to contribute the same amount without such assurance.[3]

Poverty relief, then, is another example of a good that will be under-demanded if people act individually and independently. Each person may be tempted to free-ride on the contributions of others. Or each may reason that his or her small contribution will do little to relieve the communal problem. If aid to the poor is expanded by government intervention, most

3. Milton Friedman, *Capitalism and Freedom* (Chicago: University of Chicago Press, 1962), p. 191.

Perspectives in Economics: The Myth of the Elderly Poor

Robert D. Hershey, Jr.

If anything is as powerful as an idea whose time has come, it is probably the mythology encrusting an idea that is passe. Last fall [1984], in the face of 12-digit budget deficits, President Reagan found himself forced to promise that, while almost everything else would be slashed, not a penny would be cut from Social Security—not even from future benefits. It was a clear demonstration of the extent to which elderly Americans have come to occupy a special place in the national psyche.

There was a time, 20 or 30 years ago, when the elderly were, in fact, worse off as a group than younger people and were the subject of legitimate, solicitous concern. Since then, however, various benefits for the elderly have increased so much that their poverty rate is now actually lower than that of the rest of the population. Their incomes have more than kept up with inflation over the last 15 years, while those of people who live on wages and salaries have fallen behind it.

Yet, the notion persists that the typical older American is someone to be pitied. He or she, according to the stereotype, is likely to be not only suffering from loneliness and expensive illness but also living on a "fixed" income, invariably deemed inadequate for a decent standard of living. Of course, many elderly people are still poor, but familiar tales of old women existing on cat food appear to have been greatly exaggerated. On the whole, figures show, people over 65 no longer have a bum deal.

The annual report of the President's Council of Economic Advisers, just issued [1985], makes a major effort to dispel some of the myths. Although it amounts to a defense of the Administration's plans to save money on such programs as Medicare, Medicaid, Federal pensions and subsidized housing of particular benefit to the elderly, it is also a serious and important piece of analysis. Policy makers need to consider the prospect that in 35 years the entire country is expected to have the same percentage of people over 65 as Florida has today.

Although there is unceasing debate over how to carve up the national economic pie, there is no doubt whatever that the elderly have made huge gains. Between 1950 and 1983, for example, median annual wages and salaries rose 451 percent, while the average monthly Social Security benefit jumped 905 percent, more than twice as much. The Consumer Price Index during this period rose 312 percent.

Since 1970, income levels of the elderly climbed relative to the rest of the population because Social Security benefits rose 46 percent, after adjustment for inflation, while the buying power of people earning wages and salaries fell 7 percent. "Younger families have had to work more to keep up with

people will be better off. The poor will receive more income, and the relatively well-to-do will avoid some of the costs of isolating themselves from the poor. (See Chapter 30 for more information on the externality argument for government activities.)

Redistribution of Income as Social Insurance and Political Reward

Poverty relief programs may also be construed as a form of social insurance that people purchase through government. If voters are uncertain about inflation," the report says. "Older families have not."

The error of equating old age with a low standard of living becomes still more evident when factors other than cash income are considered. About two-thirds of the elderly, for example, pay no income tax. The poorest receive a 15 percent credit against tax liability, while people over 65 get a $1,000 exemption and those over 55 get preferential tax treatment on the capital gain from a sale of one principal residence. Nearly three-quarters of elderly householders own their own home, half of them without a mortgage. And in spite of lower poverty rates, the elderly are more likely to get at least one type of means-tested benefit than other people. When the market value of food stamps, housing aid and medical benefits is counted, the 1983 poverty rate was found to be only 3.3 percent.

The report from the Council of Economic Advisers also rebuts the notion the elderly suffer more from inflation than the rest of us. This "common perception," it says, "is not supported by recent evidence." Nor have most of the elderly been forced to retire because of poor health or mandatory retirement laws. Nonetheless, the relative prosperity of the aged—many of them continue to save and accumulate more assets—is far from uniform. Blacks and the very old are more likely than others to be poor. Over all, financial hardship among the aged is less a matter of growing old than a result of the factors that lead to low incomes at any age—education, for example, or work history. The main exception to this is elderly women who are widowed or divorced and who have a remarriage rate only one-seventh as high as elderly men.

But the Social Security system is a great leveler. Some people complain that Social Security taxes are regressive and unfair because the poor pay a higher proportion of their incomes than the rich. But the benefits are highly progressive, with the poor getting a better return on their investment than the rich. Activists for the elderly, quick to denounce the budget cuts being proposed this week, seem to recognize that some myths are being challenged. "There is the perception among a growing number of Washington policy makers that older Americans are well off," the American Association of Retired Persons said in a statement last month. "This," it insisted, "simply is not the case."

The battle has now been joined.

Robert D. Hershey, Jr., "Economic Scene: Modern Myths about the Elderly," *New York Times*, February 6, 1985, p. 26. Copyright © 1985 by the New York Times Company Reprinted by permission.

their future earning power, they may be willing to support protective relief programs. In other words, their motivation would not be a concern with social justice, but a desire to guard against potential personal hardship.

If individual votes are thought of as small claims against the nation's total income, poverty relief programs can be seen as a voter's attempt to cash in on the nation's prosperity through political clout. Relief programs may represent one of the services politicians provide to their constituents. If so, the scope of such services will mirror the size of the constituency that benefits from them. While for some, income redistribution may be a moral imperative, for others it may simply be good politics.

Perspectives in Economics: The Misuse of Statistics on the Elderly Poor

Paul Davidson

[R. D. Hershey's article—see box—is a sign] of the Administration's latest trial balloon to place the burden of reducing the deficit on the backs of the elderly who were the working poor and middle class during their laboring years. (The rich and healthy elderly, such as the President and his California cronies, need not worry—their after-tax incomes will continue to rise.)

The basis of this latest push on the elderly is the Administration's Council of Economic Advisers' statistical study, which says that the elderly are no longer "a relatively disadvantage group," since between 1950 and 1983, Social Security benefits jumped 905 percent, wages rose 451 percent, and the consumer price level rose 312 percent. Thus, it would appear that the elderly's real Social Security income rose twice as fast as that of the average wage-and-salary family.

These statistics are particularly misleading because they seem to support the "implication" that Social Security (and Medicare?) need not be considered sacrosanct in the foolish search for sacrificial welfare-state lambs to reduce the Reagan deficit. Why should the Consumer Price Index be used as the deflator to suggest higher "real" gains by Social Security recipients vis-a-vis average wage-and-salary families? The C.P.I. may reflect the market basket of the typical working-class family, but it is clearly biased in its composition against the elderly—whose health requires a major portion of their budgets to be spent for hospital and doctor bills, pharmaceuticals, nursing homes.

We know that medical costs, since 1950, have skyrocketed relative to the other components of the consumer market basket. Thus, if we were to compute a C.P.I. for the "elderly," and if it were to measure the elderly's cost-of-living, it would be heavily weighted by medical costs and would probably have risen at a rate more than twice the C.P.I. for the average salary-recipient family. Accordingly, in "real" terms Social Security beneficiaries would not have had any significant increase since 1950 relative to working families. Moreover, for many "average" wage-and-salaried families,

Methods of Relieving Poverty

There are many different ways of aiding the poor. This section examines the effects of four broad categories of aid: in-kind transfers of food, housing, medical care, and education; cash transfers; minimum wage and rent controls; and job training.

Regardless of their purpose, all relief programs tend to change people's incentives to work, invest, and buy subsidized goods and services. Most have two distinguishable effects, an income effect and a relative price effect. When the poor are given more income, their opportunities change. They can choose to have more or less of various goods and services—including leisure. At the same time, aid changes the relative prices of goods and services. As rational consumers, the poor will buy more of the goods whose relative price has fallen, and less of the goods whose relative price has risen. The following discussion will consider the incentive effects of different types of aid and compare their relative efficiency.

medical expenses are a smaller percentage of the budget, often either elective (e.g., obstetrics, cosmetic surgery) or fully covered by third-party insurance (including major medical) paid in whole or part by employers. These employer-paid medical-insurance costs are therefore not included in the statistics of average wages and salaries. This omission biases downward the reported growth of average wages and salaries since 1950; hence we can be reasonably certain that wages (including health insurance benefits) rose more than the 451 percent reported, and used by the Council of Economic Advisers as the baseline to dispel the "myth" that the elderly are still disadvantaged.

The elderly, once they retire, must contribute a significant portion of their Social Security payments to Medicare and then buy supplementary Blue Cross–Blue Shield (or other third-party insurance) from remaining income. Even with this paid-for insurance, the elderly are, at most, covered only for "usual" doctor fees in the area as calculated by Medicare. But with past freezing of doctor payments by Medicare, the elderly in most urban areas find that almost none of the doctors accept the sum that Medicare says is the usual fee for service. Hence the elderly, unless they are destitute, are still liable for large medical bills over and above third-party insurance coverage.

Finally, until the elderly are "pauperized," Medicare will not accept liability for the cost of medical services not covered by third-party insurance available to the elderly. The elderly—especially if they are not part of the truly wealthy—because of their different health status are still a disadvantaged group. Their twilight years are especially threatening; government should reduce their fears and contingent liabilities—not increase them.

Paul Davidson, "The Statistical Assault Against the Elderly," *New York Times*, February 14, 1985, p. 24. Copyright © 1985 by the New York Times Company. Reprinted with permission.

In-Kind Transfers

Instead of cash grants, government often provides aid in the form of specific commodities, called in-kind transfers. Strictly speaking, an **in-kind transfer** is any good or service provided by government to a select group of citizens. In-kind transfers include grants of subsidized or free food, housing, and education.

In-kind transfer: any good or service provided by government to a select group of citizens.

Food

Of the several government food programs, the food stamp program is by far the largest, in terms of both tax dollars spent and number of people affected. In 1985 the federal government expected to spend slightly more than $11 billion on food stamps for approximately twenty million citizens.

Under the food stamp program the poor are given government coupons, or "stamps," to use in buying food. The value of the stamps provided

Table 29.6. Food Stamp Benefits for a Family of Four, July 1984

Monthly Net Income (1)	Food Stamp Value (2)	Total Purchasing Power [(1) + (2)] (3)
$ 0	$264	$264
100	234	334
200	204	404
300	174	474
400	144	544
500	114	614
600	84	684
700	54	754
800	24	824
850	0	850

Source: *U.S. AFCD and Food Stamp Programs Manual* (June 13, 1984), chap. 4.

Break-even income level: that income level at which a government subsidy is no longer available.

varies with family size and income. The bigger the family, the higher the allotted value of the stamps. For a family of a given size, the higher its income, the lower the allotted value. At some stipulated break-even income level, the subsidy falls to zero. The **break-even income level** is the income level at which a government subsidy is no longer available.

Table 29.6 shows how the food stamp program works for a family of four. A family earning a zero net (adjusted) income would receive the maximum subsidy, $264 worth of stamps a month.[4] The subsidy falls as net income rises, reaching zero at an adjusted income level of $850 a month. The food subsidy raises the family's total adjusted income, shown in column 3. Notice that the program tends to equalize the incomes of people within the low-income group it serves. After the subsidy, a family whose adjusted income was $500 a month (column 1) has only $70 more in total purchasing power (column 3) than a family whose adjusted income was $400 but who received a larger subsidy. A $100 difference in presubsidy income has dwindled to a $70 difference in purchasing power. Thus the program slightly reduces the incentive of the poor to work and earn income.

Many people favor food stamps as a means of helping the poor because they believe poor people might use unrestricted cash grants to buy cigarettes and liquor. But although food stamps cannot be used to buy such products directly, they may indirectly enable recipients to increase their consumption of liquor or any other good. In any case, statistics show that the poor generally spend a lower percentage of their incomes on tobacco and alcohol

---

4. The gross monthly family income is adjusted by subtracting a standard deduction of $95 and certain expenses, such as child care (up to a maximum of $134) and utilities (up to a maximum of $150). Given the adjustments, a family can earn some money and still receive the maximum amount of food stamps.

than do higher-income groups. The poor cannot use food stamps directly to buy something they might want more than extra food—for instance, continuing education. For that reason food stamps are less valuable to the poor than cash grants.

Housing

Sometimes government constructs and manages housing units for low-income people. Such public housing projects typically have effects similar to those of food stamp programs. Housing transfers reduce the relative price of housing to the poor, causing them to demand more housing than they otherwise would. They also increase the total effective income of the poor. But because the aid is given as a specific good or service, its value to the poor is not quite as great as an equivalent cash grant. The poor must accept the type and size of housing the government provides, instead of something they may want more.

There is one important difference between food stamps and public housing programs. Everyone who qualifies for food stamps receives them. But the number and the size of public housing units is determined by government, depending on specific appropriations. Generally, the quantity demanded for subsidized housing has exceeded the quantity supplied. Far more people want to get into public housing projects than can be accommodated. Long waiting lists are common in many parts of the nation.

In other words, public housing programs provide a significant benefit to a relatively small portion of the people who need it. Rent increases could permit better maintenance and encourage the construction of new housing units for those still on the waiting list. But since the law prevents project managers from raising rents, little can be done to alleviate the shortage, unless the taxpayers are willing to provide additional funds.

Education

Transfers in the form of elementary and high-school education typically go to all families, not just the poor. Most nations provide free elementary education to all children. In some countries, private schools offer parents who can afford them the opportunity to purchase a better education for their children. But most children go to government-run schools, because the subsidized price of this in-kind transfer is close to zero.

All students in government-provided schools get much the same treatment (though some limited programs for exceptional students are offered). How much students learn often depends more on what they bring to school—their innate abilities and their home experiences—than on school curricula. Studies suggest that children from high-income families do much better than those from low-income families. Thus this government transfer can be more valuable to high-income students than to low-income students.[5]

---

5. Howard P. Tuckman, *The Economics of the Rich* (New York: Random House, 1973), chaps. 9 and 10. Tuckman suggests that public education is a tool that the wealthy use to maintain and expand their share of the nation's wealth.

The discrepancy is even more noticeable in the case of higher education, which is often cited as a government program that takes from the poor and gives to the well-off.[6] High-income students gain more than low-income students from any given investment of resources by the state. Moreover the resources invested by the state tend to be rationed so that high-income students get more of them than the poor do. That is, a relatively large portion of the poorest students—those who have the lowest expected lifetime income—are typically not eligible for higher education in the better state universities and colleges. They simply cannot meet the entrance requirements. Those who do qualify for higher education must often go to schools in which the state invests relatively little. This is redistribution to the upper-income group.

Like the food stamp program, government subsidies of higher education raise the real incomes of those who are aided. They also increase the supply of college and university openings and depress the cost of tuition, room and board, and other fees. The public tends to assume that the implied increase in real income will be spent on additional years of education or additional courses. After all, the subsidy lowers the relative price of a college education, and the demand curve for education slopes downward, like all other demand curves. But the additional real income can also be spent at least partially on better housing, entertainment, or spring vacations. Indeed, most of the benefits of the subsidy may go to parents, who normally pay for their children's education. Thus educational subsidies may wind up supporting a house, a boat, or an additional investment that parents might not otherwise be able to afford. Still, the subsidy does change the relative price of an education, inducing parents and students to purchase more of that good than they might otherwise—the central objective of the program.

Cash Transfers

Cash transfer: a money grant provided by government to a select group of citizens.

A **cash transfer** is a money grant provided by government to a select group of citizens. If given a choice between a cash grant and an equal dollar value of food stamps, the poor would prefer to receive cash. The same is true for other forms of in-kind aid. Educational benefits can be received only by going to school, whereas dollars can be used to buy a wide variety of goods and services. Because cash represents greater choice, we should expect the poor to be better off with an amount of cash equal to the cost of an in-kind subsidy. Therefore a cash grant can provide the same level of assistance as a nominally larger educational or other type of subsidy. (This point is supported by graphic analysis in Appendix A.)

---

6. For opposing views on this subject, see W. Lee Hanser and Burton A. Weisbrod, "The Distribution of Costs and Benefits of Public Higher Education: The Case of California," *Journal of Human Resources*, 4 (Spring 1969), 176–91; and Joseph A. Pechman, "The Distributional Effects of Public Higher Education in California," *Journal of Human Resources*, 5 (Fall 1970), pp. 361–70.

Table 29.7. Hypothetical Negative Income Tax Schedule

Pretransfer Income (1)	Cash Grant or Transfer (2)	Total Disposable Income [(1) + (2)] (3)
$ 0	$5,000	$ 5,000
1,000	4,500	5,500
2,000	4,000	6,000
3,000	3,500	6,500
4,000	3,000	7,000
5,000	2,500	7,500
6,000	2,000	8,000
7,000	1,500	8,500
8,000	1,000	9,000
9,000	500	9,500
10,000	0	10,000

Cash grants can be made to the poor in many ways. One method, the negative income tax, has received considerable attention over the past two decades. The **negative income tax** is an income redistribution system under which people below a break-even income level receive cash grants. The lower their income, the higher the grant. Most income earners are subject to a positive income tax. That is, they pay part of their income to the government. The negative income tax, as the name suggests, is a cash payment from the government to people with low incomes. The greater the gap between a family's income and the stipulated break-even level, the higher the supplement.

Table 29.7 shows one of many possible negative income tax schedules. Under this plan, every poor family receives a minimum disposable income of $5,000, even if no one in the family works. This minimum is often referred to as the guaranteed income level. The **guaranteed income level** is the income level below which a family's or individual's income will not be allowed to fall. In effect it is the government income subsidy at a zero adjusted earned income level. With every rise in income of $1,000 (column 1), the government cash transfer drops $500 (column 2). At an income level of $10,000, the break-even level, no cash transfer is made. Above the break-even level, a family would be expected to pay part of its additional income to the government.

The negative income tax imposes a hidden, or implicit, marginal tax on the income of the poor. An **implicit marginal income tax** is the amount by which a government subsidy is reduced when earned income rises. This tax is often stated as a rate, or percentage, of additional earned income. When a family's income rises by $1,000, for instance, the government effectively taxes away 50 percent of the increase by reducing the family's cash transfer by $500. Like the food stamp program, therefore, this system carries a built-in disincentive to work. To keep costs down

Negative income tax: an income redistribution system under which people below a break-even income level receive cash grants. The lower the income, the higher the grant.

Guaranteed income level: the income level below which a family's or individual's income will not be allowed to fall. In effect, the government income subsidy at a zero adjusted earned income level.

Implicit marginal income tax: the amount by which a government subsidy is reduced when earned income rises.

Perspectives in Economics:
The Threatened Social Security System

The Social Security system has enjoyed widespread support since its establishment during the Great Depression. Designed originally to provide workers with monthly benefits on retirement at age sixty-five, the program has been expanded over the years to include dependents' and survivors' benefits, and disability and health care insurance. Social Security now covers over 90 percent of the work force. In 1984 nearly $175 billion in benefits was paid—about 20 percent of total federal expenditures.

The system is both an insurance and a welfare program. As insurance, Social Security payments were intended to replace part of the earnings workers lost when they retired. The program was therefore financed through a special payroll tax, assessed against part of a worker's income. The payroll tax was essentially an insurance premium, entitling participants to a government annuity in their old age, based to a limited extent on the amount paid into the system.

Social Security benefits are not based solely on taxes, however. Some benefits are paid on the basis of need, regardless of an individual's contributions to the plan. For example, benefits favor low-income workers. And workers with dependents can receive more benefits than single workers with identical employment histories.

Social Security has been criticized on several grounds. First, it is a regressive tax, one that places the heaviest burden on the low-income group it was designed to help. If the Social Security system had never been established, the nation's elderly poor would most likely be provided for through welfare programs, which are financed by the progressive income tax. As it is, elderly poor people who qualify for public assistance in addition to Social Security receive less than they would without the Social Security program. Yet they were taxed heavily in their working years for the privilege of receiving Social Security. And the poor tend to be taxed longer than the rich, who can delay entering the labor force by extending their schooling. And because low-income and minority groups typically have shorter life-spans, they do not collect benefits as long as the rich.

Second, the goals of welfare and insurance are financially incompatible. Social Security cannot provide extensive welfare benefits and still remain a sound insurance program. The taxes collected by the Social Security Administration are not saved and invested, but are paid out almost immediately

and concentrate benefits on the truly poor, any negative income tax system is likely to bear a rather high implicit marginal tax rate. (See the Appendix A on the disincentives of poverty relief, at the end of this chapter, for an extended discussion of this point.)

Minimum Wage and Rent Controls

Other common means of trying to help the poor are minimum wage laws and government-administered rent controls. Minimum wage laws, as we saw in Chapter 26, are less than effective because they tend to boost wages above equilibrium, thus reducing the number of available jobs. Though they raise the incomes of those who retain their jobs, others end up to those receiving benefits. People who retired in the early days of the program, most of whom were not poor, received enormous windfalls from Social Security, paid for by younger people.

At first this redistribution of income worked, because many workers were paying into the program and relatively few were collecting benefits. But today the system is threatened by financial insolvency. In 1950, there were sixteen workers for each beneficiary. Today that ratio is just three to one, and it may decline to two to one by the year 2035. The average retiree today receives five times more in benefits than he or she has paid into the program, even after allowing for the interest those payments could have earned if invested. Many younger workers will be less fortunate. They will receive a low rate of return on their taxes, probably less than if they had invested their money elsewhere.

Some economists argue that Social Security discourages working and saving. If individuals view the payroll tax as a form of forced saving, they are likely to reduce their personal saving for retirement. And if Social Security payments raise their marginal tax rate, they are likely to work fewer hours. These adverse effects of Social Security may be overstated, however. Social Security may simply have replaced the private, pay-as-you-go support systems once operated by families. And to the extent that Social Security enables people to retire earlier, it may encourage them to save more to achieve that goal.

Regardless of the system's past effects, Social Security now promises more in future benefits than can be delivered by its expected collections. Various proposals have been advanced to put the system back on a sound footing. In 1983 Congress took steps that will delay bankruptcy of the system until sometime in the twenty-first century. Payroll taxes have been raised; coverage has been extended to new groups of workers; cost-of-living adjustments have been delayed; benefits above certain thresholds will be taxed; and the retirement age will be gradually raised. Future shortfalls might be financed by either slowing the growth of future benefits or finding new sources of revenue. More radical proposals would eliminate the program's welfare function, transferring that responsibility to traditional welfare programs. Some people would even transfer the program's insurance function to private retirement funds, abolishing the government-run Social Security system in the process.

earning nothing. Since the poor tend to be less productive than other workers, they are often the first to be laid off when minimum wage rates are established or raised.

Rent controls tend to create a housing shortage. People will always want more rent-controlled housing than there are units available. Thus landlords can be selective in choosing tenants. They will tend to choose those most likely to pay their rent consistently—that is, high-income rather than low-income families. Landlords may also reduce the amount they spend on maintenance, and allow their apartment buildings to deteriorate. Some may simply close up their rental units and move to other areas, where they can charge higher rents. Finally, rent controls discourage the construction of new housing units, if the new units are subject to rent control.

Job Training

Many people are poor because they do not have the skills to obtain jobs that offer more than a subsistence income. Others are impoverished, some temporarily but some more or less permanently, because of the changing structure of the economy. If the demand for certain goods and services—for example, steel—declines, workers in the affected industries may be left without a job and with few other opportunities to use their skills.

Government has attempted to relieve poverty that results from changes in the job market in two principal ways. First, it provides a publicly financed employment service, which tries to increase the flow of information on job openings from employers to potential employees. These programs reduce the cost of a job search for those who are out of work, especially those with limited skills. Second, it has established job training programs for the underprivileged, such as the Jobs Corp and various summer employment programs for youths and displaced workers. Under the Job Partnership Training Act, begun in 1984, the federal government allocated nearly $2 billion for grants to state programs that provide summer jobs in the public sector or subsidize private jobs offering training to the unskilled and displaced.

Employment programs are justified on the grounds that they speed up the reemployment process, increase people's incomes, and thus raise tax revenues. Similarly it is argued that job training programs remove people from the welfare rolls, increase workers' capacity to earn a livelihood, and therefore raise tax revenues. Because millions of workers are helped by these programs, we should expect some of the funds to increase workers' and businesses' incomes. But by raising taxes, these programs may also reduce employment opportunities elsewhere.

Problems of Poverty Relief

Aid to low-income groups tends to reduce their incentive to earn an income. The poor may not pay much in taxes, for they do not earn much. But because most welfare benefits drop as earned income rises, a poor family's total spendable income does not rise much with an increase in earnings.

Consider food stamp benefits (Table 29.6). If the monthly earnings of a family of four rise by $100, from $500 to $600, its spendable income rises only $70 (from $614 to $684 a month). In effect, $30, or 30 percent of the family's additional earnings, is taxed away by the government. When expressed as a percentage of the increase in earned income, these lost benefits are called the implicit marginal tax rate. The **implicit marginal income tax rate** is the amount by which a government subsidy is reduced when earned income rises, stated as a percentage of the additional earned income. In Table 29.6, the rate is constant up to a monthly net income of $800 (near the break-even income level). No matter how much a poor person earns, he faces the same implicit marginal tax rate.

Implicit marginal income tax rate: the amount by which a government subsidy is reduced when earned income rises, stated as a percentage of the additional earned income.

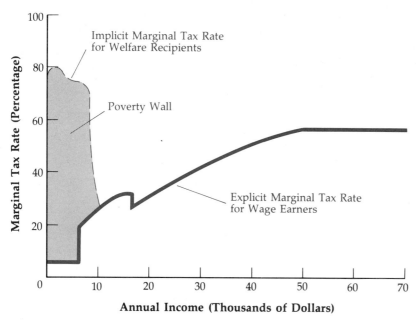

Figure 29.1. The Poverty Wall, 1976.
In 1976 the explicit marginal tax rate on earned income ranged from 5.85 percent on the first $6,100 to above 55 percent on income over $49,800. But because welfare benefits decrease with increases in earned income, people with low incomes faced an implicit marginal tax rate of up to 80 percent. This high implicit tax rate, which discourages the poor from working, has been called the poverty wall.
Source: Reprinted from *Welfare: The Political Economy of Welfare Reform in the United States* by Martin Anderson with permission of the publishers, Hoover Institution Press. Copyright © 1978 by the Board of Trustees of the Leland Stanford Junior University.

A major problem with the welfare system in the United States is that poor people generally qualify for a number of programs. Each program's benefits go down as income goes up. If a poor family earns $100 of additional income each month, its benefits from Aid to Families with Dependent Children, food stamps, housing, and Medicaid programs will all be cut back. Thus the negative incentive effect of the implicit marginal tax is compounded. Many poor pay a very high implicit marginal tax rate—in most cases close to 100 percent, and sometimes more. The result is that working does not increase their spending power noticeably, if at all.

In Figure 29.1, the upward-sloping curve represents the explicit tax rate levied on families of various income levels through the income and social security taxes. In 1976, people who earned less than $6,100 paid 5.85 percent of their income in social security taxes. Beyond $6,100, the explicit tax rate went up, peaking above 55 percent for an income of $49,800. That is, government taxed away $61 of every $100 of extra income over $49,800—a sizable disincentive to high-income earners. Yet many of the poor faced

Table 29.8. Earned Income from Wages and Family Spendable Income After Welfare Benefits, Los Angeles, 1983

Gross Monthly Wages ($) (1)	Net Monthly Spendable Income ($) (2)	Increase or Decrease in Spendable Income ($)[a] (3)	Implicit Marginal Tax Rate (%) (4)
$ 0	$1,261	n/a	n/a
100	1,304	$ 43	57%
200	1,341	37	63
300	1,366	25	75
400	1,391	25	75
500	1,419	28	72
600	1,429	10	90
700	1,423	−5	105
800	1,418	−5	105
900	1,420	2	98
1,000	1,432	12	89
1,100	1,253	−178	278
1,200	1,215	−39	139
1,300	1,217	2	98
1,400	1,256	39	61
1,500	1,294	38	62
1,600	1,330	37	63

[a] May not correlate exactly with data on net family spendable income because of rounding.
Sources: County of Los Angeles, Department of Social Security, Department of Social Services, and Housing Authority; and Arthur B. Laffer, "The Tightening Grip of the Poverty Trap," *Poverty Analysis* (Washington, D.C.: Cato Institute, 1984), p. 5.

an even greater disincentive. Their implicit marginal tax rate peaked at 80 percent—meaning that they gained only $20 in spendable income for every additional $100 earned. This extremely high disincentive is sometimes referred to as the poverty wall.

Because most welfare programs are administered by the states, both benefits and implicit marginal tax rates vary from place to place. Table 29.8 summarizes the net spendable income available to families of four on welfare in Los Angeles in 1983.[7] Column 3 shows the increase or decrease (−) in spendable income from each extra $100 of earned income. Column 4 shows the implicit marginal tax rate. The lowest marginal tax rate was 57 percent; the highest, a staggering 278 percent. Families whose monthly income rose from $1,000 to $1,100 lost so much in reduced welfare benefits that their spendable income actually fell by $178. They were worse off when they earned more.

7. Benefits from four programs are included: Aid to Families with Dependent Children, food stamps, MediCal (California's Medicaid program), and a housing program.

Generally, any aid based on income, family size, and family structure (like the food stamp program and the negative income tax) has significant incentive or disincentive effects. If benefits are based on money earnings, the poor can be expected to spend less time on earning an income and more time on home projects—for instance, growing their own food. If benefits are based on number of children, the poor are likely to have larger families. And if aid is conditional on the absence of a male breadwinner, poor families may break up more frequently than they would otherwise.

The table below shows a hypothetical schedule of cash grants given to poor people in three different family structures.

Family Structure	Cash Grant
1 adult	$3,000
1 adult, 2 children	4,000
2 adults, 2 children	5,000

If a family of two adults and two children stays together, it will receive $5,000. But if the parents separate (or give the appearance of having separated) and one parent takes both children, their total aid will rise from $5,000 to $7,000. In general, when aid is based on special characteristics such as income or family size, the poor can be expected to adjust marginally to meet the qualifications. Thus policymakers must be careful how they design welfare programs. If the implied tradeoffs are recognized, the weaknesses described above can be avoided.

The Difficulty of Overcoming Poverty

Many poor people face a kind of Catch-22 in their struggle to overcome poverty. To raise their wages, they need to improve their job skills. To accomplish that goal they need education and work experience. Yet many poor people are women with dependent children. Working or attending school takes them from their children and they must provide substitute care, which can cost $2 an hour or more. In 1985 the minimum wage was $3.35 an hour. Allowing for day care, transportation costs, and the higher food and clothing costs associated with employment, a job may offer no net economic gain to a poor woman with children—especially considering the disincentives built into the welfare system.

To help women escape from this poverty trap, society could increase the supply of day-care centers, which might lower the price of child care. The government could subsidize day-care centers or reimburse the working poor for their day-care expenditures. A subsidy to day-care centers might increase the supply curve of child care from S_1 to S_2 in Figure 29.2(a). The market price for care would fall from P_2 to P_1, and the number of children cared for would go up, from Q_1 to Q_2. The cost of the government subsidy is shown by the vertical distance between the two supply curves, ab.

If the government gave the child care subsidy to parents, the demand for day care would rise by the amount of the subsidy (ab), from D_1 to D_2

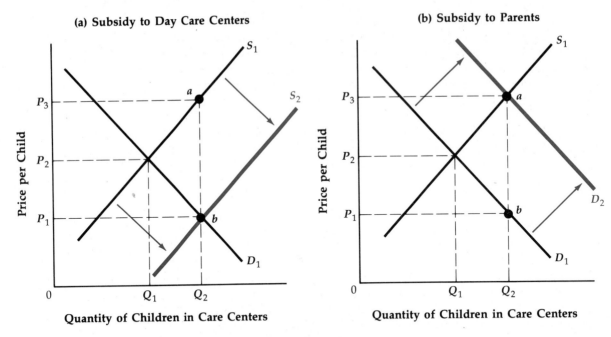

(a) Subsidy to Day Care Centers

(b) Subsidy to Parents

Figure 29.2. Subsidized Child Care.
The government can subsidize child care in two ways. It can support day care centers (part (a)), shifting the supply curve for child care from S_1 to S_2. Then the price of child care will fall, from P_2 to P_1, and the number of children cared for will rise from Q_1 to Q_2. Or the government can subsidize parents of children enrolled in day-care centers (part (b)). In that case the demand for child care will rise from D_1 to D_2, increasing the market price from P_2 to P_3. The subsidy will cover the increase in price, which is equal to the vertical distance ab. Parents will pay only P_1, and the number of children cared for will rise from Q_1 to Q_2.

in Figure 29.2(b). Again the number of children cared for would rise from Q_1 to Q_2. But the market price, instead of falling, would rise, from P_2 to P_3. Though the poor would have to pay a higher price, it would be partly covered by the subsidy ab. After deduction of the subsidy, the effective price to the poor would be lower, P_1.

A second way of increasing the availability of child care, and thus lowering its price to the poor, would be to eliminate the many government regulations that restrict the supply of day-care services. Such regulations include building codes that increase the construction costs of the centers and standards that specify everything from the qualifications of the day-care staff to the services (dietary, educational, and health) that must be provided. The elimination of such restrictions, some argue, would reduce the cost of day care, increase the supply, and lower the price. Even if the quality of the service were to fall, reducing demand from D_1 to D_2 in Figure 29.3, the supply should increase more—say from S_1 to S_2. Thus the quantity of places available should increase slightly, from Q_1 to Q_2, and

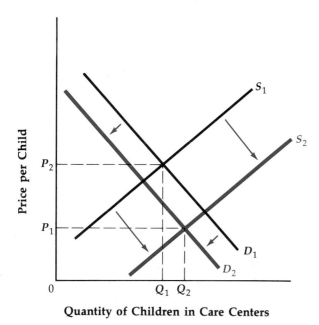

Figure 29.3. The Effects of Regulation on Child Care Services.
Regulation increases the cost of providing child care; thus it limits the supply and
drives up the price. Eliminating regulations should therefore increase the supply
of child care, from S_1 to S_2. Even if the reduced quality of care causes demand for
the service to fall, from D_1 to D_2, consumers should be better off. As long as
supply increases more than demand falls, the change should lower the market
price of child care. Here the price falls from P_2 to P_1, and the number of children
cared for increases from Q_1 to Q_2.

the price should drop from P_2 to P_1—at no extra cost to the taxpayer. (If
the supply did not increase by more than the fall in demand, day-care
operators would not be able to accept the reduced market price of their
service, and no changes would be undertaken.)

Whether the work-related benefits to poor parents—and the reduced
welfare costs to society—justify reducing the quality of day care is a
debatable question, of course.

**Summary and
Extensions**

We have discussed the distribution of income in the United States, and
some of the reasons for income differences. We have also examined the
rationale for government attempts to relieve poverty, as well as the
disincentive effects of specific programs. And we have tried to suggest
ways economics can be used to think through the tradeoffs involved in
helping the poor.

Many government redistribution programs are not really intended to help the poor. Often the purpose is to redistribute income among the middle- and upper-income groups—or sometimes to move it from the poor to the rich. One of the major challenges government faces in helping the poor is to prevent the exploitation of relief programs by those who do not need them.

Major Conclusions

1. The distribution of income in the United States is uneven. A small number of high-income people takes home a substantial share of the nation's total income, while a fairly large group of lower-income people receives a disproportionately low share.
2. In current dollar terms, the median family income of most groups rose during the 1970s and early 1980s. In constant dollar terms, however, it has dropped; median family income was lower in the 1980s than at any time during the 1970s.
3. The distribution of the nation's earned income has not changed very much in recent decades.
4. The poverty rate rose slightly in the early 1980s. Thirty-five million people, or 15.2 percent of the U.S. population, were officially counted as poor in 1983. Poverty statistics are based on a definition of the poverty income level that is deficient in several respects, however.
5. Poverty has a number of causes. People may be poor because of low productivity, sexual or racial discrimination, choice of life style, or poor economic conditions generally.
6. Poverty relief can be justified on the economic ground that aid to the poor is a public good, which only government can provide efficiently. It can also be seen as a form of social insurance, or simply as the outcome of practical politics.
7. Poverty can be relieved through either in-kind or cash transfers. The poor would prefer cash transfers, because cash gives them more choice in their purchases. Thus a smaller cash transfer would give the poor the same value as an in-kind transfer, while reducing the burden on taxpayers.
8. Because government transfer programs incorporate a high implicit marginal tax rate, they tend to reduce poor people's incentive to earn additional income.

9. Government policymakers face difficult tradeoffs in their choice of methods to aid the poor. To reduce the disincentives of the poor to earn additional income, they may have to raise the break-even income level or lower the guaranteed income level more than would be desirable on purely social grounds. Some people who do not need help would receive it, or some who need it would not receive enough.

1. We have considered several economic explanations for government aid to the poor. Can you think of others?
2. How do food stamps affect the ability of the poor to purchase education or training that will increase their productivity and earned income? How does the implicit tax on the income associated with the food stamp program affect the return on an investment in education or training? The amount of education or training a poor person is likely to seek?
3. List the advantages and disadvantages of in-kind transfers and cash grants. If you were poor, which method would you prefer? Explain.
4. "Because the poor have very little education, they are the ones who can benefit most from it. The return on education is greater to them than to the rich. Therefore public support of education for the poor is unnecessary." Do you agree? Why or why not?
5. Government aid to the poor can be a means by which the rich reduce the external costs imposed on them by the presence of poverty. If that is the basis for government action, which would be preferable, in-kind transfers or cash grants? What factors must be considered in this decision?
6. Predict the effects of the food stamp program on:
   a. The real incomes of those who qualify
   b. The quantity of food bought by the nonpoor
   c. The price of food
   d. The quantity of food produced
   e. The real income of nonpoor farmers
   f. The real disposable income of nonpoor taxpayers
7. Suppose the government wishes to reduce the number of nonpoor people who benefit from a negative income tax, without reducing aid to the truly poor or increasing the implicit marginal tax rate. Can such an objective be accomplished? If not, what improvements could the government achieve?

Appendix A:

More on the Disincentives of Poverty Relief

The practice of scaling down welfare benefits as earned income rises creates an implicit marginal tax on additional earned income that discourages the poor from working. Why not lower the implicit marginal tax rate?

Figure 29.A1 gives the answer. The 45-degree line that extends out from the origin indicates points of equal distance from each axis—that is, points at which spendable income equals earned income. At point y, for example, a poor person earns and can spend $5,000 annually. At points above the line, spendable income exceeds earned income. For instance, at point x, a poor person earns $5,000 annually and can spend $7,500. He receives a subsidy equal to $y - x$, or $2,500.

Suppose the government establishes a negative income tax with a guaranteed annual income level of $5,000, or SI_1. The break-even earned income level is $10,000, or EI_1. A person who earns nothing will receive a subsidy of $5,000 a year. As his earned income rises the subsidy will decline, until it reaches zero at $10,000. Curve SI_1 shows the spendable income of people in this program at various earned income levels. They lose $500 in subsidies for every $1,000 of additional earned income. That is, they face an implicit marginal tax rate of 50 percent.

If policymakers want to reduce the implicit marginal tax rate on an earned income of $10,000 to less than 50 percent, they must either reduce the guaranteed spendable income level or raise the break-even earned income level. If they raise the break-even earned income level—to $15,000, or EI_2, for example—curve SI_1a will shift to SI_1b. But then more people—all those with earned incomes up to EI_2—will receive benefits. Moreover, all the people covered originally will receive larger subsidies. A person with an income of $5,000 would receive $8,000 instead of $7,000 in spendable income (point z instead of point x), for example. The total increase in the government's poverty relief expenditures would equal the shaded area in the figure bounded by SI_1ab.

Figure 29.A1. Policy Tradeoffs of a Negative Income Tax.
With a guaranteed income of SI_1 ($5,000) and a break-even earned income level of
EI_1 ($10,000), the implicit marginal tax rate on the poor is 50 percent. If policymakers
attempt to reduce the implicit tax rate by raising the break-even income level,
however, the government's poverty relief budget will rise by the shaded area SI_1ab.
A higher explicit tax burden will fall on a smaller group of taxpaying workers.

This increase in expenditures will place a greater tax burden on taxpaying
workers. Yet because more workers are covered by the negative income
tax, the increased tax burden will be shared by fewer people. Thus the
explicit marginal tax rate on high-income workers will rise—lowering their
incentive to work and earn additional income.

If the government reduces the guaranteed income level, say from SI_1 to
SI_0, a different problem will result. On the new curve SI_0a, the poor will
receive less government aid at each earned income level. They may have
more incentive to work under such an arrangement, but will they have
enough to live on?

Thus policymakers face difficult tradeoffs between the goal of helping the poor and the goal of minimizing the disincentive to work. To provide adequate aid, they may have to raise the break-even income level high enough that people who are not strictly poor benefit. Yet to reduce aid to people who are not truly poor, they would have to lower the break-even income level—thus increasing the implicit tax rate on the poor. Or, to keep the implicit marginal tax rate down, they could lower the guaranteed income level—decreasing the benefits that go to the truly poor.

Our graphic analysis suggests that there may be economic as well as altruistic limits to the government's ability to transfer income from the rich to the poor. As more and more income is allocated to the poor, either the guaranteed income and/or break-even income level must go up. If only the guaranteed income level is raised, the implicit marginal tax rate facing the poor increases. If that problem is avoided by raising the break-even income level, more people will be covered by poverty relief, and the taxes paid by the remaining workers will go up. Increased aid to the poor thus should have three consequences. A higher explicit tax burden will fall on fewer taxpayers. Because of this burden, higher-income groups will have less incentive to work. And lower-income groups, because of the higher implicit tax rate, will also be less inclined to work.

Appendix B:
Cash Versus In-Kind Transfers— An Analysis Based on the Budget Line and Indifference Curves

A cash grant will raise the welfare of the poor more than an in-kind transfer of equal value. Figure 29.A2 illustrates a poor family's budget line for higher education and housing, H_3E_3. Without subsidies, this family can buy as much as E_3 units of education (and no housing) or H_3 units of housing (and no education). Because the family wants both housing and higher education, it will probably divide its income between the two, choosing some combination like point a, or E_1 education and H_1 housing.

Suppose that the government decides to subsidize the family's higher education purchases through reduced university tuition. Its action lowers the total price of education, pivoting the family's budget line out to H_3E_5. The result is that the family can now consume more of both items, education and housing. The family will probably move to some combination like b, H_2 housing and E_2 education. Its education consumption has gone up and the additional housing purchased represents an increase in income equal to the vertical distance between b and c.

Suppose the family were given the cash equivalent of bc instead. The additional money would not change the relative prices of higher education and housing, as the reduced tuition program did. But it would shift the budget line from H_3E_3 to a parallel position, H_4E_4 (dashed line). The relative price of housing is lower on H_4E_4 than on H_3E_5. Thus the family would tend to prefer a point like d, where it could consume more housing and less education, to b, their preference under the reduced tuition program. And if the family would prefer d to b, both of which are available on line H_4E_4, we must presume that they would prefer cash to an in-kind subsidy.

Figure 29.A2. Budget Line: Cash Grants Versus Food Stamps.
If the price of education is reduced by an in-kind subsidy, a family's budget line will pivot from H_3E_3 to H_3E_5. The family will move from point a to point b, where it can consume more food and housing. But if the family is given the same subsidy in cash, its budget line will move from H_3E_3 to H_4E_4. Since the relative price of housing is lower on H_4E_4 than on H_3E_5, the family will choose a point like d over b. Since b was the family's preferred point on H_3E_5, but they prefer d to b, we must presume they also prefer cash to a food subsidy.

This point can be seen even more clearly with the help of indifference curves. In Figure 29.A3, in the absence of government relief, the family's indifference curve will be I_1, and it will choose point a. If government subsidy reduces the price of education, the family's utility level rises and

Figure 29.A3. Indifference Curves for Two Relief Programs.
A subsidy that reduces the price of food alone will move a family from indifference
curve I_1 to I_2. The family will move from point a on budget line H_3E_3 to point b on
line H_3E_5. But a cash subsidy will move the family to an even higher indifference
curve, I_3. They will choose point d on budget line H_4E_4.

its indifference curve shifts to I_2. It will move to point b, the intersection
of I_2 and the subsidized budget line H_3E_5. But if the same transfer is made
in cash, the family moves to an even higher indifference curve, I_3. It then
chooses point d, where I_3 and H_4E_4 meet.

Part IX

Applications of Microeconomic Theory

**Central
Question**

*How do external costs
and benefits justify
government intervention
in the market?*

Chapter 30

Market Failures: External Costs and Benefits

In its broadest definitional sense, collective action is the enactment and enforcement of law. The justification for all collective action, for government, lies in its ability to make men better off. This is where any discussion of the bases for collective action must begin.

James Buchanan

*H*ow much should government involve itself in the marketplace? This question touches on one of the most important economic issues of our time: the division of responsibility between the public and private sectors. In general, economic principles would suggest that government undertake only functions that it can perform more efficiently than the market.

Economics provides a method for evaluating the relative efficiency of government and the marketplace. It enables us to identify which goods and services the market will fail to produce altogether, and which it will produce inefficiently. We saw in Chapter 4 that such market failures have three sources: monopoly and monopsony power, external costs, and external benefits. Now, using the principles and graphic analyses developed in earlier chapters, we will take a closer look at external costs and benefits and at government attempts to capture them and correct market failures. (See Chapters 23 and 27 for discussions of monopoly and monopsony power.)

External Costs and External Benefits

In a competitive market, producers must minimize their production costs in order to lower their prices, increase their production levels, and improve the quality of their products. Consumers must demonstrate how much they will pay for a product, and in what amount they will buy it. In a competitive market, production will move toward the intersection of the market supply and demand curves—Q_1 in Figure 30.1. At that point, the marginal cost of the last unit produced will equal its marginal benefit to consumers.

To the extent that the market moves toward equilibrium in supply and demand, it is efficient in a very special sense. So long as the marginal benefit of anything people do is greater than the marginal cost, people are presumed to be better off. In Figure 30.1, for each loaf of bread up to Q_1, the marginal benefit of consumption (as shown by the demand curve) exceeds the marginal cost of production (as shown by the supply curve). Because the marginal cost of a loaf of bread is the value of the most attractive alternative forgone, people must be getting more value out of each of those loaves than they could from any alternative good. By producing exactly Q_1 loaves—no more and no less—the market extracts all possible surplus or excess benefits from production (see the shaded area on the graph) and divides them among buyers and sellers. In this sense the production and distribution of economic resources can be said to be efficient.

These results cannot be achieved unless competition is intense (perfect), buyers receive all the product's benefits, and producers pay all the costs of production. To the extent that such optimum conditions are not achieved, the market fails. Part of the excess benefits shown by the shaded area in the figure will not be realized by either buyers or sellers.

When exchanges between buyers and sellers affect people who are not directly involved in the trades, they are said to have external effects, or to generate externalities. Externalities, as we saw in Chapter 4, are the

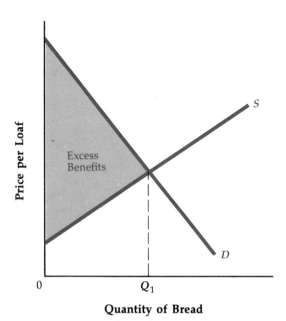

Figure 30.1. Marginal Benefit Versus Marginal Cost.
The demand curve reflects the marginal benefits of each loaf of bread produced.
The supply curve reflects the marginal cost of producing each loaf. For each loaf
of bread up to Q_1, the marginal benefits exceed the marginal cost. The shaded
area shows the maximum welfare that can be gained from the production of bread.
When the market is at equilibrium (when supply equals demand), all those benefits
will be realized.

positive or negative effects that exchanges may have on people who are
not in the market. They are third-party effects. When such effects are
pleasurable they are called external benefits. When they are unpleasant,
or impose a cost on people other than the buyers or sellers, they are called
external costs. The effects of external costs and benefits on production and
market efficiency can be seen with the aid of supply and demand curves.

External Costs

Figure 30.2 represents the market for a paper product. The market demand
curve, *D*, indicates the benefits consumers receive from the product. To
make paper, the producers must pay the costs of labor, chemicals, and
pulpwood. The industry supply curve, S_1, shows the costs on which paper
manufacturers must base their production decisions. In a perfectly competitive market, the quantity of the paper product that is bought will be
Q_2, and the price paid by consumers will be P_1.

But producers may not bear all the costs associated with production. A
by-product of the production process may be solid or gaseous waste

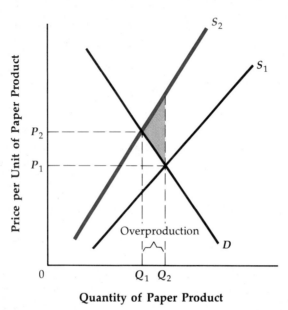

Figure 30.2. External Costs.
Ignoring the external costs associated with the manufacture of paper products, firms will base their production and pricing decisions on supply curve S_1. If they considered external costs, such as the cost of pollution, they would operate on the basis of supply curve S_2, producing Q_1 instead of Q_2 units. The shaded area shows the amount by which the marginal cost of production of $Q_2 - Q_1$ units exceeds the marginal benefits to consumers. It indicates the inefficiency of the private market when external costs are not borne by producers.

dumped into rivers or emitted into the atmosphere. The stench of production may pervade the surrounding community. Towns located downstream may have to clean up the water. People may have to paint their houses more frequently or seek medical attention for eye irritation. Homeowners may have to accept lower prices than usual for their property. All these costs are imposed on people not directly involved in the production, consumption, or exchange of the paper product. Nonetheless, these external costs are part of the total cost of production to society.

In a perfectly competitive market, in which all participants act independently, survival may require that a producer impose external costs on others. An individual producer who voluntarily installs equipment to clean up pollution will incur costs higher than those of its competitors. It will not be able to match price cuts, and so may be run out of business. And some producers may not care whether they cause harm to others by polluting the environment. Even socially concerned producers cannot afford to care too much about the environment.

The supply curve S_2 incorporates both the external production costs of pollution and the private costs borne by producers. If producers have to bear all those costs, the price of the product will be higher (P_2 rather than P_1), and consumers will buy a smaller quantity (Q_1 rather than Q_2). Thus the true marginal cost of each unit of paper between Q_1 and Q_2 is greater than the marginal benefit to consumers. If consumers have to pay for external costs, they will value other goods more highly than those units. In a sense, then, the paper manufacturers are overproducing, by $Q_2 - Q_1$ units. The marginal cost of those units exceeds their marginal benefit by the shaded triangular area.

Other examples of external costs that encourage overproduction are the highway congestion created by automobiles and the noise created by airplanes in and around airports. The argument can also be extended to include less obvious costs, like the death and destruction caused by speeding and reckless driving. If government does not penalize such negligent behaviors, people will produce them, at a potentially high external cost to others. In the same way, adult bookstores, X-rated movie houses, and massage parlors impose costs on neighboring businesses. Their sordid appearance scares away many people who might otherwise patronize legitimate businesses in the area. And to the extent that free public education reduces the burden of supporting children, it too can impose an external cost. For just as failure to charge for pollution encourages overproduction of paper, public expenditures on education can contribute to overpopulation.

External Benefits

Sometimes market inefficiencies are created by external benefits. Market demand does not always reflect all the benefits received from a good. Instead, people not directly involved in the production, consumption, or exchange of the good receive some of its benefits.

To see the effects of external benefits on the allocation of resources, consider the market for flu shots. The cost of producing vaccine includes labor, research and production equipment, eggs, and transportation. Assuming that all those costs are borne by the producers, the market supply curve will be S in Figure 30.3.

Individuals receive important personal benefits from flu shots. The fact that many millions of people pay for them every year shows that there is a demand, illustrated by curve D_1 in Figure 30.3. But in getting shots for themselves, people also provide external benefits for others. By protecting themselves, they reduce the probability that the flu will spread to others. But when others escape the medical expenses and lost work time associated with flu, those benefits are not captured in the market demand curve, D_1. Only in the higher societal demand curve, labeled D_2, are those benefits realized.

Left to itself, a perfectly competitive market will produce at the inter-section of the market supply and market demand curves (S and D_1), or

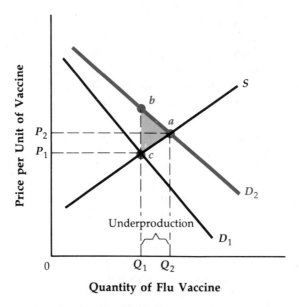

Figure 30.3. External Benefits.
Ignoring the external benefits of getting flu shots, consumers will base their purchases on demand curve D_1 instead of D_2. Fewer shots will be purchased than could be justified economically—Q_1 instead of Q_2. Because the marginal benefit of each shot between Q_1 and Q_2 (as shown by demand curve D_2) exceeds its marginal cost of production, external benefits are not being realized. The shaded area abc indicates market inefficiency.

at point c. At that point the equilibrium price will be P_1 and the quantity produced will be Q_1. But if external benefits are considered in the production decision, the marginal benefits of flu shots between Q_1 and Q_2 (shown by the demand curve D_2) will exceed their marginal cost of production (shown by the supply curve). In other words, if all benefits, both private and external, were considered, Q_2 shots would be produced and purchased at a price of P_2. At Q_2, the marginal cost of the last shot would equal its marginal benefit. Social welfare would rise by an amount equal to the triangular shaded area abc.

Because a free market can fail to capture such external benefits, government action to subsidize flu shots may be justified. On such grounds governments all over the world have mounted programs to inoculate people against diseases like smallpox. The external benefit argument has also been used to justify government support of medical research. It can also be extended to services such as public transportation. City buses provide direct benefits to their passengers but also benefit motorists and pedestrians by reducing traffic congestion. And in many ways, education provides external benefits to the general population. An informed and articulate citizenry raises both the level of public discourse and the general standard of living.[1] Public parks and environmental programs can also provide external benefits that are not likely to be realized privately, because of their high cost to individuals. Again, government action may be required to supplement private efforts.

The Pros and Cons of Government Action

More often than not, exchanges between buyers and sellers affect others. People buy clothes partly to keep warm in the winter and dry in the rain. But most people value the appearance of clothing at least as much as its comfort. We choose clothing because we want others to be pleased or impressed (or perhaps irritated). The same can be said, to some extent, of the cars we purchase, the places we go to eat, the records we buy, even the colleges we attend. We impose the external effects of our actions deliberately as well as accidentally.

The fact that externalities are involved in economic transactions does not necessarily mean that government should intervene. First, the economic distortions created by externalities are often quite small, if not inconsequential. So far our examples of external costs and benefits involved possibly significant distortions of market forces. But in Figure 30.4, the supply curve S_2, which incorporates both private and external costs, lies only slightly to the left of the market supply curve, S_1. The difference between the market output level, Q_2, and the optimum output level, Q_1, is small, as is the market inefficiency, shown by the shaded triangular area. Therefore little can be gained by government intervention.

This limited benefit must be weighed against the cost of government action. Whenever government intervenes in any difficulty, agencies are set up, employees are hired, papers are shuffled, and reports are filed. Almost invariably, suits are brought against firms and individuals who have violated government rules. In short, significant costs can be incurred in redressing small market inefficiencies. If the cost of government intervention exceeds the cost of the market's inefficiencies, government action will actually increase inefficiency.

A second reason for limiting government action is that it generates external costs of its own. If government dictates the construction methods to be used in building homes, the way mothers deliver their babies, or the hair lengths of government workers, the people who set the standards impose a cost—which may be external to them—on those who do not share their standards. We may agree with some government rules, but strenuously object to others. On balance, such government intervention is as likely to hurt us as help us.

---

1. The ratio of public to private benefits varies by educational levels. Elementary school education develops crucial social and communication skills; its private benefits are virtually side effects. At the college level, however, the private benefits to students may dominate the public benefits. Thus elementary education is supported almost entirely by public sources, while college education is only partially subsidized.

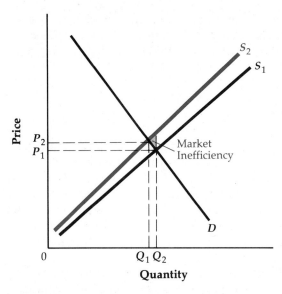

Figure 30.4. Is Government Action Justified?
Because of external costs, the market illustrated above produces more than the efficient output. But market inefficiency, represented by the shaded triangular area, is quite small—so small that government intervention may not be justified on economic grounds alone.

Government dictates have sometimes attained Big Brother proportions in the educational system. For instance, until the late 1960s, the University of Virginia had a dress code that required male students to wear coats and ties. Colleges routinely set the hours by which students should return to their dormitories, and expelled those who rebelled. At the University of California, students were once forbidden to engage in on-campus political activity. Costs are imposed on those who must obey such rules. The more centralized the government that is setting the standards, the less opportunity people will have to escape the rules by moving elsewhere.

In certain markets, government action may not be necessary. Over the long run, some of the external costs and benefits that cause market distortions may be internalized. That is, they may become private costs and benefits. Suppose the development of a park would generate external benefits for all the businesses in a shopping district. More customers would be attracted to the district, and more sales would be made. An alert entrepreneur could internalize those benefits by building a shopping mall with a park in the middle. Because the mall would attract more customers than other shopping areas, the owner could benefit from higher rents. To the extent that shopping centers can internalize such externalities, economic efficiency will be enhanced—without government intervention.

When Walt Disney built Disneyland, he benefited merchants in the Anaheim area. Other businesses quickly moved in to take advantage of the external benefits—the crowds of visitors—spilling over from the amusement park. Disney did not make the same mistake twice. When he built Disney World in Orlando, he bought enough land so that most of the benefits of the amusement park would stay within the Disney domain. Inside the more than six thousand acres of Disney-owned land in Florida, development has been controlled and profits captured by the Disney corporation. Though other businesses have established themselves on the perimeters of Disney World, their distance from its center makes it more difficult for them to capture external benefits from the amusement park.

Methods of Reducing Externalities

Government action can undoubtedly guarantee that certain goods and services will be produced more efficiently. The benefits of such action may be substantial, even when compared with the costs. In such cases, only the form of government intervention remains to be determined. Government action can take several forms: persuasion; assignment of communal property rights to individuals; government production of goods and services; regulation of production through published standards; and control of product prices through taxes, fines, and subsidies. Economists generally argue that if government is going to intervene, it should choose the least costly means sufficient to the task at hand.

Persuasion

External costs arise partly because we do not consider the welfare of others in our decisions. Indeed, if we fully recognized the adverse effects of our actions on others, external costs would not exist. Our production decisions would be based as much as possible on the total costs of production to society.

Thus government can alleviate market distortions by persuading citizens to consider how their behavior affects others. Forest Service advertisements urge people not to litter or to risk forest fires when camping. Other government campaigns encourage people not to drive if they drink, to cultivate their land so as to minimize erosion, and to conserve water and gas. Although such efforts are limited in their effect, they may be more acceptable than other approaches, given political constraints.

Assignment of Property Rights

As we saw in Chapter 4, when property rights are held communally or left unassigned, property tends to be overused. So long as no one else is already using the property, anyone can use it without paying for its use.

Costs that are not borne by users, of course, are passed on to others as external costs. When public land was open to grazing in the West 150 years ago, for instance, ranchers allowed their herds to overgraze. The external cost of their indiscriminate use of the land has been borne by later generations, who have inherited a barren, wasted environment.

Thus the assignment of property rights can eliminate some externalities. If land rights are assigned to individuals, they will bear the cost of their own neglect. If owners allow their cattle to strip a range of its grass, they will no longer be able to raise their cattle there. And the price of the land will decline with its productivity.

Some resources, such as air and water, cannot always be divided into parcels. In those cases, the property rights solution will not work well, if at all.

Government Production

Through nationalization of some industries, government can attempt to internalize external costs. The argument is that because government is concerned with social consequences, it will consider the total costs of production, both internal and external. On the basis of that argument, governments in the United States operate schools, public health services, national and state parks, transportation systems, harbors, and electric power plants. In other nations, governments also operate major industries, such as the steel and automobile industries.

Government production can be a mixed blessing. When other producers remain in the market, government participation may increase competition. But sometimes it means the elimination of competition. Consider the U.S. Postal Service, which has exclusive rights to the delivery of first-class mail. As a government agency, the Post Office is not permitted to make a profit. Because of its monopolistic position, however, it may tolerate higher costs and lower work standards than competitive firms.

Some government production, such as the provision of public goods like national defense, may be unavoidable. But in most cases, direct ownership and production may not be necessary. Instead of producing goods with which externalities are associated, government could simply contract with private firms for the business. That is precisely how most states handle road construction, how several states handle penal systems, and how a few city governments provide ambulance, police, and fire-fighting services.

Taxes and Subsidies

Government can deal with some external costs by taxing producers. Pollution can be discouraged by a tax on either the pollution itself or the final product. Taxing the pollution emitted by firms internalizes external costs, increasing total costs to the producer. Imposing such taxes should have a twofold effect in reducing pollution. First, many producers would find the cost of pollution control cheaper than the pollution tax. And second, the tax would raise the prices of final products, reducing the number of units consumed—and hence reducing the level of pollution.

The size of the tax can be adjusted to achieve whatever level of pollution is judged acceptable. If a tax of $1 per unit produced does not reduce pollution sufficiently, the tax can be raised to $2. In terms of Figure 30.2, the ideal tax would be just enough to encourage producers to view their supply curve as S_2 instead of S_1. The resulting cutback in production from Q_2 to Q_1 would eliminate market inefficiency, represented by the shaded area abc.

Theoretically, the government could achieve the same result by subsidizing firms in their efforts to eliminate pollution. It could give tax credits for the installation of pollution controls or pay firms outright to install the equipment. Until 1985, the federal government used tax credits to encourage the installation of fuel-saving devices, which indirectly reduced pollution.

Production Standards

Alternatively, the government could simply impose standards on all producers. It could rule, for example, that polluters may not emit more than a certain amount of pollutants during a given period. Offenders would either have to pay for a clean-up or risk a fine. A firm that flagrantly violated the standard, might be forced to shut down.

Choosing the Most Efficient Remedy for Externalities

Selecting the most efficient method of minimizing externalities can be a complicated process. To illustrate, we will compare the costs of two approaches to controlling pollution, government standards versus property rights.

Suppose five firms are emitting sulfur dioxide, a pollutant that causes acid rain. The reduction of the unwanted emissions can be thought of as an economic good whose production involves a cost. We can assume that the marginal cost of reducing sulfur dioxide emissions will rise as more and more units are eliminated. We can also assume that such costs will differ from firm to firm. Table 30.1 incorporates these assumptions. Firm A, for example, must pay $100 to eliminate the first unit of sulfur dioxide and $200 to eliminate the second. Firm B must pay $200 for the first unit and $600 for the second. Although the information in the table is hypothetical, it reflects the structure of real-world pollution clean-up costs. The technological fact of increasing marginal costs afflicts firms when they clean up the air as well as when they produce goods and services.

Suppose the Environmental Protection Agency (EPA) decides that the maximum acceptable level of sulfur dioxide is ten units. To achieve that level, the EPA prohibits firms from emitting more than two units of sulfur

Table 30.1. Cost of Reducing Sulfur Dioxide Emissions

	A	B	C	D	E
Cost of eliminating:					
First unit	$ 100	$ 200	$ 200	$ 600	$1,000
Second unit	200	600	400	1,000	2,000
Third unit	400	1,800	600	1,400	3,000
Fourth unit	800	5,400	800	1,800	4,000
Fifth unit	1,600	16,200	1,000	2,200	5,000

Cost of Reducing Pollution by Establishment of Government Standards		Cost of Reducing Pollution by Sale of Pollution Rights	
Cost to A of eliminating 3 units	$ 700	Cost to A of eliminating 4 units	$1,500
Cost to B of eliminating 3 units	2,600	Cost to B of eliminating 2 units	800
Cost to C of eliminating 3 units	1,200	Cost to C of eliminating 5 units	3,000
Cost to D of eliminating 3 units	3,000	Cost to D of eliminating 3 units	3,000
Cost to E of eliminating 3 units	6,000	Cost to E of eliminating 1 unit	1,000
Total cost	$13,500	Total cost	$9,300

dioxide each. If each firm was emitting five units, each will have to reduce its emissions by three units. The total cost of meeting the limit of two units is shown in the lower half of Table 30.1. Firm A incurs the relatively modest cost of $700 ($100 + $200 + $400). But firm B must pay $2,600 ($200 + $600 + $1,800). The total cost to all firms is $13,500.

What if the EPA adopts a different strategy and sells rights to pollute? Such rights can be thought of as tickets that authorize firms to dump a unit of waste into the atmosphere. The more tickets a firm purchases, the more waste it can dump and the more cleanup costs it can avoid.

Remember that the EPA can control the number of tickets it sells. To limit pollution to the maximum acceptable level of ten units, all it needs to do is sell no more than ten tickets. Either way, whether by pollution standards or rights, the level of pollution is kept down to ten units. But the pollution rights method allows firms that want to avoid the cost of a clean-up to bid for tickets.

The potential market for such rights can be illustrated by conventional supply and demand curves, as in Figure 30.5. The supply curve is determined by EPA policymakers, who limit the number of tickets to ten. Since in this example the supply is fixed, the supply curve must be vertical (perfectly inelastic). Whatever the price, the number of pollution rights remains the same. The demand curve is derived from the costs firms must bear to clean up their emissions. The higher the cost of the cleanup, the more attractive pollution rights will be. As with all demand curves, price and quantity are inversely related. The lower the price of pollution rights, the higher the quantity demanded.

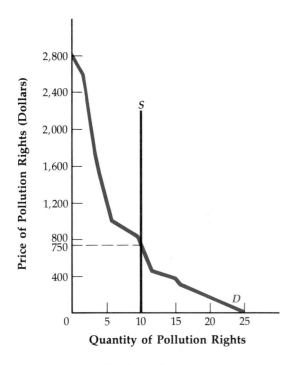

Figure 30.5. Market for Pollution Rights.
Reducing pollution is costly (see Table 30.1). It adds to the costs of production, increasing product prices and reducing the quantities of products demanded. Therefore firms have a demand for the right to avoid pollution abatement costs. The lower the price of such rights, the greater the quantity of rights that firms will demand (see Table 30.2). If the government fixes the supply of rights at ten and sells those ten rights to the highest bidders, the price of the rights will settle at the intersection of the supply and demand curves—here, $1,500.

Table 30.2 shows the total quantity demanded by the firms at various prices. At a price of zero, the firms want twenty-five rights (five each). At a price of $201, they demand only twenty-one. A wants only three, for it will cost less to clean up its first two units (at costs of $100 and $200) than to buy rights to emit them at a price of $201. B wants four rights, for its cleanup costs are higher.

Given the information in the table, the market clearing price—the price at which the quantity of pollution rights demanded exactly equals the number of rights for sale—will be something over $1,400—say $1,500. Who will buy those rights, and what will the cost of the program be?

At a price of $1,500 per ticket, firm A will buy one and only one ticket. At that price, it is cheaper for the firm to clean up its first four units (the cost of the cleanup is $100 + $200 + $400 + $800). Only the fifth unit, which would cost $1,600 to clean up, makes the purchase of a $1,500 ticket worthwhile. Similarly, firm B will buy three tickets, firm C none, firm D two, and firm E four.

Perspectives in Economics: Emerging Markets in Pollution Rights

The sale of pollution rights is a less costly way of controlling pollution than the establishment of government standards. For a given cost, the sale of pollution rights will produce cleaner air than the set standard method. Yet some people are disturbed that government should sell rights to the air. There is no reason, however, that rights must be sold by the government. Instead, the government can set a standard, allocate pollution rights to existing firms, and allow them to sell the rights. The cost savings will be approximately the same as if the government had auctioned off the rights.

Suppose the government decides to divide ten pollution rights among five producers—two to each producer. The producers pay nothing for the rights and are free to resell them among themselves. Table 30.1 shows the possibilities of such a system, from the producers' point of view.

Under the government standard system, firm E must eliminate three units of sulfur dioxide, even though the cost of the third unit is prohibitively high at $3,000. Firm E should be willing to pay anything less than $3,000 to avoid eliminating that last unit. Firm A is required to eliminate three units of pollution, but could eliminate a fourth at a cost of only $800. Obviously, a trade can be struck between A and E. E will pay A as much as $3,000 for the right to emit the third unit of pollution, while A will clean up the extra unit for any sum over $800. If the price of pollution rights is set by market forces at $1,500 per unit, E will save $1,500 ($3,000 − $1,500) and A will earn $700 ($1,500 − $800). The overall cost of meeting the officially established standard will drop by $2,200 (the $3,000 E saves minus the extra $800 cost incurred by A).

But additional trades can also be made. It will cost E $2,000 to eliminate its second unit of pollution. Thus E will find it worthwhile to buy a second pollution right from A or C. B and D should also be willing to bargain for rights held by A and C. Competition among E, B, and D will move the price of rights toward the equilibrium price of $1,500 achieved when the government sells rights (see Figure 30.5). The end result will be the same as if the government had sold the rights at an auction initially. The total cost of the cleanup will be $9,300, $4,200 less than under a uniform standard system. The only difference is that this way, the government does not receive any of the income from the sales. Instead, firms A and C reap the benefits.

Rights that were distributed free by the government are now enriching some of the lucky owners. Such a redistribution of the wealth may seem unjust—but the injustice does not result from the market exchanges, but from the way the rights were distributed. As noted earlier, there is no compelling economic reason for giving away the rights to the air, any more than for giving away rights to the national forests. Ethical questions must be confronted before distribution of rights, not after. Once the system has been set up, economic analysis can show only that resources will be saved, and income and output raised, through market exchanges in existing rights.

The cost of any cleanup must be measured by the value of the resources that go into it. The value of the resources is approximated by the firms' expenditures on the cleanup—not by their expenditures on pollution tickets. (The tickets do not represent real resources, but a transfer of purchasing power from the firms to the government.) Accordingly, the economic cost of reducing pollution to ten units is $9,300: $1,500 for firm A, $800 for B, $3,000 each for C and D, and $1,000 for E. This figure is significantly less than the $13,500 cost of the cleanup when each firm is

A real-world market for pollution rights is now beginning to emerge. For several years, Standard Oil of Ohio wanted to build a pipeline terminal near Long Beach, California, where oil brought down by tanker from Alaska's North Slope could be unloaded. The terminal would cause a pollution problem, however, and the pollution level in that area was already at the maximum legal limit. So Standard set out to secure the rights it needed from other companies in the area. By equipping three dry-cleaning stores with pollution control devices, Standard hoped to obtain enough rights to build the terminal. The company has made a similar arrangement with California Edison.

Similarly, in the late 1970s, Volkswagen of America, Inc. (VW), began producing Rabbits in Pennsylvania. The firm was able to open its new factory because of a special arrangement with the state of Pennsylvania. The state wanted the plant both for its jobs and for the tax revenues it would generate, but it wanted to avoid further pollution. So it agreed to reduce its own hydrocarbon emissions by changing the process it used to pave roads, and gave some of its emission rights to VW. The state is now paying more to pave its roads, but presumably the increase in tax revenues and decrease in welfare payments have made the trade worthwhile.

In the early 1980s, General Electric was faced with a choice of shutting down a plant in Louisville, Kentucky; paying for pollution control equipment; or failing to comply with emissions standards. General Electric paid $60,000 to lease several hundred tons of emissions reductions that International Harvester deposited in the Louisville "emissions bank." The purchase of the emissions rights reportedly saved GE approximately $1.5 million in capital costs and $3,000 in annual operating costs.[1]

These trades of pollution rights are not the straightforward monetary transactions that were described previously, but such deals may soon be possible. Entrepreneurs are currently investigating the idea of pollution rights agencies (similar to real estate firms) that would bring buyers and sellers of rights together.

Should this newly emerging market be controlled? To the extent that the rights to anything—land, public services, trademarks—must be defined and guaranteed, the market for pollution rights must be controlled by government. For instance, to ensure that official pollution levels are maintained, government must monitor the amount of pollution in the atmosphere. If government fails to enforce the pollution rights it has distributed, the atmosphere will revert back to its old status of communal property.

1. For discussions of the emerging market in pollution rights, see Bruce Yandle, "The Emerging Market in Air Pollution Rights," *Regulation* (July–August 1978), pp. 21–29; and Michael H. Levin, "Building a Better Bubble at EPA," *Regulation* (March–April 1985), pp. 32–42.

required to eliminate three units of pollution. Yet in each case, fifteen units are eliminated. In short, the pricing system is more economical— more cost-effective or efficient—than setting standards. And because it is more efficient, it is also the more economical way of producing goods and services. More resources go into production and less into cleanup.

The idea of selling rights to pollute may not sound attractive, but it makes sense economically. When the government sets standards, it is giving away rights to pollute. In our example, telling each firm that it

Table 30.2. Demand for Pollution Rights

Price	Quantity
$ 0	25
101	24
201	21
401	19
601	16
801	14
1,001	11
1,401	10
1,601	9
1,801	7
2,001	6
2,201	5
3,001	4
4,001	3
5,001	2
5,601	0

must reduce its sulfur dioxide emissions by three units is effectively giving them each permission to dump two units into the atmosphere. One might ask whether the government should be giving away rights to the atmosphere, which has many other uses besides the absorption of pollution. Though some pollution may be necessary to continued production, that is no argument for giving away pollution rights. Land is needed in many production processes, but the Forest Service does not give away the rights to public lands. When pollution rights are sold, on the other hand, potential users can express the relative values they place on the right to pollute.[2] In that way, rights can be assigned to their most valuable and productive uses.

Summary and Extensions

As we saw in Chapter 4, a market economy will overproduce goods and services that impose external costs on society. It will underproduce goods and services that confer external benefits. Sometimes, but not always, government intervention can be justified to correct for externalities. To be worthwhile, the benefits of action must outweigh the costs.

---

2. Note that the system allows environmental groups as well as producers to express the value they place on pollution rights. If environmental groups think ten units of sulfur dioxide is too much pollution, they can buy some of the tickets themselves and then not exercise their right to pollute.

Some ways of dealing with external costs and benefits are more efficient than others. Even when government intervention in the market is clearly warranted, the method of intervening must be carefully selected.

Major Conclusions

1. In private markets, external costs encourage overproduction; external benefits encourage underproduction. Government action can narrow such gaps between actual and efficient output levels.
2. Not all market inefficiencies should be alleviated by government action. Government action incurs costs that may well exceed its benefits.
3. Government can deal with external costs and benefits through (a) persuasion, (b) assignment of property rights, (c) government production, (d) taxes and subsidies, and (e) production standards.
4. In setting pollution standards, government effectively gives firms the right to pollute up to a point. So long as the cost of reducing pollution differs from firm to firm, there will be a market for those pollution rights. Firms that are less efficient in reducing pollution will want to buy rights from firms that are more efficient. Such trades offer a more economical—less costly—way of achieving official pollution standards.

Questions to Ponder

1. The existence of external costs is not in itself sufficient reason for government intervention in the production of steel. Why not?
2. List five goods or services not discussed in this chapter that are produced by the federal government. Give an economic explanation for government production of those goods.
3. "Population growth will lead to increased government control over people's behavior." Do you agree or disagree? Explain.
4. Developers frequently buy land and hold it on speculation; in effect they "bank" land. Should firms be permitted to buy and bank pollution rights in the same way? Would such a practice contribute to overall economic efficiency?
5. "If allowing firms to trade pollution rights lowers the cost of meeting pollution standards, it should also allow government to tighten standards without increasing costs." Do you agree or disagree? Why?
6. If businesses are permitted to sell pollution rights, should brokers in pollution rights be expected to emerge? Why or why not? Would such agents increase the efficiency with which pollution is cleaned up?
7. If pollution rights are traded, should the government impose a price ceiling on them? Would such a system contribute to the efficient allocation of resources?
8. Compared with the allocation of cattle, how well would you expect the market system to work in allocating pollution rights?
9. If you were a producer, which method of pollution control would you favor, the setting of government standards or the auction of pollution rights by government? Why?

Central Question

What are the economic consequences of government controls?

Chapter 31

Government Controls: Price Controls and Consumer Protection

*Without bandying jargon or
exhibiting formulae, without
being superficial or
condescending, the scientist
should be able to communicate
to the public the nature and
variety of consequences that
can reasonably be expected to
flow from a given action or
sequence of actions. In the case
of the economist, he can often
reveal in an informal way, if
not the detailed chain of
reasoning by which he reaches
his conclusions, at least the
broad contours of the
argument.*
E. J. Mishan

*E*arlier chapters showed how the competitive and monopolistic market models illuminate the economic effects of market changes, such as an increase in the price of oil. This chapter will examine the use of government controls to soften the impact of such changes. We will consider three types of government control: excise taxes, price controls, and consumer protection laws. As we saw in the last chapter, the cost of capturing external costs and benefits determines the economic effectiveness of government controls.

Who Pays the Tax?

The general public is convinced that consumers bear the burden of excise taxes. They believe producers simply pass the tax on to consumers as higher prices. Yet every time a new (or increased) excise tax is proposed, producers lobby against it. If excise taxes could be passed on to consumers, firms would have little reason to spend hundreds of thousands of dollars opposing them. In fact, excise taxes do hurt producers.

Figure 31.1 shows the margarine industry's supply and demand curves, S_1 and D. In a competitive market, the price will tend toward P_2 and the quantity sold toward Q_3. If the state imposes a $0.25 tax on each pound of margarine sold and collects the tax from producers, it effectively raises the cost of production. The producer must now pay a price not just for the right to use resources, such as equipment and raw materials, but for the right to continue production legally. The supply curve, reflecting this cost increase, shifts to S_2. The vertical difference between the two curves, $P_3 - P_1$, represents the extra $0.25 cost added by the tax.

Given the shift in supply, the quantity of margarine produced falls to Q_2 and the price rises to P_3. Note, however, that the price increase $(P_3 - P_2)$ is less than the vertical distance between the two supply curves $(P_3 - P_1)$. That is, the price increases by less than the amount of the tax that caused the shift in supply. Clearly, the producer's net price has fallen. If the tax is $0.25, but the price paid by consumers rises only $0.20 ($1.20 − 1.00), the producer loses $0.05. It now nets only $0.95 on a product that used to bring $1.00. In other words, the tax not only reduces the quantity of margarine producers can sell, but makes each sale less profitable.

Butter producers have a clear incentive to support a tax on margarine. When the price of margarine increases, consumers will seek substitutes. The demand for butter will rise, and producers will be able to sell more butter and charge more for each pound.

Is there any situation in which producers' profits will not be affected by an excise tax? Only if people will buy the same quantity of a good regardless of its price. That is, the demand curve for the product must be vertical, or perfectly inelastic (see Figure 31.2). Again, the vertical distance between the two supply curves represents the tax. Because of the tax, the price rises from P_1 to P_2. But if the quantity sold remains at Q_1, the producer's net price remains at P_1. This case is primarily of theoretical interest, for most real-world goods obey the law of demand (so that consumers buy less when price rises). But the extreme case does show that the more

Figure 31.1. The Economic Effect of an Excise Tax. An excise tax of $0.25 will shift the supply curve for margarine to the left, from S_1 to S_2. The quantity produced will fall from Q_3 to Q_2; the price will rise from P_2 to P_3. But the price increase, $0.20, will not cover the added cost to the producer, $0.25.

Figure 31.2. The Effect of an Excise Tax When Demand Is Perfectly Inelastic. If the demand for a product is perfectly inelastic (vertical), the quantity produced will not change when supply decreases from S_1 to S_2 in response to the added cost of an excise tax. Producers will be able to pass the entire tax on to consumers as a price increase.

inelastic the demand for a product, the greater the price increase caused by an excise tax. (The elasticity of demand, as we saw in Chapter 18, depends on the number of viable substitutes for a product.)

Price Controls

Price controls are by no means a modern invention. The first recorded legal code, the four-thousand-year-old Code of Hammurabi, included regulations governing the maximum wage, housing prices, and rents on property such as boats, animals, and tools. And in 301 A.D., the Roman Emperor Diocletian issued an edict specifying maximum prices for everything from poultry to gold, and maximum wages for everyone from lawyers to the cleaners of sewer systems. The penalty for violating the edict was death. More recently, wage and price controls have been used both in wartime (during the Second World War and the Korean War) and in peacetime. President Richard Nixon imposed an across-the-board wage-price freeze in 1971. Prime Minister Trudeau imposed controls on the Canadian economy in 1975. President Jimmy Carter controlled energy prices in 1977 and later proposed the decontrol of natural gas.

Wage and price controls are almost always controversial. Like attempts to control expenditures, they often create more problems than they solve. We will examine both sides of the issue, starting with the argument in favor of controls.

The Case for Price Controls

The case for price ceilings on particular products is complex. On the most basic level, many people believe that prices should be controlled to protect citizens from the harmful effects of inflation. When prices start to rise, redistributing personal income and disrupting the status quo, it seems unfair. Price controls may seem especially legitimate to people, like the elderly, who must live on fixed incomes, and have little means of compensating for the effects of price increases on goods like oil and gas.

Unearned Profits

Many proponents of price controls view the supply curve for a controlled good as essentially vertical. They believe that a price rise will not affect the quantity produced. Consumers will get nothing more in the way of goods, but producers will reap a windfall profit. Instead of an incentive to produce more, profit is seen as an economic rent—an exploitative surplus received by companies fortunate enough to be in the market at the right time.

Concentration of Industry

A technical argument for price controls is most often advanced by economists and public officials. Many economists maintain that a significant segment of the business and industrial community—the larger firms that control a sizable portion of industry sales—no longer responds to the forces of supply and demand. Firms in concentrated industries like steel, automobiles, paper, and tobacco can override market forces by manipulating their output so as to set price levels. And they can manage the demand for their products through advertising campaigns. With market forces ineffective, control must come from the government. Price controls are the only way to avoid the production inefficiencies and inequitable distribution of income that result from concentration of industry. As John Kenneth Galbraith, a leading advocate of price controls, has put it, "Controls are made necessary because planning has replaced the market system. That is to say that the firm and the union have assumed the decisive power in setting prices and wages. This means that the decision no longer lies with the market and thus with the public."[1]

---

1. John Kenneth Galbraith, *Economics and the Public Purpose* (Boston: Houghton Mifflin, 1973), p. 315.

Figure 31.3. The Effect of Price Controls on the Monopolistic Production Decision. In a free market, a monopolistic electric utility will produce Q_m kilowatts and will sell them for P_m. If the firm's price is controlled at P_1, however, its marginal revenue curve will become horizontal at P_1. The firm will produce Q_1—more than the amount it would normally produce.

Monopoly Power

Market theory suggests that price controls can cause monopolistic firms to increase their output. Figure 31.3 shows the pricing and production tendencies of a monopolistic electric utility. Without price controls, a firm with monopoly power will produce Q_m kilowatts and sell them at P_m. But if the government declares that price too high, it can force the firm to sell at a lower price—for example, P_1. At that price the firm can sell as many as Q_1 kilowatts. With the price controlled at P_1, the firm's marginal revenue curve for Q_1 units becomes horizontal at P_1a. Every time it sells an additional kilowatt, its total revenues will rise by P_1.

As we stressed in Chapter 22, the firm's ideal production level is that point at which marginal cost equals marginal revenue. If the firm cannot perfectly equate marginal cost and marginal revenue, it should strive to come as close as possible. With the maximum price controlled at P_1, the firm can increase its revenues by selling up to Q_1 units, which is all demand will permit. At that point marginal revenue approaches but does not equal marginal cost (MC). (To equate marginal revenue with marginal cost, the firm would have to expand production past Q_1, the limit consumers will buy.) Notice that Q_1 is greater than Q_m, the amount the firm would produce under a free but monopolized market. In short, price controls can cause a firm with market power to expand production. (Some exceptions to this rule will be described later.)

The Case Against Price Controls

Just as the case for price controls is tied closely to the existence of monopoly power, the case against controls rests heavily on the competitive market model. Economists who oppose controls feel that competition is sufficient to govern business behavior, including pricing decisions. Opponents of controls also stress the individual's right to act without government interference—a right they see as crucial to a society's ability to adjust to social and environmental change.

When we say that the prices of certain products should be controlled by government, what do we mean by "government"? Can government as we know it consistently reflect the public interest? Is government immune to human failings? Opponents of price controls emphasize that the pricing decisions made by any government agency will reflect the will of its staff. Personal preferences will loom large in their decisions on what constitutes a just price and a just allocation of goods and services. Political considerations may also play a role. Firms with a talent for political maneuvering will have an advantage under a price control system. In other words, competitive behavior is not necessarily reduced by price controls, though its form of expression may be changed.

If price controls are complemented by a system of government allocation of supplies, strikes, demonstrations, and violence may also influence government decisions. During the energy crisis of 1973–1974, and again in 1978, the federal government regulated the allocation of crude oil between gasoline and diesel fuel producers. When truckers received less fuel than they claimed they needed, independent drivers struck, threatening to paralyze the nation's commerce unless they got more fuel at lower prices. To ensure cooperation among drivers, the strikers blocked roads, vandalized the equipment of nonstrikers, and shot at drivers who ventured out on the road. One trucker was killed, and others were seriously injured. And at least for a short time, such tactics were productive. The government agreed to earmark more crude oil for diesel fuel production and to lower the federal excise tax on diesel fuel. (Courts later declared those decisions illegal.)

Shortages and the Effective Price of a Product

In a competitive market, any restriction on the upward movement of prices will lead to shortages. Consider Figure 31.4, which shows supply and demand curves for gasoline. Initially, the supply and demand curves are S_1 and D, and the equilibrium price is P_1. But suppose the supply of gasoline shifts to S_2, and government officials, believing that the new equilibrium price is unjust, freeze the price at P_1. What will happen to the market for gasoline?

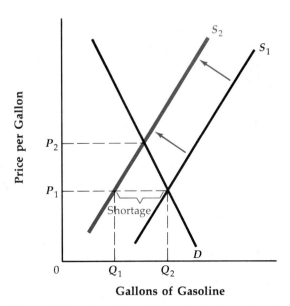

Figure 31.4. The Effect of Price Controls on Supply.
If the supply of gasoline is reduced from S_1 to S_2, but the price is controlled at P_1, a shortage equal to the difference between Q_1 and Q_2 will emerge.

At price P_1, which is now below equilibrium, the number of gallons demanded by consumers is Q_2. But the number of gallons supplied is much lower, Q_1. A shortage of $Q_2 - Q_1$ gallons has developed. As a result, some consumers will not get all the gasoline they want. Some may be unable to get any.

Because of the shortage, consumers will have to wait in line to get whatever gasoline they can. To avoid a long line, they may try to get to the service station early—but others may do the same. To assure themselves a prime position, consumers may have to sit at the pumps before the station opens. And in winter, waiting in line may mean wasting gas to keep warm. The moral of the story: although the pump price of gasoline may be held constant at P_1, the effective price—the sum of the pump price and the value of time lost waiting in line—will rise.

Shortages can raise the effective price of a product in other ways. With a long line of customers waiting to buy, a service station owner can afford to lower the quality of his service. He can neglect to clean windshields or check oil levels, and in general treat customers more abruptly than usual. As a result, the effective price of gasoline rises still higher. During the energy crises of 1973–1974 and 1978, some service station owners started closing on weekends and at night. A few required customers to sign long-term contracts and pay in advance for their gasoline. The added interest cost of advance payment raised the price of gasoline even higher.

Figure 31.5. The Effect of Rationing on Demand.
Price controls can create a shortage. For instance, at the controlled price P_1, a shortage of $Q_2 - Q_1$ gallons will develop. But by issuing a limited number of coupons that must be used to purchase a product, government can reduce demand and eliminate the shortage. Here rationing reduces demand from D_1 to D_2, where demand equals the supply at the controlled price.

Black Markets and the Need for Rationing

Besides such legal maneuvers to evade price controls, some businesses may engage in illegal fraud or black marketeering. During the winter of 1973–1974, a good many gasoline station owners filled their premium tanks with regular gasoline and sold it at premium prices. At the same time, a greater-than-expected shortage of heating oil developed. Truckers, unable to get all the diesel fuel they wanted at the controlled price, had found they could use home heating oil in their trucks. They paid home heating oil dealers a black market price for fuel oil, thus reducing the supply available to homeowners. As always, government controls bring enforcement problems.

To assure fair and equitable distribution of goods in short supply, some means of rationing is needed. If no formal system is adopted, supplies will be distributed on a first-come, first-served basis—in effect, rationing by congestion. The usual method of distribution is to issue coupons that entitle people to buy specific quantities of the rationed good at the prevailing price. By limiting the number of coupons, government reduces the demand for the product to match the available supply, thereby eliminating the shortage and relieving the congestion in the marketplace. In Figure 31.5, for example, demand is reduced from D_1 to D_2.

The coupon system may appear to be fair and simple. But how are the coupons to be distributed? Clearly the government will not want to auction off the coupons, for that would amount to letting consumers bid up the price. Should coupons be distributed equally among all consumers? Not everyone lives the same distance from work or school. Some, like salespeople, must travel much more than others. Should a commuter receive more gas than a retired person? If so, how much more? Should the distribution of coupons be based on the distance traveled? (And if such a system is adopted, will people lie about their needs?) These are formidable questions that must be answered if a coupon system is to be truly equitable. By comparison, the pricing system inherently allows people to reflect the intensity of their needs in their purchases.

Once the coupons are distributed, should the recipients be allowed to sell them to others? That is, should legal markets for coupons be allowed to spring up? If the deals made in such a market are voluntary, both parties to the exchange will benefit. The person who buys coupons values gasoline more than her money. The person who sells his coupons may have to cut back on driving, but he will have more money to buy other things. He must value those other things more than his lost trips, or he would not agree to make the exchange. The fact that the coupons have a market value shows that price controls have not really eliminated the shortage.

Furthermore, if the coupons have a value, the price of a gallon of gasoline has not really been held constant. If the price of an extra coupon for one gallon of gasoline is $0.50 and the pump price of that gallon is $1.25, the total price to the consumer is $1.75 ($0.50 + $1.25). The existence of a coupon market means that the price of gasoline has risen. In fact, the price to the consumer will be greater under a rationing system than under the pricing system. This is because the quantity supplied by refineries will be reduced.

Perhaps the most damaging aspect of a rationing system is that the benefits of such a price increase are not received by producers—oil companies, refineries, and service stations—but by those fortunate enough to get coupons. Thus the price increase does not provide producers with an incentive to supply more gasoline. (If the increase went to producers, their higher profits would encourage them to search for new sources of oil and step up their production plans.)

Consumer Protection

Less than one hundred years ago the general rule of the marketplace was caveat emptor—"let the buyer beware." The individual consumer was held responsible for the safety, quality, and effectiveness of his purchases. The seller could assume liability for the safety and effectiveness of goods and services, but only through a contract endorsed by both parties. The same rule applied to contracts: the buyer was responsible for what he signed. Though consumers could sue sellers for breach of contract or for fraud, no government agency would initiate the suit. Nor did government protect citizens in other ways from the products they bought.

Perspectives in Economics: Water Rights and Water Markets

Terry L. Anderson

Mark Twain wrote, "Whiskey is for drinkin'—water is for fightin'." In the American West, water has always been a matter of survival. It was the cause of many frontier skirmishes, and it may provoke conflict again. *Newsweek* warned recently that "drought, waste, and pollution threaten a water shortage whose impact may rival the energy crisis." And former Secretary of the Interior James Watt said, "The energy crisis will seem like a Sunday picnic when compared to the water crisis."

Unless Americans change their ways, a water crisis is inevitable. In economic terms, the quantity of water demanded is greater than the quantity available, and there is little time to adjust either amount. The reason for the imbalance is that the government has been keeping prices below market-clearing levels. In most places in the United States, water is cheaper than dirt. Nowhere in the nation do water prices reflect the true scarcity of the resource.

In Southern California, for example, water is in short supply. Yet Los Angeles residents pay only $0.60 per thousand gallons—a quantity that costs the residents of Frankfurt, Germany, $2.80. It is not surprising, therefore, that each person in the United States consumes an average of 180 gallons a day, compared with 37 gallons in Germany. Water prices are actually lowest in the arid Southwest, where residents of El Paso and Albuquerque pay $0.53 and $0.59, respectively, per thousand gallons, compared with $1.78 in Philadelphia. In many U.S. cities the real price of water has fallen in recent decades, despite the threat of shortages.

Agricultural users, who consume over 80 percent of the water in western states, enjoy extremely low prices. Throughout the nation the price of irrigation water ranges from about $0.009 to $0.09 per thousand gallons. In 1981, the average price of covering one acre of land in California's Central Valley with one foot of water was $5.00, or less than $0.02 per thousand gallons. Supplying that amount of water cost the government as much as $325. According to a 1980 study by the Department of the Interior, government subsidies covered between 57 and 97 percent of the cost of water projects.

Pricing water at market rates could help to solve the water crisis. Water consumption—whether for industrial, municipal, or agricultural use—is highly responsive to price changes. For example, the

During this century, however, product liability has gradually shifted from the consumer to the producer and the seller. Both court decisions and changes in the law have contributed to this shift. Consumer protection is now seen by many as a government function.

The Case for Consumer Protection

The argument for relieving consumers of product liability resembles the argument for regulation of utilities in many respects. Both cases hinge on the costs of gaining information and the problems created by external benefits and costs and monopoly power.

quantity of water used in industrial processes varies considerably around the world, depending on prices. Where water is expensive, electric power is produced using as little as 1.32 gallons per kilowatt hour. Where water is cheap, production requires as many as 170 gallons per kilowatt hour. One study of urban water consumption showed that a 10 percent increase in the price of water decreased the quantity of water demanded about 4 to 13 percent.

Pricing water more realistically will require changes in the laws governing water use, as well as the creation of an effective water market. Like any market, a water market will depend on well-defined, well-enforced property rights. If water rights are secure and people can trade them, prices will quickly come to reflect the true scarcity of the resource. During the late nineteenth century, such a system evolved in the American West. Rights were defined on a first-come, first-served basis, and institutions arose through which owners of rights could seek out the highest and best use of the resource. The system offered incentives that encouraged some people to deliver water wherever it was demanded. Thousands of miles of ditches were constructed, and millions of acres blossomed, as a result of entrepreneurial efforts to deliver water. Over time, however, legislators, bureaucrats, and judges have tinkered with the system. Legal restrictions now limit the transfer of water, and its use is determined by politicians, not by the market.

One place where a water market might encourage more efficient water use is the Imperial Irrigation District (IID) in Southern California. The IID receives its water from the U.S. Bureau of Reclamation, at subsidized rates. Its water could be conserved if ditches were lined, waste water recovered, and the timing of irrigation changed. All those measures would be costly to farmers, however. And at present low prices, farmers have little incentive to invest in conservation. Recently, the Municipal Water District (MWD) of Southern California, thwarted in its effort to obtain water from Northern California, has begun negotiating for water from the IID. The MWD is willing to fund improvements in farmers' irrigation systems in return for the water those improvements would save. If such a trade could be accomplished, everyone would be better off.

External Benefits

In our earlier discussion of business regulation, we developed an explanation of the external benefits of shock-absorbing bumpers (see page 556). When two cars collide, both cars will sustain less damage and both drivers less injury if just one of the cars is equipped with protective bumpers. Thus people who do not buy protective bumpers can benefit from others' investments. To the extent that car buyers ignore the benefits others may receive from their purchases, the quantity of shock-absorbing bumpers sold will be less than the socially desirable or economically efficient amount.

This analysis of external benefits can be extended to include the concept of consumer protection. Suppose the supply curve in Figure 31.6 is the

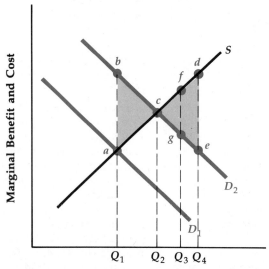

Quantity of Shock-Absorbing Bumpers

Figure 31.6. The External Benefits of Consumer Protection.
Private demand for shock-absorbing bumpers is shown by the demand curve D_1; total demand (private plus public, or external, benefits), by D_2. The vertical distance between the two curves represents the social benefits from each bumper. In a free market, Q_1 bumpers will be sold. If *all* benefits are considered, however, the efficient output level will be Q_2. By requiring people to purchase Q_2 bumpers, government can capture the external benefits shown by the shaded area *abc*. If the government requires consumers to buy more than Q_2 bumpers, however, excess costs will be incurred. If Q_4 bumpers are purchased, their excess social cost, shown by the shaded area *cdc*, will offset their social benefits (*abc*). The *net* social gain will be zero.

industry's marginal cost curve for protective bumpers. The demand curve D_1 represents consumer demand based on the private benefits to consumers, while D_2 represents private plus public (external) benefits. Under competitive conditions, the quantity produced and sold in the marketplace will be Q_1—even though up to Q_2, the total benefits of bumpers exceed their cost. The private benefits of the bumpers are small enough that many people cannot justify purchasing them.

Graphically, the vertical distance between the two demand curves, *ab*, represents the external benefits per bumper sold that are not being captured by the market. Government can close this gap by setting product standards. By requiring new cars to have shock-absorbing bumpers, government effectively increases demand from D_1 to D_2. It forces people to expand their purchases from Q_1 to Q_2, thus capturing the external benefits shown by the shaded area *abc*.

This approach can be extended to a wide range of goods and services that offer significant external benefits, from safety caps for drugs to protective devices for explosives. But this argument does not justify unlimited government intervention. We cannot conclude, for example, that all automobiles must have shock-absorbing bumpers. Such a requirement might result in the purchase of far more than Q_2 bumpers. And beyond Q_2, the marginal cost of safety bumpers is greater than their marginal benefit. An excess burden, or net social cost, is incurred when the public must purchase more than Q_2.

If the public is required to purchase Q_4 bumpers, for instance, the excess burden will be equal to the shaded area *cde*. This social cost of extending purchases to Q_4 just equals the social benefits of extending purchases to Q_2 (shown by the area *abc*). Consequently, there is no real *net* social benefit in moving to Q_4. If the required number of bumpers is greater than Q_2 but less than Q_4, some net social benefit will be realized. At Q_3, the excess social cost *cfg* is smaller than the social benefit *abc*. Some net benefit will be realized.

Up to a point, then, consumer protection can be socially beneficial. But society can end up purchasing too much of a good thing. It is possible to make the world so safe that few resources are available for any other purpose.

Nevertheless, governments tend to require safety devices for all products in a category. Determining the optimum quantity is so difficult and costly that a blanket rule is preferable. Yet as opponents of consumer protection point out, the blanket rule itself may be extremely costly, if it requires more than the socially beneficial quantity to be produced. Ultimately, the question comes down to the actual costs and benefits of particular product standards.

External Costs

The argument for consumer protection based on external costs is closely related to the argument for pollution control (see Chapter 30). If the consumers who use a product do not bear all the costs associated with its use, they will tend to consume more of the good than is socially desirable. In the process they will impose a cost on others. For example, a person who buys a spray deodorant incurs a private cost equal to its money price. But if the release of the chemicals used in aerosol sprays has a harmful effect on the earth's ozone layer, as many scientists believe, the use of such products imposes an external cost on nonusers. At the very least, the public incurs a risk cost from the use of aerosol sprays.

Curve D in Figure 31.7 shows the market demand for spray deodorant. The supply curve S_1 shows the marginal cost of producing the good, not counting the ozone effect. In a competitive market, the quantity of spray deodorant purchased will be Q_2. If producers have to compensate those who bear the external costs of their product, however, their supply curve will shift to S_2, and the quantity purchased will drop to Q_1. The vertical distance between the two supply curves represents the external, or ozone, cost of each can sold. By including this cost in the price of the product, the government reduces social costs by the shaded area.

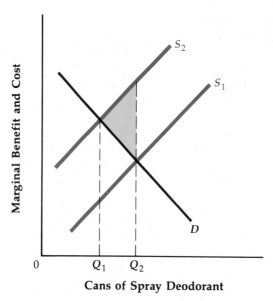

Figure 31.7. The External Costs of Consumer Protection.
Curve S_1 represents the supply curve for spray deodorant, not including external costs. Curve S_2 represents the total cost, including harm to the earth's ozone layer. Thus the vertical distance between S_1 and S_2 shows the social cost of producing each can of spray deodorant. In a free market, Q_2 cans will be produced—more than the efficient level, Q_1. Government can eliminate overproduction by internalizing the external costs of production, shown by the shaded area.

This argument does not necessarily imply that spray cans should be banned. The extent of government regulation should depend on the degree of external cost. If the use of spray cans will ultimately cause the destruction of life on earth, then the external costs are quite high and a complete ban is in order. If costs are lower, a less stringent policy might be appropriate.

Monopoly Power

Consumer advocates suspect that some firms use their market power to restrict the variety of products available to consumers and to reduce their quality, safety, and effectiveness. The monopolist, in other words, can choose not only what price and quantity of a given product to offer, but what features it will have. Left to itself, the monopolistic firm will maximize profits by finding that one combination of price, quantity, and product features that minimizes costs and maximizes revenues.

Consumer advocates argue that most consumers want safer, more effective products than they can now obtain and are willing to pay competitive prices for them. They see consumer protection laws as a means of forcing monopolistic producers to provide what the public wants.

Information Costs

The complexities of modern technology can be overwhelming. Proponents of consumer protection argue that consumers cannot hope to comprehend the ins and outs of the dozens of products they must consider, from color televisions to prescription drugs. For instance, the production of cereals and meats is so far removed from common experience that consumers have little idea what chemicals may be added during processing. Without adequate information and the technical ability to comprehend it, consumers cannot make rational choices based on true costs and benefits. Therefore they must be protected by product safety experts.

This line of reasoning resembles the argument for a standard requiring shock-absorbing bumpers. Like the bumpers, consumer information benefits far more people than those who pay for it. That is, there are external benefits associated with its provision. To that extent, the market demand for information, like the market demand for protective bumpers, will not fully reflect its social benefits. The quantity of information produced and purchased will fall short of the efficient level. By intervening in the market to supplement the information flow, government can increase social welfare.

The Case Against Consumer Protection

Some of the arguments against consumer protection have already been mentioned. In this section we will reemphasize them and highlight some additional points. As these arguments and counterarguments suggest, consumer protection is a complex issue, and it is difficult to find an efficient solution to the problem.

Competition as a Form of Consumer Protection

No one can reasonably expect to be protected against all the whims and exploitative efforts of businesses. The cost of complete protection would be prohibitive, and the benefits often too small to justify the cost. Thus we should not expect the market system to protect consumers completely against unsafe products and services. The relevant question is whether the market or government is more complete or efficient in accomplishing the task of consumer protection.

Nor are consumers as powerless as consumer protection advocates maintain. Though one person can do little to coerce producers into providing safer, more effective goods and services, collectively consumers have considerable power of persuasion. They can offer to pay for a safer product—and there is some price that profit-maximizing entrepreneurs will accept for such a product. Or they can turn to different producers to obtain what they want. If producers do not offer what consumers want, if they repeatedly produce shoddy merchandise, more and more consumers will move to other producers or purchase substitute goods. For example, if the Coca-Cola Company persisted in selling drinks that had lost their carbonation, consumers could move to Pepsi, 7-Up, or other substitute

Perspectives in Economics: Seat-Belt and Air-Bag Laws

Robert Valero

Each year more than 40,000 people are killed in traffic accidents on America's highways, and over 300,000 suffer serious injuries. In addition to the human suffering, the estimated financial toll of the carnage is staggering. High automobile insurance premiums have become a financial burden to millions of Americans. And automobile accidents cost the federal government $7.5 billion annually in Medicaid, Social Security, welfare, and workers' compensation payments—to say nothing of lost tax revenues. States and localities pay an additional $3.5 billion.

Partly because of these costs, in 1966, Congress authorized the secretary of transportation to set federal motor vehicle safety standards. But though the need for motor vehicle safety is undisputed, it is not clear exactly what standards should be adopted. Given existing technology, the government has several alternatives. It could continue to allow people to choose whether to use safety seat belts. It could mandate the use of seat belts and impose penalties for noncompliance with the law. Or it could require the installation of automatic protection systems, such as air bags or automatic seat belts, in all automobiles.

The public has resisted using safety devices. Seat belts have been standard equipment in automobiles since 1968, but only 12.5 percent of Americans use them voluntarily. Air bags were offered briefly by one major auto manufacturer,

drinks. The fear of losing customers helps keep producers in line, pressuring them to offer the goods customers want.

Differences in Risk Taking

Some people are more willing than others to assume the risk that goods and services may be defective, ineffective, or unsafe. They differ in the personal value they place on avoiding risk. Thus some will participate in dangerous sports like hang gliding; others would not dare. And some people will take a chance on buying a used car or toaster, while others would always insist on (and pay more for) new merchandise. If surveys are correct, most drivers are willing to accept the risk of driving without seatbelts—though a few would not go around the block without them. Everything else held equal, people with a strong aversion to risk will demand safer products than those who prefer to take their chances.

Such differences in the willingness to assume risk may reflect differences in economic circumstances. Some believe that the demand for safer products is positively related to income. People with low incomes patronize greasy-spoon restaurants, accepting the risk of food poisoning. They may reason that they are better off by eating cheaply than by spending more to protect their health.

If all consumers were willing to accept the same degree of risk, it would be relatively easy to protect them through product standards. Government regulators would simply determine the level of risk acceptable to all, and but were dropped because of poor consumer response. Many drivers fear that air bags could inflate at inappropriate times, blocking their view and possibly causing an accident. Some have even argued that by reducing the risk of injury or death from auto crashes, air bags and seat belts encourage reckless driving.

Advocates of seat belts and air bags cite studies showing that the use of safety devices would cut highway fatalities in half. In countries that require the use of seat belts, reductions in the number of fatalities have been dramatic. Similar legislation is being considered in many places in the United States. Air bags, on the other hand, have been found to be effective in head-on collisions, but not in rear-end or side crashes.

The issue of automatic crash protection has been before the Department of Transportation, Congress, and the Supreme Court for nearly two decades now. The original regulations, written in 1970, have been amended many times. In 1984, Secretary of Transportation Elizabeth Dole issued a new rule requiring the gradual phase-in of protection for all passenger cars manufactured for sale in the United States. But the requirement will be dropped if states representing two-thirds of the nation's population enact mandatory seat-belt laws before April 1989. As a result, manufacturers have mounted an intensive lobbying campaign in support of seat-belt laws.

set their standards accordingly. Of course, consumer choice would be restricted. Some ineffective or less safe products would no longer be offered for sale. In the real world, as we have observed, consumers differ in their risk aversion. Uniform standards would force those who are comparatively efficient in coping with risk, or who have no real aversion to risk, to buy safer products. Assuming that safety is not a free good, the cost to consumers would increase—and in economic terms, that amounts to a misallocation of resources. People who do not have children, for example, must still pay for child-proof caps on drug bottles.

If full liability for product safety and effectiveness were shifted to the producer, the same type of problem could develop. Again, consumers would be unable to choose their preferred level of risk. For when producers assumed the risk, they might decide to discontinue certain product lines, to avoid lawsuits and damage claims. Or they might buy insurance to cover their newly acquired risk cost, raising the price to the consumer. In effect consumers would be forced to buy insurance against unsafe or defective products. They no longer have the option of insuring themselves, perhaps at a lower price.

The Needs of the Poor

Many people support consumer protection because of their concern for the poor, who may be unable to afford the information necessary to an informed choice. The poor may also be the least capable of understanding technical product information, and the least able to endure the losses associated with defective goods and services. But opponents of consumer protection point out that the poor often prefer to buy low-quality goods and services because they are less expensive. They rationally pay less so they may have more of other goods and services. If less safe products are removed from the shelves, then, the burden of consumer protection falls disproportionately on the poor.

Summary and Extensions

The market system can perform the very valuable service of rationing scarce resources among those who want them. It alleviates the congestion that develops when resources, goods, and services are rationed by other means. But markets are not always permitted to operate unobstructed. Government has objectives of its own, objectives that are determined collectively rather than individually. We have seen how government can use its power to tax to raise government revenues or reallocate market demand. Government power can also be used to eliminate externalities or reduce monopoly power. Whether the use of such controls is considered good or bad depends to a significant extent on one's personal values and circumstances. In a free market system, price controls and consumer protection will always be controversial.

Major Conclusions

1. If an excise tax is imposed on a commodity like margarine, the price of the product will rise, and consumers will buy less. Furthermore, the new price will not compensate producers for the full amount of the tax. Therefore producers have an incentive to oppose excise taxes.

2. Proponents of price controls make the following arguments. (a) Government control of prices is necessary to prevent erosion of citizens' purchasing power—especially among people living on fixed incomes. (b) Price increases have little effect on the quantity of goods produced. Therefore government should control prices to prevent firms from earning windfall profits. (c) Large corporations control the market, not vice versa. Therefore, government intervention is necessary to check their power. (d) When price controls are imposed on monopolistic firms, they can actually expand production.

3. Opponents of price controls make the following major arguments. (a) Competition lends sufficient control to the market; government intrusion is unnecessary. (b) Government control is an affront to individual freedom. (c) Control of market prices will lead to competition among the controlled for special treatment by government officials.

4. Price controls invariably lead to shortages and black markets. They raise the effective price of a product and generally require cumbersome rationing systems to ensure the equitable distribution of goods.

5. The case for consumer protection laws rests on the following arguments. (a) Consumers need special protection when external benefits and costs are involved in the production or consumption of goods and services. (b) Consumers need protection against the abuses of monopoly power. (c) Consumers need protection because they cannot understand the complexities of modern production.

6. The case against consumer protection laws rests on the following arguments. (a) Even imperfectly competitive markets provide consumers with a rationally determined measure of protection. (b) People differ in their willingness to accept risk—that is, to use products that are not perfectly safe. Consumer protection laws invariably reduce the option of buying products of lower quality at lower prices. (c) Consumer protection laws discriminate against the poor, who because of their low incomes tend to buy lower-quality products, by forcing them to pay higher prices for the goods they buy.

1. Is a tax on margarine efficient in the economic sense of the term? Why would margarine producers prefer to have an excise tax imposed on both butter and margarine? Would such a tax be more or less efficient than a tax on margarine alone?

2. If punishment for crime is a kind of tax on those who engage in illegal activity, what effect would the legalization of marijuana have on its supply and demand? What would happen to the market price? The quantity sold? Illustrate with supply and demand curves.

3. In areas where beer and liquor cannot be sold legally, bootleggers support the ban on alcohol. Explain the logic of their position, using supply and demand curves.

4. If in a competitive market, prices are held below market equilibrium by government controls, what will be the effect on output? Explain.

5. In a monopolistic market, price controls can lower prices while raising output. If prices are lowered too much, would a monopolistic producer reduce production?

6. How would price controls affect a firm's incentive to innovate? Explain.

7. "If prices are controlled in only one competitive industry, the resulting shortage will be greater than if prices were controlled in all industries." Do you agree? Explain.

8. "Price controls can be more effective in the short run than in the long run." Explain.

Questions to Ponder

What are the sources of American farmers' economic difficulties, and why are food prices higher than they need to be?

Chapter 32

Agriculture and Government Agricultural Policy

Egg prices have always gone in cycles. Once a hen starts her laying cycle of 60 weeks, she keeps on producing. There's no tap short of the soup plant that will shut off the supply. This makes the supply curve very price inelastic in the short run, and economic theory tells us that in such a situation any shift in demand produces a very sharp change in prices.
Patrick Howe

*M*ost farm commodities, such as wheat, cotton, and potatoes, are sold in highly competitive markets. Thousands of buyers and farmers come together to determine prices in almost all lines of produce. Consumers benefit from the competitiveness of agriculture, for they receive more of the foods they want at lower prices. But farmers must cope with some problems that characterize competitive markets. In the short run, the prices of agricultural goods respond rapidly to the forces of supply and demand. Prices can change substantially over a growing season—that is, between the time a crop is planted and the time it is harvested and marketed. Moreover, in recent decades agricultural technology has become increasingly sophisticated and expensive. Many farmers have faced the difficult choice of retooling or being forced out of business.

Only rarely have farmers been able to collude to control competitive forces. That is, any efforts to join together to restrict output, divide the market, raise prices, and increase their incomes have not succeeded for very long. There are just too many farmers to form a workable cartel. Thus it is understandable that farmers have turned to government for assistance. The U.S. Department of Agriculture has used tax dollars to subsidize agricultural production. Farmers in turn have produced more of some commodities than could possibly be sold on the market. Faced with a surplus, the Department of Agriculture has paid farmers to take land out of production.

Not surprisingly, many of these government forays into the agricultural market began in the 1930s, when farm families represented 30 percent of the population and commanded more than proportional representation in federal and state legislatures. Today the farm population is much smaller, and legislative apportionment more nearly reflects the distribution of population in rural areas. At the same time consumers have become more aware of the adverse consequences of government agricultural policies. As a result legislators have begun to talk of returning agriculture to a free-market status. This chapter will examine the predicament of farmers, and the usefulness of government policy in alleviating it.

Short-Run Problems of Farming

Several characteristics inherent in farming can create short-run problems for farmers. First, the short-run demand for most farm products tends to be highly inelastic. That is, consumers are relatively unresponsive to price changes. They are unwilling or unable to use substitutes when prices go up, and there is a limit to how much food one can eat when prices go down. As a consequence, prices can fall substantially with even a small increase in supply, depressing the farmer's revenues. Suppose the supply of wheat increases, dropping the price per bushel from $4.00 to $3.00. If the quantity purchased rises only from 1 million to 1.1 million bushels, total revenues fall from $4 million (1 million bushels × $4.00) to $3.3 million (1.1 million bushels × $3.00).

Second, modern farming requires substantial investment in land and equipment. Thus farmers must incur significant fixed expenses, such as mortgage debt, whose repayment depends on the sale of future crops. By harvest time, most of these expenses are sunk costs and cannot be considered in the decision to harvest. They therefore have little or no influence in determining the short-run supply of any crop on the market.

Only the costs of harvesting and transporting the crop to market enter into the farmer's decision on how much to harvest. Even at very low prices, the revenues acquired from a harvest will usually cover those costs. But they may well not cover the farmer's entire costs, including the sunk costs of planting, land, and equipment.

Assume, for example, that a farmer has spent $10,000 in preparing his land and planting it with corn. Assume further that the cost of the harvest is $1,000. If at harvest time the market price of corn is $2.50 a bushel, and the farmer has three thousand bushels to sell, total revenues from the sale will be $7,500—more than enough to justify the $1,000 cost of the harvest. Total costs, however, are $11,000, so the farmer loses $3,500 for the year. Still, he is better off selling the crop than leaving it in the field. If the crop is not harvested and taken to market, all the costs incurred before the harvest—$10,000—will be lost. Only if expected revenues fall short of harvest costs will a farmer leave a crop to rot in the fields.

Farmers can store some of a harvest in the hope that prices will rise, but storage can be expensive. And there is no guarantee that prices will rise; they may fall further. Meanwhile, by delaying the sale of a crop, a farmer postpones repayment of his debts, adding to the interest he owes. For these reasons, the short-run supply of most farm commodities tends to be highly inelastic. The quantities available change very little with changes in market price.

Given the inelastic supply and demand for farm products, factors like climate, over which farmers have no control, can cause substantial changes in the prices and income farmers receive. If good weather produces a bumper crop, farmers may be worse off than if bad weather lowers production. Figure 32.1 shows the highly inelastic demand and supply curves characteristic of the short-run market for most farm products. Given the demand shown by D, if the weather is poor and the supply of corn is restricted to S_1, the equilibrium price of corn will be $5, and 13 million bushels will be sold. Farmers will receive total revenues of $65 million ($5 × 13 million bushels).

But if the weather is favorable, the supply of corn will shift out to the right, to S_2. The equilibrium price will drop to just $2.50 a bushel, and 14 million bushels will be sold. Total revenues will fall from $65 million to $35 million ($2.50 × 14 million bushels). And because farmers' production costs change very little with good weather, the difference between revenues and costs (that is, profit) will also fall. Farmers may not lose money at $2.50 a bushel, but they clearly prefer a market supply curve of S_1 to S_2. In 1985, because of good weather and a bumper crop of California grapes used for raisin production, the price of raisin grapes was depressed to the point that grapes were left to rot on the vines.

Figure 32.1. Effects of an Increase in Supply on Farmers' Revenues.
Because of the inelasticity of the demand for corn, an increase in the supply of
corn from S_1 to S_2 will cause a substantial short-run decrease in price (from \$5 to
\$2.50 a bushel). Total revenues will drop from \$65 million for 13 million bushels
to \$35 million for 14 million bushels.

Most farmers appear to hope for good weather. They express concern
about dry spells or cold snaps that limit their harvests. Although our
analysis has shown that poor growing conditions can favor farm profitability, the individual farmer, viewing the market from his own geographical
location, may still prefer good weather, for two reasons. First, there is
always the danger that the poor weather he experiences may not occur
elsewhere. If farmers elsewhere have good growing conditions, the total
harvest may be large and prices fairly low. Since the individual farmer
afflicted with bad weather will have little to sell, his revenues will be
extremely low. Good weather, on the other hand, means that he will
harvest more. And since his own output has little influence on the market
price, his revenues will be greater. If he sells five thousand bushels at
\$2.50, for example, he will earn more than if he harvests only three
thousand bushels at the same price.

At least in the short run, then, profitability would seem likely to be
highest for farms located in a limited geographical area that enjoys good
weather while poor conditions prevail elsewhere. In recent years, for
example, American farmers have benefited from crop failures in other
nations, like the Soviet Union. But even repeated crop failures elsewhere

may yield only short-lived financial benefits. For if more farmers enter the market, attracted by high profits, in the long run expanded production will increase supply and lower the market price.

To sum up the short-term problem of farming, small changes in the size of the expected harvest can cause significant fluctuations in price. Small, unexpected changes in demand can have the same effect, because of the inelasticity of supply. The potential for price fluctuation may be greater in agriculture than in many other markets, because of the special properties of food—perishability, for instance.

But the element of uncertainty in farming should not be overemphasized. There is uncertainty in any production process in which costs are incurred well before the sale of the product. The risks taken by companies in the personal computer business, for instance, may equal or exceed those taken by farmers. Producers in such industries incur a long-run risk cost that tends to restrict their long-term supply. In the long run, then, the price of farm commodities should be expected to compensate for the risks involved in farming.

Long-Run Problems of Farming

Over the years the prices of many farm commodities have risen. But their relative prices—that is, the ratios of farm prices to nonfarm prices—have tended to fall. The prices of nonfarm goods have simply risen faster than those of farm goods.

Productivity gains have been a major factor in this relative decline in farm prices. With improved technology, American farmers have been able to grow more crops with fewer resources. Stimulated by government research programs and the competitiveness of the farm sector, productivity growth in farming historically has been almost twice that of the nonfarm sector.

In itself, growth in productivity is not bad. Farmers who took advantage of the new methods have been able to cope with rising costs for labor and fertilizer. They have had to pay more to raise their crops, but they have produced more as well. Their increased productivity has allowed them to accept lower relative prices for their output. But farmers who have been less aggressive in innovating have faced a price-cost squeeze. When their costs increased but their productivity did not, their net income—revenues minus costs—evaporated. Many have been forced to seek employment outside farming—a trend clearly visible in Table 32.1. Others, unwilling or unable to adjust to another life, have stayed on their farms, eking out a subsistence-level income with outmoded equipment.

Agriculture today is so competitive and technologically advanced that individual farmers are hard pressed to keep pace. More and more, farming is becoming the province of institutional investors. Meanwhile, government has tried in various ways to control the supply or prop up the low prices created by advances in productivity. We will examine three types of government programs: price supports, acreage allotments and set-asides, and target prices.

Table 32.1. Long-Run Decline of Employment in Agriculture, 1929–1984

Year	Civilian Labor Force (in Thousands)	Agriculture Workers (in Thousands)	Percent of Civilian Labor Force in Agriculture
1929	49,180	10,450	21.9
1940	55,640	9,540	20.0
1950	62,208	7,160	12.1
1960	69,628	5,458	8.2
1970	82,771	3,462	4.4
1980	106,940	3,364	3.1
1984	113,544	3,321	2.9

Source: *Economic Report of the President* (Washington, D.C.: U.S. Government Printing Office, 1985), p. 266.

The Price Support Program

Suppose the long-run supply and demand for wheat are represented by curves S and D in Figure 32.2. The market price will be P_1, the price at which supply equals demand. But suppose the government decides that price is too low for farmers to make a decent living, and passes a law establishing a minimum wheat price of P_2?

The Creation and Purchase of a Surplus

When wheat is sold at the higher price of P_2, Figure 32.2 shows, consumers will buy less wheat—Q_1—yet producers will expand production to Q_3. A surplus will emerge: producers will offer more than buyers are willing to take. Some farmers may not be able to sell any wheat. Others will be unable to sell as much as they would like. All will have an incentive to sell their wheat illegally—and will be able to find customers if they sell below price P_2. To hold the price at P_2, then, government must incur the cost of enforcing its ruling. It must also cope with the problem of dividing the market, so that each farmer sells a reasonable portion of wheat.

To prevent illegal sales of wheat below the support price, government may have to enter the market as a buyer of last resort. That is, it may have to guarantee farmers a price of P_2 if they cannot get it on the market. In effect the government takes the surplus off the market, eliminating the competitive pressure to lower prices and forcing market buyers to pay P_2 for the remaining wheat. Since the 1930s, the Department of Agriculture has supported the prices of wheat, cotton, feed grains, dairy products, peanuts, rice, milk, and tobacco in just this way.

Some farmers have benefited from the relative stability of government price supports. (How much and how long they have benefited is a question to which we will return.) But government price supports for wheat have

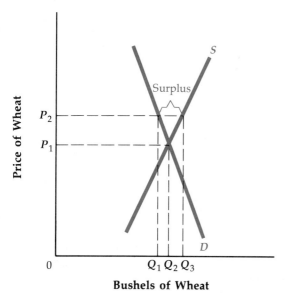

Figure 32.2. Effect of a Government Price Support.
The market price is P_1, at the intersection of the supply and demand curves. If the government raises the price to P_2, it will create a market surplus equal to $Q_3 - Q_1$. It must then buy the surplus from farmers, using government funds.

also meant that consumers have to pay more for bread. Price supports have also increased the cost of feed grains, lowering the supply of cattle and raising meat prices. They have meant higher prices for cotton and thus higher clothing costs. And because price supports have increased the production of supported commodities, fewer resources have been available for the production of other crops. Supplies of nonsupported commodities have been restricted, and prices have been higher than they would otherwise have been. Finally, the funds used to pay for price supports have come from general tax revenues. Thus federal taxes have been used to raise the price of groceries.

Disposal of the Surplus

Once the government has bought surplus commodities from the farmer, it must decide what to do with them. The options are surprisingly restricted. Government cannot sell in the domestic market what it has purchased at P_2, because market demand has already been satisfied at the support price. That was the reason for the government purchase in the first place. If it offers the commodities at a price below P_2, buyers will purchase from the government rather than farmers. Farmers will be unable to dispose of even Q_1 in the marketplace, and will sell what remains to the government.

Perspectives in Economics: The Financial Crisis in Agriculture

B. H. Robinson

A financial storm that began on the nation's farms in 1979 hit the Midwest with gale force in the mid-1980s. The new farm debt crisis was as grave as that of the Great Depression. With low crop prices and weak demand, combined with high production costs, mountainous surpluses, cash-flow problems, and heavy debt, many farmers had problems repaying their debts. As more and more farms failed, several farm-based banks went down with them.

At the heart of the crisis was the extra debt many farmers had assumed. Farm debt increased fourfold during the 1970s—a rate of increase unparalleled in recent history. By 1984 farm debt had risen to $215 billion, twice the level of 1970. At the same time debt-asset ratios increased from about 16 percent to 22 to 28 percent. And the number of farms with debt-asset ratios above 40 percent was alarming. Studies suggested that over a third of all farms in the United States were carrying debt-asset ratios over 40 percent, and that about 18 percent of all farmers were in trouble.

Unlike many other businesses, farms do not generate enough cash flow to support that much debt. In fact, farm income, both real and nominal, has declined precipitously in recent years, worsening the crisis. From 1974 to 1984, farmers' annual interest costs increased from less than $4 billion to almost $22 billion—over half their net farm income.

Some kinds of farms have been hit harder than others. The biggest farms, those with sales over $500,000, usually produce specialty crops that are not traded internationally. They generally have well-established lines of credit. Small, noncommercial farms, by far the most numerous, are not in serious financial trouble either. Most of their debt is supported by income from off-farm sources. Commercial family farms—which produce the bulk of traditional agricultural commodities, like wheat, corn, cotton, and tobacco—are the ones with the most serious financial problems. But all farms are experiencing a decline in net worth because of mounting debt and falling land values.

Farmers' current difficulties can be traced to three root causes: inflation, government monetary

Thus if the government attempts to sell the surplus below the support price, it may end up buying almost the entire crop.

Part of the crop can be given away—and that has been done through both domestic and foreign aid programs. But the government must be careful to give only to people who would not otherwise be in the market for that food. If it gives to those who would otherwise buy, market demand will fall, leaving more surplus for the government to absorb.

If the government tries to sell its holdings in the world commodity markets, U.S. farmers' exports may decline. Other nations may complain that the United States is dumping its excess crops on them, depressing prices in their markets. They may retaliate by dumping their surpluses on U.S. markets, or by imposing higher tariffs on U.S. exports. Finally, and fiscal policy, and international exchange rates. In 1979 the federal government shifted from an expansionary to a contractionary monetary policy in order to reduce inflation. At the same time, the government's growing budget deficits increased borrowing in financial markets, putting upward pressure on interest rates. Farmers with high debt-asset ratios were hurt by rising interest rates, but hurt even more by falling inflation rates. When nominal interest rates moderated in the early 1980s as a result of anti-inflationary policies, real interest rates (the nominal interest rate minus the inflation rate) did not moderate. Instead, as inflation slowed down, real interest rates jumped from the 1 to 2 percent level of the 1970s to over 8 percent by the mid-1980s.

To make matters worse, in the early 1980s, a worldwide recession dampened demand for U.S. agricultural commodities. At the same time, the relatively high interest rates available in the United States stimulated foreign investment. As investors sought to acquire dollars on the international financial market, the value of the dollar rose. The new, higher exchange rates raised the prices of U.S. exports beyond competitive levels. The price of wheat, for instance, rose from $3 per bushel to as much as $9 per bushel, simply because of exchange rates. Unfortunately, these price increases occurred just as U.S. production was expanding in response to domestic farm programs and increased efficiency of production. The result was a tremendous surplus of farm products.

Together, reduced demand for food and high real interest rates drove down farmers' demand for capital items, particularly land. Between 1981 and 1984, farm land values dropped over 20 percent, eroding farmers' debt security and pushing their debt-asset ratios up even further.

Without significant government intervention—and that does not appear likely—agriculture is headed for major disruptions in the next few years. Many farms, particularly commercial family farms, will go out of business. For many individuals, the dislocation will be devastating. But given a changing world market, the upheaval is probably unavoidable.

consumers in the United States may object to the sale of wheat or other crops abroad for less than the going price at home.

Another way of eliminating a surplus is to destroy it. For some crops, destruction may be unavoidable. For example, when supported prices for eggs in Canada encouraged U.S. farmers to ship eggs there illegally, an oversupply quickly developed. The excess supply had to be purchased by the Canadian government and later, when it was organized, by the Canadian Egg Marketing Agency. Of course, eggs are highly perishable and cannot be stored very long in their natural state. In one instance, 28 million of them rotted and had to be destroyed. When millions of people throughout the world are starving, politicians and agricultural officials find it difficult to support such destruction.

Perspectives in Economics: A Lemon of an Agricultural Policy

James Bovard

Federal regulations sentence a half-billion fresh lemons to rot each year. A federal marketing order is driving up lemon prices 30% to 40%, driving down per-capita fresh-lemon consumption, and sacrificing lemon growers to Sunkist, the dominant power in the Western lemon industry. A new shrink-wrap process could revolutionize lemon marketing, reduce lemon prices and end the excuse for government supply control. But Sunkist—and, so far, the U.S. Department of Agriculture—has effectively prohibited the new technology.

Arizona farmers are desperately awaiting a USDA decision that could allow them to shrink-wrap their winter lemons and delay marketing them until June and July, when prices are higher and consumers are thirstier. But Sunkist, which controls 80% of the summer lemon industry, wants to prevent Arizona growers from postponing the selling of their lemons and breaking Sunkist's stranglehold on the summer lemon market. USDA Secretary John Block recently addressed Sunkist's directors in a closed meeting in Los Angeles, and Arizona growers are worried that Mr. Block may promise to continue sacrificing them to the corporate giant.

All lemons grown in California and Arizona are covered under Federal Marketing Order 910. Federal restrictions require California and Arizona growers to grow three or four lemons to earn the right to sell one lemon on the domestic fresh market. The marketing order is supposedly justi-fied by the lemon's highly perishable nature. But federal marketing restrictions have made the lemon market far more unstable, inequitable and unprofitable.

Order 910 began in 1941 ostensibly to help save the small family grower. But since 1954, the number of growers has fallen from 8,012 to 2,079. Order 910 is also supposed to stabilize lemon prices. But fresh-lemon prices fluctuate far more than most fruit prices.

Restrictions on domestic marketing also force growers to dump their crops at a loss on the export market. Japanese consumers often receive high-quality American lemons for lower prices than Americans pay—one farm subsidy few congressmen brag about. Exports to Canada, on the other hand, are covered by federal restrictions, and growers need the Lemon Administrative Committee's (LAC) permission to sell north of the border. Because of restrictions on U.S. exports, American lemon prices in Canada are artificially high, and foreign competitors are rapidly trimming the U.S. market share.

While the USDA restricts domestic producers' right to sell lemons to U.S. consumers, no such barriers exist for foreign producers. Inflated U.S. fresh-lemon prices have encouraged huge increases in production in Spain, Chile and elsewhere. Imports are soaring—and American growers are gnashing their teeth as their lemons rot while foreign lemons roll in.

Government may choose to store the excess supply for emergency use. Some crops, like wheat, can be held to soften the consequences of natural disasters. But if support prices are held continually above market level, stored commodities will accumulate beyond the level required for disaster relief, and the government will incur spiraling storage costs. That is exactly what has happened in the United States. At one time, the cost of storing supported crops ran well over $1 million a day. Over the years some of the crops in storage have rotted. Taxpayers would have been better off if the government had paid farmers to bury their crops in the fields.

Order 910 is especially perverse because the three districts covered by it harvest their crops at different times of the year. Lemon prices are sometimes twice as high in the summer as in the winter—thanks largely to the vagaries of the LAC. Southern California controls the LAC, and prevents northern Californian growers from holding their fruit for sale during the high-demand summer months.

While Order 910 forced Southern California growers to abandon 3% of their crop in 1981–82, Arizona growers left 16% of their crop rotting on trees and northern California growers lost 28% of their crop. A Small Business Administration study concluded, "There is a wide disparity in average net on-tree returns between [Arizona and southern California]—as much as three to one in some years." Arizona growers have had to stand by and watch their lemons freeze on the trees because they had not received government permission to harvest.

Federal regulations give Sunkist control of the lemon industry. Six of the 12 voting members of the LAC are Sunkist affiliates. Sunkist can veto any proposals it doesn't like. The SBA concluded that "the LAC's annual marketing policy statement originates at Sunkist."

Sunkist's control is threatened by the new shrink-wrap technology. Lemons shrink-wrapped in a plastic coating do not dehydrate like unwrapped lemons and can be stored for six months or more.

Shrink-wrap ends the perishability problem—thereby ending the justification for federal marketing controls.

But the USDA so far has effectively blocked shrink-wrap's use. Lemons must be sent to market within a few weeks of harvest, regardless of market prices or demand. The number of fresh lemons a grower is allowed to sell is determined by the weekly prorate. The grower can automatically sell his prorated shares; any shrink-wrapped lemons he sells count against his quota, so he has no incentive to go to extra expense to sell his allotment.

Several growers are lobbying the USDA to grant an exemption from marketing controls to test out the shrink-wrap lemon sales. But Sunkist and the LAC are fighting any innovation.

The shrink-wrap decision will be a precursor of whether the second Reagan administration will sacrifice the free market to its Western political friends. If the USDA continues banning shrink-wrap, then we can look forward to four more years of nonsensical agricultural policy, dislocation on the farms and higher grocery prices, all courtesy of Uncle Sam. But if the USDA admits the obvious and grants a large exemption for shrink-wrap (or gets rid of all marketing restrictions), then consumers may not have to go completely sour on the USDA after all.

James Bovard, "Can Sunkist Wrap Up the Lemon Industry?" *Wall Street Journal* (January 24, 1985), p. 30.

Acreage Allotment and Set-Aside Programs

Because price supports generate surpluses, programs that limit food production might seem an attractive alternative. Limited production is the concept behind acreage allotment and set-aside programs. Because the demand for most agricultural commodities is inelastic, farmers can improve their welfare by cooperating to restrict production and raise prices.

Although cartels are prohibited in most sectors of the economy, they are specifically permitted in farming by the Clayton Act of 1914. Yet it is very difficult for farmers to restrict production through collusion. Several million of them are spread over a large geographical area. Thus the costs of agreeing to restrict output, and of effectively enforcing that agreement, are high—so high that long-term working agreements have been rare.

Besides the cost of communication, there is the tendency to cheat, as in any cartel. Farmers are intelligent business people; they can see the benefits of reducing the market supply of a particular product. But at the same time, individual farmers can see that the price will not be affected if one or two farmers ignore the agreement. An individual farmer will be better off if everyone cuts back on production, but he will be even better off if he alone continues to produce as before while everyone else cuts back. Moreover, the individual farmer may hesitate to cut back if he fears that others will not. Hence attempts to collude tend to be nipped in the bud.

Frustrated farmers have occasionally vented their anger by dumping milk in a ditch or shooting their livestock. Such demonstrations can be a useful means of bringing pressure to bear on the government. But without collective action, such tactics will not materially improve the farmer's lot. In most markets, individual farmers cannot affect the market price even by destroying their entire crop.

Thus the attraction of government programs to restrict production. With its powers of enforcement, government can compel farmers to behave as a unified group. With tax revenues it can pay farmers to reduce the supply of food, and avoid going into the market as a buyer. In doing so it raises market prices, and therefore the short-run incomes of farmers. In Figure 32.3, the desired price is P_2 but the market supply of wheat is S_1. Government raises the price from the equilibrium level of P_1 by reducing the supply to S_2. Farm revenues rise from P_1Q_2 to P_2Q_1.

Government can restrict the supply of farm commodities in three ways. It can use acreage allotments to limit the number of acres each farmer can plant. It can establish production quotas. And it can simply pay farmers to produce less. Each method is a means of dividing the restricted quantity among individual farmers.

Acreage Allotments

Through acreage allotments, government restricts the number of acres that can be planted in a given crop in some predetermined manner. In the case of tobacco, acreage allotments were distributed to farmers, in proportion to each one's historical land use. Acreage allotments resemble crop marketing quotas, which fix the quantities farmers can take to market. But there is one important difference. Acreage allotments restrict only the amount of land farmers can use. They are free to cultivate that land as intensely as they wish, using extra fertilizer and labor to increase its productivity.

For this reason, acreage allotment programs are less reliable than marketing quotas as a way of limiting production. With marketing quotas, it is certain that no more than a given number of pounds of walnuts or bushels of oranges will be coming onto the market. With acreage allotments,

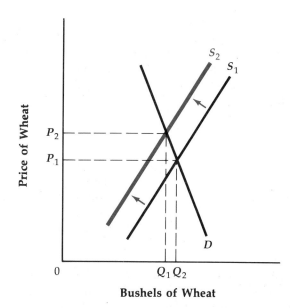

Figure 32.3. Effect of Government Restrictions on Supply.
A reduction in the supply of wheat from S_1 to S_2 will increase the price from P_1 to P_2. Because of the inelasticity of the demand curve D, farmers' revenues will increase from P_1Q_2 to P_2Q_1.

farmers can produce more than government intended by spending more on other resources. For the same reason, we should expect the cost of producing wheat, corn, or tobacco to be higher under acreage allotment programs than under marketing quotas. Fertilizer is a more expensive resource than land, so using relatively less land and more fertilizer will increase the cost of producing a crop. By contrast, under market quotas the farmer cannot benefit by raising output. His sole objective will be to minimize the costs of production.

Soil Bank and Set-Aside Programs

In 1956 President Dwight Eisenhower initiated what came to be known as the soil bank program (now defunct). The Department of Agriculture paid farmers to take part of their land out of production. (Under acreage allotments, no payments are made; farmers are simply prohibited from using more than a certain number of acres.) Farmers benefited both through the direct payments they received for not producing and through higher prices for what they did produce. The supply did not drop in proportion to the number of acres taken out of production, however. Farmers tended to take their worst land out of production and to farm their remaining land more intensely.

Today, so-called set-aside programs are used to discourage farmers from producing. To qualify for government price supports, farmers must agree to set aside or take out of production a certain number of acres. Since price supports are a form of money payment, the set-aside program has much the same effect as the old soil bank program. It restricts supply and raises the price of supported crops.

Payment in Kind (PIK)

In 1983 the Reagan administration began a program that paid farmers in kind for their set-asides. That is, surplus wheat, corn, sorghum, or rice from government storage was used to compensate farmers for taking their land out of production. Farmers were free to sell the commodities they received from the government.

The primary purpose of the PIK program was to reduce both federal price support payments, which had increased by 500 percent between 1981 and 1983, and federal storage costs. Organizers of the program believed that it would not raise food prices to consumers. Unfortunately, drought brought crop shortages and rising prices in many farm states in the summer of 1983. The PIK program had kept eighty million acres of farmland standing idle that summer, aggravating the shortage. And though higher prices for feed grains helped grain farmers, they hurt growers of cattle, hogs, and chickens. The PIK program was scaled down and finally terminated after the 1984 growing season.

The Target Price System

With passage of the Agricultural and Consumer Protection Act (1973), the federal government began to move from price supports to so-called target prices. For certain commodities, the government declared it would no longer raise the market price by purchasing surplus crops. Instead, it would announce target prices for various crops and let the market seek equilibrium, given what farmers chose to produce. If the market cleared below the target price, the government would pay farmers the difference. For example, if the target price for a bushel of wheat was $5, but the market would pay only $4.50, the government would give farmers an additional $0.50 for each bushel sold.

Under the new scheme consumers found market prices lower than under price supports. But as taxpayers, they still had to foot the bill for the farm subsidy. The system also continued to contribute to inefficiency in the agricultural sector, for it encouraged farmers to produce beyond the point at which the marginal cost of an additional bushel equaled the marginal benefit. The program did, however, reduce the government's purchases of surplus crops.

These points became clear in an analysis of market supply and demand. Figure 32.4 shows the difference between the old support price system and the target price system. Suppose the government determines that price P_t is the appropriate price for a bushel of wheat. Under the support

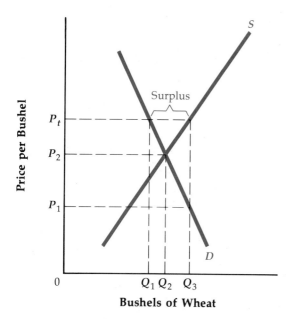

Figure 32.4. The Effect of a Target Price System.
If the government guarantees farmers a target price of P_t, they will produce Q_3 bushels of wheat—a quantity that will not clear the market until the price has fallen to P_1. Consumers will enjoy a lower price and a greater quantity of wheat than under a price support system, in which the government takes the surplus crop off the market. But the target price system is inefficient in the sense that the marginal cost of each bushel beyond Q_2, as indicated by the supply curve, is greater than its marginal benefit, as indicated by the demand curve. Consumers end up paying for the subsidy, $P_t - P_1$, in the form of higher taxes.

price system, farmers would supply Q_3 bushels and the government would have to buy the surplus, $Q_3 - Q_1$. Under the new system, the government guarantees farmers the target price P_t, but does not act as a buyer of last resort. Farmers still provide Q_3 bushels, a quantity that does not clear the market until the price has fallen to P_1. The government makes up the difference, paying farmers $P_t - P_1$ for each bushel sold. Taxpayers are still saddled with a heavy tax burden: $Q_3 \times (P_t - P_1)$. But they get more wheat—Q_3 instead of Q_1—at a lower price—P_1 instead of P_t. Note, however, that the marginal cost of producing each bushel beyond Q_2 is greater than its marginal benefit.

The Long-Run Effects of Government Agricultural Programs

Farmers can receive significant short-term gains from federal agricultural programs. But will they gain in the long run? The answer is a qualified no. Unless government controls the rental and sale of farm property, the benefits of farm programs will tend to become capitalized, or incorporated

Perspectives in Economics: Farm Exports and U.S. Agricultural Policy

Clifford M. Hardin

The most dramatic change in U.S. agriculture over the past two decades has been the rapid growth in farm exports. In the 1970s, U.S. farmers responded to a boom in the foreign demand for grains with huge increases in production. By the mid-1980s, the United States was exporting about a fourth of its feed grains, half of its soybeans, and 60 percent of its wheat, as well as substantial shares of its rice and cotton.

The expansion in export demand during the 1970s was fueled not only by the relatively low value of the U.S. dollar, but by improved economic conditions throughout the world. Consumers almost everywhere wanted to improve the quality of their diets. As their personal incomes rose, they demanded more animal protein. Since several pounds of grain are needed to produce a pound of animal products, much more grain was demanded than would have been required if people were consuming cereals in preference to meats.

The U.S. grain export boom ended in 1982, when favorable weather conditions and high price supports induced U.S. farmers to set new production records. Simultaneously, a worldwide recession set in, prompting a record rise in the value of the U.S. dollar. As U.S. exports became more expensive to foreign purchasers, their dollar value dropped. Between 1981 and 1983 total exports fell from $44 billion to $35 billion, contributing to the largest grain surplus in history. Rigidities in the Agricultural Act of 1981 locked the surplus into a farmer-owned reserve for the next three years, only postponing the devastating effect it would have when it finally came onto the market. For the first time in more than forty years, the price of farmland fell. Farmers who had borrowed heavily at high interest rates suddenly found themselves in a financial squeeze.

In response to flaws in the Agricultural Act of 1981, and the need to return government grain stocks to the market, the Reagan administration developed the PIK program. But by paying farmers in kind for reducing production, PIK reduced more than the government surplus. Almost immediately into the market prices of farms, farm equipment, marketable acreage allotments, and land leases.

For example, if an acreage allotment program makes tobacco growing more profitable in the short run, the demand for farms with acreage allotments will rise, and so will the price of those farms. Farmers will have to make a greater investment to get into tobacco farming than before. But the rate of return on that larger investment may be no higher than they could have realized without the allotment program.

Suppose a farmer can buy a small tobacco farm for $50,000 before an allotment program is set up. If the yearly profit on the farm is $5,000, the annual rate of return on the farmer's investment is 10 percent. Now suppose the government restricts the supply of tobacco through allotments, and the price of tobacco rises. The farmer's profit may rise to $10,000. If the farm's profitability doubles, we should expect its selling price to rise, for it will be more in demand among buyers. If farmers were willing to accept a 10 percent return on their investment before the allotment program, after the PIK program was begun, farmers in foreign countries expanded production. Canadian farmers planted more wheat; Argentinian farmers planted more corn. By cutting back U.S. production, government policy encouraged foreign producers to increase their share of the world market—and reduce the U.S. share.

The PIK program was only the latest in a series of government actions that encouraged foreign competition in the markets for U.S. farm products. In 1972, soybeans were included in President Richard Nixon's temporary price control program. The ceiling applied only to soybeans sold in the United States, however, not to exports. When it became evident that the whole crop would be exported, leaving none for domestic use, an embargo was placed on soybean exports. That sudden action caused Japan, then the largest customer for U.S. soybeans, to turn to Brazil for its soybean imports. President Jimmy Carter's embargo of grain and soybean shipments to the Soviet Union following the Russian invasion of Afghanistan in 1979 further encouraged foreign production. At other times during the 1970s, the United States attempted to reduce the world supply of farm products unilaterally by curtailing the acreage under cultivation at home. Each time such actions were taken, farmers in foreign countries were encouraged to expand their production.

In the future, the U.S. government must recognize that U.S. farm products that are heavily involved in international trade are highly vulnerable to foreign competition. Any cutback in U.S. production will lead to expanded foreign production. Thus any attempt to achieve political objectives by curtailing grain exports will be futile, indeed probably counterproductive, especially over the long run. Foreign producers will gladly fill the market void left by the curtailment of U.S. exports.

Adapted from Clifford M. Hardin, *Toward a New Farm Policy* (St. Louis, Mo.: Center for the Study of American Business, 1985).

---

we should expect them to accept the same return now. The price of the farm can therefore rise to ten times its profitability, or $100,000.

Thus the establishment of the allotment program offers considerable benefits to the person who happens to own a tobacco farm already. His wealth increases as much as $50,000. Because more land can be opened up for farming, the price of the existing farm may not rise quite so high as to reduce the rate of return all the way back to preallotment levels. But we should expect the price to move upward, and the rate of return on investment to move back down toward the preallotment level.

If landowners have to pay more for their land, or can sell it for a higher price because of the allotment, rental payments on land must also be raised. For the opportunity cost of holding on to land is greater at the higher price. But that is not all. If allotments are detached from the land and marketed in the same way as stocks and bonds, as they have been in recent years, farmers will have to buy both land and allotment rights just to get into business. Again the minimum investment increases.

Target price and soil bank programs can also increase the demand for farmland, raising the price of land and reducing the rate of return to the competitive level that existed before government intervention. For this reason we should expect farmers to resist the phase-out of farm programs. Many have already bought their farms at prices inflated by government programs. The elimination of farm subsidies would depress the demand for farm property, lowering the real wealth of those who assumed farm programs would continue indefinitely.

Farm Programs as a Method of Income Redistribution

The effect of government agricultural policies has been to redistribute income, from consumers and taxpayers to farmers. But as a method of income distribution, farm programs are neither direct nor necessarily equitable. Using tax dollars to increase the price of bread benefits both rich and poor farmers—and makes the poor as well as the rich pay higher prices for bread. In the process, the government encourages farmers to waste valuable resources—seed, fertilizer, labor, land, and equipment.

Redistribution of income through higher food prices is not only haphazard; it is a regressive form of taxation. Poor people spend a larger proportion of their incomes on food than the nonpoor. Therefore higher food prices reduce their real purchasing power more than that of other groups. Indeed, the food stamp program is in part an attempt to relieve the burden that government agricultural programs have placed on the poor. There would be less support for food stamps, and the taxes to pay for them, if government policy had not raised the price of groceries.

Because the United States has restricted its food supply, furthermore, world food prices have been kept high. Fewer mouths have been fed, and whole populations have experienced more starvation or malnutrition than they would otherwise. Certainly the United States has given away a great deal of food, but it is not clear that our giveaway programs have helped as much as our restricted supplies have hurt.

The fairness of the distribution of the benefits of farm programs is as questionable as the distribution of the burdens. Price supports and soil banks tend to help wealthy farmers more than poor ones. If a price support system raises the price of wheat $0.50 a bushel, the farmer who produces several hundred thousand bushels of wheat will reap a greater subsidy than the farmer who produces only a few thousand bushels. And the larger a farmer's landholdings, the more land he can take out of production in return for subsidy payments. Since farmer's wealth and income are directly related to farm output and acreage, farm programs based on output and acreage tend to aid affluent farmers more.

Finally, as we have said, any short-run benefits of government agricultural programs may dissipate over the long run as they are capitalized in the value of farm assets. Thus benefits go largely to those fortunate enough to own farms at the time programs are initiated. If government wants to help low-income farmers, a fairer alternative may be to give income grants to the truly needy.

U.S. agricultural policy is a good example of how government efforts to help one group of citizens can impose a substantial cost on others. Efforts to increase the incomes of farmers have raised the market prices of many foods, reducing consumers' purchases. The effect, then, has been to reduce the real incomes of consumers. At the same time, taxes have been collected to buy and store surplus products, and to persuade farmers not to produce. This redistribution of income from consumers and taxpayers to farmers does not always help the poor at the expense of the rich.

Even farmers themselves do not always benefit from farm programs. Government programs may increase farm profits, but if they also inflate the purchase prices of farms, farmers' rate of return on their investment may be no higher than it would have been without the programs. To the extent that government agricultural policy has stabilized farmers' incomes, thus reducing the risks of farming, it may actually have depressed farmers' rates of return.

Agricultural policy also illustrates the difficulties government can encounter in withdrawing from the business of income redistribution. If the government cancels target price or set-aside programs, the demand for and prices of farmland will fall. Many farmers will sustain capital losses; others will regret debts they incurred in expectation of continued government support. The political implications, especially in states with large farm constituencies, are obvious.

Summary and Extensions

Major Conclusions

1. In the short run, the prices of agricultural goods tend to fluctuate widely because of (a) the inelasticity of demand for most agricultural goods; (b) the inelasticity of supply of some agricultural products; (c) the competitive nature of agriculture; and (d) unpredictable changes in the weather.
2. At harvest time, supplies of crops tend to be highly inelastic with respect to price, mainly because most costs by then have become sunk costs.
3. The farm population has dwindled over the decades, in part because of technological change. New machinery and fertilizers have improved productivity, pushing relative prices down and increasing competition. Some farmers have been unable to stay in business.
4. In the 1930s, the government instituted price supports to help farmers. The program resulted in large surplus stocks of agricultural commodities, which the government had to buy and store at taxpayers' expense.
5. To avoid the accumulation of a surplus, the government has tried other methods of reducing the supply and increasing the prices of agricultural commodities. Acreage allotment programs attempt to push up crop

prices by restricting the number of acres farmers can plant. Soil bank programs pursue the same objective by paying farmers to take land out of production. The set-aside program requires farmers to take land out of production as a condition of receiving price supports. And the now defunct PIK program paid farmers in kind for taking land out of production.

6. The target price system guarantees farmers a minimum price for their crops, but allows the market price to fall in order to clear the market. Under this system government need not buy and store market surpluses.

7. Many of the benefits of government farm programs have been capitalized into the prices of farms and farm equipment. Thus farmers may earn a higher profit (or incur a lower loss) because of government programs; but they must also make a greater investment, or meet a higher lease payment, because of government intervention in the market.

1. Is an agricultural policy that keeps the price of sugar above equilibrium efficient in the economic sense of the term?
2. If the price of sugar is supported through purchases by the Department of Agriculture, must the United States also restrict the importation of sugar from foreign countries? Why or why not?
3. Are the long-run demand and supply of corn likely to be more or less elastic than the short-run demand and supply?
4. Suppose that throughout the world soybean farmers harvest a poor crop. What will happen to the price of soybeans? To the incomes of soybean farmers? What may happen to the price of soybeans the following year, if the new crop is just as poor?
5. If the government raises its target price for wheat, what will happen to the market clearing price?
6. Suppose the federal government simply declares that purchases and sales of wheat cannot be made below officially established prices. What will happen to the wheat market?

Questions to Ponder

*How is government
policy determined, and
what are the economic
effects of
that process?*

Median voter

Chapter 33

Public Choice: The Economics of Government

I have no fear, but that the
result of our experiment will
be, that men may be trusted to
govern themselves without a
master. Could the contrary be
proved, I should conclude,
either that there is no God, or
that he is a malevolent being.

Thomas Jefferson

*P*revious chapters have discussed the effects of various government policies on the market system. We looked at government efforts to control the external costs of pollution. We considered the economic impact of price controls and consumer protection laws on the market for final goods and services. And we examined the effects of government agricultural policy. Throughout the analysis we have focused on assessing the economic efficiency of government policy. We said little about how government policy is determined, or why government prefers one policy to another.

In this chapter, we will shift our focus to the functioning of government itself. Using economic principles, we will examine the process through which government decisions are made and carried out in a two-party democratic system, and consider its consequences. Today, when government production accounts for a substantial portion of the nation's goods and services, no student of economics can afford to ignore these issues.

The Central Tendency of a Two-Party System

In a two-party democratic system, elected officials typically take middle-of-the road positions. Winning candidates tend to represent the moderate views of the many voters who are neither liberals nor conservatives. For this reason there is generally little difference between Republican and Democratic candidates. Even when the major parties' candidates differ strongly, as Ronald Reagan and Walter Mondale did at the start of their 1984 presidential campaign, they tend to move closer together as the campaign progresses.

Figure 33.1 illustrates politicians' incentives to move toward the center. The bell-shaped curve shows the approximate distribution of voters along the political spectrum. A few voters have views that place them in the wings of the distribution, but most cluster near the center. Assuming that citizens will vote for the candidate who most closely approximates their own political position, a politician who wants to win the election will not choose a position in the wings of the distribution.

Suppose, for instance, that the Republican candidate chooses a position at R_1. The Democratic candidate can easily win the election by taking a position slightly to the left, at D_1. Though the Republican will take all the votes to the right of R_1 and roughly half the votes between R_1 and D_1, the Democrat will take all the votes to the left. Clearly the Democrat will win an overwhelming majority.

The smart politician, therefore, will choose a position near the middle. Then the opposing candidate must also move to the middle, or accept certain defeat. Suppose, for instance, that the Republican candidate chooses position R, but the Democrat remains at D_1. The Republican will take all the votes to the left of R and roughly half the votes between R and D_1. She will have more than the simple majority needed to beat her Democratic opponent. In short, both candidates will choose political positions in the middle of the distribution.

Politicians can misinterpret the political climate, of course. Even with polls, no one can be certain of the distribution of votes before an election.

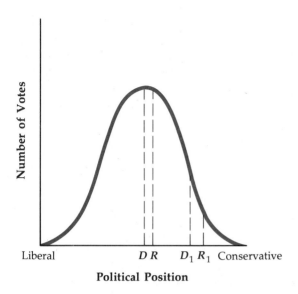

Figure 33.1. The Political Spectrum.
A political candidate who takes a position in the wings of a voter distribution, such as D_1 or R_1, will win fewer votes than a candidate who moves toward the middle of the distribution. In a two-party election, therefore, both candidates will take middle-of-the-road positions, such as D and R.

Just as producers find the optimum production level through trial and error, politicians may suffer several defeats before finding the true center of public opinion. But inevitably, political competition will drive them toward the middle of the distribution, where the median voter group resides. The **median voter** is the voter in the middle of the political distribution.

Median voter: the voter in the middle of the political distribution.

The recent history of presidential elections illustrates how politicians play to the views of the median voter. After an election in which the successful candidate won by a wide margin, the losing party has moved toward the position of the winning party. After Barry Goldwater lost by a wide margin to Lyndon Johnson in 1964, the Republic party made a deliberate effort to pick a more moderate candidate. As a result, the contest between Richard Nixon and Hubert Humphrey in 1968 was practically a dead heat. And after George McGovern was defeated by Richard Nixon in 1972, Democrats realized they too needed a less extreme candidate. Their choices in 1976 and 1984, Jimmy Carter and Walter Mondale, were more moderate.

The Economics of the Voting Rule

So far we have been assuming that a winning candidate must receive more than 50 percent of the vote. But although most issues that confront civic bodies are determined by simple-majority rule, not all collective decisions are made on that basis, nor should they be. Some decisions are too trivial for group consideration. The cost of a bad decision is so small that it is uneconomical to put the question up for debate. Other decisions are too important to be decided by a simple majority. Richard Nixon was elected president with only 43 percent of the popular vote in 1968 (when a third-party candidate, George Wallace, took almost 14 percent), but Nixon's impeachment would have required more than a majority of the Senate and the state legislatures. In murder cases, juries are required to reach unanimous agreement. In such instances, the cost of a misguided decision is high enough to justify the extra time and trouble required to achieve more than a simple majority.

The voting rule that government follows helps determine the size and scope of government activities. If only a few people need to agree on budgetary proposals, for example, the effect can be to foster big government. Under such an arrangement, small groups can easily pass their proposals, expanding the scope of government activity each time they do so. But under a voting rule that requires unanimous agreement among voters, very few proposals will be agreed to or implemented by government. There are very few issues on which everyone can agree, particularly when many people are involved.

A unanimity rule can be exploited by small groups of voters. If everyone's vote is critically important, as it is with a unanimous voting rule, then everyone is in a strategic bargaining position. Anyone can threaten to veto the proposed legislation unless he is given special treatment. Such tactics increase the cost of decision making.

Government represents people's collective interest. But the type of voting rule used determines the particular interests it represents, and the extent to which it represents them.

The Inefficiencies of Democracy

As a form of government, democracy has some important advantages. It disperses the power of decision making among a large number of people, reducing the influence of individual whim and personal interest. Thus it provides some protection for individual liberties. Democracy also gives political candidates an incentive to seek out and represent voters' interests. Competition for votes forces candidates to reveal what they are willing to do for various interest groups. Like the market system, however, the democratic system has some drawbacks as well. In particular, democracy is less than efficient as a producer of some goods and services.

The fact that the democratic form of government is inefficient in some respects does not mean that we should replace it with another decision-making process, any more than we should replace the market system, which is also plagued by inefficiencies. Instead, we must measure the costs of one type of production against the other, and choose the more efficient means of production in each particular case. We must weigh the cost of externalities in the private market against the cost of inefficiencies in the public sector. Because neither system is perfect, we must choose carefully between them.

Table 33.1. Costs and Benefits of a Public Park for a Five-Person Community

Individuals (1)	Dollar Value of Benefits to Each Person (2)	Tax Levied on Each Person (3)	Net Benefit (+) or Net Cost (−) [(2) − (3)] (4)	Vote For or Against (5)
A	$200	$100	+$100	For
B	150	100	+ 50	For
C	125	100	+ 25	For
D	50	100	− 50	Against
E	25	100	− 75	Against
Total	$550	$500		

Median Voter Preferences

When you buy a good like ice cream in the marketplace, you can decide how much you want. You can adjust the quantity you consume to your individual preferences and your ability to pay. But if you join with your neighbors to purchase some public service, you must accept whatever quantity of service the collective decision-making process yields. How much of a public good government buys depends not only on citizens' preferences, but on the voting rule that is used.

Consider police protection, for instance. Perhaps you would prefer to pay higher taxes in return for a larger police force and a lower crime rate. Your neighbors might prefer a lower tax rate, a smaller police force, and a higher crime rate. But public goods must be purchased collectively, no matter how the government is organized. If preferences differ, you cannot each have your own way. Under a democracy, the preferences of the median voter group will tend to determine the types and quantities of public goods produced. If you are not a member of that group, the compromise that is necessary to a democracy inflicts a cost on you. You probably will not receive the amount of police protection you want.

The Simple-Majority Voting Rule

Any decision that is made less than unanimously can benefit some people at the expense of others. Because government expenses are shared by all taxpayers, the majority that votes for a project imposes an external cost on the minority that votes against it. Consider a democratic community composed of only five people, each of whom would benefit to some degree from a proposed public park. If the cost of the park, $500, is divided evenly among the five, each will pay a tax of $100. The costs and benefits to each taxpayer are shown in Table 33.1. Because the total benefits of the project ($550) exceed its total costs ($500), the measure will pass by a vote of three to two. But the majority of three imposes net costs of $50 and $75 on taxpayers D and E.

When total benefits exceed total costs, as in this example, decision by majority rule is fairly easy to live with. But sometimes a project passes even though its cost exceeds its benefits. Table 33.2 illustrates such a situation. Again the $500 cost of a proposed park is shared equally by five people. Total benefits are only $430, but again they are unevenly distributed. Taxpayers A, B, and C each receive benefits that outweigh a $100 tax cost. Thus, A, B, and C will pass the project, even though it cannot be justified on economic grounds.

It is conceivable that many different measures, each of whose costs exceeded its benefits, could be passed by separate votes under such a system. If all the measures were considered together, however, the package could be defeated. Consider the costs and benefits of three proposed projects—a park, a road, and a school—shown in Table 33.3. If the park is put to a vote by itself, it will receive majority support from A, B, and C. Similarly, the road will pass with the support of A, C, and E, and the school will pass with the support of C, D, and E. But if all three projects are considered together, they will be defeated. Voters A, B, and D will reject the package (see column 4).

Many if not most measures that come up for a vote in a democratic government benefit society more than they burden it. And voters in the minority camp can use "logrolling" (vote trading) to defeat some projects that might otherwise pass. For instance, voter A can agree to vote against the park if voter D will vote against the school. Our purpose is simply to demonstrate that, in some instances, the democratic process can be less than cost efficient.

Political Ignorance

In some ways, the lack of an informed citizenry is the severest problem in a democratic system. The typical voter is not well informed about political issues and candidates. In fact, the average individual's welfare is not perceptibly improved by knowledge of public issues.

A simple experiment will illustrate this point. Ask everyone in your class to write down the name of his or her congressional representative. Then ask them for the name of the opposing candidate in the last election. You may be surprised by the results. In one survey, college juniors and seniors, most of whom had taken several courses in economics, political science, and sociology, were asked how their U.S. senators had voted on some major bills. The students scored no better than they would have done by guessing.[1] In the United States as a whole, most voters do not even know which party controls Congress.[2] And public opinion polls

---

1. Richard B. McKenzie, "Political Ignorance: An Empirical Assessment of Educational Remedies," *Frontiers of Economics* (Blacksburg, Va.: University Publications, 1977).
2. Donald E. Stokes and Warren E. Miller, "Party Government and the Saliency of Congress," *Public Opinion Quarterly*, 26 (Winter 1962), 531–46.

Table 33.2. Costs and Benefits of a Public Park for a Five-Person Community, Alternative Schedule

Individuals (1)	Dollar Value of Benefits to Each Person (2)	Tax Levied on Each Person (3)	Net Benefit (+) or Net Cost (−) [(2) − (3)] (4)	Vote For or Against (5)
A	$140	$100	+$ 40	For
B	130	100	+ 30	For
C	110	100	+ 10	For
D	50	100	− 50	Against
E	0	100	− 100	Against
Total	$430	$500		

Table 33.3. Costs and Benefits of a Park, a Road, and a School for a Five-Person Community

Individuals	Park (1)			Road (2)			School (3)			Total, 3 Projects (4)		
	Benefit	Cost	Vote	Benefit	Cost	Vote	Benefit	Cost	Vote	Benefit	Cost	Vote
A	$120	$100	For	$250	$ 200	For	$ 50	$ 400	Against	$ 420	$ 700	Against
B	120	100	For	50	200	Against	50	400	Against	220	700	Against
C	120	100	For	250	200	For	500	400	For	870	700	For
D	50	100	Against	50	200	Against	500	400	For	600	700	Against
E	50	100	Against	250	200	For	500	400	For	800	700	For
Total	$460	$500		$850	$1,000		$1,600	$2,000		$2,910	$3,500	

indicate that most voters greatly underestimate the cost of programs like Social Security.[3]

If voters were better informed on legislative proposals and their implications, government might make better decisions. In that sense, political information is a public good that benefits everyone. But as we have seen before, in large groups people have little incentive to contribute anything toward the production of a public good. Their individual contributions simply have little effect on the outcome.

To remain politically free, people must exercise their right to determine who will represent them. The result is that they often cast their votes on the basis of impressions received from newspaper headlines or television commercials—impressions carefully created by advertisers and press secretaries.

---

3. Edgar Browning, "Why the Social Insurance Budget is Too Large in a Democracy," *Economic Inquiry*, 13 (September 1974), 373–88.

Special Interests

The problem of political ignorance is especially acute when the benefits of government programs are spread more or less evenly, so that the benefits to each person are relatively small. But benefits are not always spread evenly; subgroups of voters—farmers, labor unions, or civil servants—often receive more than their proportional share. Members of such groups thus have a special incentive to acquire information on legislative proposals. Farmers can be expected to know more about farm programs than the average voter. Civil servants will keep abreast of proposed pay increases and fringe benefits for government workers. And defense contractors will take a private interest in the military budget.

Congressional representatives, knowing they are being watched by special-interest groups, will tend to cater to their wishes. As a result, government programs will be designed to serve the interests of groups with political clout, not the public as a whole.

Cyclical Majorities

In their personal lives, most people tend to act consistently on the basis of rational goals. If he prefers good A to good B, and good B to good C, the rational individual will choose A over C repeatedly. But collective decisions made by majority rule are not always consistent. Consider a community of three people, whose preferences for goods A, B, and C are as follows.

Individual	Order of Preference
I	A, B, C
II	B, C, A
III	C, A, B

Suppose these three voters are presented with a choice between successive pairs of goods, A, B, and C. If the choice is between good A and good B, which will be preferred collectively? The answer is A, because individuals I and III both prefer it to B. But if A is pitted against C, which will be preferred? The answer is C, because individuals II and III both prefer it to A. Since the group prefers A to B and C to A, one might think it would prefer C to B. But note that if C and B are put up to a vote, B will win. A cyclical, or revolving, majority has developed in this group situation. This phenomenon can lead to continual changes in policy in a government based on collective decision making.

Although there is no stable majority, the individuals involved are not acting irrationally. People with perfectly consistent personal preferences can make inconsistent collective choices when acting as a group. Fortunately, the larger the number of voters and issues at stake, the less likely a cyclical majority is to develop. Still, citizens of a democratic state should recognize that the political process may generate a series of inconsistent or even contradictory policies.

The Efficiencies of Competition Among Governments

In the private sector, competition among producers keeps prices down and productivity up. A producer who is just one of many knows that any independent attempt to raise prices or lower quality will fail. Customers will switch to other products or buy from other producers, and sales will fall sharply. To avoid being undersold, therefore, the individual producer must minimize its production costs. Only a producer who has no competition—that is, a monopolist—can afford to raise the price of a product without fear of losing customers.

These points apply to the public as well as the private sector. The framers of the Constitution, in fact, bore them in mind when they set up the federal government. Recognizing the benefits of competition, they established a system of competing state governments loosely joined in federation. As James Madison described it in *The Federalist* Papers, "In a single republic, all the power surrendered by the people is submitted to the administration of a single government; and the usurpations are guarded against by a division of the government into distinct and separate departments."[4]

Under the federal system, the power of local governments is checked not just by citizens' ability to vote, but by their ability to move somewhere else. If a city government raises its taxes or lowers the quality of its services, residents can go elsewhere, taking with them part of the city's tax base. Of course, many people are reluctant to move, and so government has a measure of monopoly power. But competition among governments affords at least some protection against the abuses of power.

Local competition in government has its drawbacks. Just as in private industry, large governments realize economies of scale in the production of services. Garbage, road, and sewage service can be provided at lower cost on a larger scale. For this reason, it is frequently argued that local governments, especially in metropolitan areas, should consolidate. Moreover, many of the benefits offered by local governments spill over into surrounding areas. For example, people who live just outside San Francisco may benefit from its services, without helping to pay for them. One large metropolitan government, including both city and suburbs, could spread the tax burden over all those who benefit from city services.

Consolidation can be a mixed blessing, however, if it reduces competition among governments. A large government restricts the number and variety of alternatives open to citizens and increases the cost of moving to another locale by increasing the geographical size of its jurisdiction. Consolidation, in other words, can increase government's monopoly power. As long as politicians and government employees pursue only the public interest, no harm may be done. But in fact, the people who run government have interests of their own. So the potential for acheiving greater efficiency

---

4. Alexandèr Hamilton, John Jay, and James Madison, *The Federalist: A Commentary on the Constitution of the United States*, no. 51 (New York: Random House, Modern Library, 1964) pp. 338–39.

Perspectives in Economics: Differences in Health Care Systems—A Public Choice Perspective

Cotton M. Lindsay

In most industrialized nations health care is financed by the government. Health care services are organized in a variety of ways. In Britain and the Soviet Union, physician and hospital services are produced by the government. Government agencies decide which hospitals to expand, how many orthopedic surgeons and urologists to hire at each, and so on. In West Germany and Denmark, the government leaves the allocation of health services to the market. Doctors are free to practice anywhere they choose, and hospitals are allowed to make their own investment decisions. The government simply pays the bills.

The way the governments organize their health sector has a significant effect on the overall allocation of resources. When the government is in the business of producing health care, decisions are made by disinterested civil service employees or by politicians sensitive to public opinion. On the other hand, when the government offers insurance, decisions are made by people who are ill and want medical attention. It is not surprising that the results of the two systems differ markedly.

In Britain, where Parliament must approve the budget for the National Health Service, decisions tend to reflect the needs of the majority of voters—most of whom are healthy and do not want the government to spend a great deal on health care. Voters who appear at the hospital door needing medical care receive only as much care as Parlia-

through consolidation could easily be lost in bureaucratic red tape. Studies of consolidation in government are inconclusive. But it seems clear that consolidation proposals should be examined carefully.

The Economics of Government Bureaucracy

Bureaucracy is not limited to government. Large corporations like General Motors and AT&T employ more people than the governments of some nations. They are bigger than the major departments of the federal government—though no company, of course, is as large as the federal government as a whole. Yet corporate bureaucracy tends to work more efficiently than government bureaucracy. The reason may be found in the fact that it pursues one simple objective—profit—that can be easily measured in dollars and cents.

Certainly the reason cannot be that stockholders are better informed than voters. Most stockholders are rationally ignorant of their companies' doings, for the cost of becoming informed outweighs the benefits. Even in very large corporations, however, some individuals hold enough stock to make the acquisition of information a rational act. Often such stockholders sit on the company's board of directors, where their interest in ment has paid for. In the United States, where the government is an insurer rather than a producer of health, the sick decide how much to spend on health care. If patients demand more hospital space and the government will pay the bills, hospitals simply expand to provide that space. Indeed, because government pays the bills, people seek even more care than they would be willing to pay for themselves. Even for apparent necessities like medical care, demand curves slope downward.

Because of the difference in interests of the people making the decisions in the two cases, economists would expect government-organized health systems to spend less than insurance-based health systems. And that is precisely what hap-

pens. Production costs, and therefore prices, may differ from place to place, and exchange rates may further distort spending data, making comparisons of nominal expenditures misleading. But we can ask what proportion of their gross national product various nations devote to health. Britain's National Health Service cares for citizens' health on a budget amounting to only about 6 percent of the nation's GNP. But West Germany, where health care is insured rather than delivered by the government, about 13 percent of GNP is spent on health. And in the United States, when Congress adopted a special health insurance plan covering the elderly and the poor, health spending increased from 6 to 10 percent of GNP in one decade.

increasing the value of their own shares makes them good representatives of the rest of the stockholders. The crucial point is that this informed stockholder has one relatively simple objective—profit—and can find out relatively easily whether the corporation is meeting it. The voter, on the other hand, has a complicated set of objectives and must do considerable digging to find out whether they are being met.

Because most corporations function in competitive markets, furthermore, the stockholder's drive toward profit is reinforced. General Motors knows that its customers may switch to Toyota if it offers them a better deal. In fact, stockholders can sell their General Motors stock and buy stock in Toyota. Thus corporate executives make decisions on the basis of the consumer's well-being—not because they wish to serve the public good, but because they want to make money.

Government bureaucracies, on the other hand, tend to produce public goods and services for which there is no competition. No built-in efficiencies guard the taxpayer's interests in a government bureaucracy. Both government bureaucrats and corporate executives base their decisions on their own interests, not those of society. But competition ensures that the interests of corporate decision makers coincide with those of consumers. No such safeguards govern the operations of government bureaucracies. Bureaucracies are constrained by political, as opposed to market, forces.

Figure 33.2. Bureaucratic Profit Maximization.
Given the demand for police service, D, and the marginal cost of providing it, MC, the optimum quantity of police service is Q_2. But a monopolistic police department interested in maximizing its profits will supply only Q_1 service at a price of P_2. (A monopolistic bureaucracy interested in maximizing its size would expand police service to Q_3.)

From the economist's point of view, one of the advantages of the profit-maximizing goal of competitive business is that it permits one to make predictions. Though some business people pursue other goals—personal income, respect in the business—their behavior can generally be well explained in terms of the single objective, profit. There is no single goal like profit that drives the government bureaucracy. Different bureaucracies pursue different objectives. We do not have time or space to consider all the possible objectives of bureaucracy, but we will touch on three: monopolistic profit maximization; size maximization; and waste maximization.

Profit Maximization

Assume that police protection can be produced at a constant marginal cost, as shown by the horizontal marginal cost curve in Figure 33.2. The demand for police protection is shown by the downward-sloping demand curve D. If individuals could purchase police service competitively at a constant price of P_1, the optimum amount of police service would be Q_2, the amount at which the marginal cost of the last unit of police service equals its marginal benefit. The total cost would be $P_1 \times Q_2$ (or the area $0P_1aQ_2$), leaving a consumer surplus equal to the triangular area P_1P_3a.

Police protection is usually delivered by regional monopolies, however. That is, all police services in an area are supplied by one organization. These regional monopolies have their own goals and their own decision-making process, which do not necessarily match the individual taxpayers'. If police service must be purchased from such a profit-maximizing monopoly, service will be produced to the point where the marginal cost of the last unit produced equals its marginal revenue: Q_1. The monopolist will sell that quantity above cost at price P_2, making a profit equal to the rectangular area P_1P_2ed.

At the monopolized production level, there is still some surplus—the triangular area P_2P_3e—left for consumers. But they are worse off than under competitive market conditions. They get less police protection (Q_1 instead of Q_2) for a higher price (P_2 instead of P_1).

This analysis presumes that the police are capable of concealing their costs. If taxpayers know that P_2 is an unnecessarily high price, the outcome will be the same as under competition. They will force the police to produce Q_2 protection for a price of P_1.

Size Maximization

In fact, a government bureaucracy is unlikely to take profit as its overriding objective, if only because bureaucrats do not get to pocket the profit. Instead, government monopolies may try to maximize the size of their operations. For if a bureaucracy expands, those who work for it will have more chance of promotion. Their power, influence, and public standing will improve, along with their offices and equipment.

What level of protection will a police department produce under such conditions? Instead of providing Q_1 service and misrepresenting its cost at P_2, it will probably provide Q_3 service—more than taxpayers desire—at the true price of P_1. The bill will be $P_1 \times Q_3$, or the area $0P_1bQ_3$ in Figure 33.2. Note that the net waste to taxpayers, shown by the shaded triangular area abc, exactly equals the consumer surplus, P_1P_3a. By extending service to Q_3, the police have squeezed out the entire consumer surplus and spent it on themselves.

Waste Maximization

Instead of maximizing the amount of service they offer, bureaucrats may choose to maximize waste. They can increase their salaries, improve their working conditions, or reduce their workloads. All such changes increase the cost of providing a given amount of service.

Figure 33.3 shows how far a bureau can go in increasing the cost of, or budget for, its services. The marginal cost curve MC_1 is the minimum cost of providing additional police protection. The optimum quantity of police protection is therefore Q_2, the same as in Figure 33.2. But if the police pad their costs, the marginal cost curve will shift up to MC_2. The bureau's

Figure 33.3. Bureaucratic Waste Maximization.
Given a demand for police service D and a marginal cost of providing it MC_1, the optimum quantity of police service will be Q_2. A monopolistic bureaucracy, however, may seek to maximize waste by inflating its costs to MC_2. It will supply Q_2 units of police protection at a tax price of P_2 instead of P_1. The shaded area abc shows the waste created, which exactly equals the consumer surplus P_2P_3a.

budget climbs from $P_1 \times Q_2$ to $P_2 \times Q_2$. Note that beyond Q_1, the marginal cost of additional police service is now greater than its marginal benefit, indicated by the demand curve. Again, the police are wasting taxpayers' money, as shown by the shaded triangular area abc. By moving their cost curve to MC_2, they have managed to extract all the consumer surplus (shown by the triangular area P_2P_3a) and to spend it on unnecessary frills.

In real life, most bureaucratic monopolies may pursue both size maximization and waste maximization. For each unit of service they provide, they will try to expand both the size of their operation and the funds spent on it. But they do have to make tradeoffs between the two objectives. Whenever they expand their size, they must forgo a certain amount of expansion in their cost per unit of service. There is, after all, only so much consumer surplus that can be extracted from the system.

Figure 33.4 shows one possible combination of size and budget maximization. In this case the department chooses to expand its service from Q_1 to Q_2. Having done so, it can expand its cost per unit only to MC_2. Again, the shaded triangular area that indicates waste, abc, just equals the consumer surplus P_2P_3a.

Fortunately government bureaucracies do not usually achieve perfect maximization of size or waste. For one thing, most legislatures have at least some information about the production costs of various services.

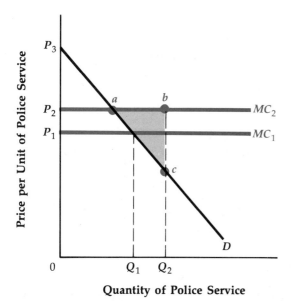

Figure 33.4. Size and Waste Maximization Combined.
The monopolistic bureaucracy may choose to increase both its size and the cost of its service. Any increase in one must come at the cost of the other, however, for together the two increases must not exceed the consumer surplus. Here net waste, shown by the shaded triangular area abc, is divided between size and cost increases. The area between the two marginal cost curves MC_1 and MC_2 represents waste maximization. The area below the marginal cost curve MC_1 represents size maximization. The whole area abc exactly equals the consumer surplus, P_2P_3a.

And bureaucrats may not be willing to do the hard work necessary to exploit their position fully. If bureaucracy does not manage to capture the entire consumer surplus, citizens will realize some net benefit from their investment.

Making Bureaucracy More Competitive

What can be done to make government bureaucracy more efficient? Perhaps the development of managerial expertise at the congressional level would encourage more accurate measurement of the costs and benefits of government programs. But cost-benefit analysis alone will not necessarily help. As long as special-interest groups, including those of government employees, exist, the potential for waste can be substantial.

A better solution to bureaucratic inefficiency may be to increase competition in the public sector. In the private marketplace, buyers do not attempt to discover the production costs of the companies they buy from. They simply compare the various products offered, in terms of price and quality, and choose the best value for their money. A monopoly of any kind, of course, makes that task difficult if not impossible. But the existence of even one competitor for a government bureaucracy's services would allow some comparison of costs. The more different sources of a service, the flatter the demand curve faced by each source, and the more efficient it must be to stay in business.

How exactly can competition be introduced into bureaucracy? First, proposals to consolidate departments should be carefully scrutinized. What appears to be wasteful duplication may actually be a source of competition in the provision of service. In the private sector, we would not expect the consolidation of General Motors, Ford, and Chrysler to improve the efficiency of the auto industry. If anything, we would favor the breakup of the large firms into separate, competing companies. Why then should we merge the sanitation departments of three separate cities?

A second way to increase the competitiveness of government services is to contract for them with private producers. Many government activities that must be publicly financed need not necessarily be publicly produced. In the United States, highways are usually built by private companies but repaired and maintained by government. Competitive provision of maintenance as well as construction might reduce costs. Other services that might be "privatized" are fire protection, garbage collection, and education.

Finally, competition can be increased simply by dividing a bureaucracy into several smaller departments with separate budgets, thus increasing competition. Such a change would reduce the costs citizens must bear to move to an area that offers better or cheaper government services. The loss (or threat of loss) of constituents can put pressure on government to improve its performance.

Summary and Extensions

This chapter has used cost-benefit analysis to develop an economic model of government. In government as well as private industry, producers in a monopolistic market position will tend to exploit the lack of competition for their service. A government bureau that has no competitors are in an enviable bargaining position vis-à-vis legislators and taxpayers. As the sole producer of a service, it can charge higher prices and deliver poorer service than competitive producers would.

In many cases, then, the performance of government bureaucracies can be improved by the introduction of competition for their services. Where possible, alternative sources of a government-provided good or service should be encouraged. If government bureaus have to compete with other producers by lowering their prices or increasing the quality of their service, they will be forced, like private producers, to reveal not just what they want to do, but the limit of what they will do for the consumer's business.

The democratic system provides checks and balances to control the exploitation of power in government. Voters can vote not to re-elect officeholders who abuse the public trust. They may not do so reliably, however, because of imperfect information. The fact that democracy is not a completely efficient system does not mean that a nondemocratic form of government is preferable.

1. In a two-party democracy, political candidates will tend to represent the interests of the median voter group.
2. The simple-majority voting rule can minimize the cost of reaching collective agreement. But it is not the only possible voting rule, nor does it minimize the cost of all collective agreements. Some issues are too important to be decided by simple majority; others are too trivial to require voters' attention.
3. Democracy is inefficient in several respects. (a) Individual citizens must accept whatever quantity of a public good the government provides, as established by the median voter group. They cannot adjust their consumption to suit their individual preferences. (b) Under the simple-majority voting rule, government programs can be authorized even if their total cost exceeds their total benefit. They may be rejected even if their benefits exceed their costs. (c) Voters have little incentive to become informed about candidates' political positions or the consequences of government policy. (d) Special-interest groups receive a disproportionate share of political influence. (e) Cyclical majorities can create inconsistent or even contradictory policies.
4. Decentralized forms of government, like the federal-state arrangement in the United States, foster efficiency in the public sector by providing citizens with alternatives to their local government.
5. Public bureaucracies can become too large, both because legislators do not know the true cost of government services and because bureaucrats benefit personally from government expansion. Instead of maximizing profits, bureaucratic governments will tend to maximize government size and waste.
6. Government efficiency can be increased by the introduction of competition into the provision of public services. That goal can be accomplished either by increasing the number of departments that provide a service or by requiring government to compete with private firms.

1. Is it desirable, in your opinion, that government generally adopts policies intended to please the median voter group? Why or why not?
2. It is sometimes said that a rational decision must be based on perfect information. Would it be rational for a voter to acquire perfect information about politics? Would it be possible?
3. What effect does increased competition have on the slope of an individual firm's demand curve? Why? How does a change in the slope of a firm's demand curve affect its efficiency? How do these effects apply to government bureaucracy?
4. "Competition forces producers to reveal what they are willing to do at the limit, not just what they want to do." How does this statement apply to government bureaucracy, and to legislators' ability to control it?
5. Write down all the government-provided services you can think of. Which of them *must* be provided by government bureaucracy? Which could be provided through competitive contract?

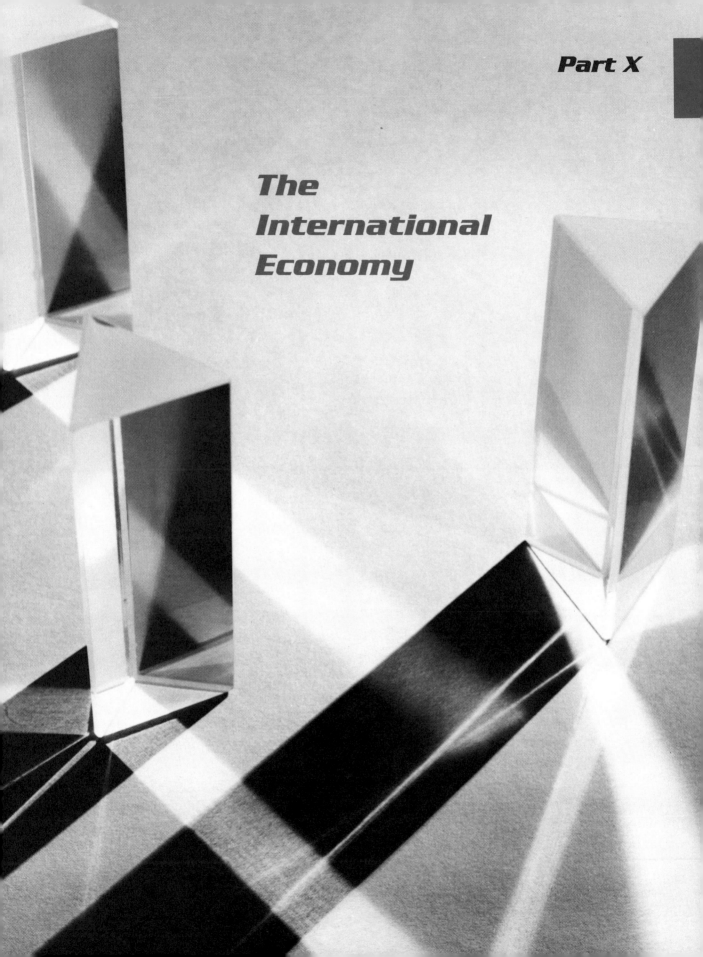

Part X

The International Economy

Central Question

How and to what extent do nations benefit from international trade?

Key Terms

International balance of payments

Merchandise trade balance

Current account

Current account deficit

Current account surplus

Capital account

Capital account surplus

Capital account deficit

Absolute advantage

Merchandise trade surplus

Merchandise trade deficit

Tariff

Quota

Chapter 34

International Trade

It can be of no consequence to
America, whether the
commodities she obtains in
return for her own, cost
Europeans much, or little
labor; all she is interested in,
is that they shall cost her less
labor by purchasing than by
manufacturing them herself.
David Ricardo

*N*ations never really trade; people do. This simple point is important, for it allows us to approach international trade as an extension of models already developed, rather than a completely new topic. Earlier discussions focused on the local or national marketplace. In this and the following chapter, our marketplace will be the world.

Of course, there are differences between international and domestic trade—enough to make international economics an important subdiscipline of the profession. Some differences are obvious, like the many different national currencies involved in international exchange. Others go largely unrecognized. An intangible but significant factor is the difference in people's attitudes toward domestic and international trade. As Abraham Lincoln is supposed to have said, "Domestic trade is among us; international trade is between us and them." Yet people all over the world trade with each other for the same reason: they stand to gain from the transaction.

Understanding that trade is between people, not nations, is important for another reason. If we focus solely on gains from trade to nations, we may overlook the distributional effects of international commerce—the gains and losses to individuals. As we will see, while international trade increases a nation's total income, it reduces some individuals' incomes and increases others'. To evaluate objections to free trade among nations in proper perspective, we must recognize these hidden gains and losses.

Objections to free trade can be explained easily in terms of market theory. A major principle of economic theory is that each individual competitor has a vested interest in reducing competition. Competition forces product prices down and spurs product development, restricting business income. Thus it is natural for domestic firms to seek protection from their foreign competitors. But protection only increases the prices consumers must pay. Carried to an extreme, protection based on the narrow interests of particular sectors of the economy can reduce everyone's income. On this basis rests the case for free international trade.

After examining the advantages of international trade from a purely national perspective, we will look at the distributional, or individual, effects. The chapter closes with a discussion of the pros and cons of protectionism.

Collective Gains from Trade

The benefits of international commerce to the United States are revealed in the international balance of payments statistics. The **international balance of payments** is a summary statement of all international transactions between one nation—for example, the United States—and the rest of the world. International transactions include exports and imports of goods, services, gifts, interest and dividend payments, and travel expenditures, as well as the flows of financial capital (purchases of stocks and bonds and real capital assets) across national boundaries. The bulk of the United States' international transactions are exports and imports, which are summarized in the merchandise trade balance. The **merchandise trade balance** is the difference between the dollar value of goods (raw materials,

International balance of payments: a summary statement of all international transactions between one nation—for example, the United States—and the rest of the world.

Merchandise trade balance: the difference between the dollar value of goods—raw materials, agricultural and manufactured products, and capital and consumer products—imported and exported.

Table 34.1. International Transactions, 1983 (in billions of dollars)

Merchandise trade	
Exports	$200.3
Imports	−261.3
Investment income	
Receipts	77.0
Payments	−53.5
Net military transactions	.5
Net travel	−4.6
Other services	8.7
Balance on goods and services	−$32.9
Remittances, pensions, and gifts	−8.7
Balance on current account	−$41.6
International capital flows	
U.S. investments abroad (capital outflows)	−$49.5
Foreign investments in the United States	81.7
Balance on capital account	$32.3
Statistical discrepancy	9.3
Balance of current account, capital account, and statistical discrepancy	$ 0.0

Source: *Economic Report of the President* (Washington, D.C.: U.S. Government Printing Office, 1985), pp. 344, 345.

Current account: the record of all the nation's international transactions other than capital flows and statistical discrepancies, including its merchandise trade, its investment income, its military transactions, its travel expenditures, its other services, and its remittances, pensions, and gifts.

Current account deficit: the dollar amount by which a nation's imports of goods and services, interest and dividend payments to foreigners, gifts to foreigners, travel expenditures abroad, and other remittances to foreign nations exceed its exports of goods and services, interest and dividend receipts from foreign nations, gifts from abroad, foreign travel expenditures in this nation, and other remittances from abroad.

agricultural and manufactured products, and capital and consumer products) imported and exported. In 1983 the United States exported goods and services valued at $200.3 billion, or approximately 6 percent of its GNP (see Table 34.1). It imported $261.3 billion worth of goods and services, or almost 8 percent of its total production. Imports exceeded exports by $61 billion.

The difference between exports and imports was offset by other international transactions. In 1983 Americans received approximately $77 billion in interest and dividends from investments in foreign nations. Foreigners, on the other hand, received only about $53.5 billion in interest and dividends from investments in American businesses and securities. American tourists spent $4.6 billion more abroad than foreign tourists spent here. But "other services" sold to foreigners exceeded "other services" to Americans by $8.7 billion. When remittances, pensions, and gifts were added, the United States had a current account deficit equal to $41.6 billion.

The **current account** is the record of all the nation's international transactions other than capital flows and statistical discrepancies, including its merchandise trade, its investment income, its military transactions, its travel expenditures, its other services, and its remittances, pensions, and gifts. A **current account deficit** is the dollar amount by which a nation's

Current account surplus: the dollar amount by which a nation's exports of goods and services, interest and dividend receipts from foreigners, gifts from foreigners, foreign travel expenditures in this nation, and other receipts from abroad exceed the nation's imports of goods and services, interest and dividend payments to foreigners, gifts to foreigners, travel expenditures abroad, and other remittances to foreign nations.

Capital account: the record of U.S. investments abroad and foreign investments in the United States.

Capital account surplus: the dollar amount by which foreign investments in the United States—that is, capital inflows—exceed U.S. investments abroad—that is, capital outflows.

Capital account deficit: the dollar amount by which U.S. investments abroad—that is, capital outflows—exceed foreign investments in the United States—that is, capital inflows.

imports of goods and services, interest and dividend payments to foreigners, gifts to foreigners, travel expenditures abroad, and other remittances to foreign nations exceed its exports of goods and services, interest and dividend receipts from foreign nations, gifts from abroad, foreign travel expenditures in this nation, and other remittances from abroad. In contrast to the 1980s, during the 1960s and 1970s, the United States frequently ran a current account surplus. A **current account surplus** is the dollar amount by which a nation's exports of goods and services, interest and dividend receipts from foreigners, gifts from foreigners, foreign travel expenditures in this nation, and other receipts from abroad exceed the nation's imports of goods and services, interest and dividend payments to foreigners, gifts to foreigners, travel expenditures abroad, and other remittances to foreign nations.

Part of the income received from the sale of American goods abroad went into purchases of foreign stocks and bonds and overseas investment by U.S. firms. Such investments are not included in current account statistics, because they are not imports. Instead, they are included in the nation's capital account. The **capital account** is the record of U.S. investments abroad and foreign investments in the United States. In 1983 Americans invested $49.5 billion abroad, while foreigners invested $81.7 billion here. Thus the nation ran a capital account surplus of $32.3 billion. A **capital account surplus** is the dollar amount by which foreign investments in the United States—that is, capital inflows—exceed U.S. investments abroad—that is, capital outflows. In contrast to the 1980s, during the 1960s and 1970s, the United States frequently ran a capital account deficit. A **capital account deficit** is the dollar amount by which U.S. investments abroad—that is, capital outflows—exceed foreign investments in the United States—that is, capital inflows.

Many of the imports Americans bought were finished products like automobiles and television sets, their Japanese or German origins clearly identified. Other imports were raw materials, like crude oil and tin, or parts used in the production of other goods, like transistors and auto parts. Some of the imported raw materials were used to make products that were ultimately exported to other countries. More will be said about export-import balances in the following chapter. The point here is that all these international transactions were undertaken for mutual gain. Americans who bought foreign goods did so because they offered a better price-quality package than their U.S. counterparts. Americans who invested in foreign countries did so because they expected to earn a higher rate of return than would be possible on U.S. properties.

The gains from international trade are clearest when there is no domestic substitute for an imported good. For example, the United States does not have any known reserves of chromium, manganese, or tin. For those basic resources, which are widely used in manufacturing, American firms must rely on foreign suppliers. The gains from trade are also clear for goods that are very costly or difficult to produce in the United States. For example, cocoa and coffee can be raised in the United States, but only in a greenhouse. Obviously it is less costly to import coffee in exchange for some other good, like wheat, for which the U.S. climate is better suited.

Foreign competition also offers benefits to the American consumer. By challenging the market power of domestic firms, foreign producers who market their goods in the United States reduce product prices and expand domestic consumption. Foreign competition also increases the variety of goods available. Without competition from the twenty or more foreign automobile producers who sell in the American market, the three or four U.S. automakers would each get a much larger percentage of the market. They would be less hesitant to raise their prices if consumers had fewer alternative sources of supply. Collusion among major manufacturers would also be much more likely without the presence of foreign competitors.

International trade also promotes specialization, whose benefits are fairly clear. By concentrating on producing a small number of goods and selling to the world market, a nation can reap the benefits of greater efficiency and economies of scale. Resource savings that are not obvious at first may be gained. Indeed, after considering the following example, some readers may doubt that international trade can be mutually beneficial.

Consider a world in which only two nations, the United States and Japan, produce only two goods, textiles and beef. Assume that the United States produces both textiles and beef more efficiently than Japan. That is, with the same resources, the United States can produce more beef and more textiles than Japan can. It has an absolute advantage in the production of both goods. An **absolute advantage** in production is the capacity to produce more units of output than a competitor can for any given level of resource use.

Table 34.2 shows such a situation. With the same labor, capital, and other resources, the United States can produce thirty units of textiles; Japan can produce twenty-five. If the same resources are applied to beef production, the United States still outproduces Japan, by ninety units to twenty-five. Under such conditions, one might think that trade with Japan could not possibly benefit the United States. But the relevant question is not how efficient the United States is in absolute terms, but whether the people of the United States can make a better deal by trading with Japan than they can make by trading among themselves.

Absolute advantage: the capacity to produce more units of output than a competitor can for any given level of resource use.

Table 34.2. Comparative Cost Advantages, Beef and Textiles, United States and Japan

	Maximum Units of Textiles (Zero Beef Units)	Maximum Units of Beef (Zero Textile Units)	Domestic Cost Ratios in Each Nation	Mutually Beneficial Trade Ratio, Both Nations
United States	30	90	1 textile costs 3 beef	1 textile trades for 2 beef
Japan	25	25	1 textile costs 1 beef	

Perspectives in Economics: The Balance on Current Account

Edward L. Hudgins

International economic transactions can be measured in several ways. The merchandise trade balance includes the dollar value of imports and exports. The balance on current account, a more complete measure, includes investment income receipts and payments and other minor transactions as well.

During the twenty-five years following World War II, the United States ran yearly surpluses in its merchandise trade. A **merchandise trade surplus** is the dollar amount by which exports of goods exceed imports of goods. Between 1946 and 1970, exports averaged $4 billion more than imports. Total exports increased from $11.8 billion to $42.5 billion, while imports went from $5 billion to $40 billion.

Except for two years since then, however, the United States has run a steadily increasing merchandise trade deficit. A **merchandise trade deficit** is the dollar amount by which imports of goods exceed exports of goods. Between 1977 and 1982, the deficit averaged $30 billion. In 1983 it climbed to $61 billion, and in 1984 doubled again to reach $123 billion.

During the same period, the balance on current account was more favorable. Ever since World War II, interest income from U.S. investments abroad has exceeded interest payments on foreign investments in the United States. In fact, the surplus interest income has usually been greater than the trade deficit. But from 1977 to 1979, the United States ran deficits on current account of $7.96 to $15.4 billion. That was nothing, however, compared with the staggering deficits of 1983 and 1984 (see Figure 34.1).

The major cause of these deficits in the balance on current account was an increase in imports. After a general decline during the 1970s, the U.S. dollar regained much of its historical strength abroad, allowing Americans to purchase more imports. The surplus of investment income receipts also decreased in these years, in part because of increased investment in the United States by both Americans, who began to invest less abroad, and by foreigners, who began to invest more in the United States.

Some economists see the deficit on current account as a problem. As long as the investment

To determine which is the better deal we must compare the costs of production. If each nation produces and trades the products in which it has a comparative cost advantage, trade can raise both their incomes. Remember that a comparative advantage is the capacity to produce a product at a lower cost than a competitor, in terms of the goods that must be given up. The United States may have an absolute advantage in the production of both beef and textiles, but it may have a comparative advantage only in the production of beef. In other words, the United States must forgo fewer units of textiles to obtain a unit of beef than Japan. Having a comparative advantage in beef necessarily means the United States cannot have a comparative advantage in textiles—a point that will become clear shortly.

In a sense, the United States trades with itself every time it produces either beef or textiles. If it produces beef, it incurs an opportunity cost: it gives up some of the textiles it could have produced. If it produces textiles, it gives up some beef. In Table 34.2, every time the United States produces

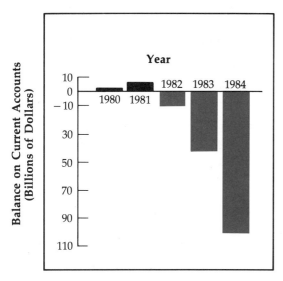

Figure 34.1. U.S. Balance on Current Account, 1980–1984.
In 1980 and 1981 the United States recorded a small surplus on current account. By 1984, however, the nation was running a record deficit of $101.6 billion on current account—more than twice its deficit in 1983.
Source: U.S. Department of Commerce, *Survey of Current Business* (July 1985).

income surplus matches the trade deficit, they maintain, excess imports can be covered. But if the United States does not earn the equivalent of its excess imports in net investment income, it is in effect buying on credit. In the long run the United States will become a debtor nation, unable to import goods or to attract investment capital because of its high debt payments.

But other economists feel a deficit on current account reflects a passing situation, not an economic problem that demands government action. Excess imports, they argue, may be considered as paid for by the increased buying power of the dollar. That is, the strong dollar has benefited Americans by lowering the prices of imported goods. If too many dollars flow out of the United States, furthermore, the dollar will decrease in value. Over the long run, exports will increase and imports will decrease. Finally, excess dollars that flow out of the United States in payment for imports may well return in the form of foreign investment. Such an inflow of capital would help, not harm, American industry.

one unit of textiles, it gives up three units of beef. (It can produce either thirty units of textiles or ninety of beef—a ratio of one to three.) Thus the United States can benefit by trading beef for textiles if it can give up fewer than three units of beef for each unit of textiles it gets from Japan.

Japan, on the other hand, gives up an advantage of one unit of beef for each unit of textiles it produces. If Japan can get more than one unit of beef for each unit of textiles it trades, it too can gain by trading. In short, if the trade ratio is greater than one unit of beef for one unit of textiles but less than three units of beef for one unit of textiles, trade will benefit both countries. The United States will gain because it has to give up fewer units of beef—two, perhaps, instead of three—than if it tried to produce the textiles itself. It can produce three units of beef, trade two of them for a textile unit, and have one extra beef unit left over. Or it can trade all three units of beef for one and one-half units of textiles. Japan can produce one unit of textiles and trade it for two units of beef, gaining one textile unit in the process.

Table 34.3. Mutual Gains from Trade in Beef and Textiles, United States and Japan

	United States	Japan	Total, U.S. and Japan
Production and consumption levels before international trade	15 textiles 45 beef	3 textiles 22 beef	18 textiles 67 beef
Production levels in anticipation of international trade (complete specialization assumed)	0 textiles 90 beef	25 textiles 0 beef	25 textiles 90 beef

At an exchange ratio of 2 beef for 1 textile, United States and Japan agree to trade 40 beef for 20 textiles.

	United States	Japan	Total, U.S. and Japan
Consumption levels after international trade	20 textiles 50 beef	5 textiles 40 beef	25 textiles 90 beef
Increased consumption (before-trade consumption levels subtracted)	5 textiles 5 beef	2 textiles 18 beef	7 textiles 23 beef

Both nations can gain from such a trade because each is specializing in the production of a good for which it has a comparative cost advantage. Even though the United States has an absolute cost advantage in both products, Japan has a comparative advantage in textiles. One unit of textiles costs Japan one unit of beef; the same unit of textiles costs the United States three units of beef. Similarly, the United States has a comparative cost advantage in the production of beef. One unit of beef costs the United States only one-third unit of textiles; it costs Japan a whole unit. If each specializes in the commodities for which it has a comparative cost advantage, the two nations can save resources for use in further production.

Table 34.3 shows the gains in production each nation can realize under such an arrangement. Before trade, the United States produces 15 units of textiles and 45 of beef; Japan produces 3 units of textiles and 22 of beef. Total production is therefore 18 units of textiles and 67 units of beef. With trade, the United States produces 90 units of beef and Japan produces 25 units of textiles. At an international trade ratio of 1 unit of textiles to 2 units of beef, suppose the two nations agree to trade 40 units of beef for 20 units of textiles. The United States gets more beef—50 units as opposed to 45—and more textiles—20 units as opposed to 15. Japan also gets more of both commodities. Through specialization, total world production has risen from 18 to 25 units of textiles and from 67 to 90 units of beef. Both nations can now consume more of both commodities. In a very important sense, the world's aggregate real income has increased.

The same gain in aggregate welfare is shown graphically in Figure 34.2. On the left-hand side of the figure, the U.S. production possibilities curve extends from 30 units of textiles on the horizontal axis to 90 units of beef

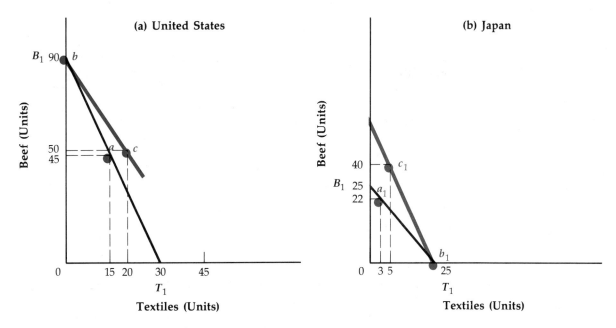

Figure 34.2. Production Gains from International Trade.
The United States can produce any combination of beef and textiles along its production possibilities curve B_1T_1 (left-hand panel). Without trade, it will choose to produce at point a, 45 units of beef and 15 units of textiles. If given the opportunity to trade two units of beef for one unit of textiles, however, the United States will specialize completely in beef (point b) and trade beef for textiles along the color line. Through trade, the United States moves from a to c, exporting 40 units of beef (90 units produced minus 50 consumed) and importing 20 units of textiles. In the process the nation increases its consumption of both beef and textiles, from 45 units of beef and 15 units of textiles to 50 units of beef and 20 units of textiles. (The color line does not intersect the horizontal axis because the United States cannot get more than 25 units of textiles from Japan.)

At the same time trade permits Japan (right-hand panel) to shift its consumption from the black production possibilities curve to the color curve. By producing at b_1 and exporting 20 units of textiles in exchange for 40 units of beef, Japan too can expand its consumption, from a_1 to c_1.

on the vertical axis. Japan's production capability is shown on the right. Without trade, the United States chooses to produce at point a, 15 textile units and 45 beef units. But at an exchange ratio of 2 beef units for 1 textile unit, the United States can move up and to the left on its production possibilities curve. At the extreme, it will produce at point b, 90 units of beef and no textiles. It can then trade along the color outer line, exchanging 40 beef units for 20 textile units (point c). Through trade, the United States realizes a gain in aggregate welfare represented by the distance between points a and c. In other words, international trade permits the United States to consume at a point beyond its own limited production possibilities curve (the black line in the graph). In the same way, Japan realizes a gain in welfare equal to the difference between its consumption before trade, a_1, and its consumption after trade, b_1.

The Distributional Effects of Trade

As we have seen, even a nation that has an absolute advantage in every production process can benefit from trade. In reality, no such nation exists, but that just underscores the point that even in the unlikeliest conditions we can make the case for free trade. If voluntary trade takes place, furthermore, we must assume that both parties gain. Why else would they agree to the arrangement?

Yet international trade remains a controversial subject, for while nations gain from trade, individuals within those nations may not. Individual gains tend to go to the firms that produce goods and services for export.

Gains to Exporters

Exporters of domestic goods gain from international trade because the market for their goods expands, increasing demand for their products. The increase in their revenue can be seen in Figure 34.3. When the demand curve shifts from D_1 to D_2, producers' revenues rise from P_1Q_2 (point a) to P_2Q_3 (point b). The increase in revenues is equal to the shaded L-shaped area $P_2bQ_3Q_2aP_1$. Producers benefit because they receive greater profits, equal to the shaded area above the supply curve, P_2baP_1. Workers and suppliers of raw materials benefit because their services are in greater demand, and therefore more costly. The cost of producing additional units for export is equal to the shaded area below the supply curve, Q_2abQ_3.

This graphic suggests why farmers supported the sales of wheat to the Soviet Union that began in the early 1970s. They complained loudly when the U.S. government suspended sales temporarily for political reasons. But many consumers and members of Congress objected to the wheat sales, on the ground that they would increase the domestic price of wheat and therefore of bread. In a narrow sense, consumers of exported products have an interest in restricting their exportation. Yet in the broad context of international trade, restrictions can work against the private interests of individuals, including even consumers of bread. Trade is ultimately a two-way street. To import goods and services that can be produced more cheaply abroad than at home, a nation must export something else. No nation will continually export part of what it produces without getting something in return. To the extent that exports are restricted to suit the special interests of some group, imports of other commodities also are restricted. Restrictions on the exportation of wheat may hold down the price of bread, but they can also increase the price of imported goods, like radios and television sets.

Losses to Firms Competing with Imports

While consumers gain from increased imports, domestic producers may lose from increased competition. Foreign producers can gain a foothold in the domestic market in three ways: (1) by providing a better product than

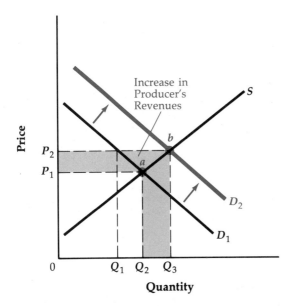

Figure 34.3. Gains from the Export Trade.
The opening up of foreign markets to U.S. producers increases the demand for their products, from D_1 to D_2. As a result, domestic producers can raise their price from P_1 to P_2 and sell a larger quantity, Q_3 instead of Q_2. Revenues increase by the shaded area $P_2bQ_3Q_2aP_1$.

domestic firms; (2) by selling essentially the same product as domestic firms, but at a lower price; and (3) by providing a product previously unavailable in the domestic market. Most people welcome the importation of a previously unavailable product. But producers who face competition from foreign suppliers have an incentive to object to importation. If imports are allowed, the domestic supply of a good increases. Domestic competitors will sell less, and they may have to sell at a lower price. In short, the employment opportunities and real income of domestic producers decline as a result of foreign competition.

Figure 34.4 shows the effects of importing foreign textiles. Without imports, demand is D and supply is S_1. In a competitive market, producers will sell Q_2 units at a price of P_2. Total receipts will be $P_2 \times Q_2$. But the importation of foreign textiles increases the supply to S_2, dropping the price from P_2 to P_1. Because prices are lower, consumers increase their consumption from Q_2 to Q_3 and get more for their money.

But domestic firms, their employees, and their suppliers lose. Because the price is lower, domestic producers must move down their supply curve (S_1) to the lower quantity Q_1. Their revenues fall from P_2Q_2 to P_1Q_1. In other words, the revenues in the shaded L-shaped area $P_2aQ_2Q_1bP_1$ are lost. Of this total loss in revenues, owners of domestic firms lose the area above the supply curve, P_2abP_1. Workers and suppliers of raw materials lose the area below the supply curve, Q_2abQ_1. This is the cost domestic

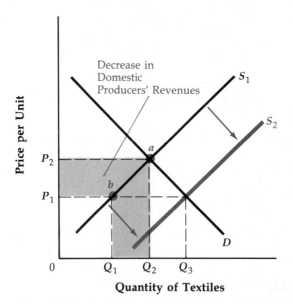

Figure 34.4. Losses from Competition with Imported Products.
The opening up of the market to foreign trade increases the supply of textiles from S_1 to S_2. As a result, the price of textiles falls from P_2 to P_1, and domestic producers sell a lower quantity, Q_1 instead of Q_2. Consumers benefit from the lower price and the higher quantity of textiles they are able to buy. But domestic producers, workers, and suppliers lose. Producers' revenues drop by an amount equal to the shaded area P_2abP_1. Workers' and suppliers' payments drop by an amount equal to the shaded area Q_2abQ_1.

firms would incur in increasing production from Q_1 to Q_2, the payments that would be made to domestic workers and suppliers in the absence of foreign competition. If workers and other resources are employed in textiles because it is their best possible employment, the introduction of foreign products can be seen as a restriction on some workers' employment opportunities.

The Effects of Tariffs and Quotas

Because foreign competition hurts some individuals, domestic producers, workers, and suppliers have an incentive to seek government restrictions on imports. Two forms of protection are commonly used, tariffs and quotas. A **tariff** is a special tax on imported goods. A **quota** is a limit on the amount of a good that can be imported.

Tariff: a special tax on imported goods.

Quota: a limit on the amount of a good that can be imported.

If tariffs are imposed on foreign goods, the supply of textiles will decrease—say from S_2 toward S_1 in Figure 34.4—and the price of imports will rise. Domestic producers will raise their prices too, and domestic production will go up. If the tariff is high and all foreign textiles are excluded, the supply will shift all the way back to S_1. A small tariff will have a more modest effect, shifting the supply curve only partway back toward S_1. The price of textiles will rise, and domestic producers will expand their production, but imports will continue to come into the country.

A quota has the same general effect as a tariff. It reduces the market supply, raises the market price, and encourages domestic production. There are three main differences between quotas and tariffs, however. First, quotas firmly restrict the amount of a product that can be imported, regardless of market conditions. A quota may specify how much oil may be imported each day or how much sugar each year. Tariffs, on the other hand, permit any level of importation for which consumers are willing to pay. Thus if demand for the product increases, imports may rise.

The first Reagan administration imposed quotas on steel, copper, textiles, and autos from Japan. In 1984 the so-called voluntary restraint program forced Japan to restrict auto sales in the United States to 1.84 million cars. Because Japanese supply was not allowed to keep pace with the rapidly expanding U.S. demand, the price of Japanese cars rose, more expensive models were imported, and consumers faced longer waiting lists for Japanese cars. In addition, the prices of American cars rose. These consequences led to the termination of the voluntary restraint program in 1985.

The second major difference from tariffs is that quotas are typically specified for each important foreign producer. Otherwise, all foreign producers would rush to sell their goods before the quota was reached. When quotas are rationed in this way, more detailed government enforcement is required. Tariffs place no such restriction on individual producers.

Finally, quotas enable foreign firms to raise their prices and extract more income from consumers. One economist estimated that the Reagan administration's voluntary restraint program permitted Japanese auto producers to raise their prices high enough to take an additional $2 billion out of the American market.[1] Tariffs, on the other hand, force foreign firms to lower their prices to offset the increase from the tariff. They also generate income for the federal government.

Because of the private benefits to be gained from tariffs and quotas, we should expect an industry to seek them so long as their market benefits exceed their political cost. Politicians are likely to expect votes and campaign contributions in return for tariff legislation, and producers will usually make the necessary contributions, because the elimination of foreign competition promises increased revenues. The difference between the increase in profits due to import restrictions and the amount spent on political activity can be seen as a kind of profit in itself.

Consumers, on the other hand, have reason to oppose tariffs or quotas on imported products. Such legislation inevitably causes prices to rise. Consumers typically do not offer very much resistance, however, because the effects of tariffs and quotas are hard to perceive. Unlike a sales tax, the cost of a tariff is not rung up separately at the cash register. And many consumers do not reason through the complex effects of a tariff on

---

1. Robert Crandell, "Import Quotas and the Automobile Industry: The Costs of Protectionism," *Brookings Review* (Summer 1984), pp. 8–16.

consumer prices. In fact, many, if not most, consumers accept the proposition that what is good for the textile, automobile, steel, or copper industry is good for the nation and themselves. "Buy American" slogans and advertisements emphasizing the need to preserve American jobs are generally effective in swaying public opinion.

As a group, consumers have less incentive to oppose tariffs than industry has to support them. The benefits of a tariff accrue principally to a relatively small group of firms, whose lobby may already be well entrenched in Washington. These firms have a strong incentive to be fully informed on the issue and to make campaign contributions. But the harmful effects of a tariff are diffused over an extremely large group of consumers. The financial burden borne by any one consumer may be very slight, particularly if the tariff in question is small, as most tariffs are. As a result, the individual consumer has little incentive to become informed on tariff legislation or to make political contributions. Though consumers as a whole may share an interest in opposing tariffs, collective action must still be undertaken by individuals. And individuals will not incur the cost of organizing unless they expect to receive compensating private benefit.

At some level of increased cost, of course, consumers will find the necessary incentive to oppose tariff legislation. For this reason Congress rarely passes tariffs high enough to make importation totally unprofitable. But even low tariffs reduce the nation's real income while redistributing it toward protected sectors. The size of the pie is reduced, but the protected few get a bigger slice.

The Case for Free Trade

We have seen how international trade can increase the total incomes of the nations engaged in it. By extension, we can conclude that anything that restricts the scope of trade between nations generally reduces their real incomes. To the extent that trade is a two-way street—that exports trade for imports, at least in the long run—a reduction in imports brings a reduction in exports. From our imports the Japanese get the dollars they need to buy American exports. If we reduce our imports, they will have fewer funds with which to buy from us. For this reason, U.S. farmers, who sell approximately one-third of their crops in foreign markets, actively opposed the protectionist movement led by textile, steel, and copper firms in the first half of the 1980s.

Yet what is true for one sector of the economy is not necessarily true for all. If all sectors are protected by tariffs, it is possible (but not inevitable) that all experience a drop in real income. Figure 34.5 illustrates the case of an economy with two industries, automobiles and textiles. Both industries must compete with imports. If neither seeks protection, both will operate in cell I, at a combined real income of $50 ($20 for the textile industry and $30 for the automobile industry). If the textile industry seeks protection but the auto industry does not, they will move to cell II, where tariffs raise the textile industry's income from $20 to $23. The automotive

	Textile Industry Without Tariff Protection	Textile Industry With Tariff Protection
Automobile Industry Without Tariff Protection	Cell I Real Income, Textile / Real Income, Auto ———— / ———— $20 / $30	Cell II Real Income, Textile / Real Income, Auto ———— / ———— $23 / $25
Automobile Industry With Tariff Protection	Cell III Real Income, Textile / Real Income, Auto ———— / ———— $15 / $34	Cell IV Real Income, Textile / Real Income, Auto ———— / ———— $17 / $26

Figure 34.5. Effects of Tariff Protection on Individual Industries: Case 1.
If neither the textile nor the automobile industry obtains tariff protection, the economy will earn its highest possible collective income (cell I). But each industry has an incentive to obtain tariff protection for itself. If the textile industry alone seeks protection (cell II), its income will rise while the auto industry's income falls. If the auto industry alone seeks protection, its income will rise while textile income falls. If both obtain protection, the economy will end up in cell IV, its worst possible position. Income in both sectors will fall.

sector's income falls to $25, so that the two industries' combined real income falls to $48. Consumers get fewer textiles at a higher price.

Similarly, if the auto industry seeks protection while the textile industry does not, the economy will move from cell I to cell III. Again, total real income falls from $50 to $49, but this time the auto industry is better off. Its income rises from $30 to $34, while the textile industry's income falls to $15. Obviously, if one industry seeks protection, the other has an incentive to follow suit. If the textile industry counters with a tariff of its own, the economy will move from cell III to cell IV, and the industry's real income will rise from $15 to $17.

Without some constraint on both sectors, then, each has an interest in seeking protection regardless of what the other does. Yet if the economy winds up in cell IV, total real income will be lower than under any other conditions: only $43. Obviously the best course for the economy as a whole is to prohibit tariffs altogether. And in an economy with only two sectors, the cost of reaching an agreement is manageable. In the real world, however, there are many economic sectors, and the costs of reaching a decision are much greater.

In Figure 34.5, both industries end up with lower real incomes in cell IV. But in reality, the effects of multiple tariffs will be different in different sectors of the economy. Although total real income will fall, several sectors may realize individual gains. Consider Figure 34.6. Though total real income falls from cell I ($50) to cell IV ($48), the auto sector's income rises (from $30 to $31). In this case the textile sector bears the brunt of tariff protection, and the auto sector has a compelling interest in obtaining protective tariffs. The sectors of the economy that are most adept at manipulating the political process will be least willing to accept free trade.

Thus the case for free trade is a subtle one. As always, special-interest groups—entrepreneurs, labor organizations, consumer groups—will pursue their individual interests, competing for favors and benefits the same way they compete in the marketplace. Yet if all are to be treated equally by government, we must choose between free trade for all and protection for all. Economists generally choose free trade for all, because of its obvious benefits to the nation as a whole. There are some legitimate exceptions to that rule, such as the required domestic production of public goods, which are discussed below. Yet even trade restrictions necessary for the public good are abused by those who would secure protection for private purposes.

The Case for Restricted Trade

Proponents of tariffs rarely argue publicly that they will serve private interests, raise prices, and reduce the availability of goods. Instead, they typically advocate tariffs as the most efficient means of accomplishing some national objective. Any private benefits that would accrue to protected industries are generally portrayed as insignificant side effects.

But though most arguments in favor of tariffs camouflage the underlying issues, one is partially valid. It has to do with the maintenance of national security.

The Need for National Security

Protariff arguments based on national security stress the need for a strong defense industry. If imports are completely unrestricted, certain industries

	Textile Industry Without Tariff Protection	Textile Industry With Tariff Protection
Automobile Industry Without Tariff Protection	Cell I Real Income, Textile — $20 Real Income, Auto — $30	Cell II Real Income, Textile — $23 Real Income, Auto — $25
Automobile Industry With Tariff Protection	Cell III Real Income, Textile — $15 Real Income, Auto — $34	Cell IV Real Income, Textile — $17 Real Income, Auto — $31

Figure 34.6. Effects of Tariff Protection on Individual Industries: Case 2.
In this more realistic case, the auto industry gains from tariff protection, even if both sectors are protected (cell IV). The textile industry's income falls from $20 (cell I) to $17 (cell IV). But the auto industry's income rises from $30 (cell I) to $31 (cell IV). Thus the auto industry has no incentive to agree to the elimination of tariffs.

needed in time of war or other national emergency could be undersold and run out of business by foreign competitors. In an emergency, the United States would then be dependent on possibly hostile foreign suppliers for essential defense equipment. (Although the nation could convert to production of war-related goods, the conversion process might be prohibitively lengthy and complex.) Tariffs may create inefficiencies in the allocation of world resources, but that is one of the costs a nation must bear to maintain a strong national defense.

Given the unsteady popularity of U.S. foreign policy and the uncertain support of allies, this argument has some merit. Other nations, like Israel, have found that they cannot count on the support of all their allies in time of war. Because France disagreed with Israeli policy in the Middle East, it held up shipment of spare parts for planes it had sold to Israel earlier. The United States could conceivably find itself in a similar position if it relies on foreign firms for planes, firearms, and oil.

Special-interest groups can easily abuse the national defense argument for tariffs. The textile industry, for example, promotes itself as a ready source of combat uniforms during wartime. Even candle manufacturers have petitioned Congress for increased tariff protection, on the grounds that candles are "a product required in the national defense."[2] In years past, U.S. oil producers, contending that a healthy domestic oil industry is vital to the national defense, have lobbied for protection from foreign oil imports. But although few would dispute the need for a reliable source of oil in wartime, the effects of a tariff are not entirely straightforward. By making foreign oil more expensive, a tariff increases consumption of domestic oil. Since oil is a finite resource, a tariff can ultimately make the United States more dependent on foreign energy sources in time of emergency.

Recent history illustrates the danger of dependence on foreign suppliers. In 1973, the OPEC oil cartel used U.S. dependence on its oil reserves as a bargaining tool in its efforts to reduce U.S. support for Israel. President Gerald Ford responded in 1974 by supporting a tariff on imported oil, to stimulate exploration for new domestic energy reserves. If the United States could become energy independent by the end of the 1980s, Ford argued, it would reduce the threat of political blackmail from the Middle East. And in 1983, for the same reason, the Reagan administration granted tariff protection to specialty steel products, which are used extensively in high-technology defense systems.

Other Arguments

Most of the other arguments in support of tariffs are weak from a practical as well as a theoretical perspective. It is sometimes argued that because workers are paid less in foreign countries, U.S. industries cannot hope to compete with foreign imports. But trade depends on the relative costs of production, not absolute wage rates in various nations. U.S. wages may be quite high in either absolute or relative terms. But if U.S. workers are more productive than others, the costs of production can be lower in the United States than elsewhere.

The important point is what tariffs do to trade. In an earlier example of trade in textiles and beef, the United States was more efficient than Japan in the production of both products. That is, generally speaking, fewer resources were required to produce those goods in the United States than in Japan. Very possibly, the incomes of textile and beef workers would be higher in the United States than in Japan. But because Japanese firms had

---

2. "Petition of the Candlemakers—1951," in *Readings in Economics*, ed. Paul Samuelson (New York: McGraw-Hill, 1973), 7th ed., p. 237.

a comparative cost advantage in textiles (measured in terms of the number of units of beef forgone for each textile unit), they were able to undersell textile firms in the United States. If the U.S. imposed tariffs or quotas on imported textiles because Japan had a comparative advantage in that product, it would destroy the basis for trade between the two nations. Reducing imports will tend to reduce exports, at least in the long run.

A second questionable argument for tariffs is based on the faulty idea that the United States loses when money flows overseas in payment for imports. As Abraham Lincoln is reported to have said, "I don't know much about the tariff, but this I do know. When we trade with other countries, we get the goods and they get the money. When we trade with ourselves, we get the goods and the money."

Lincoln was clearly right when he said he did not know much about the tariff. He failed to recognize the real income benefits of international trade, which are reduced by tariffs. He seems to have confused the nation's welfare with its monetary holdings. It is true that if Americans buy goods from abroad, they get the goods and foreigners get the money.[3] But what are foreigners going to do with the money they receive? If they never spend it, Americans will be better off, for they will have gotten some foreign goods in exchange for some paper bills, which are relatively cheap to print. At some point, however, foreign exporters will want to get something concrete in return for their labor and materials. They will use their dollars to buy goods from U.S. manufacturers. Again, trade is a give-and-take process, in which benefits flow to both sides.

A third argument often made is that foreign nations impose tariffs on U.S. goods; unless we respond in kind, foreign producers will have the advantage in both markets. This argument has a significant flaw. By restricting their imports, foreign nations reduce their ability to sell to the United States and other nations. To buy Japanese goods, for instance, Americans need yen. They get yen by selling to Japan. If Japan reduces its imports from the United States, Americans will have fewer yen to buy Japanese goods. So the Japanese are restricting their own exports with their tariffs. They harm themselves as well as Americans. If Americans respond to their actions by imposing tariffs of their own, they will reduce trade even further. The harm is compounded, not negated.

One sound reason for increasing tariffs is to strengthen our bargaining position in international trade conferences. By matching foreign restrictions, the United States may be able to force a multilateral reduction of tariffs. To the extent that all tariffs are reduced by such a strategy, world trade will be stimulated.

According to the fourth argument, tariffs increase workers' employment opportunities. If the government imposes tariffs on imported goods, the demand for American goods will rise. More workers will have jobs and can spend their income on goods and services produced by other Americans.

---

3. Actually, the transaction may not involve the transfer of paper money. It is more likely—as explained in the next chapter—that payment will be made by transferring funds from one bank account to another. The importer's bank balance will drop, and the exporter's bank balance will increase.

Perspectives in Economics: The Pros and Cons of Textile Protection

Import controls are a highly controversial issue in states like North and South Carolina, where foreign competition seriously threatens the textile industry, which dominates the local employment market. The following are typical arguments for and against protection, as advanced by representatives of the textile industry and the Reagan administration. They illustrate not only the different viewpoints Americans may take on such an issue, but the extent to which opponents often talk at cross-purposes.

The Case for Import Restrictions

The U.S. government has an obligation to encourage private enterprise to provide jobs for American citizens. We cannot remain a world power, or provide assistance to our allies and to developing countries, if our basic industries are crippled by competition from state-supported foreign industries. Currently the American market is inundated with textiles produced in countries where labor is much cheaper than in the United States. We aren't asking for protection—just the opportunity for fair competition with foreign producers.

Specifically, the government should:

Roll back import quotas to 1983 levels.

Reduce by one-third the import quotas of the Big Six: Taiwan, South Korea, Hong Kong, China, Japan, and Italy.

Limit imports to no more than 20 percent of domestic sales in every category.

Enforce to the letter restrictive trade agreements already on the books.

Work to establish worldwide quotas that would curb overall import growth, allowing imports to grow no faster than domestic markets.

Establish an enforceable import licensing system, with strong penalties for violations of agreements.

Reciprocate promptly when other nations restrict the importation of American products.

It is true that in the short run, more workers are likely to be hired because of tariffs. But in the long run reduced imports will result in reduced exports. The market for U.S. goods will shrink, increasing unemployment in the export industries.

Furthermore, if Americans reduce their demand for foreign goods to increase employment in the United States, their domestic recession will be transmitted to other nations. With fewer sales of foreign goods, fewer workers will be needed in foreign industries. Foreign governments may retaliate by imposing tariffs of their own. Tariffs will temporarily increase their employment levels and can be used as a bargaining tool in trade negotiations as well. The end result will be a reduction in total worldwide production and real income.

Finally, tariff advocates sometimes claim that new industries deserve protection, because they are too small to compete with established foreign firms. If protected by tariffs, these new industries can expand their scale of production, lower their production costs, and eventually compete with foreign producers. But it is very difficult for a government to determine which new industries may eventually be able to compete with foreign rivals. Over the long period of time that an industry needs to mature,

Reduce the budget deficit, which is keeping the value of the dollar artificially high and encouraging imports.

These steps would allow U.S. companies time to modernize and produce better-quality products and consumer service; to develop new uses for products; and to work with the state and federal governments to encourage product research.

The Case Against Import Restrictions

Protection from imports is obviously beneficial to parts of the textile industry, but by no means all of it. And measures that may be good for the textile industry are not necessarily good for the general economy. The benefits of trade protectionism are received by executives, stockholders, and workers in the textile industry—at the expense of other Americans. For protectionism drives up the prices of both foreign and domestic textiles, de-

pressing consumers' real incomes. And many consumers earn less than those who benefit from protection.

Tariffs and quotas in one industry, like textiles, increase the costs of other industries, like ready-made apparel. Because they inspire retaliation by other countries, they make it more difficult for still other industries—for example, the soybean industry—to export their products. Protectionism also reduces the incentive of producers to increase their productivity and maintain their competitiveness. It retards economic diversification, encouraging a nation to stake its economic future on industries that are not fully competitive. In short, protectionism destroys American jobs just as surely as it saves them.

The U.S. textile industry buys a great deal of machinery from abroad, because foreign-made machinery is a better buy than domestically made machinery. The case against protectionism is simply a case for granting all consumers the same right to buy from abroad.

conditions, including the technology of production, may change significantly. For a so-called infant industry to become truly competitive, furthermore, it must develop a comparative cost advantage, not just economies of scale.

Moreover, the mere likelihood that a firm will eventually be able to compete with its foreign rivals does not in itself warrant protection. Not until firms have become established will consumers receive the benefit of lower prices. In the interim, tariff protection hurts consumers by raising the prices they must pay. Proponents of protection must be able to show that the future benefits to be gained by establishing an industry exceed the current costs of protecting it.

Finally, if a firm can expand, cover all its costs of production, and eventually compete with its foreign rivals, private entrepreneurs are not likely to miss the opportunity to invest in it. Through the stock and bond markets, firms with growth potential will be able to secure the funds they need for expansion. If a firm cannot raise capital from private sources, it may be because the return on the investment is too low in relation to the risk. Why should the government accept risks that the private market will not accept?

Summary and Extensions

The schedule of tariffs applied to goods coming into the United States is now larger than the Los Angeles telephone directory. Surely all those tariffs were not imposed in pursuit of the national interest, as in the maintenance of a strong defense industry. Most probably reflect the political influence of special-interest groups.

The case against such special-interest tariffs was wittily stated by the nineteenth-century French economist Frederic Bastiat. Pretending to represent the candle manufacturers of his day, he wrote to the French Chamber of Deputies in 1845:

> Gentlemen:
> . . . We are subjected to the intolerable competition of a foreign rival, who enjoys, it would seem, such superior facilities for the production of light, that he is enabled to *inundate* our *national market* at so exceedingly reduced price, that, the moment he makes his appearance, he draws off all customs for us; and thus an important branch of French industry . . . is suddenly reduced to a state of complete stagnation. This rival is no other than the sun.
>
> Our petition is, that it would please your honorable body to pass a law whereby shall be directed the shutting up of all windows, doors, skylights, shutters, curtains, in a word, all openings, holes, chinks, and fissures through which light of the sun . . . penetrates into our dwellings.[4]

Bastiat suggests that passage of his proposed law would be consistent with the Chamber's attempts to check the importation of "coal, iron, cheese, and goods of foreign manufacture, merely because and even in proportion as their price approaches zero."

Clearly, tariffs force consumers to pay more for domestic goods. To that extent they reduce aggregate real income. Unfortunately, because they benefit special-interest groups—and because the political process is easily exploited by special-interest groups—tariffs, like taxes, are probably inevitable.

Major Conclusions

1. When two nations trade with each other, both parties gain from the transaction.
2. Even if one nation has an absolute advantage in the production of all goods and services, trade between nations can be mutually beneficial.

---

4. Frederic Bastiat, "A Petition," *Economic Sophisms* (Irvington-on-Hudson, N.Y.: Foundation for Economic Education, 1964; originally published 1845), pp. 56–60.

3. Although nations as a whole always gain from international trade, not all individuals do. Firms that produce for export can gain from foreign trade, along with their employees. But free trade can hurt firms that must compete with foreign producers. And consumers who buy products that are exported must pay higher prices than they would in the absence of trade.

4. Tariffs and quotas reduce the supply of goods on the market, raising prices and encouraging domestic production.

5. Producers who face foreign competition can benefit substantially from, and have a private interest in, tariff or quota restrictions on imports. Consumers have little incentive to oppose tariff legislation, for the cost of opposition is generally greater than the benefit to be gained from it (slightly lower prices).

6. Tariffs and quotas on imports reduce international trade, and therefore the aggregate incomes of the nations that engage in international commerce.

7. Tariffs and quotas sometimes serve the national interest, especially where national defense and security are concerned. Most other arguments in favor of tariffs are seriously flawed.

Questions to Ponder

1. Using supply and demand curves, show how a U.S. tariff on a foreign-made good will affect the price and quantity sold in the country of origin.

2. How will an import quota on sugar affect the price of sugar produced and sold domestically? Sugar produced domestically and sold abroad?

3. If a tariff is imposed on imported autos and the domestic demand for autos rises, what will happen to auto imports? If a quota is imposed on imported autos and the demand for autos increases, what will happen to auto imports?

4. Given the following production capabilities for cheese and bread, which nation will export cheese to the other? What might be a mutually beneficial exchange rate for cheese and bread?

	Cheese		Bread
France	40 units	or	60 units
Italy	10 units	or	5 units

5. "Tariffs on imported textiles increase the employment opportunities and incomes of domestic textile workers. They therefore increase aggregate employment and income." Evaluate this statement.

Central Question

How do firms based in nations with different currencies engage in international trade?

Key Terms

International exchange rate

Depreciation of the dollar

Appreciation of the dollar

Floating (flexible) exchange rate system

Fixed exchange rate system

Chapter 35

International Finance

The goal of every science is a
conceptual model which shows
how the pieces of its universe
are related. Economists seek to
become the Copernicuses of the
international financial system,
but their task is complicated
since this system has changed
substantially in the last one
hundred years and continues to
change.

Robert Aliber

*P*eople rarely use barter in trade. Exchanging one toy for two pens or three pots for the rear end of a steer simply is not practical. Because the bartering seller must also be a buyer, buyers and sellers may have to incur very substantial costs to find one another, even in the domestic market. When people are hundreds or thousands of miles apart, and separated by national boundaries and foreign cultures and languages, as they are in international trade, barter would be all the more complicated. We rarely see exporters acting as importers, exchanging specific exports for specific imports.

In the domestic economy, money reduces the cost of making exchanges. The seller of pots needs only to find a buyer willing to pay with bills, coins, or a check. He does not have to accept goods that may be difficult to store, use, and trade. In the international economy too, money facilitates trade, but well over a hundred different national currencies are in use. The French have the franc; the Japanese, the yen; the Americans, the dollar. To deal with this complication, a system of international exchanges emerged in which importers pay for the goods they buy in their own currency, but the exporters they deal with receive payment in their currency. How this system works, and the problems inherent in it, are the subjects of this chapter.

The Process of International Monetary Exchange

Imagine you own a small gourmet shop that carries special cheeses. You may buy your cheese either domestically—cheddar from New York, Monterey jack from California—or abroad. If you buy from a domestic firm, it is easy to negotiate the deal and make payment. Since the price of cheese is quoted in dollars and the domestic firm expects payment in dollars, you can pay the same way you pay other bills—by writing a personal check. Only one national currency is involved.

Purchasing cheese from a French cheese maker is a little more complicated, for two reasons. First, the price of the cheese will be quoted in francs. Second, you will want to pay in dollars, but the French cheese maker must be paid in francs. Either you must exchange your dollars for francs, or the cheese maker must convert them for you. At some point, currencies must be exchanged at some recognized exchange rate.

International Exchange Rates

International exchange rate: the price of one national currency stated in terms of another national currency.

Before you buy, you will want to compare the prices of French and domestic cheeses. You must convert the franc price of cheese into its dollar equivalent. To do that, you need to know the international exchange rate between dollars and francs. The **international exchange rate** is the price of one national currency (like the franc) stated in terms of another national currency (like the dollar). In other words, the international exchange rate is the dollar price you must pay for each franc you buy. Table 35.1 gives the dollar prices of several foreign currencies as of the end of February,

Table 35.1. Selected International Exchange Rates (dollar prices of foreign currencies), February 28, 1985.

	Dollar Price of Foreign Currency
British pound	$1.0825
Canadian dollar	0.7246
French franc	0.0982
Japanese yen	0.0039
Spanish peseta	0.0055
Swedish krona	0.1060
West German mark	0.2996

Source: *Wall Street Journal*, March 1, 1985, p. 39.

1985. The franc was then worth almost $0.10, and the British pound cost a little more than $1.08.

Once you know the current exchange rate, conversion of currencies is not difficult. Assume that you want to buy F5,000 (read "5,000 francs") worth of cheese, and that the international exchange rate between dollars and francs is $0.10 (that is, $1 sells for F10). F5,000 at $0.10 apiece will cost you $500.

The international exchange rate determines the dollar price of the foreign goods you want to buy. A different exchange rate would have changed the dollar price of cheese. For instance, suppose the exchange rate rose from $0.10 = F1 to $0.20 = F1. In the jargon of international finance, such a change represents a depreciation (sometimes called a devaluation) of the dollar. A **depreciation of the dollar** (or any other national currency) is a reduction in purchasing power in terms of other national currencies. The dollar is now cheaper in terms of francs: it takes fewer francs (F5) to buy a dollar than previously (F10).

The same change represents an appreciation of the franc. An **appreciation of the dollar** (or any other national currency) is an increase in purchasing power in terms of other national currencies. Each franc will now buy a larger fraction of a dollar—$0.20 as opposed to $0.10. From the perspective of the gourmet shop, the important point is that at the higher exchange rate, the dollar price of the cheese purchase is $1,000 ($0.20 × 5,000). If the exchange rate fell from $0.10 = F1 to $0.05 = F1, the price of the French cheese would decline to $250.

As you can see, your willingness to buy French cheese depends very much on the franc price of cheese and the exchange rate. If the franc price of cheese increases or decreases, your dollar price increases or decreases. Changes in the dollar price of francs have a similar effect. If the dollar depreciates (that is, if the price of francs in dollars rises), the dollar price of French cheese rises. Very likely you will be inclined to import less, since at the higher price your customers will buy less. If the dollar appreciates (that is, if the price of francs falls), the dollar price of French

Depreciation of the dollar (or any other national currency): a reduction in purchasing power in terms of other national currencies.

Appreciation of the dollar (or any other national currency): an increase in purchasing power in terms of other national currencies.

Table 35.2. The Effects of Depreciation and Appreciation of the Dollar on U.S. Exports and Imports

	Depreciation of Dollar	Appreciation of Dollar
Price of exports	Decrease	Increase
Total dollar value of exports	Increase	Decrease
Price of imports	Increase	Decrease
Total dollar value of imports	Decrease	Increase

---

cheese falls. Very likely you will import more, since you can lower your own price and sell more. In general, a depreciation of the dollar discourages imports; an appreciation of the dollar encourages imports. (The results of changes in the international rate of exchange are summarized in Table 35.2.)

During the first half of this decade the U.S. dollar appreciated in relation to most major currencies. The dollar price of the French franc, for instance, began to tumble in the early 1980s, falling from about twenty-four cents in 1980 to just above eleven cents in late 1984 (see Figure 35.1). As the dollar value of the franc fell, French goods and travel in France became less expensive for Americans. U.S. goods and foreign travel in the United States became more expensive for the French.

The Exchange of National Currencies

Assume you have figured the dollar price of cheese using the exchange rate and find it satisfactory. Since your American customers pay for their groceries in dollars, that is the only currency you have to make the payment. Yet cheese makers in France need francs to pay for their groceries. Therefore the French cheese exporter must ultimately be paid in francs.

How can you make payment in dollars while the French exporter is paid in francs? A bank will exchange your dollars for you. Banks deal in national currencies for the same reason that business people trade in commodities: to make money. An automobile dealer buys cars at a low price with the hope of selling them at a higher price. Banks do the same thing, except that their commodities are national currencies. They buy dollars and pay for them in francs or yen, with the idea of selling them at a profit.

If you pay for your French cheese in dollars, you write a check against your checking account and send it to the French firm.[1] The French cheese maker will accept the check knowing that your dollars can be traded for francs (that is, sold to a French bank) at the current rate of exchange. If

---

1. Instruments of exchange other than checks are often used in international transactions. The process, however, is the same.

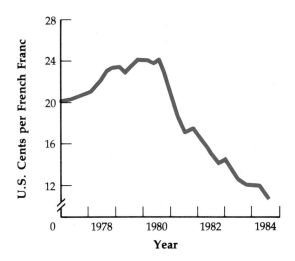

Figure 35.1. The Changing Dollar Price of the Franc.
The dollar price of the French franc has fluctuated considerably in recent years. From a high of about 24 cents in 1979, it fell to just above 11 cents in the third quarter of 1984.

the exchange rate is $0.10 = F1, and you have sent the cheese maker a check for $500, the exporter will receive F5,000 for your check from the French bank. Remember that banks, even foreign ones, have accounts with other banks, just as individuals do. The French bank will deposit your check with its U.S. banker. Your bank balance will fall, and the French bank's balance at the U.S. institution will rise. Then the French bank will sell (or trade) the dollars it has on account for francs.

In the process of buying and selling dollars, the French bank may make a profit. Suppose, for example, that the French bank buys dollars from the French cheese maker at a rate of $0.10 = F1 (or $1 = F10), paying F5,000 for $500. It can then sell its dollars to a French importer for a higher franc price—say $0.09 = F1 (or $1 = F11.11). It will receive F5,555 for its $500—a net gain of F555.

This hypothetical purchase of French cheese leads to an important observation. Any U.S. import, be it cheese or watches, will increase the dollar holdings of foreign banks. So will American expenditures abroad, whether for tours or for foreign stocks and bonds. Americans must have francs for such transactions; therefore they must offer American dollars in exchange. In most instances, foreign banks end up holding the dollars that Americans have sold.

In the same way, U.S. exports reduce the dollar holdings of foreign banks. Exports are typically paid for out of the dollar accounts of foreign banks. Foreign expenditures on trips to the United States or on the stocks and bonds of U.S. corporations have the same effect. They reduce the dollar holdings of foreign banks and increase the foreign currency holdings of U.S. banks. If American expenditures abroad exceed foreign expenditures here, the dollar holdings of foreign banks will rise—and vice versa.

If American expenditures abroad exceed foreign expenditures here for a long time, foreign banks will eventually accumulate all the dollars they can reasonably expect to use—that is, to sell back to their citizens for the purchase of American goods. Foreign banks then have several options. First, they may sell their dollar holdings to other foreign commercial banks in exchange for francs, marks, or krona. Second, they may sell their dollars to their government—or, more properly, to their government's central bank (for example, the Bank of France).

But the market may already be saturated with dollars. No one, including the central bank, may want to buy dollars at the going price, $0.10 = F1 in our illustration. In that case, foreign banks can induce people to buy dollars by lowering their price. For instance, they can alter the exchange rate from $0.10 = F1 to $0.15 = F1. In so doing they increase the price of francs and decrease (depreciate) the price of dollars.

A change in the exchange rate will have several effects, all tending to reduce the number of dollars coming onto the international money market. As explained earlier, the change will make French goods more expensive for Americans to buy. Thus it will tend to reduce U.S. imports, and accordingly the number of dollars that must be exchanged for foreign currencies. Depreciation will also tend to reduce the price of American goods to foreigners. For instance, at an exchange rate of $0.10 = F1, the franc price of a $1 million American computer is F10 million. At an exchange rate of $0.15 = F1, the franc price of the same computer is F6.66 million— a substantial reduction in price. To buy American goods at the new lower franc price, the French will increase their demand for dollars. Again, the quantity of dollars being offered on the money market will fall, and the growth in foreign dollar holdings will be checked.

Determination of the Exchange Rate

National currencies have a market value—that is, a price—because individuals, firms, and governments use them to buy foreign goods, services, and securities. There is a market demand for a national currency like the franc. Furthermore, the demand for the franc (or any other currency) slopes downward, like curve D in Figure 35.2. To see why, look at the market for francs from the point of view of a U.S. resident. As the dollar price of the franc falls, the price of French goods to Americans also falls. As a result Americans will want to buy more French goods. They will require a larger quantity of francs to complete their transactions.

The supply of francs coming onto the market reflects the French people's demand for American goods, services, and securities. To get American goods, the French need dollars. They must pay for those dollars with francs, and in doing so they supply francs to the international money market. As the dollar price of the franc rises, the price of American goods to the French falls. To buy a larger quantity of American goods at the lower franc price, the French need more dollars; they must offer more francs to get them. Therefore the quantity of francs supplied on the market

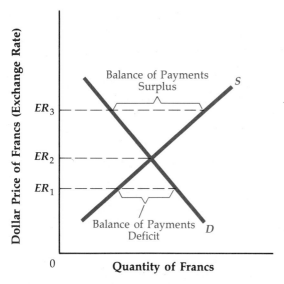

Figure 35.2. Supply and Demand for Francs on the International Currency Market. The international exchange rate between the dollar and the franc is determined by the forces of supply and demand. If the exchange rate is below equilibrium at ER_1, the quantity of francs demanded, shown by the demand curve, will exceed the quantity supplied, shown by the supply curve. Competitive pressure will push the exchange rate up. If the exchange rate is above equilibrium at ER_3, the quantity supplied will exceed the quantity demanded, and competitive pressure will push the exchange rate down. Thus the price of a foreign currency is determined in much the same way as the price of any other commodity.

rises. Thus the supply curve for francs slopes upward to the right, like curve S in Figure 35.2.

The buyers and sellers of francs make up what is loosely called the international money market in francs. Banks are very much involved in such markets. They buy francs from the sellers (suppliers) and sell to the buyers (demanders). As in other markets, the interaction of suppliers and demanders determines the market price. That is, given the supply and demand curves in Figure 35.2, in a competitive market the dollar price of the franc will move toward the intersection of the supply and demand curves. The equilibrium price, or exchange rate, will be ER_2, the price at which the quantity of francs supplied exactly equals the quantity of francs demanded.

At the market equilibrium point there is no build-up of dollars or francs in the accounts of foreign banks. French and U.S. banks have no reason to modify the exchange rate to encourage or discourage the purchase or sale of either currency. To use a financial expression, the net balance of payments coming into and going out of each nation is zero.

If the exchange rate is below equilibrium level—say ER_1—the quantity of francs demanded will exceed the quantity supplied (see Figure 35.2).

An imbalance in the balance of payments will develop. Or in the jargon of international finance, the United States will develop a balance of payments deficit—a shortfall in the quantity of a foreign currency supplied. (This is a conceptual definition. When it comes to defining the balance of payments deficit in a way that can be measured by the Department of Commerce, economists are in considerable disagreement.)

As in other markets, this imbalance will eventually right itself. Because of the excess demand for francs, French banks will accumulate excess dollar balances. French banks will have more dollars than they can sell and fewer francs than they need. Competitive pressure will then push the exchange rate back up to ER_2. People who cannot buy francs at ER_1 will offer a higher price. As the price of francs rises, French goods will become less attractive to Americans, and the quantity of francs demanded will fall. Conversely American goods will become more attractive to the French, and the quantity of francs supplied will rise.

Similarly, at an exchange rate higher than ER_2—say ER_3—the quantity of francs supplied will exceed the quantity demanded (see Figure 35.2). A balance of payments surplus—an excess quantity of a foreign currency supplied—will develop. The surplus will not last forever, however. Eventually the exchange rate will fall back toward ER_2, causing an increase in the quantity of francs demanded and a decrease in the quantity supplied. In short, in a free foreign currency market, the price of a currency is determined in the same way the prices of other commodities are determined.

Market Adjustment to Changes in Money Market Conditions

By modifying exchange rates to correct for imbalances in payments, the money market can accommodate vast changes in the economic conditions of nations engaged in trade. A good example is the way the market handles a change in consumption patterns.

Suppose American preferences for French goods increase for some reason. The demand for francs will rise, because Americans will need more francs to buy the additional French goods they desire. If, as in Figure 35.3, the U.S. demand for francs shifts from D_1 to D_2, the quantity of francs demanded at the old equilibrium exchange rate of ER_1 will exceed the quantity supplied. Those who cannot buy more francs at ER_1 will offer to pay a higher price. The exchange rate will rise toward the new equilibrium level of ER_2. As the dollar depreciates in value, the imbalance in payments is eliminated.

Now suppose Americans' real incomes rise. Assuming that consumption goes up with real income, they will be likely to demand more foreign imports, both directly and in the form of domestic goods that incorporate foreign parts or materials. Either way, an increase in real incomes leads to an increase in the demand for foreign currencies. Again the demand for francs will rise, as in Figure 35.3. The exchange rate will rise with it to bring the quantity supplied into line with the quantity demanded.

Figure 35.3. Effect of an Increase in Demand for Francs.
An increase in the demand for francs will shift the demand curve from D_1 to D_2. At the initial equilibrium exchange rate, ER_1, a shortage will develop. Competition among buyers will push the exchange rate up to the new equilibrium level, ER_2.

A change in the rate of inflation can have a similar effect on the exchange rate. If the inflation rates are about the same in two nations that trade with each other, the exchange rate between their currencies will remain stable, *ceteris paribus*. Because the relative prices of goods in the two nations stay the same, people will have no incentive to switch from domestic to imported goods, or vice versa. If one nation's inflation rate exceeds another's, however, the relative prices of foreign and domestic goods change. If prices increase faster in the United States, for example, Americans will want to buy more foreign goods and fewer domestic goods. Foreigners, on the other hand, will have an incentive to buy more goods from their own countries, where prices are not rising as fast as in the United States. In sum, a higher U.S. inflation rate spells a rise in the demand for foreign currencies, a fall in their supply, and a depreciation of the dollar.

Figure 35.4 illustrates the process. As U.S. demand for foreign goods rises, the demand curve for francs shifts outward, from D_1 to D_2. But as foreign demand for U.S. products falls, the supply curve for francs shifts to the left, from S_1 to S_2. At the initial equilibrium exchange rate of ER_1, a shortage of francs will develop. The exchange rate will rise to ER_2, eliminating the shortage and reestablishing balance in the money market. At the higher rate, Americans must pay a higher dollar price for foreign goods. The rise in the exchange rate has evened out the difference in the two nations' inflation rates.

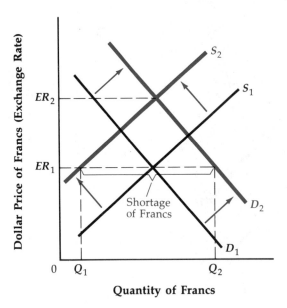

Figure 35.4. Effect of an Increase in Inflation on the Supply and Demand for Francs.
If the rate of inflation is higher in the United States than in France, the demand for francs will rise from D_1 to D_2, while the supply of francs will contract from S_1 to S_2. The dollar price of francs will rise from ER_1 to ER_2.

Control of the Exchange Rate: The Fixed-Rate System

Floating (flexible) exchange rate system: an international monetary exchange system in which the prices of currencies are determined by competitive market forces.

Fixed exchange rate system: an international monetary exchange system in which the prices of currencies are established and maintained by governments.

So far our analysis of the international money market has assumed a floating, or flexible, system of exchange. A **floating (flexible) exchange rate system** is one in which the prices of currencies are determined by competitive market forces. Until 1971, however, international exchange rates were controlled by governments. Rates were not permitted to move in response to changes in supply and demand. Because rates were fixed for long periods of time by government decree, this system is generally referred to as a fixed exchange rate system. A **fixed exchange rate system** is one in which the prices of currencies are established and maintained by governments. Though the fixed-rate system is no longer in use among major nations, it merits some discussion because of its historical importance.

The fixed exchange rate has one advantage over the floating rate: it is stable. Because even a small change in the exchange rate can cause significant losses to people who have already concluded business deals, a flexible exchange rate can increase the risks involved in international trade. For example, suppose you agree to purchase cheese at an exchange rate of $0.10 = F1. You promise to pay the exporter $500, and the French cheese maker expects to receive F5,000. But by the time you send the check, the exchange rate has moved to $0.11 = F1. The exporter will now receive only F4,545 ($500 ÷ 0.11). He loses F455.

If the exchange rate moves in the opposite direction, of course, the exporter will gain. In addition, the French cheese maker can hedge against short-term losses by agreeing, at the time he closes the deal, to sell the proceeds at a given exchange rate, perhaps a fraction of a cent less than the current rate of $.10 = F1. In long-term deals, however, traders inevitably risk losing money because of changes in exchange rates. They incur a risk cost that is translated into higher prices. Under a fixed-rate system, exchange rates move only periodically. The risk cost is reduced, and the prices of foreign goods can be lower.

Like any other form of price control, however, control of foreign exchange rates creates its own problems. If the exchange rate is fixed—at ER_1 in Figure 35.3, for example—and the supply and demand curves remain stable, there is no problem. But neither is there any need for government to fix the rate. It will remain at ER_1 as long as the supply and demand curves for currency stay put.

Problems can develop when market conditions change but the exchange rate is fixed. If the demand for francs increases from D_1 to D_2 in Figure 35.3, a shortage of francs will develop on the international money market. Those who want francs at the fixed price will be unable to get all they want. The government may have to ration the available francs and police the market against black marketeering. For if black markets are not controlled, the price of currency will rise—illegally perhaps, but it will rise nonetheless. In the end the exchange rate will not really be controlled.

Monetary Adjustment Under the Fixed-Rate System

Under the conditions just described, the United States government can keep the exchange rate fixed if it finds some way to fill the gap between the quantity of francs supplied and demanded. Under the fixed exchange system, governments hold currency reserves for just this purpose. Accordingly, the U.S. government sells some of its francs at the officially established price (ER_1 in Figure 35.3), eliminating the upward pressure on the exchange rate. To do so, however, the government must have collected reserves at times when the quantity of francs supplied exceeded the quantity demanded. During such periods the government generally buys the excess francs with dollars specially created for the purchase.

If a shortage of francs persists, however—if the imbalance in the balance of payments is fundamental rather than temporary—it can only be corrected by a shift in market conditions. An increase in the demand for U.S. goods, for instance, might correct a persistent imbalance. Until market conditions change, maintaining sufficient currency reserves can become a real problem. A persistent shortage of currencies, often referred to as a liquidity problem, can be remedied temporarily in several ways.

Perspectives in Economics: The World Debt Crisis

Early in the 1980s, American news magazines began carrying articles on the dramatic rise in debt owed by third-world nations, including Brazil, Mexico, and Argentina. And indeed, when measured in current U.S. dollars, the growth of those three countries' debt was staggering (see Figure 35.5). Between 1972 and 1981 their combined debt grew at an average annual rate of 26 percent. In just nine years, their total debt expanded eight times. No wonder that two of those nations, Argentina and Mexico, were occasionally unable to meet their interest payments.

Soon policymakers began to fear that some countries might default on their debt. The Reagan administration involved itself in the controversy when it became known that several U.S. banks, including the Chase Manhattan Bank of New York, had made sizable loans to the governments of foreign countries. Concerned that default might bankrupt these banks, weakening public confidence in the entire banking system, the U.S. government in 1983 agreed with other members of the International Monetary Fund to an increase in IMF loans. The action gave debt-strapped third-world nations more funds at lower interest rates. (IMF loans are made at below-market rates.)

Critics opposed the administration's efforts to ease the debt burden of foreign countries on several grounds. First, they charged, the IMF loans represented a thinly disguised bailout of U.S. banks that had made bad loans. In effect, U.S. tax dollars had been made available to other nations through the IMF, enabling them to pay the interest they owed U.S. banks.

Second, many banks had charged high interest rates on their foreign loans to compensate for the risk of default. Even if several of their loans went bad, income from their other loans should be sufficient to cover their losses.

Third, the seriousness of the debt crisis had been overblown. A nation's ability to repay its debt may be gauged by the ratio of its debt to its gross national product. Though the debt burdens of Brazil, Mexico, and Argentina rose in comparison with their GNP during much of the 1970s, their debt-GNP ratios began to fall toward the end of the decade (see Figure 35.6). They continued to fall or held steady through 1981.

Fourth, default would not enable a nation to walk away from its debt. It would simply require the debtor nation to find some other way of covering its debt payments besides current tax collections. A nation in default could sell some of its assets, whether land or nationalized industries. Or it could convert its debt to an equity interest in its assets. After all, debtor nations had used much of their borrowings to expand their capital base. From that perspective, the debt crisis was really a crisis in their willingness—not their ability—to make good on their debts.

Fifth, the government's remedy for the presumed debt crisis—subsidized loans from the IMF—could foster a real debt crisis. Low-interest loans might encourage debtor nations to go so far into debt that they could not extract themselves without further aid from the IMF—and indirectly, from U.S. taxpayers.

Proponents of government aid to developing countries, on the other hand, maintained that the third-world debt crisis was real. Many developing countries had had difficulty earning the money to make payments on their debt. Third-world nations tend to rely heavily on agricultural exports, whose prices were depressed in the early 1980s. From that perspective, IMF loans could be seen as a way of helping debtor nations through temporary hard times.

Proponents of aid charged also that U.S. banks and even some governments had urged developing countries to go into debt in the 1970s. Policymakers had apparently reasoned that greater debt meant greater demand for goods and services in developing countries—and thus greater sales of goods and services to them. The OPEC oil price hikes had also increased the indebtedness of third-world nations. To meet the rising oil prices of the mid-1970s, developing countries had to sell more goods and services abroad. At the same time, OPEC

Figure 35.5. Debt in Selected Third-World Nations, 1972–1981.
In current U.S. dollars, Brazil's debt rose from approximately $6 billion to $44 billion from 1972 to 1981. In the same period, Mexico's debt jumped from slightly under $4 billion to $42 billion. Argentina's debt grew more modestly, from just over $2 billion to over $10 billion.
Source: Jon Osborne, "Paper Crisis," *Reason* (May 1984), p. 31.

Figure 35.6. Debt as a Percentage of GNP in Selected Third-World Nations, 1972–1981.
Mexico's debt-to-GNP ratio jumped dramatically between 1972 and 1977, and then fell sharply after 1978. Brazil's debt-to-GNP ratio grew more gradually until 1980, then turned slightly downward. During the same period Argentina's debt-to-GNP ratio fluctuated.
Source: Jon Osborne, "Paper Crisis," *Reason* (May 1984), p. 32.

countries were earning substantially more from their oil exports than they wanted to spend on imports. They had money available for overseas investment, which they channeled to both third-world and developed nations through U.S. banks.

The controversy over what should be done to help developing countries manage their debt arose partly because people interpreted the facts differently. The magnitude of the problem, and the capacity of third-world nations to handle it, remain matters of debate. So does the question of who should be held responsible for the debt—the developing countries that incurred it, or the banks that made the loans to them.

Gold Reserves

For centuries governments have used gold as an international monetary reserve, defining their national currencies in terms of it. The U.S. government might establish the price of gold at $35 an ounce, for example; the French government, at F350 an ounce. In case of a currency shortage, these gold reserves can be used to fill the gap between quantity supplied and demanded. If a shortage of francs develops on the money market, for instance, the U.S. government can sell some of its gold to France and receive F350 for each ounce. The government can then sell the francs on the money market, filling the gap at the official exchange rate.

In practice, the process may not work exactly that way. Given the shortage of francs, foreign banks may continue to exchange francs for dollars and then sell their dollars to the Bank of France, which will exchange them for gold. The final outcome is the same, however. Gold is traded for francs, and the shortage of francs is eliminated.

Conversely, if there is a shortage of dollars, the French government can keep the price of the dollar from rising above the official level by selling some of its gold to the United States. It then exchanges (sells) its dollars for francs.

Currency Reserves

From the 1930s until 1971, when exchange rates were allowed to float, most nations kept a combination of gold and currency as monetary reserves. Many kept the U.S. dollar, which has come to be accepted throughout the world as a form of exchange. A Brazilian exporter, for example, might accept dollars from a German importer, because he is confident that they can be converted into Brazilian currency.

Foreign banks too have been willing to hold large amounts of dollars, partly because of the dollar's acceptability in business transactions and partly because banks know foreigners will always demand a large variety of U.S. goods. Before 1971, banks could trade their dollars in for gold at any time. Since gold was more expensive to store, however, they chose to hold dollars. Note that these foreign banks got their dollars from the sale of goods and services to Americans. To the extent that they still hold them for the purpose of carrying out other transactions, people in the United States have struck a tremendous deal. They have traded money— a paper product relatively cheap to produce—for foreign textiles, automobiles, and appliances, which are much more expensive to produce.

The International Monetary Fund (IMF)

The International Monetary Fund (IMF) was created at the close of the Second World War to expand international reserves further. By depositing part of its gold reserves and a specified amount of its currency in the IMF, a nation receives the right to borrow other foreign currencies at a modest interest rate. It can then use those currencies to fill a gap between outgoing and incoming foreign payments. Borrowing rights are restricted to 125 percent of a nation's deposit with the IMF.

Suppose the United States' deposit is $1 billion. At the established exchange rates, the United States can borrow as much as $1.25 billion worth of francs, pounds, yen, or any other currency. When its need for extra reserves has slackened, the United States can pay back the currencies it has borrowed. The method works well. Over the years member nations have raised their deposits at the IMF, increasing the quantity of foreign currencies they can borrow.

Currency Swaps

At times nations have increased one another's currency reserves simply by trading their currencies. For instance, the United States might agree to swap some of its dollars for West German marks. Each nation then has more of the other's currency available to cover a balance of payments deficit, should one occur. In addition, during periods of international monetary crisis, when buyers and sellers of a particular currency no longer accept the official exchange rate, nations can lend money to each other. The borrowed funds can be used to fill a balance of payments gap and prevent the exchange rate from rising.

Reserves acquired through currency swaps are meant to be used only to correct temporary imbalances in a nation's international accounts, or to get it through financial difficulties. During periods when incoming payments exceed outgoing payments, nations are expected to rebuild their depleted reserves. In the 1960s, however, the system failed to work as expected. Some nations, particularly the United States and Great Britain, failed to correct their persistent balance of payment deficits. Once they got additional reserves, they used them up. In effect, the United States and Britain were using currency swaps to trade their paper currency for the goods and services of other nations.

To correct a fundamental imbalance of payments, a nation might adopt anti-inflationary policies or impose tariffs on imports. It might also take measures to improve the competitiveness of its industry. (More will be said on this subject later.)

Special Drawing Rights (SDRs)

Gold has been used for centuries as an international reserve. But it is expensive to mine and store. To use gold as a currency reserve, a nation must not only get it out of the ground, but go to the trouble and expense of storing it. And it must maintain expensive security systems to prevent the gold from being stolen. Though gold has an important role in international finance, its benefits come at considerable expense to all who use it.

Gold reserves have another disadvantage: they increase only as new gold is mined and distributed. Yet growth in world trade can quickly widen the gap between a nation's outgoing and incoming payments. If the exchange rate is to be held constant, the growing gap must be filled with a larger quantity of reserves. Unfortunately, growth in world trade can easily outstrip not only growth in gold reserves, but growth in reserves from other sources.

Fearing that currency imbalances might impede world trade, and recognizing the expense of increasing world gold reserves, members of the IMF developed plans for a new monetary reserve system, called Special Drawing Rights (SDRs) in the 1960s. Unlike other reserves, SDRs are merely bookkeeping entries in the IMF accounts. Once a nation has an SDR account, it can use SDRs to settle imbalances in any currency. It can sell some of its SDRs to France for francs (or to Germany for marks), and use the francs (marks) to fill the balance of payments gap. Because SDRs can be used much as gold is used, they are sometimes called paper gold.

Even though SDRs are only bookkeeping entries, they are a form of international money. The members of the IMF have agreed to accept SDRs in settlement of their accounts, just as they accepted gold in the past. Just as the general acceptability of the U.S. dollar gives the bills in your wallet value in domestic transactions, the general acceptability of SDRs gives them value. Money is what people will generally accept in trade.

Correcting a Persistent Balance of Payments Deficit

International reserves of gold, foreign currencies, and SDRs are useful in solving temporary balance of payment problems. But if outgoing payments exceed incoming payments for long, a nation's reserves will eventually run out. It will not be able to prop up the value of its currency without resorting to elaborate corrective measures, most of which are either economically inefficient or politically unacceptable.

Tax increases, expenditure decreases, and a reduction in the growth of the money stock may help to reduce inflation temporarily, but at the cost of a drop in total real income. The lower inflation rate will make domestically produced goods more attractive, both at home and abroad. And a lower aggregate real income will mean people will have less to spend, both on domestic goods and on imports. This reduced demand for foreign goods will be translated into a reduced demand for foreign currencies. As a result, the gap between the supply of and demand for any particular foreign currency will narrow, reducing the short-run balance of payments deficit. Many economists believe this was precisely the policy President Dwight Eisenhower followed during his term of office (1953–1961). Politically it is a controversial approach. By lowering total real income and production, this method of correcting a balance of payments deficit can add to the nation's unemployment. Though a reduction in the inflation rate may seem attractive, increased short-term unemployment is a high price to pay for an improved balance of payments.

Tariffs on imported goods and/or restrictions on the flow of funds into foreign investments are another way of correcting a persistent balance of payments deficit. Both approaches tend to reduce the immediate demand for foreign currencies. Though these policies have been used by almost all governments at one time or another, they expose citizens to all the

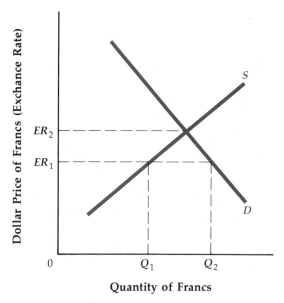

Figure 35.7. Balance of Payments Deficit.
Given a supply of francs equal to S and a demand for francs equal to D, an exchange rate of ER_1 will cause a balance of payments deficit equal to the difference between Q_2 and Q_1. At ER_1, the exchange rate is below equilibrium; more francs are demanded than supplied. Depreciation of the dollar through a rise in the exchange rate, from ER_1 to ER_2, will eliminate the deficit.

negative effects of restrictions on international trade described in the preceding chapter.

After all else has been tried, a nation may be forced to depreciate its currency. Given a fixed exchange rate of $\$0.10 = F1$, for instance, the United States could correct a balance of payments deficit by depreciating the dollar (or revising the exchange rate upward) to $\$0.20 = F1$. The rules of the IMF provide for such a change, which would make U.S. exports more attractive to foreigners and foreign imports less attractive to Americans. Thus it would reduce the quantity of francs demanded and increase the quantity of francs supplied on the international money market. In Figure 35.7, with the exchange rate at ER_1, the balance of payments deficit is the difference between the quantity of francs demanded, Q_2, and the quantity supplied, Q_1. At ER_1, the exchange rate is below equilibrium. Depreciation of the dollar moves the exchange rate up toward the equilibrium rate of ER_2, reducing the gap between supply and demand.

The Demise of the Fixed-Rate System

In August 1971, President Richard Nixon withdrew the United States' commitment to maintain fixed exchange rates between the dollar and other national currencies. In so doing, he allowed the overvalued U.S. dollar to seek a new equilibrium level and to move, or float, with changes in money market conditions. The demise of the fixed exchange rate system—sometimes called the adjustable peg system, since nations could adjust the rates periodically—was inevitable. The United States had run a balance of payments deficit almost every year since 1950. Its gold reserves, valued at $35 an ounce, had dwindled from a high of $23 billion in 1950 to $12 billion in 1971. At the same time, about $80 billion had accumulated in foreign bank accounts. Although many of those dollars were necessary to the transaction of world trade, it was becoming clear that the market was saturated with overvalued dollars.

In the mid-1960s, moreover, people had begun to expect depreciation of the dollar and the British pound. Every year or so there would be a run on the dollar or the pound. Panicky investors would try to exchange their dollars or pounds for some other currency, like German marks. Such crises became progressively more frequent in the late 1960s and early 1970s. By August 1971, they had so destabilized the fixed exchange rate system that it was certain to be abandoned. The only question was the timing of the change to a floating exchange rate system.

Fear of depreciation can disrupt the international money market for two reasons. First, depreciation of a currency reduces the value of foreign holdings of that currency in terms of other world currencies. For example, at an exchange rate of $0.10 = F1, a $100 bank account is worth F1,000. At $0.20 = F1, however, that same $100 is worth only F500. To avoid a loss from an expected depreciation, people will try to sell the currency in question and buy others. In other words, at times of international monetary crisis, the demand for undervalued foreign currencies like francs will increase. The greater demand for francs will widen the gap between the quantity demanded and the quantity supplied, thus increasing the amount of reserves needed to bring the quantity supplied into line with the quantity demanded.

Second, speculators will try to make a profit on any expected depreciation of a currency. If a person holding dollars can buy francs at $0.10 apiece and sell them back at $0.20, he will make a profit of $0.10 on each franc. This speculative activity increases the demand for francs, again widening the gap between the quantity demanded and the quantity supplied. During the 1950s and 1960s, when the British experienced substantial balance of payments deficits, speculation in the pound was active.

Summary and Extensions

A stable set of international exchange rates is needed for the smooth operation of international trade. Continual and significant variations in exchange rates introduce an unwanted element of risk into international commerce, reducing the volume of trade. But control of exchange rates through a fixed rate system has serious practical defects.

Under a floating exchange rate system, exchange rates vary in response to changes in consumer taste and the technology of production. Such fluctuations are not only useful but necessary. Exchange rates also vary with changes in domestic and foreign inflation rates and national income levels. In short, the international monetary system mirrors the stability or instability of the world's national economies. If the nations of the world are pursuing inappropriate domestic policies, they cannot expect the international monetary system to remain stable.

Major Conclusions

1. The international exchange rate affects the relative prices of domestic and foreign products.
2. Changes in the exchange rate will change the relative prices of foreign and domestic products, altering import and export levels. Specifically, depreciation of the dollar will lower imports to the United States and increase exports from the United States. Appreciation of the dollar will have the opposite effect.
3. Under a floating exchange rate system, international exchange rates are determined by the interaction of supply and demand.
4. Changes in consumer tastes, in total real income, and in the rate of inflation can alter the exchange rate.
5. Under a fixed exchange rate system, nations use gold and currency reserves, loans from the International Monetary Fund, currency swaps, and special drawing rights to fill gaps between the quantity of a currency supplied and the quantity demanded.
6. A fixed exchange rate system lessens the risk involved in trade, but tends to create balance of payment problems. The United States dropped the fixed exchange rate in 1971.

Questions to Ponder

1. If a nation appreciates its currency in relation to other national currencies, what will be the effect on other nations' exports and imports? On the willingness of that nation's citizens to invest abroad?
2. Will a tax on imports and a subsidy on exports have the same effect on trade as depreciation of a nation's currency?
3. Suppose the exchange rate between the pound and the dollar is fixed. If both the United States and Great Britain double the price of gold in terms of their own national currencies, what will be the effect on trade between the two nations? Assuming that other nations hold the price of gold in their own currencies constant, how will the change in the dollar and pound prices of gold affect trade between the United States and Britain and the rest of the world?
4. Develop cases for and against the fixed exchange rate system.
5. Do you agree that if a nation runs a persistent balance of payments surplus—that is, if its outgoing international payments fall consistently short of its incoming payments—it is trading goods and services for foreign currencies? Why might a nation be unwilling to incur an extended balance of payments surplus?

Central Question

*What are the major
forms of economic
organization, and how
do they differ?*

Key Terms

Mercantilism

Capitalism

Communism

National economic planning

Socialism

Chapter 36

Comparative Economic Systems

[I]nappropriate, wasteful, and
sometimes harmful
commodities have been
produced and sold as the
logical embodiment of the
accepted principle which in a
capitalist economy governs
what is produced—the
maximization of profit.
Barry Commoner

*I*n his *Wealth of Nations* in 1776, Adam Smith explained how the invisible hand of self-interest, tempered by competition, could effectively satisfy society's economic needs. The American economic system rests largely on Smith's theory. Our supermarkets, shopping centers, fast-food chains, and computer companies are bastions of free enterprise. Yet the federal government frequently thrusts a visible hand into the operations of the market, setting standards, propping up prices, interfering with imports, or encouraging employment.

In the Soviet Union, on the other hand, the economy is carefully controlled. Still, financial incentives must be employed to stimulate production, and many goods are sold on the open market. Not long ago, in fact, many economists believed that over time the United States and the Soviet Union, like a married couple, would come to resemble each other more and more.[1] Recent years have given little evidence that the Soviet hierarchy is relaxing its control of the economy, however. And the United States seems to be moving away from government intervention, particularly in transportation, communication, and banking.

At the same time, the economies of Western Europe are showing signs of economic ambivalence. Under Margaret Thatcher's Conservative government in Great Britain, government interference has sometimes taken precedence over the free market. In France, the Socialist regime of Francois Mitterrand has retreated from some traditional socialist objectives. History is similarly ambiguous. In ancient times, trade stretched far across the Mediterranean. Yet the Code of Hammurabi and the construction of the pyramids in Egypt attest to persistent government efforts to manipulate and control economic activity.

This chapter explores some of the various "isms" under which government control and free enterprise blend in the modern world. Despite some important differences, there are many startling similarities in the way various economies operate.

Mercantilism

The fading of the Middle Ages in Europe brought the gradual consolidation of nation-states, a process that transformed Western society. Particularly in England and France, but later in Germany and Italy, sovereigns wrought dramatic changes. They fostered the development of roads and canals, struck down internal tariffs that hindered trade along rivers, and stabilized systems of coinage. As fragmented and self-sufficient feudal fiefdoms gave way to more centralized political units, commerce blossomed.

While these changes spurred economic development, they were politically motivated. Their ultimate goal was to help sovereigns achieve control. Each new nation aimed to export more goods than it imported, in order

---

1. Neil H. Jacoby and James E. Howell, *European Economics—East and West: Convergence of Five European Countries and the United States* (Cleveland: World Publishing, 1967).

to enrich its sovereign's treasury. To achieve their desired balance of trade, nations granted monopoly rights to corporations. The formal name for such a policy is mercantilism. **Mercantilism** was a system of economic organization that flourished between 1500 and 1800. It was designed specifically to promote a desired balance of trade through monopoly of production and trading rights.

The Balance of Trade

Students of American history will recall that the British government discouraged manufacturing in its colonies. It preferred to extract raw materials, ship them to the homeland, enhance their value through the manufacturing process, and return finished goods to the colonies.

When exports outweigh imports, the nation is giving up more goods than it gets in return. You may wonder why sovereigns pursued that goal. As Adam Smith wrote in 1776, "If a foreign country can supply us with a commodity cheaper than we ourselves can make it, better buy it of them with some part of the produce of our own industry, employed in a way in which we have some advantage."[2] But there was method in the royal madness. What the sovereigns coveted was the money income, generally in the form of silver or gold, that made up the difference between their nations' exports and imports. Such funds could be taxed. The ample revenues they provided would equip large armies or support the construction of palatial royal estates.

David Hume first pointed out the fallacy in this reasoning. Adding an increased flow of hard currency to the domestic money supply would simply inflate prices. That in turn would discourage foreigners from buying British products, which would become more expensive in relation to their own. British exports would drop. Simultaneously, foreign items would become relatively more attractive to the British. Their imports would increase. The two trends would eventually combine to eliminate the trade surplus, cutting off the inflow of gold and silver. In the meantime, however, the sovereign would have enhanced his treasury—a victory of narrow personal interests over the general welfare.

Monopoly Corporations

The establishment of monopoly corporations under mercantilism was designed to assure the surplus of exports that sovereigns desired. For a fee, rulers created special corporations and granted them exclusive control over trade with specific royal colonies. Such chartered companies were particularly appealing to the English monarchs, who found Parliament

Mercantilism: a system of economic organization that flourished between 1500 and 1800, designed to promote a desired balance of trade through monopoly of production and trading rights.

---

2. Adam Smith, *An Inquiry into the Nature and Causes of the Wealth of Nations* (New York: Modern Library, 1937), p. 424.

persistently tightfisted in its support of royalty. In 1601, Queen Elizabeth I chartered the East India Company, granting it for fifteen years the power to "have, use and enjoy the whole entire and only trade and traffic . . . to and from the said East Indies and to and from all the islands, posts, havens, cities, towns and places aforesaid." The charter was repeatedly renewed, until in 1661 it became perpetual. Similar monopoly privileges were granted to settlers of the colonies and to those who would manufacture such items as glass, salt, and soap in England. Royal policy even required that many imports and exports be transported on the nation's own ships. The famous Navigation Acts of 1651 and 1660 served that purpose.

Of all the European rulers, the Dutch relied least on royally chartered monopolies. And it was the Dutch economy, the one with fewest government constraints, that expanded most rapidly in the mercantilist era. At the other extreme, the French government, under Louis XIV's minister of finance, Jean Baptiste Colbert, not only created great monopolies for producing such items as tapestries, but rigorously controlled product quality to enhance the products' export value. All such policies, though supposedly designed to promote the wealth of the nation, clearly enhanced the wealth of the sovereign and of investors in privileged companies more than the welfare of the people.

In the late 1600s, the influence of mercantilist thought began to wane. Following the Glorious Revolution in 1688, the British Parliament abolished the sovereign's right to create monopolies, for emerging commercial interests yearned to trade freely. By the late 1700s, American colonists so despised the confining monopoly power of royal corporations that the framers of the Constitution decided to avoid even mentioning corporations in that document, hoping that none would be created.[3] Not surprisingly, few corporations gained federal charters. Instead, virtually all corporations in the new nation were established by the states. In fact, states vied with one another for the economic development corporations would bring by making corporate charters easier and easier to obtain. Incorporation became so easy that corporations quickly lost all their monopoly privileges. Today's corporate charters certainly do not grant General Motors, IBM, Xerox, and RCA immunity from the forces of competition.

Modern Mercantilism

Despite the founding fathers' hostility to monopoly rights, vestiges of mercantilism persist in the United States today. A good example is trade barriers that seek to limit foreign competition in the production of everything from steel, copper, cars, and textiles to golf carts, plastic mattress handles, canned pears, and ice cream sandwich wafers. These modern barriers are designed not to provide revenue for the Treasury,

---

3. A. A. Berle, Jr., *Economic Power and the Free Society* (Santa Barbara, Calif.: Center for the Study of Democratic Institutions, 1957), p. 4.

but to limit the supply and raise the price of protected products. But the general effect is the same: favored producers can sell their products at a higher price. Other vestiges of mercantilism limit entry into certain activities, such as the practice of medicine and law. In some cities, cab drivers must be licensed. The supply of licenses is limited so strictly that in recent years, licenses have sold for $84,000 and more.

Obviously, then, government and business are not natural enemies. They are often in cahoots. When the Carter administration deregulated the protected truck and airline industries, firms fought vigorously to maintain their privileged positions. Even under the conservative Reagan administration, attempts have been made to create new monopoly privileges. A bill submitted to Congress recently would have allowed beer producers to create exclusive monopolies for the distribution of their products. As one congressional representative wrote, "Beer wholesalers apparently are uncomfortable about the uncertainty that accompanies a competitive marketplace."[4] Finally, much like the British Navigation Acts, the Jones Act limits shipping between two American ports to American ships—although foreign vessels often offer lower rates and better service.

Thus, though the days of the exclusive royal charter are long gone, political leaders still serve their constituencies by granting exclusive monopoly privileges and protecting domestic industries. Nationalistic restrictions and favoritism are still with us.

Capitalism and Its Critics

Mercantilism did not disappear overnight. Nor did Adam Smith's arguments about the power of the invisible hand have overwhelming impact. In the newly formed United States, Secretary of the Treasury Alexander Hamilton argued that tariffs on foreign imports were needed to protect fledgling industries at home. But in England, the Industrial Revolution wrought drastic changes in the economic environment. By the early 1800s, steam engines and innovations in textile manufacture combined to move production out of the home and into the factory. To finance production on such a large scale, producers needed large amounts of capital. A new economic system, called capitalism, quickly emerged. **Capitalism** is an economic system based on private property and free enterprise, in which few or no government barriers to trade or restrictions on entry into business or the professions discourage competition.

Capitalism is, of course, the philosophical basis for the free market system that exists today in the United States and many other nations. In its pure form, it has never enjoyed unqualified support anywhere. English writers like William Blake deplored the "dark, satanic mills" that fouled the air over the English countryside. "Supply-and-demand,—Alas!" wrote

Capitalism: an economic system based on private property and free enterprise, in which few or no government barriers to trade or restrictions on entry into business or the professions discourage competition.

---

4. Charles E. Schumer, "A Beer Bill to Mug Consumers," *Wall Street Journal*, February 22, 1984, p. 32.

Perspectives in Economics: The Competitive Japanese Economy

Katsuro Sakoh

Japan has experienced remarkable economic success since the end of World War II. In 1981 Japan's GNP surpassed that of the Soviet Union, making it the second-largest economy in the world. By 1984 its current dollar GNP had climbed to $1,251 billion, compared with $3,820 billion in the United States—a nation with twice its population. In terms of GNP per capita, Japan ranked tenth in the world.

The driving forces of Japan's phenomenal success have been private entrepreneurs and a well-educated labor force. Unlike European governments, the Japanese government has tried to avoid owning and operating major industries. Instead, it has concentrated on keeping taxes low by holding down expenditures on social welfare, quality of life, and national defense. (Japan's tax-revenue-to-GNP ratio is the lowest of the developed nations.) This relatively low tax burden has allowed the Japanese to achieve a high rate of saving—20 percent, or almost three times that of Americans. In turn, high savings have produced a high rate of capital investment and rapid technological improvements in the private sector.

This free market environment enabled Japan to shift quickly from an agricultural orientation in the 1950s to an industrial orientation in the 1960s and a service orientation in recent years. Today, 57 percent of Japanese workers are employed in service industries—only 12 percentage points less than in the United States. Contrary to popular perception, these changes in economic structure have been carried out mostly by small private companies rather than by government direction. In the private sector as a whole, nearly 70 percent of the labor force works for companies with fewer than 200 employees. Almost all the workers in agriculture; more than three-quarters of the workers in construction, wholesale, retail, and personal service industries; and more than half of the workers in manufacturing are employed by small companies. The majority—perhaps two-thirds—of these workers are not guaranteed permanent employment.

Japan has achieved its economic success despite some formidable obstacles. The nation is small, the size of Montana, with no fossil fuels and few natural resources. To survive and grow, it must import most of its raw materials. During the oil crises of 1973 and 1978, Japan suffered high inflation, severe economic recession and negative growth rates, and large balance of trade deficits. As a result of that recession, the government is carrying a huge budget deficit. In 1983 Japan's debt-to-GNP ratio was 51 percent, compared with 43 percent in the United States.

Though Japan is heavily dependent on foreign trade for its well-being, trade is not the main source of its phenomenal economic growth. Japan's export-to-GNP ratio was only 13 percent in 1984—much lower than the ratio in any major industrial nation except the United States.[1] During the two oil crises of the 1970s, the buying power of Japan's exports deteriorated more than 30 percent. But the nation overcame that handicap by investing heavily in energy-saving measures and more productive technology. Once more, Japan became competitive in the world market. Like its rapid recovery from the devastation of World War II, Japan's strength today is due to its imaginative, hard-working, consumer-oriented private sector.

1. The figures are 48 percent for the Netherlands; 27 percent for West Germany; 25 percent for Canada; 20 percent for the United Kingdom; and 7 percent for the United States.

Thomas Carlyle in 1843.[5] And in 1862 John Ruskin complained, "To this . . . professed and organized pursuit of Money . . . is owing *All* the evil of modern days."[6] Today, the writings of environmentalist Barry Commoner and economist John Kenneth Galbraith, among others, reflect a wariness toward the free market and the quest for profit. But of all the critics of capitalism, none is more notable than the man who made *capitalism* a household word: the German economist Karl Marx.

Marxian Communism

Marx (1818–1883) did not favor a return to a traditional economy. Indeed, he commended capitalists for rescuing "a considerable part of the population from the idiocy of rural life."[7] But though he accepted the writings of the classical economists Adam Smith and David Ricardo, he viewed capitalist activities as at best a temporary necessity. To Marx, capitalism was merely a brief period of transition between a grim past and the more prosperous future. For Marx had observed a more fully developed capitalism than had Adam Smith, one in which the blessings of the division of labor were obscured by the curse of unemployment. It was unemployment that Marx saw as the fatal weakness of capitalism.

Marx's ideas are often summed up in the phrase "dialectical materialism." The word *dialectic* is derived from the Greek word for the process of developing philosophical ideas. Ancient Greek philosophers originated the technique of posing an idea, or hypothesis, against a contrasting idea, or antithesis. Through discussion thinkers would eventually merge the two ideas to create a new idea, or synthesis. But the process did not end there. The synthesis became the new hypothesis, and a new antithesis spawned a new synthesis.

In the early nineteenth century, the German philosopher Friedrich Hegel applied the concept of dialectics to historical development. He suggested that human evolution could be seen as a continuous process of hypothesis, antithesis, and synthesis. Marx extended the idea by specifying social classes as the opposing forces in the dialectical process. Medieval lords and serfs, pitted against each other, had been replaced by the bourgeois capitalists and the paid laborers ("proletariat") of modern times. Marx noted that each historical era had its own peculiar mode of production—the windmill of earlier times had given way to the steam engine. Thus the dialectical process had a distinctly economic, or material, base.

---

5. Quoted in Neil H. Jacoby and James E. Howell, *European Economics—East and West: Convergence of Five European Countries and the United States* (Cleveland: World Publishing, 1967), p. 2.
6. Quoted in Bernard Murchland, *Humanism and Capitalism: A Survey of Thought on Morality* (Washington: American Enterprise Institute for Public Policy Research, 1984), p. 7.
7. Karl Marx and Friedrich Engels, *The Communist Manifesto* (New York: Appleton-Century-Crofts, 1955), p. 14.

Like Hegel, Marx saw human history as a broad upward sweep through time. In London, where he took refuge from political persecution at home, Marx developed his theory. He started with the classical labor theory of value. For Adam Smith, that theory had meant emancipation from the mercantilist belief that the value of the world's output was rigidly fixed and could not increase. Trade was not a zero-sum game, Smith saw; what France gained, England would not necessarily lose. But the opening words of *The Wealth of Nations*, "Labour . . . supplies . . . all the necessities and conveniences of life," meant something quite different to Marx. He took the idea one step further and argued that only labor created value. The capitalist was an unnecessary parasite who had freed workers from bondage to the land, but was unnecessary to their future advancement.

The capitalist was, of course, the owner of the means of production: the machinery and tools that workers used. Forces of competition compelled capitalists then and now to acquire more and more capital. To purchase it, Marx charged, capitalists paid workers less than the value of their output—a tendency David Ricardo had already described. Capitalists did not live on the surplus revenues; instead, they used it to purchase more capital.

Meanwhile, instead of benefiting from the improved productivity created by new equipment, workers lost their jobs. As more and more of them were fired, they joined the "reserve army of the unemployed," a ready source of eager labor that depressed wages. Because workers were unable to buy the output of the new factories, capitalists would suffer wrenching business failures. Eventually, Marx believed, the reserve army of the unemployed would become so large and so desperate that it would rise up and overthrow the remaining capitalists in a bloody revolution. Such a violent transition had marked the advent of capitalism in France, and Marx expected history to repeat itself. The coming revolution would usher in the new and final era of communism. **Communism**, as conceived by Marx, was a classless society governed by workers that would emerge from the downfall of capitalism. In practical terms, communism is an economic system in which virtually all the means of production are owned and controlled by the state.

In the period after the revolution, which Marx called the dictatorship of the proletariat, property rights would be abolished and a new society would emerge. Since workers would no longer be the slaves of capitalists, they would spontaneously become more productive. And since the state—like religion—had merely been a device to suppress the workers, it would eventually wither away. Although Marx dwelt only briefly on the nature of the new society, he apparently believed that it would be both productive and satisfying. According to his famous slogan, production and distribution would be based on the principle "from each according to his ability, to each according to his need."

Marx may have been wrong about the threat that capital posed to labor, and naive to believe that a totally classless society was possible. But for many oppressed peoples, his writings have served as a beacon of hope and inspiration. And for many communist leaders, from Lenin to Mao to Castro, his writings have provided the foundation for new revolutionary

Communism: as conceived by Marx, a classless society governed by workers that would emerge from the downfall of capitalism. In practical terms, an economic system in which virtually all the means of production are owned and controlled by the state.

goals. Still, what is called communism today, especially in the Soviet Union, is very unlike the ideal state Marx envisioned. The economist Joseph Schumpeter once remarked that "There is, between the true meaning of Marx's message and . . . [Soviet] practice and ideology, at least as great a gulf as there was between the religion of humble Galileans and the practice and ideology of the princes of the church or the warlords of the Middle Ages."[8]

Soviet Communism

In the late nineteenth century, Russia was governed by a repressive monarchy whose abuses encouraged revolutionary activity. There were some spurts of economic development in the 1890s and the early twentieth century, but industry was largely directed and controlled by government, and the economy remained overwhelmingly agricultural. On the eve of the Communist Revolution, then, czarist Russia had not nearly reached the stage of capitalist development that Marx had predicted would precede a workers' revolution.

Nevertheless revolutionary uprisings occurred in early 1917. They were largely a spontaneous reaction to Russia's devastating losses in the First World War. A provisional regime set up under Alexander Kerensky seemed to offer the possibility of a more democratic government. But then a man named Lenin appeared on the scene.

Leninism

Lenin, whose real name was Vladimir Ilyich Ulyanov, was a native Russian whose father had taught mathematics and physics. As a young man Lenin had been exiled to Siberia because of his efforts to promote more power for the working class. He believed that revolution should be brought about by the concerted effort of a small group of professionals. In 1903, at a meeting in London, his determination on that point had split the Russian revolutionary party in two. Lenin's smaller group had adroitly termed itself the Bolsheviks, which means "majority." The other group became known as the Mensheviks, or the minority.

In 1917 Lenin was in exile again, this time in Switzerland. There he aided the Germans in a devious plan to neutralize their enemy on the eastern front. By helping Lenin return to Russia, Winston Churchill observed, the Germans deployed "the most grisly of all weapons" in a war already distinguished by the use of poison gas and flame throwers. "They transplanted Lenin in a sealed truck like a plague bacillus from Switzerland into Russia."[9]

8. Joseph A. Schumpeter, *Capitalism, Socialism, and Democracy*, 3d ed. (New York: Harper & Row, 1950), p. 3.
9. Quoted in Alan Moorehead, *The Russian Revolution* (New York: Perennial Library, Harper & Row, 1965), p. 171.

In October 1917 Lenin led the Bolsheviks in overthrowing Kerensky's provisional government. As the Germans had hoped, he withdrew Russia from the war, thus eliminating one of their enemies. But several years of struggle were required before Lenin could consolidate his control of the country. During this period of "war communism," industry was nationalized, wages were equalized, and crops were confiscated to feed the army and urban workers. By 1921, when Lenin finally claimed political success, the economy was faltering so badly that he was forced to retreat temporarily from his ideological objectives. His New Economic Policy (NEP) provided more freedom to farmers and small businessmen, in an effort to restore production to previous levels.

This new, more open society did not last, for in January 1924 Lenin died without designating his successor. Joseph Stalin and Leon Trotsky fought for control and by 1928 Stalin was victorious.

Stalinism

National economic planning: the process of deciding collectively on national economic objectives, and of developing policies and programs for accomplishing those objectives.

Stalin's overriding goal was the rapid industrialization of the Russian economy through national economic planning. **National economic planning** is the process of deciding collectively on national economic objectives, and of developing policies and programs for accomplishing those objectives. To achieve his end Stalin set up Gosplan, the Soviet central planning agency. In the first of a series of five-year plans, bureaucrats in Gosplan established mandatory economic goals for various sectors of the economy. The last vestiges of the NEP program were swept away, and the secret police regained the pervasive control they had held first under the czars and then during the period of war communism.

Whereas Lenin had come to believe that greater freedom was the key to enhancing agricultural output, Stalin rejected that view. He abolished private farms and combined them into huge collectives, running some like factories in which workers earned wages. Farmers did not gain the benefit of improvements in productivity. Instead, most of the food was earmarked for workers in urban areas, to support their construction and factory work. In essence, farmers were forced to accept subsistence wages to support the rapid accumulation of capital in industry—an ironic reincarnation of the capitalist system Marx had condemned.

At least initially, Stalin's plans for raising farm productivity through collectivization backfired. The peasants so resented the new system that they retaliated by destroying their crops and slaughtering their livestock. Such discord was inconsistent with Marx's prediction of a placid and productive postrevolutionary society. Conflict was supposed to be the result of class distinctions, and classes had presumably been wiped out. So Stalin resolved the dilemma by blaming the difficulties of forced collectivization on the *kulaks* (prosperous peasant farmers who had done well for themselves under the NEP). Eventually he announced that the kulaks would be "liquidated," and several thousand of them were shot.[10]

---

10. Calvin Hoover, *Memoirs of Capitalism, Communism, and Nazism* (Durham, N.C.: Duke University Press, 1965), pp. 111–14.

Stalin's repressive policies did not last, but neither did Soviet agriculture flourish. Eventually Soviet planners had to establish incentives to stimulate production. Instead of paying equal wages to all, they rewarded more productive workers. In recent years peasants have been allowed to farm small plots of land near their homes and to sell the produce in local markets. Peasants naturally tend to use these plots to produce agricultural items whose market value is high—milk and eggs, for instance. Still, the productivity of the privately farmed land testifies to the value of incentives. The collectively farmed lands, which produce less valuable foodstuffs like wheat, are not nearly so productive. In recent years, the Soviets have had to import grain regularly from capitalist nations.

The lack of a profit motive also presented problems in Soviet industry. Managers of Soviet plants were expected to meet quotas, not to satisfy the demands of customers. A factory manager who had been told to produce a million pairs of shoes could satisfy his quota most easily by making all of them the same size—and many managers did just that. Knitting factories made caps but not sweaters, because caps were easier to make. Lampshade factories made all their products one color—orange. And in the lighting fixtures industry, where quotas were established in terms of weight, a small number of extremely heavy products was produced.

Such tales may be exaggerated, but they demonstrate the problem of establishing an effective system of incentives. While the Soviet government can take pride in its military and space technology, it has not been able to match Western economies and Japan in the production of consumer goods and services. Competition with the United States spurs Soviet military and space achievements. The lack of competition holds back the Soviet consumer products sector.

Marx's classless society has not yet emerged in the Soviet Union. The ruling class has privileges that workers do not. A reporter who lived in the Soviet Union observed that special stores reserved for the elite "insulate the Soviet aristocracy from chronic shortages, endless waiting in line, rude service, and other daily harassments that plague ordinary citizens. Here the politically anointed can obtain rare Russian delicacies like caviar, smoked salmon, the best canned sturgeon, export brands of vodka or unusual vintages of Georgian and Moldavian wines, choice meat, fresh fruits and vegetables in winter that are rarely available elsewhere."[11]

Soviet industry may have become even more inefficient in recent years. During his brief tenure as premier, Yuri Andropov tried earnestly to improve productivity, but there are few signs that he was successful. Suggestions that the Soviet economy is tottering on the brink of collapse are probably exaggerated, however. Like their czarist predecessors, party members enjoy power and privileges they will not readily forgo. And there are no strong signs of unrest among the Soviet people. In fact, the similarities between czardom and communism in Russia are so great that one is reminded of the old French proverb: the more things change, the more they stay the same.

---

11. Hedrick Smith, *The Russians* (New York: Quadrangle, New York Times Book Co., 1976), p. 26.

Perspectives in Economics: A Traveler's View of Emerging Capitalism in China

Laurence S. Moss

Ten years ago no one imagined China would reach out to embrace capitalist economic methods. During Mao Zedong's Cultural Revolution, bands of teenagers had roamed China's countryside, burning books, destroying historical monuments, and dragging reluctant counterrevolutionaries through the streets. Thousands of citizens were forced to renounce their bourgeois-capitalist ways and close their flourishing commercial institutions.

Today the news media are filled with reports of China's return to capitalism. It is not yet clear how far the dismantling of China's centrally planned economy will proceed. But Premier Deng Xiaoping, China's pragmatic new leader, has obviously set out to accomplish what Mao would never have allowed: the liberalization of trade and the toleration of Western lifestyles.

The change in government policy has been most dramatic in the agricultural sector. In 1958, Mao's Great Leap Forward literally abolished most private landholding, consolidating farm management in huge regional collectives. The merging of small peasant farms and village lands was supposed not only to help in the mechanization of farming and the improvement of productivity, but to foster the spiritual rebirth of the Communist people. Unfortunately, the move did not produce the promised results. The stifling of personal incentives disrupted the whole economy for most of a decade.

Starting in 1980, however, the Chinese government declared a series of agricultural reforms that amounted to wholesale abandonment of collective land management. Most provincial landholdings were abolished, and small village and family farms were restored to their former owners. Farmers are now required to turn over only part of their output to the government. Any surplus is theirs to consume or to trade for cash in the cities. Government officials also encouraged the development of an agricultural futures market by allowing farmers to contract ahead of time for delivery of their crops. The idea was to give farmers an incentive to vary the composition of their output as market conditions warranted.

Trade works best when buyers and sellers can communicate easily with one another. In most Chinese cities the government has now granted sidewalk space to traders, and even blocked off traffic on selected streets. Traders still need licenses, but they are said to be relatively easy to acquire. In hopes of making a profit, a person may set up a trading booth and offer beans, clothing, ginseng roots, or dried beetles to passing shoppers. In one outdoor market in the city of Guangzhou, Western travelers recently saw a vendor offer several packages of Wrigley's chewing gum at premium prices. Another vendor, equipped with a dentist's chair, white apron, and surgical pliers,

Democratic Socialism

Between the command economy of the Soviet Union and the market system of the United States lies another form of economic organization that, much like mercantilism, involves partial government control of the economy. Under mercantilism, monarchs created monopolies and then left merchants and manufacturers relatively free to operate them, within certain guidelines. Under socialism, the government actually gets into the offered to pull aching teeth for passers-by who found the wait at the state hospital painfully long.

The free market principles operating in the open air markets can also be observed in Chinese factories. Managers are encouraged to negotiate Western-style contracts promising bonuses if a job is completed under budget and penalties if deadlines are not met. In Guangzhou the manager of a jade factory is now allowed to negotiate contracts with business people from Hong Kong without the approval of the Central Communist Party in Beijing (Peking). Only the small bureaucracy of Guangzhou province watches over his dealings. Contracts with foreigners are more likely to be approved if they provide employment for Chinese laborers or help to augment the state-owned Bank of China's foreign exchange holdings. Among other companies J. R. Reynolds (tobacco), Gillette (razor blades), Foxboro (automatic controls), and IBM (computers) have entered into joint ventures in China. To foreign travelers, the most obvious joint ventures are the smart high-rise hotels, some with indoor pools and revolving restaurants, that cater to the thousands of tourists who visit China each day.

In addition to the opportunities now available to entrepreneurs, a private labor market provides extra disposable income to many Chinese citizens. Tourists who read Chinese report seeing hand-painted signs along the roadways offering wages for after-hours labor on construction projects. Taxicab drivers in Beijing say that after they have paid a fixed sum to the government, they are free to work for themselves. Workers use their extra earnings to purchase television sets and refrigerators, or to establish small businesses in the open air market.

Chinese citizens' ability to reorganize production methods or reallocate capital in response to changing market conditions is more limited. The days of total police control of citizens' movements seem to be over. Individuals can now travel freely within each of China's provinces, without signing in and out of police stations. As a result, some middleman activity is possible. Goods can be moved from countryside to city to even out maladjustments in supply and demand. But can individuals start a labor union and strike? Can entrepreneurs issue stocks or engage in other sophisticated venture capital arrangements? In 1985 the government allowed a company in Shanghai to offer stock, but it is not yet clear whether that action was the harbinger of a new China or only a tentative experiment. Only time will tell whether Chinese capitalism will last.

See also Laurence S. Moss, "Capitalism in China" (Babson Park, Mass.: Economics Department, Babson College, 1985).

---

business of production. **Socialism** (sometimes called democratic socialism) is an economic system in which the government owns major plants in industries such as coal, transportation, steel, and banking, and operates them in the public interest.

Socialist philosophy tends to reflect Marx's belief that capitalist profits are unearned. Public ownership of industry thus allows unearned profits to be turned over to the public. (Of course, members of the general public can and do hold shares in capitalist corporations. And in return for their

Socialism (or democratic socialism): an economic system in which the government owns major plants in industries such as coal, transportation, steel, and banking, and operates them in the public interest.

profit, capitalists do take risks in funding production.) Another socialist goal has been the elimination of the exploitation of labor.[12] The theory is that if industry is owned publicly, profits can be used to improve working conditions and promote a more equitable distribution of income.

In the United States, the postal service has always been owned by government. Today public elementary and secondary schools and land-grant colleges are all run by state, county, or local governments. (The historian Arnold Toynbee once called the American public schools the most socialistic system of education in the world.) In the 1930s, the federal government entered the electricity business by establishing the Tennessee Valley Authority. More recently it has taken control of ailing railroads to establish Amtrak and Conrail. Still, outright government ownership of plant and equipment is relatively limited.

In Europe, industry has been far more extensively socialized. At the end of the Second World War, Britain's new Labour government nationalized several major industries. In Austria at about the same time, a substantial segment of industry that had been confiscated by the Nazis during the war was placed under government control. More recently, governments in Norway, Sweden, and France have assumed ownership of many industries.

One study of nationalization estimated the percentages of industry owned by the public in several Western European nations as follows:[13]

Austria	65%
France	55
Italy	45
Norway	40
Sweden	30
Great Britain	25
West Germany	20

The Effects of Nationalization

Originally, industries were nationalized in order to prevent the exploitation of workers and to distribute unearned profits. Over the years, however, motivations have changed. Government officials began taking over industries simply because they were failing. In Britain, Rolls Royce was nationalized not by a Labour administration with socialist leanings, but by a Conservative government. Similar moves have become common in Norway and Sweden.

In a free-market economy, persistent losses are usually taken as a signal that a firm should reorganize or go out of business. Of course, during recessions and sometimes for other reasons, producers may endure

---

12. Upton Sinclair described turn-of-the-century labor conditions in wrenching detail in his novel *The Jungle* (1906). See the afterword by Robert B. Downs to the Signet edition (New York: New American Library, 1960).
13. R. Joseph Monsen and Kenneth D. Walters, *Nationalized Companies: A Threat to American Business* (New York: McGraw-Hill, 1983), p. 17.

temporary losses, expecting better times. But continued losses suggest that the firm is producing the wrong product or managing resources inefficiently. Like a thermostat that turns on the furnace when the temperature in a building falls too low, losses reveal a need for change.

Sometimes unprofitable companies can be rescued by astute managers. For instance, Lee Iacocca turned Chrysler from a failing enterprise into a profitable company. His efforts were assisted by government loan guarantees (which critics maintain was a wasteful use of funds). If nothing else, the example shows there are other ways for government to restore a company's profitability besides outright ownership. John Kenneth Galbraith, an economist who favors the nationalization of failing industries, insists that once a company has been nationalized, it should be run according to strict principles of profit and loss. The manager appointed by the state "must have extensive autonomy in decision-making. . . . [Public management] must be held accountable for results by the orthodox standards of cost and return. This is not a capitalist test of efficiency; it is the universal and only test."[14]

What sounds good in theory does not necessarily work in practice, however. Scholars have found that "the government as owner is interested in whether the company contributed to the nation's export drive, whether it managed to avoid laying off employees, and whether it kept domestic prices under control. One rarely hears about the state-owned company's return on investment, its return on capital, or the profitability of its assets."[15] Thus macroeconomic goals—the mercantilist desire to promote exports, the Keynesian urge to achieve high employment, and the monetarist aim to suppress inflation—tend to replace the profit motive in state-run companies.

Political considerations also influence the management of publicly owned firms. When the chairman of British Steel announced plans to reduce employment because of lagging demand in 1975, the secretary of industry objected, and the chairman was replaced. More recently, Conservative Prime Minister Margaret Thatcher refused to fund a new factory for a state-owned microelectronics firm unless it were located in Wales, where unemployment is high. Such political intervention raises costs, which either consumers or taxpayers must ultimately pay for. It also "creates chaos for the managers of nationalized firms."[16] Too often, the short-term interests of politicians conflict radically with the long-run goals of industry.

Nowhere is the conflict between political and economic goals more obvious than in government attempts to deal with inflation. It has been charged that "state companies tend to nearly freeze their prices in the year before national elections and then raise them rapidly in the following year."[17] Even in nonsocialist nations like the United States, politicians

---

14. John Kenneth Galbraith, quoted in R. Joseph Monsen and Kenneth D. Walters, *Nationalized Companies: A Threat to American Business* (New York: McGraw-Hill, 1983), p. 71.

15. Ibid., p. xi.

16. Ibid., p. 42.

17. Ibid., p. 44.

Perspectives in Economics: Yugoslavia, a Modified Communist Economy

Russell Shannon

Perhaps no nation has a paper currency more appropriate to its economy than Yugoslavia. Instead of a monarch or a president, the face of the 10 dinar note shows a smiling factory worker outfitted with cap, gloves, and shovel. On the back of the note, a sprawling industrial complex belches smoke into the air. For a nation whose industries are publicly owned and guided by workers' committees, the bill seems fitting.

A nation only a bit larger than Wyoming, Yugoslavia has a population density similar to that of industrial states like Ohio and Pennsylvania. Though it is a communist nation, its economy resembles a free market system more than the centrally planned system of the Soviet Union.

In the state-owned factories, self-management by workers is the rule. Workers are elected to a council, which may then select a management committee. The council or committee makes basic decisions about production, pricing, and pay. Profits are divided among workers or reinvested in the operation. Firms tend to be market oriented, because the workers suffer if their products do not satisfy consumers. And workers are paid according to the value of their output. Although parts of this arrangement seem to resemble the free market system, Yugoslavs insist that their approach is true to the Marxist ideal of a dictatorship of the proletariat.

Worker management has produced moderately successful results for the Yugoslavs. From 1952 to 1965, Yugoslavia's per capita growth in GNP was second only to Japan's. In 1980 its output, $73.2 billion worth, almost equaled that of Iran, a nation with half as many more people. Compared with other nations, however, Yugoslavia's per capita GNP, $3,000 in 1980, was small. In the same year, the communist nations of East Germany, Czechoslovakia, and Hungary produced per capita GNPs of $5,000 to $8,000. And the free market nations of Japan, France, and West Germany enjoyed GNPs of $9,000 to $12,500 per capita. Yugoslavia has also been plagued by persistently high inflation—50 percent or more a year—and high unemployment.

Worker-run industries have certain problems. A group of basically untrained, inexperienced managers often cannot run an enterprise efficiently on

sometimes resort to this practice. President Richard Nixon imposed comprehensive wage and price controls just before the presidential campaign of 1972. As a result, the American economy was plagued by shortages. In his memoirs, Nixon admitted that "the . . . decision to impose [controls] was politically necessary and immensely popular in the short run. But in the long run I believe that it was wrong. The piper must always be paid, and there was an unquestionably high price for tampering with the orthodox economic mechanism."[18]

Small wonder that the income statements of nationalized firms are often awash in a sea of red ink. As one book put it, "In the state firm, there is

---

18. Richard M. Nixon, *Memoirs of Richard Nixon* (New York: Grosset and Dunlap, 1978), p. 521.

a day-to-day basis. In practice, factories must be run by a general director selected by the worker management committee. Directors are supposed to serve limited terms, but frequently retain control for many years. Workers' personal interests may also bias their business decisions. Workers commonly prefer to distribute profits among themselves rather than to reinvest them in the business. As a result, funds for new equipment or for research and development are usually scarce. At the same time, workers may be so anxious to preserve their jobs that they keep an operation going when it is no longer useful to society. And discipline is so lax in worker-run factories that the nation's output is seriously reduced.

Yugoslavia's economic problems probably originate as much in its historical circumstances as in its Marxist ideology, however. Split for centuries between the Austro-Hungarian Empire in the north and the Ottoman Empire in the south, the nation was not united until near the end of World War I. Yugoslavia is a nation of two alphabets, three religions, four languages, five ethnic groups, and six republics. Substantial economic disparities be-

tween the northern and southern regions intensify the natural rivalries and conflicts among these groups. For these reasons the central planning approach used in most communist economies simply will not work in Yugoslavia. It was tried in the 1940s under Marshal Tito's government, but failed miserably. The decentralized organization of local workers' groups fits the fragmented nature of Yugoslav society much better.

In 1980 the death of President Tito, one of the few unifying influences in the nation, left Yugoslavia in a precarious situation. As one observer worried, "So extensive is the autarky of the republics that there is now less economic cooperation and exchange among the various Yugoslav republics than among the members of the Common Market."[1] Even under the best of economic systems, the many barriers to Yugoslavia's prosperity, symbolized by the four languages printed on its currency, might still thwart the nation's prospects.

1. Milovan Djilas, "Yugoslav Unity Fragments Without Tito," *Wall Street Journal*, March 13, 1985, p. 35.

a bottom line, but it is political, not financial."[19] The same conclusion also applies to economic planning in a socialist economy.

The Effects of Economic Planning

Early socialists argued that capitalists took a narrow personal view in their production decisions, preferring individual gain to the general good of society. Government planning, they suggested, would improve economic performance. As the eminent Polish economist Oskar Lange put it, under

19. R. Joseph Monsen and Kenneth D. Walters, *Nationalized Companies: A Threat to American Business* (New York: McGraw-Hill, 1983), p. 128.

socialism, "the Central Planning Board has a much wider knowledge of what is going on in the whole economic system than any private entrepreneur can ever have."[20]

It is probably true that a group of planners can have broader knowledge than a single capitalist. But in a competitive economy of many producers, both actual and potential, the collective knowledge of producers far exceeds that of any planning board. Even with the best of intentions, then, government planning may be more prone to error than the market process.

Consider the case of Japan, which was at roughly the same stage of development as Russia at the turn of the century. Japan's economic growth has now far outstripped the Soviet Union's. Many believe that Japan's central planning agency, the Ministry for International Trade and Industry (MITI), is largely responsible for the nation's success. Yet MITI actively discouraged two Japanese firms, Honda and Toyo Kogyo, from entering the automobile industry. Both have nevertheless achieved great success. As one scholar has noted, in Japanese manufacturing, "cement, paper, glass, bicycles, and motorcycles are huge success stories, even though MITI did little to help or hinder them."[21]

Those who envy Japan's industrial prowess, then, should not credit it to economic planning. The might of MITI is a myth. There is no evidence that state ownership and central control of the economy will produce more efficient results than the free market system. Instead, it might well produce improvements in job security; redistribution of income; and personal gain for politicians.

Summary and Extensions

In recent years, the governments of Western Europe have been nationalizing ailing industries at an unprecedented rate. The election of a Conservative government in Britain has done little to reverse the trend. In the United States the Reagan administration, supposedly committed to the free market, has restricted imports of steel, textiles, sugar, cars, and motorcycles. And it has slowed the process of deregulation in the trucking industry.

Perhaps Marx was correct, then. Capitalism may be only a temporary phase in the world's economic development. Yet instead of moving toward a new utopian order, the world seems to be reverting back to old mercantilist policies. Whether the party in power is Socialist or Conservative, Republican or Democrat, seems to make little difference. A recent article on French socialist policy was headlined "Mercantilism for the 21st Century."[22]

---

20. Oskar Lange, *On the Economic Theory of Socialism* (New York: McGraw-Hill, 1964), p. 89.
21. Arthur T. Denzau, *Will an "Industrial Policy" Work for the United States?* (St. Louis: Center for the Study of American Business, Washington University, 1983), p. 10.
22. *Business Week*, January 10, 1983, p. 54.

Marx saw the capitalist economy as the servant of producers' self-interest. But the free market economy has proved far more responsive to consumers—and has limited their freedom less—than the planned economy of the communist state.[23] For though capitalism is based on producers' self-interest, in the long run the producers' interest is to satisfy their customers. As Adam Smith wrote, "Consumption is the sole end and purpose of all production."[24] Both mercantilism and socialism shift the focus away from consumers, replacing the invisible hand of self-interest with the visible and often clumsy hand of government.

Major Conclusions

1. Mercantilism is a system of trade restrictions designed primarily to produce a favorable balance of trade and a horde of gold that can be used to enlarge the powers of government or of private interests. Although the heyday of mercantilist policy was from 1500 to 1800, vestiges of the system exist today as restrictions on foreign imports and on entry into various occupations and industries.
2. Communism, as conceived by Karl Marx, has never existed and will probably never emerge as a viable economic system.
3. Socialism, an economic system that relies heavily on state ownership and control of major sectors of the economy, has flourished in many European countries. Elements of socialism can also be found in the United States.
4. Most industrial economies are a mixture of free market activity and government control.
5. Replacing capitalism with government control is not necessarily in the national interest. Government control is apt to mean lower productivity and greater power for special-interest groups and politicians.

Questions to Ponder

1. Mercantilists often argued that government control of production was necessary to maintain product quality. Who should determine what degree of quality is proper, the government or the consumer?
2. Are restrictions on imports really in the national interest?
3. Explain Hume's theory that attempts to control a nation's balance of trade would always fail.
4. Although Marx argued that the purchase of new capital equipment eliminates jobs, studies show that new equipment actually creates jobs. Explain how that can happen.
5. How does the history of agricultural production in the Soviet Union illustrate the value of incentives? Does Soviet industry have incentive problems?

23. Calvin B. Hoover, *The Economy, Liberty, and the State* (New York: Twentieth Century Fund, 1959), p. 18.
24. *An Inquiry into the Nature and Causes of the Wealth of Nations* (New York: Modern Library, 1937), p. 625.

*What are the major
problems facing under-
developed countries
seeking to increase
their national income
and wealth?*

Economic growth
Economic development

Chapter 37

Economic Growth and Development

The bourgeoisie, during its rule of scarce one hundred years, has created more massive and more colossal productive forces than have all preceding generations together. Subjection of Nature's forces to man, machinery, application of chemistry to industry and agriculture, steam navigation, railways, electric telegraph, clearing of whole continents for cultivation, canalization of rivers, whole populations conjured out of the ground— what earlier century had even a presentiment that such productive forces slumbered in the lap of social labor?
Karl Marx

*M*ost of the nations of the world can be classified as rich or poor, have or have-not. Among the have-nots—a category that includes most of the world's countries—are China and India, which together represent more than a third of the world's population. Mass poverty exists in these societies. People often lack basic food, clothing, or shelter, and have little opportunity to obtain the education taken for granted in developed countries. The enormous gap between poor nations and rich increases the potential for world conflict.

This chapter examines the reasons why some countries are far more developed economically—and therefore richer—than others. Less developed countries share certain characteristics, such as low income, high population growth, and technological underdevelopment, that are linked to their economic difficulties. We will also explore some theories of what conditions are required for economic development to occur. And we will look at the obstacles to economic growth, such as inadequate rates of saving. Finally we will consider some of the proposed remedies for economic underdevelopment.

Prerequisites for Growth and Development

Economic growth: the expansion of a nation's capacity to produce the goods and services its people want.

The terms economic growth and economic development are often used interchangeably, but they have slightly different meanings. **Economic growth** is the expansion of a nation's capacity to produce the goods and services its people want. Since the productive capacity of an economy depends fundamentally on the quantity and quality of its resources, as well as on its level of technology, economic growth must involve the expansion and improvement of those factors of production. Especially important are the accumulation of capital through saving and investment; improvements in human skills; and technological advances.

Economic development: the enhancement of a nation's capacity to produce through the creation of new kinds of output.

Economic development is the enhancement of a nation's capacity to produce through the creation of new kinds of output. It includes but goes beyond the improvements in technology and skills that promote economic expansion.

An economy can have economic growth without economic development, but not vice versa. A nation that relies on oil exports for much of its income can increase its growth rate by pumping more oil. But its economic development may be minimal unless new industries and outputs are created. Development of those new industries requires investment, which must be funded by increases in oil exports. The distinction is similar to the difference between growth and development in human beings. Growth generally means increases in height or weight. Development means changes in learning capacity, physical coordination, or the ability to adapt to new circumstances. The second depends, at least in a person's early years, on the first.

There are a number of prerequisites for economic growth and development. Most of the developed countries have at least several of the following.

1. Sufficient quantity and quality of labor. The existence of a large labor force in itself does not guarantee growth and development—India is an excellent case in point. A labor force must have the education and job skills to deal with new products and methods of production.
2. Sufficient quantity and quality of capital in the form of raw material, machines, and equipment. The supply of capital depends on the level of saving, which is the difference between income and consumption. In countries where people exist at a subsistence level, there is little difference between income and consumption. Thus capital is generally in short supply in the less developed countries.
3. Sufficient quantity and quality of natural resources. This factor is helpful but not crucial. The United States' vast natural resources obviously contributed to its economic development. But Japan, which has few natural resources, has attained a high level of growth and development, because of high savings and the quality of its labor force.
4. A sufficiently high level of technology (the knowledge of how to convert resources into goods and services). Technology is generally more important to the efficiency of production than to the introduction of new goods or the improvement of existing goods. Different combinations of land, labor, and capital simply require different levels and types of technology.
5. Favorable sociocultural factors. It has been said that the Protestant work ethic, which applauds hard work, diligence, and thrift, was partly responsible for the economic development of the United States.[1]

Characteristics of Less Developed Countries

Three-fourths of the world's population lives in less developed countries, which include most of the nations of Latin America, Africa, and Asia. Some of these countries are in more advanced stages of economic development than others. Though Mexico is far less developed than the United States, the average Mexican citizen enjoys much better living conditions than the average farmer in Bangladesh. Mexico's per capita income is only one-sixth that of the United States, but it is fifteen times greater than that of Bangladesh. Nevertheless, some characteristics are common to the less developed countries. These include low per capita income and a more inequitable distribution of income than that of developed countries.[2]

Income

Countries are sometimes classified as developed or less developed on the basis of their GNP per capita—a rough measure of the value of goods and

---

1. Max Weber, *The Protestant Ethic and the Spirit of Capitalism* (New York: Scribner, 1930).
2. See also Harvey Leibenstein, *Economic Backwardness and Economic Growth* (New York: Macmillan, 1957), pp. 40–41.

Table 37.1. GNP per Capita for Selected Countries, by Level of Development

Poorest Countries		Poor Countries		Early-Stage Developing Countries	
Country	Per Capita Income	Country	Per Capita Income	Country	Per Capita Income
Bangladesh	$140	Indonesia	$ 580	Malaysia	$1,860
Ethiopia	140	Egypt	690	South Korea	1,910
Zaire	190	Thailand	790	Chile	2,210
India	260	Philippines	820	Brazil	2,240
China	310	Nigeria	860	Mexico	2,270
Pakistan	380	Nicaragua	920	Algeria	2,350
Kenya	390	Ivory Coast	950	Portugal	2,420
Sudan	440	Guatemala	1,130	Argentina	2,520

services produced and available to the average person.[3] Among the poorest countries of the world by this measure are China, India, Bangladesh, and Pakistan. Together they include almost 40 percent of the world's population but produce less than 2 percent of the world's gross national product. The annual GNP per capita for those countries is less than 5 percent of the U.S. level, which was $13,160 in 1982. Bangladesh had a GNP per capita of only $140 in 1982, or about 1 percent of Sweden's. The poverty represented by that abstract figure shows up tangibly in nutritionally inadequate diets, primitive and crowded housing, the absence of medical services, and the general unavailability of schooling.

Table 37.1 shows per capita GNP in countries at various stages of development. The first category, the poorest countries—those with per capita incomes of $500 or less—includes both China and India, the two largest countries in the world. In the second category, Indonesia and Nigeria, with per capita GNPs between $500 and $1,000, are still not much better off than China and India. Sixty percent of the world's population lives in countries that would fall in one of these two categories. In the third category, which includes Mexico and Brazil, countries have higher incomes and at least some industrial base. These countries are in the early stages of economic development. The fourth category includes areas in

3. The United Nations classifies countries as either more developed or less developed. More developed regions comprise all of Europe, the United States, Canada, Australia, Japan, New Zealand, and the Soviet Union. All other regions are classified as less developed. There is not much difference, however, between the per capita income of Portugal, which is considered more developed, and the per capita income of Mexico, which is considered less developed.

| Later-Stage Developing Countries | | Developed Countries | |
Country	Per Capita Income	Country	Per Capita Income
South Africa	$2,670	Soviet Union	$ 5,940
Yugoslavia	2,800	United Kingdom	9,660
Venezuela	4,140	Japan	10,080
Greece	4,290	Canada	11,320
Israel	5,090	France	11,680
Hong Kong	5,340	West Germany	12,460
Spain	5,430	United States	13,160
Singapore	5,910	Sweden	14,010

Note: The average per capita income of all developed countries is $9,190; the average per capita income of all less developed countries is $750.
Source: The World Bank, *World Development Report 1984,* Table 1, pp. 218–19.

an advanced stage of development, like Hong Kong and Spain. And the highest category includes the Soviet Union and the developed market economies of the United States, Japan, and Western Europe.

Some countries with high per capita GNPs defy classification. Kuwait's per capita GNP is $19,870, higher than that of the United States or Sweden. But Kuwait relies on oil exports for its income. Its high per capita income does not reflect advanced economic development. Nor does per capita GNP tell us anything about income distribution. In fact, income is distributed less equally in the less developed countries than in developed countries, as Table 37.2 shows. In Mexico, for example, the top 10 percent of households received about 40 percent of the national income. The bottom 60 percent of households received only about half that amount, 22 percent. In Japan, the top 10 percent of families received about the same amount of income as the bottom 40 percent. Particularly in the poorest of the less developed countries, there is no middle class. An enormous gulf separates rich and poor.

Over time, economic growth and technological development can lead to greater equality in income distribution. But time is not on the side of most less developed countries. In these countries, rapid population growth tends to cancel out increases in national income per capita.

Economic Growth Versus Population Growth

Economic growth is important to a nation's development for several reasons. It increases the amount of goods and services available to consumers for personal use. It expands the supply of resources available for capital formation. And it gives government the resources it needs to

Table 37.2. Income Distribution in Selected Countries, Less Developed and Developed (percentage share of household income, by quintile)

Country	Year	First Fifth	Second Fifth	Third Fifth	Fourth Fifth	Last Fifth	Top 10 Percent
Less Developed							
India	1976	7.0%	9.2%	13.9%	20.5%	49.4%	33.6%
Kenya	1976	2.3	6.6	11.5	19.2	60.4	45.8
Peru	1972	1.9	5.1	11.0	21.0	61.0	42.9
Malaysia	1973	3.5	7.7	12.4	20.3	56.1	39.8
Panama	1970	2.0	5.2	11.0	20.0	61.8	44.2
Brazil	1972	2.0	5.0	9.4	17.0	66.6	50.6
Mexico	1977	2.9	7.0	12.0	20.4	57.7	40.6
Argentina	1970	4.4	9.7	14.1	21.5	50.3	35.2
Developed							
United Kingdom	1979	7.0	11.5	17.0	24.8	39.7	23.4
Japan	1979	8.7	13.2	17.5	23.1	36.8	21.2
Finland	1977	6.8	12.8	18.7	24.9	36.8	21.2
West Germany	1978	7.9	12.5	17.0	23.1	39.5	24.0
Sweden	1979	7.2	12.8	17.4	25.4	37.2	21.2
Norway	1979	6.3	12.9	18.8	24.7	37.3	22.2

Source: The World Bank, *World Development Report 1984*, Table 28, pp. 272–73.

discharge its social responsibilities. Table 37.3 shows the average annual growth rates for selected countries, developed and undeveloped, from 1960 to 1982. With few exceptions, growth rates were higher in the developed countries.

In the low-income countries, especially those of Africa, slow growth accentuates and perpetuates poverty. In the poorest country in the world, Chad, income per capita declined significantly from 1960 to 1982. Three other poor countries, Zaire, the Sudan, and Zambia, had static economies. India, with one of the largest populations in the world, grew at a rate of only 1.3 percent annually. To make matters worse, in countries like India, population gains often offset economic growth. Because their resources are consumed at home, poor countries have little to export to earn the income necessary for economic development.

Although the overall rate of population growth has been declining worldwide since the late 1970s, the population is still growing year by year. In 1982 world population increased by 82 million people, bringing the total to 4.7 billion—twice as many as twenty years ago.[4] Current projections suggest the world's population will be about 6.5 billion by the

---

4. "Population Bulletin of the United Nations," No. 14-182, Department of International Economic and Social Affairs (New York: United Nations), 1983.

Table 37.3. Average Annual Growth Rate of GNP Per Capita, Selected Countries, 1960–1982 (percent)

Less Developed			Developed		
	Per Capita Income	Growth Rate		Per Capita Income	Growth Rate
Chad	$ 80	−2.8	Italy	$ 6,680	3.4
Bangladesh	140	0.3	United Kingdom	9,660	2.0
Ethiopia	140	1.4	Austria	9,880	3.9
Zaire	190	−0.3	Japan	10,080	6.1
India	260	1.3	Belgium	10,760	3.6
Haiti	300	0.6	Finland	10,870	3.6
China	310	5.0	Netherlands	10,930	2.9
Pakistan	380	2.8	Australia	11,140	2.4
Sudan	440	−0.4	Canada	11,320	3.1
Indonesia	580	4.2	France	11,680	3.7
Zambia	640	−0.1	West Germany	12,460	3.1
Nigeria	860	3.3	Denmark	12,470	2.5
Peru	1,310	1.4	United States	13,160	2.2
Chile	2,210	0.6	Sweden	14,040	2.4
Brazil	2,240	4.8	Norway	14,280	3.4
Mexico	2,270	3.6	Switzerland	17,010	1.9

Source: The World Bank, *World Development Report 1984*, Table 1, pp. 218–19.

end of this century. Almost all the increase will come in Latin America, Africa, and Asia, where birth rates are high and mortality rates are declining. These are the countries that can least afford population increases. The population of China and India is projected to increase by 450 million persons by the year 2000. The population of Bangladesh and Pakistan is likely to increase by 150 million.

Table 37.4 shows past population growth rates and projected future rates for selected countries, along with per capita GNP, which reflect a country's capacity to support an increase in population. The countries with very low per capita GNP tend to be those with the highest population growth rates. Income and population growth are inversely related. Sweden, which had a per capita GNP of $14,040 in 1982, has one of the lowest population growth rates in the world. It is projected to have about the same population in the year 2000 as it did in 1982. Bangladesh, which had a per capita GNP of $140 in 1982, is projected to have 64 million more people by the year 2000.

Social Services

There are two kinds of capital, social overhead capital and physical capital. Social overhead capital includes the structure and equipment required to

Table 37.4. Population Growth, Past and Projected, Selected Countries, 1970–2000

Country	Per Capita GNP, 1982	Annual Average Population Growth		Population (millions)	
		1970–1982	1980–2000	1982	2000
Bangladesh	$ 140	2.6%	2.9%	93	157
India	260	2.3	1.9	717	994
China	310	1.4	1.0	1,008	1,196
Pakistan	380	3.0	2.7	87	140
Indonesia	580	2.3	1.9	153	212
Egypt	690	2.5	2.0	44	63
Nigeria	860	2.6	3.5	91	169
Malaysia	1,860	2.5	2.0	15	21
Brazil	2,240	2.4	2.0	127	181
Mexico	2,270	3.0	2.3	73	109
Algeria	2,350	3.1	3.7	20	39
Italy	6,840	0.4	0.1	56	58
United Kingdom	9,660	0.1	0.1	56	57
West Germany	12,460	0.1	−0.1	62	60
United States	13,160	1.0	0.7	232	259
Sweden	14,040	0.3	0.1	8	8

Source: The World Bank, *World Development Report 1984*, Table 1, pp. 218–19; Table 19, pp. 254–55.

support and develop human resources—housing, hospitals, and schools. Physical capital consists of directly productive capital: the plant and equipment used in industry and agriculture. Neither kind of capital can be created without a supply of savings. Yet as we have seen, incomes are too low to permit much saving in poor countries. Inevitably, the low rate of saving translates into a low rate of capital formation. The result is that poor countries cannot afford the medical services and educational facilities needed to improve the quality of their labor forces.

Table 37.5 shows the difference among countries in medical and educational services. In Bangladesh, there is one physician to 10,940 persons; in the United States, one to every 520. In Uganda, only 5 percent of high-school-age people are in school, and only 1 percent of college-age people are in college. In Japan, the figures are 92 percent and 30 percent, respectively.

Agriculture and Technology

One of the most fundamental characteristics of the less developed countries is that a high percentage of the population is employed in agriculture. In most of these countries it would be possible to reduce the number of workers employed in agriculture without changing technology and still

Table 37.5. Health and Education in Selected Countries, Developed and Less Developed

Country	Population per Physician	Percentage of Age Group in Secondary Schools	Percentage of Age Group in Higher Institutions
Bangladesh	10,940	15%	3%
Ethiopia	58,490	12	1
Uganda	26,810	5	1
India	3,690	30	8
China	1,810	44	1
Pakistan	3,480	17	2
Kenya	7,890	19	1
Indonesia	11,530	30	3
Nigeria	12,550	16	3
Guatemala	16,710	16	7
Italy	340	73	27
Japan	780	92	30
United States	520	97	58
Sweden	490	85	37
Soviet Union	270	96	21
Canada	550	93	37

Source: The World Bank, *World Development Report 1984*, Table 24, pp. 264–65; Table 25, pp. 266–67.

obtain the same output. Farming techniques are primitive, tools and equipment limited. Modern equipment is neither easy to import nor highly demanded. And agricultural output consists mostly of high-calorie cereals and raw materials. Relatively little protein food is produced, since it requires more acres per calorie than cereals do.

Table 37.6 shows the percentage of the labor force employed in agriculture, industry, and services in various countries. In a poor country like Bangladesh, 74 percent of the working-age population is employed in agriculture, compared with 2 percent in the United States. In the highly developed countries, employment in the service industries actually exceeds employment in manufacturing. The United States is such a postindustrial economy: employment in services far exceeds employment in industry and agriculture combined.

Technologically, many less developed countries are divided between two coexisting modes of production. One is modern, capital intensive, export oriented, and often foreign owned and managed. The other is traditional, labor intensive, dedicated to supplying the home market or the family, and domestically owned.[5] The first is technologically advanced

---

5. Bruce Herrick and Charles P. Kindleberger, *Economic Development*, 4th ed. (New York: McGraw-Hill, 1983), p. 520.

Table 37.6. Labor Force Participation Rates in Agriculture, Industry, and Services, Selected Countries

Country	Per Capita GNP (1982)	Percentage of 1980 Labor Force Employed in		
		Agriculture	Industry	Services
Bangladesh	$ 140	74%	11%	15%
Ethiopia	140	80	7	13
India	260	71	13	16
China	310	69	19	12
Niger	310	91	3	6
Pakistan	380	57	20	23
Sudan	440	78	10	12
Indonesia	580	58	12	30
Thailand	790	76	9	15
Syria	1,680	33	31	36
Brazil	2,240	30	24	46
Mexico	2,270	36	26	38
Greece	4,290	37	28	35
Italy	6,340	11	45	44
West Germany	12,460	4	46	50
United States	13,160	2	32	66

Source: The World Bank, *World Development Report 1984*, Table 1, pp. 218–19; Table 2, pp. 220–21; and Table 21, pp. 258–59.

and highly productive. The second is technologically dated and underproductive. In small cottage industries, each worker may perform every step in the production process.

This technological dualism can create social divisions, for new products and production methods often require people to change their beliefs and ways of living. Workers accustomed to different modes of production will have different values and different economic goals.

Theories of Economic Development

Over time economists have developed a considerable body of thought on the conditions necessary for economic development. We will summarize some of the more important theories here.

Classical Theory

The classical economists of the late eighteenth and early nineteenth centuries—Adam Smith, David Ricardo, Thomas Malthus, and John Stuart Mill—saw technological progress as the key to development. Increasing mechanization permitted the efficient division of labor, improving productivity. Such technological progress depended in turn on the accumulation of capital, which itself depended on the level of profits.

Classical economists worried that profits were linked to population growth. As profits increased, employment and total wages paid would rise with them, encouraging workers to have more children. (It was assumed that an unlimited amount of labor, including child labor, was available at a subsistence wage.) Population growth would tend to absorb profits, creating a drag on economic development. To feed the growing population, farmers would have to put marginal land into use or till the best land more intensively. Diminishing returns would cause prices to rise, pushing up labor costs. Profits would go down, and the accumulation of capital would decline. To stay ahead of the population growth, therefore, technology would have to improve continually.

Marxist Theory

The German economist Karl Marx contended that economic conditions were the basic forces that shaped society. Marx saw technological change as the prime mover in the development of medieval feudalism into industrial capitalism. But capitalism was merely one stage in the evolution of society toward its final form: the communist state.

Like the classical economists, Marx believed that economic development depended on technological progress, which depended on the accumulation of capital and ultimately on profits. But he saw wages as the key to the whole process. Marx argued that labor was the sole source of value in the productive process. Capitalists would try to pay labor a subsistence wage and claim the surplus value for themselves. Eventually consumption would decline, causing recurrent economic crises. Ultimately economic instability would wreck the capitalist system, preparing the way for the new communist society.

Rostow's Takeoff Theory

Probably the most prominent of recent theories of economic development is Walt Rostow's takeoff theory.[6] According to Rostow, nations pass through five stages in the process of economic development.

1. *The traditional society.* In this first stage, most resources are concentrated in agriculture. There is no cumulative, self-reinforcing process of material improvement, such as exists in industrial societies. As a result there is little social mobility. All societies before the Renaissance were traditional societies.

2. *Prerequisites for takeoff.* In the second stage, the prerequisites for sustained, systematic social change are created. At least part of the

---

6. Walt Whitman Rostow, *The Stages of Economic Growth: A Non-Communist Manifesto* (New York: Cambridge University Press, 1971).

population in traditional societies must abandon its fatalistic outlook on life. There must be entrepreneurs willing to take risks in finance and manufacturing. Social respect must come to depend on economic achievement rather than inherited status. Finally, a leading sector—mining, petroleum, or some other industry—must propel the takeoff.

3. *Takeoff.* In this stage, which lasts twenty to thirty years, the pace of social and economic change suddenly accelerates. The process is fueled by an increase in the percentage of the gross national product that is saved and invested, and by the establishment of manufacturing. Social customs, governmental forms and practices, and economic institutions continue to evolve.

4. *The drive to maturity.* This is a period of self-sustaining increases in gross national product, both overall and per capita. During this stage, which lasts about sixty years, industry acquires the most advanced technology available. Manufacturers become capable of producing whatever they wish, subject only to the constraints of the market and the availability of resources.

5. *Mass consumption.* The last stage of economic development is one of mass consumption of durable goods and services. The production of such goods and services enables most of the population to attain a high living standard.

Rostow's theory has been criticized on several counts. It does not fit historical fact very closely. Some countries' economies do not take off suddenly, but develop steadily over a long period of time. The theory is also vague on what causes growth in each stage, and what distinguishes one stage from the next. Nevertheless Rostow's theory offers valuable insight into the changes that must occur before a nation in the traditional stage of development can develop economically.

Other Theories

Two other theories of economic development deserve brief mention. The *big push theory* offers a potential solution to the vicious circle of low income, low saving, low investment, low productivity, and low income. The idea is that a large infusion of investment, primarily from foreign sources, into different industries will enlarge markets, creating support industries. As industries buy from each other, the economy will grow, income and saving will rise, and the circle will be broken.

The *dependency theory* relates the problems of the less developed countries to their former colonial status. Most less developed countries were once possessions of mercantilist nations like Spain, England, France, the Netherlands, and Portugal. Their natural resources were exploited by the mother countries, and they were prevented from developing technologically. These colonies eventually achieved independence, but they remained economically and psychologically dependent on Europe. Many of the new African countries still rely on foreign military and financial advisers, for example.

Perspectives in Economics: The Value of Children in Less Developed Countries

Martin Schnitzer

If population growth is an obstacle to economic development, why are birth control programs difficult to implement in less developed countries? For one thing, traditional cultural barriers must be overcome. To the male head of the household, a large family may be a symbol of social prestige. And religion may prohibit the use of contraceptives.

But economic factors also play a part. A large family can mean economic security for parents, for each additional child represents an earning asset. The economic motive is especially strong in agricultural areas, where farmers need extra labor to work the land. Parents also depend on children to care for them in their old age. Thus the monetary benefits of having many children may far outweigh the costs.

In the developed countries, it is usually the other way around. As living standards increase, it costs more to provide the goods and services needed to raise children. In addition there is the opportunity cost of raising children—the amount of time parents put into caring for children, compared with other uses they could have made of that time. A woman who leaves the labor force to have children may lose considerable income. No wonder people with high incomes want fewer children than people with low incomes. The alternative uses for their time—making money, enjoying leisure pursuits— are quite attractive.

Obstacles to Economic Development

Economic development has been proceeding slowly or not at all in many of the less developed countries. Per capita GNP is not only low, but stagnant. In some countries, during some periods, it has actually fallen. The fact is, economic development is an extremely elusive objective. Among the most significant obstacles to its achievement is overpopulation.

Overpopulation

Perhaps the chief obstacle to economic development in less developed countries is people. Because people provide the most important factor of production, labor, one might conclude that more people would obviously mean more GNP. That assumes access to large amounts of natural resources and capital, however. More people mean not only more labor and output, but more mouths to feed. The more people, the less capital and natural resources per capita. Unfortunately, many less developed countries are experiencing runaway population growth.

Table 37.7. Birth and Death Rates and Population Doubling-Time for Selected Countries, Developed and Less Developed, 1982

Developed Countries	Birth Rate (thousands)	Death Rate (thousands)	Doubling-Time (years)
All countries	16	9	112
Soviet Union	20	10	68
United States	16	9	100
Japan	13	6	102
West Germany	10	12	—
East Germany	14	14	—
Italy	11	10	408
United Kingdom	13	12	693
France	15	10	151
Canada	15	7	85
Sweden	11	11	3465

Population Doubling

In 1798 the English clergyman Thomas Malthus published *An Essay on the Principle of Population*. Malthus took a pessimistic view. He suggested that the world's population was growing faster than its food supply. On the basis of scattered empirical evidence, including data from the North American colonies, Malthus calculated that populations tended to double every twenty-five years, in geometric progression, whereas the food supply tends to increase arithmetically. For example:

Year	0	25	50	75	100	125	150	175	200
Population	1	2	4	8	16	32	64	128	256
Food	1	2	3	4	5	6	7	8	9

Malthus based his proposition on two assumptions that have subsequently been disproved: first, that technological change could not increase the food supply faster than the population was increasing; second, that population growth could be limited only by an increase in the death rate. Nevertheless there was some truth in Malthus's predictions. It took over four thousand years of recorded history for China to reach a population of 500 million, but then only a little more than three decades to increase to one billion. And it is true that whatever a nation's size, natural resources, and level of development, a large population and a high birth rate will bring increasing problems in the future.

Table 37.7 shows the birth and death rates and the time required for a doubling of population for selected countries. The United States, with a

Less Developed Countries	Birth Rate (thousands)	Death Rate (thousands)	Doubling-Time (years)
All countries	32	11	33
China	21	8	54
India	34	14	36
Indonesia	34	13	33
Brazil	31	8	30
Bangladesh	49	18	22
Pakistan	43	15	25
Nigeria	49	17	21
Mexico	32	6	26
Philippines	32	7	27
Vietnam	34	10	30

Source: Mary M. Kent and Carl Haub, "1984 Population Data Sheet" (Washington, D.C.: Population Reference Bureau, April 1984).

birth rate of 16 per 1,000 and a death rate of 9 per 1,000, will double its population in 100 years.[7] Mexico, with a birth rate of 32 per 1,000 and a death rate of 6 per 1,000, will double its population in just 26 years. West Germany and East Germany, with negative and zero rates of growth respectively, will never double their population unless their growth increases. Worldwide, the population doubling-time for developed countries is 112 years; for less developed countries, it is 33 years. The gap is even wider if we compare Western Europe (442 years), with Africa (24 years). And again we see the link between economic growth and population growth. In 1982, the GNP per capita for Africa was $810; it was $12,000 for Western Europe.

Urbanization

Urbanization compounds population problems through congestion. Overcrowding in cities promotes pollution, unemployment, and a greater demand for human services. The increased stress can cause disease—not only communicable diseases like tuberculosis but heart disease, cancer, and other ailments attributable to a breakdown in the body's immunity. The problems of urbanization are particularly acute in less developed countries, which lack the financial resources to provide remedial services.

By the end of this century, at least twenty-two of the world's cities will have populations of more than ten million. Sixty will have more than five

7. Mary M. Kent and Carl Haub, "1984 World Population Data Sheet" (Washington, D.C.: Population Reference Bureau, April 1984.

million.[8] Most of these, like Mexico City, now the second largest city in the world, are located in the less developed countries.

Food Shortages

The larger a nation's population, the greater its demand for food. In most overpopulated countries, the strong demand for food has left little saving and has hampered industrial development. The rural population competes with a rising tide of urban consumers for the limited agricultural output.

Here again we see the vicious circle of poverty in operation. The inability to industrialize reduces the potential of less developed countries to earn money from exports, which could be used to import additional food. Food shortages produce nutritional deficiencies and ultimately ill health. And poor health reduces productivity, output, and income.

Lack of an Infrastructure

Infrastructure is a broad concept that includes the highways, railways, airports, sewage facilities, housing, and other social amenities provided in developed areas. Once in place, the infrastructure encourages both economic and social development. Because less developed countries generally do not have infrastructures, industrial firms will not normally locate plants there. Products manufactured for mass consumption simply cannot be distributed and used without transportation and communication facilities, skilled labor, and waste disposal plants.

Schools

Educational facilities are a key component of an area's infrastructure. Because education is directly related to the quality of life, it constitutes a form of social capital. A low literacy rate can retard economic development. A high literacy rate can assist it.

Literacy is directly related to a country's stage of economic development. There is a positive correlation between a low standard of living and a high rate of illiteracy. It has been estimated that one-third of the world's people are illiterate,[9] and that most of them live in countries with high birth rates, large populations, and little money to spend on education. This general lack of educational opportunities reinforces the distribution between the haves and the have-nots, perpetuating class differences as well as slowing economic development.

8. United Nations, Department of International and Social Affairs, *Population Bulletin of the United Nations*, No. 14, 1983, p. 24.
9. United Nations, Department of International and Social Affairs, *Population Bulletin of the United Nations*, No. 14, 1983, p. 25.

Roads

A system of roads is vital to economic and social development. Without roads, transportation becomes much more expensive. The cost of air transport is prohibitively high for most products, and railroad networks serve only a limited number of major access points.

Poor countries usually do not have the resources to develop and maintain an adequate road system. Their limited capital is simply insufficient to surmount natural barriers to transportation. For example, the lack of highways across the Sierra Madre and Andes mountains has long inhibited the east-west development of Mexico and South America. Transportation is especially hard to develop in countries dominated by mountain ranges, like Bolivia and Peru.

Other Facilities

Dams, bridges, and waste disposal and communication facilities are vitally important assets that less developed countries usually lack. Dams provide the water supply and electric power necessary for economic and social development. Bridges create more efficient transportation by directly linking areas separated by water bodies. Waste disposal facilities control communicable diseases like cholera and typhoid fever, which can be spread by rats and other animals that feed on garbage dumped in city streets. Finally, communication facilities must be reliable enough to allow the transaction of business on a regular basis. In the less developed countries, government-owned telephone and telegraph services are notoriously inefficient.

Other Obstacles

Low Savings Rate

Savings are an important prerequisite for capital formation, for they free resources for use in the production of plant and equipment. An inability to raise capital is therefore a serious obstacle to economic development. Here again less developed countries are caught in a vicious circle. Small savings mean a small capital stock and a small gross national product. If GNP is small, almost all of it will be consumed in subsistence goods like food, leaving little to be saved. Capital formation will remain low, along with the standard of living and the rate of economic development.[10]

The unequal distribution of income in less developed countries exacerbates the saving problem. The vast majority of workers in these countries do not earn enough income to accumulate any savings. Instead, a minority

---

10. Ragnar Nurkse, *Problems of Capital Formation in Underdeveloped Countries* (New York: Oxford University Press, 1953).

of households receives most of the income. In Mexico, for example, the top 10 percent of income earners receives about 40 percent of the national income. In Brazil, the top 10 percent receives about 50 percent of the nation's earnings. Members of this privileged group could provide the saving necessary for capital formation, but they usually invest their money in real estate, which offers them a quick, high return on investment, or in foreign assets. Swiss bonds, which cannot be expropriated by a new government, may be extremely attractive to investors living in politically unstable countries.

Limited Range of Exports

The less developed countries tend to export agricultural products, raw fuels, and metals. Many depend on a single product for most of their export income. About 80 percent of Nigeria's total export earnings is from oil, for instance. Needless to say, such dependence on one commodity can make a country extremely vulnerable to the ups and downs of the marketplace.

When oil prices were high in the early 1970s, for example, Nigeria's income increased. It ran a surplus in its balance of payments and used foreign earnings to improve its living standards. Increased public spending improved Nigeria's infrastructure, bettering its opportunities for development. During the early 1980s, however, world demand for oil began to decline. Oil prices fell by about $6 per barrel from a peak of $35 in 1980. As revenues from oil exports declined, Nigeria developed a deficit in its balance of payments. It must now pay off a large foreign debt incurred when oil prices were high, with earnings received when prices are low.

Countries that depend on the export of agricultural products and minerals are usually at a disadvantage in trade with developed countries. The terms of trade—that is, the quantity of exports required to pay for a given amount of imports—tend to favor the developed countries. Brazilian coffee and Mexican oil, for example, are much more subject to shifts in price than American computers or Japanese cars. The demand for agricultural products and minerals tends to be inelastic, so that when prices fall, they are not offset by an increase in demand. When coffee prices decline, then, Brazil will have to give up more income to import the same number of computers or cars. At the same time, America and Japan will give up less income to acquire Brazil's coffee.

Sociocultural Factors

Sociocultural factors can also impede economic development.[11] In countless ways, culture influences individual and group behavior, determining how and when things will be done. Status distinctions based on education,

---

11. For a discussion of sociocultural factors and their impact on development, see Edmund Leach, *Social Anthropology* (New York: Oxford University Press, 1982); and W. Arthur Lewis, *The Theory of Economic Development* (Homewood, Ill.: Irwin, 1955).

caste, politics, religion, or sex can hold back employment of productive labor. Language differences can make communication and job training difficult. But culture can also contribute to development. If the use of machinery and equipment creates an industrial culture that is alien to the old agrarian ways, the new culture will speed the transition to a developed economy. Cultural conformity keeps groups of people working together, either for or against new ideas and ways of living.

Cultural attitudes and values underlie population problems as well as productivity rates. The norm in most less developed countries is to have large families. Religious prohibitions on birth control contribute to this pattern, but so do the limited social roles of women. Women in these countries occupy a secondary position that allows them little education or opportunity for work outside the home.

Status distinctions and religious values are also important determinants of economic advancement. Business has a lower status than other professions in some less developed societies. And economic development often conflicts with religious tradition. The overthrow of the Shah of Iran in 1979 was led largely by a fundamentalist Moslem clergy in revolt against Western materialism. Finally, traditional tribal conflicts can hamper development.

Remedies for Economic Underdevelopment

There is no easy way for poor countries to become rich overnight. Many problems must be overcome, notably population growth. The mismatch between population growth and income growth in many less developed countries works against economic development.

Changes in the developed countries' economic and financial policies could relieve some of the difficulties of the less developed countries. Foreign trade can be an instrument of growth. If governments of the developed countries would drop some of their import restrictions, less developed countries would be able to earn more income. Through foreign aid programs, developed countries could also lend funds for investment to developing countries.

Foreign Aid

Foreign aid is the transfer of income from rich nations to poor nations for the purpose of promoting their economic development. The transfer may be made as outright grants or as loans carrying lower interest rates and longer repayment periods than usual. (In 1982, the average interest rate for public borrowing in Bangladesh was 1.5 percent, and the average length of repayment was thirty-nine years.) Foreign aid may also take a variety of physical forms, from technical assistance to food supplies. Military assistance may be considered a form of foreign aid, although its impact on economic development is debatable.

Since the end of the Second World War, a battery of international financial institutions has sprung up to assist less developed countries in developing their economies. Among these are the International Bank of Reconstruction and Development (IBRD), the International Development Association (IDA), and the International Finance Corporation (IFC). All these organizations attempt to promote economic and social progress through the creation of modern economic and social infrastructures. All three make loans to countries or firms for such purposes as roads, irrigation projects, and electric generating plants. The IFC, for example, makes loans to firms, on the condition that the project benefit the economy of the less developed country and have a reasonable prospect of making a profit. Finally, the World Health Organization (WHO), an agency of the United Nations, assists less developed countries in improving their health services.

Besides these international institutions, the United States and other developed nations have their own programs of assistance for less developed countries. The Overseas Private Investment Corporation (OPIC), an American agency, provides direct loans for development projects at low interest rates. And the Export-Import Bank (Eximbank), though originally created for other purposes, has recently allocated most of its funds for the use of less developed countries. In addition, most Western European countries provide technical or financial assistance to the less developed countries.[12] In the Third World, or politically nonaligned, countries of Africa, Asia, and the Middle East, the Soviet Union is increasingly providing technical and capital assistance. Economic aid to those countries is now a major factor in the contest for power between the United States and the Soviet Union.

Foreign aid is not a miracle cure for economic underdevelopment. Military aid can do little to promote economic development, unless it permits a country to divert defense funds to more productive uses. The benefits of aid may end up in the hands of a few, instead of reaching a broad segment of the population. And if aid is used for consumption instead of investment, it will generate few lasting economic benefits. Moreover, many foreign aid projects take time to develop. Not all produce directly marketable output immediately.

Other Solutions

In the last three decades many less developed countries have made substantial economic and social progress. In general, this development has come about in one of three ways.

1. Exportation of a major resource, with no real progress toward industrialization. The Arab oil-producing countries have achieved very high per capita incomes through their oil exports, for example.

---

12. Foreign aid as a percentage of gross national product varies considerably by country. In 1983, for example, 0.24 percent of the U.S. GNP went to foreign aid, compared with 1.10 percent for Norway. Japan contributed 0.33 percent of its GNP to foreign aid, West Germany 0.48 percent.

Perspectives in Economics: Mexico's Economic Development Problems

Martin Schnitzer

Mexico is a nation of both extreme wealth and extreme poverty, of vast mineral resources but little arable land. It has one of the fastest-growing steel industries in the world, and is strategically located next door to the world's largest consumer market, the United States. Even though Mexico's advantages could make it one of the world's most prosperous nations, 40 percent of its labor force is unemployed or underemployed. Its population is growing at the alarmingly high rate of 2.5 percent a year. And its financial position is getting worse. From 1982 to 1984, inflation increased to rates of more than 100 percent, and the peso lost more than three-fourths of its value against the dollar. Mexico's foreign debt, around $90 billion, is now among the highest in the world. At the same time export revenues, which are based mostly on oil, are declining.

Mexico's economy is a combination of public and private enterprise. A government-owned monopoly, Pemex, produces all the oil in Mexico. The revenue from oil exports goes to finance a wide variety of development schemes, including a national support system for agriculture and a plan to generate electricity using nuclear reactors. Because in 1982 the government nationalized the banking industry, it now controls access to financial credit. It also influences the geographical location of private firms through its control of the infrastructure, such as ports and roads. In some industries, such as steel, government enterprises compete directly with private firms. Finally, the government controls access to imported goods through exchange controls and import licensing.

Despite government efforts, several factors work against the realization of Mexico's economic potential. The first is overpopulation. Unemployment and underemployment is already high, particularly in the cities. The nation will be hard pressed to find jobs for the 800,000 new workers that will join the labor force each year in the near future. Second, extreme inequality in the distribution of income and wealth limits saving and promotes social unrest. And finally, corruption, another potential cause of unrest, is widespread in Mexico's one-party political system. (Political corruption was a prime factor in Fidel Castro's rise to power in Cuba.)

2. Industrialization and protective tariffs and quotas. The Mexican government, for example, has encouraged manufacturing both directly, through controls on investment and trade, and indirectly, through taxes, subsidies, and other measures influencing resource and product prices. At the same time it has restricted imports to limit the competition faced by new industries.

3. Industrialization and the export of manufactured goods. Japan and South Korea have pursued this approach successfully. Both nations have relied mainly on the incentives of the market system, with some direction and control from the state. A high rate of investment has been a major contributor to economic growth in these nations.

These methods may not be relevant to the poorest countries in the world, which have little of value to export and little potential for industrialization. Investment in India and other poor countries is limited by their inability to absorb capital; by low levels of saving; and by adverse foreign exchange rates. Less developed countries cannot control many of the factors that influence their development prospects—such as the economic well-being of the developed countries, their source of trade and foreign aid.

In the end the key to development may lie in the right combination of government policy and private enterprise initiative. Some East Asian countries have succeeded this way. Government policies have expanded exports by keeping exchange rates competitive, while restricting imports on the basis of price. They have maintained high real interest rates, which have encouraged saving and ensured that investment is directed to the areas of highest return. Yet in these countries resources are allocated by the market, to ensure their most productive use. In China, the government recently introduced a series of measures to restructure the economy and increase the rate of development. Business enterprises are to have greater autonomy; there will be greater reliance on the market to determine output; and government monopolies will be broken up through competition.

Summary and Extensions

Almost half the world's population lives in countries with a GNP per capita of $500 a year or less. Another 500 million people live in countries with a per capita income of between $500 and $1,500 a year. These countries are in the beginning stages of economic development. Yet many countries with higher per capita incomes, like Mexico and Brazil, are by no means modern industrial economies. Similarly, in the oil-exporting countries, per capita incomes are high, but the level of development is low.

Less developed countries face many challenges in their efforts to advance. The first is to attract enough investment, either through saving or aid, to provide a satisfactory rate of economic growth. They must also build an infrastructure that provides the services necessary for industrial development. Negative sociocultural attitudes must also be overcome. Probably the most important obstacle to conquer is high population growth. If population grows rapidly, most of a nation's investment must be devoted to maintaining per capita income at current levels rather than to increasing it.

Major Conclusions

1. Although the terms economic growth and economic development are often used interchangeably, they have different meanings. Economic growth involves an expanded capacity to produce goods and services. Economic development involves growth through a reorganization of the resources used and the goods and services produced.
2. Economic growth and development depend on (a) the quantity and quality of a nation's labor force, capital stock, and natural resources;

(b) a nation's level of technology; and (c) socioeconomic factors, such as religion, that influence what goods are produced and how.

3. The per capita GNP of many underdeveloped countries, like India and China, is only a small fraction of the per capita GNP of industrialized countries, like Japan and the United States.

4. In less developed countries, the national income tends to be concentrated more heavily in the hands of high-income earners than in developed countries.

5. Less developed countries typically have lower growth rates than developed countries.

6. The rate of population growth tends to be higher in less developed than in developed countries.

7. In less developed countries a much higher percentage of the labor force is employed in agriculture than in developed countries.

8. There are a number of theories of economic growth and development. (a) Classical theory focuses on the role of capital accumulation in growth and development. (b) Marxist theory focuses on the role of expanding technology and the capitalist incentive to accumulate ever increasing amounts of capital. (c) Rostow's takeoff theory divides growth into five stages, from the early traditional society to the mass consumption society.

9. The major problems facing less developed countries in their efforts to grow and develop include (a) overpopulation and relatively high rates of population growth; (b) an inadequate infrastructure; (c) concentration on the exportation of only a few products or commodities; and (d) a low rate of saving and investment.

10. Remedies for the economic problems of less developed countries include (a) control of population growth; (b) foreign aid; and (c) greater reliance on market incentives in the allocation of scarce resources.

Questions to Ponder

1. On what basis is a country classified as less developed?
2. What are the typical features of a less developed economy?
3. Distinguish between economic growth and economic development.
4. Describe Rostow's theory of the stages of economic development.
5. What is the typical attitude toward family size in traditional societies? Why?
6. What do you consider the most important obstacle to economic development in the less developed countries? Why?
7. Give some examples of sociocultural factors that block economic development.
8. Why are less developed countries at a disadvantage in their trade with developed countries?
9. When and how are people a liability rather than an asset in achieving economic development?

Glossary

A

Absolute advantage the capacity to produce more units of output than a competitor can for any given level of resource use.

Aggregate demand the presumed negative relationship between the general price level and the total quantity of goods and services that consumers, business, and government want to buy.

Aggregate supply the presumed positive relationship between the general price level and the total quantity of goods and services produced in the economy during a given period.

Appreciation of the dollar (or any other national currency) an increase in purchasing power in terms of other national currencies.

Automatic stabilizer a tax or expenditure that increases total planned spending in times of recession and lowers it in times of economic expansion, without special action on the part of the administration and Congress. Also known as nondiscretionary fiscal policy.

Average fixed cost total fixed costs (FC) divided by the number of units produced (Q). Or, $AFC = FC \div Q$.

Average tax rate the percentage of total income that is paid in taxes. Obtained by dividing total taxes paid by total taxable income.

Average total cost the total of all fixed and variable costs divided by the number of units produced (Q). Or, $ATC = TC \div Q = AFC + AVC$.

Average variable cost total variable costs (VC) divided by the number of units produced (Q). Or, $AVC = VC \div Q$.

B

Bonds a long-term debt obligation of a corporation, generally traded on the open market.

Book profit the profit shown on a company's accounting books.

Break-even income level that income level at which a government subsidy is no longer available.

Budget deficit the amount by which outlays exceed receipts during a given accounting period.

Budget line a curve that shows all the combinations of two goods a consumer can buy with a given amount of income.

Budgetary (or fiscal) policy the manipulation of federal expenditures and taxes to promote a high and stable level of employment and production, price level stability, and economic growth. Also known as discretionary fiscal policy.

Budget surplus the amount by which receipts exceed outlays during a given accounting period.

Business cycle a recurring swing in general economic activity; a smaller pattern of ups and downs within a major long-term trend.

C

Capital (investment goods) any output of a production process that is designed to be used later in other production processes. Plant and equipment—things produced to produce other things—are examples of these manufactured means of production.

Capital account the record of U.S. investments abroad and foreign investments in the United States.

Capital account deficit the dollar amount by which U.S. investments abroad—that is, capital outflows—exceed foreign investments in the United States—that is, capital inflows.

Capital account surplus the dollar amount by which foreign investments in the United States—that is, capital inflows—exceed U.S. investments abroad—that is, capital outflows.

Capitalism an economic system based on private property and free enterprise, in which no government barriers to trade or restrictions on entry into business or the professions discourage competition.

Cartel an organization of independent producers intent on thwarting competition among themselves through the joint regulation of market shares, production levels, and prices. The principal purpose of such anticompetitive efforts is to raise prices and profits above competitive levels.

Cash transfer a money grant provided by government to a select group of citizens.

Circular flow of income the integrated flow of resources, goods, and services between or among broad sectors of the economy, like producers, consumers, and government.

Common access resources resources owned in common instead of privately by individuals. Thus individuals may not be excluded from their use.

Common stock a set of ownership rights in a corporation that entitles the investor to a share of any profits remaining after all other obligations have been met.

Communism as conceived by Karl Marx, a classless society governed by workers that would emerge from the downfall of capitalism. In practical terms, an economic system in which virtually all the means of production (not just some, as in socialism) are owned and controlled by the state.

Comparative advantage a relatively lower cost of production, or the capacity to produce a product at a lower cost than a competitor, in terms of the goods that must be given up.

Competition the process by which market participants, in pursuing their own interests, attempt to outdo, outprice, outproduce, and outmaneuver each other.

Conglomerate a firm that results from the merging of several firms from different industries.

Constant dollar (or real) gross national product gross national product adjusted for price changes.

Consumer equilibrium a state of stability in consumer purchasing patterns in which the individual has maximized his or her utility. Unless conditions—income, tastes, or prices—change, the consumer's buying patterns will tend to remain the same.

Consumer price index (CPI) the ratio of the cost of specific consumer items in any one year to the cost of those items in the base year, 1967. Used to gauge price trends in the consumer products sector of the economy.

Consumption function the assumed direct relationship between the national income level and the planned consumption expenditures of households.

Consumption goods goods that are produced to be used and enjoyed more or less immediately by their purchasers.

Corporate income taxes government revenues collected on a corporation's computed profits, as reported on its profit and loss statements.

Corporation a legal entity, created by government charter, with the right to conduct business in its own name, much as an individual does. A corporation can buy and sell, sue and be sued in its own name rather than the names of its owners.

Cost (opportunity cost) the value of the most highly preferred alternative not taken. Also called real cost. (Compare to money cost.)

Cost-benefit analysis the careful calculation of all costs and benefits associated with a given course of action.

Cost-push inflation a general rise in prices that occurs when restrictions are placed on the supply of one or more resources, or when the price of one or more resources is increased.

Cost structure the way various measures of cost (total cost, variable cost, and so forth) vary with the production level.

Current account the record of all the nation's international transactions other than capital flows and statistical discrepancies, including its merchandise trade, its investment income, its military transactions, its travel expenditures, its other services, and its remittances, pensions, and gifts.

Current account deficit the dollar amount by which a nation's imports of goods and services, interest and dividend payments to foreigners, gifts to foreigners, travel expenditures abroad, and other remittances to foreign nations exceed its exports of goods and services, interest and dividend receipts from foreign nations, gifts from abroad, foreign travel expenditures in this nation, and other remittances from abroad.

Current account surplus the dollar amount by which a nation's exports of goods and services, interest and dividend receipts from foreigners, gifts from foreigners, foreign travel expenditures in this nation, and other receipts from abroad exceed the nation's imports of goods and services, interest and dividend payments to foreigners, gifts to foreigners, travel expenditures abroad, and other remittances to foreign nations.

Cyclical unemployment unemployment that is caused by downswings of the business cycle—that is, by a broad-based reduction in the overall level of spending in the economy. Lasts for a period of weeks or months.

D

Decrease in demand a decrease in the quantity demand at each and every price, represented graphically by a leftward, or inward, shift of the demand curve. Also a decrease in the price buyers are willing and able to pay for each and every quantity demand.

Decrease in supply a decrease in the quantity producers are willing and able to offer at each and every price, represented graphically by a leftward, or inward, shift of the supply curve. Also an increase in the price producers are willing and able to accept for each and every quantity supplied.

Demand the assumed inverse relationship between the price of a good or service and the quantity consumers are willing and able to buy during a given period, all other things held constant.

Demand for labor the assumed inverse relationship between the real wage rate and the quantity of labor employed during a given period, everything else held constant. Derived from worker productivity and the market price of the product produced.

Demand-pull inflation a general rise in prices that occurs when total planned expenditures increase faster than total production.

Depreciation of the dollar (or any other national currency) a reduction in purchasing power in terms of other national currencies.

Discount rate the interest rate the Federal Reserve charges on loans to member banks.

Diseconomies of scale increases in per-unit cost due to an increase in the rate of production when the use of all resources is expanded; increases in the long-run average cost. Diseconomies of scale occur when an increase in resource inputs is not matched by a proportionate increase in output.

Disposable income personal income minus personal income tax payments.

Dissaving any net withdrawal from accumulated past savings, or any net increase in borrowing. Same as negative saving.

Duopoly an oligopolistic market shared by only two firms.

E

Econometric model a statistical equation or set of equations that describes economic data.

Econometrics the science of the statistical testing of economic theories and predictions.

Economic development the enhancement of a nation's capacity to produce through the creation of new kinds of output. Includes but goes beyond the improvements in technology and skills which promote economic growth.

Economic growth the expansion of a nation's capacity to produce the goods and services its people want. Caused by additions to or improvements in the technology of production.

Economic losses the amount by which the accounting expenses, the opportunity cost of capital, and the risk cost of doing business exceed a company's revenue.

Economic profit the amount left after all costs, including the opportunity cost of capital and the risk of losing money, have been deducted from company revenues. Normally zero.

Economic rent any payment received for the use of a resource or factor of production that exceeds its opportunity cost.

Economics the study of how people cope with scarcity—with the pressing problem of how to allocate their limited resources among their competing wants so as to satisfy as many of those wants as possible.

Economies of scale decreases in per-unit cost due to an increase in the rate of production when the use of all resources is expanded; decreases in the long-run average cost. Economies of scale occur when an increase in resource inputs brings a proportionally greater increase in output during a given period of time.

Efficiency the maximization of output through careful allocation of resources, given the constraints of supply (producers' costs) and demand (consumers' preferences). The achievement of efficiency means that consumers' or producers' welfare will be reduced by an expansion or contraction of output.

Elastic demand a relatively sensitive consumer response to price changes. If the price goes up or down, consumers will respond with a strong decrease or increase in the quantity demanded.

Elasticity coefficient of demand (E_d) the ratio of the percentage change in the quantity demanded to the percentage change in price. E_d = percentage change in quantity ÷ percentage change in price. Measures buyer response to price changes.

Employer cartel any organization of employers that seeks to restrict the number of workers hired in order to lower wages and increase profits.

Entrepreneur an enterprising person who discovers profitable opportunities and organizes, directs, and manages productive ventures. Entrepreneurs are often considered to be a resource in themselves. Distinguished from labor because they manage other resources.

Equation of exchange $(MV = PQ)$ a statement of mathematical equality between the product of the money stock (M) and the velocity of money (V) and the product of the price level (P) and the national output level (Q).

Equilibrium income level the income level at which producers have no reason to change their output level. Reached when leakages equal injections, or when total spending equals total output.

Equilibrium price the price toward which a competitive market will move, and at which it will remain once there, everything else held constant. The price at which the market "clears"—that is, at which the quantity demanded by consumers is matched exactly by the quantity offered by producers.

Equilibrium quantity the output (or sales) level toward which the market will move, and at which it will remain once there, everything else held constant. Reached when the quantity demanded equals the quantity supplied (at the equilibrium price).

Excess reserves the amount of a bank's reserves equal to the total reserves minus the required reserves.

Excise taxes taxes levied on specific products or services, for specific purposes. Normally stated as a percentage of the purchase price.

Exclusive dealership an agreement between a manufacturer and its dealers that forbids the dealers from handling other manufacturers' products. Declared illegal in the Clayton Act.

Explicit cost the money expenditure required to obtain a resource, product, or service.

External benefits benefits of production and consumption that are received by people not directly involved in the production, consumption, or exchange of a good. Positive effects on some third party. Also known as spillover benefits.

External costs costs of production and consumption that are imposed on people not directly involved in the production, consumption, or exchange of a good. Negative effects on some third party. Also known as spillover costs.

Externalities the positive (beneficial) or negative (harmful) effects that market exchanges have on people who do not participate directly in those exchanges. Third-party, or "spillover," effects.

F

Fiat money a medium of exchange or store of value that cannot be redeemed for anything other than a replica of itself. (A fiat dollar can be exchanged only for another dollar. It is money simply because the government states that it is money.)

Final goods and services those goods and services that are purchased for consumption rather than for further processing or resale.

Fiscal policy the manipulation of federal expenditures and taxes to promote a high and stable level of employment and production, price level stability, and economic growth. Also known as budgetary policy or discretionary fiscal policy.

Fixed cost any cost that does not vary with the level of output.

Fixed exchange rate system an international monetary exchange system in which the prices of currencies are established and maintained at some fixed level or within some fixed range by governments.

Floating (flexible) exchange rate system an international monetary exchange system in which the prices of currencies are determined by competitive market forces.

Frictional (transitional) unemployment unemployment that occurs when people move from one job to another requiring similar skills. Generally temporary, lasting only a few days or weeks. Caused by normal shifts in the supply of and demand for products.

Full-bodied commodity money a medium of exchange or store of value that has some intrinsic value as a consumer good or factor of production. Money that has some economic use apart from its monetary value.

Full employment the employment level that occurs when the quantity of labor demanded equals the quantity of labor supplied at a market-determined real wage rate. Estimated at about 93 to 96 percent of the labor force.

Full wage rate the sum of the money wage rate and the monetary equivalent of the nonmonetary benefits of a job.

G

General sales tax a tax on most, but not necessarily all, consumer purchases.

Gross national product (GNP) the current market value in dollars of all final goods and services produced in the economy in a given period.

Guaranteed income level the income level below which a family's or individual's income will not be allowed to fall. In effect, the government income subsidy at the zero adjusted earned income level.

H

Horizontal merger the joining of two or more firms in the same market—for example, two car companies—into a single firm.

Human capital the acquired skills and productive capacity of workers.

I

Imperfect price discrimination the practice of charging a few different prices for different consumption levels or different market segments (based on location, age, income, or some other identifiable characteristic). A fairly common practice.

Implicit cost the forgone opportunity to do or acquire something else, or to put one's resources to another use.

Implicit marginal income tax the amount by which a government subsidy is reduced when earned income rises.

Implicit marginal income tax rate the amount by which a government subsidy is reduced when earned income rises, stated as a percentage of the additional earned income.

Increase in demand an increase in the quantity demanded at each and every price, represented graphically by a rightward, or outward, shift in the demand curve. Also an increase in the price buyers are willing and able to pay at each and every quantity demanded.

Increase in supply an increase in the quantity producers are willing and able to offer at each and every price, represented graphically by a rightward, or outward, shift in the supply curve. Also an increase in the price producers are willing and able to accept for each and every quantity supplied.

Indifference curve a curve that shows the various combinations of two goods that yield the same level of utility.

Inelastic demand a relatively insensitive consumer response to price changes. If the price goes up or down, consumers will respond with only a slight decrease or increase in the quantity demanded.

Inferior good or service any good or service for which demand falls with an increase in income, or rises with a decrease in income.

Inflation a rise in the general level of prices over a period of time.

Injection (inflow) an inflow of income into the circular flow. Investment, government expenditures, and exports are injections.

In-kind transfer any good or service provided by government to a select group of citizens.

Interest a payment for deferred consumption, which in a competitive lendable funds market tends to reflect the productivity of capital. Normally expressed as a percentage or rate, as in interest rate.

Interest rate the annual payment for deferred consumption, expressed as a percentage of the dollar amount loaned (which is equal to the deferred consumption).

Interlocking directorate the practice of having the same people serve as directors of two or more competing firms.

Intermediate goods and services goods and services that are purchased for further processing or resale.

International balance of payments a summary statement of all international transactions between one nation—for example, the United States—and the rest of the world. International transactions include exports and imports of goods and services, gifts, interest and dividend payments, and travel expenditures, as well as the flows of financial capital (purchases of stocks and bonds and real capital assets) across national boundaries.

International exchange rate the price of one national currency (like the franc) stated in terms of another national currency (like the dollar).

Investment the purchase of capital goods—plant, equipment, and inventory—that can be used in the production of other goods and services.

Investment function the assumed relationship between national income and total planned expenditures on plant, equipment, and inventory.

Investment goods (capital) any output of a production process that is designed to be used later in other production processes. Plant and equipment—things produced to produce other things—are examples of these manufactured means of production.

Irrational behavior behavior that is inconsistent or clearly not in the individual's best interests, and that the individual recognizes as such at the time of the behavior.

Isocost curve (from the Greek word *iso*, meaning "same") a curve that shows the various combinations of resources that can be employed at a given expenditure (cost) level and given resource prices.

Isoquant curve (from the Greek word *iso*, meaning "same") a curve that shows the various technically efficient combinations of resources that can be used to produce a given output level.

L

Labor any way in which human energy, physical or mental, can be usefully expended.

Labor force all persons sixteen years of age or older who are willing and able to work and who are counted as either unemployed or employed. Labor force = number unemployed + number employed.

Labor force participation rate   the number of people employed divided by the number of people in the labor force.

Land   One of the four major resource categories. Includes the surface area of the world and everything in nature—minerals, chemicals, plants—that is useful in the production process.

Law of demand   the assumed inverse relationship between product price and quantity demanded, everything else held constant. If the relative price of a good falls, the individual will buy more of the good. If the price rises, the individual will buy less.

Law of diminishing marginal returns   the law that if successive units of one resource—labor, fertilizer, or any other resource—are applied to a fixed quantity of another resource—land, for instance—then at some point in the production process, the added output gained from each additional unit of the variable resource will begin to diminish.

Law of diminishing marginal utility   the rule that as more of a good is consumed, its marginal utility or value relative to the marginal value of the good or goods given up diminishes.

Leading indicator   an index of business activity that tends to move up or down several months before measures of general economic activity, like real GNP, do so.

Leakage (outflow)   a withdrawal or outflow of income from the circular flow. Saving, taxes, and imports are leakages.

Linear regression   a statistical technique used to find the equation describing the straight line that comes closest to the plotted points of a curve.

Liquidity   the ease with which any asset can be converted into another form, especially into money.

Long run   the period during which all resources (and thus costs of production) can be changed—either increased or decreased. Calendar time varies from firm to firm and industry to industry.

Long-run equilibrium   the price-quantity combination that will exist after firms have had time to change their production facilities (or some other resource that is fixed in the short run).

Luxury good or service   any good or service for which demand rises faster than income.

M

M1   the total of the public's (as opposed to the banks') holdings of currency (paper bills and coins), demand deposits at commercial banks, traveler's checks, and other bank accounts against which checks can be written, such as NOW (negotiable order of withdrawal) and ATS (automatic transfer services) accounts.

M2   M1 plus savings accounts and small (less than $100,000) time deposits and certificates of deposit, plus money market accounts and other highly liquid assets.

Macroeconomic policy   the manipulation of taxes, federal expenditures, and the money supply to promote a high and stable level of employment and production, price level stability, and economic growth.

Macroeconomics   the study of the national economy as a whole, or of its major components. Macroeconomics deals with "the big picture," not the details, of the nation's economic activity.

Marginal cost   the additional cost incurred by producing one additional unit of a good, activity, or service.

Marginal cost of labor   the additional cost to the firm of expanding employment by one additional worker.

Marginal product   the increase in total output that results when one additional unit of a resource—for example, labor, fertilizer, or land—is added to the production process.

Marginal propensity to consume   the percentage of any change in income that consumers are inclined to spend.

Marginal propensity to save   the percentage of any change in total income that consumers are inclined to save.

Marginal rate of return on investment   the additional income earned from an additional purchase of capital goods.

Marginal revenue   the additional revenue a firm acquires by selling an additional unit of output.

Marginal tax rate   the percentage of any additional income that is subject to taxation.

Marginal utility   the additional satisfaction received from consuming one additional unit of a good or service.

Market   the process by which buyers and sellers determine what they are willing to buy and sell, on what terms. That is, the process by which buyers and sellers decide the prices and quantities of goods to be bought and sold.

Market demand   the summation of the quantities demanded by all consumers of a specified good or service at each and every price.

Market (nominal) interest rate   the total payment that can be expected on a loan, expressed as a percentage of the loan. Also called the money interest rate.

Market shortage   the amount by which the quantity demanded exceeds the quantity supplied at a given price. Graphically, the shortfall in supply that occurs at any price below the intersection of the supply and demand curves.

Market surplus   the amount by which the quantity supplied exceeds the quantity demanded at a given price. Graphically, the excess supply that occurs at any price above the intersection of the supply and demand curves.

Mean family income   the average family income level, or the total income of all families divided by the total number of families.

Median family income   the midpoint of the family income distribution, above and below which an equal number of families fall.

Median voter   the voter in the middle of the political distribution.

Mercantilism   a system of economic organization that flourished between 1500 and 1800, designed to promote a desired balance of trade through monopoly of production and trading rights.

Merchandise trade balance   the difference between the dollar value of goods—raw materials, agricultural and manufactured products, and capital and consumer products—imported and exported.

Merchandise trade deficit   the dollar amount by which imports of goods exceed exports of goods.

Merchandise trade surplus   the dollar amount by which exports of goods exceed imports of goods.

Microeconomics   the study of the individual markets—for corn, records, books, and so forth—that operate within the broad national economy.

Monetary policy   the manipulation of the rate of growth of the nation's money supply to promote price level stability and a high and stable level of employment and production.

Money   any generally accepted medium of exchange or trade that also serves as a store of purchasing power.

Money cost   a monetary measure of the benefits forgone when a choice is made. (Compare to real cost.)

Money illusion   the mistaken belief that an increase in the market price, stated in dollars, represents an increase in real price (in the price of the good or service relative to other items).

Money stock   the sum of all identified forms of money held by the public (as opposed to the banks) at a given point in time.

Monopolistic competition   a market composed of a number of producers whose products are differentiated and who face highly elastic, but not perfectly elastic, demand curves.

Monopoly   a sole seller of a good or service. Because a monopoly has no competitors, it can cut back on production (thus limiting the quantity supplied), charge higher prices, and reap greater profits than other firms.

Monopoly power   the ability of a firm to raise the market price of its good or service by reducing production.

Monopsony   the sole buyer of any good, service, or resource. (Should not be confused with monopoly, the single seller of a good or service.)

Monopsony power   the ability of a producer to alter the price of a resource like labor by changing the quantity employed.

Multiplier   the ratio of a change in national income to the change in total planned expenditures that stimulated it: m = change in Y ÷ change in TPE. Magnifies the effect of relatively small changes in total planned expenditures on national income.

N

National economic planning   the process of deciding collectively on national economic objectives, and of developing policies and programs for accomplishing those objectives.

National income   the total payment made to owners of productive resources for the use of those resources during a given period. Equals the total income earned by all resources employed during the same period. Also equals the total cost of producing the goods and services included in the net national product.

Natural monopoly   an industry in which long-run marginal and average costs decline with increases in production, so that a single firm dominates production.

Natural rate of unemployment   the minimum percentage of the labor force that is unemployed because of structural problems in the economy and transitional movement among jobs.

Negative income tax   an income redistribution system under which people below a breakeven income level receive cash grants. The lower the income, the higher the grant.

Net national product (NNP)   gross national product minus an allowance for replacement of worn-out plant and equipment (called the capital consumption allowance). Because replacement of old equipment has been subtracted, net national product is a better measure of the real growth of production than gross national product.

Nominal (market) interest rate   the total payment that can be expected on a loan, expressed as a percentage of the loan. Also called the money interest rate.

Normal good or service   any good or service for which demand rises with an increase in income, and falls with a decrease in income.

Normative economics   that branch of economic inquiry that deals with value judgments—with what prices, production levels, incomes, and government policies ought to be.

O

Oligopoly   a market composed of only a handful of producers—as few as two and as many as twelve or more—whose pricing decisions are interdependent.

Open market operations   the purchase and sale by the Federal Reserve of U.S. government securities, which can be bills, notes, or bonds.

Opportunity cost   the value of the most highly preferred alternative not taken. Also called real cost. (Compare to money cost.)

Opportunity cost of capital   the return that might have been realized on the best alternative investment not undertaken.

P

Paradox of thrift   the theory that if people attempt to save more, they will end up earning less in the aggregate, and saving no more (and possibly less) than before.

Partnership   a business venture owned and managed by two or more persons.

Peak   the phase of the business cycle that occurs when general economic activity is no longer rising.

Perfect competition   a market composed of numerous sellers and buyers of an identical product, such that no one individual seller or buyer has the ability to affect the market price by changing the production level. Entry into and exit from a perfectly competitive market is unrestricted.

Perfectly elastic demand   a demand that has an elasticity coefficient of infinity. Expressed graphically as a curve horizontal to the X axis.

Perfect price discrimination   the practice of selling each unit of a given good or service for the maximum possible price. Under perfect price discrimination, the seller's marginal revenue curve is identical to the seller's demand curve.

Personal income   that part of national income that is paid to individuals as opposed to businesses.

Personal income taxes   government revenues collected from individual earnings, after allowance for certain exemptions and deductions.

Phillips curve   a graphical representation of the presumed inverse relationship between unemployment and inflation.

Planned investment   anticipated, scheduled purchases of plant, equipment, and inventory.

Positive economics   that branch of economic inquiry that is concerned with the world as it is rather than as it should be. Deals only with the consequences of changes in economic conditions or policies.

Poverty income threshold   the income level below which people are classified as being poor. The minimum income believed necessary for basic subsistence.

Precautionary demand for money   the desire to hold money balances in order to finance unexpected or emergency purchases of goods and services.

Preferred stock   a set of ownership rights in a corporation that entitles the investor to a fixed share of profits after taxes.

Present value   the value of future costs or benefits in terms of current dollars.

Price   whatever a person must give up in exchange for a unit of goods or services purchased, obtained, or consumed. A rate of exchange, typically expressed in dollars per unit.

Price ceiling   a government-determined price above which a specified good cannot be sold. Usually a legal price that is set by the government below the equilibrium price.

Price discrimination   the practice of varying the price of a given good or service according to how much is bought and who buys it.

Price elasticity of demand   the responsiveness of consumers, in terms of the quantity purchased, to a change in price.

Price floor   a government-determined price below which a specified good cannot be sold. Usually a legal price that is set by the government above the equilibrium price.

Price searcher   a consumer or producer large enough in relation to the entire market that its purchases and sales will affect the market price. Through its consumption or production decisions, the price searcher helps to determine the market price. From the various price-quantity combinations available, it chooses that one combination that maximizes utility or profit. Also called a price maker.

Price taker a consumer or producer so small in relation to the entire market that its purchases and sales cannot affect the market price. The price taker must either accept or reject the market price, deciding how much to buy or sell on the assumption that the market price will not change.

Private goods goods that are bought or produced and used by people as individuals or as members of small voluntary groups.

Private sector all the economic transactions undertaken voluntarily by individuals, either alone or in association with others. Also known as the nongovernment sector.

Production possibilities curve a graphical representation of the various combinations of goods that can be produced when all resources are fully and efficiently employed. Sometimes called a production possibilities frontier or a product transformation curve.

Progressive tax system any means of collecting government revenues in which the percentage of income that is paid in taxes rises with income.

Property rights legally defined and permissible uses, both private and collective, of resources, goods, and services.

Property tax a tax on specified assets, usually real estate, cars and boats, household goods, bank account balances, and stocks and bonds.

Proportional tax system any means of collecting government revenues in which all income earners pay the same tax rate (the same percentage of their income in taxes).

Proprietorship any business venture owned and run by a single individual.

Public goods goods that are bought or produced and used by large groups of people or by governments. Public goods can benefit many people at once.

Public sector the activities of federal, state, and local government. Government decisions are normally made collectively, either by voters in a referendum or by Congress, and are financed primarily by forced taxation.

Pure interest rate the return one can expect from an investment in the absence of risk and inflation.

Pure monopoly a single seller of a product for which there are no close substitutes. Protected from competition by barriers to entry into the market.

Q

Quasi-rent the difference between the price of a resource and its opportunity cost, when the opportunity cost is not zero.

Quota a limit on the amount of a good that can be imported.

R

Rate of return on investment the income earned from the purchase of capital, expressed as a percentage of the purchase price.

Rational behavior consistent behavior that maximizes an individual's satisfaction.

Real (constant dollar) gross national product the gross national product adjusted for price changes.

Real wage rate the nominal or money wage rate (the number of dollars a person earns per hour or day) adjusted for inflation or deflation. Measures a worker's actual purchasing power.

Recession a downward movement in general economic activity, especially in national production and employment. (A downward movement in real GNP must last for two quarters to be classified by the U.S. Department of Commerce as a recession.)

Recovery an upward movement in general economic activity, especially in national production and employment.

Regressive tax system any means of collecting government revenues in which the percentage of income that is paid in taxes declines as income rises.

Representative commodity money certificates or notes that can be converted into given quantities of a specific commodity, like gold or silver.

Reserve deposits the accounts that banks hold in Federal Reserve Banks. (A bank's reserve deposit balance plus its vault cash equals its total reserves.)

Reserve requirement that portion of a bank's reserves that cannot be used to create money (that is, to make loans).

Reserves the cash a bank has in its vault plus its deposits at the Federal Reserve Bank.

Resources things used in the production of goods and services. Also referred to as factors of production or inputs.

Right-to-work laws a state statute that allows unionized firms to hire nonunion workers, and to continue to employ them whether or not they join the existing union.

Risk cost the loss that can be anticipated because

of the failure of a certain percentage of a firm's ventures.

S

Saving that portion of income not spent. Represents forgone expenditures on real goods and services.

Saving function the assumed direct relationship between national income and the amount of income saved (not spent on goods and services).

Say's law the macroeconomic principle that supply creates its own demand—that is, that the production of a supply of products creates an equal demand for goods and services.

Scarcity the fact that we cannot all have everything we want all the time. Put simply, there isn't enough of everything to go around.

Short run the period during which one or more resources (and thus one or more costs of production) cannot be changed—either increased or decreased. Calendar time varies from firm to firm and industry to industry.

Short-run equilibrium the price-quantity combination that will exist so long as producers do not have time to change their production facilities (or some other resource that is fixed in the short run).

Socialism an economic system in which the government owns major plants in industries such as coal, transportation, steel, and banking, and operates them in the public interest. Sometimes called democratic socialism.

Specialization of labor the process of dividing and assigning different production tasks to individuals with differing skills and talents.

Speculative demand for money the desire to hold money balances in anticipation of a decrease in the price of other assets and in anticipation of future profits.

Stagflation the combination of persistently high rates of unemployment and inflation.

Structural inflation a general rise in prices that occurs when producers cannot shift production in response to changes in the structure of the economy. Changes in the demand for a product, in the technology of its production, and in the competition producers face can all cause structural inflation.

Structural unemployment unemployment that occurs with major changes in the skills needed by workers. Caused by changes in the structure of industry due to technological innovation or changes in the relative competitiveness of an industry.

Sunk cost a cost incurred in the past, which cannot be altered by current decisions.

Supply the assumed relationship between the quantity of a good producers are willing and able to offer during a given period and the price, everything else held constant. Generally, because managerial costs tend to rise with expanded production, this relationship is presumed to be positive.

Supply of labor the assumed positive relationship between the real wage rate and the number of workers (or worker-hours) offered for employment during a given period, everything else held constant. Depends on the opportunity cost of workers' time.

T

Tariff a special tax on imported goods.

Technology the knowledge of how resources can be combined in productive ways.

Theory a set of abstractions about the real world.

An economic theory is a simplified explanation of how the economy, or part of the economy, functions or would function under specific conditions. A good theory must predict and explain outcomes.

Total cost the sum of fixed costs (*FC*) and variable costs (*VC*) at each output level. Or, $TC = FC + VC$.

Total expenditure function the relationship of total planned expenditures to national income, normally assumed to be a direct relationship. (Total expenditures equal consumption spending plus investment spending plus government spending plus exports minus imports.)

Transactions demand for money the desire to hold money balances in order to carry out anticipated purchases of goods and services.

Transitional (frictional) unemployment unemployment that occurs when people move from one job to another requiring similar skills. Generally temporary, lasting only a few days or weeks. Caused by normal shifts in the supply of and demand for products.

Trend a long-run directional change, up or down, in some economic variable—for example, real GNP.

Trough the bottom of the business cycle, the point at which general economic activity ceases to fall.

Tying contract an agreement between seller and buyer that requires the buyer of one good or service to purchase some other product or service. Declared illegal in the Clayton Act.

U

Unemployment rate the ratio of the number of people estimated to be unemployed to the number of people estimated to be in the labor force, stated as a percentage. Unemployment rate = number unemployed ÷ labor force.

Union shop a place of employment where a worker, once employed, must join the recognized union as a condition of continued employment.

Unitary elastic demand a consumer response to a price change in which the percentage change in price exactly matches the percentage change in quantity demanded. A change in price therefore does not alter consumer expenditures.

Unplanned investment unanticipated, unscheduled purchases of plant, equipment, and inventory.

Usury laws a legislated upper limit on the interest rates that lending institutions may charge to borrowers.

Utility the satisfaction a person receives from the consumption of a good or service, or from participation in an activity.

V

Variable cost any cost that changes with the level of output.

Variable rate mortgage a mortgage whose interest rate is adjusted periodically to agree with some market interest rate—for example, the rate on a specific type of government or corporate bond.

Velocity of money the average number of times a dollar is used during a given period.

Vertical merger the joining of two or more firms that perform different stages of the production process into a single firm.

Very long run the time period during which the technology of production and the availability of resources can change because of invention, innovation, and discovery of new technologies and resources.

Index

Boldfaced page numbers indicate the first occurrence of key terms; page numbers followed by (tab) indicate information from tables; page numbers followed by (fig) indicate figures; and page numbers followed by n indicate material from notes.

Business and Economic Indicators

Employment, Wages, Productivity

Prices, Inflation Rates

Year	Population (thousands)	Civilian Labor Force (thousands)	Civilian Un-employment (thousands)	Civilian Unem-ployment Rate (percent)	Average Gross Hourly Earnings, Current Dollars— Total Private Non-agricul-tural	Output per Hour Business Sector (1977 = 100)	Con-sumer Price Index (1967 = 100)	Annual Inflation Rate (percent change in CPI, Dec. to Dec.)	Annual Inflation Rate, GNP Deflator
1929	121,767	49,180	1,550	3.2				0.2	0.0
1933	125,579	51,590	12,830	24.9				.5	−2.1
1939	130,880	55,230	9,480	17.2				−.5	−.8
1940	132,122	55,640	8,120	14.6				1.0	2.2
1941	133,402	55,910	5,560	9.9				9.7	7.5
1942	134,860	56,410	2,660	4.7				9.3	9.9
1943	136,739	55,540	1,070	1.9				3.2	5.3
1944	138,397	54,630	670	1.2				2.1	2.4
1945	139,928	53,860	1,040	1.9				2.3	2.4
1946	141,389	57,520	2,270	3.9			58.5	18.2	15.7
1947	144,126	59,350	2,311	3.9	$1.131	43.7	66.9	9.0	12.9
1948	146,631	60,621	2,276	3.8	1.225	46.1	72.1	2.7	6.9
1949	149,188	61,286	3,637	5.9	1.275	46.7	71.4	−1.8	−.9
1950	152,271	62,208	3,288	5.3	1.335	50.4	72.1	5.8	2.1
1951	154,878	62,017	2,055	3.3	1.45	51.8	77.8	5.9	6.6
1952	157,553	62,138	1,883	3.0	1.52	53.5	79.5	.9	1.4
1953	160,184	63,015	1,834	2.9	1.61	55.2	80.1	.6	1.6
1954	163,026	63,643	3,532	5.5	1.65	56.1	80.5	−.5	1.2
1955	165,931	65,023	2,852	4.4	1.71	58.3	80.2	.4	2.2
1956	168,903	66,552	2,750	4.1	1.80	58.9	81.4	2.9	3.2
1957	171,984	66,929	2,859	4.3	1.89	60.4	84.3	3.0	3.4
1958	174,882	67,639	4,602	6.8	1.95	62.3	86.6	1.8	1.7
1959	177,830	68,369	3,740	5.5	2.02	64.3	87.3	1.5	2.4
1960	180,671	69,628	3,852	5.5	2.09	65.2	88.7	1.5	1.6
1961	183,691	70,459	4,714	6.7	2.14	67.4	89.6	.7	.9
1962	186,538	70,614	3,911	5.5	2.22	69.9	90.6	1.2	1.8
1963	189,242	71,833	4,070	5.7	2.28	72.5	91.7	1.6	1.5
1964	191,889	73,091	3,786	5.2	2.36	75.6	92.9	1.2	1.5
1965	194,303	74,455	3,366	4.5	2.46	78.3	94.5	1.9	2.2
1966	196,560	75,770	2,875	3.8	2.56	80.8	97.2	3.4	3.2
1967	198,712	77,347	2,975	3.8	2.68	82.6	100.0	3.0	3.0
1968	200,706	78,737	2,817	3.6	2.85	85.3	104.2	4.7	4.4
1969	202,677	80,734	2,832	3.5	3.04	85.5	109.8	6.1	5.1
1970	205,052	82,771	4,093	4.9	3.23	86.2	116.3	5.5	5.4
1971	207,661	84,382	5,016	5.9	3.45	89.3	121.3	3.4	5.0
1972	209,896	87,034	4,882	5.6	3.70	92.4	125.3	3.4	4.2
1973	211,909	89,429	4,365	4.9	3.94	94.8	133.1	8.8	5.8
1974	213,854	91,949	5,156	5.6	4.24	92.5	147.7	12.2	8.8
1975	215,973	93,775	7,929	8.5	4.53	94.6	161.2	7.0	9.3
1976	218,035	96,158	7,406	7.7	4.86	97.6	170.5	4.8	5.2
1977	220,239	99,009	6,991	7.1	5.25	100.0	181.5	6.8	5.8
1978	222,585	102,251	6,202	6.1	5.69	100.5	195.4	9.0	7.4
1979	225,055	104,962	6,137	5.8	6.16	99.3	217.4	13.3	8.6
1980	227,738	106,940	7,637	7.1	6.66	98.8	246.8	12.4	9.2
1981	230,019	108,670	8,273	7.6	7.25	100.7	272.4	8.9	9.6
1982	232,309	110,204	10,678	9.7	7.68	100.9	289.1	3.9	6.0
1983	234,496	111,550	10,717	9.6	8.02	103.7	298.4	3.8	3.8
1984	236,634	113,544	8,539	7.5	8.33	107.4	311.1	4.0	3.7